DERMOT LUCEY

MODERN EUROPE

AND THE WIDER WORLD

FOURTH EDITION

g GILL EDUCATION

Gill Education
Hume Avenue
Park West
Dublin 12
www.gilleducation.ie

Gill Education is an imprint of M.H. Gill & Co.

ISBN: 978-0-7171-78988

Design and layout: Design Image, Ireland
Illustrations: Jeremy Bays, www.art-work-shop.co.uk; and Designit Creative Consultants Ltd., Dublin

At the time of going to press, all web addresses were active and contained information relevant to the topics in this book. Gill Education does not, however, accept responsibility for the content or views contained on these websites. Content, views and addresses may change beyond the publisher or author's control. Students should always be supervised when reviewing websites.

The paper used in this book is made from the wood pulp of managed forests. For every tree felled, at least one tree is planted, thereby renewing natural resources.

For permission to reproduce photographs, the authors and publisher gratefully acknowledge the following:
© Advertising Archive: 383, 395, 396T, 441; © Alamy: 3, 5, 6, 10, 13, 18, 23, 31, 32, 35, 40, 41, 45TR, 45BL, 50, 52, 53, 54CR, 55, 58, 61R, 63, 68, 76, 77, 81, 82, 84, 86, 88TL, 89, 94, 96, 97, 98TL, 103, 105, 106TL, 106CL, 109, 110, 112, 122, 123, 124, 125, 132, 134R, 136, 137, 138, 141, 142, 143, 145BR, 145BL, 148BR, 149, 152BL, 156B, 157, 159, 160T, 168, 169TR, 180CL, 181, 193TL, 196, 207, 208CL, 211, 212B, 218, 221, 227CR, 239, 246, 255, 257T, 256, 288, 289C, 295TL, 296, 301TR, 302, 308, 309, 315, 324CL, 328CL, 329, 331, 333, 339, 355BR, 368, 376B, 382, 384, 412B, 414, 415, 443, 458, 463, 480B; © Associated Press: 355TR, 355BL, 377; © INTERFOTO/Alamy: 44; Courtesy of BASF: 28; © Bridgeman Images / Archives Charmet: 169TL; © Bridgeman Images / British Library: 139; © Bridgeman Images / Collection Gregoire: 45BR; © Bridgeman Images / Look and Learn: 148CL; © Bridgeman Images / SZ Photo: 227TL, 227TR; © Bridgeman Images / The Stapleton Collection: 88BR; © British Cartoon Archive/Express Syndication Ltd: 247; © British Cartoon Archive / Solo Syndication / Associated Newspapers Ltd: 185, 229B; © Getty Images: 2, 11, 39, 61T, 98TR, 111, 113, 117, 118, 128, 144, 145CR, 146, 152TL, 156T, 158, 160BR, 161, 163, 164, 165, 166, 172, 173, 178TL, 191, 192CL, 194, 200, 201, 203, 205BR, 208TL, 209BL, 209BR, 210, 227BL, 227BR, 228, 229T, 231, 232L, 234TL, 235, 237, 244T, 244B, 252, 254, 254, 258, 259, 260, 262, 270, 271, 266, 267, 274, 275, 276, 277, 281TR, 282TR, 282BL, 283, 285B, 289B, 292CL, 293, 294TL, 299, 304, 305, 310BR, 313, 316, 316, 317TL, 317TC, 317TR, 317BL, 323BR, 323BL, 324BL, 325TR, 327, 328BR, 330, 335, 336T, 340, 341, 343, 344, 345, 346, 352, 355TL, 356TL, 356TR, 357, 358, 369, 363T, 364, 369, 372T, 374, 376T, 379, 380, 386, 387, 388, 390, 391, 394B, 396B, 397, 398, 399, 401, 403TL, 405, 406, 410, 411, 412T, 417, 419, 420, 421, 422, 424, 427, 429, 433, 435, 442, 444, 446, 450, 453, 455BR, 456, 457, 461, 464, 468, 469, 475, 476; ©iStock Editorial / Getty Images: 372B; Courtesy of gracesguide.co.uk: 151; © Hagley Museum and Library: 394T; © The Herb Block Foundation: 362, 365, 436; Courtesy of Imperial War Museum: 22, 106CR, 107; Courtesy of John F. Kennedy Presidential Library and Museum: 482; © David King Library: 174; Courtesy of TUC Library Collections / London Metropolitan University: 54CL; © Library of Congress Prints and Photographs Division Washington: 306BR; © Magnum Photos / Elliott Erwitt: 413; © Magnum Photos / Thomas Hoepker: 426; © Magnum Photos / Eve Arnold: 428; © Mary Evans Picture Library: 25, 37, 60, 87, 100, 101, 190C, 192TL, 193BL, 193CR, 193BR, 200, 202TR, 202BL, 202BR, 205TR, 209CL, 209CR, 209T, 213T, 220, 257B, 284, 290, 292TL, 294BL, 297, 298, 301BR, 306TL, 314; © Mike Luckovich / Creators Syndicate: 393; © Mirrorpix: 234BL, 234BR, 285T, 310BL, 317BC, 317BR; © NASA: 466, 479, 480C; © Punch: 282TL; Courtesy of Charles Rotkin: 404; © REX/Shutterstock: 49, 193CL, 195, 199, 202CR, 213B, 217, 232R, 281CR, 452, 455TR, 471; Courtesy of simplicissimus.info: 134L; © Sputnik Images: 169TC; Courtesy of Tamiment Library and Robert F. Wagner Labour Archive: 436BR; © Topfoto: 64, 171, 212T, 227CL, 287, 363B, 445; © Victoria and Albert Museum: 170; © Paul Weir Cloud: 251; Courtesy of Wikimedia: 177, 416, 447.

The authors and publisher have made every effort to trace all copyright holders, but if any have been inadvertently overlooked we would be pleased to make the necessary arrangement at the first opportunity.

Contents

PART 3: THE UNITED STATES AND THE WORLD, 1945–89

Note:

The sections of this book, parts 1 to 3, cover Topics 2, 3 and 6 of the syllabus. They will be labelled Topic 2, Topic 3 and Topic 6 on your exam paper.

TOPIC 2: NATION STATES AND INTERNATIONAL TENSIONS, 1871–1920

PERSPECTIVE	ELEMENTS	CASE STUDIES
Politics and administration	The Second Reich and the changing balance of power; Anglo- and Franco-German tensions; Bismarck's foreign policy. The structures of European diplomacy; the New Imperialism and colonial rivalries; Wilhelm II and Weltpolitik. Serbia as a fulcrum of Great Power rivalry. The Second International. The outbreak of war in 1914; the conduct of war; war and revolution; the Peace Settlement.	The naval policy of Wilhelm II
Society and economy	Economic growth and social tensions: industrialisation in Germany and its impact on society; industrialisation and economic crisis in Tsarist Russia; the impact of war on society and economy.	Women in the workforce during World War I
Culture, religion and science	Expression of national identity through literature and the arts; the literature of World War I. Church/State tensions in Germany and Italy. Anti-Semitism in France and Russia. Key developments in science, technology and medicine.	The invention and early history of the motor car

In their study of the topic, students should become aware of the role of certain key personalities.

Another 'key' to developing understanding will be learning to identify the main issues through a familiarity with certain key concepts.

KEY PERSONALITIES

Students should be aware of the contribution of the following to the developments listed under the elements above:
Otto von Bismarck; Wilhelm II; Douglas Haig; Woodrow Wilson; the Krupp family; Rosa Luxemburg; Wilfred Owen; Leo XIII; Marie Curie; Karl Benz.

KEY CONCEPTS

Balance of power; nationalism; the New Imperialism; world war; war of attrition; conscription; self-determination; war guilt; anti-Semitism

DIFFERENTIATION – HIGHER AND ORDINARY

While students at both levels will study the same topics, for Ordinary Level students a particular emphasis will be placed on Key Personalities and Case Studies associated with their topics. Higher Level students will be expected to study all aspects of topics to a greater depth and to develop a greater level of conceptual understanding.

TOPIC 3: DICTATORSHIP AND DEMOCRACY IN EUROPE, 1920–45

PERSPECTIVE	ELEMENTS	CASE STUDIES
Politics and administration	Origins and growth of the Fascist regimes in Europe; the Nazi state in peace and war. Communism in Russia: the regimes of Lenin and Stalin; the Stalinist state in peace and war. France: the Third Republic, 1920–40, and the Vichy state 1940–44. Wartime alliances, 1939–45.	Stalin's Show Trials
Society and economy	Economic and social problems of the inter-war years, with particular reference to Britain and Germany. The Soviet alternative. Society during World War II: The Home Front; rationing/evacuees; refugees; collaboration/resistance. Anti-semitism and the Holocaust.	The Jarrow March, October 1936
Culture, religion and science	Nazi propaganda – state control and use of mass media. Church-state relations under Mussolini and Hitler. Anglo-American popular culture in peace and war: radio and cinema. The technology of warfare.	The Nuremberg Rallies

In their study of the topic, students should become aware of the role of certain key personalities.

Another 'key' to developing understanding will be learning to identify the main issues through a familiarity with certain key concepts.

KEY PERSONALITIES

Students should be aware of the contribution of the following to the developments listed under the elements above:
J M Keynes, Adolf Hitler, Benito Mussolini, Vladimir Ilyich Lenin, Josef Stalin, Winston Churchill, Joseph Goebbels, Leni Riefenstahl, Bing Crosby, Charlie Chaplin.

KEY CONCEPTS

Inflation, the Depression, protectionism, collectivisation, Communism, Fascism, dictatorship, personality cult, totalitarianism, democracy, propaganda, anti-Semitism, herrenvolk Reichskirche, the Holocaust, collaboration, resistance, lebensraum, blitzkrieg.

DIFFERENTIATION – HIGHER AND ORDINARY

While students at both levels will study the same topics, for Ordinary Level students a particular emphasis will be placed on Key Personalities and Case Studies associated with their topics. Higher Level students will be expected to study all aspects of topics to a greater depth and to develop a greater level of conceptual understanding.

TOPIC 6: THE UNITED STATES AND THE WORLD, 1945–89

PERSPECTIVE	ELEMENTS	CASE STUDIES
Politics and administration	US politics: structures and tensions – federal government and the states; the separation of powers. The Presidency from Roosevelt to Reagan. Domestic factors in US foreign policy: McCarthyism, the anti-war movement, race relations. US foreign policy, 1945–72: Berlin, Korea, Cuba, Vietnam. Decline of Cold War certainties, 1973–89: withdrawal from Vietnam, détente, SALT and Star Wars.	Lyndon Johnson and Vietnam, 1963–68
Society and economy	Sources of the US economic boom; the war, public investment and international financing, 1945–68. The development of the US industrial structure: the multinational corporation, 1945–68. The Vietnam War; the federal deficit; domestic recession; international competition from Japan and Europe, 1968–89. Demographic growth; affluence – consumerism, leisure, the role of work, the changing role of women and the family. Troubled affluence: racial conflict, urban poverty, drugs and crime.	The Montgomery Bus Boycott, 1956
Culture, religion and science	Consensus? 1945–68: Hollywood – the American Dream; the 'red scare'. Collapse of consensus, 1968–89: youth culture, 'counter-culture' and multiculturalism. Religion in modern American culture; the mass media in modern American culture; mass higher education. Advances in military, space and information technology.	The Moon Landing, 1969

In their study of the topic, students should become aware of the role of certain key personalities.

Another 'key' to developing understanding will be learning to identify the main issues through a familiarity with certain key concepts.

KEY PERSONALITIES

Students should be aware of the contribution of the following to the developments listed under the elements above:
Harry Truman, Joe McCarthy, Martin Luther King, Lyndon Johnson, the 'Organisation Man', Betty Friedan, Norman Mailer, Muhammad Ali, Billy Graham, Marilyn Monroe.

KEY CONCEPTS

Corporate capitalism, globalisation, internationalism, imperialism, consumerism, technological development, the military-industrial complex, discrimination, liberalism, presidential bureaucracy, mass media, public opinion, fundamentalism, moral majority, feminism.

DIFFERENTIATION – HIGHER AND ORDINARY

While students at both levels will study the same topics, for Ordinary Level students a particular emphasis will be placed on Key Personalities and Case Studies associated with their topics. Higher Level students will be expected to study all aspects of topics to a greater depth and to develop a greater level of conceptual understanding.

① Nation States and International Tensions, 1871–1920

In this section, you should understand:
• The role of Bismarck in the Second Reich.
• Bismarck's internal and foreign policy.

Germany Before 1871

Otto von Bismarck

In the early 19th century, the country we know today as Germany was made up of a confederation of 39 states, known as the **German Confederation**. Each state had its own ruler.

The two largest states were **Austria** and **Prussia**, and they competed for power as the dominant German state. In two wars in the 1860s, **Otto von Bismarck**, Prime Minister of Prussia, defeated Denmark and Austria. The victory over Austria led to the creation of the **North German Confederation**, dominated by Prussia. It also ensured that a united Germany would not include Austria.

In a third war, the **Franco-Prussian War, 1870–71**, Bismarck defeated France and united Germany as the German Empire. Prussia, the largest, richest and most highly populated state, became the dominant state in the newly united German Empire.

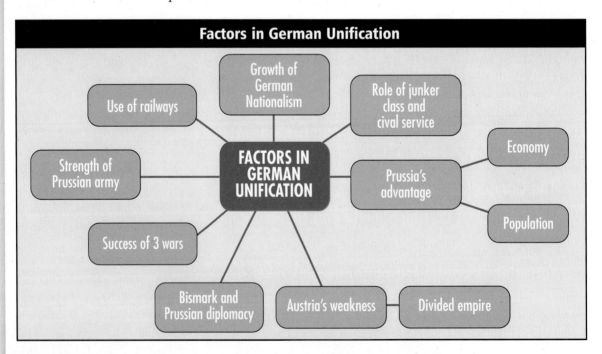

Factors in German Unification

- Use of railways
- Growth of German Nationalism
- Role of junker class and cival service
- Strength of Prussian army
- **FACTORS IN GERMAN UNIFICATION**
- Prussia's advantage
- Economy
- Population
- Success of 3 wars
- Bismark and Prussian diplomacy
- Austria's weakness
- Divided empire

What was the Impact of the Franco-Prussian War?

The Franco-Prussian war, which began in 1870, came to a sudden end in early 1871. Earlier, France had been defeated in the **Battle of Sedan**, which resulted in the capture of the French Emperor, **Napoleon III**. Then on 28 January 1871, Paris surrendered to a besieging Prussian army. Four months later, in May, Germany and France signed the **Treaty of Frankfurt**, which brought the war to a final conclusion.

The Treaty of Frankfurt: The terms of the Treaty of Frankfurt imposed strict conditions on France:

- France had to pay a **war indemnity** (money paid for damage or loss) of **5 billion francs** over three years.
- The German army remained in France until the indemnity was paid.
- The provinces of **Alsace and Lorraine** were annexed (taken over) by Germany. This resulted in continued **French bitterness** towards Germany. Bismarck's view was: 'We cannot look to the French temper for our guarantees. What the French nation will never forgive is their defeat as such. In German hands Strasbourg and Metz will take on a purely defensive character.'

As a result of defeat in the war, **France** lost its dominant political and military position in Europe. This was now taken by Germany. The defeat and the treaty resulted in a French desire for **vengeance**, especially over Alsace-Lorraine, which contributed to **hostility** between the two countries until after World War II, and influenced the causes of both World War I and World War II.

German unification: Even before the war ended, **Wilhelm I** of Prussia was crowned Kaiser (Emperor) of the German Empire in a ceremony on 18 January 1871 in the palace of Versailles. As a result of the French threat in the war, south German states joined with Prussia and the North German Confederation to create a united **Germany**.

Wilhelm I of Prussia

QUESTIONS ?

1. How did Bismarck unite Germany?
2. What were the terms of the Treaty of Frankfurt?
3. Why did France want vengeance against Germany?

Wilhelm I was proclaimed Kaiser of Germany in a ceremony in Versailles, France.

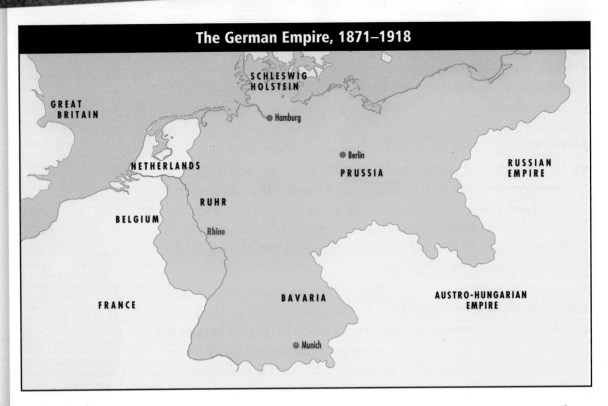

The German Empire, 1871–1918

The German Constitution: Bismarck wrote the German Constitution to ensure the dominance of Prussia in the new country, and the dominance of his landowning *Junker* class in Prussia:

The role of the Kaiser: The new Empire was a **federal state** with the states retaining local powers. However, the King of Prussia (Wilhelm I) was Kaiser of Germany and the Prime Minister of Prussia (Bismarck) was Chancellor of Germany. The Kaiser had power to appoint and dismiss ministers who were responsible only to him. He had control of foreign affairs, though in Wilhelm's case he left the running of foreign affairs to Bismarck. **Bismarck's success** in unifying Germany and in maintaining Prussian power ensured that he would be the most powerful politician in Germany for the foreseeable future.

The Reichstag (lower house of parliament): The Reichstag was elected by universal male suffrage (vote) but it could not appoint or dismiss the Chancellor and his ministers. The Reichstag could veto (reject) the military budget, and laws had to be passed by it but it could not initiate new laws. Bismarck had to get support from the main parties in the Reichstag to ensure the passage of his laws.

The Bundesrat (upper house) was made up of representatives of the states. But Prussia had 17 seats out of 58 and it could veto any proposals.

Given the power of the emperor and the structure of the Reichstag and Bundesrat, it was clear that Bismarck intended to maintain the power of Prussia and block any proposals for change. It was largely a case of '**rule from above**'.

The **success of the Prussian army** in three wars made it a model for other armies to follow over the next forty years. It based its success on mass-reserves and a standing army. The army and reserves were **mobilised** rapidly according to detailed plans drawn up by the **Prussian General Staff**. Huge numbers of troops were moved into place by a railway system designed for the purpose. The increased size of armies and their transport by trains meant **war plans** had to be drawn up well in advance of war. This contributed to the **causes** of World War I (see pp. 72–76).

The German economy: The unification of the country contributed to the growth of the German economy. Very soon Germany became the most powerful economy in Europe, even passing out Britain. (See German industrialisation pp. 27–32)

The balance of power and Bismarck's foreign policy: The unification of Germany changed the balance of power in Europe. Germany now became the dominant power but Bismarck did not want any further war. He **feared France** because he had deposed it from its previous dominant position and had taken Alsace-Lorraine from it. As a result, his policy for the next twenty years was to **isolate** the country to ensure it could not ally with other large powers, particularly Austria and Russia.

See Bismarck's foreign policy, p 9–14.

**KEY CONCEPT
BALANCE OF POWER:** When no one country is able to dominate others, when countries are roughly equal in power.

QUESTION ❓

How did Bismarck use the German constitution to ensure the dominance of Prussia?

Develop notes on the role of Bismarck in German affairs, 1871–90.

EXAM QUESTION ❓

Which did Bismarck manage better, Germany's internal or external affairs? Argue your case, referring to both (2008)

KEY PERSONALITY: OTTO VON BISMARCK

Bismarck became **Chancellor** of Germany and the Prussian king, Wilhelm I, became Kaiser (Emperor) of Germany in the newly unified Germany in 1871.

Bismarck had definite **aims** in **domestic policy**. He wrote the German **constitution**, in which he ensured that Prussia had the greatest influence in the new Germany (p. 4).

Bismarck feared the power of the Catholic Church so he attacked the Church and the Catholic Centre Party in the **Kulturkampf** (p. 5). He next took on the socialists, especially the main socialist party, the **Social Democratic Party** (SPD). Here he developed a 'carrot-and-stick' approach (see p. 7). In doing so he developed **state socialism** and created the most comprehensive welfare system in Europe at the time (see p. 7). He also contributed to the growth of the **German economy** (p. 29). In **foreign policy**, Bismarck did not want to involve the united Germany in another war. He believed that the greatest danger came from France so his main aim in foreign policy was to **isolate France**. One way of doing this was to maintain good relations with Austria and Russia (see p. 9–14). Bismarck also reluctantly took an interest in colonial affairs but he wanted to ensure that **colonial conflict** would not lead to war in Europe (pp. 12–13).

Bismarck's downfall came with the reign of a new Emperor, Wilhelm II (p. 14).

Church–State Tensions – the Kulturkampf

In his **domestic policy** in the new German Empire, Bismarck aimed to maintain Prussian power in Germany; he believed that German greatness depended on this. He also believed that the *Junker* class was the best class of people to run Prussia and Germany. He also wanted to maintain his own power.

His **immediate aim** was to consolidate the unity of the new state he had created. Apart from drawing up the German constitution, he also developed a national bank, a national currency and a commercial code for trade and industry.

Bismarck harassed **minority groups** – 'enemies of the state' or *Reichsfeinde* – and tried to reduce their influence and win support from the wider German people. The two main groups he attacked were the **Catholic Church** and the **Socialists**.

Origins of the Kulturkampf

The Kulturkampf ('struggle for civilisation') was a conflict between Bismarck and the Catholic Church. In the **decree of papal infallibility, 1870** the pope, Pius IX, said he could not make mistakes in matters of faith and morals. Bismarck feared that Catholics in Germany – almost 40 per cent of the population – would owe their allegiance

? QUESTION

Why did Bismarck attack the Catholic Church?

(loyalty) to an outside power (the pope), rather than the Empire. Catholics were dominant in Bavaria and the Rhineland, close to Austria and France, respectively, two 'Catholic' powers which Bismarck had just defeated. He said, 'It is not a matter of a struggle between belief and unbelief. It is a matter of the conflict between monarchy and priesthood. What is a stake is the defence of the state.'

Bismarck also feared the growth of the Catholic **Centre Party**. The Party won 57 seats in parliament, and he worried that their growth in popularity might lead them to link up with the defeated 'Catholic' powers of Austria and France. The party also favoured a **more decentralised Germany**, giving more power to each of the provinces.

Bismarck also needed a '**new enemy**' to get support behind him. He could not get outside enemies now, because Germany was united; so he selected the Catholics in order to unite the rest of Germany behind him. In his attack on the Catholic Church, Bismarck got the support of the **National Liberals** who disliked the publication of Pope Pius IX's *Syllabus of Errors* (1864) which condemned many principles which Liberals supported.

Progress of the Kulturkampf

The attack on the Catholic Church began in 1872. First, diplomatic relations were cut between Germany and the Vatican. Then the **Jesuits**, a major Catholic religious order, were expelled from Germany. The **Pulpit Law** (1871), which banned all clergy from preaching about politics in their sermons, was also used against Catholic priests. A final imperial law was passed in 1875 when civil marriages were made compulsory. But the Kulturkampf was mainly a **Prussian conflict**. The main legal attack came in 1873, in Prussia. There, **Falk**, minister of ecclesiastical (church) affairs, passed the **May or Falk Laws**. All schools were put under state supervision. There were state regulations regarding the training and licensing of clergy, and priests had to pass a state exam.

The Catholic Church and laity (worshippers who were not priests) resisted strongly. Catholic clergy and bishops were imprisoned. By 1876 most of the Prussian Catholic bishops were in prison or in exile, over 1,000 parishes had no priests and almost 1,800 priests were also in prison or in exile. Catholic newspapers were shut down, and many Catholic civil servants were dismissed.

The Kulturkampf came to a sudden end from 1878 onwards. Most of the May Laws were repealed, and Falk was dismissed as minister for ecclesiastical affairs in 1879.

Why Did the Kulturkampf End?

Bismarck realised that he was not winning his battle with the Catholic Church. Catholic clergy were supported by their laity, and the Centre Party, instead of declining, increased its seats in the Reichstag from 57 to 95. By 1878, the German economy was going into recession,

Between Berlin and Rome, Bismarck (left) confronts the Pope, 1875.

and Bismarck needed the support of the Centre Party to pass laws on the new policies of **protectionism** (tariffs on imports). His main supporters up to this, the National Liberals, favoured free trade and opposed protectionism.

As well as this, the royal family and the Protestant churches were against religious persecution; the churches feared that the laws could be turned on them next. Instead of consolidating support behind him, Bismarck realised he was dividing Germany. Bismarck availed of the election of a new Pope, **Leo XIII**, who was more conciliatory than the previous pope, Pius IX, to end the Kulturkampf.

Did Bismarck Achieve his Aims?

The Kulturkampf showed there was a limit to Bismarck's power. While he maintained his own power and Prussian power in Germany, he could not crush the Catholic Church or the Centre Party. But he realised the limitations of his power and was prepared to change policy and look for Centre Party help when it suited him. In the process, though, he caused severe tensions in Germany and divided his people.

Why did Bismarck Attack the Socialists?

Another reason for Bismarck's change of policy with the Catholics in the late 1870s was his wish to take on a new 'enemy of the state', the **socialists**. The policy of the main socialist party, the **Social Democratic Party** (*Sozialdemokratische Partei Deutschlands*, SPD), was to take power from the *Junkers* and the industrialists. The state (or government) would take over industry and the workers would share profits. In the **Gotha Programme** (1875), the SPD wanted 'to extinguish all social and political inequality'. As German industrialisation spread, Bismarck feared that a growing working class would increase the support for the SPD. By 1878, Bismarck knew he had to get the support of the **Centre Party** to bring in protectionism and to pass **anti-socialist laws** so he had to stop his attacks on the Centre Party and attack the socialists instead. He used the occasion of two failed attempts on the life of the Kaiser, Wilhelm I, to do this.

How did Bismarck Attack the Socialists?

Bismarck used the **carrot-and-stick** approach to try to defeat socialism. In the 'stick' part he used the **Exceptional Laws** (anti-socialist laws) in 1878 to break up the SPD.
- Socialist meetings and newspapers were banned.
- Socialist leaders were arrested.

In the 'carrot' part, Bismarck tried to win the support of the working class by bringing in '**state socialism**'. He said, *'The action of the state is the only means of arresting the socialist movement. We must carry out what seems justified in the socialist programme and can be realised within the present framework of state and society'*. He introduced **sickness insurance** (1883) and **accident insurance** (1884) for workers. In 1889, he introduced old-age **pensions** for workers over 70. This was the most comprehensive social welfare programme of any country in the 19th century (see p. 31).

Did Bismarck Defeat the Socialists?

Bismarck failed to stop the growth of the Social Democratic Party. Its membership almost trebled between 1884 and 1890, while the number of socialist seats in the Reichstag grew from nine in 1878 to 35 in 1890. However, some historians believe that

QUESTIONS
1. How did Bismarck persecute the Catholic Church?
2. Why did he end the Kulturkampf? Was he successful in the Kulturkampf?

QUESTIONS
1. What danger did Bismarck see in the socialists?
2. What was the carrot-and-stick approach to attacking the socialists?
3. Was Bismarck successful?

Bismarck's state socialism had the effect of dampening down any threat to the state from the working class.

A more serious outcome of Bismarck's attack on the socialists was that it led to his own **downfall**. A new Kaiser, **Wilhelm II**, was opposed to Bismarck's attacks on the socialists, and the socialist laws were allowed to lapse in 1890. By 1912 the SPD had become the **largest party** in the Reichstag.

HOMEWORK EXERCISES

1. Study the documents and answer the questions below.

DOCUMENT A

The question we currently deal with, in my opinion, is falsely described, ... if one regards it as a confessional (religious, doctrinal) one. It is mainly a political one; it is not about the struggle, as our Catholic fellow citizens are told, of a Protestant dynasty against the Catholic Church, it is not a struggle between believers and unbelievers, it is the age-old struggle between kingship and priesthood, a power struggle as old as mankind, older than the appearance on earth of our Saviour, ... the power struggle which shaped the German history in the Middle Ages, leading to the disintegration (break-up) of the German Empire, in the form of the conflict between emperors and popes, ... This power struggle is subject to the same conditions as any other struggle; ... It is a matter of defense of the state, ... Because in this world the state claims both authority and priority.

Bismarck on the reasons for the Kulturkampf, Speech in the Prussian House of Lords, March 1873

DOCUMENT B

The Kulturkampf was a *failure*. The Centre Party won strength in the Reichstag elections of 1874, despite government hostility. Bismarck recognised his mistake and attempted to rectify it. In 1878 Pope Pius IX was succeeded by the more conciliatory and diplomatic Leo XIII, and shortly afterwards Bismarck opened negotiations with the Vatican to put an end to the Kulturkampf. He had strong political reasons for doing so. In the course of the Kulturkampf he had gained a healthy respect for the strength and organisation of the Catholic Church and for the political power represented by the Centre party. By striking a bargain with the Church about the Kulturkampf laws, he hoped to gain the support of the Centre party for his own political purposes.

Edited extract from N. Rich, *The Age of Nationalism and Reform*, 1850–1890 (1977)

A. (i) According to Document A, what is 'falsely described'?
   (ii) What is the 'age-old struggle', according to Bismarck?
   (iii) What is at stake in this power struggle, according to Bismarck?
   (iv) Why does Document B say the Kulturkampf was a 'failure'?
   (v) Why was Bismarck able to 'open negotiations' with the Vatican, according to Document B?
   (vi) Did Bismarck admire the Centre Party? Explain.

B. (i) What types of documents are Documents A and B? Explain your answer.
   (ii) Which document is more reliable as a source on Bismarck's Germany?
   (iii) Give one opinion from Document A, and one fact from Document B.

C. From your understanding of Bismarck's career,
   (i) Do you believe the reasons for the Kulturkampf given by Bismarck in Document A? Explain.
   (ii) Can you outline 'the political purposes' mentioned in Document B that Bismarck had in mind for ending the Kulturkampf?

ORDINARY LEVEL

2. What problems were caused by Bismarck's relations with the Catholic Church in Germany? (2013)

HIGHER LEVEL

3. What problems were posed by Church-State relations in Germany? (2011)

4. How did European states manage relations with the churches and/or religious minorities such as the Jews during the period, 1871–1914? (2015)

In this section, you should understand:
- The aims of Bismarck's foreign policy.
- How Bismarck's foreign policy was implemented.
- How successful Bismarck's foreign policy was.
- Wilhelm II's Weltpolitik.
- The naval policy of Wilhelm II.

Bismarck's Foreign Policy

The Balance of Power

The unification of Germany, and also Italy at the same time, changed the balance of power in Europe. Germany was now the most powerful country in Europe. France was angry, because it had been defeated in the Franco-Prussian War and the provinces of Alsace-Lorraine had been taken by Germany. Many French people wanted *revanche* (revenge for lost territory). Britain was more interested in its empire in Asia and Africa. It followed a policy of **splendid isolation** by not intervening on the Continent unless the balance of power was upset and there was a danger to Britain.

Bismarck's Aims in Foreign Policy

As far as Bismarck was concerned, Germany had no further territorial ambitions – *'when we have arrived in a good harbour, we should be content to cultivate and hold what we have won'*. Bismarck wanted to maintain Germany **united and supreme** in Europe – he believed that Germany would break up if it fought another war. Now his aim was to prevent any events in Europe from disrupting the country he had created. This would mean preventing a European War, especially a war between Austria-Hungary and Russia. In such a situation, Germany would be forced to take sides and the other country (Austria-Hungary or Russia) would look elsewhere for an ally (friend), very likely France. For this reason, Bismarck needed to **isolate France**, which wanted revenge for the loss of Alsace-Lorraine.

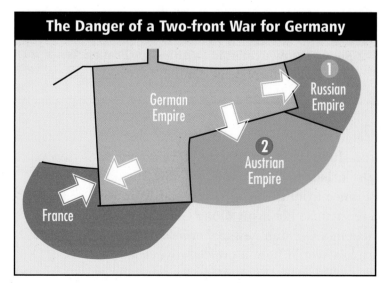

The Danger of a Two-front War for Germany

German Empire

① Russian Empire

② Austrian Empire

France

A diagrammatic representation showing the danger of a two-front war to Germany which Bismarck realised could happen if France got help from either (1) the Russian Empire or (2) the Austrian Empire.

QUESTIONS ❓

1. How did the balance of power in Europe change after the Franco-Prussian War?
2. What were Bismarck's aims in foreign policy?

Bismarck's Foreign Policy in Action

The First Dreikaiserbund (League of the Three Emperors), 1873

Bismarck was able to use the rise of nationalism and the danger posed by the new republic in France, as well as the events of the **Paris Commune**, to bring the three leading conservative monarchs in Europe together. The **First Dreikaiserbund** brought together the German Empire, Austro-Hungarian Empire and the Russian Empire. They were united against the disruptive forces of **nationalism** and **socialism** which endangered their power. They agreed to:

- Maintain existing borders in Europe.
- Fight socialism and republicanism (which was born in France).

The Three Emperors: Tsar Alexander III of Russia, Kaiser Wilhelm I of Germany and Emperor Franz Josef of Austria-Hungary.

The Three Emperors, or the Ventriloquist of Varzin; who is pulling the strings? What is the cartoon suggesting? Is the cartoon biased?

PUNCH, OR THE LONDON CHARIVARI—September 20, 1884.

THE THREE EMPERORS;
OR, THE VENTRILOQUIST OF VARZIN!

This was a **gentleman's agreement**, not an alliance (it did not commit them to go to war for each other). But Bismarck achieved his aims because France was isolated, and Austria-Hungary and Russia were tied to Germany.

Neither Austria-Hungary nor Russia was now available as allies for France. By creating this informal League, Bismarck hoped to prevent conflict between Austria-Hungary and Russia over Eastern Europe.

The 'War-in-Sight' Crisis, 1875

But Bismarck was not always successful in manipulating the foreign policy of Europe, as became clear in the '**war-in-sight**' crisis two years later. By now, Bismarck was angered by the quick recovery of France from the Franco-Prussian War. He was also concerned when France began to reorganise her army along German lines.

Prompted by Bismarck, an article in a German newspaper asked, '**Is war in sight?**' This gave the impression that Germany would fight a preventative war.

Instead of the French retreating again, they appealed to Britain and Russia for protection. Britain and Russia warned Bismarck about the dangers of war. Bismarck was forced to **retreat** – he said that the rumours about war were false. The crisis was over, but it ended in defeat for Germany. It also showed the dangers posed to Germany by a Russian intervention.

Difficulties in the Balkans – Bismarck as 'Honest Broker'

The First Dreikaiserbund came under pressure from conflict in the Balkans between Austria-Hungary and Russia. The Turkish Empire, which had controlled large parts of that area, was collapsing. There was a series of uprisings there in the 1870s against Turkish rule.

Both Russia and Austria-Hungary saw opportunities to extend their influence there. Russia wanted control of the **Dardanelles** (the sea route from the Black Sea to the Mediterranean Sea) to ensure a warm water port. Austria was also interested in the Balkans since some of the **nationalities** there were also part of the Austrian Empire. Russia declared war on Turkey in 1877 in support of national uprisings in Bulgaria and Serbia. It easily defeated Turkey and imposed the **Treaty of San Stefano** (1878) on the country; it reduced the size of European Turkey and created a Russian-dominated state in Bulgaria.

Austria-Hungary was angry about the Russian advance; it feared its interests in the Balkans were threatened. Britain was also concerned that Russian influence was extending into the Mediterranean.

Bismarck stepped in to keep the peace between Austria-Hungary and Russia: he held the **Congress of Berlin** (1878) which was attended by all the major powers in Europe. Here he tried to act as an 'honest broker' in the dispute between Austria and Russia. In the **Treaty of Berlin**, the Congress reversed the terms of the Treaty of San Stefano by splitting up Bulgaria and reducing Russian influence in the Balkans.

The Congress of Berlin, held in 1878, was attended by all major powers in Europe.

The Congress of Berlin emphasised Bismarck's status in Europe and confirmed Berlin as the centre of **European diplomacy**. Bismarck had also managed to preserve the peace. But Russia was now upset, and it felt it was opposed by 'a European coalition under the leadership of Prince Bismarck'. The Congress coincided with the imposition of protective tariffs in Germany against Russian wheat imports in 1879. Not surprisingly, the First Dreikaiserbund came to an end.

The Dual Alliance Between Germany and Austria-Hungary (1879)

Bismarck now felt it was time to strengthen the relationship between Germany and Austria-Hungary, a relationship that was popular in Germany at this time. Bismarck wrote, '*German kinship, historical memories, the German language, all that makes an alliance with Austria more popular in Germany than an alliance with Russia.*'

? **QUESTIONS**

1. What was the First Dreikaiserbund?
2. How did Bismarck deal with the 'war-in-sight' crisis?
3. Why was the Congress of Berlin held?
4. Was it successful?

In the **Dual Alliance** (1879), Germany and Austria-Hungary agreed to help each other if either was attacked by Russia. If one country was attacked by a country other than Russia, the other would remain neutral. This helped Bismarck to achieve his foreign policy aims, because:

- Germany was still supreme in Europe.
- War between Austria-Hungary and Russia was less likely.

However, Russia was not allied to anyone now, so there was a **danger** that it could become friendly with France. There was also another danger – that Austria-Hungary might feel it would get the backing of Germany in a war against Russia. So Austria-Hungary could get overconfident, advance into the Balkans and drag Germany into a war.

Very soon, the Dual Alliance became the **Triple Alliance** when Italy joined in 1882. Bismarck encouraged French colonisation in North Africa, which led to conflict between France and Italy. This gave Bismarck the chance of persuading Italy to join the Triple Alliance, which further increased French isolation.

The Second Dreikaiserbund (1881)

Russian fear of being isolated diplomatically encouraged the country to join again with Germany and Austria-Hungary. This also suited Bismarck who wanted to keep Russia away from France. In the **Second Dreikaiserbund**, each country would remain neutral if one of them was involved in a war with a fourth power. As well as this, Austria-Hungary and Russia reduced tensions in the Balkans by recognising each other's **sphere of influence**.

Bismarck had again achieved his aims, because France was isolated from Russia, and there was no danger France would attack Germany on its own. However, by the mid-1880s, the growth of Russian influence again in the Balkans threatened war between itself and Austria-Hungary. As Russian influence was once again reversed, Russia refused to renew the Second Dreikaiserbund (1887).

BISMARCK AND COLONIES

Bismarck was **opposed** to colonies for Germany. He saw them as expensive luxuries. He also did not want colonies to cause conflict between Germany, Britain and France. His interest was in making Germany the most powerful state in Europe, rather than being distracted by colonies, as he saw it.

'Colonies will become a cause of weakness of Germany, because the colonies could be defended only by a strong navy. But the geographical position of Germany is such that it does not need to be a first-class naval power. Many colonies have been offered to me but I have refused to accept them.'

However, in the early 1880s a rise of nationalist pride in Germany brought colonies to the forefront. The **German Colonial Association** was founded in 1882 and it promoted German acquisition of colonies. Some Germans saw colonies as a **symbol** of German power. Others promoted the idea of **new markets** and locations for German emigration. Some also grew **jealous** of the European powers acquiring vast areas of Africa, in particular.

Bismarck was **forced to change** his anti-colonial policy in 1884–85 because of the need for parliamentary support for his legislation. As a result, in 1884–85 Germany acquired colonies in South-West Africa, East Africa and islands in the Pacific Ocean. However, Bismarck favoured minimal German government involvement in these colonies and instead preferred to leave their exploitation to private companies (see also The Berlin Conference, p. 61).

But just as suddenly as Bismarck had become interested in colonies, he lost interest. By 1887, he was concerned that colonies put a strain on relations with Britain. Indeed, he offered to give away South-West Africa to Britain, but was refused.

Even though Bismarck's interest in colonies was minimal, in the space of a couple of years he had acquired the bulk of Germany's colonial territories. As he had feared, the later **policy of Wilhelm II** – *Weltpolitik* (world policy) – upset the balance of power in Europe and created the alliances that ultimately led to World War I.

This cartoon from 1884 shows Bismarck happy in Europe with social reform as other countries are busy 'down there'.

The Reinsurance Treaty (1887)

Instead, the **Reinsurance Treaty** (1887) was agreed between Germany and Russia. This was Bismarck's way of ensuring that Russia would not move any closer to France. He achieved this by getting agreement with Russia that each country would stay neutral in war unless Russia attacked Austria-Hungary or Germany attacked France.

Since Russia would not attack Austria-Hungary backed up by Germany, Bismarck prevented war between Austria-Hungary and Russia. He also kept France isolated because Germany had no intention of attacking France. By the Reinsurance Treaty, Bismarck kept **Germany supreme** in Europe.

Which did Bismarck manage better, German internal or external affairs? Argue your case, referring to both.
- [Intro: Brief background on unification of Germany]
- German Constitution
- Kulturkampf
- Attack of the Socialists
- German industrialisation
- First Dreikaiserbund
- War-in-Sight
- Honest Broker – Congress of Berlin
- Dual Alliance
- Second Dreikaiserbund and Reinsurance Treaty
- Berlin Conference – Colonies
- Conclusion – which did he manage better?

QUESTIONS

1. What was the Second Dreikaiserbund?
2. Why did Bismarck agree the Reinsurance Treaty with Russia?
3. Did Bismarck achieve his aims in foreign policy?

The Downfall of Bismarck

In 1888, Wilhelm I died, and was succeeded as Kaiser by his grandson, **Wilhelm II**. Wilhelm was headstrong and a firm believer in the divine right of kings, and in his own power. It was inevitable he would clash with Bismarck, who up to this had held great power in Germany.

Wilhelm disagreed with Bismarck's foreign policy and with his approach to the socialists. They clashed over the renewal of the anti-socialist laws, and Bismarck was forced to resign in March 1890. One historian wrote, *'Bismarck left his successors a troubled system, designed by and for one man, over which even he had lost full control.'* (Blackbourn)

Overall Assessment of Bismarck's Foreign Policy

Bismarck achieved his aims in his handling of foreign policy from 1871 to his fall from power in 1890:

- He kept Germany supreme in Europe.
- He prevented war, particularly between Austria-Hungary and Russia.
- He isolated France.

But the policy was very much his own policy and it was not clearly understood by those who followed him, particularly **Wilhelm II**, who did not realise how the balance of power operated in Europe at that time. One of Wilhelm's first actions, for example, was to allow the **Reinsurance Treaty** with Russia to lapse in 1890, even though Russia wished to continue with it. Wilhelm naively assumed that ideological differences and lack of common interest would keep **republican France** and **tsarist or autocratic Russia** apart. However the failure to renew the Reinsurance Treaty set the groundwork for a later **Franco-Russian alliance** – the **Dual Alliance** of 1894, which Bismarck had worked constantly to prevent.

HOMEWORK EXERCISES

Draw a table in your notes with a heading **Bismarck's Foreign Policy**.

Insert bullet-pointed notes under the following headings, giving a row to each agreement.

Bismarck's Foreign Policy			
Treaties/ agreements	**Countries involved**	**Overall terms**	**Success or failure?**

1. Study the documents and answer the questions below.

DOCUMENT A

The Chancellor (Bismarck) refuses all talk of colonies. He says we haven't an adequate fleet to protect them, and our bureaucracy is not skillful enough to direct the government of such territories. The Chancellor also alluded to my report on the French plans for Morocco, and he thought we could only rejoice if France annexed it. She would then be very occupied, and we could let her expand in Africa as compensation for the loss of Alsace-Lorraine.

> An extract from the Memoirs of Prince von Hohenlohe, at different times Foreign Secretary and later Chancellor of Germany (1907)

DOCUMENT B

The colonial question may bedevil (upset) our relations with England for a considerable period … It is precisely the liberals and democrats who want colonies. I am far from supposing that this is the reason why the Chancellor has suddenly made the colonial question a part of his political programme. But if the need arises, he will use it as a means of combating foreign influences. …The Chancellor is right to pursue a colonial policy. Had he not embarked upon it, it would have remained a slogan for the opposition.

> Diary of F. von Holstein, senior official in the German Foreign Office, 1884

DOCUMENT C

There were now no points of difference between England and Germany. He had never favoured the colonial idea himself, but opinion in Germany ran so strongly in favour of colonial enterprise (business, projects) that he could not refrain (abstain) from turning the colonial stream into the main channel of his parliamentary policy.

> Official of the British Foreign Office, notes of conversation with Bismarck, 1885

A. (i) According to Document A, why was Bismarck opposed to colonies?
   (ii) Who wanted colonies, according to Document A?
   (iii) According to Document A, why was Bismarck happy that France was involved in Morocco?
   (iv) Why is the author of Document B concerned about colonial policy?
   (v) Why does he favour Bismarck's involvement in colonies?
   (vi) According to Document C, why did Bismarck pursue a colonial policy?

B. (i) Are these documents **primary** or **secondary** sources? Explain.
   (ii) Which document would you consider the **most reliable**? Explain.
   (iii) Are each of the documents **useful** for understanding Bismarck's policy towards the colonies? Explain.

C. (i) From your knowledge of the course, how accurate a prediction did Document B make about relations between England and Germany?
   (ii) From your knowledge of the course, why did 'opinion in Germany' run 'so strongly in favour of colonial enterprise'? (see Ch. 8, New Imperialism)

   (iii) Summarise Bismarck's policy on colonies in bullet-point notes.

ORDINARY LEVEL

2. Write a short **paragraph** on one of the following:
   (i) Bismarck and the Dreikaiserbund
   (ii) The Downfall of Bismarck
   (iii) Bismarck's dealings with Russia

3. Write a **long answer** on one of the following:
   (i) How did Bismarck keep France isolated from other countries?
   (ii) How successful was Bismarck in maintaining good relations between Austria-Hungary and Russia?

4. How did Bismarck conduct German foreign policy between 1871 and 1890? (2017)

HIGHER LEVEL

5. How successful was Otto von Bismarck as Chancellor of Germany?

6. How successful was Bismarck's foreign policy?

Wilhelm II and Weltpolitik

Wilhelm II, The Kaiser took a close interest in foreign affairs. He promoted a policy of *Weltpolitik* (making Germany a **world power**). This was in contrast to the more European-centred policy of Bismarck.

This change in policy partly reflected Wilhelm II's restless personality. He was not content to confine German ambitions to Europe. Instead, he wanted to increase Germany's (and his own) status. He also wanted Germany to gain from large markets in colonies. In this he was encouraged by pressure groups such as the **Pan-German League** and the **Colonial Society** who supported this policy. Industrialists feared that the German economy would run out of resources and markets. *'Our vigorous national development, mainly in the industrial sphere, forced us to cross the ocean.'* A further reason was the desire to unite the country behind the new policy and to cover over the internal divisions in the country. As one historian said, *'Weltpolitik came into existence as a red herring of the ruling classes to distract the middle and working classes from social and political problems at home.'*

Wilhelm and colonies: Wilhelm II also wanted to gain colonies to satisfy national pride: he wanted 'a place in the sun'. In 1891, Germany under Wilhelm gained Chinese Kiaochow. Later he bought the Marianas and Caroline Islands in the Pacific, and he acquired part of the Samoa Islands. These gains showed that the German navy wanted to create a **worldwide network** of bases and coaling stations.

Increasing Tensions

Next, Wilhelm intervened in South Africa; he praised the Boers for their resistance to the Jameson Raid in the **Kruger Telegram**. He also supported the Boers in their war with the British. These increased tensions with **Britain** (see pp. 63–64).

Wilhelm also increased **French and German rivalry**. In the **First Moroccan crisis** (1905), Wilhelm visited Tangier and promised support for Morocco against France. He demanded an international conference to discuss the position of Morocco. At the conference at **Algeciras** (1906), Britain sided with France, and Germany lost influence.

In the **Second Moroccan crisis** (1911) Germany sent the gunboat *Panther* to Agadir to protect Germans living there. He then demanded the French Congo in return for recognising French control of Morocco. Wilhelm had to back down when Britain supported France (see p. 64).

Wilhelm's policy of *Weltpolitik* began the process of moving France and Britain closer together as they feared the aggressive nature of that policy.

> *'The chief real criticism to be made of the Kaiser is that, instead of seeing this danger and using his influence to restrain German appetites, he shared those appetites and indeed increased them, particularly by his determination to give Germany a navy of which it could be proud and by his frequently tactless and aggressive public statements.'*
>
> *www.britannica.com*

The policy of *Weltpolitik* resulted in:

1. The growth of the German Navy.
2. The acquisition of colonies.
3. Conflict or tension with Britain.
4. A contribution to the causes of the First World War.

ANGLO-GERMAN TENSIONS, 1871–1914

In the second half of the 19th century, Britain was mainly concerned with its empire, which was spread across the globe. It followed a policy of '**splendid isolation**' in relation to European affairs: it would intervene on the continent of Europe only if one country became too powerful. But Britain was satisfied with the balance of power in Europe under Bismarck's control so it rarely intervened there. This all changed when Wilhelm II came to power in 1890. **Disraeli**, British Prime Minister, co-operated with Bismarck at the **Congress of Berlin** (1878), called to sort out problems in the Balkans. Both men pressurised Russia to agree to the Congress and to limit its gains in the Balkans (see p. 11).

Britain and Germany also co-operated at the **Berlin Conference** (1884–5) and agreed on **spheres of influence** in the 'scramble for Africa'. Bismarck wanted to ensure that colonies would not lead him into conflict with Britain (see Berlin Conference, p. 61).

But Britain and Germany came into conflict when Wilhelm II became Kaiser in 1890, (see p. 16, pp. 20–26, pp. 63–64). The issues which caused tensions between them were:

● Wilhelm's *Weltpolitik*.

● His naval policy.

● His interference in the Boer War.

As Britain realised that it needed **allies** in Europe because of increased tension with Germany, the policy of 'splendid isolation' came to an end. Britain made an alliance with Japan (1902) to protect it against Russia in Asia.

Britain was rejected by Germany when it sought agreement in 1899–1900. Britain signed the **Entente Cordiale** with France, then signed a **naval agreement** with them.

Britain and France were brought closer together by the two **Moroccan crises**, and driven further away from Germany (see Moroccan Crises, p. 64).

In 1907, Britain and France created the **Triple Alliance** with Russia. Britain entered the First World War to protect Belgium against Germany (see Causes of the First World War p. 72).

QUESTIONS ?

1. What was Wilhelm's policy of Weltpolitik?
2. Why did he want more colonies?
3. How did he increase tensions with France and Britain?

Develop your own notes on Anglo-German tensions, 1871–1914 using the guidelines here.

This is an extract from notes of a conversation with Bismarck, written by a British diplomat in 1885. Study it and answer the questions that follow.

> He (Bismarck) said that Mr Gladstone might become Prime Minister again, a man with whom it was impossible to do business.
>
> But the policy Bismarck had followed on colonial matters in Africa was not inspired by any feeling of hostility towards England. He had sided with France on colonial matters in Africa in order to reduce the hatred of France towards Germany.
>
> However, this policy did not have the desired effect because France was as hostile as ever towards Germany. In fact France was ready to seize any opportunity of attacking Germany in order to regain Alsace-Lorraine.
>
> P. H. Currie, a member of the British Foreign Office, on 28 September 1885.

1. What was Bismarck's opinion of the British leader, Mr Gladstone?

2. Why had Bismarck sided with France on colonial matters in Africa?

3. Did Bismarck's support for France produce the desired effect on France? Explain your answer.

4. Why was France 'ready to seize any opportunity' of attacking Germany?

5. How does the above extract help you understand the relationship between Germany and France at the end of the 19th century? (2008)

EXAM QUESTION

What was the naval policy of Kaiser Wilhelm II, and how did it affect relations with Britain? (2007)

KEY PERSONALITY: WILHELM II

Wilhelm II became Kaiser of Germany in 1888. He immediately came into conflict with his chancellor, Bismarck, over Bismarck's attack on the socialists and Bismarck's foreign policy. Bismarck was forced to resign (see p. 14).

Social reform under Wilhelm II: Wilhelm wanted to undermine workers' support for socialism by improving working conditions (see p. 31). **Wilhelm II and Weltpolitik:** Wilhelm II took a close interest in foreign affairs. He promoted a policy of Weltpolitik (making Germany a world power) (see p. 16). **Wilhelm and the German Navy:** Wilhelm II wanted to expand the German Navy as part of his Weltpolitik (world policy). (See Case Study: The Naval Policy of Wilhelm II, pp. 20–26.)

Wilhelm was supported in his views by Admiral von Tirpitz, who was appointed secretary for the navy. Wilhelm's policy of expanding the German Navy upset the British. As a result of Wilhelm's naval policy, two armed camps faced each other – the Triple Alliance and the Triple Entente (see p. 72). **Wilhelm and colonies:** Germany wanted to gain colonies to satisfy national pride; the Kaiser wanted 'a place in the sun'. His actions here increased tensions with Britain and France (see p. 16, pp. 63–64) **Wilhelm and the First World War:** When Franz Ferdinand, heir to the Austrian throne, was assassinated by Serbian nationalists, Austria was backed up by Germany in the form of a 'blank cheque' from Wilhelm. This led Austria to declare war on Serbia and it later led to German mobilisation for war.

Utterly convinced of his right to rule, Wilhelm always overestimated his capacity for wise political judgment. His dismissal of Chancellor Bismarck in 1890 and ambitious aim to make Germany a world power disrupted the established balance of the European order.
http://www.iwm.org.uk

Develop your own notes on Wilhelm II using the guidelines here.

During the First World War, Germany suffered a great deal from the British blockade of its ports. By 1918, people were angry with Kaiser Wilhelm II because he refused to make peace. Sailors in the German Navy mutinied at Kiel. The mutiny spread to other parts of Germany. Wilhelm abdicated (gave up the throne) on 9 November 1918 and went into exile in the Netherlands.

Differences between Bismarck's Foreign Policy and Wilhelm II's Foreign Policy	
Bismarck's *Realpolitik*	**Wilhelm's *Weltpolitik***
Germany as a European power	Germany as a world power
Avoid a two-front war	Not concerned about a two-front war
Maintain friendly relations with Austria and Russia	Not interested in maintaining good relations with Russia
Keep France isolated	Not concerned about French isolation
Not interested in developing a strong navy	Expand the German navy to compete with the British navy
Maintain good relations with Britain	Saw Britain as main competitor for world power

HOMEWORK EXERCISES

ORDINARY LEVEL

1. This is an edited extract from an interview which Wilhelm II gave to the Daily Telegraph, in 1908, while on a visit to England. Read it and answer the questions which follow.

    You English are mad, mad, mad.

    I have declared that my heart is set on peace. But your press bids the people of England to refuse my friendship.

    Germany has a worldwide commerce (trade) which is rapidly expanding. Germany must have a powerful fleet, to protect that commerce, in even the most distant seas.

    A. How does Wilhelm II insult the English?
    B. Why does Wilhelm II criticise English newspapers?
    C. What claims are made for Germany's commerce?
    D. According to Wilhelm II, why does Germany need a powerful fleet?
    E. What action did Britain take in response to the naval policy of Wilhelm II? (2011)
    F. Write a **short paragraph** on **one** of the following.
        (i)   The naval policy of Wilhelm II.
        (ii)   Bismarck's foreign policy
        (iii) Wilhelm II's policy of *Weltpolitik*

2. Write a **long answer** on **one** of the following.
    A. What was the naval policy of Wilhelm II and how did it affect relations with Britain? (2007)
    B. What was the naval policy of Wilhelm II and how did it affect one or more countries? (2012)
    C. What was Wilhelm II's naval policy and why did it alarm the British government? (2017)

HIGHER LEVEL

3. In what ways did the naval policy of Wilhelm II and/or Franco-German tensions contribute to the outbreak of World War I? (2007)

4. Who was more effective in handling German affairs, Bismarck or Wilhelm II? Argue your case, referring to both. (2009)

5. What impact did German foreign policy have on the changing balance of power in Europe, 1871–1914? (2010)

6. How did Wilhelm's policy of Weltpolitik affect international relations? (2012)

7. How did German foreign policy develop under Bismarck and Wilhelm II? (2014)

8. During the period, 1871–1914, would you agree that Wilhelm II's foreign policy was more provocative than Bismarck's? Argue your case, referring to both in your answer. (2016)

The Naval Policy of Wilhelm II

Wilhelm II wanted to expand the German Navy as part of his *Weltpolitik* (world policy). Wilhelm believed that command of the sea would increase the power of Germany. He was influenced by the ideas in Admiral Mahan's book *The Influence of Sea Power upon History* (1890), which argued that a country's greatness depended on its command of the seas in war, and its successful use for trade in peacetime.

SOURCE 1 – WILHELM 'S ROLE IN THE EXPANSION OF THE GERMAN NAVY

Wilhelm's vital role in the formation of a powerful German Navy cannot be overstated. The Kaiser harboured a personal fascination for navies originating with his childhood when he used to look upon the British Royal Navy fleet with awe and reverence. His own personal passion for navies 'was the customary blend of absurdity and energetic enthusiasm' often exhibited for example by Wilhelm's donning of an admiral's uniform in public, his obsession with learning the technical details of British Royal Navy ships, and his repeated readings of Alfred Thayer Mahan's influential maritime study *The Influence of Sea Power upon History*. Thus as Germany rose in power it was no accident that Wilhelm decided the country needed a strong navy. Furthermore, this navy was to be the instrument, or perhaps more correctly, the enforcer of Wilhelmine *Weltpolitik*.

Chris Petersen, *'A Place in the Sun': The Effect of Great Power Psychology on German Weltpolitik in the Wilhelmine Era*, http://christopher-petersen. blogspot.ie/2012/04/my-research-paper.html

> List Wilhelm's reasons for expanding the German navy, according to this source.
>
> What is meant by the phrase the navy would be 'the enforcer of Wilhelmine Weltpolitik'?

SOURCE 2 – A SPEECH BY KAISER WILHELM II OF GERMANY TO THE NORTH GERMAN REGATTA ASSOCIATION, 1901

In spite of the fact that we have no such fleet as we should have, we have conquered for ourselves a place in the sun. It will now be my task to see to it that this place in the sun shall remain our undisputed possession, in order that the sun's rays may fall fruitfully upon our activity and trade in foreign parts, that our industry and agriculture may develop within the state and our sailing sports upon the water, for our future lies upon the water. The more Germans go out upon the waters, whether it be in races or regattas, whether it be in journeys across the ocean, or in the service of the battle flag, so much the better it will be for us.

For when the German has once learned to direct his glance upon what is distant and great, the pettiness which surrounds him in daily life on all sides will disappear.

Quoted in C. Gauss, *The German Kaiser as Shown in His Public Utterances* (New York: Charles Scribner's Sons, 1915)

> What does Wilhelm II see as 'my task'? How will Germans benefit from Wilhelm's policy, according to himself?

The Role of von Tirpitz

Wilhelm was supported in his views by **Admiral von Tirpitz**, who was appointed secretary for the navy in 1897. Tirpitz believed that Germany should undertake a world policy *'because in the new great national undertaking and the economic boom associated with it lies a strong calming influence against educated and uneducated social democrats.'*

Von Tirpitz persuaded the Reichstag and the German people to support the expansion of the navy, using **propaganda** to convince people of its importance. He distributed copies of Mahan's book as part of his political campaign for the passage of the Reichstag Navy Laws.

He said the German Navy should be large enough to deter the enemy from attacking because of fear of the damage it would do. This was his '**Risk Theory**'. As the German Navy got bigger, Von Tirpitz believed that Britain would try to avoid war with Germany or at least make agreements which favoured Germany.

Von Tirpitz was also aware of what his policy of expanding the navy would involve. In a memo in 1897 to Wilhelm II he said, *'For Germany, the most dangerous enemy at the present time is England. It is also the enemy against which we most urgently require a certain measure of naval force as a political power factor.'*

? CASE STUDY QUESTION

What book influenced Wilhelm II's naval policy? How did Admiral von Tirpitz help Wilhelm? What was von Tirpitz's 'Risk Theory'?

Pressure Groups

Pressure groups such as the **Pan-German League** and **German Navy League** (or German Naval Association) also wanted to expand the German Navy. The Pan-German League founded in 1891 was calling for 'world power status' for Germany in 1894. It favoured an aggressive foreign policy and it opposed what it regarded as anti-national movements. The German Navy League was founded in 1898 and it was partly funded by the German government. By 1900, it had over 270,000 members and this was increased to over 1 million by 1908. It reflected the interests of heavy industry, shipyards, trade and commerce. One of its most prominent members was **Alfred Krupp**. It mobilised public opinion in favour of expanding the German navy.

Timeline of German Naval Expansion, 1897–1914

- 1891 Pan-German League founded
- 1897 Admiral von Tirpitz appointed Secretary of State for the Navy by William II

  Planned strength of the German Navy
  - 19 battleships
  - 12 large cruisers
  - 30 light cruisers
- 1898 First Naval Law
  German Navy League founded
- 1900 Second Naval Law

  - 38 battleships
  - 14 large cruisers
  - 38 light cruisers
  - 96 torpedo boats
- 1904 Anglo-French Entente Cordiale
- 1906 Third Naval Law
  British Dreadnought launched
  Germany planned Dreadnoughts
- 1907 Anglo-French-Russian Triple Entente
- 1908 Germany speeding up dreadnought construction

  - 41 battleships
  - 18 large cruisers
  - 144 light cruisers
  - 72 submarines
- 1912 Further speeding up of German dreadnought construction
- 1914 First World War

The Navy Laws

In line with Wilhelm's policy of *Weltpolitik*, the Reichstag passed a series of Navy Laws for the building of battleships, cruisers and other boats.

- In 1898, the **First Navy Law** planned a force of 19 battleships, 12 heavy cruisers and 30 light cruisers to be built by 1904.
- In 1900, the **Second Navy Law** planned doubling the navy to 38 battleships, 20 armoured cruisers and 38 light cruisers.

At the conclusion of the programme, the strength of the German Navy would be 2:3 in comparison to the British Navy. This had serious implications for Britain. These laws were added to by later laws in 1906, 1908 and 1912.

? CASE STUDY QUESTION

What was the First and Second Navy Law?

British Reaction

The German naval expansion upset the British. In 1909, Sir Edward Grey, the British Foreign Secretary, explained: *'There is no comparison between the importance of the German Navy to Germany, and the importance of our navy to us. Our navy is to us what their army is to them. To have a strong navy would increase Germany's prestige and influence, but it is not a matter of life and death to them as it is to us'*. The new German policy led to a direct clash with Britain in spite of the fact that Britain was the one country that Germany had no disagreement with over European issues. British naval policy followed the **'two-power standard'**, that is, its navy should be larger than the combined size of the next two largest navies. In was clear by the **Second Navy Law** (1900) that the 'two-power standard' was in danger from Wilhelm's naval policy.

WHAT INFORMATION CA YOU GET FROM THE SOURCE?

 WHAT CAN YOU TELL ABOUT THE SOURCES?

| Analysing Documents Posters | Is this a **primary** or a **secondary** source? | Is this a **reliable** source? | Is this a **useful** source? | Is this source **biased** or **objective**? | How **persuasive** is this source? | What **features** of this source impress you? | What **features** of this source do not impress you? |

What heavy cruiser is featured in this poster?

What merchant ship is featured in this poster?

What information is provided in the poster concerning careers in the Imperial Navy?

Apart from the poster, how does the German Naval Association advertise information about careers in the navy and merchant navy?

How would this poster promote Wilhelm II's naval policy?

Explain your answer in each case.

A poster from Deutscher Flotten-Verein [German Navy League/German Naval Association] from 1913 advertising careers in the Navy and Merchant Navy

Translation of Text: German Naval Association.

H.M. light cruiser 'Breslau.' Steam trawler. Training ship of the German Training Ship Association. Trawler. H.M. heavy cruiser 'Gneisenau.' 'Hapag' steamship at the Rotesand lighthouse. Compass. Full-rigged sailing ship. Barque. Anchor. H.M. ship of the line 'Kaiserin.' Ship's propeller. Brig. Schooner. Buoy. North German Lloyd's steamship at the quay in Bremerhaven. Large torpedo boat. Torpedo. Torpedo tube. Submarine. The gun used aboard ships of the line.

Careers in the Navy and Merchant Navy

A. Navy [details of the different jobs available in the navy follow]. B. Merchant Navy [details of the different jobs available in the merchant navy follow]. Information about all careers including desk careers, the conditions of admission, the nature, duration and cost of preliminary training, and about the posts, pay and allowances is given in the books 'Guide to Careers in the Imperial Navy' (price 50 pfennigs) and 'Guide to Careers in the Merchant Navy' (price 30 pfennigs), published by the German Naval Association. Both publications can be found in school libraries, or can be obtained from the office of the President of the German Naval Association [address]. In addition the annually published calendar of the German Naval Association contains a shortened guide to careers in the Navy and Merchant Navy; it can be obtained from the office of the President of the German Naval Association [address] in return for sending in 50 pfennigs.]

Source: http://www.iwm.org.uk/collections/item/object/28999

British Alliances

The British policy of 'splendid isolation' was now abandoned.

- In 1902, in the **Anglo-Japanese Alliance**, Britain and Japan committed themselves to protect each other's interests in China and Korea, and to stay neutral in a war involving another power.
- In 1904, Britain joined with France in the **Entente Cordiale**. Even though this was mainly an agreement over colonies, it brought Britain and France closer together.
- In 1907, in the **Anglo-Russian Convention**, Britain and Russia agreed to settle a series of disputes in central Asia.

Britain was now involved in the **Triple Entente**, which was opposed in Europe by the **Triple Alliance** of Germany, Austria-Hungary and Italy. Europe was now divided into two armed camps, largely due to the influence of Wilhelm's expansionary policy.

CASE STUDY QUESTIONS

1. What was Britain's 'two-power standard'?
2. How did Wilhelm's naval policy endanger Britain's 'two-power standard'?
3. How did Britain end its policy of 'splendid isolation'?

Dreadnoughts and the Naval Race

Britain also began the expansion of its own navy by building '**dreadnoughts**' – ships that were larger and faster than all other ships. In 1906, Britain launched *Dreadnought*, the first of these new battleships. It made all previous battleships obsolete because of its advantages of speed, fire-power and protection (Sources 3 and 4).

SOURCE 3 – ADVANTAGES OF THE DREADNOUGHTS

Fast steam-turbine engines

Thick armour plating

Guns on rotating turrets can fire shells over 9 km

Heavy calibre guns

How did the advantages of the new dreadnoughts make all previous battleships obsolete (out of date)?

SOURCE 4 – THE NAVAL RACE BETWEEN BRITAIN AND GERMANY

For centuries a central tenet (principle) of British foreign policy had been the preservation of British Royal Naval supremacy in the seas based first of course on security for the homeland because of its geographical handicap as an island nation and second as an instrument of protection for its widely flung colonies. Therefore, any perceived attempt to change or challenge British naval supremacy would immediately be construed as a threat by Great Britain. And so not surprisingly Great Britain began to interpret German naval development in such a fashion. This resulted in a naval arms race between the two powers with the result that by 1912 England came out just slightly ahead in the number of its Dreadnought class battle ships versus similar German versions. This naval arms race between England and Germany did more to create hostility between the two powers than did any other factor before the First World War.

Chris Petersen, *'A Place in the Sun': The Effect of Great Power Psychology on German Weltpolitik in the Wilhelmine Era*

http://christopher-petersen.blogspot.ie/2012/04/my-research-paper.html

> Why did Britain depend on naval supremacy? Why did Britain see German naval expansion as a threat?

Germany responded by building its own dreadnoughts. This began a **naval race**. Since dreadnoughts made all previous battleships out of date, Britain's 'two-power standard' was in even greater danger now because what mattered was the number of dreadnoughts.

Increasing Tensions

A number of incidents led to increased tensions between Germany and Britain. First, Germany rejected a British proposal for naval disarmament. This put an end to the hope of improving relations with Britain. Then Wilhelm gave an interview to the *Daily Telegraph* in 1908 which justified why Germany wanted a large navy (Source 5).

Further, Britain faced a '**naval scare**' in 1909 which increased pressure on the government to build more dreadnoughts. New information led the British Admiralty to believe that the Germans were secretly building dreadnoughts at a faster rate than their published naval laws suggested they would. The increased German numbers would not only break Britain's 'two-power standard', but might even put Germany ahead of Britain. This led to a public outcry in Britain with people demanding more dreadnoughts be built: 'We want eight and we won't wait.' This intensified the naval race and heightened tensions between Germany and Britain (Source 6).

War Plans

These increasing tensions and other important factors, such as the **Moroccan Crises**, brought Britain and France closer together. By 1912, both countries agreed that the British Navy would defend the Atlantic and North Sea coasts, while the French Navy would defend the Mediterranean.

 CASE STUDY QUESTION

What was the 'naval scare' of 1909? How were Britain and France drawn closer together?

The Impact of Wilhelm's Naval Policy

- As a result of Wilhelm's *Weltpolitik* and his naval policy, **two armed camps** faced each other in Europe – the Triple Alliance and the Triple Entente.
- As part of the Triple Entente, Britain and France went further and began to co-operate on **war plans**, both naval and land.
- Germany built up **huge debts** in creating its navy. By 1914, the expansion of the Russian army forced Germany to invest in its army, and slow down the building of

dreadnoughts. By the beginning of the war, British dreadnoughts outnumbered Germany's by 29 to 17 so they could retain naval supremacy.

- In spite of the large navies which had been created by 1914, there was only one very serious sea battle in the First World War, the **Battle of Jutland** in 1916. Even though the German fleet did more damage than the British one, the German Navy stayed in port for the rest of the war. A mutiny in the German navy in Kiel in 1918 contributed significantly to Germany's surrender in November 1918 (see p. 111).

> **? CASE STUDY QUESTION**
>
> How did Wilhelm's naval policy contribute to the formation of alliances in Europe?

SOURCE 5 – WILHELM II'S INTERVIEW WITH THE DAILY TELEGRAPH, 1908

… You English, are mad, mad, mad as March hares. What has come over you that you are so completely given over to suspicions quite unworthy of a great nation? … But, you will say, what of the German Navy? Surely, that is a menace to England! Against whom but England are my squadrons being prepared? If England is not in the minds of those Germans who are bent on creating a powerful fleet, why is Germany asked to consent to such new and heavy burdens of taxation? My answer is clear. Germany is a young and growing empire. She has a worldwide commerce which is rapidly expanding, and to which the legitimate ambition of patriotic Germans refuses to assign any bounds. Germany must have a powerful fleet to protect that commerce and her manifold interests in even the most distant seas. She expects those interests to go on growing, and she must be able to champion them manfully in any quarter of the globe. Her horizons stretch far away.

Source: The interview of the Emperor Wilhelm II, (London) *Daily Telegraph*, 28 October 1908.

> How does Wilhelm II justify the creation of a larger German Navy? What do you think British reaction to the interview would be?

> Is this cartoon propaganda? What is the message of the cartoon? Based on your knowledge of Wilhelm's foreign and naval policies, how would a German of the time view this cartoon?

L'INGORDO TROP DUR

French postcard from WW1 showing Kaiser Wilhelm II biting into the world. The text reads 'The glutton (over eater) – too hard.'

SOURCE 6 – THE NAVAL RACE – THE NUMBER OF DREADNOUGHTS BUILT BY BRITAIN AND GERMANY, 1906–14

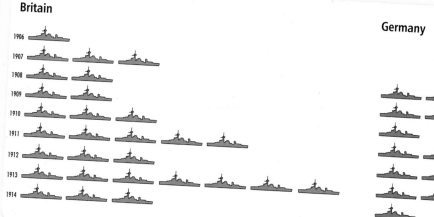

Britain

Germany

1906
1907
1908
1909
1910
1911
1912
1913
1914

> How many dreadnoughts had each country built by 1914? What was the danger to Britain of Germany building dreadnoughts?

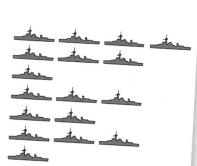

SOURCE 7 – VON TIRPITZ'S INFLUENCE

For all his great abilities, one is tempted to describe Tirpitz as the evil genius of German foreign relations from 1898 onwards …. His naval plans succeeded in putting an end to any remaining hopes the German government might have about winning an alliance with Great Britain.

Source: G. Craig, Germany, 1866–1945

SOURCE 9 – HISTORIANS' VIEWS ON GERMAN NAVAL POLICY

Germany's blundering attempts to exert influence on the world stage merely strengthened the forces of opposition to German ambitions in Europe. Britain responded to the direct German challenge in two ways: firstly by increasing the size of its own navy and introducing the revolutionary new battleship, the Dreadnought; and secondly by making agreements with other powers.

Source: C. Culpin and R. Henig, Modern Europe, 1870–1945

SOURCE 8 – THE GERMAN PEOPLE BEHIND A POLICY OF A STRONG NAVY

In the centre of Wilhelm's political plans stood the construction of a great fleet. This, it seemed, was the only way of catching up with Britain as a world power and getting recognised by the other world powers as an equal. The fleet, combined with economic power, was to furnish the basis to support Germany's claim for a revision of the colonial status quo … When the Sino-Japanese War of 1895, the Spanish-American of 1898 and the Boer War of 1899–1902 seemed to prove beyond all question the importance of sea-power as a *sine qua no*n (an essential condition) of world power, the goal of the creation of a strong navy as the expression of Germany's claims was adopted by industry and popularised by new forms of mass propaganda until it became axiomatic (obvious) for the whole German people.

Source: Franz Fischer, Germany's aims in the First World War

 CASE STUDY QUESTIONS

1. Do the historians in Sources 7, 8 and 9 support the conclusions of The Impact of Wilhelm's Naval Policy (p. 24)?
2. Do all sources agree on who bore greatest responsibility for the naval policy?
3. What is your view on the overall impact of Wilhelm's naval policy?

DOCUMENTS-BASED QUESTION

1. Study the document and answer the questions below.

A. In this edited extract the *Daily Mail* newspaper comments (5 February 1903) on what it sees as a growing threat from Germany. Read it and answer the questions below.

   While great naval power in the hands of Britain cannot be a menace, in the hands of Germany it will be a great peril to the world.

   The recent history of Germany is one of daring aggression.

   The lack of space at home forces Germany to conquer the colonies of others, or perish.

   (i) What claim is made for British naval power?
   (ii) What claim is made for German naval power?
   (iii) From the extract, what was a feature of the recent history of Germany?
   (iv) According to the extract, why must Germany conquer the colonies of others or perish?
   (v) What was the Dreadnought?
   (vi) Is this extract a primary or a secondary source? Explain your answer.
   (vii) Is this source reliable? Explain your answer.
   (viii) Is this source useful? Explain your answer.

B. Write a short **paragraph** on **one** of the following:
   (i) Wilhelm II's *Weltpolitik*
   (ii) The German Navy Laws
   (iii) British reaction to the naval policy of Wilhelm II

C. Write a **long answer** on one of the following:
   (i) How did naval race develop between Germany and Britain, and what were its consequences?
   (ii) What was the naval policy of Kaiser Wilhelm II, and how did it affect relations with Britain during the period, 1890–1914?
   (iii) How successful was Wilhelm's foreign policy (including his naval policy)?

HIGHER LEVEL

2. How did German foreign policy develop under Wilhelm II? (2014)
3. During the period 1871–1914, how did the naval policy of Wilhelm II contribute to international tensions? (2015)
4. To what extent did Wilhelm II's foreign policy contribute to the causes of World War I?

In this section, you should understand:
- Why and how Germany was industrialised at the end of 19th century.
- The impact of German industrialisation.

Why Did the German Economy Grow so Rapidly?

The German economy expanded rapidly after the country was united in 1871. By 1914 Germany had the largest economy in Europe.

Economic Comparisons between Germany, Britain and France in 1870 and 1890						
Millions/million tons	Germany		Britain		France	
Population	41	50	32	38	36	38
Coal	38	89	118	184	13	26
Iron	2.9	8	14.0	14.0	2.6	3.5
Steel	0.3	2.2	0.6	3.6	0.08	0.6

Between 1870 and 1890, Germany closed the gap rapidly between Britain and itself in coal, iron and steel production. France was falling further behind.

Population growth: German unification created a market of 41 million people in 1871. The population continued to grow so that by 1890 it had increased to 50 million. By 1910, the population had risen to 65 million. This growth provided more workers and a larger market, which encouraged large-scale investments in new companies and inventions.

Bismarck helped to create a **unified market** – he ensured the passage of laws which made trade easier – a new currency, and a national code for trade and commerce.

Raw materials: Germany was rich in raw materials such as coal, iron ore and potash; the Ruhr had rich coalfields while iron ore was mined from the captured provinces of Alsace-Lorraine. Coal production was well behind Britain in 1871 but it had closed the gap by 1890 (see box) and by 1914 Germany had almost caught up, 279 million tons to 292 million tons. The invention of the **Thomas-Gilchrist steel-making process** (1878) enabled Germany to use its low-grade iron ore. Large deposits of **potash** made Germany the world's main producer in the 19th century and it became the basis of the fertiliser industry.

Germany was able to benefit from the industries of the **First Industrial Revolution** – coal, iron and steel – and also from the **Second Industrial Revolution** of the late 19th century with newer industries such as chemicals and electricity.

Tariffs: From the late 1870s, Bismarck introduced a **protectionist policy** whereby tariffs (taxes on imports and exports) were used to protect German industry and agriculture from foreign competition.

The BASF-chemical factories in Ludwigshafen, Germany, 1881, an example of the growth of new industries in Germany.

? QUESTION

Why did the German economy grow rapidly at the end of the 19th century and the beginning of the 20th century?

Cartels: German **cartels** (large industrial companies with monopolies), e.g. in steel, electrical and chemical industries, made large profits. Between 1875 and 1890 over 200 cartels were set up. They produced their goods behind tariff walls and sometimes benefitted from dumping goods cheaply onto foreign markets. They introduced **mass-production technology** and developed **laboratories** for research. The greater mechanisation increased productivity in textiles, coal and iron and steel industries.

Banking: A well-developed banking system, headed by the central bank, the *Reichsbank*, provided loans for industry and the state. The loans boosted the growth of railways and the development of new chemical and electrical industries.

Education: Schools and universities provided a highly educated workforce. The new electrical and chemical industries benefitted from research, and many trained scientists were employed in these industries.

How Did the Economy Grow?

German unification led to a **boom** in the early 1870s as Germany benefitted from the French indemnity (security) and the banks made credit easily available. However, in 1873 this boom came to a sudden end, and Germany experienced a **recession** during the rest of the 1870s. Workers suffered cuts in wages and rising unemployment; in Berlin in 1879, 25 per cent of the industrial workers were unemployed. However, production levels in the economy recovered by 1880. Thereafter, the German economy grew to become the largest in Europe by 1914.

German railways in 1880

The growth of the German rail network by 1880. What role did railways play in the growth of German industry?

- The railways expanded from 11,000 km in 1860 to 61,000 km in 1910. Railway construction increased demand for coal, iron and steel. The railways reduced the cost of transport and created a wider market.

- The **electrical industry** grew with the production of generators, trams and the building of power stations. **Siemens** invented the dynamo in 1866, and, by 1913, Siemens and AEG dominated the German electrical industry which produced half of the world's trade in electrical goods.

- The **chemical industry** produced dyes, fertilisers and explosives. Apart from the supplies of potash, intensive research was encouraged and **synthetic products**, such as dyes, were developed as by-products of coal. By 1914, Germany produced three-quarters of the world's chemical dyes. Some of these synthetic products, such as ammonia for explosives, were useful when German supplies were cut off during World War I.

- **Coal output** continued to grow, and **steel production** surpassed that in Britain, rising from 1.5 million tons in 1880 to over 13 million tons in 1910.

- German **imports and exports** began to rival Britain's. Imports increased by 150 per cent between 1890 and 1913, while exports almost doubled in the same period. To cope with this increase, Germany's merchant navy expanded to 3 million tons by 1914. While this was far behind the size of the British merchant navy, it was three times greater than that of the USA.

- **Agriculture**, however, did not prosper to the same extent as industry. While protectionism (tariffs) was used to reduce imports of wheat and mechanisation used to increase productivity, by 1900 it was cheaper to import American grain due to the development of large ocean-going steamers and lower transport charges.

How Did Industrialisation Impact on German Society?

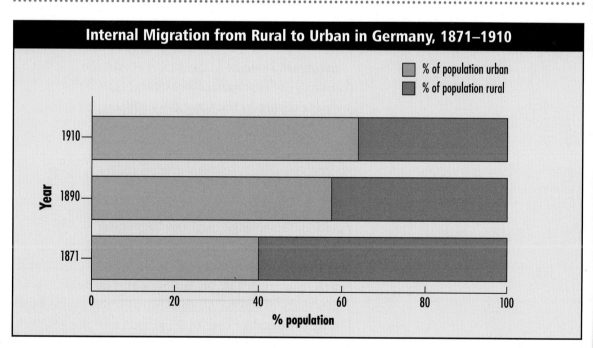

Internal Migration from Rural to Urban in Germany, 1871–1910

% of population urban
% of population rural

Migration

Internal migration: There was a shift in population from rural to urban as the new industries attracted more workers. Also growing mechanisation in the rich estates of Prussia reduced the demand for labour in the countryside. As a result, the urban population grew from 36 per cent in 1871 to 60 per cent in 1910 (see graph).

Emigration was also affected by industrialisation. The growth in jobs attracted

---

Bismarck played a role in the growth of German industry and economy:
- He united Germany, which provided a greater population and market.
- Victory in the Franco-Prussian War meant that the iron and coal resources of Alsace-Lorraine could be used for the benefit of Germany.
- He brought in customs duties, which protected industry and agriculture.
- Bismarck ensured the passage of laws which made trade easier – a new currency, and a national code for trade and commerce.
- Bismarck introduced laws to cover sickness and accident insurance and old age pensions.

QUESTION

Which industries in Germany were successful towards the end of the 19th century?

QUESTIONS

1. What was the main change in the balance between the rural and urban population in Germany between 1871 and 1910?
2. Why did this change occur?

emigrants, such as Polish Catholics, to Germany. But also the depression in the 1870s resulted in increased German emigration, particularly to the USA. More than 800,000 people – mostly farming and factory workers – left Germany between 1880 and 1885, 220,000 in 1881 alone. This emigration continued up to 1890 but as the economy expanded again it slowed considerably after that.

Urbanisation

Many of the larger cities grew rapidly – **Berlin** more than doubled its population between 1870 and 1910. The eight cities with populations of more than 100,000 in 1871 increased to 48 cities with more than 100,000 people by 1910. This was partly due to the internal German **migration** – in 1910, 60 per cent of Berlin's population was born outside the city. But it was also due to the **natural increase** of a young population marrying early.

Working and Living Conditions

The rapid industrialisation and the growth of cities meant that housing and social facilities could not keep up with population growth. As a result, **working and living conditions** were bad, as workers and their families lived in slums and tenements or 'rental barracks', often paying high rents.

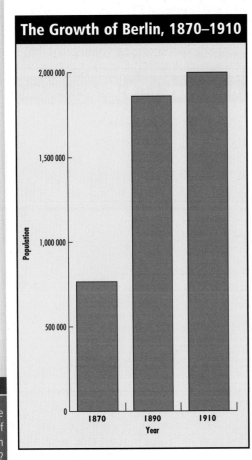

The Growth of Berlin, 1870–1910

'In Berlin the conditions are specially bad, and the average number of persons inhabiting one tenement has risen from 60.7 in 1880 to 66.0 in 1885. Subletting is extremely frequent … One instance is given of a household taking in 34 night lodgers … it is still the opinion of experienced observers … that the evils existing in the large towns of England are less crying than in Germany.'

Source: T. S. Hamerow, The Age of Bismarck, Documents and interpretations (1973)

Not surprisingly, in such conditions with inadequate sewage facilities and water supply, there were occasional outbreaks of **cholera** and **typhus**. But even more of the working class died each year from TB, pneumonia and other infectious diseases. All this contributed to the **high infant mortality** rate of 25 per cent in the 1870s.

Hygiene and living conditions improved as the century progressed so that the average life expectancy of working class men and women increased from 36 and 38 respectively in the 1870s to 45 and 48 respectively by the early 1900s. This was helped by the fall in infant mortality to 15 per cent in 1912.

? QUESTION

What were the main effects of industrialisation on German society?

Social Reform

Social reform under Bismarck: As industrialisation spread and the working class numbers increased, Bismarck introduced a major programme of social reform, often called '**state socialism**'. This was one part of his attack on the **Social Democratic Party** (SPD) (see p. 7).

- In 1883, the **Sickness Incurrence Act** was passed – it provided insurance cover for workers who got sick. Workers paid two-thirds of the contribution, and employers one-third.
- In 1884, the **Accident Insurance Act** was passed – it covered medical treatment for workers in case of an accident. Employers paid the full contribution.
- In 1889, **old age pensions** and **disability cover** were brought in for workers. The cost was covered equally by the government, the workers and the employers. Pensions were paid to workers at 70.

By 1914, 15 million Germans were covered by sickness insurance, 28 million were covered by accident insurance and 1 million got pensions.

Social reform under Wilhelm II: Wilhelm wanted to undermine the workers' support for socialism by improving working conditions.

Wilhelm supported the **Workers' Protection Act** of 1891. This law set up stricter regulations to ensure greater workplace safety, banned work on Sundays, introduced a maximum working day of eleven hours for women and ten hours for workers under 16 years of age. It also prohibited night work by women and children under the age of 16, banned those under the age of 13 from working in industry, and encouraged the establishment of worker's committees in factories to address disputes. As a result, industrial tribunals were set up to settle disputes between employees and employers.

KEY PERSONALITY: THE KRUPP FAMILY

The Krupp family were the main producers of armaments in Germany.

Alfred Krupp was in charge of the family business from 1850 until his death in 1887. He was known as the 'Cannon King'. He built up the business by pioneering the Bessemer steel-making process on the Continent and introduced the open-hearth method of steel casting in 1869. He also took over mines in Germany and France. This helped him develop the vertical 'mixed company' by adding power and transportation to his company.

Krupp believed in the superiority of the breech-loading cannon over muzzle loaders. He was proved correct when Krupp guns helped Prussia to defeat France in the Franco-Prussian War in 1870–71.

The company expanded rapidly. By the late 1880s arms manufacture accounted for 50 per cent of Krupp's total production. By the time of his death, Alfred employed 20,200 people. Alfred Krupp's great business success was based on the quality of the products, the use of new steelmaking techniques, good organisation of the company, and the development of a loyal and skilled workforce.

Krupp invested in subsidised housing for his workers and their families. The housing schemes or 'colonies' as they were called, were separate villages that included parks and schools. Various benefits insured the workers in case of illness or death.

Breech-loading cannon, 1882

This aerial view shows the Krupp settlement in Essen, which provided housing for Krupp employees.

The Krupp family business expanded again under Alfred's only son, Friedrich. His expertise was in finance rather than in technical developments. During his time the numbers employed rose to over 40,000. Like his father, Friedrich Krupp declined a title of nobility.

Friedrich Krupp expanded the range of products to include armour plate, ships, submarines and diesel engines. Krupp benefited from the huge expansion of the German Navy under Wilhelm II. As a member of the German Navy League, Krupp supported Wilhelm's policy of Weltpolitik.

Friedrich Krupp committed suicide in 1902, when he was exposed in German newspapers as a homosexual who entertained under-age Italian boys.

His eldest daughter Bertha inherited the company in 1902 at the age of 16. As Bertha Krupp was still a minor, her mother Margarethe exercised her rights as owner until Bertha reached the age of majority and married. In 1906 Bertha married Gustav von Bohlen, who took over the management of the firm. The marriage had been arranged because it was deemed impossible at the time for a large company to be run by a woman. The Kaiser announced at the wedding that Gustav would now use the name Krupp.

Krupp manufactured the 16.5-inch (420-mm) howitzer Big Bertha (named after his wife), which was used in the shelling of Liège in Belgium at the beginning of the First World War. Krupp supplied other arms and ammunition to the German Army during the war.

In 1918, they produced the Paris Gun. This was a huge railway gun – the largest in the war – which was used to shell Paris. About 250 people were killed by its shells, but its impact was mainly psychological. By the end of the war, Krupp employed 168,000 workers.

The Big Bertha being used in World War I.

What was the importance of the Krupp family for the industrial development of Germany? (2007)

After the war Krupp was widely criticised within Germany for the profits he had made from the war. Krupp was forced to give up armaments production by the Treaty of Versailles. Instead, the company diversified into agricultural equipment, vehicles and consumer goods. However, it secretly continued to work on artillery through subsidiaries in the Netherlands and Sweden.

HOMEWORK EXERCISES

1. Study the document and answer the questions below.

    The Krupp family business, already an early global player in the [production of seamless, no-weld railroad carriage wheels], then also benefited from weapons manufacturing. The company was a key supplier of gun and mortar shells, as well as cannons, as early as the Franco-Prussian War of 1871. Much of Germany's military superiority was due to Krupp's steel cannons, earning Alfred [Krupp] the dubious nickname of 'Krupp, the cannon king.'

    Steel wheels and weaponry brought the Krupp family enormous growth, expanding the company from four employees, when it was founded to 75,000 when Alfred Krupp died in 1887. More than 20,000 of these were in Essen.

    The Krupp management also tried to demonstrate social responsibility. It took care of permanent employees and trained them. Hospitals, schools and libraries were set up for good workers.

    This was not just charity – it also demonstrated some far-sighted business acumen (shrewdness). Only the best workers received the coveted benefits. 'The permanent staff was never more than 10 per cent of the workforce,' says [Ruhr] museum director Grütter.

    These privileged workers kept their jobs even during bad times, and their special training ensured high productivity and expertise. This model also served as a constant incentive to the rest of the workers.

    The Krupp dynasty - glorified and vilified, http://www.dw.com/en/the-krupp-dynasty-glorified-and-vilified/a-15867835

A. (i)   What products brought 'the Krupp family enormous growth', according to the source above?

    (ii) What role did the Franco-Prussian War play in the history of Krupps?

    (iii) What 'social responsibility' did the company show, according to the source?

    (iv) How did the 'social responsibility' show 'far-sighted business acumen'?

B. (i)   Is this source **primary** or **secondary**? Explain.

    (ii) Is this source more about the 'glorification' of the Krupps? Explain.

    (iii) Investigate why and when Krupps were 'vilified'. Explain.

C. (i)   From your knowledge of the course, what aspects of the Krupps story from 1871 to 1920 are not mentioned in this source?

ORDINARY LEVEL

2. A. Write a **short paragraph** on **one** of the following:

        (i) The success of German industry, 1871–1914

        (ii) Social reform under Bismarck and Wilhelm II

    B. Write a **long answer** on the following:

        (i) What was the impact of industrialisation on German economy and society, 1871–1914?

HIGHER LEVEL

3. How did industry develop in Europe, 1870–1914, and what was its impact on society? (2016)

4. During the period 1871–1914, what was the impact of industrialisation and the invention and early history of the motor car? (2017)

INDUSTRIALISATION AND ECONOMIC CRISIS IN TSARIST RUSSIA, 1871–1914

In this section, you should understand:
• How Russia was industrialised.
• The impact of industrialisation on Russian society.
• How and why the 1905 Revolution occurred.
• The impact of Stolypin's reforms.

Russia in the 1870s

By 1870, the Russian Empire was Europe's largest country. However, only some of the country was in Europe; most of it was in Asia. Not surprisingly, this huge empire had many different nationalities, cultures and languages. Both the size of the country and the many different nationalities made Russia a difficult country to rule.

In 1871, the Russian Empire was ruled by the **Tsar**. He was an *'autocratic and unlimited monarch; God himself ordains and all must bow to his supreme power.'* However, the Tsar had to work with the Russian nobility and his appointed ministers. Where there was a strong Tsar like **Alexander III**, policy and action could be directed effectively. But where there was a weak Tsar like his son, **Nicholas II**, who could not make up his mind, this could lead to disorder and uncertainty.

? QUESTION

How does this diagram illustrate the power of the Tsar in Russia?

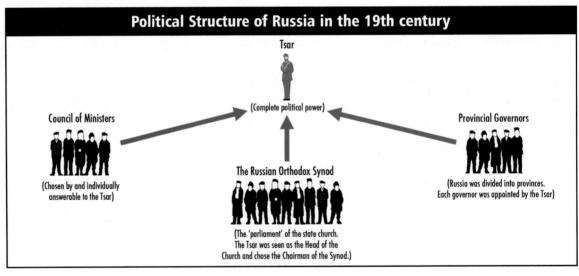

Political Structure of Russia in the 19th century

Tsar

(Complete political power)

Council of Ministers

(Chosen by and individually answerable to the Tsar)

The Russian Orthodox Synod

(The 'parliament' of the state church. The Tsar was seen as the Head of the Church and chose the Chairman of the Synod.)

Provincial Governors

(Russia was divided into provinces. Each governor was appointed by the Tsar)

? QUESTION

Why was Russia a difficult country to rule? Who had the supreme power? What disadvantages did the peasants suffer?

There was **very little industry** in Tsarist Russia. Over 90 per cent of the people were **peasants** (farmers). Peasants had only been **emancipated** (freed from serfdom – having to serve landowners) in 1861, and they still suffered by having to make **redemption payments** to pay for their freedom along with having to pay **heavy government taxes**.

Industrialisation Under Count Witte

The main industrialisation of Russia began in the 1880s during the reign of **Alexander III** (1881–94). It continued during the reign of the next Tsar, Nicholas II. The person mainly responsible for this industrialisation was **Count Witte**, who was minister of finance from 1892 until 1903.

Witte believed that economic policies were necessary to save Russia and to create a **modern state.** He said, *'If we do not take energetic and decisive measures so that our industry will be able to satisfy the needs of Russia … then the rapidly growing foreign industries will break through our tariff barriers and establish themselves in our fatherland.'*

He believed that the **government** should take an active part in industrialising Russia. He used **tariffs** (customs duties) to protect Russian industry from outside competition (**protectionism**). He brought the Russian rouble into the **gold standard** (based on a fixed quantity of gold) to give financial stability. He also encouraged **foreign loans**. Money from France, Britain and Germany was invested in railway construction, mining, oil production and banking. Foreign capital also brought **foreign expertise** such as engineers and financiers who helped with the industrialisation in Russia. Foreign capital was matched by **increased taxes** in Russia to pay for industrial development. The government also encouraged the peasants to sell large amounts of grain which was then exported to pay for **foreign debts**.

Count Witte

The Railways

The key to industrialisation was the expansion of the railways, especially the building of the **Trans-Siberian railway**. Railway construction began in the reign of Tsar Alexander II, but expanded rapidly under the rule of Alexander III.

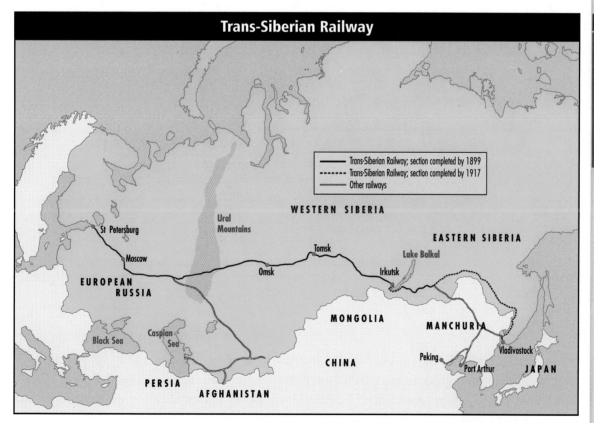

Trans-Siberian Railway

Timeline of the Tsars

— 1855 Alexander II became Tsar

— 1861 Emancipation of the serfs

— 1881 Alexander II assassinated
Alexander III became Tsar

— 1892 Witte became Finance Minister

— 1894 Nicholas II became Tsar

— 1904 Russo-Japanese
—05 War

— 1905 Russian Revolution

— 1914 First World War began

— 1917 Feb: Revolution – abdication of Nicholas; Provisional Gov. took over
Oct: Bolshevik (Communist) Revolution

— 1918 Russian Civil War began

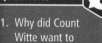

QUESTIONS

1. Why did Count Witte want to industrialise Russia?
2. What policies did he follow to help with industrialisation?

The Trans-Siberian railway was begun in 1891. It linked European Russia and the Far East. Some sections were not completed until 1915. During the Russo-Japanese war in 1904–05, it was very difficult to get supplies from the industrial areas in European Russia to the location of the war in the Far East.

The Development of Russian Railways	
1881	21,228 km
1891	31,219 km
1900	53,234 km
1914	70,156 km

There was 1,600 km of track in 1864; by 1903 it had increased to over 50,000 km. The railways connected cities and made it easier to export grain from the ports. The expansion of the railways also led to the growth of the coal and iron and steel industry.

? QUESTION

What were the benefits of an increased railway network in Russia?

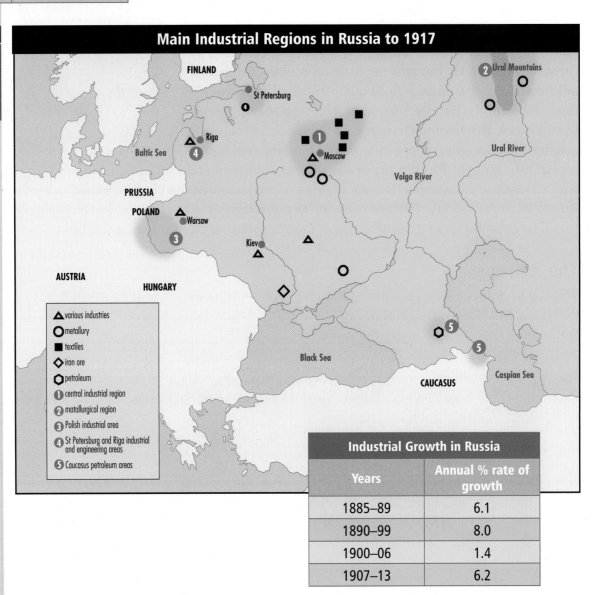

Industrialisation was concentrated in four main regions: around St Petersburg, around Moscow, in Poland (then part of the Russian Empire) and the Donbas and Krivoi Rog in the south, with some developments in the Ural Mountains.

Industrial Growth in Russia	
Years	Annual % rate of growth
1885–89	6.1
1890–99	8.0
1900–06	1.4
1907–13	6.2

What Were the Effects of Industrialisation on Russia?

The **population** of Russia grew rapidly. It grew from 97 million in 1880 to 165 million in 1914. Cities also grew in particular, as migrants were attracted to the them for industrial work. The population of St Petersburg (later Petrograd), for example, doubled between 1891 and 1914 from 1 million to 2 million.

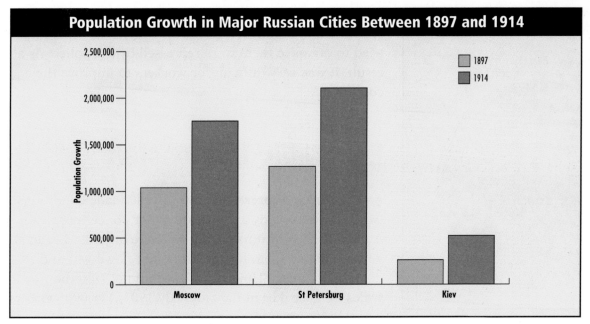

Population Growth in Major Russian Cities Between 1897 and 1914

The number of **urban industrial workers** (working class) increased rapidly – to almost 3 million in the early 20th century. Half of the workers worked in large factories with more than 1,000 workers. Some worked in very large factories, such as a textile factory in Moscow with over 20,000 workers, or the **Putilov** iron and steel works in St Petersburg with more than 40,000 workers. These large numbers made it easier to organise workers for strikes and political action. These were **key factors** in the revolutions that happened in 1905 and 1917.

The **workers** suffered. Their wages were low and their **working conditions** were bad; they worked long hours, often more than 11 hours a day, and could be fined and punished for various reasons. One witness reported, '*I often watched the crowds of poorly clad* (clothed) *and emaciated* (thin) *figures of men and girls returning from the mills* (factories).' There was a shortage of houses, so there was **overcrowding** with as many as 10 people living in one room and taking turns to sleep. Some workers were kept in barrack-style buildings, purpose-built by their employers.

1. What is the message of the cartoon? Is it effective propaganda?
2. Is this a reliable source?

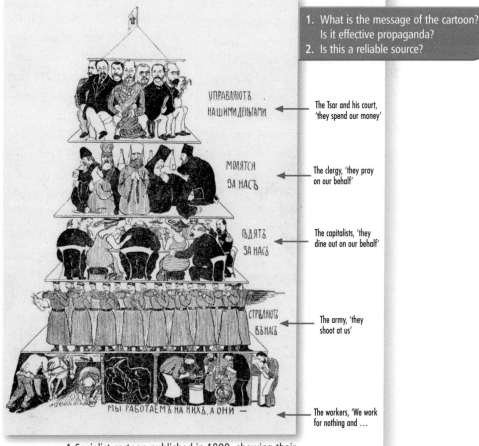

The Tsar and his court, 'they spend our money'

The clergy, 'they pray on our behalf'

The capitalists, 'they dine out on our behalf'

The army, 'they shoot at us'

The workers, 'We work for nothing and …'

A Socialist cartoon published in 1900, showing their view of the Russian social class under the Tsars.

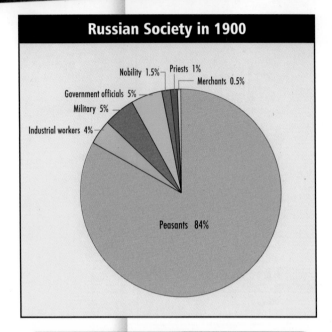

Russian Society in 1900

- Priests 1%
- Merchants 0.5%
- Nobility 1.5%
- Government officials 5%
- Military 5%
- Industrial workers 4%
- Peasants 84%

POLITICAL GROUPS IN RUSSIA

The Liberals: The Liberals came from the **educated middle classes**. They wanted the Tsar to share power with an elected parliament (**Duma**). They also wanted to modernise Russia to keep up with the main European powers.

The Social Revolutionary Party (SRs): This was formed in 1901. It drew its main support from the peasants. Its main policy was that **all land** should be shared by the peasants, not owned by the big landowners. The SRs sometimes used violence, including **assassination** of government officials.

The Social Democratic Party: This was based on the teachings of Karl Marx. He said **industrial workers** should own the **means of production** and create a **communist society**. The Social Democrats believed that **capitalism** would be overthrown by a workers' revolution. The Social Democrats split into two groups called **Mensheviks** and **Bolsheviks**. The Mensheviks said the party should depend on the broad support of the people. The Bolsheviks, led by **Lenin**, said that an **elite group** should plan and carry out **revolution**.

(?) QUESTIONS

1. How did economic and social conditions contribute to anger amongst the peasants and workers?
2. What were the main political groups?
3. How did the Russo-Japanese War contribute to the 1905 Revolution?

Polluted water supplies led to cholera and typhus epidemics. Trade unions were banned and workers who tried to organise them were repressed by the police. As a result, it was very difficult for workers to improve their conditions.

Economic Depression

An **economic depression** around 1900 made conditions worse for everybody and led to further police repression. A number of **pogroms** (see p. 46) were organised against **Jews** to blame them for the economic slowdown and to distract attention. However, this could not stop the widespread strikes in the cities. By 1903, 138,000 workers had taken part in 550 strikes.

In the **countryside**, peasants found it difficult to cope with the heavy burden of taxation. There was a rapid rise in rural population – it increased by 50 per cent between 1860 and 1897 – and farms got smaller. They depended mostly on **manual labour**, with very few animals or tools, and only occasionally wooden ploughs. Peasants had to sell more of their grain to pay for **redemption payments** and **heavy taxes**, and families often went hungry. The average life expectancy was less than 40 years.

Poor harvests between 1897 and 1901 worsened conditions and caused **famine**. This increased the frustration and anger amongst peasants, which led to local uprisings against landlords and government officials in some areas. In early 1905, more than 3,000 peasant uprisings were put down by government troops.

There was a growth of **revolutionary groups**:

- The **Social Revolutionaries** used terrorist methods to achieve socialism.
- The **Social Democrats** (Bolsheviks and Mensheviks) encouraged revolution among the working classes.
- The **middle classes** demanded a parliament.

The **Russo-Japanese war** worsened conditions as communications and transport of goods and food were disrupted. In 1904–05, prices rose and food became scarce. By 1905, worsening social and economic conditions in the cities and the countryside led to considerable anger with the Tsarist government of Nicholas II. These conditions provided the background to a **spontaneous revolution** in 1905. Other factors provided the spark which unleashed the anger that was building up in Russia.

The Progress of the 1905 Revolution

The 1905 Revolution was sparked off by **Bloody Sunday**, when 150,000 demonstrators marched to the Winter Palace in St Petersburg to petition **Tsar Nicholas II** for better conditions. They were led by **Father Gapon** and many wore their best clothes and carried images of the Tsar. Instead of getting help from Tsar Nicholas, who fled to another palace, the crowd was charged by **Cossacks** (people from Ukraine and Russia famed for their horsemanship) and fired on by other soldiers. Up to 1,000 people were killed. Bloody Sunday destroyed the image of the Tsar as father of his people. Some newspapers reported: *'In many towns in Russia the portrait of the Tsar has been removed from public buildings to prevent its being injured.'* (New York Herald).

A Crowd of petitioners, led by Father Gapon, face a wall of soldiers and Cossacks in St Petersburg on 22 January 1905.

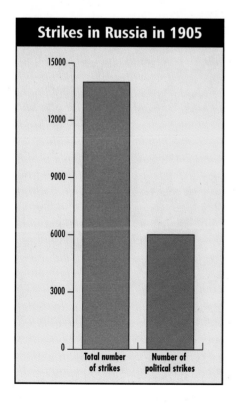

Strikes in Russia in 1905

Workers responded with increased **strikes**. By the end of 1905, almost the entire industrial workforce had been on strike at some time or other. The individual strikes became a **general strike** from September to October 1905.

Striking workers set up **soviets**, or workers' councils, to organise themselves. The most important of these was the **St Petersburg Soviet**, led by **Leon Trotsky**, which controlled much of the city.

Defeats in the Russo-Japanese war added to the discontent. There was national humiliation when the great Russian Baltic Fleet was defeated by the Japanese Navy in the **Battle of Tsushima** in May 1905. Further defeat in the **Battle of Mukden** undermined credibility in the ruling class.

Defeats and worsening conditions led to a series of **mutinies**. The most famous was the mutiny on the battleship Potemkin, but there were also mutinies in army units as well. However, the main army stood firm behind the Tsar and all mutinies were put down.

October Manifesto

When peasant revolts and strikes spread, Nicholas gave in and reluctantly issued the **October Manifesto**. He granted a **Duma**, or national assembly, and promised freedom of speech, religion and civil rights.

The October Manifesto split the revolutionary leaders as middle class liberals supported these reforms. This allowed the Tsar and the army to get back control. The general strike came to an end, the St Petersburg Soviet was closed down and an attempt at armed uprising in Moscow was put down by the army with 1,000 deaths. In all, it has been estimated the revolution resulted in about 14,000 deaths.

What Were the Results of the 1905 Revolution?

The Tsar and the nobility still held onto power, supported by the army. However, the Tsar had to share power with a newly formed Duma (parliament). This was enshrined in the **Russian Constitution of 1906**, where it said no laws could be enacted without the approval of the Duma. However, the Tsar still had full power to appoint and dismiss ministers, and to dismiss the Duma for any reason.

Tsar Nicholas II, seen here with his family, was a weak-minded ruler of Russia. He said, 'I will always give in, and in the end am made a fool, without will and without character.'

QUESTIONS

1. How was the 1905 Revolution 'spontaneous'?
2. How did the revolution spread?
3. Why was the Tsar able to hold onto power?

Stolypin's Repression and Reforms

Peter Stolypin became Prime Minister in 1906. He imposed **harsh repression** on Russia to restore law and order. Between October 1906 and May 1907, there were more than 1,100 hangings – '**Stolypin's Neckties**'. There were also many thousands convicted of political crimes. Hundreds of newspapers and over 600 trade unions were closed down. Stolypin's actions put an end to the disturbances.

How did Agriculture and Industry Improve under Stolypin?

Stolypin also realised that **social and economic reform** was needed. He wanted to **modernise Russian agriculture** and to create a **middle-class peasantry** which would be loyal to the Tsarist regime.

In 1906, he freed peasants from control of their **communes**. He instructed the **Peasants' Land Bank** to provide loans for peasants who wanted to buy the farms. He also abolished **redemption payments**. Furthermore, he encouraged some peasants to move to undeveloped land in Siberia.

As a **result** of Stolypin's policies, the peasant ownership of land rose from 20 per cent in 1905 to 50 per cent in 1915. As well as this, agricultural production rose from 46 million tons in 1906 to 62 million tons in 1913. Some **historians** have argued that if the First World War had not interrupted the progress of Russian agriculture, Russia would have developed into a stable democracy with a loyal peasantry.

Under Stolypin, Russian **industry** continued to grow up to the start of the First World War (1914). The railways expanded and the iron and steel industry grew – by the outbreak of the war, Russia was the fourth-largest producer of steel, coal and iron. However, Stolypin did little to improve industrial workers' living and working conditions. This partly accounts for the series of strikes and protests which covered Russia between 1912 and 1914. The industrial unrest only came to an end with the outbreak of the First World War.

Peter Stolypin, Prime Minister of Russia from 1906 until his assassination in 1913. His agricultural reforms brought prosperity to the countryside.

See War and Revolution – The Russian Revolutions, 1917, p. 116

Economic Crisis During the First World War

The First World War created serious **economic problems** in Russia. Imports of raw materials almost stopped. The army took over the railways, so there was a shortage of transport to take food and goods to the cities. New taxes, shortages and increased government printing of money caused rapid **inflation** (price rises).

In the **countryside** men were conscripted into the army (made to join), so there was a shortage of labour to work on the farms. More women and children were employed to keep industry going in the cities. There were also longer working hours.

In the **cities**, food prices rose and there was a shortage of fuel. Strikes increased as workers demanded increased wages. These conditions contributed to the causes of the **Russian Revolutions in 1917**.

QUESTIONS

1. What were Stolypin's industrial policies?
2. What were Stolypin's agricultural policies?
3. How did World War I impact on the Russian economy?

HOMEWORK EXERCISES

1. Study the documents and answer the questions below.

DOCUMENT A

A third of Russia lives under emergency legislation. The numbers of the regular police and of the secret police are continually growing. The prisons are overcrowded with convicts and political prisoners. At no time have religious persecutions of Jews been so cruel as they are today. In all cities and industrial centres soldiers are employed and equipped with live ammunition to be sent out against the people. Autocracy is an outdated form of government that may suit the needs of a central African tribe but not those of the Russian people who are increasingly aware of the culture of the rest of the world.

An open letter by writer and improving landlord, Leo Tolstoy, to the Tsar Nicholas II in 1902

DOCUMENT B

Lord, we workers, our children, our wives and our old helpless parents have come, Lord, to seek truth, justice and protection from you. We are impoverished and oppressed, unbearable work is imposed upon us, we are despised and not recognised as human beings. We are treated as slaves who must bear our fate and be silent.

We ask very little: to reduce the working day to eight hours and to provide a minimum wage of a rouble a day. Officials have taken the country into a shameful war. We working men have no say in how the taxes we pay are spent. Do not refuse to help your people. Destroy the wall between yourself and your people.

Father Gapon's Petition to the Tsar in 1905

A. (i) According to Document A, whose numbers are continually growing?

(ii) Who are being persecuted, according to Document A?

(iii) What is an outdated form of government?

(iv) Who is seeking 'truth, justice and protection' from the Tsar, according to Document B?

(v) What are the people asking of the Tsar in Document B?

B. (i) Are these classified as **primary** sources? Explain.

(ii) Are these documents **biased** or **objective**? Explain.

(iii) Are these documents **propaganda**? Explain.

(iv) Which document is more **emotional**? Explain.

C. (i) Is one document concerned more with political conditions and the other with economic conditions? Explain.

(ii) How do these documents help you understand the causes of the 1905 Revolution? Explain.

(iii) What aspects of the causes of the 1905 Revolution do they not mention? Explain.

ORDINARY LEVEL

2. Write a **short paragraph** on one of the following:

(i) Industrialisation and economic crisis in Tsarist Russia

(ii) The role of the railways in Tsarist Russia

(iii) The causes of the 1905 Revolution

(iv) Stolypin's reforms

HIGHER LEVEL

3. What was the impact of war and revolution on Russia, 1900–1920? (2017)

In this section, you should understand:
- The rise of anti-Semitism in France.
- Anti-Semitism in the Panama Scandal.
- Anti-Semitism in the Dreyfus Affair.
- The rise of anti-Semitism in Tsarist Russia.
- Anti-Semitism in the reign of Tsar Nicholas II.
- The Beilis Case.

Anti-Semitism in France, 1871–1920

> **KEY CONCEPT**
> **ANTI-SEMITISM:**
> Hatred of Jews.

The **Third Republic** in France was set up when Emperor Napoleon was captured in the Franco-Prussian War. There was conflict between those who supported the Republic, and the Monarchists and the right wing, who were opposed to it. At the time there were about **80,000** Jews in France, which represented 0.25 per cent of the French population. They largely lived in cities and towns, and ranged from poor workers to a small group of elite bankers, such as the **Rothschild family**. Jews became the target for many discontented groups in France at the end of the 19th century.

Rise of Anti-Semitism

Some **right-wing groups** developed anti-Semitic views for several reasons – religious, racial and economic. *La Croix*, a popular publication by the Augustinians (a Catholic religious order), blamed Jews for the death of Christ and for the declining Catholic influence in France. They attacked new education laws as 'a real Jewish trick played on the French people.' They also blamed 'Jewish money power', and in particular the Rothschilds, for the collapse of the Catholic Union Generale bank in 1882 which ruined many small farmers. *La Croix* now saw Jewish conspiracy theories in many news stories.

An equally serious contribution to anti-Semitism was journalist Édouard Drumont's book, *La France Juive* (Jewish France), published in 1886. Drumont's book went through 200 editions in 15 years. He claimed that racial theory supported the superior Aryans against the inferior Jews. He also claimed that the Jews were conspiring to enslave France.

The collapse of *Union Generale* and the Paris Stock Exchange in 1882 signalled a wider **economic recession** in France which lasted about 15 years. It was worsened by cheaper American and Russian grain imports and a decline in the wine and silk industries. There were also internal changes in the economy which resulted in many small businesses suffering from economic competition. Small businesses and shopkeepers became angry as larger retailers and department stores threatened their livelihoods. Many of those who suffered believed that the economic conditions were due to **Jewish financiers and speculators** (traders).

QUESTIONS

1. How large was the Jewish population in France in the 1870s?
2. What were the main ideas of the anti-Semitic press?
3. What part did the economic recession of the 1880s and early 1890s play in the growth of anti-Semitism?

The Panama Scandal

These rising anti-Semitic views were confirmed for many by the **Panama Scandal** which became public in 1892. Thousands of French people invested their life savings in a company which was building the Panama Canal. It was headed by **Ferdinand de Lesseps** who was already famous for building the Suez Canal. However, the company went bankrupt as it ran into problems with malaria and difficult building conditions. It persuaded the French government to invest in the company but this only delayed the collapse. It soon emerged that **two Jewish financiers** with German names had bribed politicians to get parliamentary permission to issue shares for the company.

More anti-Semitism

EXAM QUESTION

How did the Panama Scandal contribute to anti-Semitism in France?

More than 500,000 people and their families were angry because they had lost money. This gave rise to **anti-Jewish feeling** which Édouard Drumont spread in his newspaper *La Libre Parole* (The Free Word). His front page featured caricatures of the Jews, portrayed with hook-noses gloating over Christ's Crucifixion. After a later trial seemed to be too lenient on those guilty of taking bribes in the Panama Scandal, Drumont claimed this as further proof of Jewish control of the French economy. The anti-Semitic feeling whipped up by the Panama Scandal contributed significantly to the Dreyfus Affair.

**KEY CONCEPT
NATIONALISM:** The political belief that all people can be divided into nations and that each nation should have its own government.

The Dreyfus Affair

The Panama Scandal was a prelude to a much more serious case of anti-Semitism which occurred with the **Dreyfus Affair**. In 1894, Alfred Dreyfus, a Jewish officer, was convicted of spying for Germany. His decorations were torn off in a public ceremony as the crowd shouted, 'Death to the Jew!' He was sent to Devil's Island – a prison off the coast of South America.

When the spying continued, the army was unwilling to reopen the case. But Colonel **Picquart**, who became head of French Intelligence, decided that Colonel Esterhazy was the spy. Eventually the army was forced to try the real spy, Colonel Esterhazy, but he was found not guilty in 1896.

Dreyfus was stripped of his medals and his sword broken in a public ceremony in January 1895.

Zola's 'J'Accuse'

The Dreyfus Affair became a national and international scandal with the publication of an open letter, *'J'Accuse'*, in 1898 by the writer, Emile Zola, in which he accused the Army of a cover-up and a serious miscarriage of justice. This divided France. The **Dreyfusards**, comprised of the left wing, Republicans and Jews, favoured justice for Dreyfus and supported the Third Republic. The **Anti-Dreyfusards**, comprised of the right wing, Monarchists, anti-Semites and the Catholic Church, supported the army. They believed in French pride and some saw the affair as a Jewish plot.

The Dreyfus Case was reopened, and Dreyfus was tried again in 1899. Even though Colonel Henry, former head of Intelligence, admitted forging evidence against Dreyfus, Dreyfus was found guilty, though given a shorter sentence. He was eventually pardoned in 1906 by the president of France and reinstated in the French Army.

How did the Dreyfus Affair impact on Anti-Semitism?

The Dreyfus Affair heightened anti-Semitism in France in the 1890s and early 1900s. *La Libre Parole*, which earlier in the 1890s said that Jews in the Army were a danger to national security, claimed that Dreyfus was part of a **Jewish conspiracy** to deliver France to its greatest enemy, Germany. Zola's letter sparked off anti-Semitic rioting in 60 French towns which continued on and off for 18 months. In some cases, crowds of up to 4,000 people attacked Jewish businesses and synagogues. The anti-Semitism of the Dreyfus Affair was intensified by Jewish immigration from Tsarist Russia, where Jews were attacked in pogroms (see p. 47).

Charles **Maurras** founded *L'Action Française* in 1898 and published a journal which became a daily newspaper ten years later. He attacked Dreyfus and continued his anti-Semitism after the Dreyfus Affair had died down.

Anti-Semitism came to the surface again in France in the 1930s, during the Stavisky Affair (see p. 266). During the Second World War, **Vichy France** co-operated with Nazi Germany in sending Jews to labour and extermination camps (p. 275).

Zola's *J'Accuse..!* on the front page of liberal newspaper L'Aurore in 1898.

QUESTIONS (?)

1. What caused the Dreyfus Affair? How did the Dreyfus Affair give rise to anti-Semitism in France?
2. How serious was the anti-Semitism during the Dreyfus Affair?
3. How long did the Dreyfus Affair last?

A cover of Édouard Drumont's anti-Semitic newspaper *La Libre Parole* from 1893 shows a caricature of a Jew taking over the world, money falling from his pockets.

A painting of anti-Semitic rioting in Paris shows young people burning an effigy of Alfred Dreyfus.

45

Anti-Semitism in Tsarist Russia, 1871–1920

There were about 5 million Jews in Russia in 1897, which made up about 4 per cent of the population. They were largely confined to the **Pale of Settlement** – an area to the west and south-west of Russia where they were allowed to settle.

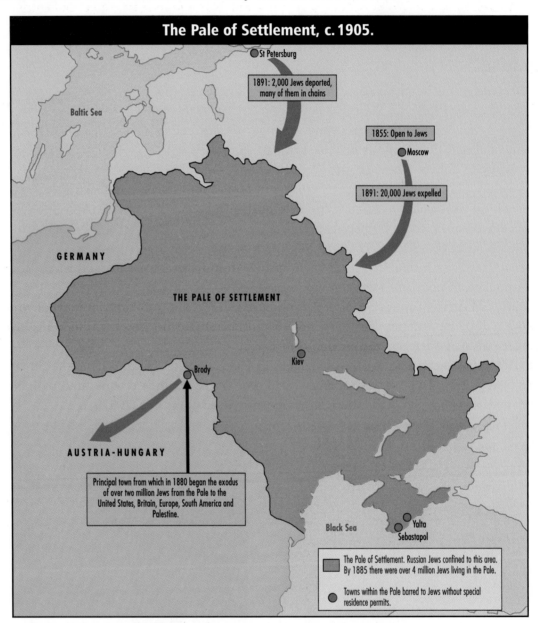

The Pale of Settlement, c. 1905.

St Petersburg

1891: 2,000 Jews deported, many of them in chains

Baltic Sea

1855: Open to Jews

Moscow

1891: 20,000 Jews expelled

GERMANY

THE PALE OF SETTLEMENT

Kiev

Brody

AUSTRIA-HUNGARY

Principal town from which in 1880 began the exodus of over two million Jews from the Pale to the United States, Britain, Europe, South America and Palestine.

Black Sea
Yalta
Sebastapol

The Pale of Settlement. Russian Jews confined to this area. By 1885 there were over 4 million Jews living in the Pale.

Towns within the Pale barred to Jews without special residence permits.

Growth of Anti-Semitism

During the reign of **Alexander II** (1855–81) some restrictions on Jews were eased, and some Jewish merchants were allowed to live and trade in other areas of Russia. However, during the reigns of **Alexander III** (1881–92) and **Nicholas II** (1892–1917) there was severe repression of the Jews. This began when the assassination of Alexander II in 1881 was blamed on Jews, even though there was little evidence to support it.

Anti-Semitism partly arose from the views of the **Orthodox Church** that the Jews were the killers of Christ. This was the view held by **Pobedonostsev**, the Tsar's religious adviser, and he probably influenced both Alexander III and Nicholas II to have anti-

QUESTIONS

1. What was the Pale of Settlement?
2. What was the influence of Pobedonostsev?

Semitic views. The growth of anti-Semitism coincided with the rise of Russian nationalism towards the end of the 19th century. Anti-Semitism was also used as a way to distract people during economic depression, and to provide an 'explanation' for it.

Pogroms

After the assassination of Alexander II in 1881 was blamed on some Jews, **pogroms** were organised against the Jews. A **pogrom** was an attack by a mob on Jewish areas of towns, where they looted, raped, burned and killed. There were attacks in Kiev, Warsaw and Odessa, for example. Between May 1881 and 1905, there were an estimated 215 pogroms.

The police and army allowed these pogroms to go ahead, and very often co-operated with them. The **Holy League**, an extreme nationalist and anti-Semitic group, supported them. Very often gangs were brought in by train to carry out the pogrom. Pobedonostsev encouraged the pogroms.

How did the Policy of 'Russification' Affect the Jews?

Alexander III brought in a policy of '**Russification**' – the repression of cultures of non-Russian people, and the imposition of the Russian culture and language. All minorities suffered under this policy, but the Jews suffered most.

Apart from the pogroms, new **regulations** were imposed on Jews, to lessen 'the injurious influence of their economic activity', and to protect Christians.

- Jews were banned from living in all rural areas of the Pale.
- The number of Jews at university was limited.
- Jews were banned from trading on Christian holy days. As a result, Jews lost business and went bankrupt, or sold out cheaply.
- Jews who lived outside the Pale were harassed and expelled.

QUESTIONS

1. What were pogroms?
2. How did the Jews suffer under the policy of 'Russification'?

The Reign of Nicholas II

More Anti-Semitism During the Reign of Nicholas II

The attacks on the Jews became even more intense during the reign of Nicholas II. The ***Protocols of the Elders of Zion*** were published in Russia in the early 20th century. These documents revealed a **supposed Jewish plot** to take over the world. The stories were used to spread anti-Semitism in Russia and elsewhere – but they were forgeries, written by the Russian secret service.

Officials were aware of **Nicholas II's hatred of the Jews**, and used this fact to support more pogroms. Some of the most serious pogroms occurred in the early 20th century. One such pogrom was the serious attack in **Kishinev** in 1903, spurred on by anti-Semitic stories in a local newspaper. There were about 50 killed, hundreds injured and many homes and businesses destroyed.

Fresh pogroms took place during the **Russo-Japanese War**, and after the 1905 Revolution, in which some Jews played a part. In October 1905 more than 500 people were killed in Odessa.

Some of these pogroms were organised by the **Black Hundred**, an organisation which united anti-Semites and nationalists. One of its members was Tsar Nicholas. They founded the **Union of Russian People** in 1905, during the 1905 Revolution, as their front organisation. They claimed to be the voice of 'Great Russian nationalism', supported the power of the Tsar, and publicised anti-Semitic views. Within a year they had 300,000 members, and the organisation was involved in a series of pogroms that year.

How Pogroms Happened

Khrushchev, who was Soviet (or Russian) leader from 1958 to 1964, explained what happened in pogroms: '*Some of the miners were telling how the 'yids' [Jews] marched around calling the Russians abusive names, carrying banners ... a rumour started that there had been a decree that for three days you could do whatever you wanted to the Jews. For three days there was no check on the looting. After the three days were up, the police started to restore order ... all the pillage and murder went unpunished.*'

There was widespread **reaction abroad** to the pogroms, especially in Britain and the USA, and Russia's reputation was badly damaged. In 1911, the US ended a commercial treaty with Russia over its anti-Semitism.

The Beilis Case

The **Beilis Case** (1911–13) highlighted how the state in Russia was involved in anti-Semitism. When the mutilated body of a 12-year old boy was discovered near Kiev in 1911, the **Black Hundred** spread the rumour that the boy was killed by Jews as part of a **ritual blood sacrifice**. The police arrested **Mendel Beilis**, a Jewish worker, in spite of evidence that the boy was killed by a gang of thieves. His case became worldwide news. People in Russia were **divided** over the issue, and the Jewish community in Russia saw this case as an attack on all of themselves.

The police and the state proceeded with the trial in 1913. The prosecution brought in a Catholic priest as an expert on Jewish law who swore that the Jews carried out ritual murders prior to the Passover. The government pressurised lawyers and judges to find Beilis guilty – but he was cleared. Beilis later left Russia to live in Palestine, but then moved to America.

What was the Jewish reaction to Anti-Semitism in Russia?

Emigration: The pogroms and anti-Semitic restrictions, along with general social and economic conditions, led to mass Jewish emigration from Russia, especially to the USA, Western Europe and South America. In the 30 years up to 1914, about 3 million Jews left the Russian Empire. The arrival of Jews in France in the 1890s increased anti-Semitic feeling there and contributed to the controversy over the **Dreyfus Affair** (p. 44).

? QUESTIONS

1. What was *The Protocols of the Elders of Zion*?
2. How did pogroms intensify in the reign of Nicholas II?
3. What effect had the Russo-Japanese War on pogroms?

Revolutionary politics: Jews were attracted to socialist and revolutionary politics. In 1897, the **Jewish Workers' Party**, known as the **Bund**, was founded. It later formed part of the **Russian Social Democratic Party** but spilt in 1903 when Lenin took control. The Bund sought equal political and economic rights for Jews within Russia and was opposed to Zionism. It created self-defence groups in the early 20th century to protect against pogroms.

Zionism: The Zionist movement grew out of the belief that anti-Semitism existed throughout society and the only way for Jews to escape from it was to set up their own state. In 1882, a Jewish writer in Odessa, in the Ukraine, published a pamphlet abroad which called for the establishment of a Jewish national territory in either Palestine or America. This was widely discussed by Jews in Russia.

This was followed by **Theodor Herzl's** *The State of the Jews*, published in 1896. Herzl, an Austro-Hungarian Jew, argued that the Jews had their own nationality, and that they should have their own state. He proposed that Jews should either go to Palestine or to Argentina to set up that state. The next year, 1897, Herzl organised the **First Zionist Congress** in Basle, Switzerland. The Basle Programme said, *'Zionism seeks to establish a home for the Jewish people in Palestine secured under public law.'* Zionism was ultimately successful in setting up the state of Israel in 1948, after the Second World War and the Holocaust (see pp. 217–18).

An American Tail, an animated movie from 1986, tells the story of a Ukrainian-Jewish family of mice who are forced to emigrate to America after a pogrom in their village in 1885.

The First World War and Revolution

At the beginning of the First World War, **Cossack forces** attacked Jews, claiming they were German spies. The Russian government was forced to **abolish the Pale of Settlement temporarily** because the main battles of the Eastern Front were located there, and hundreds of thousands of Jews fled further into Russia. When the Tsarist government of Nicholas II fell in March 1917, one of the first acts of the new Provisional Government was the abolition of all laws discriminating against Russian citizens on the basis of religion or nationality; in this way, the Jews were emancipated. A number of the Bolshevik (Communist) leaders in the Bolshevik Revolution of November 1917 were Jewish. This fact was used later by **Mussolini** in Italy and **Hitler** in Nazi Germany to link Jews with the spread of Communism.

QUESTIONS (?)

1. What did the Beilis Case highlight in Russia?
2. What were the effects of the rise of anti-Semitism in Russia?

HOMEWORK EXERCISES

ORDINARY LEVEL

1. Write a **short paragraph** on one of the following:
   (i) Anti-Semitism in France and Russia
   (ii) The Dreyfus Affair
   (iii) The Beilis Case in Tsarist Russia

HIGHER LEVEL

2. How did European states manage relations with the churches and/or religious minorities (e.g. the Jews) in the period, 1871–1914? (2008)

3. What was the impact of anti-Semitism in France and/or Russia, 1871–1914? (2009)

4. What was the impact of anti-Semitism in France and Russia, 1871–1920? (2014)

5. What problems were posed by Church-State relations in Germany and/or Anti-Semitism in France? (2011) (2015)

In this section, you should understand:
- How Church-State conflict arose in Italy.
- How Pope Leo XII handled Church-State relations.

The rift between the Catholic Church and Italy began before the final unification of Italy in 1870. The rift continued after 1870 and it was not finally resolved until the Lateran Treaty of 1929.

Origins of Church-State Conflict

The process of unification caused serious conflict between the newly unified state and the Pope, **Pius IX**. Pius IX had been very angry when most of the Papal States were taken in 1860 – he excommunicated (excluded from the Church) the King of Italy and his ministers, and appealed for outside help. In 1870, the final area around Rome was taken from the Pope and Rome became the capital of Italy. Pope Pius IX was confined to the Vatican City – he became the **prisoner** of the Vatican – and he refused to recognise the new Italian State.

The Italian government passed the **Law of Guarantees** (1871). This recognised the independence of the Vatican, guaranteed the safety of the Pope, and gave the Vatican a separate post and telegraph service. But the Pope still refused to recognise the law. The rift between the Pope and the new Italian State was now greater than ever.

The actions of the government in the 1860s contributed in other ways to the growing gap between Church and State. In 1865–66, the Kingdom of Italy passed laws which suppressed religious orders (and extended to Rome in 1873). Pius responded with ***Non Expedit*** ('It is not expedient' [appropriate]), when he ordered Italian Catholics not to take part in parliamentary politics, either by voting or standing for election. The Pope explained that the oath taken by deputies might be interpreted as approving the takeover of Church property and territory.

Pius IX had already widened the gap between the Catholic Church and the State in Italy when he published ***The Syllabus of Errors*** in 1864 which listed '80 of the principal errors of our time'. Pius was opposed to the main ideas of the time – liberalism and progress – and the Syllabus said Catholics could not accept these ideas. The conflict between the Catholic Church under Pius IX continued after unification until Pius died in 1878.

Pope Pius IX reigned as Pope for 30 years.

Later Italian governments tried to limit the influence of the Catholic Church with **anti-clerical laws**:

- Civil marriages were the only legal marriages.
- Male religious orders were disbanded.
- 4,000 houses were closed down and confiscated by the State.

Later laws outlawed Catholic charities.

Catholic Lay Organisations

The Catholic Church encouraged the growth of **lay Catholic organisations**, separate from the State. The pope, **Leo XII**, published the encyclical (papal document) *Rerum Novarum* ('Of New Things'), which encouraged the growth of a Catholic social movement.

In 1897 the Italian government **banned** all Catholic organisations. But Pope Leo XIII did not protest strongly, and this opened the way for better relations between Church and State.

They were brought closer together because of the danger of socialism. **Giollitti**, Prime Minister of Italy, allowed Catholic organisations to regroup. The Pope allowed Catholics to vote in some elections in 1904 where a socialist might be elected. A further relaxation of *Non Expedit* took place in 1909 when Catholics voted in 150 constituencies. The Pope eventually allowed Catholics to vote and to contest elections in 1919.

The anti-clerical laws helped the Catholic Church in some ways:

- **Priests** had to be properly trained as teachers.
- The **nuns** were not affected by the laws, so their numbers grew and they controlled nursing.

Unification of Italy

	Kingdom of Sardinia
	Acquired in 1859–60
	Acquired in 1866
	Acquired in 1870

FRANCE
SWITZERLAND
AUSTRIAN EMPIRE
SAVOY (France 1860)
Milan
VENETIA
LOMBARDY
Venice
Turin
FRANCE
PIEDMONT
PARMA
KINGDOM OF SARDINIA
MODENA
Genoa
Florence
TUSCANY
PAPAL STATE
Adriatic Sea
CORSICA
Rome
KINGDOM OF SARDINIA
Naples
KINGDOM
OF
Tyrrhenian Sea
THE
TWO
Mediterranean Sea
SICILIES
SICILY
AFRICA

Italy was united in stages between 1859 and 1870. Most of the Papal States were taken from the Pope in 1860. In 1870, the area around Rome was taken from the Pope to end the unification process. The Pope retained control of the Vatican State within the city of Rome.

QUESTIONS

1. What were the origins of the conflict between Church and State in Italy?
2. How did Pius IX deal with the Italian State?

QUESTION

When and how did relations between the Catholic Church and the Italian government improve?

The dispute between the Italian State and the Catholic Church was eventually settled by the **Lateran Treaty** in 1929.

KEY PERSONALITY: POPE LEO XIII

Leo XIII was pope from 1878 to 1903. Pope Leo's predecessor, Pius IX, had a controversial papacy. He published the Syllabus of Errors, which condemned the main ideas of the time. He was also in conflict with various governments.

Although he continued some of the trends of Pius IX, Leo XIII was a more diplomatic Pope. He improved relations with many governments. He negotiated with Bismarck to bring an end to the Kulturkampf in Germany (see p. 5). Exiled bishops were allowed to return and diplomatic relations between Germany and the Vatican were renewed (see p. 7). In France, he encouraged Catholics to recognise the Third French Republic. This improved relations with the French government (Raillement), but it did not prevent the separation of Church and State that occurred after his death.

Leo also tried to improve conditions for Catholics in Tsarist Russia, with some success. He was accepted as an arbitrator by Germany and Spain over the ownership of the Caroline Islands.

However, relations did not improve with the Italian government for some time. Pope Leo continued Pius IX's Non Expedit (which banned Catholics from taking part in Italian elections). But by the early years of the 20th century, the rise of socialism in Italy and elsewhere seemed to make the liberalism of the Italian State more welcome. In the circumstance, Non Expedit was relaxed in 1904 and Catholics were allowed to vote in elections if it meant defeating a socialist candidate. Five years later, in 1909, Non Expedit was dropped in 150 constituencies and this resulted in a significant rise in the Catholic vote.

Leo XIII issued many encyclicals. These provided guidance for Catholics on issues such as Christian marriage, Freemasonry, and the rosary, and on political issues. The most famous encyclical was Rerum Novarum in 1891. In this, Pope Leo:

- Was critical of the weaknesses of capitalism and socialism.
- Stressed the rights and duties of capital and labour.
- Said workers should get a living wage which 'should be sufficient to maintain the wage earner in reasonable and frugal comfort'.

This encyclical encouraged Catholic social action, especially in Italy.

During his papacy, Leo XIII succeeded in gaining great prestige for the papacy.

1. Where did Pope Leo XIII improve relations between the Catholic Church and governments?
2. Did he improve relations with the Italian government?
3. What was the message of *Rerum Novarum*?

HOMEWORK EXERCISES

ORDINARY LEVEL

1. Write a **short paragraph** on **one** of the following:
   (i) How Church-State conflict grew under Pope Pius IX
   (ii) How attempts were made to improve Church-State relations in Italy under Pope Leo XIII
2. Write a **long answer** on **one** of the following:
   (i) Why was the career of Pope Leo XIII important in the history of the Catholic Church? (2008)
   (ii) How did Pope Leo XIII try to ease social tensions in industrial Europe? (2016)
   (iii) How did Pope Leo XIII influence affairs in Europe? (2017)

HIGHER LEVEL

3. How did Church-State relations develop in Germany and in Italy between 1871 and 1914?

In this section, you should understand:
• How the Second International was developed.
• The issues on which there was disagreement.

The **First International** (the International Working Men's Association) was founded in London in 1864. It began the idea of international socialist and working-class co-operation. It was dominated by **Karl Marx**, whose ideas formed the basis for Communism. The First International ended in the mid-1870s.

MARX'S IDEAS ON THE DEVELOPMENT OF A COMMUNIST SOCIETY

● Capitalism – the private ownership of the means of production – leads to inequalities in society.
● The bourgeois (middle class) control capitalist society.
● History is a struggle between classes which will inevitably lead to the revolutionary (violent) overthrow of capitalist society.
● The proletariat (working class) will take control of the means of production.
● Later, government will fade away and a classless society based on common ownership – a Communist society – will be created.

Karl Marx, who wrote *The Communist Manifesto* (1848) and *Das Kapital*, provided much of the theory which was the basis for discussion and disagreement by the First and Second International.

Foundation of the Second International

The **Second Workers' International** was founded in 1889. It was a loose federation of national socialist and Communist parties and trade unions in various European and non-European countries. It expelled **anarchists** at their second congress in 1896 because they continually disrupted debates, and refused to accept parliamentary democracy.

At their **First Congress** in Paris in 1889 (on the anniversary of the French Revolution), there were 384 delegates from 20 countries, which later expanded to more than 400 delegates. The French delegation was largest, with 206 delegates followed by 81 delegates representing the German socialist and labour movement. England was represented by a delegation of 19, including William Morris (socialist activist), Eleanor Marx-Aveling (Karl Marx's daughter), and Keir Hardie (later one of the founders of the Labour Party in Britain). The Russian revolutionary movement was represented by six delegates, including Georgi Plekhanov, a Russian Marxist and one of the founders of the Social Democratic Party in Russia.

The Second International **agreed** on:
● The solidarity of the working class.
● The overthrow of capitalism.

- The condemnation of imperialism (colonialism), militarism and war.

The Second International also demanded:

- The eight-hour working day.
- Better help for health and education.
- Taxation of the rich.

Paul Lafargue, Karl Marx's son-in-law, welcomed the delegates to the first meeting of the Second International in Paris: *We gather here not under the banner of the tricolour or any other national colours, we gather here under the banner of the red flag, the flag of the international proletariat.*

Delegates to the seventh congress of the Second International in Stuttgart, Germany.

A delegate card from the 1896 congress held in London. A very large British delegation attended, including 159 from trade unions, 26 from trades councils and five from women's organisations. The Social Democratic Federation sent 121, the Independent Labour Party 117, and the Fabian Society, three.

The Second International held a series of conferences in **different countries** in Europe between its foundation in 1889 and the outbreak of the First World War. It established a permanent office in Brussels in 1900. By 1910, about 900 delegates attended the congress in Copenhagen, representing workers from 23 countries. The parties of the Second International celebrated **May Day** each year with a special demonstration for the labour movement.

Gradual Reform or Revolution?

There was conflict between different groups in the Second International about the methods of achieving the aims of the Labour movement. **Eduard Bernstein**, a leader of the German Social Democratic Party, said in his book, *Evolutionary Socialism* (1899), that socialists should try to achieve **gradual reforms** instead of waiting for the socialist revolution and the collapse of capitalism. He said workers were getting better off, not worse off, as Marx had said.

? QUESTIONS

1. What did the Second International agree on at the First Congress?
2. Who participated in the Second International?

Bernstein was attacked by other socialists, including **Rosa Luxemburg** (see Key Personality p. 113). They called him a **'revisionist'**, and said the class struggle made the social revolution inevitable. The German Social Democratic Party and revolutionary Marxists in the Second International rejected Bernstein's ideas, reaffirming the Marxist doctrine of the class struggle and the inevitability of class revolution. But Bernstein's ideas were later to bring the Social Democratic Party to power in Germany after World War II.

Should Socialists Participate in Government?

Further conflict arose amongst the Second International when Alexandre **Millerand**, a socialist, became a minister of the French government in 1899.
Some of the Second International argued that socialist parties should not co-operate with bourgeois (middle-class) parties to run the country. Others argued that they should do so, in order to bring in some reforms.

August Bebel, the leader of the German Social Democrats, argued against co-operation, while **Jean Juarès**, leader of the French Socialists, argued in favour. He said the German Social Democrats were trying to impose their tactics and ideas on all others. The **Amsterdam Congress** in 1904 voted against socialists co-operating with middle-class parties. Those who opposed came largely from countries with authoritarian regimes where socialists were unlikely to share power. Those who favoured socialists participating in government came largely from countries with liberal democratic systems where there was a possibility that socialists would share power.

What Should Socialists do in the Event of War?

A further area of conflict arose over what should be done in the event of a war. This issue first arose in the case of the **Russo-Japanese War**, 1904–05. It eventually became a clash between **socialism** and **nationalism**, and nationalism won out. Some socialists demanded a reduction in armaments, and an international court to settle disputes between countries. They called on all labour movements to do everything to prevent war, because workers' interests lay in preventing war or ending it quickly. They favoured a general strike and sabotage of the war effort.

Others, like **Lenin** and **Rosa Luxemburg**, believed that war would weaken the capitalist state and make it easier for a socialist revolution to succeed. If war broke out, they wanted to rouse the people to partake and speed up the end of the capitalist system.

Eduard Bernstein, German Social Democratic Party, who promoted the idea of evolutionary (rather than revolutionary) socialism.

QUESTIONS

1. What did the Second International decide on between evolutionary and revolutionary socialism?
2. Did the Second International agree that socialists should participate in government?

End of the Second International

QUESTIONS

1. What did socialists decide to do at the outbreak of World War I?
2. What were Lenin's and Luxemburg's views about the war?

However, when the **First World War** broke out, all the main socialist parties supported their governments except those in Serbia and Russia. Nationalism had won out. This led to the **collapse** of the Second International. The **minority** of the Second International who opposed the war met in Switzerland in 1915. They called for an immediate end to the war, and peace with 'no annexations, no indemnities'. But they had no impact on the progress of the war.

While the Second International was successful in creating co-operation amongst a wide number of socialist groups, it ultimately failed because each of the groups and parties reflected conditions in their own countries.

HOMEWORK EXERCISES

ORDINARY LEVEL

1. Write a **short paragraph** on one of the following:
   (i)   The aims and organisation of the Second International
   (ii) Debates and conflicts within the Second International over the development of socialism

2. Write a **long answer** on the following:
   (i)   How did the Second International represent workers interests between its foundation in 1889 and its collapse in 1915?

HIGHER LEVEL

3. How did the Second International view the development of capitalism and socialism, and why did it fail to achieve its aims?

In this section, you should understand:
- The causes of the New Imperialism.
- How the New Imperialism affected relations between European powers.

What was New Imperialism?

Imperialism is the control and rule of colonies by more powerful countries. 'Old' imperialism refers to the age of exploration in the 15th and 16th centuries. The **New Imperialism** refers to an upsurge of imperialism at the end of the 19th and beginning of the 20th centuries. It was mostly confined to Africa (the 'Scramble for Africa') and Asia. European countries expanded their existing empires by taking control of more than 10 million square miles of new territories in the 40 years from 1870 onwards. This rapid expansion has led to a debate among historians about the **causes** of the New Imperialism.

> **KEY CONCEPT**
> **NEW IMPERIALISM:** The colonial expansion of mainly European powers, but also Japan and the USA, which took place at the end of the 19th and the beginning of the 20th centuries. It is called 'New' to distinguish it from the colonial expansion of the Age of Exploration in the 15th and 16th centuries.

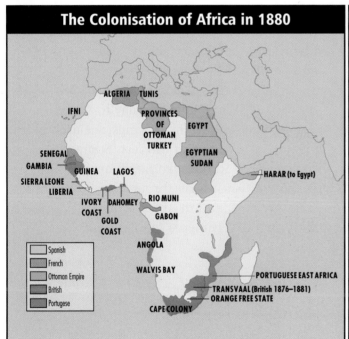

The Colonisation of Africa in 1880

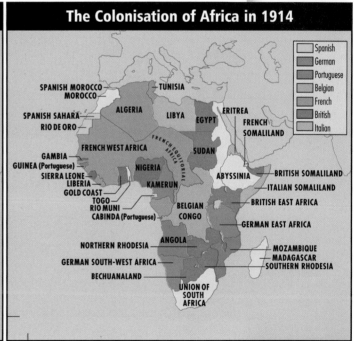

The Colonisation of Africa in 1914

1. How do these maps show how rapidly Africa was colonised between 1880 and 1914?
2. Which European countries had the largest colonies in Africa?

Causes of the New Imperialism

Geographical Explorations

Much of the interest in Africa was inspired by geographical explorers who opened up the **'Dark Continent'**. Explorers came from Britain (David Livingstone and Henry Morton Stanley), France (Jean-Baptiste Marchand) and Germany (Carl Peters). They searched for the sources of great rivers such as the Nile, and explored great lakes. Their

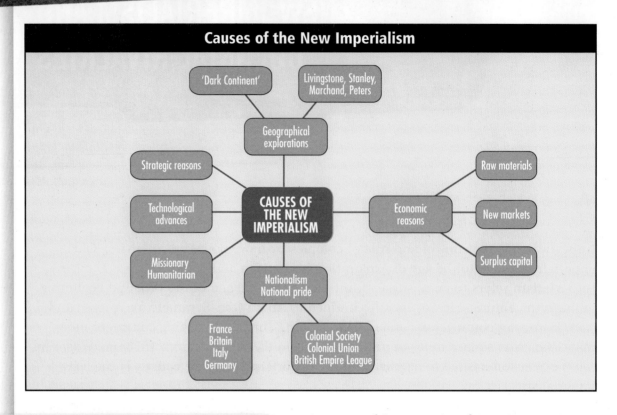

Causes of the New Imperialism

- 'Dark Continent'
- Livingstone, Stanley, Marchand, Peters
- Geographical explorations
- Strategic reasons
- Technological advances
- Missionary Humanitarian
- **CAUSES OF THE NEW IMPERIALISM**
- Economic reasons
  - Raw materials
  - New markets
  - Surplus capital
- Nationalism National pride
  - France Britain Italy Germany
  - Colonial Society Colonial Union British Empire League

David Livingstone went on three explorations in Africa. He wanted to end slavery and spread Christianity. These trips made him a national hero. On the third journey, there was no contact with him for a number of months so Henry Stanley was sent to find him. When they met in the middle of Africa in 1871, Stanley said, 'Dr Livingstone, I presume?'

stories created **interest** in Africa. On returning to Britain, after one period of exploration, Livingstone conducted many speaking tours and published his bestselling account, *Missionary Travels and Researches in South Africa* (1857). In a later journey to Africa, Stanley was sent to find Livingstone and their meeting aroused great interest. Some explorers, such as Cecil Rhodes from Britain and Carl Peters, got possession through local treaties of large areas of land in Africa which they wanted their own governments to take over.

Economic Reasons

Some historians have argued that **economic reasons** were the main cause of the new imperialism. They say that European capitalism had advanced to the stage that it needed new sources of raw materials, new markets and new outlets for **surplus capital**. In the case of raw materials, Europe was going through the Second Industrial Revolution and developing new industries, such as chemicals and cars. Some of the sources of the new **raw materials** were in Africa and Asia. Rubber for tyres came from the Congo and the Amazon, and further afield in Malaysia. **King Leopold** of Belgium, for example, took over the Congo and exploited its rubber supplies. However, older industries were still important. Egypt and India provided raw cotton for Lancashire cotton factories. Africa and Asia also provided plentiful supplies of other materials such as ivory, copper, gold and diamonds. The need for **new markets developed** because the

Industrial Revolution had spread to many countries in Europe. Markets in Europe were now saturated (full) and in the 1870s and 1880s, **protectionism** was spreading. India provided a huge market for Lancashire cotton. Another country, China, with a population of 400 million, was also attractive to outside countries as a market. As the French Prime Minister Jules Ferry said, *'Europe's consumption is saturated. It is essential to discover new consumers in other parts of the world.'*

Surplus Capital

J.A. Hobson in *Imperialism, A Study* and Lenin in *Imperialism, the Highest Stage of Capitalism*, argued for the role of surplus capital (money) in developing New Imperialism. Both stressed that surplus capital in Europe needed new investments. This money, they maintained, was invested in plantations, ports, shipping and railways in Africa and Asia. Countries then took over these areas in Africa and Asia to protect the sources of raw materials, the new markets and the investments. As Hobson said, *'Aggressive imperialism ... is a source of great gain to the investor who cannot find at home the profitable use he seeks for his capital, and insists that his Government should help him to profitable and secure investments abroad.'*

However, historians have pointed out that many areas which were colonised had **little economic value**. France took over the Sahara Desert, and Germany took over South West Africa, which was mostly desert. Indeed, European countries invested very little of their capital in their new colonies. Britain invested mostly in the USA and Latin America; France only invested 10 per cent of its capital in colonies, while Germany only invested 2 per cent.

Nationalism and National Pride

Some historians have argued for the importance of **nationalism and national pride** in the development of imperialism. After 1871, **France** wanted to compensate for defeat in the Franco-Prussian War. A French politician, Gambetta, said, *'To remain a great nation or to become one, you must colonise.'* Bismarck encouraged France to get involved in Tunisia and, overall, France colonised more than 4 million square miles of land. **Britain** boasted it had an 'empire on which the sun never sets', while **Italy** wanted to attain great-power status after its unification in 1870.

Many associations used arguments for **national pride** to encourage their governments to take over colonies. The **Colonial Society** in Germany, the **Colonial Union** in France and the **British Empire League** were examples of these. They used the popular press to highlight rivalries and increase competition. As British Prime Minister, Lord Salisbury, said, *'the diplomacy of nations is now conducted quite as much in the letters of special correspondents, as in the despatches (reports) of the foreign office.'*

Missionary and Humanitarian Causes

Some believed that Europeans should improve the lives of the native people by abolishing slavery and spreading Christianity and European medicine. They did this for **missionary and humanitarian reasons**. Two-thirds of all Catholic missionaries were French. Dr David Livingstone, the British explorer, was a missionary and medical doctor. He was sent to Africa by the British government as an explorer 'to open a path for commerce and Christianity'. Others, however, based their actions on **Social**

QUESTIONS ?

1. How did geographical explorations inspire the New Imperialism?
2. What contribution did economic causes make to the causes of the New Imperialism?
3. Of the economic causes, which would you regard as most important: raw materials, new markets or surplus capital?

KEY CONCEPT
NATIONALISM: The political belief that all people can be divided into nations and that each nation should have its own government.

Darwinism. They said Darwin's ideas on evolution also applied to the development of races – they claimed that white races developed greater civilisations because they were the 'fittest to survive', compared to black or yellow races. As a result, the white races needed to develop colonies to maintain their great power status.

Technological Advances

Advances in **technology** made it easier for Europeans to conquer lands and to control them. This included:

- **Military technology**, such as rifles and machine guns, to overcome native tribes and countries.
- Developments in **transport technology**, with faster steamships and railways to transport soldiers.
- An increase in **goods** for import and export.

In the late 19th century, Cecil Rhodes proposed the **Cape to Cairo** railway to open up the African continent to further British colonialism. In Russia, the **Trans-Siberian railway** allowed the government to extend its influence into eastern Asia. These developments were combined with the **telegraph** for faster communications over greater distances. Finally, **quinine** (a medicine) was used for controlling malaria, which opened up tropical areas of central Africa and Asia to colonisation.

Strategic Reasons

Some decisions on colonialism were based on **strategic reasons**. Britain, for example, was concerned about protecting the route to the 'Jewel in the Crown' – India. This involved creating bases round the Cape of Good Hope and acquiring part-ownership of the Suez Canal. This led to British occupation of Egypt in 1882 to put down a nationalist uprising, and full control of the canal. Similarly, German control of the port of Kiaochow in China, the Marianas, Caroline Islands and part of the Samoa Islands was developed to provide a worldwide network of bases for their steam ships.

What is the message of the cartoon? Does it support Rhodes's proposal?

The Rhodes Colossus shows Cecil Rhodes, the British coloniser, straddling the entire African continent. He proposed the development of a railway and telegraph line from Cape Town to Cairo to open up central Africa to British control.

? QUESTIONS

1. What did associations such as The Colonial Society in Germany contribute to the causes of the New Imperialism?
2. Explain the contribution of missionary and humanitarian causes to the New Imperialism.
3. How did technological advances contribute to the New Imperialism?
4. Which would you consider more important as a cause of the New Imperialism – technological advances or strategic reasons

Colonial Rivalries and the Berlin Conference, 1884–85

A painting shows the first meeting of the Berlin Conference on 15 November 1884, with Bismarck as a central figure.

In 1876, King Leopold of Belgium set up the **International African Association**. He employed the explorer, Henry Stanley, to explore and lay claim to the lands around the Congo River in central Africa. This brought Leopold into conflict with France and Portugal over control of the Congo River. To prevent the conflict getting worse, Bismarck called the **Berlin Conference**, 1884–85, to overcome colonial rivalries. He wanted to prevent disputes in Africa causing war in Europe (see pp. 12–13).

The Berlin Conference agreed that:

- **Spheres of influence** should be set up – once a country conquered an area, it became part of its sphere of influence.
- **Slavery** was **outlawed**.
- The **Congo** was given to Leopold.

The conference speeded up the process of carving-up Africa – '**the Scramble for Africa**' – so that by 1900, European states claimed 90 per cent of African territory. The agreement in Berlin also achieved its main aim, which was **to prevent war** between European states over colonial affairs: it was largely responsible for the peaceful carve-up of Africa.

According to this cartoon, what is the attitude of the Berlin Conference to Africa and colonisation? Is this a primary or a secondary source for the New Imperialism?

EXAM QUESTION (?)

Why was the Berlin Conference called in 1884–85, and what was agreed there?

British and French Rivalry

Britain and France had different reasons for advancing colonisation. **Britain** developed colonies to protect the trade route to India, and provide raw materials for industry and markets for products of its Industrial Revolution. It also wanted to protect investment in Africa, increase national pride, and spread missionary and humanitarian work.

On the other hand, economic reasons were less important for **France**. France developed colonies to increase national pride because of the loss of Alsace-Lorraine in the Franco-Prussian War (see p. 3). The French Army also wanted to regain its pride after its defeat in that war. As well as this, France was an active missionary country – thousands of French Catholic missionaries led the way into Africa.

Conflict over Sudan and Fashoda

Both countries came into conflict in the **Fashoda Affair** in 1898. Prior to this, in 1882, Britain had taken over Egypt and the Suez Canal when the French did not join them in putting down a nationalist uprising there. Britain now claimed Sudan and the headwaters of the Nile, to the south of Egypt.

French imperialists also wanted to extend the French empire from western Africa to the east. Captain **Marchand** tried to do this when he marched for almost two years from French West Africa to Fashoda on the Nile. He claimed it for France. Lord Kitchener challenged him at **Fashoda** with a much bigger army (220 against 2,000 soldiers). The commanders passed the problem back to London and Paris to resolve. The dispute resulted in a **war scare** and a heated debate in Europe.

How does the map illustrate the conflict between Britain and France?

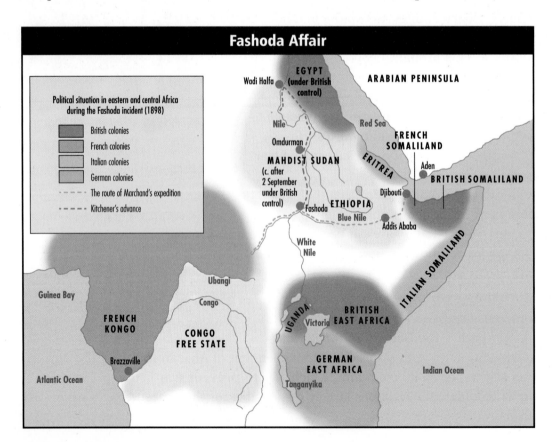

Fashoda Affair

Political situation in eastern and central Africa during the Fashoda incident (1898)

- British colonies
- French colonies
- Italian colonies
- German colonies
- The route of Marchand's expedition
- Kitchener's advance

At the time, the French Army was in chaos after the **Dreyfus Affair** (see p. 44). The French also needed allies in Europe against Germany, so they gave in to Britain. The **Fashoda Affair** almost caused a war, because public opinion in each country was angry; but instead it brought Britain and France closer together. The Affair showed that European politics were often more important than colonial affairs. It eventually led to the signing of the **Entente Cordiale** between the two countries in 1904, as both countries recognised that they were isolated in Europe in the face of growing German power. In the Entente, Britain and France agreed to resolve issues which divided them in relation to Egypt, Morocco and other areas of colonial disagreement in the world.

QUESTIONS ?

1. What caused the Fashoda affair?
2. How was it resolved?
3. What does the Fashoda Affair tell you about relations between European countries and imperial conflict?

British and German Rivalry – South Africa and the Boer War

Britain controlled the Cape Colony in South Africa. The **Boers** (Dutch farmers) controlled the Orange Free State and the Transvaal. There was conflict between the two sides because of different languages and cultures, and because of diamonds and gold found in the Boer provinces.

The **Jameson Raid** (1895–96) was organised by Cecil Rhodes to attack the Boer republics; the raid failed and this led to further tension. The Boers then attacked the British colonies and so began the **Boer War** (1899–1902).

Germany was a late starter in the colonial race because Bismarck was opposed to colonies – he said they were 'expensive luxuries' (See pp. 12–13). But a new emperor, Kaiser Wilhelm II, wanted to develop Germany as a world power (*Weltpolitik*) in opposition to Britain. Germany also wanted to expand to satisfy national pride; the Kaiser wanted 'a place in the sun'. German business interests such as the **German Colonial Society** encouraged imperialism because they wanted profits.

> **'The Kruger Telegram'**
> **Kaiser Wilhelm II's telegram of congratulations to Paul Kruger for defeating the Jameson Raid**
> I express to you my sincere congratulations that you and your people, without appealing for the help of friendly powers, have succeeded, by your energetic action against the armed bands which invaded your country as disturbers of the peace, in restoring peace and in maintaining the independence of the country against attack from without.

The Kruger Telegram

Kaiser Wilhelm II intervened in events in South Africa. In the **Kruger Telegram** (sent to Paul Kruger, President of the Transvaal Republic), he praised the Boers for resisting the Jameson Raid in which 65 British irregular forces were killed and the remaining 600 attackers captured. German newspapers applauded the telegram but it increased **tensions** with Britain, where it was seen as both a threatening letter and interfering in the British sphere of influence. Consequently, it led to an upsurge of anti-German feeling in Britain.

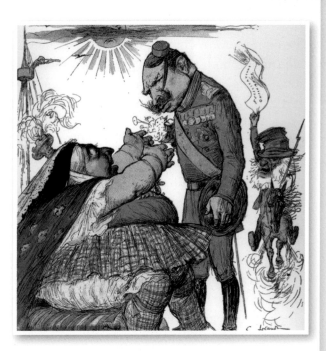

A cartoon on the front of French satirical magazine Le Rire shows Kaiser Wilhelm meeting Queen Victoria while, in the background, Paul Kruger waves the telegram he received from the Kaiser congratulating him on resisting the British in the Jameson Raid.

QUESTION

How did events in South Africa increase tensions between Britain and Germany?

To what extent did colonial rivalries contribute to international tensions, 1871–1914?

- Introduction; brief – role of national pride and strategic reasons in Age of Imperialism
- Colonial rivalries and Berlin Conference
- British and French rivalry – Fashoda
- British and German rivalry – South Africa and Boers
- French and German rivalry – Morocco
- Colonial rivalry in Asia – Russia and Japan
- Settling colonial rivalry – Britain and Russia
- Conclusion: contribution to causes of World War I?

QUESTIONS

1. What was agreed in the Entente Cordiale between Britain and France?
2. How did the Kaiser interfere in the First Moroccan Crisis?
3. How did he interfere in the Second Moroccan Crisis?
4. How did both crises affect relations between Britain, France and Germany?

The main British newspaper, *The Times*, denounced the telegram, saying, 'England will concede nothing to menaces and will not lie down under insult.' The Kaiser was forced to retract in a letter to his grandmother, Queen Victoria, but it was too late. The British were left wondering about the instability of the German Kaiser. Later events in Europe and Africa only reinforced British attitudes towards the Kaiser and Germany.

French and German Rivalry – Morocco

Cartoon portraying the Second Moroccan Crisis, when Wilhelm II sent a German warship to Agadir to intimidate the French.

Imperial conflict increased differences between France and Germany. Morocco in North Africa was within the French **sphere of influence** but that did not prevent Kaiser Wilhelm II from intervening.

In 1904, the **Entente Cordiale** between Britain and France settled long-standing colonial rivalries between the two countries. It allowed Britain maintain its interest in Egypt, and it allowed France expand from Algeria into Morocco.

In the **First Moroccan Crisis** (1905) Kaiser Wilhelm II visited Tangier in March 1905, and promised support for Morocco against France. He demanded an international conference to discuss the position of Morocco. Wilhelm hoped that his intervention in Morocco would drive France and Britain apart. Instead, at the conference in **Algeciras** (1906), Britain sided with France and Germany lost influence. The conference recognised French influence in Morocco, and reinforced Franco-British relations as both countries grew even more suspicious of Germany. King Edward VII called it *'the most mischievous and uncalled-for event which the German emperor has ever been engaged in'*. Soon after, military leaders in Britain and France engaged in informal discussions, which developed into a more formal agreement in the event of war in Europe.

In the **Second Moroccan Crisis** (1911), French troops occupied Fez (capital of Morocco at the time), claiming to be defending the Sultan of Morocco against rioters. In response, Germany sent the gunboat *Panther* to Agadir to protect Germans living there in May 1911. Kaiser Wilhelm demanded the French Congo in return for recognising French control of Morocco, but he had to back down again when Britain supported France.

As a result of the two Moroccan crises, France and Britain drew closer together and Germany grew further apart from them. These crises reinforced the **Entente Cordiale**, which Britain and France had agreed in 1904.

Colonial Rivalry in Asia

European expansion in Asia also led to **colonial rivalry**. Britain and Germany took over islands in the south and western Pacific. European powers and the USA established centres of trade and influence in China, which was weakened by a crumbling government. While European countries competed for advantages in China, this led to a nationalist Chinese uprising, the **Boxer Rebellion**, in 1899. In spite of their rivalry, the European powers, Japan and the USA co-operated in putting down the uprising and forcing China to pay compensation.

The Russo-Japanese War, 1904–05

In the late 19th century, Russia opened up **Siberia** and built the **Trans-Siberian railway**. The country expanded into Manchuria and leased the Lioatung Peninsula from China. It came into conflict with the newly expanding eastern power, Japan, which had control of Korea.

Japan agreed the **Anglo-Japanese Alliance** with Britain in 1902 in which each country agreed not to be involved in a war with a third power. Two years later, in 1904, Japan suddenly attacked the Russian sea base at **Port Arthur**. It also defeated Russia in major land battle, the **Battle of Mukden**, in early 1905.

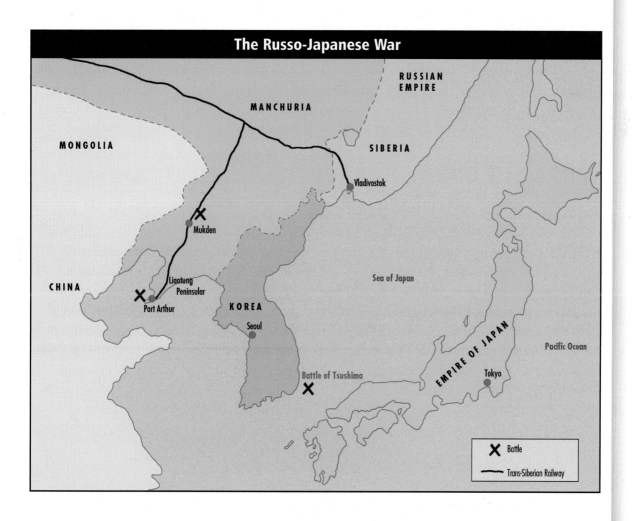

QUESTIONS

1. Did involvement in China lead to conflict between colonial powers?
2. Why was there conflict between Russia and Japan, and what was the outcome of that conflict?

Russia was forced to send its Baltic Fleet on a trip around Africa to challenge Japan. In the **Battle of the Tsushima Straits** (May 1905), the Japanese Navy defeated the Russian Navy. This was the first defeat of a European power by an Asian power. In the Treaty of Portsmouth (1905), Russia recognised Korea as being within the Japanese sphere of influence (control). It also agreed to evacuate Manchuria.

The defeat forced Russia out of the East, brought her attention back to the Balkans, further weakened the Russian government and led to the **1905 Russian Revolution**.

Why did Britain and Russia Settle Colonial Disputes?

Russia's advance into Asia at the end of the 19th century brought her into conflict with Britain which already had interests in the Middle East and in India. Their conflict centred on **Iran**, **Afghanistan** and **Tibet**. However, events in Europe dictated that Britain and Russia would settle their disagreements.

Germany's growing power and the establishment of the **Triple Alliance** of Germany, Austria-Hungary and Italy left Russia **isolated** in Eastern Europe. As well as this, Russia's **defeat** in the Russo-Japanese War forced the country to resolve issues with Britain. Britain was also concerned about Germany's growing power and needed to build up better relations with other European powers.

As a result, Britain and Russia agreed the **Anglo-Russian Entente** in 1907 which settled disagreements, particularly in Iran, and brought the countries closer together in Europe. This developed into the **Triple Entente** of Britain, France and Russia, which faced the **Triple Alliance** of Germany, Austria-Hungary and Italy.

What did Imperialism Contribute to the Causes of the First World War?

QUESTION

Why did Britain and Russia settle their colonial disputes?

Lenin argued in his publication *Imperialism, the Highest Stage of Capitalism* that capitalists' competition for markets, raw materials and investment of surplus capital would inevitably lead to conflicts which would in turn lead to a wider war. As far as Lenin was concerned it was developments in capitalism which caused the First World War. However, **historians** have challenged this view. They have shown that investment by capitalist economies in their colonies was small compared to investment in the USA. They have also said that there were many other causes to the war (see p. 72).

HOMEWORK EXERCISES

1. Draw a table in your notes with a heading **Causes of New Imperialism**. *Rank* the causes in order of importance, and provide *Reasons* for your ranking.

Causes of New Imperialism		
Causes	**Rank in order of importance**	**Reasons for your ranking**
Geographical explorations		
Economic reasons		
Nationalism and national pride		
Missionary, humanitarian		
Technological advances		
Strategic reasons		
Any other reasons?		

ORDINARY LEVEL

2. This is an extract from notes of a conversation with Bismarck, written by a British diplomat in 1885. Study it and answer the questions which follow.

> He (Bismarck) *said that Mr Gladstone might become Prime Minister again, a man with whom it was impossible to do business.*
>
> *But the policy Bismarck had followed on colonial matters in Africa was not inspired by any feeling of hostility towards England. He had sided with France on colonial matters in Africa in order to reduce the hatred of France towards Germany.*
>
> *However, this policy did not have the desired effect because France was as hostile as ever towards Germany. In fact France was ready to seize any opportunity of attacking Germany in order to regain Alsace-Lorraine.*
>
> P. H. Currie, a member of the British Foreign Office, on 28 September, 1885.

A. **(i)** What was Bismarck's opinion of the British leader, Mr Gladstone?

(ii) Why had Bismarck sided with France on colonial matters in Africa?

(iii) Did Bismarck's support for France produce the desired effect on France? Explain your answer.

(iv) Why was France 'ready to seize any opportunity' of attacking Germany?

(v) What was Bismarck's policy towards the New Imperialism? (2008)

B. Write a **short paragraph** on **one** of the following:

(i) How Economic reasons contributed to the New Imperialism

(ii) Colonial Rivalries between France and Germany

(iii) Colonial Rivalries between Britain and Germany

C. Write a **long answer** on **one** of the following:

(i) What caused the rise of New Imperialism at the end of the 19th century?

(ii) How did the New Imperialism impact on relations between European countries?

HIGHER LEVEL

3. Why did European powers seek colonies overseas during the period, 1871–1914? (2006)

4. What were the causes of the New Imperialism, and how did the New Imperialism affect Europe? (2009)

5. To what extent did colonial rivalries contribute to international tensions, 1871–1914? (2013)

6. What were the causes of the New Imperialism and how did the new Imperialism affect Europe? (2017)

THE EASTERN QUESTION: SERBIA AND GREAT POWER RIVALRY

9

In this section, you should understand:
- The attitude of the great powers towards the Balkans.
- How the Balkans Crisis and Wars developed.
- How the Balkans Wars prepared the groundwork for the causes of World War I.

'The Sick Man of Europe'

KEY CONCEPT
BALANCE OF POWER: When no one country is able to dominate others, when countries are roughly equal in power.

By the end of the 19th century, the Turkish Empire was collapsing – it was known as '**the sick man of Europe**'. It stretched across North Africa and into the Balkans. In the European section, the Turks often treated the Christian people of the Balkans savagely.

Nationalist movements in the Balkans were looking for their independence. Some countries, such as **Serbia**, already had self-government.

Great Power Rivalry

A cartoon by Leonard Raven-Hill from Punch, 2 October 1912 shows European leaders try to keep the lid on the Balkan 'powder keg' – a barrel of gunpowder ready to explode.

Other empires tried to extend their influence into the Balkans. A variety of factors brought the **great powers** into conflict over Serbia and the Balkans ('the powder keg of Europe'), which ultimately contributed to the causes of the First World War.

AUSTRIA-HUNGARY wanted to extend its influence because it was pushed out of Central Europe by German unification. It also wanted to control **Slav nationalism**, because it might lead to the break-up of its empire. 'Slavs' refers to the ethnic group to which the peoples of the Balkans belong.

RUSSIA wanted to gain influence in the Balkans, to support fellow Slavs there. It also wanted to control the **exit** through the Dardanelles from the Black Sea for its trade.

GERMANY, under Bismarck, had no direct interest in the Balkans but wanted to ensure that any conflict there would not lead to a European War. Such a war could lead to the collapse of the new German Empire, he feared.

BRITAIN also had no direct interest in the Balkans, but feared that **Russian expansion** there would threaten British interests in the eastern Mediterranean. As a result, Britain supported the Turkish Empire in its resistance to Russian expansion.

? QUESTIONS

1. Why was the Balkans the 'powder keg of Europe'?
2. Why did the great powers clash in the Balkans?

The Creation of an Independent Serbia

Serbia was a small country in the Balkans, but there were Serbs in the Austro-Hungarian Empire. Serbia gained independence from the Turkish (Ottoman) Empire in the Congress of Berlin (1878). Serbia wanted to create a **Greater Serbia** or a **South Slav state** (Yugoslavia) by incorporating other territories close by where Serbs lived, such as **Bosnia** and **Herzegovina** and **Montenegro**. This led it into conflict with other Balkan countries, with the Turkish Empire and the Austro-Hungarian Empire.

The Bosnian Crisis, 1908

After defeat in the Russo-Japanese War in 1904–05, **Russia** renewed its interest in the Balkans. This brought it once again into conflict with Austria-Hungary. The pro-Austrian king of Serbia was assassinated in 1903, and replaced by a pro-Russian king, Peter. He declared that he was following a policy of '**South Slavism**' (Yugoslavism) to instal Serbia as the economic and political leader of Slavs in the Balkans, including those within the Austro-Hungarian Empire.

The Balkans After the Congress of Berlin, 1878

AUSTRIA-HUNGARY
RUSSIAN EMPIRE
CROATIA
ROMANIA
BOSNIA SERBIA
BULGARIA
MONTENEGRO
OTTOMAN
ITALY
EMPIRE
GREECE

New leadership in **Austria-Hungary** was anxious to re-establish the dominance of the empire in the Balkans and to crush nationalist feeling within the empire. As a result, in 1908, Austria-Hungary annexed (took over) Bosnia and Herzegovina, which they had administered since 1878.

Serbia was angry and looked for Russian support, because there were Serbs in Bosnia and Herzegovina. Austria-Hungary sought and got support from Germany. They forced Serbia and Russia to accept the Austro-Hungarian takeover of Bosnia and Herzegovina.

> **KEY CONCEPT**
> NATIONALISM: The political belief that all people can be divided into nations and that each nation should have its own government.

'A Dress rehearsal for the First World War'

Serbia and Russia were **humiliated**. There was strong anti-Austrian feeling in Serbia; its ambition for a South Slav state had been stopped. This encouraged the growth of terrorist organisations, including the **Black Hand Society**. As well as the dangers developing in Serbia, **Russia** felt it could not concede any more in the Balkans. It began a military build-up to strengthen its position.

The **German** support for Austria was puzzling. Germany had involved itself in the Balkans even though it had no direct interest there. It had also supported Austria even

QUESTIONS

1. What was Greater Serbia?
2. What caused the Balkan Crisis, 1912?
3. What were the results of the crisis?

though Austria had not consulted Germany beforehand, making both countries more dependent on each other. As one historian said, *'the Bosnian crisis in the East was a kind of dress rehearsal for the First World War'* (Geiss).

The Balkan Wars

The First Balkan War, 1912

In 1911, Turkey was distracted by an unprovoked attack by Italy on Tripoli in North Africa. This provided an opportunity for the **Balkan League** of Serbia, Bulgaria, Montenegro and Greece to free the Balkans of the last of Turkish control. In 1912, the League went to war against Turkey. The League easily defeated the heavily outnumbered Turkish army which was still getting organised. The victorious League took over sections of the Turkish Empire, and Turkish territory in Europe was largely reduced to land around Constantinople.

In the **Treaty of London** (1913), which dealt with the outcome of the war, each of the great powers was opposed to the gains of the Balkan League. As a result, Serbia and Montenegro lost the extra land they gained, and Albania was created as a separate and independent state. Serbia was given part of northern Macedonia as compensation, which Bulgaria also claimed.

The Second Balkan War, 1913

Bulgaria resented the gains of Serbia and Greece in the First Balkan War, and attacked them in 1913. But Greece and Rumania helped Serbia, and Bulgaria was stopped. In the **Treaty of Bucharest** (1913), Bulgaria gave lands to Serbia and Greece. It even lost territory which it had gained from the Turkish Empire in the First Balkan War.

Results of the Balkan Wars

Serbia was the real winner in the Balkan Wars. As a result of the two wars, **Serbia** doubled its size. Its population increased by 1.5 million and its army could mobilise 400,000 men. It was now the most powerful state in the Balkans. Ominously, the wars resulted in deep **anti-Austrian feeling** in Serbia – it saw Austria as the main block in creating a Greater Serbia.

Before the wars, the **Black Hand Society** had been created in 1911 to work for a South Slav state. It was a secret society largely composed of army officers and professionals. As an 'organisation [which] prefers terrorist action', it soon planned the **assassination** of the Archduke, Franz Ferdinand of Austria-Hungary to further its cause. It was this event which triggered World War I.

Austria-Hungary's influence was lessened considerably, and it could not lose any more power. Serbs in Austrian-controlled Bosnia and Herzegovina grew increasingly restless after Serbia's success. Austria feared Serbia even more than ever – it believed that Serbia should be defeated because its success could lead to the break-up of the Austrian Empire. It was ready to resist any further Serbian advances.

As a result of the Balkan Wars, **Germany** was even more committed to Austria, which it felt was its only dependable ally. It increased the size of its army, and it assured

Austria that it could depend on German support. Kaiser Wilhelm II said to Austria, *'you can be certain that I stand behind you and am ready to draw the sword whenever your action makes it necessary.'*

The Assassination of Franz Ferdinand, 1914

Franz Ferdinand, heir to the Austrian throne, was inspecting Austrian troops in Sarajevo in June 1914. He and his wife, Sophia, were **assassinated** by a member of the **Black Hand Society**, Gavril Princip.

The Austrian government blamed Serbia and issued an **ultimatum**. Serbia was supported by Russia, and Austria-Hungary was supported by Germany. However, Serbia agreed to most of the conditions of the Austrian ultimatum.

But Austria was not satisfied, so it still declared war on Serbia. The other great powers joined in and the **First World War** began (see Chapter 10).

The Balkans, 1914

QUESTIONS (?)

1. Why did the Balkan League attack Turkey?
2. What were the results of the First War?
3. Who fought in the Second Balkan War?
4. What was the outcome of the war?
5. Who gained from the Balkan Wars?
6. Who lost? What were the lessons for the future?

HOMEWORK EXERCISES

ORDINARY LEVEL

1. **A.** Write a **short paragraph** on one of the following:
   (i) Serbia, 1871–1914
   (ii) Serbia as a fulcrum of great power rivalry

   B. Write a **long answer** on the following:
   (i) How did tensions in the Balkans lead to crises and wars in that area between 1871 and 1914?

HIGHER LEVEL

2. What were the main international tensions in Europe, 1871–1914? (2011)

3. During the period, 1871–1914, how did one or more of the following contribute to international tensions: colonial rivalries; the naval policy of Wilhelm II; Serbia and its neighbours? (2015)

4. To what extent was Serbia the fulcrum of Great Power rivalry?

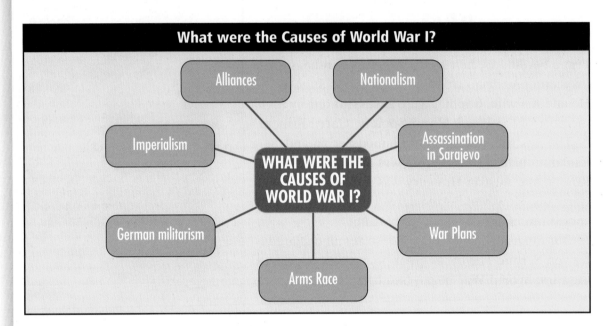

What were the Causes of World War I?

- Alliances
- Nationalism
- Imperialism
- Assassination in Sarajevo
- **WHAT WERE THE CAUSES OF WORLD WAR I?**
- German militarism
- War Plans
- Arms Race

The Alliances

There were **two alliances** of the great powers organised before the First World War. The **Entente Powers** were also known as the Allies; the **Alliance Powers** were also known as the Central Powers:

Triple Alliance	Triple Entente
Germany	France
Austria-Hungary	Russia
Italy	Britain

KEY CONCEPT
WORLD WAR: A war involving most of the largest countries in the world.

Their purpose was **defensive** – if one country was attacked, the others would come to its help. But by 1914 a local war could become a world war, because the alliance system would drag in all the great powers.

This is what happened in 1914 when Austria-Hungary declared war on Serbia. Serbia was backed up by Russia and the alliances spread the war.

Some **historians** claim the alliances were not a significant cause of the war, and that they were a loose arrangement. They point to Italy as an example – it did not join in the war until 1915 and then it favoured the Triple Entente because the Treaty of London promised it extra land.

However, other historians have pointed out that the **Moroccan Crises** and the **Balkans Crisis and Wars** (see pp. 64; 70) worsened relations between the alliances and strengthened relations within the alliances.

World War I System of Alliances

Triple Entente
Triple Alliance

NORWAY
SWEDEN
DENMARK
THE NETHERLANDS
GREAT BRITAIN
BELGIUM
GERMAN EMPIRE
RUSSIA
FRANCE
AUSTRIA-HUNGARY
ROMANIA
SERBIA
BULGARIA
ALBANIA
GREECE
SWITZERLAND
ITALY
PORTUGAL
SPAIN

QUESTIONS ?

1. What two alliances faced each other in 1914?
2. What contribution did the alliances make to the causes of World War I?

Imperialism

The great powers wanted to expand in Africa and Asia and this caused clashes between them (see pp. 61–66). In South Africa, there were clashes between **Britain** and **Germany**:

- Wilhelm II congratulated the **Boers** on defeating the Jameson Raid.
- Wilhelm II favoured the Boers during their war with Britain.

In Morocco, there were clashes between **France** and **Germany**:

- Germany supported Moroccan independence against France.

According to **Lenin** in his book, *Imperialism, the Highest Stage of Capitalism*, the First World War was the inevitable result of the development of capitalism, as capitalist countries competed for markets, raw materials and investment of surplus capital. He said that the war was a war between **capitalist powers** (see pp. 58–59).

However, some historians have rejected Lenin's analysis. They have shown that capitalist countries had much stronger trading and financial links with each other than with their colonies. They have argued that if imperialism contributed to the causes of the war, it was not the only cause of the war.

Colonial Powers of Europe, 1914		
Country	Colonial area sq. km (million)	Number of colonial territories
Britain	31.1	55
France	10.3	29
Germany	2.6	10
Belgium, Portugal, Netherlands, Italy	7.8	21

1. Based on the figures in this box, which countries were more likely to come into conflict with each other?
2. Do the figures support the idea that imperialism was an inevitable cause of World War I?

German Militarism

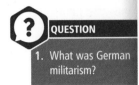

QUESTION

1. What was German militarism?

Some historians have blamed German **militarism** for causing the war. They say that German political leaders were dominated by **military leaders** who were prepared to back up Austria's threat to Serbia and **use war**, rather than diplomacy or negotiation, to achieve their aims. The army and navy were heavily populated by the *Junker* class (see p. 5) who believed that war would make Germany a great power. They also feared the growth of the Russian army at the time. Many German leaders favoured the idea of a 'preventative war', to defeat Russia before their army was fully ready about two years later. Von Moltke, German Chief of General Staff said in June 1914, *'If only things would finally boil over, we are ready – the sooner, the better for us.'*

Arms Race

In the 30 years before the war, spending on **armaments** increased by more than 300 per cent in Europe generally, headed by Germany (340 per cent increase) and Russia (260 per cent increase). There was widespread use of **conscription** (compulsory military service) following on the successful example of Prussia in the **Franco-Prussian War** in 1870–71. The use of conscription and reserves resulted in huge armies in wartime.

Germany's peacetime army could be expanded from 800,000 to 5.6 million; the French could send out 3.5 million men while Russia had 5 million available for war.

Increase in the peacetime German Army	
1880	401,650
1914	791,000

The German Army almost doubled in size between 1880 and 1914.

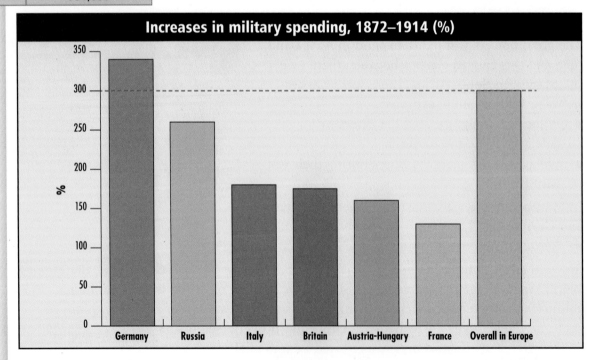

The **navies** also expanded. There was a **naval race** between Britain and Germany. After the German Navy Laws, Britain feared Germany would catch up with them, so they built **dreadnoughts**. Germany followed the British lead and built their own dreadnoughts. The **arms race** – racing to build larger armies and navies – increased tensions between the great powers and contributed to the formation of the Triple Entente to oppose the German-dominated Triple Alliance (see p. 72). (Case Study, The Naval Policy of Wilhelm II, p. 20)

Nationalism

Nationalism caused friction in different parts of Europe.

   The Balkans was considered the '**powder keg of Europe**' as the Ottoman (Turkish) Empire collapsed and countries competed for greater power and territory. Here **Austria-Hungary** was threatened by growing **Serbian nationalism** – Serbs wanted to unite with Serbs in Bosnia and Herzegovina, part of the Austrian empire, to create a Greater Serbia. **Russia** supported the Serbs in order to extend its influence into the Balkans.

   Austria wanted to crush the Serbs because they thought that if they gave in to Serbia their empire would break up. The **Balkans Crisis** in 1908 and the two **Balkan Wars** in 1912 and 1913 worsened relations between Austria and Serbia. Now Austria was ready for any opportunity to crush Serbia.

   In western Europe, **France and Germany** were in conflict over **Alsace-Lorraine**. These provinces had been taken by Germany after the Franco-Prussian War in 1870–71. The French wanted to get them back; they said they were the '**lost provinces**'. Their continued loss was a reminder of defeat in the war.

KEY CONCEPT
NATIONALISM: The political belief that all people can be divided into nations and that each nation should have its own government.

QUESTIONS

1. What was the Arms Race?
2. Why did it increase tensions?
3. Where did nationalism cause tensions between the great powers?

War Plans

War plans were needed to get the huge armies ready for battle (**mobilisation**). There were detailed railway timetables to move troops to the fronts. Some historians have argued that once the **July Crisis** occurred (below), the war plans took over in each of the great powers which undermined any diplomatic efforts to end the crisis.

'All the great powers had vast conscript armies. These armies were brought together by mobilisation. All mobilisation plans depend on the railways, and railways demand timetables. Any alteration in the mobilisation plan meant not a delay for 24 hours but for at least six months before the next set of timetables were ready.'

(A.J.P. Taylor, *How Wars Begin*.)

- The Germans developed the **Schlieffen Plan** to fight a **two-front war** against Russia and France; however, they had no plan to attack Russia on its own: only France and then Russia. They had to defeat France in six weeks to switch their armies across Germany to fight Russia, whose mobilisation plan would take longer to implement. The German plan to attack France included going through neutral Belgium.
- The **Russians had no plan** to attack Austria-Hungary on its own (partial mobilisation); only a plan to attack Austria and Germany at the same time (full mobilisation).
- The **Austro-Hungarians had war plans** to fight Serbia and Russia separately or together. But once they mobilised against Serbia, they would have to prepare for war against Russia, in case Russia supported Serbia.

QUESTIONS

1. What were the war plans?
2. Why was it difficult to stop mobilisation for war once it had started?

The Assassination at Sarajevo – the July Crisis, 1914

Austria blamed the Serbian government for the assassination of Archduke Franz Ferdinand, heir to the Austrian throne, in Sarajevo on 28 June 1914. The assassination was carried out by Gavril **Princip** of the **Black Hand Society** – a secret Serbian nationalist organisation.

- On 5 July, Austria got the full support of **Kaiser Wilhelm II** and the German government for whatever measures they intended to take against Serbia, an arrangement that was called the **'blank cheque'**.

- On 23 July, Austria issued a severe **ultimatum** to Serbia, which they had to fulfil within 48 hours. Giving in to the demands of the ultimatum would effectively mean the end of an independent Serbia. However, Serbia agreed to all the demands except the demand that Austrian police be allowed carry out investigations in Serbia.

- Austria was not satisfied with this. They **declared war** on Serbia on 28 July, and bombarded Belgrade, the capital of Serbia, the next day.

- Serbia was supported by **Russia** who did not want to back down as had happened in the Balkan Crisis of 1908. **Tsar Nicholas II** ordered partial mobilisation of his army against Austria-Hungary but only then found out that Russia had no plan for partial mobilisation. Russia had only a plan for **full mobilisation** against both Austria-Hungary and Germany.

- Russian mobilisation led to **German mobilisation**. However, Germany had no plan to mobilise against Russia on its own; it only had a plan to attack France first and then attack Russia (The Schlieffen Plan, see above). Germany issued an ultimatum to Russia to demobilise and when the ultimatum expired after 12 hours, Germany declared war on Russia on 1 August. To bring the Schlieffen Plan into effect, Germany declared war on France on 3 August.

- This brought **Belgium** into the war because the Schlieffen Plan involved the German army sweeping through Belgium to attack France. **Britain** supported France, as part of the **Triple Entente**, and Belgium, because of a commitment to protect Belgium's neutrality made in 1839. Britain declared war on Germany on 4 August. World War I had begun.

- It took just five weeks from the assassination of Franz Ferdinand to change a **local Balkan conflict** into a **European and World War**. The build-up of mistrust during the previous

An artist's reconstruction of what happened when Gavril Princip shot Franz Ferdinand and his wife, Sophia, in Sarajevo in June 1914.

? QUESTION

How was the assassination of Franz Ferdinand the spark that set off World War I?

decades over imperialism and the arms race, the structure of the alliances, the fear of nationalism, the belief in the use of war to solve problems – all of these meant that when the assassination of Franz Ferdinand occurred, the great powers, particularly Germany, Austria-Hungary and Russia, could not delay their war plans.

New York Times report on the assassination of Franz Ferdinand and his wife, 29 June 1914.

HOMEWORK EXERCISES

1. Draw up a table in a page of your notes, with the heading **Causes of World War I**. *Rank* the causes of World War I, with 1 the most important cause. Explain why you ranked them under *Reasons*.

Causes of World War I		
Cause	**Rank in order of importance**	**Reasons for ranking the cause**
The Alliances		
Imperialism		
German militarism		
Arms Race		
Nationalism		
War Plans		
Assassination at Sarajevo		
Any other reasons?		

ORDINARY LEVEL

2. Write a **short paragraph** on **one** of the following:
   (i) New Imperialism and the causes of World War I
   (ii) War Plans and the causes of World War I

3. Write a **long answer** on the following:
   (i) How did the assassination of Archduke Franz Ferdinand in Sarajevo in June 1914 spark off World War I?

HIGHER LEVEL

4. In what ways did the naval policy of Wilhelm II and/or Franco-German tensions contribute to the outbreak of World War I? (2007)

5. What were the causes of World War I? (2008)

6. What were the main international tensions in Europe, 1871–1914? (2011)

7. To what extent was nationalism the main cause of World War I?

8. Was Germany mainly responsible for the outbreak of World War I?

11 THE CONDUCT OF WORLD WAR I

In this section, you should understand:
- How the Schlieffen Plan failed.
- How trench warfare developed.
- How alternative strategies were developed to overcome the stalemate on the Western Front.
- How Germany defeated Russia on the Eastern Front.
- The part played by the war at sea and the war in the air.
- Why America entered the war, and its impact.
- Why the Allies won the war.
- The role of Douglas Haig.

The War of Movement

The **Schlieffen Plan** was developed by Germany to fight a **two-front war** against both France and Russia. Germany planned to mobilise its army faster than France, while Russia would be the slowest to mobilise.

The German Army planned to attack France first by advancing through Belgium. They would defeat France before Russia was ready. The German Army would then move to the east to attack Russia.

The German Schlieffen Plan and the French war plan, including the role of the British Expeditionary Force (BEF).

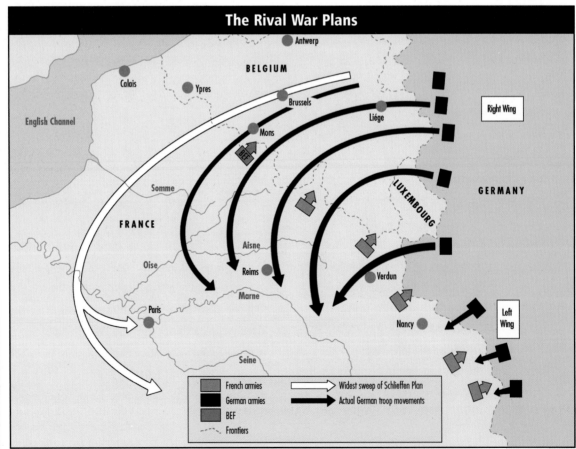

The Rival War Plans

Legend:
- French armies
- German armies
- BEF
- Frontiers
- Widest sweep of Schlieffen Plan
- Actual German troop movements

? QUESTION

What were the strengths and weaknesses of each plan?

The Schlieffen Plan in Action

The German Army attacked through Belgium, capturing the fortress of **Liége** after two weeks, and **Brussels** on 20 August. However, the Belgians slowed down the German advance. The **British Expeditionary Force** (BEF) which took up a position on the left of the French army also slowed the Germans at the **Battle of Mons** (23–24 August). But the Germans continued to advance.

The **Russians** invaded more quickly in the East than expected, so Germany had to transfer troops from the French campaign to the East. This **weakened** the attack on France. The Germans also transferred troops from the right to the left wing of their army in France to resist the French.

As a result, the German chief of staff, **Von Moltke**, was forced to change the original Schlieffen Plan. He had to swing the German army **east (inside) of Paris** rather than to the west (outside of Paris) where he would have surrounded and captured the city.

The German and French armies clashed at the **Battle of the Marne** (5–9 September). The defeat of the German army here changed the course of the war. The Schlieffen Plan **failed** and Germany faced a **two-front war**. It was also the end of the war of movement. The German Army retreated to the River Aisne and dug in (dug trenches for protection). This established the future pattern of the war with **stalemate** and **trench warfare**. As Germany dug in along the River Aisne, both sides now tried to outflank each other (move past to attack from the side) in a **race to the sea**. Neither side succeeded in outflanking the other so that by December the front lines had reached the coastline.

Casualties of the first months of the war		
Country	**Size of army**	**Casualties**
Britain	160,000	85,000
France	1,000,000	850,000
Germany	1,500,000	677,000

WHY DID THE SCHLIEFFEN PLAN FAIL?

- The Plan was too ambitious.
- The Belgians and British slowed down the advance of the right wing of the German army.
- The Russians attacked in the East sooner than the Germans expected.
- The Germans transferred troops to the East, weakening the Plan.
- The Germans transferred troops from the right wing (which did most of the fighting) to the left wing to resist the French.
- The German troops were exhausted from fighting and walking in the autumn heat.
- The German army swung inside Paris and was exposed to attack from the city.
- The German army was defeated at the Battle of the Marne and had to retreat.

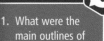

QUESTIONS

1. What were the main outlines of the Schlieffen Plan?
2. Why did it fail?

Trench Warfare and Stalemate

The initial war of movement was now over. Both sides dug **trenches**. These trench lines stretched from the English Channel to the border with Switzerland, a distance of about 800 kilometres.

Each side developed their **front line** trenches. Behind these were **support** trenches for supplies, reinforcements and communications. In between the two front lines was an area known as '**No Man's Land**,' which could range from 10 metres to hundreds of metres wide. No Man's Land, the poet Wilfred Owen said, was *'like the face of the moon, chaotic, crater-ridden, uninhabitable, awful, the abode of madness.'* Conditions in the trenches were often terrible – wet and muddy, overrun with rats and reeking of smells from dead bodies.

For much of the rest of the war, the defence was **stronger** than the offence (attack). **Rifles**, **machine guns** and **barbed wire** protected the troops in the trenches, and **reinforcements** were easily brought up to resist attacks. Over the next three-and-a-half years, from the end of 1914 to the middle of 1918, there was very little movement of the trench lines. Both sides used heavy artillery bombardments to break through the others' front lines. The assaults which followed the bombardments were usually stopped by a second line of trenches. This resulted in heavy losses for the Allied forces, for example, in the **Battles of Champagne** and **Loos** in 1915.

As stalemate (a situation where no progress could be made) took over, each side sought different means to overcome it and to achieve a **breakthrough** of the enemy lines.

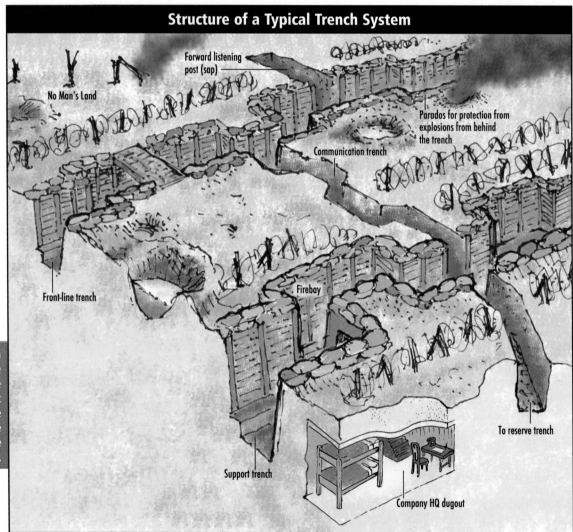

Structure of a Typical Trench System

No Man's Land

Forward listening post (sap)

Parados for protection from explosions from behind the trench

Communication trench

Front-line trench

Firebay

To reserve trench

Support trench

Company HQ dugout

> Using evidence from the drawing of the trench system and the photo, explain why it was difficult for the attackers to defeat the defenders in the trenches.

Trenches on the Somme, July 1916. One sentry keeps watch while the others sleep.

Trying to Achieve a Breakthrough

1. New Weapons

Various new weapons were developed to try to defeat the trench system.

Poison gas: Poison gas was used first by the Germans in the Second Battle of Ypres in 1915. It was directed by the wind (or later in the war fired from shells). The gas caused **panic** amongst the Allied troops and the Germans opened a gap of eight kilometres. However, this was soon closed by reinforcements.

The British next used gas in September 1915 but the wind blew it back on their own lines. Gas was a terrifying weapon but it had less impact on the conduct of the war than expected. Soldiers wore masks to counter its effects. While there were 1.25 million gas casualties, only less than 10 per cent died. Gas failed to achieve the breakthrough of the enemy lines.

Tanks: Tanks were invented by the British and **first used in 1916** in the Battle of the Somme. British commander Douglas Haig (see p. 84) used 32 tanks with limited success because the tanks were slow and often broke down. Some got caught in the muddy trenches. They were also used in small groups in support of the infantry, rather than all together.

The **first big success** for tanks occurred when almost 500 tanks were used together in the **Battle of Cambrai** in November 1917. 20 kilometres of the German front lines were broken and thousands of German troops were captured. However, the Germans won back the ground in a counter-attack when the British did not have sufficient infantry to follow up the tanks' success.

Tanks played a large part in the Allied successes in the last months of the war. But by then the German army had been weakened considerably. It took inter-war developments in both tank design and tactics before the tank came into its own in the Second World War.

Soldiers wore gas masks to counter the effect of poison gas.

Tanks had mixed results in the muddy conditions of the war.

? QUESTION

How successful were poison gas and tanks in achieving a breakthrough in the Western Front?

2. Diversionary Attack: Gallipoli, 1915

The British and French planned to attack **Turkey** to get supplies to hard-pressed Russia and to defeat Turkey, an ally of Germany. Defeating Turkey would be a morale-booster for the Allied side, while getting help to Russia would put greater pressure on Germany on the Eastern Front.

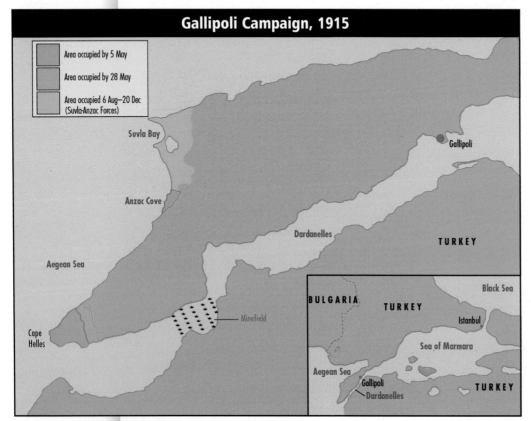

Gallipoli Campaign, 1915

Area occupied by 5 May

Area occupied by 28 May

Area occupied 6 Aug–20 Dec (Suvla-Anzac Forces)

Suvla Bay

Gallipoli

Anzac Cove

Dardanelles

TURKEY

Aegean Sea

Cape Helles

Minefield

BULGARIA

TURKEY

Black Sea

Istanbul

Sea of Marmara

Aegean Sea

Gallipoli

Dardanelles

TURKEY

The British and French planned to capture the **Gallipoli Peninsula** on the north side of the Dardanelles. This would allow them to control the Dardanelles into the Black Sea. They used a naval attack, to be followed by landings on Gallipoli by troops.

The naval attack failed due to bad planning and co-ordination; when troops landed they were forced onto the beaches, such as at Anzac Cove and Cape Hellas, where they suffered heavy casualties. The British

withdrew in December 1915 with 250,000 troops dead or wounded. It was clear now that the war could only be won on the Western Front. It also meant that no extra resources or help could be given to Russia through the Black Sea ports (See map).

3. War of Attrition: the Battle of Verdun, 1916

The new German commander, **Falkenhayn**, decided to attack the French at **Verdun**. He believed that the French would defend to the end and that Germany would wear them down (attrition) by causing them as many casualties as possible ('**bleed France white**'). This would force Britain to surrender also (See map).

The French defended Verdun for **national honour**. **Pétain**, the French commander, was ordered not to give in. The Battle of Verdun was one of the bloodiest battles of the war, as the German army fired 24 million shells into the area around Verdun. One French soldier described what he saw: *'You found the dead embedded in the walls of the trenches; heads, legs and half-bodies.'* France lost about 300,000 soldiers but Germany lost almost the same number. The British began the Battle of the Somme earlier than planned to relieve German pressure on Verdun. The French army held Verdun but it was badly weakened and this led to **mutinies** in the army in 1917.

4. The Battle of the Somme, 1916

Haig, the British commander, believed that he should use full force to break through the trench lines. He attacked the Germans at the **Battle of the Somme**, partly to relieve pressure on Verdun. He bombarded the Germans for five days to destroy the German barbed wire defending their trenches. The Germans protected themselves in **deep dugouts**, and the bombardment failed to clear the barbed wire. Thousands on the British side, including many Irishmen, were killed or wounded as they attacked across No Man's Land on the first day of the battle, 1 July 1916. The battle lasted for five months. Tanks were first used in this battle, but they had little impact.

> **KEY CONCEPT**
> **WAR OF ATTRITION:**
> A type of warfare where the purpose is to wear down the enemy. It refers in particular to warfare on the Western Front in the First World War.

> **QUESTIONS** ?
> 1. Why was a diversionary attack in Gallipoli planned?
> 2. Why did it fail?
> 3. What was the aim of the war of attrition?
> 4. Did it succeed?

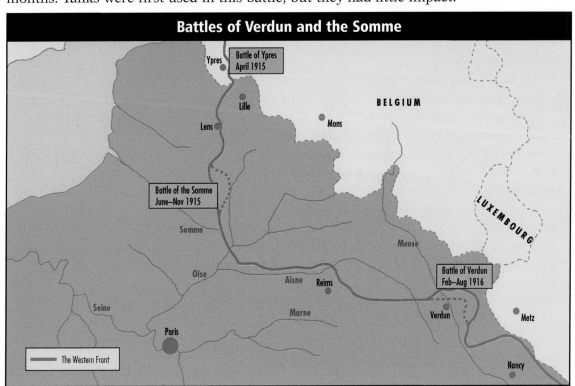

Battles of Verdun and the Somme

- Ypres — Battle of Ypres April 1915
- Lille
- Lens
- Mons
- BELGIUM
- Battle of the Somme June–Nov 1915
- Somme
- LUXEMBOURG
- Meuse
- Oise
- Aisne
- Reims
- Battle of Verdun Feb–Aug 1916
- Seine
- Marne
- Verdun
- Metz
- Paris
- Nancy
- —— The Western Front

Conditions worsened in bad weather – *'in the wilderness of mud, holding water-logged trenches or shell-hole posts, accessible only by night, the infantry lived in conditions which might be likened to those of earth-worms, rather than that of human kind.'* There were more than 600,000 Allied casualties, three-quarters of them British, and almost the same number of Germans. While neither side won, and the British failed to break through, the German army was 'completely exhausted' at its end.

KEY PERSONALITY: DOUGLAS HAIG

Douglas Haig – 'a dour Lowland Scot' – became an officer in the 7th Hussars in 1885. Haig saw active service in the colonies. He served in India and worked his way up through the ranks. He served in Sudan in 1897–8. He was also active in the Boer War, where he served under General Sir John French. Haig returned to India, where he worked in administrative posts under Lord Kitchener.

In 1906 he became director of military training at the War Office in London. Here he worked closely with the secretary of state for war, Haldane, to establish a general staff and a territorial Army. He was also responsible for organising the British Expeditionary Force (BEF), which would be used in any future European war.

When the First World War began Haig was in command of the 1st Army Corps of the BEF in France and Belgium, under the overall command of General Sir John French. He commanded his troops at the Battle of Mons and was praised for his fighting in the First Battle of Ypres (1914). Haig was promoted to full general and given command of the BEF, under French's supreme command. A year later, in December 1915, Haig replaced French and was made commander-in-chief of the British Army.

Haig disliked the type of warfare fought on the Western Front. He was mainly a cavalryman, and he thought the machine gun and tanks were overrated. He believed in a strategy of attrition – that attacking with artillery and great numbers of men would lead to a breakthrough of the German lines.

In 1916 he came under pressure from the French, who wanted him to relieve the German pressure on them during the Battle of Verdun. Haig brought forward his plans for the Battle of the Somme, which began on 1 July 1916. During the Battle of the Somme, Haig gained 12 kilometres for the loss of more than 400,000 British soldiers and 200,000 French soldiers.

There is much controversy over Haig's handling of the battle:

- David Lloyd George, later British Prime Minister, wrote in his memoirs that he considered resigning rather than permitting Haig to continue.
- Some historians said Haig's tactics of sending men against the well-defended German positions were flawed. They said the gains were at too high a price.
- Other historians said Haig's actions were forced on him by the weakness of the French.

Haig also commanded at Passchendaele (1917), which cost many British lives but weakened German resistance. He was in charge of the British advances on the Western Front in 1918, which contributed to the Allied victory in November 1918.

When the war was over Haig was made commander-in-chief of home forces until his retirement in 1921. He received a pension of £100,000 and became Baron Haig. Until he died in 1928, he devoted his time to the welfare of ex-soldiers through the Royal British Legion.

1. How experienced a soldier and leader was Haig before World War I?
2. How did he hope to achieve a breakthrough on the Western Front?
3. How successful was he in the Battles of the Somme and Passchendaele?

War on the Eastern Front

In 1914 the Russian Army mobilised more quickly than expected. This contributed to the failure of the Schlieffen Plan in the West. But Germany defeated the Russians soon afterwards at the **Battle of Tannenberg** and the **Battle of the Masurian Lakes** (1914). These battles saved Germany from invasion.

The Russians suffered a serious **defeat** in 1915. After a huge bombardment, Germany broke through Russian lines and advanced 140 kilometres, capturing Warsaw in August. Russia suffered further defeats in 1915, losing in all 1 million casualties and 1 million soldiers taken prisoner, and withdrawing about 450 kilometres.

The Eastern Front

Eastern Front 1914–18
— Farthest Russian advance 1914
— Gallipoli campaign 1915
— Front at the start of Russian Revolution 1917
— Farthest Austro-German advance 1918

Brusilov Offensive, 1916

In 1916, Russia recovered temporarily. In the **Brusilov Offensive**, Russia advanced against the Austrian army, inflicting 340,000 casualties and capturing 400,000 Austrian soldiers. However, Russia failed to take advantage of its success, and German troops were brought from the Western Front to reinforce the Austrian lines. Nevertheless, Austrian morale was destroyed and Austria was only kept in the war by 'German power'.

Revolutions

By 1917 the Russian Army was weak. Soldiers lacked arms and ammunition and some deserted (left the army). The failures of the Russian Army contributed to the revolutions in Russia in 1917. In turn, the two revolutions – March and November – ended Russia's contribution to the war. After the **November Revolution** of 1917, Lenin and the Communists signed the **Treaty of Brest-Litovsk** (1918) with Germany. This took Russia out of the war, but it lost much land to Germany.

Germany now had to fight on **only one front**. German troops were transferred to the Western Front in advance of a German effort to win the war there.

QUESTIONS

1. Who won the battles on the Eastern Front?
2. How was Russia affected by its participation in the war?

War at Sea

Battle of Jutland, 1916

Many people expected major sea battles in the First World War because of the building of dreadnoughts (see p. 23). But there was only one major sea battle – the **Battle of Jutland** in 1916, off the coast of Denmark. The British lost more ships and men – 14 ships and 6,000 men to Germany's 11 ships and 2,500 men. However, the British fleet was ready for battle again the next day and the British Navy was able to maintain its blockade of Germany. On the other hand, the German Navy retreated to their ports and stayed there for the rest of the war. Towards the end of the war, a **mutiny** amongst the German High Seas Fleet contributed to Germany's surrender.

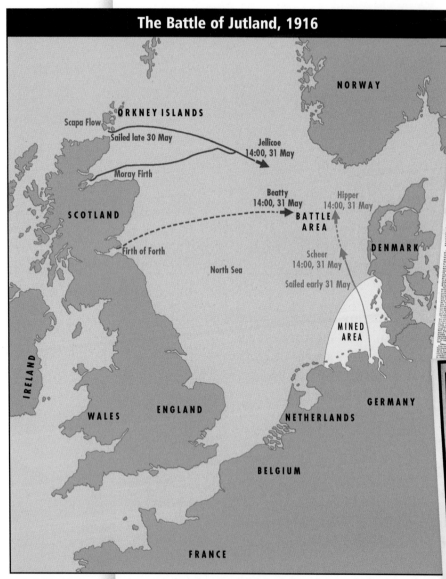

The Battle of Jutland, 1916

A New York Times headline from 8 May 1915 reports on the sinking of the Lusitania off the Irish coast.

A propaganda poster urges Irishmen to join the army to avenge the sinking of the Lusitania in 1915.

Submarine Warfare

The **main roles** of the British Navy were protecting merchant ships to ensure supplies came from America and the British Empire, and blockading enemy ports.
In contrast, Germany used **U-boats** (submarines) to sink merchant ships bringing supplies to Britain.

The Germans used **restricted** (attacking only warships) and **unrestricted** (attacking all ships) submarine warfare at different times during the war. In 1915, Germany used unrestricted submarine warfare which resulted in the sinking of some passenger ships, such as the *Lusitania* off the Old Head of Kinsale (May 1915). This resulted in President **Wilson** (USA) criticising Germany over the loss of 1,201 people, including 128 Americans.

After its failure in the Battle of Jutland, Germany relied on **submarine warfare** to defeat Britain at sea. It began unrestricted warfare again in early 1917. The German high command realised that this policy could mean war with America but they calculated that they would have defeated the British and French on the Western Front before **America** would have fully mobilised its army. Very soon, thousands of ships were sunk and Britain had only six weeks' supply of wheat left in 1917. On this occasion, however, the policy encouraged America into the war in April 1917, and fresh troops from America played a key role in the battles in 1918.

Britain **won** the war at sea by:
- Using **convoys**, which could be more easily protected by destroyers, to cross the Atlantic.
- Using depth charges to sink **submarines** and **Q-ships** (decoy ships) to entice submarines to the surface where they would be attacked.
- **Blockading** German ports with British ships and mines. Germany suffered severe shortages and this contributed to its defeat in 1918.

Some **historians** claim that Britain won the First World War because it won the war at sea. Germany failed to cut off Britain entirely from its supplies, and its unrestricted submarine warfare brought America into the war, tipping the balance in favour of the Allies on the Western Front in 1918 (pp. 98–99).

QUESTIONS ?

1. Why did Britain blockade German ports?
2. What role did German submarines (U-boats) play in World War I?
3. How important was the war at sea for the outcome of World War I?

War in the Air

The war in the air did not have a very important influence on the progress of the war. Britain used **airships** to protect merchant ships. Germany used airships (called **Zeppelins**) to bomb British cities, but Zeppelins were easy targets for aeroplanes.

The first Zeppelin raid was in 1915, and over the next three years 50 more raids were carried out against towns in England, particularly London. This was the first time civilians were bombed from the air. These airship raids resulted in almost 1,900 casualties, including 564 deaths.

The searchlight shines on a German Zeppelin (airship) dropping bombs.

'Mick' Mannock, a British pilot of Irish descent, who became a national hero.

Defensive measures carried out by Britain included better anti-aircraft guns, barrage balloons (large balloons tethered by metal cables) and more aeroplanes defending the cities. These measures brought down 30 airships and forced the Germans to use heavy **Gotha bombers** by 1918. Their impact was more severe, killing more than 800 people. Nevertheless, the impact of the bombing was exaggerated, and this influenced bombing raids during World War II.

In World War I, **aeroplanes** were very fragile. They were used for **reconnaissance** on the Western and Eastern Fronts. They faced enemy planes in **dogfights**, and some pilots became **national heroes** – Baron von Richthofen (the Red Baron) in Germany, and 'Mick' Mannock in Britain.

Aircraft development was rapid during the war, so by the time it ended, planes had become larger and could fly further. There were also more planes involved in direct bombing of enemy trenches. On the British side, the Royal Flying Corps (RFC) took 37 planes to France in 1914; by the end of the war, the RFC was combined with the Royal Naval Air Service to create the **Royal Air Force** with more than 20,000 aircraft – the largest in the world.

1917 – Major Changes in the War

In 1917, the French Army **mutinied**, and Britain was left to fight largely on its own on the Western Front. However, **Pétain** was restored as commander-in-chief of the French Army and he gradually raised morale by improving conditions of pay and forbidding major attacks. He also imposed discipline and executed 43 soldiers.

Britain fought the **Battle of Messines** and the **Third Battle of Ypres (Passchendaele)** in 1917. The British dug deep tunnels under Messines Ridge and planted explosives. A massive explosion heard in London began the attack, which had been preceded by heavy bombardments. The British achieved their objective and took over the Ridge, but suffered heavy losses.

Massive bombardments lasting two weeks before the **Battle of Passchendaele** destroyed the drainage system and turned the ground into mud. This was worsened when the weather broke and made the ground impassable to infantry and tanks. The British reached their target after three months but with the loss of 250,000 men – a similar number to the German loss.

EXAM QUESTION

What did you learn about World War I from your study of the conduct of war?
(2016)

QUESTIONS

1. What impact had airships on the war?
2. What role did aeroplanes play in the war?
3. What major changes occurred in the war in 1917?

Nevinson's *After A Push* – the scarred battlefield similar to Passchendaele.

America's Entrance to the War, 1917

At the same time, the USA joined the war in April that year because:

- American citizens had been killed in 1915 when the *Lusitania* was sunk.
- Germany tried to persuade Mexico to invade the US in the **Zimmermann Telegram**.
- Germany began a campaign of **unrestricted submarine warfare** again in early 1917.

This is an edited extract from the telegram sent by the German Foreign Minister, Alfred Zimmermann, to the German ambassador in Mexico. Study it and answer the questions which follow.

Berlin, 19 January 1917

On the first of February we intend to begin unrestricted submarine warfare.

In spite of this, it is our intention to keep neutral the United States of America.

If this is not successful, we propose an alliance with Mexico on the following basis: that we shall make war together, and together, make peace.

It is understood that Mexico is to recover her lost territories in New Mexico, Texas and Arizona.

The use of ruthless submarine warfare now promises to force England to make peace in a few months.

Zimmermann.

QUESTIONS
1. What does Germany intend to do on the first day of February?
2. If the United States does not remain neutral, what does Zimmermann propose to do?
3. What does Mexico hope to gain from an alliance with Germany?
4. What will force England to make peace?
5. Give one reason why the United States entered World War I in April 1917. (2007)

The Last Battles in 1918

America's entry into the war made up for French weakness in the West, and Russia's losses in the East. After the **Bolshevik** (Communist) **Revolution** in November 1917, and the signing of the **Treaty of Brest-Litovsk** (March 1918), Russia pulled out of the war.

Ludendorff Offensive

However, it took time for the American forces to be trained and brought to Europe. The German commander, **Ludendorff**, decided that he would attack on the Western Front before the Americans had built up their strength. He would use German troops brought from the Eastern Front to try one last major attack on the Western Front.

In March 1918, Ludendorff attacked and almost reached Paris, but the German Army was exhausted and running out of supplies. The Allied troops, helped by fresh American troops, counter-attacked and drove the Germans back. The Allies broke through the **Hindenburg Line** – a specially constructed German defensive line – and the German army continued to retreat.

QUESTIONS ?
1. Why did Ludendorff attack in 1918?
2. Why did his attack fail? Why did Germany sign an armistice?

Armistice, 11 November 1918

In Germany, there were shortages of food and supplies that led to strikes and riots. The High Seas Fleet **mutinied**. The Kaiser, Wilhelm II, went into exile in the Netherlands. Germany signed an armistice on **11 November 1918** in a railway carriage in Compiégne Forest in Northern France. The war was over and Germany was defeated.

The Pairs Gun was developed by Krupps during World War I. With its long range, it began firing on Paris in March 1918, killing 250 people over a period of four months.

Allied and Central Power Resources

Strength of Countries in 1914		
	Allied Powers	**Central Powers**
Population (millions)	265.5	115.2
Steel (million tons)	15.3	17.0
Army divisions available for mobilisation	179.3	69.0

Armed Forces of World War I			
Allied Powers		**Central Powers**	
Russia	12.0	**Germany**	11.0
British Empire	8.9	**Austria-Hungary**	7.8
France	8.4	**Turkey**	2.9
Italy	5.6	**Total** (inc. all countries)	**22.9**
USA	4.3		
Total (inc. all countries)	**42.1**		

The Results of the war

- The German, Austrian, Russian and Turkish empires **collapsed**.
- There were **revolutions** in Russia in March and November 1917; the first Communist state was set up in the second revolution.
- About 8 million soldiers were **killed**; millions more were injured or disabled.
- There was widespread **destruction** in Northern France along the Western Front.
- **Civilians** became war targets, largely due to the new technologies of the submarine and the aeroplane.
- Europe's economies **declined**. Manufacturing declined. Countries lost foreign investments and export markets. Non-European countries such as the USA and Japan benefitted.
- European countries had huge **debts** after the war. These weakened currencies and caused inflation, especially in Germany.
- A **harsh peace settlement** was imposed in Germany in the Treaty of Versailles, which contributed to the causes of World War II (see pp. 128–132).
- The war influenced the **role of women** (see Case Study: Women in the workforce during World War I, pp. 100–10).

How many were killed in the war?					
Deaths (millions)		**Wounded (millions)**		**Civilian casualties (millions)**	
Germany	2.0	Total Allied Forces	11.9	Russia	1.5
Russia	2.0	Total Central Powers	8.3	France	0.3
French Empire	1.4	**Total**	**20.2**	Britain	0.1
Austria-Hungary	1.5			Italy	0.6
British Empire	0.95			Germany	0.4
Italy	0.65			Austria-Hungary	0.5
America	0.1			Ottoman Empire	
Other countries	1.4			(inc. Armenian massacre)	4.5
Total Allied Forces	5.6			Other countries	1.28
Total Central Powers	4.4			**Total**	**9.2**
Total	**10.0**				

HOMEWORK EXERCISES

1. Study the documents on the Battle of the Somme and answer the questions below.

DOCUMENT A

The generals are commonly lambasted [scolded] for failing to capture more than a few miles of territory. But, rather than the capture of ground in what was a rural region lacking in strategic objectives, the aim of the Battle of the Somme was to fatally weaken the German Army in France. The reduced French contribution meant that such a result was never on the cards.

However, despite being inconclusive, the battle was not without result. German strategy in 1917 was detrimentally influenced by the suffering endured by the German Army on the Somme, which had not thought the Allies capable of such a sustained attack with such fearsome artillery support. Seeing no immediate hope of victory in the West, they made the fatal decision to attempt to knock Britain out of the war through a campaign of 'unrestricted' submarine warfare. This involved sinking neutral shipping heading for British ports – effectively ensuring that the chief neutral nation, the United States, would enter the war against Germany.

http://www.iwm.org.uk/history/command-on-the-somme

DOCUMENT B

Casualty figures on the Somme*

British	French	German
420,000	200,000	500,000

*The British added their casualties daily, whereas the Germans added them every ten days. The British included all wounded, dead and missing soldiers as casualties; the Germans did not record lightly wounded or missing soldiers as casualties.

DOCUMENT C

The strain during the year (1916) proved too great. The endurance of the troops had been weakened by long spells of defence under the powerful enemy artillery fire ... We were completely exhausted on the Western Front. ... The Somme was the muddy grave of the German field army and of the faith in the infallibility of German leadership ... The most precious thing lost on the Somme was the good relationship between the leaders and the led.

General Ludendorff, German commander-in chief in 1918 & Captain von Hentig of the General Staff.

DOCUMENT D

The Battle of the Somme was not responsible for the failure of the German effort to capture Verdun. The French commander-in-chief (Joffre) said in May (1916) that the Germans had already been beaten at Verdun. It is claimed that the Battle of the Somme destroyed the old German Army by killing its best officers and men. It killed off far more of our best and of the French best.

David Lloyd George, Prime Minister of Britain, writing in the 1930s.

A. (i) What was the aim of the Battle of the Somme, according to Document A?

(ii) What effect did the Battle of the Somme have on the German Army, according to Document A?

(iii) What 'fatal decision' did the Germans make, according to Document A?

(iv) According to Document B, why is it likely that German casualty figures for the Battle of the Somme are underestimated?

(v) According to Document C, how did the strain during 1916 prove too great for the German army?

(vi) After reading Document D, would you think Lloyd George favoured the British conduct of the Battle of the Somme?

B. (i) Are these **primary** or **secondary** sources? Explain.

(ii) Is the **conclusion** in Document A that fatally weakening the German Army was 'never on the cards' supported by Documents B and C? Explain.

(iii) Does Lloyd George in Document D **believe** the claim 'that the Battle of the Somme destroyed the old German Army'? Explain.

(iv) Are Lloyd George's **conclusions** supported by Documents B and C? Explain.

(v) Which document would consider the **most objective** and which document the **most biased**? Explain.

C. (i) Do these documents explain why the Battle of Somme caused so much **controversy**? Explain.

(ii) From your knowledge of the course and these documents, how **significant** was the Battle of the Somme in your view?

ORDINARY LEVEL

2. Write a **short paragraph** on **one** of the following:
   (i) Trench warfare on the Western Front
   (ii) The Battles of Verdun and the Somme
   (iii) The war at sea
   (iv) The war in the air

3. Write a **long answer** on **one** of the following:
   (i) What part did Douglas Haig play in World War I? (2007)
   (ii) What did you learn about World War I from your study of Wilfred Owen? (2017) (See p. 138)
   (iii) Why did Germany lose World War I?

HIGHER LEVEL

4. What did you learn about World War I from your study of one or more of the following: Douglas Haig; Wilfred Owen; women in the workforce? (2009)

5. What did you learn about World War I and the post-war Peace Settlement from your study of one or more of the following: the conduct of war; women in the workforce; Woodrow Wilson? (2014)

6. What did you learn about World War I from your study of the conduct of war and/or the literature of the war? (2016) (See pp. 137–39)

7. To what extent do you agree that the defeat of Germany in World War I was inevitable once the Schlieffen Plan failed?

8. What factors contributed to the defeat of Germany in World War I?

The Kapp Putsch

In June 1919, the German government was forced to sign the humiliating **Treaty of Versailles**. Ebert's government was blamed. They were called the **November Criminals**, because they had also signed the armistice in November 1918. Nationalist Germans, including Wolfgang Kapp, said they 'stabbed' the German Army 'in the back'.

The next threat to the Weimar government came from the right wing in the **Kapp Putsch** (coup d'état). In March 1920, Kapp, with the help of Freikorps militia, seized control of **Berlin** and declared himself chancellor of Germany, with the support of the former army commander, **Ludendorff**. Ebert and his government were forced to leave Berlin. Army units refused to support Kapp but also failed to support Ebert and his government. Instead, Ebert called a **general strike**. This paralysed Berlin and led to the collapse of the coup.

The new Weimar Republic had survived attacks from both the left and the right.

KEY CONCEPT
NATIONALISM: The political belief that all people can be divided into nations and that each nation should have its own government.

KEY PERSONALITY: ROSA LUXEMBURG

Rosa Luxemburg was born in Poland (then part of the Russian Empire) in 1871. She was Jewish and became involved in revolutionary activities while she was still in secondary school.

Jews and revolutionaries were persecuted in Tsarist Russia, so Luxemburg emigrated to Zürich (Switzerland) in 1889. There she studied law and political economy.

Luxemburg became involved in the Second International. She also met the leading Russian Marxists (or Communists). Luxemburg disagreed with them, and with the Polish Socialist Party, because of their support for Polish independence. Along with friends, she founded the Polish Social Democratic Party, later the Polish Communist Party.

Luxemburg criticised nationalism. Instead she stressed the international nature of socialism and the working class, underestimating the influence of nationalism.

In 1898 Luxemburg settled in Berlin and worked with the German Social Democratic Party, the largest party of the Second International. In her book, *Social Reform or Revolution*, Luxemburg disagreed with Eduard Bernstein's alternative view that Marxism or socialism would be achieved through gradual reform and parliamentary democracy (evolutionary socialism). Instead, she argued that revolution was necessary to move from capitalism to a socialist society.

Luxemburg was influenced by the Russian Revolution of 1905. She believed in the use of mass (widespread) revolutionary action. She was opposed to Lenin's view of a small, dedicated group of revolutionaries.

As World War I approached, Luxemburg criticised German militarism. She also believed that imperialism was the result of the expansion of capitalism into underdeveloped countries. She criticised the influence of imperialism on the causes of the war. At the Congress of the Second International in Stuttgart in 1909, her resolution, which demanded that all European workers' parties should unite in attempting to stop the war, was accepted.

When the First World War began, she opposed the support of the German Social Democratic Party for the German government and war effort. She organised anti-war demonstrations, and called on workers to conscientiously object to conscription. Along with Karl Liebknecht, she founded the Spartacus League. They believed that they would end the war through revolution and establish a socialist or working-class government. But during the war Luxemburg's influence was small, because she was jailed for being against the war.

As the German Revolution spread at the end of the First World War, Luxemburg and Liebknecht were released from jail in November 1918. They demanded political power for the workers' and soldiers' councils.

Luxemburg, Liebknecht and the Spartacus League joined with other groups to found the German Communist Party in January, 1919. They preferred a more democratic party to Lenin's dictatorial methods, and Luxemburg criticised the Bolshevik methods for retaining power afterwards.

When the Spartacists staged a revolt in Berlin, Luxemburg and Liebknecht were killed in January 1919 by Freikorps troops loyal to the German government.

What was Luxemburg's view about how socialism would develop? What was her view of Lenin's support for an elite group of revolutionaries? What was her view about World War I? What role did she play in the Spartacus League? How did she die?

HOMEWORK EXERCISES

1. Study the documents and answer the questions below.

DOCUMENT A

In the event of war threatening to break out, it is the duty of the workers and their parliamentary representatives in the countries involved to do everything possible to prevent the outbreak of war by taking suitable measures, which can, of course, be changed or intensified in accordance with the exacerbation [worsening] of the class struggle and the general political situation.

Should the war break out nevertheless, it is their duty to advocate its speedy end and to utilise the economic and political crisis brought about by the war to rouse the various social strata and to hasten the overthrow of capitalist class rule.

Rosa Luxemburg, speech made in Second International Congress in Stuttgart in 1907.

DOCUMENT B

I was taken to see Rosa Luxemburg … [she] differed from Lenin on several matters of revolutionary policy, and especially about the role of the Communist Party in the Workers' and Peasants' Councils, or Soviets. She did not like the Russian Communist Party monopolising all power in the Soviets and expelling anyone who disagreed with it. She feared that Lenin's policy had brought about, not the dictatorship of the working classes over the middle classes, which she approved of but the dictatorship of the Communist Party over the working classes.

Morgan Philips Price, *My Three Revolutions* (1969) http://spartacus-educational.com/RUSluxemburg.htm.

DOCUMENT C

When in January 1919 a second wave of revolt broke out, Luxemburg and (Karl) Liebknecht gave the movement their support in their *Red Flag* newspaper. In a move that is still highly controversial, the SPD (Social Democratic Party) leadership then gave right-wing paramilitaries, the Freikorps, the go-ahead to crush the left-wing revolution. On 15 January (1919), Luxemburg and Liebknecht were abducted and taken to the luxury Hotel Eden, where they were tortured. The two were then driven away separately into the nearby Tiergarten Park and murdered, Liebknecht was delivered to the city morgue while Luxemburg was shot and dumped into Berlin's Landwehr canal.

Her body was only recovered five months later after the winter ice had thawed and she was buried next to Liebknecht in the Friedrichsfelde Cemetery, the two becoming martyrs to the communist cause.

S. Dowling, *Luxemburg Still Popular 90 Years after Assassination* http://www.spiegel.de/international/germany/remembering-rosa-luxemburg-still-popular-90-years-after-assassination-a-601475.html

A. (i)   According to Rosa Luxemburg in Document A, what is the duty of the workers and their representatives if war threatens?

(ii) What does she say they must do if war breaks out?

(iii) According to Document B, how did Rosa Luxemburg differ from Lenin?

(iv) What did she fear about Lenin's policy, according to Document B?

(v)   Who did Luxemburg and Liebknecht support in the *Red Flag*, according to Document C?

(vi) Who told the Freikorps to crush the left-wing revolution?

(vii) How did Rosa Luxemburg die, according to Document C?

B. **(i)** Are the sources above **primary** or **secondary**? Explain.

    (ii) What is the difference between a '**source**' and '**evidence**'? Explain.

    (iii) Which is more factual, Document A or Document C? Explain

    (iv) Explain the difference between 'bias' and 'objectivity' using the documents.

C. **(i)** From your knowledge of the course and the documents, outline Luxemburg's views on the role and aims of socialism.

    (ii) From your knowledge of the course and the documents, can you explain why Rosa Luxemburg became a martyr 'to the communist cause' (Document C)?

ORDINARY LEVEL

2. Write a **short paragraph** on **one** of the following:

    (i) What was the impact of worsening conditions in Germany in 1918?

    (ii) What were the aims of the Spartacist Uprising and why did it fail?

    (ii) What were the aims of the Kapp Putsch and why did it fail?

3. Write a **long answer** on the following:

    (i) Why did the new German government face threats from both Left and Right, 1918–1920, and how did it overcome those threats?

HIGHER LEVEL

4. What was the impact of both war and revolution on Germany between 1918 and 1920?

In this section, you should understand:
- Why and how the Tsarist regime collapsed in March 1917.
- Why and how the Provisional Government collapsed in November 1917.
- How the Bolsheviks took power in November 1917.

In 1917, Russia experienced **two revolutions** – one in March, and the second in November. These revolutions were mainly caused by the effects of the First World War and bad social and economic conditions.

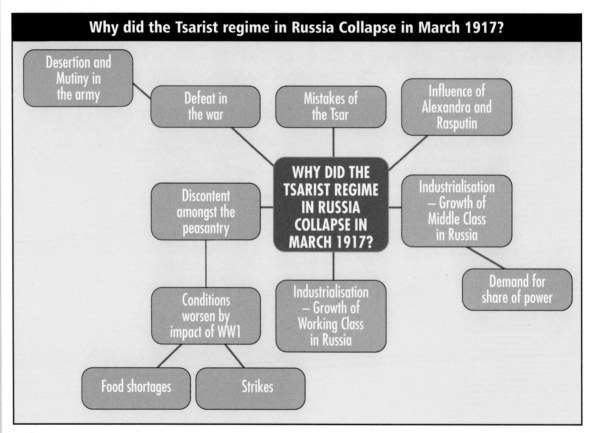

Why did the Tsarist regime in Russia Collapse in March 1917?

- Desertion and Mutiny in the army
- Defeat in the war
- Mistakes of the Tsar
- Influence of Alexandra and Rasputin
- Discontent amongst the peasantry
- **WHY DID THE TSARIST REGIME IN RUSSIA COLLAPSE IN MARCH 1917?**
- Industrialisation – Growth of Middle Class in Russia
- Demand for share of power
- Conditions worsen by impact of WW1
- Industrialisation – Growth of Working Class in Russia
- Food shortages
- Strikes

The Causes of the March Revolution, 1917

1. What were the Effects of World War One on Russia?

Russia suffered heavy defeats in battles such as **Tannenberg** and the **Masurian Lakes** (1914), and the **Brusilov Offensive** (1916). The army commanders were incompetent, the officers badly trained and the soldiers had inadequate supplies of weapons, ammunition, food and clothing. Artillery, for example, was often limited to two or three shells a day. Men sometimes went into battle without rifles.

By the end of 1916, 1.6 million Russian soldiers had been killed, 3.9 million were wounded and 2.4 million were taken prisoner. Not surprisingly, after the loss of 1 million men in the Brusilov Offensive in 1916, the army experienced **desertions** and very **low morale**.

2. What was the Impact of the War on the Home Front?

The home front experienced **shortages** of food and supplies. Mobilisation of men and horses affected food production. Most young men were at the front, so work on the land was done by older men, women and children. However, a more serious cause of the food shortage was the **mismanagement** by the army of the railways under their control in the western half of Russia. As an example, Moscow's normal supply of 2,200 railway wagons of grain in 1914 was cut to 300 wagons by the end of 1916. At the same time, Russia experienced a **severe economic crisis**. Russia mobilised 5.3 million men in August 1914 and by late 1916, 15.3 million had been mobilised by the army. The huge expense of the war was borne by higher taxes and by loans from Britain and France. In response, the government printed more money and this, along with the food shortages, contributed to rapid **inflation** with prices rising by 200 per cent between 1914 and the end of 1916. Ordinary people bore the brunt of the hardship.

EXAM QUESTION ?

How did economic crises and wars affect Tsarist Russia? (2015)

3. What Mistakes were Made by Tsar Nicholas II?

Tsar Nicholas II was not interested in politics. He was **weak-willed** and **indecisive**, and his wife, Tsarina **Alexandra**, easily influenced him. But he also believed totally in his autocratic form of government.

Due to army losses in 1915, the Tsar dismissed his uncle (Nikolai) in September 1915 and took over as **commander-in-chief** of the Russian Army. His decision to take over direct control of the army and move to the front had serious consequences for his reign. First, he was blamed directly now for the failures of the army at the front. Second, he handed over control of the government in Petrograd to his wife, Alexandra.

WHO WAS RASPUTIN?

Rasputin was a monk who seemed to have healing powers which worked with the Tsar's only son, Alexei, who suffered from haemophilia. His influence with the Tsar and Tsarina grew from about 1905 onwards. But he also had a reputation for drunkenness, sexual promiscuity and bribery.

4. How did the Influence of Alexandra and Rasputin Undermine the Tsar?

What is the message of this cartoon?

Alexandra believed in the **divine right of kings** and urged Nicholas not to give in to anybody. Her analysis of the condition of Russia in late February 1917, just before the revolution, showed how incompetent she was. She wrote to the Tsar: *'The whole trouble comes from those idlers, well-dressed people, wounded soldiers, school girls, etc. They say they have no bread, simply to create excitement. But things will settle down. They say it is all different from 1905 because they all worship you and only want bread.'*

Alexandra was deeply suspicious of the politicians in the **Duma** (assembly), and depended a great deal on the advice of **Rasputin** (see box). His influence grew stronger after the Tsar went to the front in September 1915. He contributed to the appointment of corrupt and inefficient ministers. His influence was seen as **evil** by others in the royal household.

Supporters of the Tsarist regime spread **rumours** about him and Alexandra. She was also blackened by her German origins. Some regarded the '**German woman**' as a spy and responsible for Russian defeats on the Eastern Front. They were concerned that the regime would collapse so they plotted the **assassination** of Rasputin. However, by the time he was murdered in December, 1916 it was too late – respect for the Tsar and Tsarina had been lost.

5. Why was the Growth of the political Middle Class Important?

The growth of industry in the previous 30 years in Russia and the professional classes (lawyers, engineers, doctors and teachers) increased the numbers of the middle class. Middle-class representation on *zemstva* (local and provincial councils) and the Duma gave them political experience.

The political middle class was represented by a variety of political groupings.

- The **Kadets**, or Constitutional Democrats, founded in 1905, demanded a constitutional monarchy, with a Tsar answerable to an elected assembly.
- The **Octobrists**, also founded in 1905, favoured a constitutional monarchy.
- The **Progressives**, a smaller party founded in 1908, supported a constitutional monarchy.

By August 1915 the three parties came together and formed the **Progressive Bloc**. Then they demanded a greater share of power from the Tsar, who did not want to share it. The government responded by dismissing the Duma. By late 1916, this liberal opposition had 'lost faith in the ability of this government to achieve victory.'

Working class people, in early 1900s Russia.

6. How Bad were the Conditions of the Working Class and Peasants?

There was a growing working class created by **rapid industrialisation**, but they suffered from bad working conditions – long hours, poor pay, danger of accidents. These conditions were worsened by war; the huge rate of inflation caused pay demands and strikes. Even though pay rates rose, they could not keep up with the rate of inflation.

Many Russian factories were **large-scale industrial complexes**; for example, the Putilov factory in Petrograd had 40,000 to 50,000 workers, so they were easier to organise, and they made a big impact when they went on strike.

In the **countryside**, the peasants (farmers) were emancipated in the 1860s, but had to pay **redemption payments** for their land. They were also controlled by the village *mir* (council). There was a rapid growth in population, which resulted in smaller farms and worse conditions.

The **war** affected the countryside as men were called up for war, and the burden of the work was carried now by women and older men. The seizure of horses by the army made farming work more difficult. In spite of inflated prices in the cities and towns, peasants still got low prices for their produce. Peasant **discontent** was increased by stories about their men at the front.

118

These conditions made both **workers** and **peasants** more open to the **appeals of revolutionary groups**.

Number of peasant uprisings	
1914	250
1915	160
1916	300
1917 (Jan-Feb)	700

Strikes by factory workers in Petrograd	
1914	60
1915	930
1916	1260
1917 (Jan-Feb)	1320

An average worker's wage in 1917 was 5 roubles a day. This would buy:

- In 1913, 4 bags of flour
- In 1917, ¾ of a bag of flour
- In 1913, 5 bags of potatoes
- In 1917, ¾ of a bag of potatoes
- In 1913, 20 kilograms of meat
- In 1917, 4 kilograms of meat

What Happened During the March Revolution, 1917?

The March Revolution began **spontaneously**. A series of public protests began in Petrograd which lasted for eight days and resulted in the downfall of the Tsarist system in Russia.

Workers in the **Putilov factory** in Petrograd demanded a 50 per cent increase in wages. When this was refused, the management locked out 40,000 workers, who were joined by crowds in the streets. The next day, workers were joined by thousands of women, angered by **food shortages**. By the third day, there were a quarter of a million men on strike.

The **army** played a crucial role in the downfall of the Tsar. At first, on 26 February soldiers opened fire on a crowd, killing 40 people. But this action undermined the morale of the troops and within a day thousands of soldiers of the **Petrograd garrison** had joined the striking workers. One of the generals reported, *'Due to fatigue and propaganda, the troops have laid down their arms, passed to the side of the rebels or become neutral.'*

Growing Opposition

There were also developments in the **political opposition**. Nicholas believed that the riots and strikes were not serious. He called for the Duma to be disbanded, but the Duma disobeyed his orders. Instead, the liberal members of the Duma formed a **Provisional Committee** which wanted the Tsar to abdicate.

Another development was the establishment of a **Workers' and Soldiers' Soviet (council) of Deputies**. Members were elected by workers and soldiers in their workplaces and garrisons. The **Petrograd Soviet** had great influence as it controlled the factories and services such as the railways and electricity.

Nicholas attempted to return to Petrograd but his train was blocked. He failed to get the support of the army so he was forced to **abdicate** on 2 March. The basis of the Tsarist regime was Nicholas's ability in the final resort to call on troops to put down those who resisted his authority. But that was now gone.

Nicholas abdicated in favour of his brother, but the latter refused to take the throne. The **Romanov dynasty** ended and Russia became a republic.

Provisional Government Takeover

A **Provisional Government** was formed to replace the Tsar's government, with Prince **Lvov** as its leader. However, the government had to share power with the Petrograd Soviet.

'The downfall of Tsarism in 1917 was welcomed by all classes in Russia. It was a spontaneous affair. The demonstrations were not controlled by political leaders. For the most part, opposition politicians were caught off balance by the events. As a result, there was no ready-made government waiting to take over when the Tsar abdicated.'

(A. White, Lenin's Russia)

CHANGES IN THE RUSSIAN CALENDAR

Russia used the Julian or Old Style calendar until January 1918, which was 13 days behind the Gregorian or New Style calendar, used by the rest of Europe. As a result, the **February Revolution** is also known as the **March Revolution**, and the **October Revolution** is also known as the **November Revolution**.

Timeline of the March Revolution

January
- 9 Jan   Thousands of workers went on strike and demonstrated to commemorate Bloody Sunday, 1905

February
- 14 Feb   Over 100,000 workers strike in Petrograd over food shortages and poor working conditions
- 19 Feb   Government announced that bread would be rationed from 1 March, resulting in panic buying
- 23 Feb   Women and striking Putilov workers demonstrated in Petrograd for International Women's Day
- 24 Feb   Strikes continued and grew larger
- 25 Feb   The Petrograd strike now totalled 250,000 and violence increased
- 26 Feb   The Tsar ordered the use of military force to break the strikes
            Troops fired on protestors killing 40
- 27 Feb   The Petrograd garrison mutinied, and joined the protestors
            Duma set up a Provisional Committee
            Soldiers, sailors and workers formed the Petrograd Soviet (council)
- 28 Feb   Tsar began return to Petrograd

March
- 1 March   Army refused to support the Tsar
- 2 March   Tsar abdicated in favour of his brother, Grand Duke, Michael
             The Provisional Government formed with Lvov as Prime Minister
- 3 March   Brother refused to become Tsar
             Provisional Government took over; forced to share power with the Petrograd Soviet

The November Revolution, 1917

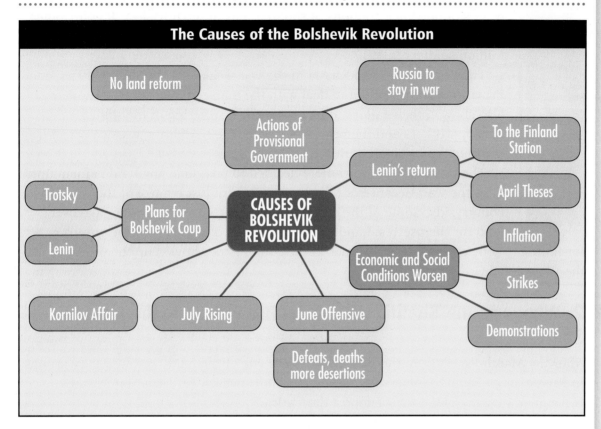

The Causes of the Bolshevik Revolution

- No land reform
- Russia to stay in war
- Actions of Provisional Government
- To the Finland Station
- Lenin's return
- April Theses
- Trotsky
- Plans for Bolshevik Coup
- **CAUSES OF BOLSHEVIK REVOLUTION**
- Inflation
- Lenin
- Economic and Social Conditions Worsen
- Strikes
- Kornilov Affair
- July Rising
- June Offensive
- Demonstrations
- Defeats, deaths more desertions

The Causes of the November Revolution, November 1917

1. How did the Actions of the Provisional Government Undermine their Support?

After the March Revolution and the downfall of the Tsar, the Provisional Government was set up. It was initially led by **Prince Lvov** but **Alexander Kerensky** became Prime Minister in July 1917. The Provisional Government faced the same problems as the Tsar, and also failed to find solutions for these.

The Provisional Government, formed from the Duma, was **weak and unstable** from the start. It had to share power with the **Petrograd Soviet** whose Order No. 1 said, '*The orders of the State Duma (Provisional Government) will be carried out only when they do not contradict the decisions of the Petrograd Soviet.*'

However, its first actions were well supported. It freed political prisoners, and allowed freedom of speech and of the press. It abolished secret courts and promised elections for a constituent assembly (parliament).

But its **failure** to end Russia's part in the war, and its refusal to bring in land reforms (by giving more land to the peasants) contributed to its downfall. The government decided to continue fighting in World War I in the hope they would defeat Germany and regain lost land. They also hoped to benefit financially from their alliance with Britain and France.

Alexander Kerensky became Prime Minister in July 1917.

Kerensky decided to launch a major offensive in June 1917, but this resulted in a severe defeat. In the **June Offensive** at least 150,000 Russians were wounded and millions of square miles of territory lost. It contributed to a collapse in morale amongst the soldiers and to the desertion of 2 million soldiers in 1917.

The decision to keep Russia in the war weakened the ability of the Provisional Government to deal with the many problems which it faced. It also showed their failure to understand the suffering of the soldiers, the factory workers and the peasants. In turn their suffering was worsened by continued participation in the war.

The Provisional Government decided to postpone any **land reform** until after the war. Because of this the government lost control of the countryside. Some of the deserting soldiers returned home to take over land for themselves. Landlords were attacked and blamed the government for failing to protect them. The disorder in the countryside showed up the weakness of the Provisional Government.

2. What was the Significance of Lenin's Return to the Finland Station?

After the March Revolution, the **Bolsheviks** were one of the many revolutionary groups in Russia. They had a membership of only 20,000. However, between March and November, they increased their support dramatically.

The first step was the **return of Lenin** from Switzerland to Russia in April 1917. Lenin, the leader of the Bolsheviks, was in Switzerland when the March Revolution broke out. He was given a **safe passage** through Germany to Russia. The Germans believed his anti-war attitude would weaken the Russian Army and people. As soon as he arrived in at the **Finland Station** in Petrograd, he criticised the Provisional Government. One journalist reported on Lenin's speech to the waiting crowd at the Finland Station: '*Suddenly, before the eyes of all of us, completely swallowed up by the routine drudgery of the revolution, there was presented a bright, blinding light … Lenin's voice heard straight from the train, was a "voice from outside".*'

Lenin greets crowds of people on his arrival in the Finland Station, April 1917.

In his *April Theses*, Lenin said the Provisional Government represented the bourgeois or middle class stage of the Marxist Revolution. He believed the Bolsheviks should move it to the final stage of a workers and peasants revolution.

Lenin demanded that the Bolsheviks plan for an **immediate revolution**. He committed the Bolsheviks to ending the war, giving land to the people and ensuring adequate food supplies. This became the catchy slogan of '**Peace, Land and Bread**' which united the demands of the working class and the peasantry.

He also called for '**All power to the Soviets**', as the Bolsheviks were using the cover of the Petrograd Soviet to increase their power.

3. What Role did Worsening Economic and Social Conditions Play in Creating the Conditions for Revolution?

All this time, economic and social conditions were worsening in Russia, particularly in Moscow and Petrograd. This contributed to the breakdown of society.

By the end of the summer of 1917, one eyewitness reported how law and order had broken down: '*Lynch law, the destruction of homes and shops, jeering and attacks on officers, unauthorised arrests, seizures and beatings up were recorded every day by tens and hundreds. In the country, burnings and destruction of country houses became more frequent.*'

Daily Bread rations per person in Petrograd in 1917 (grammes)				
	March	April	September	October
Manual workers	675	335	225	110
Others	450	335	225	110

4. How Important were the July Days?

Added to the worsening economic and social conditions was the failure of the June Offensive on the Eastern Front. All these undermined the Provisional Government and contributed to demonstrations in Petrograd in early July 1917. It seemed as if the conditions of the March Revolution were being repeated. **Lenin** believed the Provisional Government was badly shaken and ripe for overthrow. He attempted to use the collapse of the June Offensive and the demonstrations in a bid to **seize power**.

Demonstrating workers were joined by some soldiers on 3 and 4 July. There was a revolt by soldiers from the naval base of **Kronstadt**, in which 400 people were killed in two days. However, the Provisional Government, led by Kerensky, used loyal troops brought back from the front to surround the Bolshevik headquarters and force the surrender of 500 Bolsheviks inside. Lenin escaped arrest, and fled Petrograd to Finland in disguise.

These **failed July Days** were a serious blow to the Bolsheviks, and its organisation was now considerably weakened. Lenin was branded a German spy and other leaders, including Trotsky, were in jail. On the other hand, the Provisional Government had survived and strengthened its position. However, this did not last long.

Lenin without his beard.

5. What Impact had the Kornilov Affair, August 1917?

Very soon after the July Days, the **Kornilov Affair** showed up the weakness of the Provisional Government and dealt it a deadly blow.

General **Kornilov** was appointed commander-in-chief of the Russian Army after the failed June Offensive. He intended to move troops to Petrograd to protect the Provisional Government against a possible further left-wing attack.

EXAM QUESTION (?)

During the period 1900–1920, how was Russia affected by war and revolution? (2012)

However, Kerensky looked on Kornilov's move as an attempt to impose a **military dictatorship**. He called on the Petrograd Soviet for help. He armed workers in the capital and released many Bolsheviks to defend the city and the government. In all, there were about 25,000 **Red Guards**, the armed followers of the **Bolsheviks**. Kornilov was arrested and his troops failed to reach Petrograd. The affair or attempted coup increased the support and prestige of the Bolsheviks while the Provisional Government and its support collapsed. It was now totally isolated.

Bolshevik support: The Bolshevik part in the Kornilov Affair increased the support which they had already gathered. In spite of the failure of the July Days, Lenin's slogan of 'Peace, Land and Bread' had gained support for the Bolsheviks. By August 1917, they were producing 41 different newspapers and had 200,000 members, as well as an elite force of Red Guards, led by Trotsky. The Bolshevik support was demonstrated in the September elections to the Petrograd Soviet. Here the Bolsheviks obtained the majority and Trotsky became the President of the Soviet. Similarly, the Bolsheviks gained a majority in the Moscow Soviet.

6. What were the Bolsheviks Plans for Revolution?

Conditions were now ripe for the Bolsheviks to seize power. Lenin, who had returned to Petrograd in October, convinced some reluctant Bolshevik leaders that the time was now right, in spite of opposition from Zinoviev and Kamenev. **Trotsky** was put in charge of planning the revolution.

The actions of the Provisional Government decided the timing of the revolution. First, Kerensky announced elections for the Constituent Assembly for November. Lenin decided the revolution would have to be before the elections because other parties would win more seats than the Bolsheviks. Secondly, the Provisional Government began a clampdown on the Bolsheviks by arresting some supporters and closing down some Bolshevik newspapers.

As a result of these actions, **Trotsky** planned the revolution for the eve of the meeting of the Congress of the All-Russian Soviets in early November. He used the cover of the Military Revolutionary Committee of the Petrograd Soviet to undertake the revolt.

Leon Trotsky was put in charge of the Bolshevik revolution.

7. How was the Revolution Carried Out?

The revolution began at 2 a.m. on 7 November, when a blank shot was fired from a ship in Petrograd harbour, the cruiser *Aurora*. The Bolshevik Red Guards occupied key points in Petrograd – railway stations, the state bank, the post office, the telegraph exchange, power stations and key bridges. Very soon Petrograd was in the grip of the Bolsheviks.

Then the **Winter Palace**, the headquarters of the Provisional Government, was captured. The government had been weakened so much by events since they came to power in March that the Bolsheviks were able to take over quite easily. Since the Bolsheviks had a majority on the All-Russian Soviet, it endorsed the seizure of power the next day.

against German aggression. Having himself experienced two German invasions of France in 1870 and 1914, Clemenceau wanted to ensure that this would not be repeated. France had suffered severely in the war as part of the country was occupied for four years and the country suffered serious casualties (see box). The French believed that their country could only be protected by punishing Germany so that the country would remain weak.

The proportion of armed forces killed or wounded in Britain and France			
	% dead	% wounded	% unhurt
Britain	12	27	59
France	14	53	29

1. Do these figures suggest that France might have greater resentment towards Germany than Britain?
2. What other factors would explain French resentment towards Germany?

The Treaty of Versailles

In May 1919, the German delegation was presented with the terms of the Treaty of Versailles, which they had to accept. The German Reichstag (parliament) voted to accept the terms in spite of shouts of *'diktat'* or dictated peace terms.

The Terms of the Treaty
War Guilt Clause

Germany was forced to accept the **War Guilt Clause** (Article 231) and acknowledge its guilt and responsibility for starting the war.

Arising from the War Guilt Clause, the Allies imposed **reparations** on Germany. A **Reparations Commission** was set up to calculate the total figure for war damage. In 1921, it concluded that Germany should pay **£6,600** million (€7,500 million) to the victorious countries as compensation for the war damage. Reparations became the most serious issue between the countries in the immediate post-war years.

The War Guilt Clause: The Allied governments affirm, and Germany accepts, the responsibility of Germany and her allies for causing all the loss and damage to which the Allied governments and their peoples have been subjected as a result of the war.

Military Terms

Following on this, Germany faced **immediate disarmament**.
- Its army was reduced to 100,000 men.
- Conscription was banned.
- The navy could only build six battleships, and it was prevented from having submarines.
- Its air force was not allowed aeroplanes.

Land Losses

Germany lost **territory** to neighbouring countries:
- Alsace-Lorraine was returned to France; Eupen-Malmedy to Belgium and North Schleswig to Denmark; the Polish Corridor was given to Poland, and the city of Danzig, a largely German city, became a 'free city' to give Poland its only access to the sea.
- The Rhineland was **demilitarised**.
- Along with the changes in Europe, Germany had to give up all its **overseas colonies**.
- Germany was not allowed to unite with Austria.

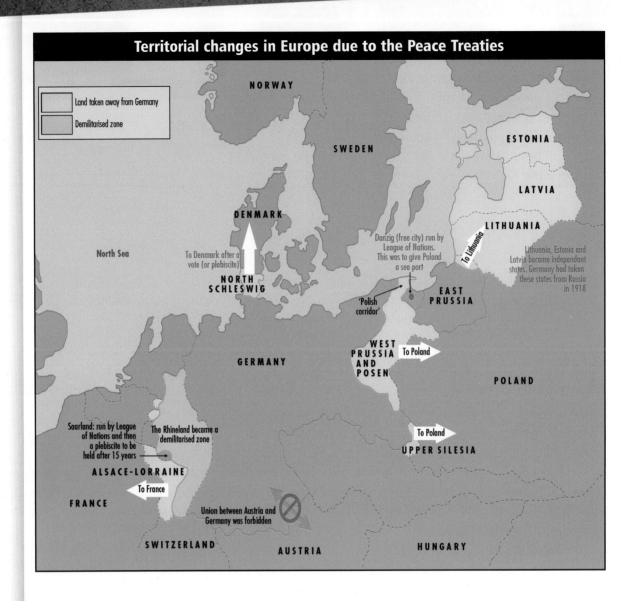

Territorial changes in Europe due to the Peace Treaties

Land taken away from Germany

Demilitarised zone

NORWAY

SWEDEN

ESTONIA

LATVIA

DENMARK

LITHUANIA

North Sea

Danzig (free city) run by
League of Nations.
This was to give Poland
a sea port

To Denmark after a
vote (or plebiscite)

NORTH
SCHLESWIG

'Polish
corridor'

EAST
PRUSSIA

To Lithuania

Lithuania, Estonia and
Latvia became independant
states. Germany had taken
these states from Russia
in 1918

WEST
PRUSSIA
AND
POSEN

To Poland

GERMANY

POLAND

Saarland: run by League
of Nations and then
a plebiscite to be
held after 15 years

The Rhineland became a
demilitarised zone

To Poland

UPPER SILESIA

ALSACE-LORRAINE

To France

FRANCE

Union between Austria and
Germany was forbidden

SWITZERLAND

AUSTRIA

HUNGARY

The Other Treaties

Other treaties were signed with Germany's allies.
- Each had to pay reparations and reduce its armed forces.
- The Austro-Hungarian and Turkish empires were broken up.

Austria – Treaty of St Germain:
- Austria lost land to Italy; Czechoslovakia was formed.

Bulgaria – Treaty of Neuilly:
- Bulgaria lost land to Greece, Yugoslavia and Romania.

Hungary – Treaty of Trianon:
- Hungary lost land to Czechoslovakia, Romania and Yugoslavia.

Turkey – Treaty of Sèvres:
- The Dardanelles was taken from Turkey, which lost land and islands to Greece.

The **League of Nations** was formed to maintain peace.

Reaction and Assessment – Why was the Versailles Peace Settlement a Failure?

Instead of the Paris Peace Conference providing peace for future generations, Europe went to war again 20 years later. As British historian, A. J. P. Taylor said, *'The Second World War was, in large part, a repeat performance of the first.'*

None of the countries were satisfied with the outcome of the conference.

- **France** was disappointed because the Treaty of Versailles was not severe enough.
- **Italy** was disappointed because it did not get Fiume or Dalmatia.
- The **USA** did not sign the Treaties because it would mean joining the League of Nations as well.
- **Germany** was bitterly disappointed because it was blamed for starting the war and forced to accept the terms.
- Some in **Britain** felt the Treaty of Versailles was too harsh on Germany.

Impact on Germany: The terms of the Treaty of Versailles were too harsh on Germany. The country could not pay reparations and this weakened its economy. The treatment of Germany helped the rise to power of Hitler (see p. 204).

Problems with Peacemaking

The leaders faced **huge difficulties** because the collapse of four empires meant that most of the land of Europe had to be regulated and reformed. This alone was a huge task apart altogether from the different approaches by each leader.

A **second cause** of the failure of the Versailles Settlement was that it caused serious German resentment at its harsh treatment. German representatives felt that the peace settlement would be based on Wilson's 14 Points. To their shock and dismay, the dictated peace resulted in the loss of 65,000 sq. km. (13 per cent) of territory and 7 million (10 per cent) of people. It also resulted in the continuing payments of reparations as a reminder of the verdict of the peace settlement.

However, in spite of these punishments, Germany still retained the capacity of rebuilding its position. For one thing, it still had 90 per cent of its economic resources. Also, its reduced territory was enhanced by the collapse of the Russian and Austro-Hungarian empires which resulted in many smaller states to the east. Once a new aggressive leader, such as Hitler, took control of Germany, its resources could still be harnessed to a **new expansionary policy**.

A **third weakness** of the peace settlement was **America's withdrawal** to isolation. The US Senate rejected America's role in a permanent peacekeeping organisation in the League of Nations. This meant the influence of the most powerful country in the world would not be involved in maintaining peace in the inter-war years.

A **further weakness** arose from criticisms by economist J. M. Keynes in his book, *The Economic Consequences of the Peace* (1920). He believed that reparations put too much weight on the German economy and in that way endangered the safety of the European economy. *'This treaty ignores the economic solidarity of Europe, and by aiming at the economic life of Germany, it threatens the health and stability of the Allies themselves.'*

However, **other economists** have challenged that view. They state the success of German productivity in the 1930s, particularly in relation to armaments, showed that Germany was well capable of repaying reparations. Nevertheless, the imposition of reparations caused serious and continuing resentment in Germany.

> The historian, Margaret Macmillan wrote, *'The mistake the Allies made ... was that, as a result of the armistice terms, the great majority of Germans never experienced their country's defeat at first hand. Except in the Rhineland, they did not see occupying troops. The Allies did not march in triumph to Berlin, as the Germans had done in Paris in 1871. In 1918, German troops marched home in good order, with crowds cheering their way.'*

1. Why did Wilson keep America out of the war in 1914? Why did Wilson bring America into the war in 1917?
2. What were his Fourteen Points?
3. How successful was Wilson at the Paris Peace Conference?
4. Why was America's participation in the League of Nations rejected by the US Senate?

KEY PERSONALITY: WOODROW WILSON

Woodrow Wilson served two terms as president of the US, from 1912 to 1921.

When the First World War began, President Wilson and America remained neutral. This followed the traditional US policy of isolation. Wilson offered to mediate between the two sides, but neither side agreed.

Americans did not want to be involved in a war in Europe. Wilson was concerned about the large number of people in America who had been born in Germany and Austria. But the sinking of the Lusitania in 1915, with the death of US citizens, hardened US opinion against Germany.

Wilson expanded the army and navy to prepare for the possibility of war. But he won re-election in 1916 with the slogan: 'He Kept Us Out of the War.'

In April 1917, Wilson took America into the war as an associated power, because:

- Germany announced a policy of unrestricted submarine warfare.
- Germany attempted to get Mexico to attack America by means of the Zimmermann Telegram (see p. 89).
- The US took some time to build up its troops in Europe, but the fresh soldiers were important in tipping the balance against the Germans in 1918.

In January 1918, Wilson announced his peace programme of **Fourteen Points**. The Fourteen Points included:

- The end of secret treaties.
- The freedom of the seas.
- The removal of trade barriers.
- Proposals for arms reductions.
- The international arbitration of all colonial disputes.
- Specific territorial claims made by Russia, France and Italy and claims for independence by the people living in areas controlled by Germany, Austria and Turkey.
- The League of Nations to settle international disputes.

Wilson worked very hard at the Paris Peace Conference to promote his peace plan. He was one of the Big Three, along with Lloyd George of Britain and Clemenceau of France; but he faced strong opposition to many of his points. Wilson ensured that the proposal for the League of Nations was included in all treaties agreed in Paris. Wilson received the Nobel Peace Prize in 1920 for his peacemaking efforts.

During the Russian Civil War, between 1918 and 1920, Wilson and the US supported the Whites with troops in a number of locations. They feared the rise of Communism in Russia. However, their intervention was unsuccessful.

In America, the Republicans now controlled the Senate, and they disliked the proposed League of Nations. They said it would drag America into future wars. Wilson, a Democrat, argued that US membership of the League was necessary for world peace.

When the Senate rejected the Treaty of Versailles, Wilson went on a nationwide tour to rouse support for it. He suffered a stroke and a week later a more serious one, which left him incapacitated. In 1921 his term as President ended, and he died in 1924.

 EXAM QUESTION

How did Woodrow Wilson influence affairs in Europe? (2017)

HOMEWORK EXERCISES

1. Study the documents and answer the questions.
A. **(i)** How fair was the Treaty of Versailles?
   (ii) Could the Allies have handled the 'peace' better?

SOURCE 1

We were told that we should acknowledge that we alone are guilty of having caused the war. I would be a liar if I agreed to this. We are not trying to avoid all responsibility for this World War. However, we emphatically deny that the German people should be seen as the only guilty party. Over fifty years the imperialism of all European states has poisoned the international situation.

Count Brockdorff, leader of the German delegation at Versailes, 7 May 1919

SOURCE 3

Germany lost:

- 10 per cent of its land.
- All of its overseas colonies.
- 12.5 per cent of its population.
- 16 per cent of its coalfields and almost half of its iron and steel industry.

The Deutsche Zeitung said: *'Today in the Hall of Mirrors the disgraceful treaty is being signed. Do not forget it! The German people will, with unceasing labour, press forward to reconquer the place among the nations to which it is entitled.'*

SOURCE 5

In agreement with the Field Marshall (Hindenberg), [Ludendorf] responded: the O.H.L. (army command) and the German army are at an end; the war can no longer be won; indeed, a total defeat can probably no longer be averted. Bulgaria has fallen. Austria and Turkey, at the end of their strength, will probably soon fall as well. Our own army is unfortunately already badly infected with the poison of Spartacist-socialist ideas. One can no longer rely on the troops.

Ludendorf, German commander-in-chief, 1918

SOURCE 2

In my opinion, it is not possible to lay the entire responsibility for the war on any single nation. By aiming at the destruction of the economic life of Germany this treaty threatens the health and prop(e)rity of the Allies themselves. By making impossible demands it leaves Europe more unsettled than it found it.

J. M. Keynes in *Economic Consequences of the Peace* (1920)

SOURCE 4

The mistake the Allies made … was that, as a result of the armistice terms, the great majority of Germans never experienced their country's defeat at first hand. Except in the Rhineland, they did not see occupying troops. The Allies did not march in triumph to Berlin, as the Germans had done in Paris in 1871. In 1918, German troops marched home in good order, with crowds cheering their way.

Margaret MacMillan, historian

SOURCE 6

The Versailles Treaty was severe, but it is amazing that it was not more so. Thanks to Wilson's insistence, Germany lost remarkably little territory, considering how thoroughly it lost the war. True, the colonies were gone, but the European losses were relatively modest. The real difficulty was not that the Treaty was exceptionally severe, but that the Germans thought it was, and in time persuaded others it was.

Sally Marks, historian

SOURCE 7

Compared to the treaties which Germany imposed on defeated Russia and Rumania in 1918, the Treaty of Versailles was relatively moderate … The Treaty of Versailles was not excessively harsh on Germany, either territorially or economically. However, the German people were expecting victory not defeat. It was the acknowledgement of defeat as much as the treaty terms themselves, which they found hard to accept.

Ruth Henig, historian

SOURCE 8

In many respects terrible terms to force upon a country. We shall have to fight another war all over again in twenty-five years at three times the cost.

David Lloyd George, politician

SOURCE 9

The Treaties were a reasonable attempt to solve an impossible problem. It was impossible because the atmosphere of 1919 meant the Allies could not be lenient towards the defeated countries. It would have been difficult to do better.

J. Traynor, I. Dawson, historians (1997)

SOURCE 10

SOURCE 11

Draw up tables in your notes and fill in the relevant information (in bullet points where necessary) from the sources above.

How fair was the Treaty of Versailles?	
Fair (List Sources)	
Why fair? (Reasons)	
Not Fair (List Sources)	
Why not fair? (Reasons)	

Which sources say that the Allies could have handled the peace better?	
List Sources	How could the Allies have handled the peace better?

Summarise your views on the Treaty of Versailles in bullet-points

In this section, you should understand:
- How literature and the arts contributed to national identity at the end of the 19th century and the beginning of the 20th century.
- The role of Wilfred Owen.

Literature and the arts flourished during the late 19th and early 20th centuries, owing to:

- The growing wealth of the middle classes and some sections of the working class.
- The spread of education.
- The growth in communications, especially newspapers and magazines.

Literature and the arts displayed many **different characteristics or features** during this time; **realism** and **social criticism** were the main ones. But the expression of **national identity** was also very significant.

Literature

Realism and social criticism, based on the portrayal of industrial or country life, were the most common features in literature. But some writers continued in the romantic or nationalist tradition.

In **England**, Rudyard Kipling highlighted the glories of the British Empire in his books and poems, such as *Kim*, *The Jungle Book*, *Puck of Pook's Hill* and *The Man Who Was*. Kipling wrote 'The White Man's Burden' originally to commemorate Queen Victoria's Diamond Jubilee but later changed it to encourage the American takeover of the Philippine Islands (1898).

> **THE WHITE MAN'S BURDEN (FIRST VERSE)**
>
> TAKE up the White Man's burden –
> Send forth the best ye breed –
> Go bind your sons to exile
> To serve your captives' need;
> To wait in heavy harness
> On fluttered folk and wild –
> Your new-caught sullen peoples,
> Half devil and half child.
>
> **Rudyard Kipling**

In **France**, Charles Peguy wrote his poems on the love of France, a blend of Catholicism and patriotism. He died later in the Battle of the Marne in 1914.

Maurice Barres, a French nationalist, wrote his trilogy – *The Novel of National Energy* – about attachment to native places. Some of his novels (e.g. *In the Service of Germany*) were used as French propaganda during the First World War.

In **Italy**, D'Annunzio was a fervent nationalist. One of his poetry collections was *In Praise of Sky, Sea, Earth, and the Heroes*. He too fought in the First World War. After the war, he led a nationalist takeover of Fiume, which had not been given to Italy at the Paris Peace Conference.

In **Russia**, Dostoevsky was an extreme nationalist. According to him, it was Russia's destiny to unite Europe under its domination. Some of his most important novels were *The Possessed* and **The Brothers Karamazov**.

135

Painting

The most influential artists of the time were **Impressionists**, who emphasised light and colour. Impressionists such as **Monet** and **Manet** wanted to capture the mood of the moment. Later the Cubists, such as Cézanne, stressed shapes.

Popular, though less able, artists formed schools of **nationalist painters**. They painted patriots in stirring scenes from their country's past, or portraits of leaders in heroic poses. They were using **art as propaganda**, to stir up national feelings and create national identity.

Music

Of all the arts, music was the most influenced by **nationalist tradition**. Music clearly played on emotions, so it was used to create national feeling and national consciousness.

There were many **patriotic songs**, **anthems** and **folk songs**. Singing became a part of public gatherings and was encouraged in state schools.

The more serious composers were also influenced by the national traditions. In **Italy**, Verdi produced a number of operas which expressed Italian national identity before Italian unification (1870). The lyrics of the *Chorus of the Hebrew Slaves* from the opera, *Nabucco* began:

> *Hasten thoughts on golden wings.*
> *Hasten and rest on the densely wooded hills,*
> *where warm and fragrant and soft*
> *are the gentle breezes of our native land!*

Italian opera composer Giuseppe Verdi.

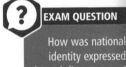

? EXAM QUESTION

How was national identity expressed through literature and the arts during the period, 1871–1920? (2010)

These are often cited as an unofficial national anthem for 19th century Italy. '*Although Italian nationalism was led to victory by soldiers like Giuseppe Garibaldi, Verdi's music provided a huge emotional boost to Il Risorgimento.*' After unification in 1870, Verdi's music continued to strengthen Italian national pride and identity.

In **Germany**, Richard Wagner based his most important works, such as *The Ring of the Nibelungen*, on Germanic legends. Wagner's career coincided with German unification and the early years of the Second Reich. He wanted to produce opera which he felt reflected German national feeling. His *Ring* cycle was written to develop a national myth for Germany which he considered important in developing national feeling and identity.

The **Russian** composer Mussorgsky was influenced by Russian folk songs. Other composers who expressed national identity through their music included **Grieg** in Norway (*Peer Gynt*); Edward **Elgar** in England with his *Pomp and Circumstance* marches; **Sibelius** in Finland, which was seeking independence from Russia (*Finlandia*); and **Dvořák**, the Czech composer.

Richard Wagner was best known for his opera compositions.

Poets and **writers** produced a great deal of literature during the First World War. This was the first war that produced 'war poets'. A whole generation of young men joined up, including many poets and writers.

People in all countries were enthusiastic when the war began. This was reflected in the early poetry and writing on the war. Many popular songs and poems were written by soldiers at the front, giving their views on their food, their friends and their generals. They often mocked or laughed at their situations.

The war poets had a **romantic and patriotic view** of the war. Two of the important poets early in the war were **Rupert Brooke** (England) and **Charles Peguy** (France).

> ### THE SOLDIER
>
> If I should die, think only this of me:
>   That there's some corner of a foreign field
> That is for ever England. There shall be
>   In that rich earth a richer dust concealed;
> A dust whom England bore, shaped, made aware,
>   Gave, once, her flowers to love, her ways to roam,
> A body of England's, breathing English air,
>   Washed by the rivers, blest by suns of home.
>
> **Rupert Brooke**

War Poets

The **early poets** welcomed the war. They saw it as a sacrifice in a just cause. Some wanted the war to get rid of the materialism of life and create a new, better world. Rupert Brooke was educated at Rugby and Cambridge. He joined the British Navy when the war broke out. He fought in the attack on Antwerp, but died of food poisoning on his way to the Dardanelles. He was buried on the island of Skyros (Greece). His war poetry was published in *1914*; in his most famous poems, '1914' and 'The Soldier', he idealised the fighting.

Rupert Brooke

The poets became **disillusioned** as the war dragged on. The slaughter of the Battle of the Somme destroyed the romantic view of war. Poets such as Siegfried **Sassoon**, Robert **Graves** and Wilfred **Owen** hated the war and wanted to show people at home what life was really like in the trenches.

Sassoon wrote angry satire about the war in poems such as 'The General' and 'Counterattack'. In 1917 he issued a statement criticising the war. After he became ill he was sent to hospital to recover; there he met Wilfred Owen and he encouraged Owen to write his poetry. Sassoon returned to the front and survived the war. Owen went back to the fighting, but was killed.

Siegfried Sassoon wrote angry satire about the war in his poems.

> **EXAM QUESTION** ?
>
> How did the literature of World War I reflect both the conduct of war and changing attitudes towards it? (2011)

Owen's poetry, such as 'Anthem for Doomed Youth', marked him as one of Britain's greatest war poets (See Key Personality p. 138).

137

Books

Most of the books written during the war had an idealistic view of the fighting. Some were written by people who were not involved in the fighting. One of the few books published by a soldier during the war was Henri Barbusse's *Under Fire*. Barbusse was a French soldier who highlighted the terrible conditions of the fighting.

It was not until after the war that soldiers had the time to write their accounts. Books by Erich Maria **Remarque** (*All Quiet on the Western Front*) and Robert **Graves** (*Goodbye to All That*) brought the conditions of the war to the public in the 1920s. They added to the **disillusionment** about war and the wish to avoid war, and contributed to the atmosphere of appeasement in Britain and France.

KEY PERSONALITY: WILFRED OWEN

Wilfred Owen was born in England in 1893. After education at the Birkenhead Institute and the University of London, he moved to France as a teacher of English. He was interested in poetry from an early age, especially the Romantic poetry of Shelley and Keats.

He enlisted in the Artists Rifles in October 1915. For the next 14 months he trained in England. He joined the Manchester Regiment as a Second Lieutenant in France in 1917. He served there for four months, five weeks of those in the front line. It was at this time he began writing poems based on his war experiences.

Owen wrote his description on No Man's Land in a letter to his mother: 'No Man's Land under snow is like the face of the moon, chaotic, crater-ridden, uninhabitable, awful, the abode of madness.'

Owen suffered shell-shock in the summer of 1917 – he had been blown into the air by a shell and fallen down a well. He was sent to Craiglockhart War Hospital in Edinburgh to recover. Here he met the poets and writers Siegfried Sassoon and Robert Graves. Sassoon advised Owen on his poetry writing. He said he should write in a more direct style.

On his return to France, over the next ten months, he wrote his most famous war poetry, including 'Anthem for Doomed Youth', 'Dulce et Decorum Est' and 'Strange Meeting'. Owen expressed the horrors of war in his poems. *'His poetry often graphically illustrated the horrors of warfare, the physical landscapes that surrounded him, and the human body in relation to those landscapes. His verses stand in stark contrast to the patriotic poems of war written by earlier poets of Great Britain, such as Rupert Brooke.'* (www.poets.org)

Within a week he had been transported to the front line in a cattle wagon and was 'sleeping' 70 or 80 yards from a heavy gun which fired every minute or so. He was soon wading miles along trenches two feet deep in water. Within a few days he was experiencing gas attacks and was horrified by the stench of the rotting dead; his sentry was blinded, his company then slept out in deep snow and intense frost till the end of January. That month was a profound shock for him: he now understood the meaning of war. *'The people of England needn't hope. They must agitate'*, he wrote home.

(http://www.warpoetry.co.uk)

ANTHEM FOR DOOMED YOUTH

What passing-bells for these who die as cattle?
    — Only the monstrous anger of the guns.
     Only the stuttering rifles' rapid rattle
Can patter out their hasty orisons.
No mockeries now for them; no prayers nor bells;
    Nor any voice of mourning save the choirs,—
The shrill, demented choirs of wailing shells;
     And bugles calling for them from sad shires.

What candles may be held to speed them all?
    Not in the hands of boys, but in their eyes
Shall shine the holy glimmers of goodbyes.
    The pallor of girls' brows shall be their pall;
Their flowers the tenderness of patient minds,
And each slow dusk a drawing-down of blinds.

Wilfred Owen

STRANGE MEETING

It seemed that out of battle I escaped
Down some profound dull tunnel, long since scooped
Through granites which titanic wars had groined.

Yet also there encumbered sleepers groaned,
Too fast in thought or death to be bestirred.
Then, as I probed them, one sprang up, and stared
With piteous recognition in fixed eyes,
Lifting distressful hands, as if to bless.
And by his smile, I knew that sullen hall,—
By his dead smile I knew we stood in Hell.
....
....
'I am the enemy you killed, my friend.
I knew you in this dark: for so you frowned
Yesterday through me as you jabbed and killed.
I parried; but my hands were loath and cold.
Let us sleep now. . . .'

Wilfred Owen

Owen's 'Dulce et Decorum Est'

http://www.bl.uk/learning

In August 1918 Owen returned to France. He felt he needed to return to serve with his men. He took part in the assault and breakthrough of the Hindenburg Line and he was awarded the Military Cross for action there.

He was killed by machine-gun fire on the Sambre Canal on 4 November 1918, one week before the war ended.

Only four of Owen's poems were published while he lived. Sassoon arranged for the publication of Owen's Collected Poems (1920). Owen is regarded as one of the greatest British war poets, although his influence was felt mainly after the war.

EXAM QUESTIONS

1. What did you learn about World War I from your study of Wilfred Owen? (2009)
2. Why was Wilfred Owen honoured, both as a soldier and as a poet, following his role in World War I? (2007)

HOMEWORK EXERCISES

ORDINARY LEVEL

1. Write a **short paragraph** on the following:
   (i)   Literature and national identity, 1871–1920
2. Write a **long answer** on the following:
   (i)   What influence had literature and the arts on shaping national identity in Europe between 1871 and 1920?
3. Write a **short paragraph** on the following:
   (i)   Literature and World War I
4. Write a **long answer** on the following:
   (i)   How does Wilfred Owen reflect changing views about the fighting during World War I?

HIGHER LEVEL

5. How was national identity expressed through literature and the arts during the period, 1871–1920? (2010)

6. What did you learn about World War I from your study of the conduct of war and/or the literature of the war? (2016)

7. How did the literature of World War I reflect changing attitudes towards the war? (2006)

In this section, you should understand:
- How science and medicine developed in the late 19th and early 20th centuries.
- The role of Marie Curie.
- How technology developed in the late 19th and early 20th centuries.
- The role of Karl Benz.
- The invention and early history of the motor car.

Science

Developments in science had a significant influence on the progress of the 20th century.

Ernest Rutherford developed the theory of radioactivity, which explained how changes in atoms occurred. He reported the existence of alpha and beta rays in uranium radiation. He developed a method of detecting a single alpha particle and a system for counting the number emitted from radium was devised. Further investigation into atoms led him to suggest the possibility of a nucleus for the atom. His work in all these areas led to him being called the 'Father of the Nuclear Age'.

Albert Einstein provided new ways of looking at space, time and gravitation. He developed his **Theory of Relativity** – that time and motion are relative to the observer. He explained the links between energy and mass ($E = mc^2$). Einstein's ideas influenced 20th century space investigations and explorations.

Rutherford's and Einstein's ideas led to the development of nuclear bombs later in the 20th century.

Albert Einstein

Medicine

Louis **Pasteur**, a French chemist, proved the connection between germs and the spread of disease (the **germ theory of disease**). He showed how the souring of milk was due to tiny organisms. This led to the development of **pasteurisation** of milk. He also developed vaccines to prevent anthrax in sheep and cattle, and rabies in humans and dogs. His work on infectious diseases saved the French silkworm industry when he devised a method which preserved healthy silkworm eggs and prevented their infection by the disease-causing organisms.

Louis Pasteur

141

Diseases

The German doctor **Robert Koch** showed how bacteria could be examined in a laboratory. He discovered the organisms of tuberculosis and cholera. This led to the discovery of further organisms that caused other diseases.

Other doctors showed how insects carried disease – in particular how the mosquito carried malaria. Yellow fever was also controlled, leading to the completion of the Panama Canal as the death rate among those working on it fell from 176 per 1,000 to just 6 per 1,000.

There were further discoveries of the **viruses** which caused measles and mumps. A German chemist, Paul **Ehrlich**, discovered a drug that controlled syphilis. His success and methods were applied to treat and control infectious diseases.

Surgery made important advances. There were major operations for stomach cancer, ulcers and appendicitis. The horrific experiences of World War I increased the knowledge and skills of surgeons as they dealt with multiple injuries.

Wilhelm **Röntgen** discovered X-rays in 1895. This was a very significant medical advance in detecting injuries and the causes of sickness. The French scientist, Henri **Becquerel**, showed that uranium gave off rays similar to those discovered by Röntgen. The phenomenon became known as **radioactivity**.

> What role did Marie Curie play in scientific discovery?

KEY PERSONALITY: MARIE CURIE

Marie Curie was born Marya Sklodowska in Poland in 1867. She dreamt of a career in science, but had to become a private tutor for some time. Marie went to Paris in 1891 for further education. She got degrees in physics and mathematics from the Sorbonne University.

She was introduced to French scientist Pierre Curie, and one year later they married. Marie and Pierre worked together on her experiments. They showed that radioactivity was a property of the atom. She also discovered two new chemical elements, radium and polonium (which she called after her native country).

Marie and Pierre Curie worked in a laboratory with bad conditions – it was often very cold in winter. They found it difficult to get loans to continue their work; but they refused to patent their findings because they wanted them to be available to other scientists for further discoveries.

In 1903 the Curies were awarded a joint Nobel Prize for Physics with scientist, Henri Becquerel, for their discovery of radioactivity. Marie was the first woman to be awarded a Nobel Prize.

In 1906, however, Pierre was knocked down by a car and killed. Marie had to rear their two children alone and continue their work. She obtained her husband's position, Professor of Physics, at the Sorbonne. She was the first woman to be appointed professor in the university.

In 1911, she was refused entry to the Academy of Sciences because of prejudice against foreigners and women. She also experienced public criticism for an affair with another married scientist at the time. Marie was awarded the Nobel Prize for Chemistry in 1913 for determining the atomic weight of radium. Now she was the first person to win or share two Nobel Prizes.

Marie was very pleased with the foundation of the Radium Institute and Pasteur Institute to continue her work. When the First World War broke out, she said that X-rays would help find shrapnel and bullets. She set up X-ray vans for this purpose. Along with her daughter, Irene, Marie worked to train people to use the X-ray vans. After the war, she returned to research.

Marie Curie died in 1934 of leukaemia due to her exposure to radioactivity during her research. Her work on radioactivity became the basis for later work on cancer treatment, dating objects in archaeology and geology, and genetics, as well as nuclear energy and the atomic bomb.

Freud and Psychiatry

Around this time Austrian neurologist **Sigmund Freud** began his work in psychiatry. Freud developed psychoanalysis, a method through which an analyst unpacks unconscious conflicts based on the free associations, dreams and fantasies of the patient. He published a series of books about his investigations. These included *The Interpretation of Dreams* (1900), *The Psychopathology of Everyday Life* (1901) and *Three Essays on the Theory of Sexuality* (1905).

The **First World War** influenced developments in medicine. In surgery, new techniques were developed. Many young doctors gained experience in surgical techniques that they used after the war. X-rays were used to determine war injuries.

Technology

Eiffel Tower

There were **significant developments** in technology between 1871 and 1920. As a result, Europeans looked with pride on the building of the Eiffel Tower; the construction of the Trans-Siberian railway, the Suez Canal and the Panama Canal; the launching of great ocean liners such as the *Titanic* and *Lusitania*; and all the developments relating to the invention of the internal combustion engine.

The invention of the internal combustion engine had a major influence on transportation and many other aspects of life. Cars, lorries and aircraft were developed using this type of engine.

KEY PERSONALITY KARL BENZ

Karl Benz was born in Germany. He worked as a mechanical engineer before setting up his first company in 1871, supplying building materials.

But his business was not successful, so Benz worked on the development of a two-stroke engine to find another source of income. His first engines were stationary internal combustion engines.

Benz began Benz and Co. in 1883 to produce industrial engines. At this time also he worked to put engines on wheels. He heard that Gottlieb Daimler was designing a four-wheeled vehicle. Benz was encouraged to work on his Motorwagen.

Benz designed the engine and also a complete three-wheeled vehicle. Benz was granted a patent in 1886, and later that year produced the first petrol-driven car or automobile. His first sale was to Emile Rogers, a Parisian engineer, in 1887.

Benz was helped by his wife, Bertha. She used her dowry to buy out Benz's partner in his first company. She also drove his first car through Mannheim in 1885. A few years later she took the longest road journey yet, by driving more than 100 kilometres from Mannheim to Pforzheim, and back.

Benz's motor-car company was successful. In 1888 he employed 50 workers to make his three-wheeled car. Soon he began producing a four-wheeled car and his workforce had increased to over 400 by 1899. His Benz Velo was very successful – it was reasonably priced and so achieved very good sales of 1,200. In 1899 alone he produced 572 vehicles. By the beginning of the 20th century, Benz and Co. was one of the world's leading car manufacturers.

In 1903 Benz retired from Benz and Co., although he remained a member of the supervisory board of the company. The Benz and Daimler companies merged in 1926 to form Daimler-Benz. Benz continued his interest in the company until his death in 1929.

What was the importance of Karl Benz for the industrial development of Germany?

Electricity

Siemens's invention of the dynamo and the construction of generators led to an increase in the production of electricity. Electricity was used to power Thomas Edison's electric light bulb, electric tramways in many cities and underground trains in large cities such as London.

Chemical Industry

The chemical industry grew rapidly, especially in Germany, as it produced new medicines, synthetic materials such as rayon, dynamite and plastic.

Communication

The telephone, invented by **Alexander Graham Bell** in America, was introduced slowly into Europe. Marconi, of Italian-Irish extraction, transmitted the first transatlantic wireless messages in 1901.

Military Technology

During the First World War technology was used to gain an advantage over the enemy. The Germans first used **poison gas** on the Western Front. It was very ineffective when it was released from cylinders, because of the wind. Shells were then developed to deliver the gas.

Early telephone

Tanks were developed by the British to overcome the strength of the defences in the trenches. The early tanks often broke down, but by 1918 tanks were beginning to have an effect on the progress of the war.

The **diesel engine** was used in submarines. The U-boats almost led to a German victory in the war.

The war in the air was carried on with **Zeppelins** (airships) and aeroplanes. They were used for bombing, reconnaissance and (for aeroplanes) dogfights.

HOMEWORK EXERCISES

ORDINARY LEVEL

1. Write a **short paragraph** on **one** of the following:
   (i) Developments in science and medicine, 1871–1920.
   (ii) Developments in technology, 1871–1920.
2. Write a **long answer** on the following:
   (i) Why was Marie Curie an important figure in the development of science and medicine? (2009)

HIGHER LEVEL

3. During the period, 1871–1920, what developments took place in one or more of the following: the motor car; science and technology; medicine? (2015)

The Invention and Early History of the Motor Car

The modern motor car was not the invention of any single person. Rather it was developed over a number of decades, with various inventors contributing to its evolution.

The early attempts at developing a fully-powered road vehicle went back to the late 18th century. These were largely steam-powered **horseless carriages**. However, even though steam-powered vehicles were not successful, their development led to improvements in other areas, such as hand brakes and steering.

CASE STUDY QUESTION

What were the main developments in the invention and early history of the motor car?

German Engineers

The full development of the motor car was advanced by the invention of the **internal combustion engine**. The successful early development of the motor car was largely due to German engineers. In 1870, **Siegfried Marcus** built an internal combustion engine fired by petrol. Further improvements came in 1876, when **Nikolaus Otto**, a German engineer, built the first workable, four-stroke, internal combustion engine. But his work was overshadowed by the work of **Karl Benz** and **Gottlieb Daimler**. They worked separately to produce the first cars with internal combustion engines.

Nikolaus Otto

See Key Personality: Karl Benz, p. 143

In 1885, Karl Benz produced a three-wheeled car with an open two-seater body. It was steered by a tiller, and it had a speed of about eight to ten miles an hour. He was granted a patent for the car, Benz Patent Motorwagen No. 1, in 1886. His wife, **Bertha**, contributed to the success of his cars. She proved the durability of his Benz Patent Motorwagen No. 3 by driving from his home base in Mannheim to Pforzheim, and back, in 1888. This also provided good publicity for Benz. This success encouraged him to produce his first cars.

SOURCE 1 – BENZ'S THREE-WHEELED CAR

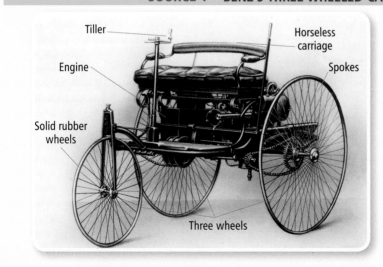

Tiller

Engine

Solid rubber wheels

Three wheels

Horseless carriage

Spokes

Bertha Benz, wife of Karl Benz, helped with the success of his cars.

What developments in motor history were made by Marcus and Otto? What was Benz's contribution to the early history of the motor car?

At the same time, Gottfried **Daimler** was working in developing his own small engine. In 1886 he fitted his engine to a four-wheel horseless carriage. A few years later, the German engineer Rudolf **Diesel** designed the engine to which he gave his name. Both Daimler and Diesel built their engines for many purposes, not just cars.

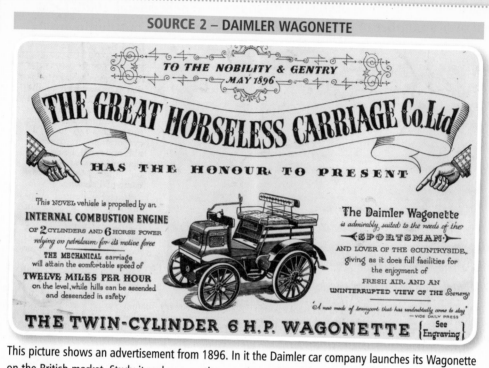

This picture shows an advertisement from 1896. In it the Daimler car company launches its Wagonette on the British market. Study it and answer the questions which follow.

1. What speed can the Wagonette do on a level road?
2. What sort of engine does it have?
3. How is it made to appeal to the lover of the countryside?
4. What evidence does the advertisement offer that it was aimed at rich people?
5. How did Karl Benz contribute to the early history of the motor car? (2013)

Improvements

Over the next 20 years improvements to the early motor car were made by inventors in other countries. These included the steering wheel, the pneumatic tyre, disc brakes and four-wheel braking. Drive shafts replaced the chain drive; disc brakes were developed in 1901, and drum brakes a year later. Number plates were added in France, and windshield wipers were patented.

Up to this also many cars were steered by a **tiller** in the centre, but in 1903 in the US, Thomas Jeffrey produced the Rambler with **standardised steering wheel** and moved it to one side (the left in America). This became the model for other car manufactures after that.

Levassor in France also made other changes which moved the car away from its horseless carriage ancestry and closer to today's cars. He moved the engine to the front of the car, used a water radiator to cool it, and installed a clutch and a gear stick to operate the gearbox.

At this time also, **motor races** were held to encourage improvements in design and to publicise motoring. The first road race was held in France in 1894, from Paris to

Rouen, which featured the first use of a steering wheel. This was followed by others, such as Paris to Bordeaux and back in 1895, which took two days at an average speed of 15 miles per hour.

SOURCE 3 – 1894 PARIS-ROUEN RACE – THE WORLD'S FIRST MOTOR RACE

On July 22, 1894, the Parisian magazine *Le Petit Journal* organised what is considered to be the world's first car race from Paris to Rouen.

Pierre Giffard, the paper's editor, promoted it as a **Competition for Horseless Carriages** (Concours des Voitures sans Chevaux) that were not dangerous, easy to drive, and cheap during the journey. The main prize was for the first across the finish line in Rouen. 102 people paid the 10 franc entrance fee.

69 cars started the 50 km (31 miles) selection event that would show which entrants would be allowed to start the main event, the 127 km (79 miles) race from Paris to Rouen. The entrants ranged from serious manufacturers to amateur owners, and only 25 were selected for the main race.

The race started from Porte Maillot and went through the Bois de Boulogne. The distance from Paris to Rouen was 127 km.

The official winners were Peugeot and Panhard as cars were judged on their speed, handling and safety characteristics, and De Dion's steam car needed a stoker which was forbidden.

The order of the finishers was as follows:

1. De Dion (Steam) - Count Jules-Albert de Dion
2. Peugeot (Petrol) - Georges Lemaitre
3. Peugeot (Petrol)
4. Panhard et Levassor (Petrol)
5. Peugeot (Petrol)
6. Le Brun (Petrol)
7. Panhard et Levassor (Petrol)
8. Panhard et Levassor (Petrol)
9. De Bourmont (Petrol)
10. Peugeot (Petrol)
11. Vacheron (Gasoline)
12. Peugeot (Gasoline)
13. Panhard et Levassor (Petrol)
14. Roger (Petrol)
15. Le Blant (Steam)

The Early History of Motoring by Claude Goodman Johnson, 1927

> What conditions were imposed on the entrants for Competition for Horseless Carriages? Why were only 25 selected for the main race? Why was De Dion not declared the winner, even though it is listed first? Which companies had the most entries in the top 15 finishers?

SOURCE 4 – 1896 LONDON-BRIGHTON RUN

The first London to Brighton run was organised by the Motor Car Club and held on the 14th November 1896.

The proceedings started with a luncheon at the Grand Banqueting Hall at the Metropole Hotel in London where some 150 guests dined.

Thirty-two cars were at the start (some estimate this to be around half of all those in the country at that time). Some of the cars that took part were:

- Panhard and Levassor Daimler carriage which won the 1895 Paris-Bordeaux-Paris Race containing Harry Lawson and Otto Mayer
- Daimler barouche containing Frederick Simms and Gottlieb Daimler
- Panhard and Levassor carriage that won the 1896 Paris-Marseilles-Paris Race
- Three Bollee motor tandem cycles ridden by Leon Bollee, Amedee Bollee and H. Duncan
- Daimler omnibus, victoria, wagonette, parcels van (belonging to Peter Robinson),
- Omnibus (belonging to Harrod's Stores, etc.)
- Two Duryea motor carriages
- Roger motor dog-cart
- Arnold motor dog-cart
- Pennington four-seat tricycle driven by Edward Joel Pennington

The weather was not good, with wind and rain and around twenty vehicles finished the run.

There was a dinner in the evening at the Metropole Hotel in Brighton. The planned parade of cars for the next day (Sunday) was abandoned owing to the bad weather.

The Early History of Motoring by Claude Goodman Johnson, 1927

> What information here shows that cars were largely confined to the very well-off in Britain in 1896? What do you notice about the brand names of the cars?

The Motor Industry

The car industry developed separately in each country: in France there were Renault, Peugeot, Citroën and De Dion-Bouton, which produced a cheaper model of car, affordable for the middle class; in Italy there was Fiat. Other smaller countries had their own producers. These manufacturers were limited by their small markets, not just in population, but also in wealth.

By 1900, **France** had developed into the world's largest producer of cars, with about 3,000 cars on the roads. Nevertheless, in spite of the rapid growth of the car industry, manufacturing processes remained largely the same. These depended on skilled workers developing and assembling parts slowly, at an average rate of about one car per worker per year.

Motor Cars in Britain

In Britain the development of the car industry was slowed up by the **Locomotives Act** or the **Red Flag Act** (1865), which set the maximum speed for cars at four miles per hour in the country and two miles per hour in towns, and insisted that cars be preceded by a man on foot waving a red flag. While the carrying of a red flag was repealed in 1878, it was not until the 1896 **Locomotives on Highways Act** that the speed limit was raised to 14 miles per hour. The annual London to Brighton race was organised to commemorate the passing of the Act. By that time there were only about 64 cars in Britain.

The Red Flag Act was not the only factor which held up car manufacturing in Britain. There were better returns from other investments.

> **What role did the Automobile Club play in promoting the use of cars?**

SOURCE 5 – THE AUTOMOBILE CLUB

The Automobile Club was formed in Britain in 1897. It later became the Royal Automobile Club. From the outset the Club became an active and virile force in the automobile movement. Its fixture list comprised tours and week-end runs, club dinners, lectures and discussions, and general meetings. It exerted its influence, with others, in preventing the introduction of vexatious clauses affecting motor vehicles in Bills seeking powers for local authorities; it assisted in opposing the Westminster Tramways Bill; and it compiled a list of motor-spirit stores. In July of the same year, moreover, an amalgamation was effected with the Self-Propelled Traffic Association (which had been previously founded by David Salomons), and the Club thereupon became the only recognised authority on automobiles in the United Kingdom.

http://www.gracesguide.co.uk

The finish of the Automobile Club's 1,000 Mile Trial in 1900. The participants included C. S. Rolls and Harvey Du Cross.

British Manufacturers

Up to the late 19th century, Britain largely depended on imported French and German cars. Then a number of manufacturers began designing and making cars in Britain. One of the first was **Frederick Lanchester** who began developing his own cars from 1895 onwards. While his cars were well built and reliable, his company went bankrupt in 1905. More successful was **Herbert Austin** who built his first car in 1895 – a three-wheeled, two-horsepower car. Very soon, Austin built a large factory near Birmingham where he produced small family cars.

This was in contrast to **F. H. Royce** and **C. S. Rolls** who produced their first luxury-style car in 1904. **Rolls-Royce** became a by-word for quality and reliability. Their top-range car, the Rolls-Royce 40/50, later called the Silver Ghost, was priced at £2,500. Their products were deliberately aimed at the upper-class market. British entrepreneurs were conscious of the class structures in the country and the need to cater for different segments.

Mass Production

The Rolls-Royce was in sharp contrast to the first mass-production car, the Model T Ford, which sold for £125 in 1908. This was the brainchild of **Henry Ford**, an American-born son of Irish emigrants. Up to this time in the early years of the 20th century, car production was largely 'one-off', with no interchangeable parts, dependent, as we have seen, on a skilled workforce. This was all changed by Henry Ford in America.

Ford used the **conveyor-belt assembly line** to produce his Model T Ford more quickly and cheaply. To achieve this it was necessary to have **standardised parts** which could be fitted by semi-skilled or unskilled workers. Ford's methods reduced assembly time to 1.5 hours per worker, and his factories in America and at Trafford Park in Manchester were producing 12 cars per worker-year in contrast to the European rate of one per worker per year. As a result, the

SOURCE 6 – MORRIS MOTOR

AFTER 400,000 MILES!
Still in Daily Use

HERE is a Morris car that is British and Proud of it. Day in, day out, it has been on the go since 1913, has travelled over 400,000 miles, and is still in daily use. Not very modern in body line, perhaps, but still a thoroughly good serviceable motor car.

And the Morris of to-day is better value, better built than was even this forerunner of what has proved to be the world's outstanding small car value.

You can't do better than buy a Morris.

Prices from £148 10s. All Models obtainable by Hire Purchase, from £37 2s. 11d. down.

AN INTERESTING COMPARISON

It is interesting to observe that the 1913 2-seater model illustrated above was listed at £199 10s. What a contrast with the 1927 Morris-Cowley Saloon which, complete with four-wheel brakes, adjustable seats, electric lighting and starting and a host of refinements, sells to-day at the remarkable figure of £195. This is striking proof of the extraordinary value presented by Morris Cars to-day.  The Morris-Cowley Saloon - £195

Write for Catalogue and full particulars of Guarantee, Hire Purchase and Service Facilities to Enquiries, Dept. P.

MORRIS

MORRIS MOTORS (1926), LTD., COWLEY, OXFORD.

Dunlop Tyres Standard.

BUY BRITISH AND BE PROUD OF IT.

How many miles has this car travelled, according to the advertisement? Why can't you do better than buy a Morris? What was Hire Purchase? What is the difference in price between the 1913 model and the 1927 model?

Model T Ford sold at a very affordable price, and by 1918, in Britain, Ford Model Ts had 40 per cent of the market.

Not surprisingly, Ford workers were **well paid** – by 1911, the workers in Manchester were paid twice the average industrial wage. Ford believed that good pay would provide a satisfied workforce but it also provided a market for his cars.

Changes in European Car Production

By 1914, European car production had changed from its earlier development. German engineering had been responsible for the invention and early development of the car in the 1880s and 1890s. But by 1900, France, which produced German engines under licence, had overtaken the Germans.

The British car industry was slow to develop but by 1913 it was overtaking the French. French production rose by one-third between 1909 and 1913, but this was exceeded by the British with a three-fold increase in the same period. While France had produced 45,000 cars by 1913, it was being caught up by Britain which produced 34,000 by then, after a very slow start. The Germans lagged far behind with only 23,000 cars produced.

Looked at in another way, there was a greater car ownership density in Britain by 1913. In Britain, there was one car to every 165 people, in France it was one to every 318 people, while in Germany it was one to every 956 people. By 1913, Britain had become the fastest-growing car market in Europe, with France being its main exporter.

Comparison with the USA

However, the European car production lagged very far behind the USA. By 1913, the USA, with 1.26 million cars in use, had four times more cars compared to Europe. This meant one car for every 77 people, well ahead of the main European countries. In 1913, Ford's factories in the US produced 200,000 cars compared to 5,000 by Peugeot, the largest French manufacturer, and 3,000 by Wolseley, the largest British manufacturer.

This was mostly due to the small, compact car, produced by assembly-line methods which dominated the US car market by 1910. American car manufacturers had greater economies of scale, which reduced their costs. On the other hand, European countries had smaller populations served by a close and efficient railway and tram network which investors and entrepreneurs had to take into account.

However, by 1914, European manufacturers began to change and move to lower priced cars. This was speeded up by the arrival of Henry Ford on the British market. He opened his **new factory in Trafford Park, Manchester** in 1911. The British press attacked his Model T Runabout as cheap and nasty but priced at £135, it was 25 per cent cheaper than the Morris Oxford, a British 'popularly priced' car introduced in 1913 to compete against the Model T. Not surprisingly, Ford sold more than 7,000 cars in Britain in 1913 which accounted for 60 per cent of cars priced below £200.

The First World War

The internal combustion engine played an important part in the First World War in cars, lorries and aircraft. The 'taxis of the Marne' took French reinforcements out of Paris to help win the Battle of the Marne. The war showed that cars needed to be made stronger and more reliable, and that standardised parts were necessary for repairs.

SOURCE 7 – DUNLOP MOTOR TYRES

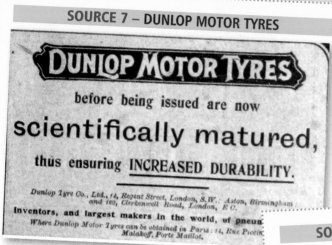

DUNLOP MOTOR TYRES before being issued are now **scientifically matured,** thus ensuring INCREASED DURABILITY.

Dunlop Tyre Co., Ltd., 14, Regent Street, London, S.W.; Aston, Birmingham and 162, Clerkenwell Road, London, E.C.

Inventors, and largest makers in the world, of pneu...

Where Dunlop Motor Tyres can be obtained in Paris: 14, Rue Piccini, Malakoff, Porte Maillot.

> What is Dunlop's message here?

> Why are the Dunlop tyres praised by Mr Cook and Mr Weigel? What feature of the tyres is Dunlop highlighting?

SOURCE 8 – DUNLOP STEEL-STUDDED TYRES

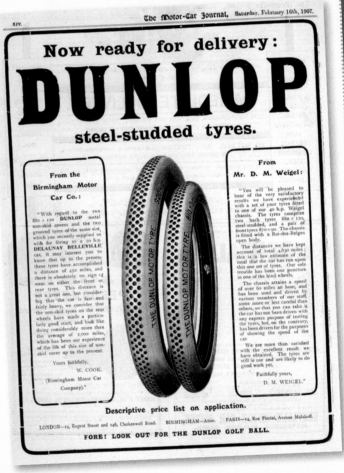

Impact of the Motor Car

Cars influenced many aspects of life but prior to World War I they only gave an indication of the changes that were ahead from the 1920s onwards.

The success of Ford's **assembly line production** spread to **other industries** so that mechanisation reduced the skills needed by factory workers. It also increased the monotony of work. The greater investment needed in the new factories led to the disappearance of smaller producers and car companies got bigger with fewer of them.

The growth of the car industry led to the growth of **spin-off industries** as car factories became more like assembly lines putting together parts made elsewhere.

An example is **Dunlop's Pneumatic Tyres**. Dunlop produced their first pneumatic tyre in Belfast in 1888. The production expanded in the 1890s, largely producing bicycle tyres. Dunlop moved production to Dublin, then to Coventry and Birmingham. In 1900, it produced its first pneumatic tyre for cars. Dunlop expanded into rubber plantations and production. By the end of World War I, it was the largest tyre manufacturer in Britain and one of Britain's largest manufacturing companies.

The car made for **noisier and more crowded** cities and towns. This impacted on cities which traced their origins back to the Middle Ages and beyond. European cities were older and their streets were narrower and therefore more easily congested than those in the US.

The chaos of London streets in the early 20th century as old and new methods of travel and transport mix.

Cars continued the **separation** of the place of work from the place of living. This began with the coming of the railways and the trams as cities grew out along lines. The car gave **greater mobility** so cities now expanded in between railway and tram lines. Workers, beginning with the well-off, could now commute to work in the city and live in the expanding suburbs.

As Henry Ford, and others, reduced the price of cars he made them more affordable for the middle class. This encouraged the spread of **instalment payments** and the growth of credit. Hire purchase became more fashionable (see advertisement, Source 6).

As a sign of the growing popularity of cars, the first Guide Michelin was published in Paris in 1900. The purpose of the guide was to provide drivers travelling in France with all the information they needed to be able to supply their car, get it repaired and find food and accommodation. It also served to advertise their products, tyres. The first Michelin Guide to the British Isles was published in 1911.

? EXAM QUESTION

This edited extract describes motoring in its early days. Read it and answer the questions which follow.

The decision to become a motorist in the early days of the motor car needed careful consideration. There was the considerable expense of buying and running a car, the unreliability of the mechanisms, no petrol stations or garages, poor roads and widespread motor phobia.

Car designs were of the open-carriage style. The absence of roof, windscreen or door meant the motorist had to dress up for protection from the elements.

By the early 1900s road dust became a problem for motorists. Night driving was out of the question because the candle or oil lamps were almost useless.

Source: Lord Montagu of Beaulieu, "The Early days of Motoring."
History Today, Vol. 36 (London: October 1986).

1. Why did early motorists have to be sure to bring enough petrol for their journey?
2. Why did the early motorist have to 'dress up for protection'?
3. By the early 1900s, what had become 'a problem for motorists'?
4. Why was night driving 'out of the question'?
5. Name one inventor who contributed to the early history of the motor car. (2017)

Other Effects

- Cars also had other impacts – they caused **death** and **injuries**. The first person killed by car in Britain was Bridget Driscoll, in August 1896. Consequently, there were calls to put more speed limits on cars to reduce the danger.

- People also protested that cars **disturbed** the quiet of the countryside, and sent dust into people's houses. Gradually, road surfaces had to be improved to reduce the dust and increase the comfort.

- Cars encouraged **day trips** and **holidays** in seaside resorts. These trips had begun with the advent of the railways. Now many more resorts, not on the railway lines, could benefit from car journeys.

From the archive, 26 August 1896: The UK's first fatal car accident

Bridget Driscoll, on a day trip to Crystal Palace, was bewildered by the car's approach, got in its way and was knocked down.

... Arthur James Edsell, the driver of the car, was cautioned by the Coroner, and elected to give evidence. He said his instructions were to drive slowly on busy days. At the time of the accident he thought he was driving about four miles an hour. He saw two women in front of him, Mrs. Driscoll being one of them, and she had an umbrella up. He rang his bell, and shouted, but just as he got up to her she seemed bewildered, and got into his way, and the car knocked her down. Witness stopped his car within a few inches of where the woman lay ...

www.theguardian.com

DOCUMENTS-BASED QUESTION

Case study to which the documents relate:

The invention and early history of the motor car

Study the documents and answer the questions below.

DOCUMENT A

While the original English motorists were typically wealthy sportsmen, it wasn't until Edward VII took up motoring (with relish) that the motor car began to gain precedence over the horse and carriage with the Marlborough House Set. The King owned several automobiles, all painted in his own royal claret, which he took for speedy runs up and down country roads. He loudly encouraged his chauffeur to pass everything and anything on the road. Surprisingly, he refused to allow his wife, Queen Alexandra, to own a motor car of her own. It was only after Alexandra borrowed motors from friends, that Edward was eventually persuaded to allow her an automobile of her own. Alexandra was the original backseat driver, growing notorious for prodding her driver violently in the back with her parasol, shouting directions. The Queen's ownership of a motor car made the machine eminently respectable, and many women took to the sport with as much alacrity (speed) as their male counterparts.

DOCUMENT B

Due to the absence of hoods or windscreens, motoring called for special clothing. Loose topcoats in leather, or special motoring coats acted as protection from weather or cold. Socially, the motor car increased the amount of time spent on leisure activities. No longer were weekend parties hasty, hectic affairs as the motor car allowed groups to speed from London to the countryside for what hostesses called 'Saturdays-to-Mondays'. General travel was made easier not only by the motor car, but also by the increased network of tramways while railways ran seaside excursions. Enthusiastic motorists added another form of leisure to the motorcar in the guise of touring. Countless books were published between 1896 and 1914, recounting motor tours in both remote and accessible places like the Hebrides and France. This new type of holidaying was incorporated into the itineraries of trusted travel agents such as Thomas Cook & Co.

Edited extracts from Evangeline Holland, *Edwardian England, A Guide to Everyday Life, 1900–1914* (2014).

1. (i) In Document A, what was the colour of the King's cars?
   (ii) In what way was Queen Alexandra the original backseat driver, according to Document A?
   (iii) According to Document B, why did early motoring need special clothing?
   (iv) What were the 'Saturdays-to-Mondays' in Document B?

2. (i) Do both documents give reasons as to why motoring became popular? Explain your answer.
   (ii) Is one document more concerned than the other with upper-class motoring? Explain your answer.

3. (i) Explain how these extracts are secondary sources.
   (ii) Are these documents reliable and useful sources?

4. What were the main trends in the development of the European motor industry up to 1914?

> ## *KEY CONCEPTS*
>
> **ANTI-SEMITISM:** Hatred of Jews.
>
> **BALANCE OF POWER:** When no one country is able to dominate others, when countries are roughly equal in power.
>
> **CONSCRIPTION:** The compulsory enlistment of young men in the armed forces during a war.
>
> **NATIONALISM:** The political belief that all people can be divided into nations and that each nation should have its own government.
>
> **NEW IMPERIALISM:** The colonial expansion of mainly European powers, but also Japan and the USA, which took place at the end of the 19th and the beginning of the 20th centuries. It is called 'New' to distinguish it from the colonial expansion of the Age of Exploration in the 15th and 16th centuries.
>
> **SELF-DETERMINATION:** The belief that each country should have its own government and should decide its own future.
>
> **WAR OF ATTRITION:** A type of warfare where the purpose is to wear down the enemy. Refers in particular to warfare on the Western Front in the First World War.
>
> **WAR GUILT:** The clause – Article 231 – in the Treaty of Versailles which said that Germany was guilty of causing the First World War.
>
> **WORLD WAR:** A war involving most of the largest countries in the world.

2

DICTATORSHIP AND DEMOCRACY IN EUROPE, 1920–45

In this section, you should understand:
- The progress of the Russian Civil War and why the Reds won.
- The role of Lenin.
- The Russian economy, 1920–24.
- Stalin's rise to power.
- Stalin's dictatorship and his use of purges and show trials.
- Stalin's transformation of the Soviet economy.
- Case Study: Stalin's Show Trials.

The Rule of Lenin

Introduction – The Communists Take Over

Lenin arrives in Moscow, 1917, at the start of the Communist Revolution in Russia.

In 1917, Russia was a huge empire ruled over by **Tsar** (emperor) **Nicholas II**, a member of the Romanov family which had ruled Russia for three hundred years. At this time, the Russian Empire was fighting the First World War (1914–18), and the chaos and destruction caused by the war led to two revolutions.

In the first revolution, in March 1917, Tsar Nicholas II was overthrown by the Provisional Government drawn from members of the Duma (parliament). Eight months later, in November, **Lenin and the Bolsheviks** overthrew the new

Develop notes on the role of Lenin in Soviet history, 1920–1924.

KEY PERSONALITY: LENIN

Lenin was born in Russia in 1870. He joined the Social Democratic Party which was the Russian Marxist or Communist party. He wanted to form a small group of elite revolutionaries to plan revolution. This group became known as the **Bolsheviks**. Lenin spent most of his time in exile in England or Switzerland. He returned to Petrograd, the capital of Russia, after the first revolution in March 1917. He began to plan the second revolution.

In the **November Revolution** 1917, Lenin and the Bolsheviks took over Russia but they had little support. They signed a peace agreement with Germany, and then in order to retain power they had to fight the opposition forces – the Whites – in the **Russian Civil War** (p. 157–61). The Bolsheviks (now called Communists) were led by Lenin and Trotsky (who organised the Red Army). Lenin was in charge of **War Communism** (p. 159). He took over the main industries and sent out Communist groups to the countryside to confiscate food from the peasants (farmers). He also set up the Cheka, a secret police, to eliminate opposition. By the end of the Civil War, Lenin had to change his policy. A revolt by the sailors in the **Kronstadt** naval base near Petrograd made him realise the severity of his policies. He now brought in the **New Economic Policy (NEP)** (p. 162) which allowed farmers to sell more of their produce for profit.

But Lenin's health was declining. In 1921, he had been shot by Dora Kaplan in an assassination attempt. He also suffered from a series of **strokes** which gradually took away his movement and speech. He was worried about who would succeed him. In his Last Testament, he preferred a collective leadership (a group sharing power) and he warned about the dangers of **Stalin**. He died in 1924. He had founded the Union of the Soviet Socialist Republics which was the **first Communist state**. His views about revolution were imitated by others during the twentieth century.

Provisional Government. Lenin wanted to introduce **Communism** into Russia, which would mean:

- The abolition of private property.
- Government control of agriculture and industry.
- A one-party dictatorship.

Lenin Holds onto Power

Having taken over the country, Lenin's biggest challenge was to hold onto power. He did this by:

- Allowing peasants to take over private land.
- Abolishing the Assembly (parliament).
- Setting up the **Cheka** (secret police) to arrest and execute those the Cheka thought were opposed to Lenin and the Bolsheviks (now called Communists).
- Taking Russia out of the First World War by making peace with Germany in the **Treaty of Brest–Litovsk**.

After Brest–Litovsk, Lenin faced his greatest threat in the Civil War.

The Russian Civil War, 1918–21

In the Civil War, the Whites opposed Lenin and his party, now called the **Communist Party**. Lenin and Trotsky led the Communists or **Reds**. Lenin concentrated on economic and political problems, while Trotsky organised the military. The Whites were composed of many different groups, such as:

- Social Revolutionaries.
- Former Tsarists who wanted to restore the Tsar.
- Supporters of the Provisional Government.
- Landlords.
- Industrialists.
- national minorities such as the Cossacks who wanted independence from Russia.

They were helped by the **Allied powers** (Britain, France, US and Japan) who wanted Russia to continue fighting in the First World War.

The Military Conflict

The Red Army was led by **Trotsky**, Commissar of War. It controlled only the centre of Russia at the beginning of the Civil War. However, this territory included the main cities of Russia (Moscow and Petrograd), the main industrial areas and the best farming land. The Red Army was attacked from all sides by the White armies but it defeated each in turn.

The East: In Siberia, the Communists were threatened by the Siberian army of General **Kolchak**. Kolchak took over territory along the Trans-Siberian railway and advanced through the Ural Mountains towards Moscow. Lenin feared

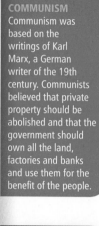

> **KEY CONCEPT**
> **COMMUNISM**
> Communism was based on the writings of Karl Marx, a German writer of the 19th century. Communists believed that private property should be abolished and that the government should own all the land, factories and banks and use them for the benefit of the people.

> In the Treaty of Brest-Litovsk, Russia lost:
> 25% of its land
> 26% of its population
> 33% of its farming land
> 80% of its coalmines
> 33% of its manufacturing industry

Trotsky played a vital role in building up the Soviet Red Army.

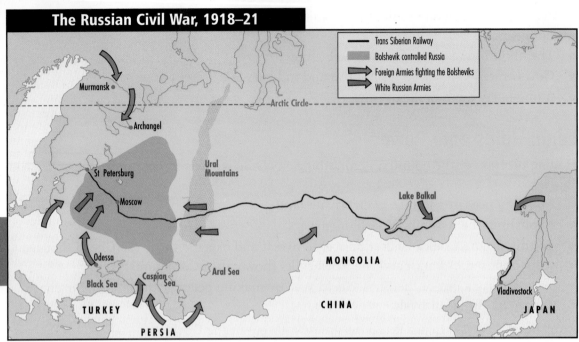

The Russian Civil War, 1918–21

— Trans Siberian Railway
■ Bolshevik controlled Russia
⇨ Foreign Armies fighting the Bolsheviks
→ White Russian Armies

Murmansk

Archangel

— Arctic Circle —

St Petersburg

Moscow

Ural Mountains

Lake Balkal

Odessa

Caspian Sea

Aral Sea

MONGOLIA

Black Sea

Vladivostock

TURKEY

CHINA

JAPAN

PERSIA

> What geographical advantages did the Reds have over the Whites?

his advance would lead to the rescue of Tsar Nicholas II and his family, who were held in Ekaterinberg. So he ordered their execution. However, Kolchak was defeated and later executed by the Reds (February 1920).

The South: General **Denikin** attacked from the south (the Crimea and the Ukraine) and came within 200 miles of Moscow, which was now the capital of the Soviet Union. But he too was defeated (October 1919). In April 1920, **Denikin** handed over control of this White Army to General **Wrangel**, and left the Crimea for Western Europe.

The North-West: General **Yudenich** advanced from the Baltic states (Lithuania, Latvia, Estonia) towards Petrograd. In 1919 he reached the suburbs of Petrograd but stubborn resistance by the Reds, encouraged by the presence of Trotsky, led to his defeat.

Allied Intervention: When the Bolsheviks (Communists) pulled Russia out of the First World War, Allied troops were landed in Murmansk and Archangel in the north, in the Crimea in the south, and in Vladivostok in the east (see map of the Russian Civil War). The Allies wanted to bring Russia back into the war. However, when the First World War ended in November 1918, the Allies were not interested in Soviet Russia and gradually withdrew their help.

So, by the beginning of 1920 Trotsky's Red Army had strengthened their position, but it had yet to face one of its greatest threats.

The Russo-Polish War, 1920–21: The Russian Civil War was complicated by the intervention of Poland. **Pilsudski**, the Polish leader, took advantage of the chaos in Russia. The Poles defeated the Reds just east of the city in the **Battle of Warsaw**. After this the Poles advanced into Russia, but peace negotiations were soon begun and concluded with the **Treaty of Riga** in March 1921. In this Treaty, Poland gained substantial territory from Russia.

Bolshevik (Communist) officers take over trains for use in the Russian Civil War.

The Last of the White Armies: By this time the Reds were distracted by another attack, the last White attack. After Denikin's failure in the south, General **Wrangel** replaced him. Wrangel took advantage of the Reds' campaign in Poland to advance into the Ukraine. However, after early successes, he was defeated by larger Red forces. Wrangel retreated to the Crimea, evacuating his troops and about 150,000 civilians to Turkey (1920). The Communist Red Army was victorious.

Why Did Lenin and Trotsky Win the Russian Civil War?

(i) Trotsky and the Red Army

Trotsky said he had to construct *'an army all over again'*. As Chairman of the **Supreme War Council**, he introduced conscription for all men between 18 and 40. By 1920 the Red Army was five million strong. To train these inexperienced soldiers, Trotsky forced former **Tsarist officers** to join the army. In some cases he took families hostage to ensure the loyalty of officers. But he also appointed **political commissars** (officers) to watch them. The commissars were loyal Communist Party workers who were responsible for the morale of the troops.

Trotsky imposed a harsh discipline on the army but he also won the respect of the soldiers by moving from front to front giving orders and raising the spirit of the troops with political speeches. He used a special armoured train equipped with a printing press for propaganda, a radio station and a telegraph office. Trotsky took advantage of internal supply lines by using the rail system which centred on Moscow and Petrograd. He could move troops around quickly to face each new threat from the Whites. One by one, Trotsky organised the Red Army to defeat the armies of Kolchak, Denikin, Yudenich and Wrangel. In these ways, Trotsky ensured that the Red Army was victorious. (See The Military Conflict on pp. 157–59.)

(ii) The Weaknesses of the White Armies

The White armies were disunited and poorly led with each group following **different aims**, so they failed to co-ordinate their attacks. Some wanted to restore the Tsar; others wanted the return of the Provisional Government; others again wanted the land returned to the landlords. Their armies were scattered far apart, and attacked at different times. They were also responsible for atrocities in the lands they conquered, including the massacre of Jews. Their soldiers were badly disciplined and were prone to drunkenness and looting. Overall they caused far more suffering to the peasants than the Red Terror of the Communists.

(iii) Lenin and War Communism

Lenin was responsible for supplying the army with weapons and food. He also had control of much of the war material produced for use in the First World War. He and Trotsky provided a **united leadership**. While Trotsky was mainly in charge of the Red Army and the military conflict, Lenin took control of economic and political problems. Lenin followed a policy of **War Communism**. With this policy, he ensured that all industry and agriculture within the Communist-controlled territory was geared solely towards the war effort. But he was also putting **Communist ideas** into practice.

Timeline of Revolution and War, 1917–24

1917	Bolsheviks seized power in Petrograd
1918	Treaty of Brest-Litovsk Civil War began War Communism End of World War I
1919–20	White armies defeated
1921	War Communism ended; NEP began
1922	Union of the Soviet Socialist Republics (USSR) set up
1924	Lenin died

Russian revolutionary poster: encouraging people to sign up immediately to join the co-operative.

159

Industry: Private trading was banned and factories with more than ten workers were taken over by the government. Production was planned and organised by the government. There was forced mobilisation of workers for industry. Strikes were also banned and strikers were shot. The control of key industries meant the Reds could produce more munitions than the Whites.

Agriculture and food supplies: Surplus crops were requisitioned (taken) by the government to feed the workers and the soldiers. Food detachments were sent to the countryside to get the food. Food was rationed and given to people depending on their contribution to the economy. Industrial workers, for example, received three times more rations than professionals, such as lawyers.

Lenin with military commanders in Red Square.

War Communism achieved its aim of **winning the war** but it caused great suffering. Industrial production declined. (See graph, Russian Production 1913–21, p. 162.) There were severe shortages of fuel, and transport ground to a halt except for the war effort. The peasants cut back in grain production so that Russia experienced famine in 1921. It is estimated that between five and seven million people died of hunger.

(iv) Use of Propaganda

The Communists used propaganda more effectively than the Whites. They used posters and leaflets to frighten the peasants and workers that the Tsar and the landlords would return under the Whites. They also appealed to Russian nationalism against the intervention of Allied armies; they were fighting for Russia against foreign invaders. The Whites, on the other hand, alienated non-Russian nationalities by claiming 'Russia One and Indivisible'.

> **KEY CONCEPT**
> PROPAGANDA is spreading information to convince people of your point of view. Governments and politicians use propaganda to achieve or retain power.

(v) The Attitude of the Peasants

The peasants did not like the Communists but they feared the Whites even more because they would bring back the landlords, as they did in some areas.

(vi) The Red Terror

The Communists used the Red Terror to force people to concentrate on the war effort and to eliminate any opposition. The **Cheka**, led by Felix Dzerhinsky, began the **Red Terror**. Any opposition to Lenin and the Communists was dealt with by violence. Peasants, striking workers, former government officials, landlords or anybody accused of co-operating with the White armies could be punished or executed. It was a systematic (organised) terror designed to ensure the continuation of Bolshevik or Communist rule. Some party officials were opposed to it but Lenin encouraged and organised the Red Terror,

Lenin sweeps away the opposition: effective Communist propaganda.

although he tried to distance himself from it as much as possible. By the end of the Civil War, it was estimated that between 12,000 and 50,000 people were killed by the Cheka and 85,000 prisoners were put into concentration camps, or into the **gulag** system of labour camps which Lenin introduced.

(vii) The Allied Withdrawal

The Allies lost interest in Russia when the First World War was over (November 1918). The Whites lost the sympathy of the Allied governments because of their atrocities, their anti-semitism and their plans to restore the Tsar. Allied armies were withdrawn and supplies of weapons dried up.

Conclusion and Results

The Red Army won the Civil War but at great cost. During the Civil War 10 million people were killed for various reasons. Besides the fighting and the terror, disease also killed many; 2 million were killed by typhus alone. In the famine of 1921, 5 to 7 million died. Compared with 1913, factory production was only one-fifth and food production was halved.

Famine: Seven million Russians died in 1921, largely due to the First World War and Civil War.

Many of the defeated Whites emigrated from Russia. Some settled in Eastern Europe but others moved to Paris, Berlin and other western cities. Soviet Russia lost many of its educated class – writers, scientists and engineers – and later suffered from a shortage of managerial talent.

Establishing a Communist Dictatorship

While the Civil War was in progress, between 1918 and 1921, Lenin established a **Communist dictatorship:**

- The newly named Communist Party grew in membership from about 250,000 in 1917 to 700,000 in 1921.
- All government power was concentrated in the hands of party members (see diagram to right).
- All opposition parties were banned, with dissenters imprisoned, exiled or shot.
- The Communist Party controlled the newspapers and radio.
- Only members of the Communist Party could get elected to the Soviets.

In March 1921, Lenin banned all factions or groups within the Communist Party. All decisions made by **Lenin and the Politburo** were binding on all members. As leader of the Communist Party, Lenin wielded great power. He had created the first **totalitarian dictatorship**.

The Communist Party

COMMUNIST PARTY

Politburo
Body of senior party members which formulated policy.

Central Committee
Main administrative body of the party. The secretary exercised great political influence.

Party Congress
Composed of representatives selected from regional and district branches. Elected members of Central Committee.

KEY CONCEPT
DICTATORSHIP is rule by one man or party. Dictators control all power. They ban other political parties, control the means of propaganda (press, radio and television), use a secret police and often imprison or kill people who oppose them.

QUESTIONS

1. Who opposed Lenin and the Communists in the Russian Civil War?
2. Who led the Red Army?
3. Why did the Allies pull out of the Civil War?
4. How did Poland threaten Russia?
5. What was War Communism?
6. Was it successful?
7. What role did the Red Terror play in the Civil War?

EXAM QUESTION

How and why did Lenin and the Communists win the Russian Civil War?

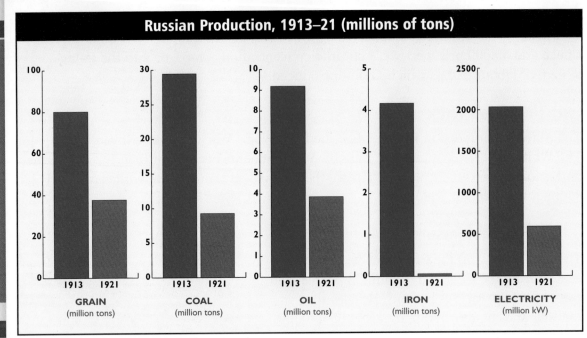

Russian Production, 1913–21 (millions of tons)

GRAIN (million tons)	COAL (million tons)	OIL (million tons)
IRON (million tons)	ELECTRICITY (million kW)	

Lenin and the New Economic Policy

Why did Lenin Introduce the New Economic Policy?

In March 1921, Lenin announced the end of War Communism and the beginning of the **New Economic Policy** (NEP). He was faced with serious discontent which undermined support for the Communist Party:

- There was widespread **famine** which in some cases led to cannibalism.
- There were **peasant risings**, against food requisitioning and the abolition of private trading.
- Workers' discontent increased as factories closed due to shortages of fuel and raw materials.
- Workers' groups demanded higher wages and better conditions.
- Strikes in **Petrograd** in early 1921 led to the imposition of martial (military) law.
- Petrograd was described as 'a city completely dead. No electricity, no heat ... people just dying.'

But the **Kronstadt rising** presented the most serious difficulties for Lenin and the Communist Party.

The Kronstadt Rising, 1921

Kronstadt was a naval base on an island near Petrograd. In March 1921 the Kronstadt sailors rose in revolt against the **Communist Party** and **War Communism**. These sailors had played a major role in the victory of the Bolsheviks in the November Revolution, 1917. Now they were very critical of the new regime brought in by Lenin.

Lenin and **Trotsky** took immediate action against the revolt because they saw the danger it posed to their survival. The sailors refused to surrender so Trotsky ordered the Red Army soldiers across the ice to crush the rising. The Kronstadt fortress fell and hundreds of prisoners were killed.

However, Lenin realised the significance of the protest and completely changed his economic policy to revive the Russian economy. The Kronstadt rising, he said, *'illuminated reality like a flash of lightning'.*

The New Economic Policy (NEP)

The **main points of the New Economic Policy** were:

- Requisitions (taking food) from the peasants were ended.
- Requisitions were replaced with a fixed tax in kind (grain).
- Peasants could sell the surplus grain.
- Private enterprise was allowed in small factories and in trade.
- Heavy industry (coal, iron, electricity, railways) – *'the commanding heights of the economy'*, as Lenin said – were still controlled by the government.
- A new currency was introduced to control inflation.
- Foreign trade was encouraged, which boosted the Soviet economy.
- Lenin encouraged the development of electrical power. *'Soviet power plus electrification equals Communism,'* he said.

Some Party members opposed Lenin's policy because they said it was **contrary** to Communist or Marxist ideas. Lenin justified his policy as a **temporary retreat** from Communism to give the Russian economy the time to recover and to ensure the survival of the Communist Party.

The Results of the NEP

The NEP lasted until 1928, and it was largely successful. It restored economic production to pre-war levels, and it lifted Russia out of the economic depression caused by World War I, the Russian Revolution and the Civil War.

- By increasing agricultural and industrial production, it helped **Lenin and the Communists survive**.
- In farming, production reached pre-war levels by 1925. Food shortages and the famine of 1921 ended. Peasant unrest declined and the richer peasants (**kulaks**) benefited.
- A new class of merchant or trader developed – **nepmen** – who controlled trade between country and towns.
- Some Communists resented the growth of nepmen, seeing them as greedy and against Communist teaching.
- Heavy industry increased production but in some areas it did not yet reach pre-war levels.

Lenin's New Economic Policy increased farming production. Richer farmers (kulaks) could afford new machinery.

Industrial and Agricultural Production in Russia under NEP, 1921–28 (million tons)				
	1921	1923	1925	1928
Grain	37.6	56.6	72.5	73.3
Coal	9	13.7	18.1	35.0
Steel	0.2	0.7	2.1	4.0
Electricity (billion kWh)	0.5	1.1	2.9	5.0

How do the figures here compare with the figures in Russian Production, 1913–21 (p. 162)?

163

QUESTIONS

1. Why did Lenin introduce the New Economic Policy (NEP)?
2. What were the main points of the New Economic Policy?
3. How successful was NEP?
4. How did Lenin die?

EXAM QUESTION

What did Lenin contribute to Communism in Russia?

- The economy slowed after 1926 and the Soviet Union needed huge investment if it was going to catch up with Western Europe and the USA.

The Death of Lenin

Lenin did not live to see the full effects of the New Economic Policy. He suffered a series of strokes in 1922 and 1923 and died in January 1924, at the age of fifty-three. His body lay in state for a week as thousands of Russian people marched past in the freezing cold. Afterwards, his body was embalmed and placed in a special mausoleum in Moscow. Petrograd was renamed Leningrad in his honour.

A cult of Lenin was developed after his death, but it is unlikely he would have wanted this. His widow, Krupskaya, said, *'Do not build memorials to him, name palaces after him, do not hold magnificent celebrations in his memory. All of this meant so little to him.'* However, the Communist Party used this **cult of personality** as a propaganda weapon to tighten their grip on the Soviet Union.

Assessment of Lenin

Lenin created the Communist Party of the Soviet Union and led it to the first Communist revolution and Communist state. He showed how a small group of dedicated revolutionaries could win a revolution. He ensured the survival of Communism in Russia after the revolution and he created a **one-party Communist dictatorship** which others later imitated.

But, he left many problems for his successor(s). Russia was still a peasant society with 80 per cent of its people earning their living from the land. It was still relatively poor compared to France, Britain and Germany. Since manufacturing industry was not fully developed it had a small working class. It was far from being a Communist society, even though it had a Communist party in charge.

Thousands of people attended Lenin's funeral.

The Rule of Stalin – The Struggle for Power

Why did Stalin win the Struggle for Power?

In December 1923, a month before he died, Lenin drafted his **Testament**. He was worried about the future leadership of the Communist Party and of the Soviet Union. In it, he wrote about the **exceptional abilities** of Comrade Trotsky. But he was critical of Trotsky's **over-confidence**. However, Lenin was more concerned about Stalin. *'Comrade Stalin, having become General Secretary, has concentrated an enormous power in his hands, and I am not sure he always knows how to use that power with sufficient caution.'* Lenin was hoping that some of the leaders would share power together. But this did not happen. Instead there was a **struggle for power**.

Trotsky Versus Stalin

The contest for Lenin's successor rested between Trotsky and Stalin. Many thought Trotsky would become the new leader because he had clear **advantages** over Stalin. He had commanded the Red Guards in the November Revolution, 1917. He had also created and led the Red Army in the Civil War. He was a great organiser and a very able speaker. But he also suffered certain **disadvantages**. He was personally arrogant and some feared he might use the army to take over Russia. He also suffered from poor health and consequently missed some important meetings where key decisions were taken. But his greatest weakness was his failure to understand where real power in the Communist Party lay.

Lenin was concerned that Stalin (right) would misuse power after his own death.

Stalin, on the other hand, was like a **grey blur** – nobody was sure what he stood for. Stalin formed alliances with other key Politburo leaders. He initially joined two other Communist leaders, **Zinoviev** and **Kamenev**, in opposition to Trotsky. All were members of the Politburo, the main ruling body of the party, and they had a strong influence over the party organisation in other ways. Zinoviev was dominant in Petrograd (Leningrad) and Kamenev was strong in Moscow. Stalin was not only **Commissar of Nationalities**, he was also **General Secretary** of the party. This gave him great influence over party membership, including organising the **Lenin Enrolment** which increased party membership with many of his own supporters. He was also able to appoint many of his supporters to key positions in the party, and to expel others. Further, he drew up a list of candidates to be sent to the Party Congress which controlled election to the Central Committee.

From left: Stalin, Rykov, Kamenev and Zinoviev defeat Trotsky after Lenin's death.

Stalin deliberately spread the cult of Lenin, beginning with the stage-management of Lenin's funeral. He was able to promote his own image as **the best, the staunchest, the truest comrade-in-arms of Lenin**. He also highlighted earlier disagreements between Lenin and Trotsky before the 1917 Revolution, thereby questioning Trotsky's loyalty to Lenin and his ideas.

Stalin was also helped by the mistakes of others. Trotsky failed to attend Lenin's funeral and also attacked Lenin's New Economic Policy. Zinoviev and Kamenev helped Stalin by refusing to publish Lenin's Testament, with its damaging verdict on Stalin.

Stalin's early victories

Stalin joined with Zinoviev and Kamenev to stop Trotsky. They agreed to keep Lenin's Testament secret because he had criticised all three, but above all Stalin. They claimed Stalin had now changed and that he should remain as General Secretary. The three also accused Trotsky of 'Bonapartist' tendencies – that like Napoleon Bonaparte, he would set up a **military dictatorship**. They also accused him of **disloyalty** to 'Leninism'. These attacks weakened Trotsky and he had to resign his position as **Commissar of War**.

Develop notes on the role of Stalin in Soviet history, 1920–45.

KEY PERSONALITY: STALIN

Stalin was born in Georgia, in the southern part of the Russian Empire, in 1879. He joined the **Bolsheviks** and was a follower of Lenin. He did not come to prominence until after the November revolution in 1917. He took part in the **Russian Civil War**, being involved in the defence of **Tsaritsyn**, which was later called Stalingrad.

After the Bolshevik (Communist) Revolution, he began a slow rise to power. He became **General Secretary** of the Communist Party. He used this position to put loyal followers in power. When Lenin died, there was a **struggle for power** between Trotsky, Kamenev, **Zinoviev, Stalin** and **Bukharin**. By 1928, Stalin was the most powerful person in the Soviet Union (pp. 164–67).

He now set about the huge **transformation** of Soviet society, through **Five Year Plans** and collectivisation (p. 171). He also made Russia into a **totalitarian state** by controlling press and radio, creating a **cult of personality** and suppressing any criticism (pp. 167–68). He organised the **Great Purges** and the **Moscow Show Trials** (p. 173, pp. 178–87).

By 1939, Stalin was aware of the dangers posed by Hitler. He signed the **Nazi-Soviet Pact** to give himself time to prepare for war (p. 286). In 1941 Hitler invaded Russia. Stalin organised the defence of the country in the **Great Patriotic War**. The **Battle of Stalingrad** was one of the turning points of the war. After that, the Russian army pushed back the German army to Berlin (p. 298). Stalin took part in the **wartime conferences** (p. 302) with Churchill and Roosevelt. He was able to take credit for playing a big part in defeating Hitler. He continued in power until his death in 1953.

? QUESTIONS

1. What did Lenin's Testament say?
2. What strengths and weaknesses did Trotsky have in the leadership struggle?
3. What advantages did Stalin have?
4. What roles did Zinoviev, Kamenev and Bukharin play in the leadership struggle?
5. What were Permanent Revolution and Socialism in One Country?
6. What happened to Trotsky?

? EXAM QUESTION

How and why did Stalin emerge as leader of the Soviet Union by 1928?

Permanent Revolution and Socialism in One Country

But the major battle between Trotsky and Stalin was fought over the future of Communism and the development of Soviet Russia. Trotsky supported the idea of **permanent revolution** in which workers in other countries would be encouraged to revolt and set up Communist states. He took the view that Communism was weak in Russia and could not be developed unless Communism was spread to other countries, particularly in western Europe.

Stalin, on the other hand, believed in *'socialism in one country'*. He said Communism should be developed in Russia first, so that the country would be a modern, powerful state, rather than encouraging world revolution.

Stalin was supported by **Bukharin**, editor of *Pravda*, the main Communist newspaper, and **Rykov**. They both favoured NEP and slow industrialisation. Stalin's policy was also supported by party members who felt that Russia had suffered enough through war and revolution from 1914 to 1921. This policy also appealed to **Russian nationalism** by aiming to make the Soviet Union into one of the greatest economic powers.

Victory for Stalin

When Zinoviev and Kamenev joined Trotsky to oppose Stalin, it was too late. The three were voted out of the Politburo in 1926, and Trotsky and Zinoviev were expelled from the party, along with 75 supporters. Trotsky was then exiled to Siberia before he was eventually banished from the Soviet Union (1931) and later assassinated in Mexico (1940) on Stalin's orders.

By the end of the 1920s, Stalin had filled all positions in the Politburo with his own supporters. He was now fully in control of the Soviet Union. He was also now in a position to radically change policy, drop Lenin's New Economic Policy and implement the rapid industrialisation and collectivisation of the country.

Struggle for power	Stalin forms alliances	Stalin's opponents	Issues	Outcome
Stage 1	Stalin, Zinoviev and Kamenev	Trotsky	To publish Lenin's Testament	Lenin's Testament kept secret Trotsky weakened
Stage 2	Stalin	Trotsky	Socialism in One Country or Permanent Revolution	Wider support for Socialism in One Country
Stage 3	Stalin, Bukharin and Rykov	Zinoviev, Kamenev and Trotsky	NEP or rapid industrialisation	Trotsky, Zinoviev expelled from Politburo and 3 of them from Party
Stage 4	Stalin	Bukharin, Rykov	Rapid industrialisation, collectivisation or NEP	Five Year Plans and collectivisation

The Stalinist State in Peace

Stalin controlled the Soviet Union through various means:

- He **controlled** the Communist Party.
- The Party **controlled** the Soviet government, the secret police and the army.
- Stalin used **propaganda**, and controlled press, radio and cinema.
- He controlled the **economy**.
- He used **terror**.

Creating a Totalitarian State

In Stalin's Russia, all adults had the right to vote. They elected the local soviets (councils) who in turn selected representatives for the higher soviets at district and provincial level. At the top there was the Congress of Soviets. The Soviet Constitution of 1936 guaranteed freedom of speech, freedom of the press and the right to work and education. However, even though this had the appearance of a democratic structure, real power lay with the Communist Party, the secret police and the army. Stalin created a **totalitarian state** where the party controlled all the people and the state.

The Party: The Communist Party grew in size from 1.3 million members in 1928 to 3.3 million in 1933. It became less a party of workers and more a party of **intelligentsia** (the educated class). The Party was controlled by the **Politburo** which was dominated by Stalin (see The Communist Party diagram p. 161). The Party then controlled press, radio and industry through members who were in positions of power in each of these.

The secret police: The Party used the OGPU, later called the NKVD, to enforce Party policy and to ensure conformity to the Party's wishes. It supervised some of the major projects of the Five Year Plans, purged the Party in the 1930s and controlled the labour force of the prison camps (gulags).

KEY CONCEPT
TOTALITARIANISM is a term which was first used in the 1920s to describe the type of government in Italy, Germany and Russia. Totalitarian governments control all aspects of life, from the actions of people to their thoughts. These governments make great use of propaganda, secret police, terror and a strong political party.

QUESTIONS (?)

1. How was the Soviet Union a totalitarian state?
2. What role did propaganda play?
3. How was the cult of Stalin developed?

The Soviet army: The army also came under the direct control of the party. Most of the army commanders were party members. At any rate, military commanders worked alongside political commissars who ensured party policy was followed.

Stalin's Use of Propaganda

Stalin saw the role of propaganda as **strengthening** the control of the Soviet state, and his own control. He used propaganda to promote the benefits of his **policies** of collectivisation and industrialisation. He also used propaganda during the Purges and Great Terror to justify the Show Trials and the persecution of 'enemies of the people' (see pp. 173–77, pp. 178–87). He believed that **all systems of communication** should be used to get his message across. This included newspapers, radio and cinema, but also art, especially posters, theatre and literature. Also, **education** was used to teach communist ideals and to glorify Stalin as leader.

Stalin used posters to develop a cult of personality. This was just one aspect of Stalinist propaganda. Other aspects included propaganda for the Five Year Plans, the Show Trials and Purges and the Second World War.

The Cult of Stalin

An important feature of Stalin's totalitarian state was the **cult of personality**. Stalin and the Communist Party deliberately promoted this worship of Stalin.

History was rewritten to make Stalin a hero of the November Revolution and the Civil War. Posters, photographs and statues of Stalin were everywhere. Cities (e.g. Stalingrad) and streets were named after him. Music, art and poetry were used to praise him. Propaganda made him the equal of Lenin; *'Stalin is the new Lenin of today.'* Soon he was exceeding Lenin in importance – he was the *'most learned of men'*, *'the fount of all wisdom'*. He was treated like a god.

The Soviet Alternative — Transforming the Soviet Economy and Society

The Five Year Plans

Why did Stalin Introduce the Five Year Plans?

In 1928, Stalin introduced the first **Five Year Plan**. This meant that the New Economic Policy was abandoned and a **centrally planned economy** was put in its place. This would ensure forced economic growth. This huge change in Soviet economic policy was due to a number of factors:

- Stalin believed that **communism** could only be developed properly in a fully industrialised society.
- The NEP had **failed** to industrialise the Soviet Union.
- Stalin wanted to get greater control of the economy so that he would have greater control of the Soviet Union.
- He wanted to **overcome** the failure of agriculture to produce enough grain for the towns.

- Stalin wanted to **modernise Russia** so that it would match the economies of the western world as quickly as possible. *'We are 50 to 100 years behind the advanced countries. Either we make good the difference in 10 years or they will crush us.'*

Propaganda in Soviet Russia: Left: in 1928 the gloating rich man calls the Five Year Plan a 'fantastic dream'; in 1933 he is angry because he is proved wrong. Middle: fulfil the Five Year Plan in four years. Right: you are now a free woman – help build socialism.

The Operation of the Five Year Plans
Industry: The First Five Year Plan, 1928–32

The economic planning was directed by the **Central Planning Commission (Gosplan)**. In industry, Gosplan decided on production targets in manufacturing, transport and raw materials. These targets were set for the regions and the factories.

The first Five Year Plan concentrated on **heavy industry** – coal, iron, gas, and electricity. Their expansion formed the basis for future industrial growth.

Overall, the targets were too high but yet by the end of 1932 significant progress was made:

- **Machinery** production increased by four-fold.
- **Oil** production doubled.
- **Electricity** almost trebled.
- **New towns** such as Magnitogorsk were constructed.

But there was also **poor quality or faulty production** because of the concentration on quantity. Workers' living and working conditions worsened; food was short and there were long queues.

Industrial Production Under Five Year Plans					
Product	Actual Production 1927-28	First Five Year Plan		Second Five Year Plan	
		Target	Actual	Target	Actual
Coal (million tonnes)	35.4	68.0	64.3	152.5	128.0
Oil (million tonnes)	11.7	19.0	21.4	46.8	28.5
Iron (million tonnes)	3.3	8.0	6.2	16.0	14.5
Steel (million tonnes)	4.0	8.3	5.9	17.0	17.7
Electricity (Billion kilowatt hours)	5.05	17.0	13.4	38.0	36.2

1. Which of the products achieved their target in 1933?
2. Which of the products achieved their target in 1937?
3. Why do you think Stalin selected these products for increased production?
4. Based on these figures, how successful were the Five Year Plans?

The Second (1933–37) and Third (1938–41) Five Year Plans

In the second Five Year Plan (1933–37) there was still concentration on heavy industry. But efforts were made to develop new metalworking industries and transport, particularly the railways. It was during the second plan that the **Moscow Underground** was built. More consumer goods – radios, washing machines etc. – were also promised.

However, during the progress of the second Five Year Plan, the troubled state of Europe resulted in more investment in armaments, and this led to a cutback in consumer goods. Production of armaments became even more important in the third Five Year Plan (1938–41) as Europe headed for the Second World War. The German invasion in 1941 shortened the life of the plan.

What were the Results of the Five Year Plans?

By 1941, the Soviet economy was **transformed**. A backward, mainly agricultural country was changed into a leading industrial power. The Russian economy grew far more rapidly than the western economies of the US, Britain and France. Russia was now the second largest economy in the world, after the US:

- Production of industrial goods almost **trebled**.
- Iron, oil and electricity production grew even faster.
- The **urban working class** grew from 11 million in 1928 to 33 million in 1938.
- The Soviet Union did not experience the Depression suffered by the West; instead there was full employment.
- Russia had a **better educated workforce** as illiteracy was wiped out and the numbers in secondary schools grew six times between 1928 and 1938.

The changes in the economy meant that Russia was now **better prepared** to face the German invasion when it came in 1941. Indeed, it can be argued that Stalin's industrialisation and modernisation saved the Soviet Union.

Enemies of the Five Year Plan, a propaganda poster from Soviet Russia, 1929.

'The enemies of the Five Year Plan:
The landowner looks like an angry dog.
The Kulak sniffs with his fat nose.
The drunkard from grief drinks to excess.
The priest howls with a piercing voice.
The money-loving journalist hisses,
The capitalist sharpens his tusks,
The Menshevik gets extremely wild.
The White Fighter used bad language.
Dogs not chained to kennels, and all who stand for the old evil, will curse the Five Year Plan and proclaim war on it, threaten it with failure, understanding that in it is their certain destruction.'

How Was This Achieved?

(i) All the authority and power of the state was used to force through industrialisation rapidly.

(ii) **The Workers:**

- Much of Stalin's success was due to the hard work and reduced living standards of the workers. Working conditions were severe and there was the risk of punishment as a **wrecker**, if targets were not met.
- **Absenteeism** from work was punished by loss of job, food rations and housing.

? QUESTIONS

1. Why did Stalin introduce the first Five Year Plan?
2. How successful was the plan?
3. How successful were the Second and Third Five Year Plans?

? EXAM QUESTION

To what extent was Soviet industry transformed by 1941?

1. Can you identify each of the people in the poster? How are they portrayed?
2. Why is each of these regarded as enemies of the Five Year Plan? What is the 'old evil'?

An **internal passport system** was introduced to prevent workers moving from job to job.

- There was a large increase in **women workers**. By 1940, forty per cent of industrial workers were women as the government set up crèches and day care centres.
- There were also incentives for workers. There were **bonus payments** for those who exceeded targets and **holidays** were paid for by the state.
- Workers were encouraged by **propaganda**. The work of **Stakhanov** is an example of this. He along with his colleagues produced 102 tonnes of coal in one shift. He became the **Hero of Socialist Labour**, and the **Stakhanovite movement** encouraged workers to follow his success.

(iii) Labour Camps: Many opponents of Stalin's rule ended up in **labour camps** or **gulags**. Here, as many as 10 million were used as **slave labour** in building roads, bridges and canals. The greatest project was the building of the 500 km canal from the White Sea to the Baltic Sea.

THE STAKHANOVITE MOVEMENT – PROPAGANDA

Industrial workers were often inefficient and ill-disciplined so the government used the work of Alexei Stakhanov during the Second Five Year Plan in a propaganda campaign to encourage harder work. Stakhanov mined 102 tonnes of coal in one shift. Later, he mined 227 tonnes in a single shift. His exploits were publicised in the press and radio, and he was on the cover of *Time* magazine. He was given a new apartment and a month's wages. Factory meetings were held throughout the Soviet Union to encourage workers to follow Stakhanov's example. Stakhanovites who exceeded production targets got better housing and free holidays. But Stakhanov's success was a set-up. He was given the best of equipment and two helpers to achieve his targets.

Summary of Five Year Plans		
First Five Year Plan	**Second Five Year Plan**	**Third Five Year Plan**
1928–32	1933–37	1938–41
Heavy industry	Heavy industry New metalworking industries Transport Some consumer goods Electricity (Some rearmament)	Heavy industry Rearmament

Collectivisation – The Revolution in Agriculture

What was Collectivisation?

The changes in industry were accompanied by equally huge changes in agriculture. Indeed the changes in agriculture contributed to the success of industry. A new policy – collectivisation – was introduced. In **collectivisation**, individual farms were taken over by the government and combined into **collective farms** in which the land was jointly

KEY CONCEPT
COLLECTIVISATION
This was the policy of Stalin's government to force the peasants (farmers) to give up their farms and form large collective farms. The work, machinery and the profits were shared.

owned and worked by the peasants. The **collectives** hired machinery from the **Machine Tractor Stations** run by the government and they had to sell quotas to the state at low prices. Some farms were combined into **state farms** where the peasants were paid as labourers. Initially Stalin encouraged voluntary collectivisation, but in 1929 he insisted on forced collectivisation.

Collectivisation: Soviet women driving tractors.

Why did Stalin Introduce Collectivisation?

Stalin introduced collectivisation for economic and political reasons.

(i) Economic Reasons: Stalin wanted to increase the output of grain to feed the workers in the industrial cities. He believed that more grain would be produced in larger farms run by the state. With larger farms, tractors and other machinery could be shared to improve efficiency. Stalin also wanted to export food to buy industrial machinery and raw materials needed for industrialisation.

(ii) Political Reasons: Many Communists disagreed with the New Economic Policy because it created a rich farming class (kulaks) who owned their own land. These Communists wanted to put their ideas into practice and this meant state control of agriculture. They supported Stalin's proposal for collectivisation.

Collectivisation in Progress

There was huge resistance to Stalin's collectivisation among the **kulaks** (or rich peasants). They slaughtered their animals and burnt or hid their grain rather than hand it over to the collectives. Food production fell and there was a **famine** in Russia in 1932–3, which killed over five million people; the Ukraine, in particular, suffered very badly.

Stalin responded with harsh measures – he said the kulaks must be **eliminated** (dekulakisation). He sent out groups from the towns to the countryside to seize grain. He had kulaks rounded up and killed or sent to labour camps (gulags).

By the middle of the 1930s the whole kulak class (about five million people) had been wiped out. But the strong resistance against collectivisation forced Stalin to make concessions. He allowed the peasants to hold onto **small private plots** around their houses.

What were the results of Collectivisation?

- Stalin's harsh methods meant that by 1940, **97 per cent** of the farms were collectivised.
- But the **cost in lives** was very great. About 10 million people died as a result of collectivisation, either because of famine or the labour camps.
- In spite of the changes, the collectives were still **inefficient**. Indeed, by the end of the 1930s, most of the country's milk and meat and half of its wool was produced on the private plots.

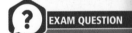

? QUESTIONS

1. What was collectivisation and why did Stalin introduce it?
2. Was collectivisation successful?

? EXAM QUESTION

How and why did Stalin transform the Soviet economy?

- Collectivisation helped the **growth of industry** – 17 million people left the countryside to work in the towns; industrial workers were sold cheap grain by the government.

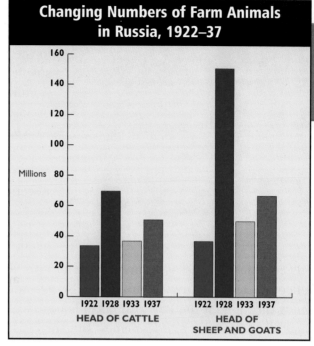

Changing Numbers of Farm Animals in Russia, 1922–37

Why were there both increases and declines in the numbers of farm animals in Soviet Russia between 1922 and 1937?

How did Stalin transform the Soviet economy and use Show Trials to consolidate his power?
- Intro: Rise to power
- Collectivisation – why? how? results?
- Industrialisation – why?
- How? – Five Year Plans – results?
- Use of propaganda/ cult of personality
  - Connect to economy and Show Trials
- Terror: Purges and Show Trials
  - Why? Who? Cruelty? Results?
  - Gulags

The Purges and Show Trials – Stalin's Use of Terror

Why did Stalin Begin the Purges?

Stalin's policies of forced **industrialisation** and **collectivisation** led to increased opposition to him in the Communist party. He was worried that his enemies were plotting against him so he wanted 'to destroy the men who might form an alternative government.' (I. Deutscher, *Stalin*, 1949) Criticisms by **Trotsky**, who was now in exile outside of Russia, angered Stalin. Stalin claimed that Trotsky was plotting with others in the country to overthrow him.

In the early 1930s, Stalin began a series of **purges** (cleaning out) of all opposition to him. He was able to create a new class of leaders loyal to him, as well as terrorise the general public. Once the purges were begun they were difficult to stop as some Party members were determined to show their loyalty and to blame others.

Show Trials in the House of Trade Unions. Posters of Marx, Engels, Lenin and Stalin.

Early Purges

The early purges were aimed mostly at those who criticised or delayed the policies of the Five Year Plans and collectivisation, or who blamed the famine of 1932–33 on these policies. **Wreckers** and **saboteurs** in factories were accused of destroying the Five Year Plans; kulaks were imprisoned, killed or exiled to Siberia for opposing collectivisation and ordinary Party members who questioned Stalin's policies were also purged. But these early purges didn't match the scale of the **Great Purge** or **Terror** begun in the middle of the 1930s.

An American newspaper published photos of Soviet leaders killed in Stalin's purges. Identify the key figures here who were executed as a result of the Show Trials. (See the Case Study: Stalin's Show Trials pp. 178–87).

The Assassination of Kirov

The assassination of **Kirov** was a major factor in the intensification of the purges. Stalin was suspicious of Kirov, who was leader of the Communist Party in Leningrad. Kirov had opposed Stalin's policies in the Politburo and won votes against Stalin. But, historians are divided on whether he ordered the assassination of Kirov in December 1934. Recent evidence from the Soviet archives suggests that the assassin did it on his own.

However, Stalin took **advantage** of Kirov's death and used it as an excuse to begin purging his enemies. The assassin and thirteen of his colleagues were shot, and over 100 others unconnected to Kirov's death were also executed. Over the next year, there was a witch hunt throughout the Party, thousands were expelled from it and hundreds were arrested, including Zinoviev and Kamenev. But this was nothing like the Great Purge which began one year later in 1936 and lasted for two years.

The Great Purge

The Great Purge or Terror began with the trial of Zinoviev, Kamenev and others – Old Bolsheviks – in August 1936. They were tried in Moscow in the first of the public trials (called **Show Trials**) and were executed. After this Stalin purged his enemies in the main institutions of the country, beginning with the Communist Party.

The Party: Members at all levels in the Party were accused of plotting against Stalin and spreading **Trotskyite** propaganda. One historian writes:

> 'The records of all members were scrutinised for dangerous tendencies. … Their fate was the same; they were unmasked by one or other of their colleagues, invited to confess before a mass meeting, were rarely found not guilty, lost their jobs, were usually deported to work camps … and their families and associates were next to be **unmasked**.'

Thousands of members were expelled from the Communist Party and over 300,000 were convicted of being 'enemies of the people' between 1934 and 1938. Also, about 70 per cent of the Central Committee of the Party was executed during the Great Purge.

The Army: Stalin next purged the Soviet Red Army. The Commander-in-chief, Tukhachevsky, an old-enemy of Stalin's during the Civil War, and 35,000 officers – half the officer corps – were either shot or jailed. These included most of the army commanders and generals. The army was the last organisation that could have stopped Stalin. Now it was weakened considerably as the Second World War approached.

The Secret Service: Not even the secret police, the NKVD, were safe. **Yagoda**, the head of the secret police, and responsible for the interrogation and execution of all the accused at the First Show Trial, was tried and executed. Stalin was dissatisfied with

Yagoda's handling of the Kirov Affair and the First Show Trial. Yagoda was replaced by **Yezhov** and targets were set for executions and exiles. Then the NKVD was purged in 1937 and newer, more sadistic agents were recruited. The Great Purge reached its peak in 1937–38 but that did not save Yezhov who was deposed in 1938 and executed in early 1940.

Minorities: Stalin also treated minorities harshly. In relation to the **Jews**, he continued Lenin's policy of closing synagogues and made serious efforts to Russianise Jews as he did with other minorities. He also punished them during the Great Terror (Purge), including some of the Old Bolsheviks who were Jewish, such as Kamenev and Zinoviev.

Many other groups, particularly the smaller nationalities, were targeted by Stalin at this time; thousands of Poles, especially, and ethnic Germans, but also even Stalin's own Georgians were arrested and shot.

Trotsky: Trotsky, who was blamed by Stalin for inciting opposition to him, was assassinated in his house in Mexico in 1940 by an agent of Stalin's.

More Trials and Purges

During this time also, there were two **further Show Trials**. In January 1937, a further 17 Communist leaders were tried and executed. This was followed in March 1938 by the last of the trials when **Bukharin**, **Rykov** and **Yagoda** along with 18 others were either shot or jailed. (See Case Study: Stalin's Show Trials, 1936–38 on pp. 178–87.)

But the Purges went far beyond the leaders and the main organisations. They reached into all areas of Soviet life. Nobody was safe. Quotas of arrests and executions were imposed by Stalin on the regions. As a consequence, millions of ordinary Russians were arrested by Stalin's secret police, the NKVD. Some were tried, some were executed, and many ended in the **slave labour camps (gulags)** in Siberia and other areas of the Soviet Union. Very often family members never heard from them again.

Why were the Purges So Cruel?

At the end of 1938, the Purges ended almost as suddenly as they began when Beria replaced Yezhov. There had been other purges in Russia during Lenin's life and earlier in Stalin's rule.

Timeline of the Purges

— 1934 Kirov assassinated; Yagoda in charge of NKVD

— 1936 First Show Trial: Kamenev and Zinoviev tried and executed; Yezhov in charge of NKVD; Great Purge or Terror began

— 1937 Second Show Trial: 17 tried; purge of the Red Army

— 1938 Third Show Trial: Bukharin, Rykov, Yagoda tried and executed; purge of NKVD; Great Purge ended

— 1939 Yezhov arrested and executed

'Visit the pyramids of the USSR': anti-Soviet cartoon published by exiled Russians living in France. What is its message?

QUESTIONS

1. Why did Stalin begin the Purges?
2. What was the Great Purge or Terror?
3. What groups were purged?
4. What were the Show Trials?

EXAM QUESTION

How did Stalin use propaganda and terror to maintain his power?

Statistics of the Great Purge

Arrests, 1937–38	–	about 8 million
Executed	–	about 1 million
Died in camps	–	about 2 million
In prison, late 1938	–	about 1 million
In camps, late 1938	–	about 7 million

The **gulags** (or slave labour camps) expanded hugely between 1929 when Stalin had established his power until his death in 1953. About 18 million went through the camps and another six million were exiled to remote places in Siberia. The camps were used both as a punishment system for what Stalin classified as **enemies of the people** but also to **provide forced labour** to work in logging, mining and construction to exploit the resources of Siberia.

But historians disagree on how to explain the **savagery and cruelty** of the Great Purge:

- Some historians say that Stalin was suffering from **paranoia** (suspicious of everybody).
- Others suggest that he was **corrupted** by great power.
- Others blame the structures laid down by **Lenin** with a one-party state and a secret police under its control. They said that it was inevitable that a totalitarian state could only operate in this way by maintaining fear amongst its people. They point to the use of gulags from early in the communist system and their continuation into the 1940s and 1950s. It was largely due to Stalin's personality and the imposition of radical changes in Soviet Russia that led to the enormous expansion during his regime.
- One historian has concluded: *'The Terror was not just a consequence of Stalin's monstrosity but it was certainly formed, expanded and accelerated by his uniquely overpowering character, reflecting his malice and vindictiveness. "The greatest delight,"* he told Kamenev, *"is to mark one's enemy, prepare everything, avenge oneself thoroughly and then go to sleep." It would not have happened without Stalin. Yet it also reflected the village hatreds of the incestuous Bolshevik sect where jealousies had seethed from years of exile and war.'* (Simon Sebag Montefiore, Stalin, The Court of the Red Tsar, 2003)

Map of the Gulags: Gulag or forced labour camps existed throughout the Soviet Union, but the largest camps lay in the most extreme geographical and climatic regions of the country from the Arctic north to the Siberian east and the Central Asian south. Prisoners were engaged in a variety of economic activities, but their work was typically unskilled, manual, and economically inefficient. The combination of endemic violence, extreme climate, hard labor, meagre food rations and unsanitary conditions led to extremely high death rates in the camps.

The Results of the Purges

1. There was now no challenge to the leadership of Stalin.

2. Stalin had destroyed the remaining leaders of the November Revolution – the **Old Bolsheviks** – and replaced them with a new generation of leaders.

3. The Red Army took time to recover from its purging. Not surprisingly, the army performed badly in the early stages of the Second World War. (See The Winter War – The Russo-Finnish War, p. 290 and The Stalinist State at War, pp. 298–301)

4. Many skilled workers, scientists and engineers were killed. This slowed down the expansion of the economy and the progress of the Five Year Plans.

A plaque showing photos of victims of the Great Purge, shot at Butovo firing range, near Moscow.

HOMEWORK EXERCISES

ORDINARY LEVEL

1. George F. Kennan, a US diplomat posted to Moscow, 1933–37, describes an encounter with a worker on a collective farm in 1936. Read it and answer the questions that follow.

    I asked the worker what type of work was he doing on the farm. He was a bookkeeper for a collective farm near Moscow, and travelled to the farm on suburban trains every day. He got 200 roubles a month, in addition to 60 kilograms of potatoes, 30 litres of milk, and some vegetables.

    How were conditions on the collective farm?

    Horrible.

    What was the trouble? Wasn't the harvest enough to go around?

    Enough to go round? There wasn't a penny left for distribution. The trouble was not the harvest. The trouble was corruption. The leaders of the farm stole everything.

    Source: Frank Costigliola (ed.) The Kennan Diaries (New York: W.W. Norton & Co. Inc., 2014).

    (i)   What job had the Russian worker?
    (ii) How did the worker travel to work each day?
    (iii) How was the worker paid?
    (iv) What was the trouble at the worker's place of work?
    (v)   Give one reason why Stalin wished to collectivise the land of Russia. (2015)

2. Write a **paragraph** on each of the following:
    (i)   Why the Reds won the Russian Civil War
    (ii) Vladimir Ilyich Lenin
    (iii) Why Stalin rose to power

3. Write a **long answer** on each of the following:
    (i)   What social and economic changes did Lenin bring about in Russia? (2010)
    (ii) What social and economic changes did Stalin bring about in Soviet Russia? (2013)
    (iii) How did Stalin use propaganda and terror to consolidate his power?

HIGHER LEVEL

1. How significant was the role of Lenin in the history of the Soviet Union between 1920 and 1924?

2. How and why did Lenin and the Communists win the Russian Civil War?

3. What did Lenin and Stalin contribute to Communism in Russia? (2008)

4. What were the main characteristics of Stalin's rule in Russia? (2012)

5. How did Stalin transform the Soviet economy and/or use Show Trials to consolidate his power? (2013)

6. How did Stalin use propaganda and terror to remain in power? (2015)

Stalin's Show Trials, 1936–38

Workers voting to demand severe punishment for 'enemies of the people'.

Introduction

During the Great Purge, three show trials were held in Moscow, where senior Communist party leaders were tried in public. They were often called **Old Bolsheviks** because they had been involved in the growth of the Bolshevik or Communist Party and in the success of the Russian Revolution in 1917. These trials were part of Stalin's efforts to ensure **greater power** for himself and to **condemn critics** of his collectivisation and industrialisation.

The First Show Trial, 1936

Background

There was an investigation of the Leningrad Communist Party after Kirov's assassination in December, 1934. As a result of this investigation, Stalin concluded that he needed to **eliminate opposition** within the Communist Party leadership. This led to the series of **Show Trials in Moscow** from 1936 to 1938.

The Trial

The first show trial – **the Trial of the 16** – was held in August 1936. **Zinoviev**, **Kamenev** and 14 other leaders were tried. Later trials followed a similar pattern to the first trial:

- accusations of treachery and plotting,
- written confessions,
- a bullying prosecutor,
- no rules of evidence, and
- a final judgment, usually of execution.

> **Show Trial:** These are public trials held by governments for political purposes. They are used for propaganda purposes. When the government establishes the guilt of the accused, it is sending out a message to its own people and foreign observers that it is following the law.
>
> **Terrorist:** a person who uses systematic (organised) terror (killings, bombings) as a means of achieving his/her aims.
>
> **Fascist:** followers of Hitler or Mussolini.
>
> **Bourgeois:** middle class.

WHO WERE ZINOVIEV AND KAMENEV?

Zinoviev and Kamenev joined with Stalin to defeat Trotsky in the struggle for power after Lenin's death. Then they split. Stalin joined with Bukharin, editor of *Pravda*, and Rykov. Stalin and his supporters were able to defeat Zinoviev and Kamenev in the Politburo.

Zinoviev and Kamenev supported Trotsky's idea of permanent or world revolution so they joined with Trotsky's supporters. But Stalin was too strong for them and Zinoviev and Kamenev were expelled from the Communist Party in 1927. Both then submitted to Stalin and they were admitted again to the Communist Party. (See The Struggle for Power, pp. 164–67)

By the middle of the 1930s, Stalin regarded them with suspicion as 'Old Bolsheviks'. They were arrested and tried for involvement in the Kirov assassination for which they were forced to admit 'moral complicity', though not guilty of the assassination. They were sentenced to five (Kamenev) and ten (Zinoviev) years in jail. While they were in jail, the preparations were made for the first of the Show Trials.

SOURCE 1 – BREAKING THE DEFENDANTS

'From the start, the rigging of the [Zinoviev] trial was closely planned by Stalin in person … Stalin would shout that Zinoviev and Kamenev were to be **given the works** until they came crawling on their bellies with confessions in their teeth. Zinoviev was influenced by threats to his family, being also subjected to the physical ordeal of a cell deliberately overheated in the height of the summer, which was additionally troublesome in view of his poor health.'

R Hingley,
Joseph Stalin: Man and Legend

What do Sources 1 and 2 tell us about Stalin's attitude to the defendants?

SOURCE 2 – ZINOVIEV ON TRIAL

Zinoviev, looking worn and haggard, only the shadow of his former self after his long imprisonment, slowly described details of the unsuccessful plot to kill Stalin two years ago. … Without any effort to defend himself, he confirmed all the prosecutors allegations, explaining that the chances of a coup seemed best in 1932 because of the unfavourable economic conditions within the country.

Reuter's Correspondent, Moscow,
The Irish Times 21 August, 1936

Why did Zinoviev plan his coup for 1932, according to this document?

In the first trial, Zinoviev, Kamenev and the others were accused of the **murder of Kirov**, the leader of the Communist Party in Leningrad, and **planning to kill Stalin**.

Even though **Trotsky** was in exile, he was as much on trial as they were. They were branded as *'terrorist groups of Trotskyites and Zinovievites'*. They were also accused of conspiring with Nazi Germany.

The secret police, the NKVD, interrogated (closely questioned) the accused and forced confessions from them. The NKVD had a great variety of ways to ensure **Zinoviev** and **Kamenev** confessed. They used forced confessions from minor Party officials against the two; they were held in isolation; they were regularly interrogated and deprived of sleep; they were subjected to beatings and threats were made against family members; The heating was turned up in their cells in midsummer; Kamenev was threatened that his son would be shot.

Zinoviev broke first and then he was used to get a confession from Kamenev. Once the confessions were signed, the defendants had to **memorise** their lines for the trial. Confessions were very important because these 'proved' that there was a conspiracy and that Stalin was right in prosecuting the offenders.

At the trial, three judges sat facing the selected audience of about 200. These included ordinary workers and international observers including journalists and diplomats. The accused sat on four rows of chairs, behind a low wooden barrier. Armed soldiers escorted the accused to their seats.

Across the room from them was the prosecutor's table. **Vyshinsky** was the prosecutor for all three trials. There were no lawyers for the defence and there was no jury. Very often the daily court sessions lasted eight hours. The only evidence produced at the trial were the **confessions** of Zinoviev, Kamenev and their co-accused. Each of the defendants was cross-examined and they made public statements admitting their guilt. (See Sources 2 and 3.)

Timeline of the Show Trials

1934 1 December – The assassination of Kirov in Leningrad

1936 19–24 August **Trial of the 16**
Trial of the 'Trotskyite-Zinovievite Terrorist Centre'
Among the sixteen sentenced to death were Zinoviev and Kamenev

1937 23–30 January **Trial of the 17**
Trial of the 'Parallel Trotskyist-Zinovievist Centre'. Among those sentenced to death were Pyatakov and Radek
11 June **Trial of the Military Leaders**
The case of the Trotskyist Anti-Soviet Military Organisation is heard by the Supreme Court.
Eight military leaders, including commander-in-chief, Mikhail Tukhachevsky, were sentenced to death and executed the following night.

1938 2–13 March **Trial of the 21**
Trial of the Anti-Soviet Right-Trotskyist Block.
Among those sentenced to death were Alexey Rykov, Bukharin, Kretinsky and Yagoda.

SOURCE 3 – VYSHINSKY'S CROSS-EXAMINATION OF KAMENEV

Vyshinsky: 'What appraisal should be given of the articles and statements you wrote in 1933, in which you expressed loyalty to the Party? Deception?'

Kamenev: 'No, worse than deception.'

Vyshinsky: 'Perfidy?' [Treachery]

Kamenev: 'Worse.'

Vyshinsky: 'Worse than deception, worse than perfidy – find the word. Treason?'

Kamenev: 'You have found it.'

Vyshinsky's summing-up speech:

'The entire people rose to their feet at the first announcement of this villainy. The entire people is trembling with rage. And I, too, as a representative of the State Prosecutor's office, add my indignant and outraged voice of a State Prosecutor to the roar of the millions! I demand that the mad dogs be shot – every single one of them!'

Transcript of the Trial

> What does Vyshinsky demand happen to the defendants?

State prosecutor, Andrei Vyshinsky.

SOURCE 4

An American newspaper cartoon from the 1930s.

> What is the message of this cartoon?

SOURCE 5 – BOLSHEVIK 'OLD GUARD', KILLED BY MACHINE THEY MADE, FIRING SQUAD FINISH TO MOSCOW TRIAL

This is the first time that members of the Bolshevik 'Old Guard' have met death at the hands of the Soviet executioners. … The world may never know how Zinoviev and Kamenev and the fourteen others met their deaths. Details of executions are not published by the Soviet authorities, as they consider the spectacle of capital punishment as barbarous. Executions which are followed by cremations are, therefore, carried out secretly. … All the property of the condemned men has been confiscated. Their execution was announced in an inconspicuous paragraph in *Pravda* this morning, and described by that paper as 'enthusiastically approved' by thousands of workers.

Reuter's Correspondent, Moscow,
***The Irish Times*, 25 August 1936**

>
> According to *Pravda*, how did people react to the executions of the Bolshevik 'Old Guard'?

? CASE STUDY QUESTIONS

1. Why did Stalin organise the Show Trials?
2. Who were tried in the First Show Trial?
3. What were the charges against them?
4. How were they made to confess?
5. Who was the prosecutor?
6. What was the outcome of the trial?

During the trial, some defendants said that the Trotskyists planned their opposition with the help of Nazi Germany. One of the defendants said: 'My connection with the Gestapo (German Secret Police) did not form any exception. This was the line of policy of the Trotskyists in accordance with Trotsky's instructions.' (*The Irish Times*, 20 August 1936)

WHAT INFORMATION CA YOU GET FROM THE SOURCE?

WHAT CAN YOU TELL ABOUT THE SOURCE?

| Analysing Documents | What does the caption tell you about this source? | Is it a primary or secondary source? | Is it objective? | Is it a reliable source? | How useful a source is it for historians of the Show Trials? | Explain your answer in each case. |

According to this source, what did Kirov stand for?

Why does the writer say 'how naive were all these hopes of ours!'?

When did Stalin decide on his 'reforms'?

What is a 'ruling caste'?

What does this source tell you about Stalin's reasons for organising the Show Trials?

Do you agree with the reasons given in this source?

This is an edited extract from Boris Nicolaevsky, *Letter of an Old Bolshevik, The Key to the Moscow Trials*, Rand School Press, New York, 1937. It was said to be written by 'a veteran member of the Bolshevik Party' and it was first published anonymously in late 1936 and early 1937 in a socialist magazine in Paris. It analyses the background to the First Show Trial.

Kirov stood for the idea of abolition of the terror both in general and inside the party. Kirov therefore strongly advocated reconciliation with those party elements who during the period of the first Five-Year Plan, had gone over to the Opposition, but who might be gotten to cooperate on the new basis, now that the 'destructive' phase was over. …Alas, how naive were all these hopes of ours! Looking back now, we find it hard to understand how we could have failed to note the symptoms which indicated that the trend was in quite the opposite direction; not toward reconciliation inside the party, but toward intensification of the terror inside the party to its logical conclusion, to the stage of physical extermination of all those whose party past might make them opponents of Stalin or aspirants to his power. Today, I have not the slightest doubt that it was at that very period between the murder of Kirov and the second Kamenev trial, that Stalin made his decision and mapped out his plan of 'reforms', an essential component part of which was the trial of the sixteen and other trials yet to come. … The determining reason for Stalin's decision was his realisation, arrived at on the basis of reports and information reaching him, that the mood of the majority of the old party workers was really one of bitterness and hostility toward him. … The conclusion he drew from all this was certainly daring: if the old Bolsheviks, the group constituting today the ruling caste in the country, are unfit to perform this function, it is necessary to remove them from their posts, to create a new ruling caste.

Source: https://archive.org/stream/LetterOfAnOldBolshevikAKeyToTheMoscowTrials/lob_djvu.txt

The prosecutor, Vyshinsky, took the defendants through their pre-arranged testimony and bullied them. All the accused were found guilty and they were shot early the next morning. The first trial had been successful from Stalin's point of view.

The Second Show Trial, 1937

Background

In late 1936, Germany and Japan formed the Anti-Comintern Pact, which represented an external threat to Soviet Russia. At the same time, a number of industrial accidents in Russia questioned the progress of the Five Year Plans.

The Trial

At the second Show Trial – **the Trial of the 17** – which lasted eight days, the defendants included **Radek, Pyatakov**

WHO WERE RADEK AND PYATAKOV?

Radek and Pyatakov were both supporters of Trotsky in the struggle for power in the 1920s. Both were expelled from the Communist Party but were allowed back in later after they admitted their 'errors'. Radek contributed to the writing of the 1936 Soviet Constitution, while Pyatakov was Deputy Head of Heavy Industries in the Five Year Plans.

and 15 others. These were all former supporters of Trotsky but they did not hold positions of great power. They were described as members of the **Anti-Soviet Trotskyite Centre**.

They faced similar accusations as Zinoviev and Kamenev faced in the first trial (See Source 6).

The trial followed a similar pattern with Vyshinsky demanding the death penalty and the defendants confessing their

SOURCE 6 – THE CHARGES IN THE SECOND TRIAL

'They were accused of conspiring with **Germany** and **Japan** to divide the U.S.S.R. between those two powers. Pyatakov (who had been deputy commissar for heavy industry) was also accused of **wrecking** and **sabotage**; he was a convenient scapegoat for the shortcomings of the industrialisation programme.'

J N Westwood, *Endurance and Endeavour: Russian History 1812–1971*

SOURCE 7 – SOVIET NEWSPAPER HEADLINES

'We demand the spies' execution!'

'No mercy for the Trotskyite degenerates, the murderous accomplices of Fascism!'

(Note: degenerate = immoral person)

 CASE STUDY QUESTIONS

1. Who were tried in the Second Show Trial?
2. What were the charges against?
3. How did the charges differ from the First Show Trial?
4. What was the outcome of the trial?

guilt. At this trial, 13 were executed and four were sent to labour camps, including Radek. Radek was killed in the camp by the NKVD.

WHO WERE BUKHARIN, RYKOV AND YAGODA?

Bukharin and Rykov worked with Stalin against Trotsky, Zinoviev and Kamenev in the struggle for power in the 1920s. Bukharin put forward the idea of 'Socialism in One Country', which Stalin claimed as his main idea in the struggle with Trotsky. Stalin and the others defeated Trotsky, Zinoviev and Kamenev. But Stalin later changed his mind and demanded rapid industrialisation and collectivisation. Bukharin criticised Stalin and lost his seat in the Politburo. He was later forced to withdraw his views. He contributed to writing the 1936 Soviet Constitution.

Rykov also lost his place in the Politburo but held onto other positions in the Communist administration until his arrest during the Great Purge.

Yagoda was the former head of the NKVD and organiser of the First Show Trial.

The Third Show Trial, 1938

Background

There was increased **international tension** with Japan expanding in the East and Germany becoming more aggressive in the West. In the Soviet Union, the **army purges** of 1937 created greater tensions, and **Yezhov**, leader of the NKVD, intensified the purges generally.

The Trial

The last of the three Show Trials – **the Trial of the 21** – was held in March 1938. **Bukharin**, **Rykov**, **Yagoda** and

18 others were tried. This trial is sometimes called the **Great Show Trial** because Bukharin and Rykov had been members of Lenin's Politburo. In Yagoda's case, this was a man who knew more about the Purges than most other people except Stalin. They were accused of:

- being members of the 'Anti-Soviet bloc of Rightists and Trotskyites'

SOURCE 8 – VYSHINSKY'S CROSS-EXAMINATION

Vyshinsky: 'Can the conclusion be drawn from this that Karakhan, with your knowledge, engaged in negotiations with Fascist circles regarding support for your treasonable activity on definite conditions? Was that the case?'

Rykov: 'Yes.'

Vyshinsky: 'And what were the conditions?'

Rykov: 'First, a number of economic concessions, and secondly the so-called dismemberment [break-up] of the USSR.'

Vyshinsky: 'Allow me to ask Bukharin. Did you know?'

Bukharin: 'I did.'

Transcript of the Trial

- **wrecking** and **sabotage** to weaken the economy
- attempting to **assassinate** Stalin.

Some doctors in the group were accused of assisting in the murders of Party members.

Before the trial, the newspapers demanded a clear verdict.

Vyshinsky questioned the defendants about their plotting. They admitted a plot involving **Fascist circles** (Germany). Some defendants moved away from the lines they had learnt, but they were quickly brought back.

Bukharin denied he was guilty of individual charges. However, as part of an agreement to save the lives of his wife and child, he still pleaded guilty to the charges in general terms. All the defendants, except three minor officials, were executed.

Reaction to the Trials

Stalin had to ensure that the trials were accepted by people, both inside and outside Russia, as legal and properly conducted. Prior to the trial, the Soviet newspapers carried full reports of the indictment (charges) of the accused. During the trials, the newspapers carried daily reports and their headlines

SOURCE 9 – STATEMENTS ON THE TRIALS

The International Assosiation of Lawyers' Statement on the Zinoviev-Kamenev Trial

'We consider the claim that the proceedings were unlawful to be totally unfounded.... We hereby categorically declare that the accused were sentenced quite lawfully.'

Report of the US Ambassador, Joseph E Davies, to the State Department

'I have talked to many if not all of the members of the diplomatic corps here, and with possibly one exception, they were all of the opinion that the proceedings established clearly the existence of a political plot and conspiracy to overthrow the government.'

What is your view of the opinions expressed here?

CASE STUDY QUESTIONS

1. Who were tried in the Third Show Trial?
2. What were the charges against them?
3. What was the outcome of the trial?

SOURCE 10 – REACTION TO THE SECOND SHOW TRIAL

In Moscow, 200,000 people, bedazzled by propaganda, massed in Red Square, despite temperatures of −27°C, bearing banners that read: 'The court's verdict is the people's verdict.' Khrushchev addressed them denouncing the 'Judas-Trotsky' … 'By raising their hand against Comrade Stalin, they raised their hand against all the best that humanity has, because Stalin is hope … Stalin is our banner. Stalin is our will, Stalin is our victory.'

Simon Sebag Montefiore,
Stalin, The Court of the Red Tsar, 2003

How do Sources 12 and 13 support the reaction in this source?

demanded severe punishment for the accused (Source 7). By the time the trials ended there was a sense of panic in Russia. The trials indicated that there was a widespread conspiracy with links to foreign countries, including Germany and Japan.

International observers were invited to the trials. These included the US Ambassador, British diplomats and reporters from the *New York Times*. They believed that the Show Trials were legal and fair (Source 9).

But other international observers did not believe in the trials. They thought they were set up by the Soviet government. The *Economist*, an influential British magazine, believed that the trials were an attempt to hide the failings of Stalin's government from the people. Some in Western Europe believed that the trials showed up weaknesses in Stalin's rule and they doubted if Soviet Russia would be capable of facing up to the growing threat from Hitler (see also Source 15).

Stalin's role

Stalin directed the Purges and Show Trials. He took a close and detailed interest in the interrogations of the accused and in the trials themselves. He directed actions within the Politburo against his enemies. He instructed **Yagoda** first, and after him **Yezhov**, to torture some to obtain confessions. *'Don't come to report to me until you have in this briefcase the confession of Kamenev,'* was one of his threats. He took pleasure in hearing the details of his opponents' reaction and suffering. He wrote some of the scripts which the defendants had to learn off, admitting their guilt, and even on occasions the summing up of the prosecutor, Vyshinsky. He signed many of the lists in the purges which authorised thousands of executions.

But that role was disguised from the people and even from those who were arrested. Instead the Purges were known in Russian as the **Yezhovshchina**, after Yezhov, the head of the NKVD (Sources 11, 12).

SOURCE 11 – YEVTUSHENKO, THE POET, REMEMBERS

'Many genuine old Bolsheviks who were arrested at this time simply refused to believe that this had happened with his [Stalin's] knowledge, still less on his personal instructions. They wrote to him. Some of them, after being tortured, inscribed "Long Live Stalin" in blood on the walls of their prison.'

SOURCE 12 – VYSHINSKY SPEAKING DURING BUKHARIN'S TRIAL, 1938

'Time will pass. The graves of the odious traitors will be overgrown with weeds, covered with the eternal contempt of Soviet people, of the whole Soviet nation. But over us, over our happy country, our sun will shine with its bright rays as clearly and joyfully as before. We, our nation, will walk as we did before, on a road cleansed of the last impurity and vileness of the past, following our beloved leader and teacher – the great Stalin – forward and ever forward, to Communism!'

Transcript of the Trial

SOURCE 13 – HISTORY BOOK

'The chief instigator and ringleader of this gang of assassins and spies was Judas Trotsky. Trotsky's assistants and agents in carrying out his counter-revolutionary instructions were Zinoviev, Kamenev and their Trotskyite underlings [assistants]. They were preparing to bring about the defeat of the USSR in the event of attack by imperialist countries; ... they had become despicable tools and agents of the German and Japanese Fascists.'

History of the Communist Party of the Soviet Union (1939)

Can you trust history books?

Assessment

The Show Trials have a special place in the general history of the Purges.

- Stalin used them to **discipline** the Soviet population, as well as close associates in the Party who feared they could be next. The Trials left him in **complete charge** of the Party and the country. He had strengthened the totalitarian system that Lenin had created.

- Stalin had eliminated the **Old Bolsheviks** in the Party and the army and replaced them with a new leadership which would be loyal to him.

- He also used the Trials as **propaganda** because, for example, various problems in Russian society could be blamed on **wreckers** or outside agents (Source 6).

- These internal and external enemies were used to create **unity** in the Soviet Union and support for Stalin as leader (Sources 6, 8).

- The Show Trials were used to increase the **intensity** of purges in the Soviet Union so that the numbers arrested, sent to gulags and killed increased during the Great Purge (or Terror) from 1936 to 1938.

- The Show Trials created a **veneer of justice** which allowed Western supporters of Stalin and the communism system to argue that a real threat and conspiracy existed.

During Stalin's lifetime, one view was expressed in Russia about the Show Trials. While speaking during the Bukharin Trial, Vyshinsky passed his judgment on 'the odious traitors' and on the future of the Soviet Union, and praised 'our beloved leader and teacher – the great Stalin'. Soviet history books provided similar views about what happened (Sources 12, 13).

SOURCE 14 – KHRUSHCHEV'S SPEECH TO THE TWENTIETH PARTY CONGRESS, 1956

'The Commission has become acquainted with a large quantity of materials in the NKVD archives and with other documents, and has established many facts relating to false accusations and glaring abuses of Soviet law which resulted in the death of innocent people. Many Party, Soviet and economic activists who were branded in 1937–8 as enemies were actually never **enemies**, spies, wreckers etc., but were always honest Communists. Often, no longer able to bear barbaric tortures, they charged themselves with all kinds of grave and unlikely crimes.'

Quoted in N Khrushchev, *Khrushchev Remembers*

SOURCE 15 – BRITISH CARTOON ON STALIN

"IT'S QUEER HOW YOU REMIND ME OF SOMEONE, JOSEF..."

What is the message of this cartoon?

WEB RESOURCES

Stalin's Terror – http://www.johndclare.net/Russ12.htm

The Great Purge – http://spartacus-educational.com/RUSpurge.htm

Moscow Trials
http://en.wikipedia.org/wiki/Moscow_Trials

Great Purge – https://en.wikipedia.org/wiki/Great_Purge

Stalin's Purges – http://www.gendercide.org/case_stalin.html

Animal Farm – http://en.wikipedia.org/wiki/Animal_Farm

Search YouTube under 'Stalin's Show Trials' and 'Stalin's Purges'.

In 1953, Stalin died and **Khrushchev** took over as leader of the Soviet Union. He set up a Commission to investigate the Purges. At the twentieth Party Congress he condemned Stalin in a wide-ranging speech, which included the findings of the Commission on the Purges and Show Trials (Source 14).

Present-day controversy

The Stalin Purges and Show Trials still cause controversy. Historians differ on their interpretations concerning what happened in the 1930s. Present-day admirers of Stalin and Trotsky also differ on what happened then.

One of those who experienced the gulags (labour camps), Alexander Solzhenitsyn, who was neither a supporter of Stalin or Trotsky, took a very different view of the Show Trials, regarding them as 'three plays'.

'Dumbfounded, the world watched three plays ... in which the powerful leaders of the fearless Communist Party ... confessed to crimes they could not in any way have committed.'

CASE STUDY QUESTIONS

1. Why did Stalin organise the Show Trials?
2. Who were tried in the First Show Trial?
3. What were the charges against them?
4. How were they made to confess?
5. Who was the prosecutor?
6. What was the outcome of the trial?

SUMMARY OF STALIN'S SHOW TRIALS, 1936–8

- Stalin organised the Show Trials because he wanted to get rid of his enemies, ensure his own power and blame others for the problems of industrialisation and collectivisation.
- The Show Trials were sparked off by the assassination of Kirov. Stalin blamed it on enemies of the people.

First Show Trial (Trial of the 16)	Zinoviev, Kamenev and 14 others	Murder of Kirov, planning to kill Stalin, plotting with Trotsky, members of Trotskyite-Zinovievite Terrorist Centre
Second Show Trial (Trial of the 17)	Radek, Pyatakov and 15 others	Conspiring with Germany and Japan, wrecking and sabotage of industry, plotting with Trotsky, members of Anti-Soviet Trotskyite Centre
Third Show Trial (Trial of the 21)	Bukharin, Rykov, Yagoda and 18 others	Attempting to assassinate Stalin, wrecking and sabotage of the economy, members of the Anti-Soviet Bloc of Rightists and Trotskyites

- In each trial, the accused were forced to confess to crimes; they learned off a prepared text or script that they followed in court.
- Stalin controlled the Show Trials – he ensured that the NKVD got written confessions; he wrote some of the script; he decided who was to be arrested and tried; and he decided the punishment.
- Many foreign observers believed the trials were legal and that there was a conspiracy against the Soviet Union.
- Soviet newspapers and radio gave huge coverage to the trials and people believed in the conspiracy.
- Results: Stalin had a greater control of the country; he got rid of likely opponents and installed younger leaders; the Show Trials were part of the Great Purge which resulted in millions of people being arrested and sent to gulags (labour camps), including Party members, Soviet army officers and ordinary people.

EXAM QUESTION

1. How did Stalin use the Purges and Show Trials to consolidate his power in the Soviet Union?
2. How did Stalin use propaganda and terror to stay in power? {2015}

DOCUMENTS-BASED QUESTION

DOCUMENT A

In September 1936, Stalin wrote a letter to two members of the Politburo, Kaganovich and Molotov, criticising *Pravda's* mistakes in the trial of the Zinovievites and Trotskyites. This is an edited extract from Stalin's letter.

To Kaganovich, Molotov.

Pravda fell flat on its face with its articles about the trial of the Zinovievites and Trotskyites. *Pravda* failed to produce a single article that provided a Marxist explanation of the process of degradation of these scum. It reduced everything to the personal element, to the notion that there are evil people who want to seize power and there are good people who hold power – and fed this paltry mush to the public.

The articles should have said that the struggle against Stalin, Voroshilov, Molotov, Zhdanov, Kosior, and others is a struggle against the Soviets; a struggle against collectivisation, against industrialisation; a struggle, consequently, to restore capitalism in the towns and villages of the USSR. Because Stalin and the other leaders are not isolated individuals but the personification of all the victories of socialism in the USSR, the personification of collectivisation, industrialisation, and the blossoming of culture in the USSR, consequently, the personification of the efforts of workers, peasants, and the working intelligentsia for the defeat of capitalism and the triumph of socialism.

They should have said that whoever fights against the party and the government in the USSR stands for the defeat of socialism and the restoration of capitalism.

Written: September 6, 1936

Source: Stalin Reference Archive (marxists.org) 2005. First Published: The Stalin-Kaganovich Correspondence (1931–36); R.W. Davies, Annals of Communism series; Yale University Press © 2003.

DOCUMENT B

Historian, Richard Overy, professor of History at the University of Exeter, writes about how local show trials were organised in Soviet Russia.

Popular justice in the Soviet Union was made visible through the many show trials that took place, not just during the Great Terror but throughout the life of the dictatorship. These could sometimes take the form of small, provincial affairs. In Western Siberia, for example, 108 show trials were conducted in 1934 alone. The difference in 1937 was the likelihood that trial would result in execution, not prison. On 3 August 1937 Stalin ordered local officials in the countryside to use the arrest of enemies as an opportunity for local show trials. Some thirty to forty trials were held in an atmosphere of rural carnival. Farmworkers were allowed a day off to go to the trials, which were lubricated with supplies of vodka. Many of those on trial were unpopular officials and experts rather than ordinary workers, which enhanced the sense of popular revenge. When the Smolensk *oblast* (provincial) committee reported to Stalin a successful rural trial late in August, he replied: 'I advise you to sentence the wreckers in Andreev *raion* (district) to shooting, and to publicise the shooting in the local press.'

Source: Richard Overy, *The Dictators: Hitler's Germany and Stalin's Russia, Penguin UK, 2005*

1. (i) According to Document A, how did Pravda *'fall flat on its face about the trial of the Zinovievites and Trotskyites'*?
   (ii) According to Document A, what was the *'struggle'* attempting to restore?
   (iii) How many show trials were held in Western Siberia in 1934, according to Document B?
   (iv) Who were allowed a day off to go to the trials?

2. (i) Do both documents show the importance of propaganda to Stalin?
   (ii) How do the documents differ in the main point they are writing about?

3. (i) Are the documents primary or secondary sources? Explain your answer.
   (ii) Which document gives you a better understanding of the role of Stalin in the show trials? Explain your answer.

4. Why did Stalin organise the Moscow Show Trials, 1936–38, and how successful were they?

20 ORIGINS AND GROWTH OF THE FASCIST REGIMES IN EUROPE

In this section, you should understand:
- The causes of Mussolini's rise to power (the rise of Fascist regimes, including Hitler later).
- Mussolini's rule in Italy.
- Church–state relations under Mussolini.
- Mussolini's foreign policy.

The Growth of Dictatorships

Many dictatorships were established in European countries between the First and Second World Wars, from 1918 to 1939. Most of southern and eastern Europe was ruled by **dictatorships**. Only in countries in western Europe, and in two in central Europe, did **democracies** survive. (See map of Dictatorships and Democracies in Europe, 1918–39.)

Characteristics of a Dictatorship
- Rule by one man (dictator) or party.
- No other political parties allowed.
- Control of the media (press).
- Police and army used to maintain control.

Characteristics of a Democracy
- Rule by the people, usually through elected representatives.
- Political parties allowed.
- Freedom of speech and a free press (media).
- Judges free to apply the rule of law.

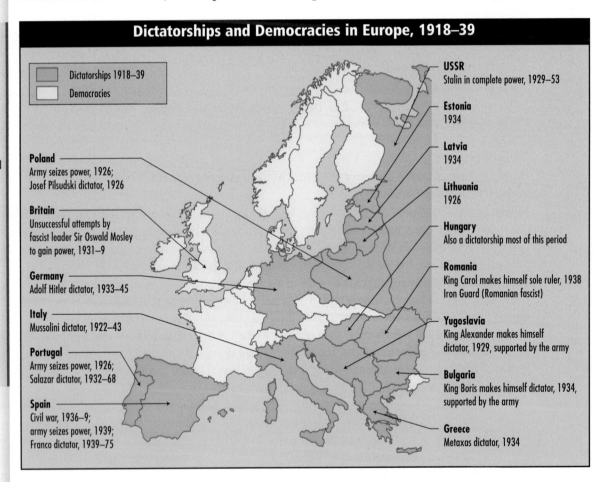

Dictatorships and Democracies in Europe, 1918–39

- Dictatorships 1918–39
- Democracies

Poland
Army seizes power, 1926; Josef Pilsudski dictator, 1926

Britain
Unsuccessful attempts by fascist leader Sir Oswald Mosley to gain power, 1931–9

Germany
Adolf Hitler dictator, 1933–45

Italy
Mussolini dictator, 1922–43

Portugal
Army seizes power, 1926; Salazar dictator, 1932–68

Spain
Civil war, 1936–9; army seizes power, 1939; Franco dictator, 1939–75

USSR
Stalin in complete power, 1929–53

Estonia
1934

Latvia
1934

Lithuania
1926

Hungary
Also a dictatorship most of this period

Romania
King Carol makes himself sole ruler, 1938 Iron Guard (Romanian fascist)

Yugoslavia
King Alexander makes himself dictator, 1929, supported by the army

Bulgaria
King Boris makes himself dictator, 1934, supported by the army

Greece
Metaxas dictator, 1934

The style of government in a dictatorship differed greatly from a democracy (see box).

Most of the European dictatorships followed these features. Sometimes the word **authoritarian** is used to describe their rule, such as **Franco's** dictatorship in Spain and **Salazar's** in Portugal.

Symbol of the Party	Germany	Italy
	The Swastika	The Fasces

Fascist Dictatorships

In many European countries, Fascist parties were popular. Mosley's Blackshirts in Britain, Belgium's Rex Party and the Falange in Spain were examples of these. However, very few Fascist parties came to power and established dictatorships. Of the few who took over government, only two lasted for any significant time. These were **Mussolini's Fascist Party** in Italy and **Hitler's Nazi Party** in Germany. They advocated a new political idea called **Fascism** or **Nazism**.

What was Fascism?

The word **Fascist** was Italian in origin. It was used by Mussolini to describe his party, the Fascist Party. It was derived from the Ancient Roman **fasces** or bundle of rods and axe which symbolised authority there. (See Characteristics of Fascism.)

Totalitarian Dictatorships

The dictatorships of Mussolini and Hitler were also **totalitarian**. In this way they were similar to Stalin's dictatorship in Soviet Russia. They believed that they should control all aspects of a person's life – social, economic, political, cultural and religious. They wanted to create a new person.

What Caused the Rise of Fascist Regimes?

The stories of the rise to power of Mussolini and Hitler differ in some respects but there were many common factors in explaining their rise to power. These were:

- The effects of the First World War.
- Economic depression.
- Unstable government and weak democracy.
- Fear of Communism.
- Strong leadership.
- Use of violence and propaganda.

Characteristics of Fascism

Fascists were:
against democracy and political parties,
against the Treaty of Versailles, anti-semitic, anti-Communist.

Fascists favoured:
Extreme nationalism – the individual was subject to the nation; the nation must expand and conquer.
Cult of the leader – everything depended on a wise leader, he must be obeyed.
Use of violence – to achieve power, the strong rule over the weak.
Racialism – the people of the nation must be kept pure.

Characteristics of Totalitarianism

- A single ideology (set of political beliefs) that everyone must follow.
- A single party led by a dictator.
- Control of propaganda (all means of communication).
- Control of police and army and the use of terror.
- Central control of the economy.

Mussolini and Fascist Italy

Mussolini became leader of Italy in 1922. His rise to power was rapid and he controlled Italy for over 20 years, until his downfall during World War II. **How can we explain his rise to power?**

What Caused Mussolini's Rise to Power?

1. Post-war Italy

At the end of the First World War (1914–18), there was great dissatisfaction in Italy with the war. Italians had joined the war in the hope of gaining more land from the defeated Austro-Hungarian Empire. At the **Paris Peace Conference**, Italy gained most of the land but failed to get **Dalmatia** and the city of **Fiume**. Italian nationalists now claimed that Italy had won the war but lost the **mutilated peace**, as they called it.

D'Annunzio, a nationalist poet and war hero, took action by capturing Fiume with a small revolutionary group. Nationalists throughout Italy supported him. But he soon turned many people against him. After 15 months in Fiume, he was expelled by the Italian army. His failure led to increased **nationalist bitterness**.

The war also affected the **Italian economy**. By 1919 the economy was in a **depressed** state. Soldiers were demobilised and there were 2 million unemployed. **Inflation** had risen by over 500 per cent between 1914 and 1920, and this wiped out wages and savings. Italians, from all different classes, felt betrayed that their sufferings during the war did not lead to improvements after the war. These conditions caused great dissatisfaction in Italy. Mussolini was able to use this dissatisfaction to gain popularity.

Hero: the Italian nationalist poet D'Annunzio took over the city of Fiume after the First World War.

2. Social and Political Discontent

There was widespread discontent in Italy because of the economic depression. In the **towns and cities**, there were large-scale strikes and workers occupied factories. They wanted higher wages and factory councils. They were inspired by socialist and Communist leadership. There was also widespread conflict in the **countryside** where peasants (farmers) and labourers took over land, often supported by priests.

Street fighting in Italy after the First World War. The chaos helped Mussolini to power.

Industrialists and landlords reacted angrily against these actions. They believed this discontent was due to the spread of Communism. They were disappointed at the failure of the Italian governments to stop the lawlessness, so they organised groups of their own to attack workers and peasants, and they got the help of Fascist squads.

3. Weak Government

The two largest parties in Italy, the Socialist Party and the Catholic Popular Party, failed to agree so Italy was ruled by **five** different **coalition governments** between 1919 and 1922. The Italian governments were shown to be weak on many occasions. They failed to control the lawlessness and to solve the political, economic and social problems. **Democracy** seemed to be failing in Italy so many people looked for a **strong leader**. Mussolini portrayed himself as that strong leader who would solve Italy's problems.

4. Mussolini's Fascist Movement

In March 1919, Mussolini founded his first **combat group** (or **fascio di combattimento**) in Milan. They were also known as **Blackshirts**. Soon other groups were set up in cities in northern and central Italy. At first they had a socialist programme but Mussolini changed that quickly after gaining only 2 per cent of the vote in elections in Milan in November 1919.

When Mussolini changed his policies to supporting the monarchy and dropping anti-clericalism (against the power of the Church in politics), he gained support. The **Fiume affair** also helped. D'Annunzio's adventure was very popular throughout Italy and Mussolini gained from his support for it.

With a more conservative and nationalist policy, Mussolini's Fascist movement grew more rapidly. By 1922 the Fascists had 3,000 groups and over 250,000 members. The membership was made up of war veterans and ex-officers, professional and landowning sons, and middle class and better-off peasant families. Mussolini got financial support from large manufacturers such as the Pirelli tyre company and the Fiat car company.

5. March on Rome

In May 1921, Mussolini's Fascists gained 35 seats in parliament and later that year he formed the **Fascist Party** out of his combat groups. Mussolini's next success was the crushing of socialist-led strikes in August 1922. It appeared as if Mussolini and the **Fascist squads** saved the country from the **red** threat while the government was helpless. This success encouraged him and his fellow leaders to organise a **March on Rome** in October 1922.

Fascist groups approached Rome from three directions. As 25,000 **Blackshirts** gathered on the edge of Rome, the Italian government was divided on what to do. But by now **King Victor Emmanuel III** was tired of all the changes in government and he also feared a civil war. He refused to bring in the army and the Prime Minister resigned. The King

After Mussolini was made Prime Minister, he led the Fascist March on Rome.

? **QUESTIONS**

1. What was Fascism? How did it differ from democracy?
2. How did each of the following help Mussolini rise to power: (i) conditions of post-war Italy (ii) social and political discontent (iii) weak government (iv) the Fascist movement (v) the March on Rome (vi) Mussolini's role?

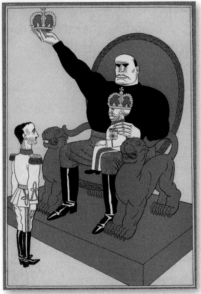

Mussolini on the throne. What is the message of the cartoon?

was left with no alternative but to appoint Mussolini as **Prime Minister**. At 39, he was the youngest Prime Minister in Italian history.

Two days after Mussolini's appointment as Prime Minister the March on Rome went ahead. It was more of a **victory parade** than a march. But Mussolini gave the impression that he had come to power in a **coup d'etat** (takeover of the state).

6. Mussolini's Role

Mussolini had played an important role in his own rise to power. Mussolini changed his policies to gain popularity. He believed that Fascism was not a system of unchanging beliefs but **a path to political power**. He made use of the discontent of the soldiers after the war. He was also a **clever propagandist** and a very able speaker. When he was offered a place in the Italian government he refused it because he knew there was no alternative to making him Prime Minister.

Mussolini was an outstanding speaker and he attracted huge crowds.

How did Mussolini Establish Dictatorship?

Mussolini's new government had only four Fascist ministers so Italian nationalists hoped to tame him. But over the next few years, Mussolini used democratic and legal means to become a **totalitarian dictator**.

Parliament – Acerbo Law

Mussolini first set about destroying the power of parliament. He began by passing the **Acerbo Law** in 1923. This law proposed that the party which got the greatest number of votes in the next election should have two-thirds of the seats. In the general election the following year, Mussolini used his Fascist groups to ensure the Fascist Party got the greatest number of votes. He enrolled his Blackshirts into a **Volunteer Militia** and this made their violence legal. He also had success in foreign policy when he got Fiume from Yugoslavia. Not surprisingly, the Fascists won 65 per cent of the vote.

Matteoti's Murder and the Aventine Secession

KEY CONCEPT
PROPAGANDA is spreading information to convince people of your point of view. Governments and politicians use propaganda to achieve or retain power.

One of Mussolini's fiercest critics was **Giacomo Matteoti**, a socialist member of parliament. He was kidnapped by a group of Fascists and brutally killed. There was widespread anger at the murder and Mussolini's position as Prime Minister seemed in great danger. However, two factors saved him. First, the socialists pulled out of parliament in protest, in what became known as the **Aventine Secession**. This only strengthened Mussolini's position and gave greater control to the Fascists. Second, King Victor Emmanuel continued to support Mussolini.

KEY PERSONALITY: MUSSOLINI

Mussolini was born in northern Italy. His mother was a schoolteacher and his father was a blacksmith. Mussolini worked at different jobs – he was a teacher, a soldier and a journalist. He was a member of the **Socialist Party** and became **editor** of their newspaper, *Avanti*. He was expelled from the Socialist Party when he wanted Italy to join the First World War. He now became more nationalistic. After the war, he founded the **fascio di combattimento** (combat groups) in 1919, and later the **Fascist Party**. His rise to power was rapid (p. 190). He became Prime Minister when the government failed to persuade **King Victor Emmanuel** to use the army against the **March on Rome** (p. 191). After becoming Prime Minister, he established a **totalitarian dictatorship** (p. 193). He set up the **corporate state**, built roads and drained marshes (pp. 196–97), and made the **Lateran Agreement** with **Pope Pius XI** (p. 195). In foreign policy, he expanded Italy's power (p. 198). After initial disagreement with **Hitler**, they grew closer through the **Spanish Civil War**, the **Rome-Berlin Axis** and the **Pact of Steel** (p. 200). During the **Second World War**, the Italian army performed badly. After the Allies invaded Italy, Mussolini was deposed. Hitler rescued him, but when he was next caught, he was shot (p. 201).

Develop notes on the role of Mussolini in Italian history, 1920–45.

Four years later a new electoral law stated that the **Fascist Grand Council**, headed by Mussolini, would nominate members of parliament. The Council drew up a list of 400 people which the electorate would vote on as a group. In this way, Mussolini had **eliminated** the power of the democratic parliament.

Dictatorship

Over the next few years he took further steps to impose dictatorship. There were constant house-to-house searches, the free press was stopped, there was harassment of political opponents, political parties were banned and the secret police, **OVRA**, was set up. Mussolini also banned trade unions and strikes. But his most important step to dictatorship was the power to **rule by decree** which he got in 1926. Over the next 17 years Mussolini signed more than 100,000 decrees.

Totalitarianism – Propaganda and Terror

But Mussolini intended to establish not just a dictatorship, but also a **totalitarian dictatorship**. He wanted to control all aspects of the lives of the people, their thoughts as well as their actions. **Fascist propaganda** played a key role in this.

   The cult of the leader: A cult of personality was developed around Mussolini. He was called **Il Duce (the Leader)**. Mussolini used photographs, newspapers, radio and newsreel film to create the image of the all-wise, all-talented leader. *'Mussolini is always*

KEY CONCEPT
TOTALITARIANISM
Totalitarian governments control all aspects of life, from the actions of people to their thoughts. These governments make great use of propaganda, secret police, terror and a strong political party.

KEY CONCEPT
CULT OF PERSONALITY In politics, the cult of personality is the worship of a leader. This involves the use of propaganda to create an image of the leader who is all-wise and powerful.

Mussolini used photographs, newspapers (and newsreel film) to create a cult of personality. What image is being created by these pictures?

right', was the motto. There was Mussolini the animal lover – he liked to be photographed with his pet lioness, **Italia**; Mussolini the sportsman – the skier, the horseman, the pilot; Mussolini the worker – the light was left on in his office all night; and Mussolini the ordinary man – he helped out cutting corn.

Mussolini's image as a **superman** was helped when he survived a number of assassination attempts.

Mussolini's image in Italy was also helped by the praise he got from foreign leaders. Churchill, later Prime Minister of Britain, said he would have worn the Blackshirt had he been an Italian.

Young Italian boys were encouraged to join the Balilla.

Education: For the Fascists, the main purpose of education was to teach children the **Fascist values** of **obedience** and **patriotism**. Children were taught that Il Duce would make Italy great again. Textbooks were changed and teachers critical of Fascism were sacked. History was rewritten to highlight the glories of the Roman Empire and only committed Fascists could teach the subject. Mussolini wanted boys to be ready for fighting and girls to be good mothers, in line with the Fascist slogan, *'War is to the male what childbearing is to the female.'*

Youth organisations: Young boys and girls had to join youth organisations outside school. From the age of four up to the age of 18, they progressed through a series of these organisations, such as the **Balilla**. After 18, the most dedicated members joined the **Young Fascists**. Fascist youth organisations concentrated on military training and Fascist ideology (beliefs), as well as sports, parades and camps. Girls' organisations were taught sewing, singing and child care in line with Fascist beliefs about the role of women in society.

Press and radio: No opposition press was allowed and the existing press and radio was made serve the Fascist regime. News reports highlighted Fascist events and successes, and Mussolini's speeches were broadcast in full. The number of radios increased from 27,000 in 1926 to over 1 million by 1939. The Fascists encouraged the production of low-cost radios because they believed the radio was an important means of maintaining contact with the people.

Sport: Sport was important to Fascists because it created fit young men and achievements in sport could be used for nationalist propaganda. Italy organised the **1934 World Cup** and won it, and retained it in 1938. In boxing, **Primo Carnera** became a national hero by winning the world Heavyweight championship.

The police state and terror: The secret police, the OVRA, was set up, along with a special court to try anybody critical of the Fascist state. Individual freedom was abolished, and political opponents were spied upon and beaten up. Over 4,000 were imprisoned and others were sent to remote islands, but only about 10 people were sentenced to death. While Mussolini's Italy was brutal and oppressive, it was not as murderous as Hitler's Germany or Stalin's Russia.

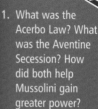

The Limits of Totalitarianism

There were limits to Mussolini's power. Even though Mussolini attempted to gain total control, many groups in Italy were able to hold onto much of their power. Very often he was satisfied by appearances. *'In reality, however, the Fascist regime fell well short of the totalitarianism claimed by its spokesmen... monarchy, industry, landowners, armed forces, and the church formed an integral part of Mussolini's regime, making it less profoundly Fascist ... and less totalitarian in scope than it pretended to be.'* (M. Blinkhorn, *Mussolini and Fascist Italy*)

Church-State Relations under Mussolini

The Catholic religion was the religion of most Italians and the head of the Catholic Church, the Pope, was based in Rome. However, relations between the Pope and the Italian state had been poor since Italy was united in 1870 and the Pope lost land to the new state.

Relations between Mussolini's government and the Catholic Church improved during the 1920s. Mussolini was anti-clerical (against the power of the Church in politics) but he knew he could not control the Church. On the other hand, the Catholic Church saw Fascism as the best hope of resisting the spread of Communism.

Mussolini took a series of steps which **improved relations**:

- He brought back compulsory religious education in primary schools.
- Crosses were allowed in the classrooms.
- He had his own civil marriage blessed by a Catholic ceremony.

Lateran Agreements, 1929

Following on the improved relations came two years of negotiations which led to the **Lateran Agreements (Treaty and Concordat) of 1929**. Three documents laid out the terms of the agreement:

- The Pope recognised the **Italian state**.
- Italy recognised the Pope's control of the **Vatican City**.
- Italy paid £30 million **compensation** for taking Rome in 1870.
- In the **Concordat**, the Catholic religion was recognised as 'the sole religion of the state'.
- The Pope appointed all the bishops of Italy, subject to Mussolini's agreement.
- The government agreed to **pay** the salaries of bishops and priests.
- **Religious instruction** was to be given in public (state) schools.

Mussolini and the Pope sign the Concordat.

This agreement was a major achievement for Mussolini following a dispute which lasted for 60 years. The agreement increased his prestige in Italy and abroad. He became more acceptable to Catholics in Italy and in the rest of Europe. Some historians regard the Lateran Agreements as Mussolini's **greatest political success**.

QUESTIONS

1. What was the Acerbo Law? What was the Aventine Secession? How did both help Mussolini gain greater power?
2. What other steps did Mussolini take to establish dictatorship?
3. How was the cult of Mussolini promoted?
4. How did Mussolini use each of the following to gain greater control of Italy: (i) education and youth organisations (ii) Press and radio (iii) sport (iv) the police state and terror

EXAM QUESTION

How did Mussolini use propaganda and terror to gain and hold onto power in Italy?

(?) QUESTIONS

1. How and why did
   Mussolini improve
   relations with the
   Catholic Church in
   the 1920s?

2. What were the
   terms of the
   Lateran Treaty and
   Concordat?

3. What issues
   caused conflict
   between Mussolini
   and the Catholic
   Church in the
   1930s?

(?) EXAM QUESTION

How did Church-state
relations develop
under Mussolini?

Further Conflicts

However, the agreement did not end the conflicts between Church and state. Mussolini was jealous of the power of **Catholic Action**, a lay Catholic organisation, which had nearly 700,000 members in 1930. In 1931, he declared that Catholic Action groups should be disbanded. However, there was strong resistance from **Pope Pius XI** who condemned Mussolini's plans. Instead, Catholic Action announced it was founding a new organisation for university students. Fascist groups attacked some Catholic Action branches but a compromise was reached which limited Catholic Action to religious activities. Relations between Mussolini and the Catholic Church were helped by agreement on the role of the family, the role of women in society and the banning of contraception and abortion by Mussolini's government.

After that, relations between Mussolini and the Catholic Church remained steady until the late 1930s. Then the Catholic Church became **critical** of Mussolini's new anti-Semitic policy and his more aggressive foreign policy (p. 198). By 1938, **Pope Pius XI** felt that Mussolini had misused the agreement with the Catholic Church. He prepared a statement that was critical of Mussolini's regime but he died before it could be issued. The new pope, **Pius XII**, wanted to keep Italy out of World War II, but Mussolini ignored his wishes. The Catholic Church also tried to protect Italian Jews by hiding them in convents and monasteries.

The strength of the Catholic Church in Italy shows the **limitations** of Mussolini's Fascism. While the Catholic Church did not openly oppose Fascism, it remained a separate organisation. Fascism was not strong enough to bring the Church under the control of the state.

How did Mussolini Deal with the Economy?

The Corporate State

The idea of the Corporate State was influenced partly by Catholic teaching. Fascists believed that the class conflict between workers and employers should be replaced by **class co-operation**. Fascists also hoped the Corporate State would increase their control of the country.

A **Ministry of Corporations** was set up in 1926 but it took over 10 years to establish the Corporate State. The economy was divided into **22 Corporations**. Each Corporation represented a major area of economic activity such as agriculture, industry and the professions. Employers, workers and the government were represented on each Corporation. They decided wages and working conditions. Finally, Parliament was abolished in 1939 and replaced by a **Chamber of Fasces and Corporations**.

Mussolini taking in the wheat in the Battle of Wheat, another of Mussolini's 'battles', this time to increase wheat production.

The Corporate State *'represented,'* as one historian said, *'a means of disciplining labour (the workers) in the interest of the employers and the state.'* It also added another layer of bureaucracy (officials and rules) and led to greater corruption and inefficiency.

Changing Economic Policies

Mussolini knew little about economics and Fascism was not an economic system like Communism. Between 1922 and 1925, Mussolini left the running of the economy in the hands of the Minister of Finance, **Alberto de Stefani**. He cut government spending, promoted free trade and benefited from the improved European economy of the time. Even though he successfully reduced unemployment to 120,000, de Stefani was fired by Mussolini and replaced with a financier and industrialist.

New Policies

This signalled a change in economic policy. **Protectionism** (duties or taxes on imports) was introduced to protect heavy industry and some agricultural products such as grain. Next, Mussolini revalued the currency to 90 lira to the £ Sterling (Quota 90). This was done for reasons of national pride but it made Italian exports dearer and damaged the economy.

By the early 1930s Mussolini was advocating a policy of **autarky** (economic self-sufficiency). This took the form of a series of **battles**. Already in 1925, Mussolini began the **Battle of Grain** – to increase grain production and make the country self-sufficient. Grain production increased steadily during the 1920s and 1930s, but often at the expense of other crops which would have been better suited to some of the land.

The Battle for Land Reclamation – a scheme for reclaiming land for grain production, accompanied the Battle of Grain. Its greatest success was the draining of the **Pontine Marshes** near Rome, which added thousands of extra acres of land and reduced malaria.

There were other advances made by the Italian economy. Electricity production was increased significantly, so also was motor car production. New motorways (**autostrada**) connected Italy's major cities and towns, much of the railway system was electrified and the mainline trains ran on time. The Fascists made good use of **propaganda** to boast about these achievements.

State Control of the Economy

As the 1930s progressed, Mussolini was more conscious of the need for **economic self-sufficiency** in preparation for war. By 1939, the beginning of the Second World War, most of Italy's shipbuilding, shipping, iron and steel industries were controlled by the state. The state owned a greater proportion of industry in Italy than in any other country outside the Soviet Union.

Who Benefited?

Some groups benefited more than others from Fascist economic policies. In particular the industrialists and larger landowners and farmers benefited. The greatest losers were the working class in the cities and the labourers in the country, in spite of the **Labour Charter** of 1927. This was a list of workers' rights – the right to good working conditions and fair wages. But the workers had no trade unions, the right to strike was

QUESTION

1. What was the corporate state and how was it set up? How successful was it?

2. What role did each of these play in Mussolini's economic policy: (i) protectionism (ii) autarky (iii) land reclamation (iv) autostrada (v) Labour Charter (vi) Dopolavoro?

abolished and unemployment rose from 110,000 in 1926 to 1 million in 1933 due to the Great Depression.

However, workers did benefit from the **Dopolavoro** (After Work) which was set up in 1925 to control leisure time. It controlled athletic and sports clubs, choirs, bands, night schools and libraries. It sponsored day outings and tours, and it promoted cinema and theatre.

How Successful was Mussolini's Foreign Policy?

Mussolini took a strong interest in foreign policy. As well as being Prime Minister, he was also Foreign Minister for much of the time between 1922 and 1939.

His declared **aims** in foreign policy were: *'I want to make Italy great, respected and feared.'* He wanted to expand the power of Italy around the Mediterranean Sea in imitation of the Roman Empire. The Mediterranean was to become **Mare Nostrum** (Our Sea).

Foreign Policy in the 1920s

Mussolini began his rule with a number of foreign policy successes. His first success was the **Corfu incident** (1923). When four Italians were killed redrawing the Greek-Albanian border for the League of Nations, Mussolini took over Corfu, a Greek island, after the Greek government refused to pay 50 million lira compensation to Italy. Mussolini continued to hold Corfu until the League ordered Greece to pay the 50 million lira which was demanded. In his second success, he acquired **Fiume** in January 1924 after negotiations with Yugoslavia.

However, after these initial successes, Mussolini spent the rest of the 1920s building up an image of an international **statesman and man of peace**. Mussolini attended the **Locarno Conference** (1925) at which Italy and other European powers, including Germany, agreed to the **Locarno Pact** which guaranteed Germany's existing borders with France and Italy. Three years later, Mussolini signed the **Kellogg-Briand Pact** outlawing war as an instrument of national policy.

Fascism for Export – the 1930s

By the 1930s, Mussolini had established full control of Italy – now he could expand. He wanted to **found an empire** and **to win glory and power**. *'The growth of empire, that is to say, the expansion of the nation, is an essential sign of vitality,'* he said. His main areas of interest were the Balkans, southern Europe and Africa.

Mussolini and Hitler Disagree

However, the first problem he faced in the 1930s was the rise to power of Hitler in Germany. While Mussolini was delighted that Fascism, **his doctrine**, was in power in another state, he was fearful of the creation of a **Greater Germany** through the union of Germany and Austria **(Anschluss)**.

Mussolini wanted to ensure the independence of Austria so he helped the Austrian Prime Minister, **Dollfuss**, break up the Nazi movement in Austria. When Dolfuss was assassinated, Mussolini sent troops to the Austro-Italian border to stop Hitler's plan to unite Germany and Austria.

Mussolini then formed the **Stresa Front** with Britain and France to oppose the break-up of treaties *'which may endanger the peace of Europe'*. Mussolini hoped the Stresa Front would limit Hitler's ambitions and that he would be able to expand his own empire in Africa. However, Mussolini's invasion of Abyssinia destroyed the Stresa Front and drove him into the arms of Hitler.

The Invasion of Abyssinia

There were a number of **reasons** for Mussolini's invasion of Abyssinia:

- Mussolini wanted to enlarge the Italian empire.
- Italians wanted revenge for a humiliating defeat by the Abyssinians in Adowa in 1896.
- Some historians suggest Mussolini wanted to distract the Italian people from economic problems at home in the middle of the 1930s.

Mussolini used a border incident with Abyssinia to build up his army and attack in October 1935. Over 400,000 Italian soldiers using tanks, planes and poison gas overran the lightly armed tribesmen of Abyssinia. Their Emperor, **Haile Selassie**, appealed to the **League of Nations**. The League condemned Italy and imposed economic sanctions. The sanctions, which excluded oil from the list, had little effect on the war and Italy took the capital, Addis Ababa, by May 1936.

Results of the Invasion

- The invasion of Abyssinia ended the **Stresa Front**. Britain and France, as key members of the League, were involved in imposing sanctions on Italy.
- The failure of the sanctions showed up the **weakness** of the League of Nations.
- At the same time, Hitler supported Mussolini, whose attitude to Hitler now changed. When he first met Hitler in Rome in 1934, he was unimpressed. But he was very impressed by German military strength after a visit there in 1937.

Other factors also drew the two countries **closer together**. One was the similarity between Fascism and Nazism, in particular, their anti-Communism. They were also drawn together by helping Franco in the **Spanish Civil War** (1936–39). In Mussolini's case he sent 75,000 men, 100 aircraft, weapons and ammunition to help Franco to victory.

Italians in Abyssinia

← Italian Campaigns 1935–6

Red Sea

ERITREA

SUDAN

FRENCH SOMALILAND

• Addis Ababa

BRITISH SOMALILAND

ABYSSINIA
(Ethiopia)

UGANDA

ITALIAN SOMALILAND

KENYA

Indian Ocean

The badly-armed Abyssinian tribesmen had little chance against the well-armed Italian army with tanks and planes.

Mussolini was very impressed with German military might when he visited there in 1937.

Agreements between Mussolini and Hitler

A series of agreements cemented their relationship:

- They first of all formed the **Rome-Berlin Axis** (October 1936), a loose agreement between the two countries.
- This was followed by the **Anti-Comintern Pact** (November 1937) with Germany and Japan to present a united front against Communism.

When Hitler invaded Austria in March 1938 to form **Anschluss**, Mussolini did not intervene.

- In May 1939, Italy and Germany signed the **Pact of Steel**. Both sides agreed to back each other in any future war.

Anti-Semitic Laws

Mussolini was now increasingly under Hitler's influence. This can be seen in the anti-Semitic laws – the **Charter of Race** – which were brought into Italy for the first time in October 1938. There was no experience of racial persecution in Italy before this and even Mussolini said he was opposed to the ideas of racial superiority. Now Jews were deprived of Italian nationality; they were not allowed to have state jobs and they were not allowed to marry non-Jewish Italians. But many Italians objected and the Pope wrote to Mussolini in protest. The anti-Semitic laws were one factor in Mussolini's **declining popularity**.

The Road to War

In March 1938, Mussolini acted as a peacemaker in **Munich** to get agreement between Germany, France and Britain over Czechoslovakia (see Chapter 24). Even though Mussolini liked to think he had **saved Europe** from war, his role in Munich was very limited.

As Europe headed for war in 1939, Mussolini realised that the Italian army was not ready. Wars in Libya (1920s), Abyssinia and Spain ensured that Italy was economically and militarily weakened. Mussolini himself said Italy would not be ready until 1943. When Hitler declared war in September 1939, Mussolini asked for huge quantities of arms and ammunition which he knew Hitler could not give him. In this way, Mussolini was able to declare Italy's **non-belligerence**.

Fascism at War – The Downfall of Mussolini

By the beginning of the Second World War, **Mussolini's popularity** was already in decline:

- Italians were worse off in the 1930s, self-sufficiency made products dearer and the standard of living fell.
- Mussolini came more under Hitler's influence and Italians did not like that.

Mussolini was drawn into the war as he envied Hitler's success in Poland and France. But this was a **fatal mistake** on his part. His army invaded southern France when Hitler had conquered Belgium and northern France. But the war exposed the **weaknesses** of Mussolini's planning and exposed his bluff:

- He made himself commander-in-chief and therefore was held responsible for Italy's defeats.
- The Italian army was badly equipped and poorly led.
- He hoped for a quick victory so he made no provision for rationing.

After Mussolini was removed from power and imprisoned in a mountain-top hotel, he was rescued by Nazi paratroopers.

Italian Defeats and the Death of Mussolini

Not surprisingly, Italy was beaten in Libya, Egypt and Greece (see Chapter 25). Mussolini failed to prepare for the Allied invasion of Sicily and Italy, and this led to his downfall. He was removed by King Victor Emmanuel and the Fascist Grand Council and imprisoned in a mountain-top hotel.

Hitler sent German commandos to rescue him. He set up a rebel Fascist government in northern Italy called the **Salo Republic**. But he was captured by Italian resistance fighters and shot. His body and that of his mistress, who was shot with him, were hung upside down in Milan. His participation in the Second World War led to his own **downfall**, and contributed to the defeat of his ally, Hitler.

Assessment of Mussolini

Mussolini was the **first** of the Fascist dictators. His tactics were later copied by Hitler to achieve power. However, Mussolini's rule was never as totalitarian as Hitler's – the king was still head of state in Italy and he eventually dismissed Mussolini. Neither could Mussolini control the Catholic Church. Mussolini's Fascist Party did not control the Italian state in the same way that Hitler's Nazi Party did in Germany.

Italian Fascism died with Mussolini. His **only long-lasting legacy** was the Lateran Agreements; his Corporate State

Mussolini was recaptured, shot dead and hung upside down in Milan, along with his mistress.

was a failure and his foreign policy led Italy into the Second World War and to his downfall. His **genius** lay in his ability to manipulate the Italian people through mass meetings, press and radio.

1. What were Mussolini's aims in foreign policy?
2. What success did Mussolini have in the 1920s?
3. What was Fascism for export? Was it a success?
4. Why did Mussolini and Hitler disagree over Austria?
5. How did they improve relations?
6. Why did Italy join World War II and what was the outcome for the country?

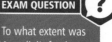
EXAM QUESTION

To what extent was Mussolini's foreign policy the main cause of his downfall?

HOMEWORK EXERCISES

ORDINARY LEVEL

1. Study the illustrations on Mussolini and answer the following questions.

   A. (i) What does the sign Il Duce mean in the first illustration?

   (ii) What does Mussolini show he can do in the other three illustrations?

   (iii) What image is Mussolini trying to create in all four illustrations?

   (iv) How effective are these illustrations as propaganda?

   B. Write a **paragraph** on **one** of the following:

   (i) Mussolini and the March on Rome

   (ii) Mussolini's relations with the Catholic Church

   (iii) Mussolini and the use of propaganda and terror

   C. Write a **long answer** on Mussolini's rise to power in Italy.

HIGHER LEVEL

2. How and why was Mussolini able to achieve power in Italy?

3. How effective were the internal and external policies of Benito Mussolini? (2011)

4. What were the characteristics of Fascist regimes in Europe in the inter-war years? (2013)

5. How did Church-state relations develop under Mussolini and Hitler? (2014)

6. How did Mussolini and/or Stalin use propaganda and terror to remain in power? (2015)

Germany in the Inter-war Years, 1920–39

Economic and Social Problems of Weimar Germany

In 1918, the Weimar Republic was established in Germany. It faced many problems. Germany was defeated in the First World War (1914–18) – some accused the Weimar government of **stabbing the army in the back** – and the government had to sign the harsh **Treaty of Versailles** imposed by the victorious Allies (Britain, France and the US):

- Germany lost territory.
- The armed forces were reduced.
- Germany had to agree a **war guilt clause**.
- Germany had to pay **reparations** of £6.6 billion.

The German Economy in the 1920s

After World War I, the German economy suffered from **high unemployment** as soldiers were demobilised. It also suffered from the reparations plan of the victorious Allies of the war. The Weimar Government printed money to pay for war debts and reparations. This contributed to increased **inflation** from 1919 to 1922.

In 1929, the Wall Street Crash led to the Great Depression. German dole queues grew as unemployment rose from 8 per cent in 1928 to 30 per cent in 1932.

Ruhr Invasion and the Collapse of the Mark

The biggest problems came when the German government could not pay reparations in 1922. As a result, French and Belgian troops invaded the **Ruhr industrial region** in January 1923 to confiscate raw materials and goods. This led to passive resistance by the Germans, the deaths of German workers, the collapse in the value of the German mark and to very rapid inflation (hyperinflation). In 1922, one dollar could buy 500 marks; by November 1923, one dollar could buy 4 trillion marks – the mark had become worthless.

The German middle class was ruined; the value of their savings and pensions collapsed and workers were made poorer. They had to bring suitcases or carts to work to take home paper money. Some lost work, but the industrialists and landowners gained; they could easily pay off loans, and as their property grew in value, some made huge fortunes.

Prosperity

A new government took decisive action to rescue the German economy. They called off the Ruhr strikes and created a **new currency** called the Rentenmark; they negotiated with the US to provide special loans and cut the reparations payments under the **Dawes Plan**.

Industrial production in Germany in the 1920s

INDUSTRIAL PRODUCTION INDEX (1928=100)

By 1928, the German economy had reached pre-war levels. The government used the loans for housing and public works, so unemployment fell to 8 per cent by 1928. As one historian wrote, *'Iron and steel, coal, chemicals and electrical goods had all reached or beaten the 1913 production figures.'* By 1929, Germany was the leading industrial country on the continent. As a result of the economic recovery, political parties such as Hitler's Nazi Party and the Communist Party saw their support fall.

But the German economic recovery was too dependent on **US loans**. This weakness was exposed by the economic crisis caused by the **Wall Street Crash** (1929) and the **Great Depression**. The economic policies of the Weimer government worsened the depression. The Weimar government cut spending and increased taxes which increased unemployment. This led to the rise of Hitler and the downfall of the Weimar Republic.

? **QUESTIONS**

1. What was the condition of the German economy after World War I?
2. Why did French and Belgian troops invade the Ruhr and what were the effects?
3. How successful was the German economy by the second half of the 1920s?
4. Why did German unemployment rise after 1929?

KEY CONCEPT
DEPRESSION is a term used to describe when an economy is doing badly; industrial production declines, factories and businesses close and there is widespread unemployment.

KEY CONCEPT
INFLATION is an increase in the prices of products, usually a large increase.

The Nazi State in Peace – Origins and Growth

What Caused the Rise to Power of Hitler and the Nazis?

1. The Wall Street Crash and German Economic and Social Problems

German economic growth in the second half of the 1920s was due largely to American loans. But, in 1929 the value of shares in the New York Stock Exchange on Wall Street collapsed. This led to an **economic depression** in America. When American banks and companies called in loans from Germany, Germany too faced economic depression.

Businesses went bankrupt, factories and mines closed and workers were laid off. In 1929, there were already 1.5 million unemployed in Germany. This rose rapidly over the next few years. By January 1932 there were 6 million unemployed, but many more were on short-time working.

The economic crisis led to poverty and hunger. Many middle-class families suffered. Some had to sell their houses, others could not afford to rent. They moved to makeshift shanty towns on the edge of cities. Many had to rely on soup kitchens for food. Some joined the Red Front (Communists) or Hitler's **Storm Troopers (SA)**. One worker explained how he became a Nazi. In the Depression, *'Hunger was the daily companion of the German working man. All people looked for better times. As for me, like many another, I lost all I possessed so, in early 1930, I joined the Nazi Party.'* (See graphs p. 206)

2. The Failure of the Weimar Republic

Already the **reputation of the Weimar Republic** was damaged among some Germans because of the Treaty of Versailles and the notion that the Weimar Republic had **stabbed the army in the back**. For this they were called the **November criminals**. The ruling classes of the old Imperial Germany who were still in power also weakened the

Republic. The judges, generals, civil servants and teachers all favoured a more **authoritarian** government and they used their positions of influence to undermine the Weimar Republic.

The actions of the Weimar government worsened the economic crisis. The **Chancellor (Prime Minister)**, **Brüning**, cut back on government spending. He reduced wages, pensions and unemployment benefit. This earned him the nickname **Hunger Chancellor** and increased dissatisfaction and disorder in the streets.

Brüning made two further mistakes. He used **President Hindenburg's** power to **rule by decree** to bring in some of his unpopular measures. This showed the failure of democracy. Brüning also called a general election for June 1930. Instead of gaining a majority, the results of the election showed a swing to **extremism** – to an increase in the popularity of Hitler and the Nazi Party, and of the Communists.

Hitler expounding his ideas at an early Nazi meeting in the Nazi headquarters in Munich. Is this a propaganda picture?

3. Hitler's Leadership of the Nazis

Hitler and the Nazis' rise to power was also due to Hitler's ability as a political leader.

Nazi Tactics and Policies: In 1923 Hitler organised the **Munich Putsch** (rising) which was a failure. After this he decided to change tactics. He now believed that the use of force was not the best way to achieve power. He intended to use democracy to destroy democracy. *'If outvoting them takes longer than outshooting them, then at least the result will be guaranteed by their own constitution.'*

He began the **reorganisation** of his party. He established branches throughout Germany and appointed regional leaders (or gauleiters). The **SA (Brownshirts)** or **stormtroopers** were a paramilitary wing of the Nazi Party. The **SS (Blackshirts)** were Hitler's bodyguards. Other branch organisations were also formed such as the **Hitler Youth** and the **Women's League**.

He shaped his **policies** to make them attractive to many different groups:

- He appealed to **nationalists** through his attack on the Treaty of Versailles – *'the disgrace of Versailles'* – and the *'November criminals'*. He also promised to unite German-speaking people in a Greater Germany.

- Hitler was very strongly **anti-Communist** and this pleased the middle class, the industrialists and the farmers. They feared a Communist state and workers' soviets, as in Russia. Hitler was able to use the violence of the SA and SS against the socialists and Communists.

- The support of **industrialists and business leaders** was important because they helped finance his elections.

- The support for the Nazi Party came mostly from the lower middle class – small merchants, farmers, craftsmen, white-collar workers and civil servants.

Hitler taking the salute at the first Nuremberg Rally in 1927.

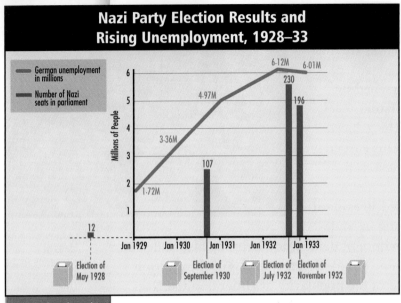

Nazi Party Election Results and Rising Unemployment, 1928–33

German unemployment in millions

Number of Nazi seats in parliament

Millions of People

6·12M 6·01M
4·97M
3·36M
1·72M

230
196
107
12

Jan 1929   Jan 1930   Jan 1931   Jan 1932   Jan 1933

Election of May 1928
Election of September 1930
Election of July 1932
Election of November 1932

What does this graph tell you about support for the Nazi Party?

Nazi Propaganda Techniques: Hitler used very effective propaganda techniques to get across his message. Hitler was an **outstanding speaker** – a Hitler speech was superb theatre. Hitler himself said, *'To be a leader means to be able to move the masses.'* He reduced his policies to simple **slogans**, *'Its [Nazi propaganda] intellectual level must be adjusted to the most limited intelligence,'* he said. *'When you lie, tell big lies.'*

The use of **uniforms, salutes and mass rallies** gave an impression of strength. They made good use of films and gramophone records (of Nazi speeches), the talker spouting forth from loudspeakers on trucks. One German explained how the Nazis fought the elections in his state. *'Hitler himself spoke at sixteen major rallies. Columns of SS troops shouted slogans and marched the villages and towns from morning to night. In every market square an SA band or Nazi minstrels played marches for hours on end.'*

Albert Speer, later Hitler's chief architect, explained how the Nazis appealed to him after listening to Hitler in 1931:

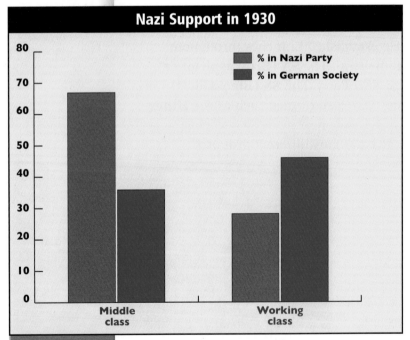

Nazi Support in 1930

% in Nazi Party
% in German Society

Middle class
Working class

What does this graph tell you about support for the Nazi Party?

'Here, it seemed to me, was hope. Here were new ideals, a new understanding, … The perils of Communism could be checked, Hitler persuaded us, and instead of hopeless unemployment, Germany could move towards economic recovery. The sight of discipline in a time of chaos, the impression of energy in an atmosphere of universal hopelessness, seems to have won [my mother] over too.'

4. Right-wing Plotting

By 1932 the Nazi Party was the **largest** in the Reichstag. Many conservative politicians believed that Hitler must be part of any government. The Nazis lost seats and votes between the elections in July and November 1932 (from 230 seats to 196 seats). Former Chancellor and leading conservative politician, **Von Papen**, now believed that Hitler was in a weaker position and that the conservatives could control him. *'I have roped him in. In two months we'll have pushed Hitler into a corner so hard that he'll be squeaking.'* In these circumstances, Von Papen persuaded **President Hindenburg** to appoint Hitler as Chancellor in January 1933. Von Papen was Vice-Chancellor and, besides Hitler, there were only two other Nazis in the cabinet. But Hitler only accepted the position provided he was allowed call a general election. Little did they know it but Hitler had outwitted them.

The Nazi State in Peace – Hitler in Power

How did Hitler Establish Dictatorship?

Hitler had come to power by largely constitutional (legal) means. But he was already planning to establish a **totalitarian state** where all aspects of life – political, social, economic and religious – would be controlled by the state.

Hitler's first step was to call a **general election** for March 1933. This became a huge propaganda campaign for the Nazis. Goebbels wrote in his diary: *'Now it will be very easy to carry on the fight as we can call on all the resources of the state. Radio and press are at our disposal. We shall stage a masterpiece of propaganda.'* This was accompanied by street violence as the **SA** clashed with the Communists. Over 400,000 SA were enlisted in the police so they now could use legal terror.

Two weeks before the election, a Dutch Communist, **van der Lubbe**, set fire to the Reichstag. Hitler exploited this by talking about the *'Communist threat'*. In the election, the Nazis increased their seats to 288 and, with the help of the Nationalist Party, Hitler had a parliamentary majority. He passed the **Enabling Law** which allowed him to **rule by decree**. Weimar democracy was at an end.

> **What were the main characteristics of Fascist regimes in Europe in the inter-war period?**
> - [Intro: Rise of Fascism]
> - Totalitarian dictatorship
> - Cult of the leader – Mussolini and Hitler
> - Wider propaganda – Italy and Germany
> - Newspapers, radio, cinema, marches, parades
> - Terror against opposition – Italy and Germany
> - Control of economy – corporate state/Four Year Plan
> - Extreme nationalism/ Racialism and Anti-Semitism
> - Aggression and war/ expansionism

KEY PERSONALITY: ADOLF HITLER

Hitler was born in **Austria** in 1889, the son of a customs official.

In Vienna he developed his **hatred** of the Jews, Communists and democracy. It was here also that he dreamt of a Greater Germany. He went to Munich and joined the German army in the First World War. He took part in 47 battles, mostly as a messenger. He was wounded twice and was also awarded the Iron Cross on two separate occasions.

After the war, he joined the German Workers' Party, soon becoming its leader and changing its name to the **National Socialist German Workers' Party**. The Party's Twenty-five Point programme emphasised anti-Semitism, extreme nationalism, racial superiority and leadership. Hitler felt the Weimar Republic was about to collapse, so he organised the **Munich Putsch**, which failed miserably.

He spent some time in jail where he dictated *Mein Kampf* (My Struggle). When he came out of jail, he reorganised the Party but Hitler had to wait for the Great Depression before he gained significant popularity (pp. 204–07). After his Party became the largest in the Reichstag, he was invited by **President Hindenburg** to become Chancellor in January 1933 (p. 206).

Over the next few years he established a **totalitarian state** under his control and that of the Nazi Party (p. 207). His campaign against the **Jews** became a significant feature of his state (p. 217). He also promoted an aggressive **foreign policy** in breaking the Treaty of Versailles and expanding Germany's borders. However, this caused the Second World War (Ch. 24).

Even though his armies were initially successful, conquering most of mainland Europe, he experienced defeat in the Battle of Britain, North Africa and, most important of all, in Russia (Ch. 25). As the Russians advanced from the east and the Americans and British from the west, Hitler committed **suicide** in his bunker in Berlin rather than be captured by the Russians (p. 309).

> Develop notes on the role of Hitler in German history, 1920–45.

Nazi 'Co-ordination'

Hitler extended his power further by a policy of **co-ordination** – by limiting or destroying the power of groups and institutions which were opposed to the Nazis:

- He **outlawed** the Communists and the SPD (Social Democrats) and seized their property.
- The Nazis were the **only political party** allowed in Germany.
- He **abolished** the elected State assemblies (parliaments) and appointed Nazi governors instead.
- Trade unions were abolished and replaced by the **German Labour Front**.
- The **press** was put under Nazi control.

Hitler's SS rounding up left-wing 'undesirables' to be questioned and searched.

The SA and the Night of the Long Knives

Next, Hitler eliminated opposition within his own party organisation in the **Night of the Long Knives**. By 1934 the **SA**, under the leadership of **Ernest Röhm**, had grown to over 2 million members. Röhm planned a **people's army** where the German army would merge with the SA with Röhm at its head. The army generals were opposed to this and Hitler needed the regular army for his plans. Hitler decided to use the SS to kill the leadership of the SA (including Röhm). Up to 400 people were killed, mostly from the SA but also some old scores were settled. The **SS under Himmler** became the most important of all Nazi organisations.

Der Führer

Hitler's next step, on the death of President Hindenburg in 1934, was to combine the offices of the Chancellor and the President. He was now called **Führer (Leader)**. *The Führer unites in himself all the sovereign authority of the Reich.'* He was now head of the armed forces and all the members had to swear a new **oath** to him, *'the Führer of the German Reich and People.'* In little over 18 months Hitler had established a **Nazi dictatorship**.

Himmler (right) used the SS, under Hitler's orders, to kill Röhm (left) and the SA leadership in 1934.

The Totalitarian State – Propaganda and Terror

The Nazis now proceeded to introduce what Goebbels called *'the national revolution'*. This resulted in Germany becoming a **totalitarian state**. Two methods were used – **propaganda and terror**.

Nazi Propaganda: Propaganda played a key role in Nazi control of Germany.

> *'Hitler's dictatorship differed in one fundamental point from all its predecessors in history... Through technical devices like radio and the loudspeaker, eighty million people were deprived of independent thought. It was thereby possible to subject them to the will of one man.'*

Albert Speer

QUESTION

How did each of the following help Hitler establish dictatorship: (i) 1933 general election (ii) Reichstag fire (iii) Enabling Law (iv) 'co-ordination' (v) Night of the Long Knives?

The Police State and the Use of Terror

As well as propaganda, Hitler used a variety of organisations to create a **police state**. The most important of these was the **SS** led by **Himmler**. The main job of the SS was to destroy opposition to Hitler and to carry out Nazi racial policies.

Of all Hitler's organisations, the **Gestapo** (Secret State Police) were the most feared by ordinary Germans. They were led by **Reinhard Heydrich** who was ruthless with all opposition. They had wide powers of arrest and they used torture to gain confessions and information.

The **police and courts** also maintained Hitler's totalitarian state. Nobody could get a **fair trial** since justice had to serve the Nazi state. Between 1934 and 1939 over 500 were tried and executed for political opposition. By 1939, over 16,000 were in jail for political offences. Many of these were held in the new **concentration camps** such as **Dachau**, near Munich. Prisoners were forced to do hard labour and punishments such as beatings were severe. The camps held **undesirables** such as Communists, intellectuals, trade unionists, tramps and Jews. During the Second World War, some of the concentration camps became **extermination camps**.

Jewish women in a Nazi concentration camp. It was not until the Second World War that some concentration camps were used for extermination.

How did Hitler deal with the Economy?

Hitler was faced with two economic challenges when he came to power – one was to reduce unemployment caused by the Great Depression (p. 204), the second was to develop self-sufficiency in raw materials (**autarky**).

Reducing Unemployment

The rising unemployment caused the discontent which brought Hitler to power. Now he needed to solve the problem. The government spent money on **public works**, the most important being 7,000 kilometres of motorways (**autobahn**). Many workers were recruited from the unemployed so the unemployment figures fell from 6 million in 1932 to 2.5 million in 1936. Further declines in unemployment occurred with the introduction of **conscription** (compulsory military training) and the **growth of heavy industry** as Germany rearmed.

An autobahn is opened in Germany with much fan fare.

The rearmament was based on the **Four Year Plan**, introduced by Hitler in 1936. It led to huge increases in coal, iron and steel production. By 1939, unemployment was

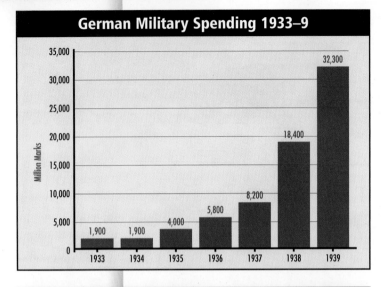

German Military Spending 1933–9

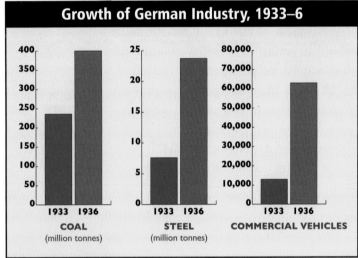

Growth of German Industry, 1933–6

COAL
(million tonnes)

STEEL
(million tonnes)

COMMERCIAL VEHICLES

? QUESTIONS

1. How did the Nazis reduce unemployment?
2. How successful were the Nazis in achieving self-sufficiency?

? EXAM QUESTION

What were the social and economic problems facing Germany, 1920–39, and how were they dealt with? (2015)

down to 200,000. Germany was much more successful than the US which reduced unemployment from 13 million (1933) to 8 million (1939) and Britain which still had 10 per cent unemployment in 1939 (see graph p. 238).

Self-sufficiency

The Plan also sought to develop **self-sufficiency** (**autarky**) in food and raw materials to prepare Germany for war. The food policy was not fully successful. There was a decline in grain and potatoes, and some foodstuffs had to be imported. In the case of raw materials there was a recycling of products and the development of synthetic products such as wool. But Germany still needed imports of oil, copper and rubber. Hitler's policy of self-sufficiency was only partly successful. Eventually Hitler would have to conquer lands in Eastern Europe to provide living space (**Lebensraum**) and supplies.

Who Benefited from Nazi Economic Policies?

The Workers

Workers benefited from the increase in jobs. Wages also increased but so did working hours. The Nazis tried to help workers by setting up two other organisations. **Beauty through Joy** aimed to improve working conditions, while the **Strength through Joy** movement was used to improve leisure time. Cheaper holidays, coach tours, concerts and cheaper sports facilities were provided. The Strength through Joy movement also encouraged the development of the **People's Car – the Volkswagen** – which ordinary Germans could own.

The Nazis and 'Big Business'

Big business gained most from German economic growth. Production came into the hands of fewer capitalists. By 1937, 70 per cent of German production was in the hands of **cartels** (monopolies). Even though the industries were owned by private individuals and companies, the overall aims of economic policy were decided by the Nazis: rearmament and self-sufficiency.

Church-State Relations in Nazi Germany

The German population was about two-thirds Protestant and one-third Catholic. Protestants were found mainly in the north of Germany, while Catholics lived in the south and west. Hitler hated **the Jewish-Christ creed**. He **condemned Christianity** for defending the weak and the lowly. But he could not openly attack it since most Germans were either Protestant or Catholic. He did not want to make martyrs of the priests. Instead he intended to use indirect methods to undermine the churches.

When he came to power, relations between the Nazis and the Catholic and Protestant churches seemed good. In his first speech as Chancellor, Hitler said he would respect the churches. *'Christianity'*, he said, *'is the unshakeable foundation of the moral and ethical life of our people.'* In return, the churches thought Hitler would be better than the Weimar Republic in maintaining family values, and defeating the 'evils of Bolshevism' (communism).

The Nazis and the Catholic Church

Hitler, a former Catholic, was suspicious of the Catholic Church in Germany because it owed its allegiance to an **outside power** – the Pope. Before Hitler came to power, Catholics also supported the Centre Party, and Catholic clergy criticised the Nazis so that Catholics were less in favour of the Nazi Party than Protestants. Hitler saw the Catholic Church as a major obstacle to creating his totalitarian state so he was determined to control it.

Concordat

For the moment, however, both sides wanted peace, so Hitler and the Church signed a **Concordat** (July 1933) soon after he came to power. Hitler promised to respect the rights of the Catholic Church – including the rights to Catholic education – if the priests stayed out of politics. This helped Hitler gain international prestige.

Yet within months, Hitler and the Nazis began openly controlling some Catholic organisations. Even though the Catholic Church complained privately to the Nazis, publicly they declared their support for them in the hope of stopping the anti-Catholic attacks.

Further Attacks

Instead, the Nazis continued their **attacks**:
- Three Catholic lay leaders were killed on the Night of the Long Knives.
- Pressure was put on Catholic youth organisations to join the Hitler Youth.
- There was a campaign to close Catholic schools and replace them with non-religious schools teaching Nazi ideas.
- Catholic priests and monks were put on trial for sexual immorality and currency smuggling. These trials became part of a huge **anti-Catholic propaganda** campaign led by Goebbels to undermine the influence of the Church.

The Nazis defended their actions by saying they were not attacks on the Catholic Church, but against churchmen involved in politics.

Papal Letter

The Pope, Pius XI, responded in 1937 with an encyclical, ***With Burning Anxiety***. This was smuggled into Germany and read at masses. The Pope criticised the Nazis' treatment of the Catholic Church and urged Catholics to resist. The Nazis responded with further attacks on Catholics. By 1939, the power and influence of the Catholic Church in Germany were severely limited.

> **KEY CONCEPT**
> **REICHSKIRCHE** Hitler wanted to unite all Protestant churches in one German national church, called the Reichskirche. This was his plan to control the Protestant religions.

In spite of these attacks, Catholics blamed them on Nazi officials rather than on Hitler himself, who was able to hide his real intentions of wiping out the influence of the Catholic Church in Germany.

Euthanasia

A further clash between the Nazis and the Catholic Church occurred during the Second World War. The Nazis began a programme of **euthanasia** (the killing of disabled or psychiatric patients). When word of this leaked out, one of the leading Catholic Churchmen, Bishop Galen, preached a strongly critical sermon in which he condemned the execution of mentally ill people. His views were reported around Germany and even abroad. Whether for this reason or others, the euthanasia programme stopped soon after.

The Nazis and the Protestant Churches

The Protestant population was divided into many different Protestant churches. Hitler wanted to unite them in one national church. He wanted to abolish 28 regional churches and create one **National Reich Church** (Reichskirche) under Nazi control. He used the **German Christians** (a National Socialist group within the Evangelical Protestant Church) to try to achieve this.

National Church

Soon after Hitler came to power, a **National Church** was established and the Nazi nominee, Ludwig Müller, was elected as Reich Bishop. Müller and his fellow German Christians introduced Nazi ideas into the Church. The clergy had to be loyal Nazis and support the superiority of the Aryan race; anti-Semitism became a feature of their preaching. 'Adolf Hitler is the new messiah' was one of the beliefs of the new Church. Pastors wore SA or SS uniforms and swastikas were hung in churches. Hitler also ordered that a copy of *Mein Kampf* be placed on the altar of each church.

Opposition in the Protestant Churches

But opposition also built up within the Protestant churches, led by **Pastor Martin Niemöller** and **Dietrich Bonhoeffer**. They were supported by 7,000 pastors, about 40 per cent of the evangelical clergy. They objected to 'Nazified Christianity'. They wanted to conduct their religion according to the Bible and not state direction, and they objected to excluding christianised Jews. This opposition founded its own Church – the **Confessing Church**, which split the evangelical churches.

Hitler set up the **Ministry of Church Affairs** in 1935. This used repressive measures against the Confessing Church. Pastors were banned, and Niemöller and about 700 other pastors were arrested. Niemöller was later sent to concentration camps until 1945.

As Hitler's power grew stronger during the 1930s, he put more pressure on the churches. They were spied upon by the **Gestapo** which had a special section to deal with them. All Confessing Church seminaries were banned, and state-funded religious schools were closed by 1939. In all, from 1933 to 1945, more than 6,000 clergymen were jailed or executed. But Hitler's actions failed to create a unified Protestant Church or to stop the opposition.

Conclusion

Overall, Hitler succeeded in weakening and controlling the Churches, but he failed to crush them. The Churches as organisations did not provide effective opposition to Hitler; only individuals provided effective opposition.

The Nazis and the Jews: Anti-Semitism and the Holocaust
Nazi Racialism

Hatred of the Jews (**anti-Semitism**) was a very important part of Hitler's ideas. This hatred formed part of his thinking on race. He said the Germans were the **master race** or **Herrenvolk**, of Aryan descent. They were depicted as blond, blue-eyed, tall and strong. As a master race, the Germans were superior to other races. They produced the great civilisations in history – the great artists, writers, thinkers and sportspeople. Hitler wanted to protect the **purity** of the German race from the *untermenschen* (subhumans), the Jews and Slavs.

Hitler and the Nazis reserved their greatest hatred and fear for the Jews. In **Mein Kampf**, Hitler said, *'The Jew is and remains a parasite, a sponger, who, like a germ, spreads over wider and wider areas.'* The Jews were regarded as the source of all evil. They were blamed for Germany's loss in the First World War and the Great Depression. They were associated with **Communism** because Karl Marx, the father of Communism, was Jewish. Nazi propaganda portrayed the Jews as rich, even though a quarter of Berlin's Jews were in poverty. But they were easy targets as a greater proportion of German bankers, lawyers, doctors and dentists were Jewish.

Nazi newspapers spread wild **stories** about the Jews. They were accused of slaughtering children and *'the blood of the slaughtered child is used by young married Jewish couples, by pregnant Jewesses, for circumcision and so forth.'*

An anti-Semitic cartoon used in a schoolbook. What is its message?

Persecution Begins

When Hitler and the Nazis came to power in 1933, they did not have a clear plan on how they would deal with the Jews. They began by excluding them from positions of social and political influence. They were barred from the civil service, universities and newspapers. Hitler ordered a boycott of Jewish shops, lawyers and doctors. There were also random attacks by the SA on Jews in the streets or on their businesses.

Systematic Persecution

However, for the first couple of years in power, Hitler moved slowly against the Jews because of the fear of upsetting world opinion and because of his need for foreign loans. But by 1935 his position at home was secure. Persecution of the Jews became more

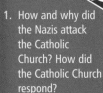

QUESTIONS

1. How and why did the Nazis attack the Catholic Church? How did the Catholic Church respond?
2. What was the disagreement about euthanasia?
3. What was the National Church? How effective was opposition to Hitler in the Protestant churches?

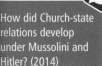

EXAM QUESTION

How did Church-state relations develop under Mussolini and Hitler? (2014)

KEY CONCEPT
HOLOCAUST: This is the word used to describe the Nazis' attempt to exterminate the Jews during the Second World War. It resulted in the death of about 6 million Jews.

KEY CONCEPT
HERRENVOLK. This was the Nazi idea of the Germans as a master race, superior to all other races.

KEY CONCEPT
ANTI-SEMITISM. The hatred for, and persecution of, the Jews. This hatred was based on religious and economic factors. Anti-Semitism became an important part of Nazi racial views.

systematic. Jews were banned from other areas of German life. They were excluded from parks, swimming pools, restaurants and public buildings. In September 1935, Hitler announced the **Nuremberg Laws**. Jews were forbidden to marry Aryans, and sexual relations between Jews and **citizens of German or kindred blood were forbidden**. Jews were also deprived of German citizenship.

Night of the Crystal Glass

During the Berlin Olympics in 1936, the Nazis reduced the persecution of the Jews and got rid of some of the anti-Jewish signs. But this was short-term.

The overcrowded conditions and the thin bodies in a Nazi concentration camp.

The worst oppression came on the **Night of the Crystal Glass (Kristallnacht)** in November 1938. The killing of a minor official in the German embassy in Paris by a Polish Jew was used as an excuse for widespread attacks on Jews by the SA. Jewish shops and synagogues were destroyed, over 100 Jews were killed and others were sent to concentration camps. Hitler imposed a fine on the Jewish community to pay for the damage.

The Holocaust

By 1939, nearly half of Germany's Jews had emigrated including the great scientist, **Einstein**. They were lucky to escape from the systematic repression and killing of the Second World War. During the war, 300,000 German Jews were joined by about 6 million more from the countries of Nazi-occupied Europe. Jews from these countries were sent to concentration camps in Germany and Poland.

From 1942, the Nazis went ahead with the **Final Solution** or extermination of the Jews. The most systematic killing was carried on in **Auschwitz** but there were other large camps at **Treblinka** and **Chelmo**. In all, six camps in Poland were involved in the scheme of **genocide** (extermination of a race or people).

Jews arrived by train and were separated into those fit for work and those unfit. The unfit were **gassed** in chambers designed like large shower rooms. The commandant of Auschwitz, Hoess, said, *'We tried to fool the victims into thinking they were going through a delousing process. Sometimes they realised our intentions and we had riots.'* The others were used as **slave labour** until they died. Jews were also used for live experiments such as operations without anaesthetic. In all about 6 million Jews were killed during the war, over 4 million of those during the Final Solution. After the war many of those responsible for the Holocaust were put on trial in Nuremberg. They claimed they were *'only obeying orders'*. (See Chapter 26, Society during the Second World War, pp. 312–20.)

QUESTION

1. Why did Hitler and the Nazis hate the Jews?
2. How did the Nazis persecute the Jews in the 1930s (before the war)?
3. What happened to the Jews during World War II (the Holocaust)?

HOMEWORK EXERCISES

1. Develop a mind-map/spider diagram of the causes of Hitler's rise to power. Explain how each of the causes you have listed helped Hitler rise to power.

2. Develop notes on the treatment of Jews in Europe, 1920–45.

ORDINARY LEVEL

3. This cartoon mocks the Nazi belief in the Aryan, or pure German, race. Study it and answer the questions which follow. (2008)

A. (i) Name the three characteristics of an Aryan, according to the cartoon.
   (ii) Why is Goering not a typical Aryan?
   (iii) Who is the Aryan teacher?
   (iv) Why would this cartoon not be published in Germany between 1933 and 1945?
   (v) What was the 'Final Solution' that was adopted by the Nazi regime after 1941?

B. Write a **paragraph** on one of the following.
   (i) Economic and social problems in Weimar Germany, 1920–33
   (ii) The Great Depression in Germany
   (iii) Anti-Semitism in Germany, 1933–45
   (iv) Hitler's relations with the Christian Churches in Germany

C. Write a **long answer** on one of the following.
   (i) Hitler's rise to power
   (ii) Hitler's dictatorship of Germany, 1933–39
   (iii) How did Joseph Goebbels use propaganda to support the Nazi state?

HIGHER LEVEL

4. Which had the greater social and economic problems during the inter-war years, Britain or Germany? Argue your case, referring to both countries. (2008)

5. How successfully did German governments deal with the social and economic problems of the period, 1920–39? (2010)

6. During the inter-war period, what conditions in Europe contributed to the growth of Fascist regimes? (2006)

7. What were the main characteristics of the Nazi state between 1933 and 1939? (2007)

8. How did dictators use propaganda and/or terror to maintain their power? (2009)

9. What contribution did Joseph Goebbels and/or Leni Riefenstahl make to Nazi propaganda? (2008)

10. How did Church-state relations develop under Mussolini and Hitler? (2014)

11. How did anti-Semitism and the Holocaust affect Europe, 1920–45? (2012)

Mass (large scale) rallies were an integral part of **Nazi organisation and propaganda**. The most important of these was the annual party rally held in Nuremberg in southern Germany each August or September. The medieval city of Nuremberg was chosen by Hitler because of its **links** with German history – it was regarded as the unofficial capital of the Holy Roman Empire and some Imperial Diets (parliaments) were held there. Hitler said it was 'the most German of German cities'.

Nuremberg was also a strong **Nazi base** – Julius Streicher, a close Party colleague of Hitler, published his anti-Semitic newspaper, *Der Sturmer*, there and through his control of the local organisation, he made Nuremberg into the 'holy city' of the Nazi movement. Another factor which helped Nuremberg was it's central location with seven railway lines converging there.

SOURCE 1 – DEUTSCHLAND UBER ALLES

'During the present week the ancient city of Nuremberg in Bavaria, will witness stirring scenes. The annual Congress of the National Socialist Party is being held there, and many thousands of enthusiastic delegates will take part in the ceremonies. Whatever may be said or thought about the Nazis, nobody can deny that they are good showmen, and that Dr Josef Goebbels is the supreme showman of them all. He has dramatised and stage-managed the Nazi movement almost from the very start. Realising that the German people love a good spectacle he has left nothing undone to provide them with spectacular fare, and during the last three years he has been advancing from strength to strength.'

The Irish Times, 8 September 1936

> What role has Goebbels played in organising the Nuremberg Rallies?

> Can you identify the different parts of the Nuremberg Rally grounds and what they were used for?

SOURCE 2 – PLAN OF NUREMBERG RALLY GROUNDS

The grounds were designed by Albert Speer. The Nazis began building them during the 1930s after Hitler came to power but they were not completed by 1939.

The First Rallies

The Nazi Party held its first rally in Munich (1923) but the second one – held in Weimar (1926) – was delayed because Hitler was jailed after the failed Munich Putsch (1924). It wasn't until 1927 that the rallies were moved to Nuremberg which became their permanent base.

The first of the Party rallies was held there in August 1927. It featured a torchlight procession, the consecration of the flags, and Hitler's speech. The next Rally, held in 1929, was on a much greater scale. This was the last Nuremberg Rally before Hitler came to power in 1933, and it preceded the Wall Street Crash and the beginning of the Great Depression.

SOURCE 3 – THE FLAG RITUAL AT THE LUITPOLD ARENA

Hitler honours the flag of the Munich Putsch in this ceremony, with the partly built grandstand in the background.

What is the significance of this ceremony?

SOURCE 4 – PLANNING

'The participants were already flooding into Nuremberg. Carefully selected months in advance, each had a number, a designated truck, a designated seat in the truck, and a designated cot in the vast tent city near Nuremberg. By the time the ceremonies began on 4 September the thousands of party members had been rehearsed to perfection.'

J Toland, Adolf Hitler

How well was the planning for the Rallies done?

CASE STUDY QUESTION

Why was Nuremberg chosen as the location of the Nuremberg Rallies? Why did the Nazis organise the rallies? What role did Albert Speer play in the organisation of the rallies?

Prior to Hitler's coming to power, the rallies were used to show the strength of the Nazi Party and to impress German public opinion. He used the rallies to denounce the Weimar Republic and criticise democracy as weak. In this way, they were instruments of Nazi propaganda.

The Nazis in Power – Expansion of the Rallies

But it was not until 1933, after Hitler came to power, that the Nuremberg Rallies took on the shape so well known to the world. Hitler declared Nuremberg to be the 'city of the Nazi Party rallies' and the resources of the German state were used to expand the annual Nazi celebration. At the 1933 Rally, **Albert Speer**, a young architect, became involved in the organisation of the rally. He constructed a huge wooden framed eagle behind the podium. The next year he was asked by Hitler to draw up an overall plan for the Nazi Party grounds, which were eleven kilometres in extent.

Site of the Rallies

The area had a series of large open spaces such as the **Zeppelin Field**, the **Luitpold Arena** and the **March Field**. The plans also included a number of large buildings such as the **Congress Hall**. These were linked by the **Great Road**, 2 kilometres long and 60 metres wide. Much progress was made in constructing the site but the construction was not completed when war broke out in 1939. (Source 2)

- The **Zeppelin Field** was built on an old airfield. It could accommodate over 100,000 spectators. Speer's design for a stone structure 'was a mighty flight of stairs topped and enclosed by a long colonnade, flanked on both ends by stone abutment… The structure had a length of thirteen hundred feet and a height of eighty feet.'

- The **Luitpold Arena** could hold 150,000 people. It was used for the mass gatherings of the SS and the SA.
- The **Congress Hall** – a huge hall based on Roman architecture.

Hitler and Speer wanted to create buildings which would last 1,000 years. They wanted to match the great buildings of past civilisations such as those of Ancient Greece and Rome. Hitler believed in Speer's theory of **'ruin value'** – that ancient ruins provided proof of the greatness of previous civilisations. Hitler also wanted his buildings to be the biggest 'to glorify his works and magnify his pride', according to Albert Speer in his autobiography, *Inside the Third Reich*. These buildings in the Party Rally grounds would demonstrate Nazi power and reflect the glory Hitler planned for Germany. They would also be suitable to mobilise large crowds and create the feeling of a great national community. (Sources 1 to 4)

SOURCE 5 – THE HITLER YOUTH

'On Sunday all Nuremberg was filled with the presence of young Germany. From the earliest hours of the morning, endless columns of Hitler Youth marched to the stadium. As always, it is a marvellous sight: In rows of 48, the youth stand with others from their area. It is a picture of discipline and strength. Other Hitler lads and girls sit in the seats around the field. Across from the Führer's platform are the choirs and music groups, and high above the watchtowers from which fanfares and drumbeats will sound. Rows of Naval Hitler Youth stand to the right and left of the Führer's platform.... A few minutes before ten a command thunders over the field. The units and detachments stiffen, then break out in thousand-fold jubilation: The Führer has arrived.'

From *The Ceremony of the Hitler Youth, 1936*

What is the evidence that this was 'a picture of discipline and strength'?

CASE STUDY QUESTION

How do Sources 4 and 5 show how the Nazis could use the organisation of the rallies for propaganda purposes?

The Themes of the Rallies – Their role in propaganda

The Rallies were used for many purposes: to glorify Hitler and thereby cement his relationship with the German people; spread Nazi ideology; celebrate Nazi achievements; mobilise the mass of the German people. They played a central role in **propagandising** Party members as well as a forum for further recruitment. (See sources 5, 6 and 7)

CASE STUDY QUESTION

What were the main locations used for the rallies in Nuremberg? How useful were they for propaganda?

One way of spreading **Nazi propaganda** was that each rally had a different theme, usually celebrating recent Nazi achievements.

- In 1933, the Nazis celebrated their rise to power in the **Rally of Victory**.

Leni Riefenstahl filmed *Victory of Faith* at this rally. Ernest Röhm, leader of the SA, featured in it so almost all copies of it were destroyed after the Night of the Long Knives.

- In 1934, the Nazis emphasised the oneness of Germany in the **Rally of Unity and Strength**.

Leni Riefenstahl filmed *Triumph of the Will* at this rally.

- In 1935, the **Rally of Freedom** celebrated breaking the Treaty of Versailles with the introduction of conscription.

Nuremberg Rally				
Year	Congress and Location	Theme	Propaganda Film (✔ the Rally was filmed)	Context
1923	1st – Munich	Germany Awake		
1926	2nd – Weimar	Refounding Congress		After Hitler came out of jail/barred from speaking in Bavaria
1927	3rd – Nuremberg	Day of Awakening	✔	First Nuremberg Rally
1929	4th – Nuremberg	Day of Composure	✔	Before the Wall Street Crash
1933	5th – Nuremberg	Rally of Victory	*Victory of Faith*	After Nazi seizure of power/Speer's involvement
1934	6th– Nuremberg	Rally of Unity and Strength	*Triumph of the Will*	After Night of Long Knives and Death of Hindenburg. Full-scale development of Rally grounds
1935	7th – Nuremberg	Rally of Freedom	*Day of Freedom*	Introduction of conscription Nuremberg Laws
1936	8th – Nuremberg	Rally of Honour	✔	Remilitarisation of Rhineland Announcement of 4 Year Plan Cathedral of Light
1937	9th – Nuremberg	Rally of Labour	✔	Reduced unemployment Cathedral of Light
1938	10th – Nuremberg	Rally of Greater Germany	✔	Annexation of Austria Conflict over Sudetenland Cathedral of Light
1939	11th – Nuremberg	Rally of Peace		Cancelled because of WWII

SOURCE 6 – AMERICAN JOURNALIST, WILLIAM SHIRER, EXPERIENCED THE POWER OF HITLER SPEAKING

'I was a little shocked at the faces,' Shirer wrote in his diary, 'when Hitler finally appeared on the balcony for a moment. They reminded me of the crazed expressions I once saw in the back country of Louisiana on the faces of some Holy Rollers… they looked up at him as if he were a Messiah, their faces transformed into something positively inhuman.'

The next morning, Shirer was among the attendees at the Rally's opening ceremony, held inside a large hall on the outskirts of Nuremberg. It was Shirer's first experience with Nazi pomp and pageantry.

'I am beginning to comprehend,' he wrote, 'some of the reasons for Hitler's astounding success. Borrowing a chapter from the Roman [Catholic] church, he is restoring pageantry and colour and mysticism to the drab lives of 20th century Germans. This morning's opening meeting… was more than a gorgeous show; it also had something of the mysticism and religious fervour of an Easter or Christmas Mass in a great Gothic cathedral. The hall was a sea of brightly coloured flags. Even Hitler's arrival was made dramatic. The band stopped playing. There was a hush over the thirty thousand people packed in the hall. Then the band struck up the Badenweiler March… Hitler appeared in the back of the auditorium and followed by his aides, Göring, Goebbels, Hess, Himmler and the others, he slowly strode down the long centre aisle while thirty thousand hands were raised in salute.'

To Shirer, the intoxicating atmosphere inside the hall was such that 'every word dropped by Hitler seemed like an inspired word from on high. Man's – or at least the German's – critical faculty is swept away at such moments, and every lie pronounced is accepted as high truth itself.'

What does Shirer think are the reasons for Hitler's success?

The **Nuremberg Laws** against the Jews were passed at a special meeting of the Reichstag in the city.

- In 1936, the Nazis celebrated the remilitarisation of the Rhineland in the **Rally of Honour**.
- In 1937, the **Rally of Labour** highlighted the reduction in unemployment since the Nazis came to power in 1933.
- In 1938, the **Rally of Greater Germany** celebrated the Union with Austria (Anschluss) in that year. (Source 8)

Hitler insisted on the return of Imperial Regalia of the old Holy Roman Empire from Vienna to Nuremberg.

Hitler also used the occasion of the rally to put pressure on Czechoslovakia (and also Britain and France) over the Sudetenland. The **Munich Conference** was held shortly after this rally resulting in the transfer of the Sudetenland to Germany.

- The Nazis named the rally in 1939 as the **Rally of Peace** but this was cancelled when the German army invaded Poland.

SOURCE 7 – LAUNCHING CAMPAIGNS

'Lloyd George [former British Prime Minister] was predictably impressed by the 1936 Party Day at Nuremberg. More spectacular than ever, it was marked by the launching of **two new campaigns: the Four-Year Plan** for economic self-sufficiency and an **anti-Bolshevik** crusade against "the powers of disorder". On a bright Sunday morning, Hitler spoke of the Bolshevik menace to 160,000 massed Brownshirts and SS men in the huge Nuremberg stadium, then drove back to the city in an open Mercedes acknowledging the plaudits of the multitude who jammed the narrow streets and hung from the dormer windows.'

J. Toland, *Adolf Hitler*

> What were the main locations used for the rallies in Nuremberg? How useful were they for propaganda?

THE PROGRAMME OF THE RALLIES

The Nuremberg Rallies were lengthened to seven or eight days from 1934. Each day was centred on a particular programme.

- Day 1: Day of Welcome
- Day 2: Day of Opening the Congress
- Day 3: Day of the Reich Labour Service
- Day 4: Day of Community
- Day 5: Day of the Political Leaders
- Day 6: Day of the Hitler Youth
- Day 7: Day of the SA and SS
- Day 8: Day of the Armed Forces

Each day was focused on speeches by various Nazi leaders along with Hitler. They used these occasions to get across Nazi ideas so that the members of the different organisations were instilled with new spirit and energy in creating the totalitarian state. They could return to their homes full of enthusiasm for Nazi policies.

SOURCE 8 – RALLY OF GREATER GERMANY

'The Party Congress at Nuremberg that year served as a dramatic prelude to the developing political crisis by its impressive display of Nazi power and discipline. The title of the 1938 festivities was appropriate: "First Party Rally of Greater Germany", as were the trappings. Hitler had brought from Vienna ... the insignia of the First Reich – the Imperial crown, the Orb of Empire, the Sceptre and the Imperial Sword. At the presentation of these symbols of imperialism he solemnly vowed that they would remain in Nuremberg.'

J. Toland, *Adolf Hitler*

> Why do you think Hitler brought the insignia of the First Reich to Nuremberg?

SOURCE 9 – SPECTACULAR

'200,000 party faithful with more than 20,000 unfurled flags crowded into Zeppelin Field and lined up with military precision. The effect of Speer's 130 giant searchlights was more breathtaking than imagined ... In the awesome silence, Hitler's voice came across the field from loudspeakers with eerie effect. "We are strong and will get stronger!" he said, and made it as much a threat as a promise.'

J. Toland, *Adolf Hitler*

> What was spectacular about the giant searchlights?

The Organisation of the Rallies

Each Rally had to be carefully planned. In 1933, 500,000 Nazis had to be accommodated in factories, public buildings and in a camp with kitchens, washing facilities and outdoor toilets. (Sources 4, 5, 6 and 7)

Features of the Rallies – Their role in propaganda

Each Rally was preceded the night before by the performance of the opera, *Die Meistersinger von Nurnberg*, by Wagner, Hitler's favourite composer. The Rally was opened with the Party Roll of Honour of those who died for the Party. Each part of the Nazi organisation presented themselves before Hitler over the six or seven days of the rally – the Hitler Youth, the German Women's League, the Reich Labour Front, the SA and the SS, as also did the Wehrmacht (the German armed forces). The ritual associated with each of these presentations played a very important part in the **propaganda** of the rally. On each day, Hitler's speech was the highlight of the occasion. (Source 10)

Apart from emphasising the themes of each rally, other features of the rallies were used for **propaganda** purposes.

Hitler cult

Triumph of the Will showed how the cult of Hitler was promoted. At the beginning, Hitler is seen descending by plane from the clouds, a modern-day saviour coming to help his people. They are worshipping him as they wait. Many other aspects of the film feature Hitler, from speaking, to meeting supporters, to participating in the ceremony of the Blood Flag (the flag sanctified by the blood of those who lost their lives in the Munich Putsch in 1923). At the conclusion of *Triumph of the Will*, he is praised by Hess who says: 'The Party is Hitler! Hitler is Germany – just as Germany is Hitler! Hitler! Sieg Heil! Sieg Heil! Sieg Heil! (resounding cheers).' (See box, *Triumph of the Will*, p. 226)

Religious experience and Ritual

Apart from presenting Hitler as saviour or messiah, another aspect of the religious element was the use of 130 searchlights by Speer from 1934 onwards to create the Cathedral of Light around the Zeppelin field at night. (Source 9)

> **? CASE STUDY QUESTIONS**
> 1. How well organised were the rallies? List three themes of the rallies.
> 2. What role did those themes play in Nazi propaganda?
> 3. What campaigns did the Nazis launch at the Nuremberg Rallies?

> **SOURCE 10 – HITLER SPEAKS**
> 'The sense of power, of force and unity was irresistible, and all converged with a mounting crescendo of excitement on the supreme moment when the Führer himself made his entry. Paradoxically, the man who was most affected by such spectacles was their originator, Hitler himself, and ... they played an indispensable part in the process of self-intoxication.'
>
> A. Bullock, *Hitler: a Study in Tyranny*

> What was the feeling like when Hitler entered to speak?

> **SOURCE 11 – RIEFENSTAHL**
> 'Hitler appointed [Leni Riefenstahl] to make films of the rallies. As the only woman officially involved in the proceedings, she had frequent conflicts with the party organisation, which was soon up in arms against her. The Nazis were by tradition anti feminist and could hardly brook this self-assured woman, the more so since she knew how to bend this men's world to her purposes. Intrigues were launched and slanderous stories carried to Hess, in order to have her ousted. But after the first Party Rally film, which convinced even the doubters of her skill as a director, these attacks ceased.'
>
> Albert Speer, *Inside the Third Reich*, Weidenfeld and Nicholson, 1970

> What difficulties did Riefenstahl face while filming *Triumph of the Will*?

> **? CASE STUDY QUESTION**
>
> How was the Cult of Hitler promoted at the rallies?

225

Ritual reinforced Nazi ideas in the minds of the people. Songs, parades and marching were the most obvious elements of the use of ritual. There was also the widespread use of flags and the consecration of Party flags. Here Hitler used the Blood Flag or Banner as a symbol of sacrifice and loyalty to the Party and touched the new flags with it.

As part of the ritual, all groups in the Nazi organisation presented themselves separately before Hitler (See Features of the Rallies). As an example, in 1936 45,000 men of the Labour Front, responsible for public works in the Third Reich, marched before the Fuhrer, carrying spades like rifles. They proclaimed, *'The hour has come when once a year we lay aside our work and appear before the Fuhrer. We stand in common work and uniform. No one is too good to work for the fatherland, and thus this service has become the duty of all.'*

Enemies

Speeches from the Nazi leaders highlighted the enemies they blamed for the problems of Germany – the Treaty of Versailles, the Bolsheviks (Communists) and the Jews.

Treaty of Versailles: National Socialism has *'succeeded in unfastening shackle upon shackle of that Treaty which at one time was meant to destroy them for all time to come.'* (*The Irish Times*, 7 September 1938)

OPENING SEQUENCE OF *TRIUMPH OF THE WILL*:
'September 4, 1934. 20 years after the outbreak of World War I, 16 years after German woe and sorrow began, 19 months after the beginning of Germany's rebirth, Adolf Hitler flew again to Nuremberg to review the columns of his faithful admirers.'

What is the message of the opening sequence of *Triumph of the Will*?

TRIUMPH OF THE WILL

In 1934, Hitler commissioned **Leni Riefenstahl** to film the Nuremberg rally. Preparations for the rally were linked with preparations for the filming. Nuremberg became a giant stage with flags, banners, marches and torches. Riefenstahl used 30 cameramen and over 100 technicians. She also used planes, cranes, roller skates and tracking rails to shoot the documentary. In all, 61 hours of footage was reduced to two hours of documentary, called the *Triumph of the Will*. 'At the premiere [of the film] she was greeted coolly by party officials but even Goebbels, her greatest critic, realised it was an outstanding achievement and, in its way, far more effective propaganda for the Führer and National Socialism than any other film yet made.' (Toland) Often regarded as one of the masterpieces of film propaganda, it was banned from public viewing for over fifty years. Now it can be viewed online. (For further information on Leni Riefenstahl, see p. 211)

What was the purpose of *Triumph of the Will*? How did Riefenstahl achieve the effects in the *Triumph of the Will*?

SUMMARY OF THE NUREMBERG RALLIES

- The Nuremberg Rallies were annual events for the Nazi Party, which usually lasted a week from 1933 onwards.
- The Nuremberg Rallies were great propaganda occasions for Hitler and the Nazi Party.
- They used them to persuade their own followers as well as the wider German public and the world.
- They used them to get across their ideas and to create unity amongst party members.
- Each rally was based on a theme, and each day was centred on the parades and speeches of one section of the Nazi organisation.
- In the 1935 rally, the Nuremberg Laws against the Jews were passed at a special meeting of the Reichstag that was held there.
- Hitler's leadership was a central feature of the rallies.
- Leni Riefenstahl was asked by Hitler to film the 1934 rally. This film was called *Triumph of the Will* and it was a very successful propaganda film.
- There was huge organisation involved in the rallies, especially since in the later ones, about half a million people attended.
- Hitler commissioned Albert Speer to design the rally grounds, but this work was not finished when war began in 1939.

WHAT CAN YOU TELL ABOUT THE SOURCES? – SCENES FROM THE TRIUMPH OF THE WILL

WHAT INFORMATION CA YOU GET FROM THE SOURCE?

Analysing Documents: Photographs

- Why were these photographs/ pictures taken?
- What do you know about the photographer/ director?
- Are they objective?
- Are they reliable sources?
- How useful are photographs and films as sources for historians of the Nuremberg Rallies?
- Explain your answer in each case.

- How is Hitler portrayed in Picture 1?
- How is support for Hitler and the Nazi Party shown in these pictures?
- How do these pictures show that the Nuremberg Rallies were well-organised?
- What aspect of Nazi ideas is shown in Picture 3?
- What symbols can be seen in these pictures?
- Explain your answer in each case.

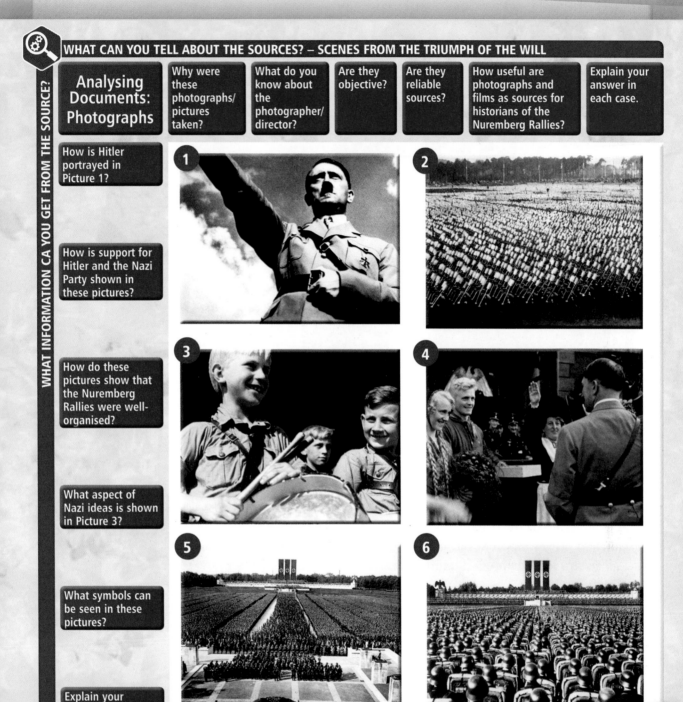

Bolsheviks (Communists): 'Bolshevism turns flourishing countrysides into sinister wastes of ruins; National Socialism transforms a Reich of destruction and misery into a healthy State and a flourishing economic life…' (Hitler's speech, 14 September 1936)

Jews: 'The nation, he said, had been cleansed of "parasites". They had begun the struggle against "the greatest enemy threatening to destroy our nation – the international Jewish enemy".' (*The Irish Times*, 7 September 1938)

THE PROPAGANDA OF *TRIUMPH OF THE WILL*

The Nazis, especially the young men, are blond and blue eyed, like the Aryan race. They are muscular and happy, but they are also shown behaving like normal young men.

The efficiency of Nazi organisation is emphasised through organising the camps, the food, the disciplined marches and parades.

Presented as a documentary, it was a propaganda film designed to convince Germany and the world of the power, strength and determination of the German people under Hitler's leadership.

R. Evans, *The Third Reich in Power*

> Do you agree with Richard Evans's conclusion on *Triumph of the Will*?

The Nuremberg Laws

In 1935, the Reichstag held a meeting in Nuremberg on the last day of the Rally. Here it passed the Nuremberg Laws against the Jews. Jews became second-class citizens; Jews were also prevented from marrying non-Jews.

German power and Unity: The architecture, the parades, the thousands marching and the scale of the organisation were deliberately done to emphasise both Nazi and German power. Speeches also highlighted German power and unity, and *Triumph of the Will* portrayed a happy and united people adoring their master.

Nuremberg – a Symbol of Nazism

The 1939 Rally, with a theme of the Party Rally of Peace, was cancelled due to the outbreak of the Second World War on 1 September 1939. By then Nuremberg had become a key symbol of the Nazis. This, along with its role as a centre of war production, led to massive Allied bombing which flattened much of the city. After the war, the US army held a victory parade there and blew up the swastika which was behind the reviewing stand. The trials of the Nazi war criminals were deliberately held in the city.

Nuremberg has now become the centre of a museum and what is left of the Nazi Party grounds have a preservation order on them. Long after the Rallies have ended, their spectacle still causes controversy.

? CASE STUDY QUESTIONS

1. Who directed *Triumph of the Will*?
2. How were (i) Hitler and (ii) the Nazis portrayed in the documentary?
3. How successful was the documentary?

The Labour-dominated Council also ensured **cross-party support** for the march, including support from the local Conservative Party. The Council did not want the march to be linked to the hunger marches organised by the National Unemployed Workers' Movement (NUWM), who had connections with the Communist Party. (See Hunger Marches, p. 237). They also called it a **crusade** rather than a march – partly to reflect the religious background of the area, but also to distance it from the hunger marches. (See Source 6 – Organisation of march).

? CASE STUDY QUESTIONS

1. Who decided to organise the Jarrow March?
2. What was the purpose of the march?
3. What did the petition say?
4. Why was it called a crusade?
5. Who supported the march?

The Progress of the Crusade

There were 11,000 Jarrow people who signed the petition, which the marchers were carrying to London in an oak box with gold lettering. Over 68,000 Tyneside people signed a further petition: 'your petitioners humbly and anxiously pray that H.M. Government realise the urgent need that work be provided for the town without further devastating delay.' (See Source 5 – Jarrow petition).

The marchers set off from the Town Hall, watched by most of the townspeople. They were led at the start by the Mayor, local councillors and **Ellen Wilkinson**, Labour Member of Parliament for Jarrow, who had encouraged the organisation of the march. They carried large banners saying **Jarrow Crusade**.

SOURCE 5 – JARROW PETITION

'To: The Honourable the Commons of the United Kingdom of Great Britain and Northern Ireland in Parliament Assembled.

The humble petition of the inhabitants of the Borough of Jarrow sheweth as follows:

During the last fifteen years Jarrow has passed through a period of industrial depression without parallel in the town's history. The persistence of unemployment has reduced us to a deplorable condition – homes are impoverished and acute distress is prevalent... your petitioners humbly and anxiously pray that H.M. Government realise the urgent need that work be provided for the town without further devastating delay, actively assist resuscitation [revival] of industry and render such other actions as may be meet.

Signed by the under-mentioned, being inhabitants of the town of Jarrow of the age of 18 years and over.'

D Dougan, Jarrow March, 1936

What are the inhabitants of Jarrow asking the government to do?

SOURCE 6 – ORGANISATION OF MARCH

'The organisation seems well nigh perfect. It includes a transport wagon – a bus bought for £20 and converted – which goes ahead with the sleeping kit, waterproofs for every man worn bandoleer fashion, 1s 6d pocket-money and two 1d stamps a week, medical attention, haircutting (and shaving for the inexpert), cobbling, accommodation at night in drill halls, schools, church institutes, and even town halls, and advance agents in the persons of the Labour agent at Jarrow, Mr. Harry Stoddart, and the Conservative agent, Mr. R Suddick, who work together in arranging accommodation and getting halls for meetings.'

With the Jarrow Marchers in the *Manchester Guardian*, 13 October 1936

Do you agree that the organisation was 'well nigh perfect'?

SOURCE 7 – SUPPORT OF MARCH

'There is no political aspect to this march. It is simply the town of Jarrow saying "Send us work". In the ranks of the marchers are Labour men, Liberals, Tories (Conservatives), and one or two Communists, but you cannot tell who's who.'

With the Jarrow Marchers in the *Manchester Guardian*, 13 October 1936

Why do you think there was 'no political aspect to this march'?

SOURCE 8 – NOT A HUNGER MARCH

'With eggs and salmon and such sandwiches as I saw today being consumed on the menu it is emphatically not a hunger-march. The men are doing well on it, and only two of them have fallen out for reasons of health in nearly 90 miles of marching.'

With the Jarrow marchers in the *Manchester Guardian*, 13 October 1936

Why was the march 'not a hunger march'?

At the end of a day's marching, the leaders presented the case of Jarrow at public meetings in the towns. Here Councillor Dave Riley, Marshall of the March, speaks and to his left is Ellen Wilkinson, M.P. for Jarrow.

Each day followed a **similar pattern**. They began around 8.45 a.m. and marched an average of 13 miles a day. Some marched army-style – 50 minutes marching and 10 minutes resting. They marched in all conditions, though they were fortunate that there were only a few days of rain along the route. Sometimes they broke the monotony by singing, led by their mouth organ band. During the day, they were fed from their transport wagon. At the end of a day's marching, they were usually warmly welcomed – and fed – in the towns where they stopped. The leaders presented the case of Jarrow at public meetings in the towns. (See Sources 7, 8, 9 and 10).

Along the way, many people praised the organisation of the march and the conduct of the men. In Barnsley, for example, the Mayor said, 'Everything that Barnsley can do for you will be done.' Apart from a hot meal of meat and potato pie, pudding and tea or coffee, some men took advantage of free seats at the cinema and others got a free drink in the local pubs. (See also Source 9 – Welcome at Harrogate).

At end of each day's marching, the leaders' speeches followed **consistent themes**: the causes of Jarrow's unemployment problems, the impact of unemployment on the town and a call on the government to provide jobs for the town. (See Source 10 – Speeches on the march).

Ellen Wilkinson, Labour M.P. for Jarrow, was a fiery speaker. Her reputation grew after the Jarrow March and she was appointed Minister of Education in the Labour government after the Second World War, when she was involved in implementing the 1944 Education Act. She also introduced free milk for all schoolchildren.

Ellen Wilkinson M.P.

One of the key speakers and leaders was local Labour M.P., Ellen Wilkinson. Known also as '**Red Ellen**', she was a former member of the Communist Party. She walked most of the way with the men, except when she attended the Labour Party conference in Edinburgh where she presented the men's case. She also attacked the National Executive of the Labour Party and the National Council of Labour which had failed to support the March. So also did the Trades Union Congress (TUC) which feared the March would be infiltrated by Communists.

SOURCE 9 – WELCOME AT HARROGATE

'Harrogate welcomed the Jarrow marchers today as cheerfully as if they were a relief column raising a siege. The music of the mouth-organ band might have been that of the bagpipes so surely did it bring the people flocking, and when the two hundred reached the Concert Rooms there were hundreds of folk drawn up on the slopes around to cheer them. The police were in attendance and there was a big banner raised saying, "Harrogate workers welcome the Jarrow marchers". At the Drill Hall, the headquarters for the night, the crowd was denser... A meeting is to be held at the Winter Gardens with Miss Ellen Wilkinson as one of the speakers. At every stopping-place there is such a meeting so that the world should know of Jarrow.'

With the Jarrow marchers in the *Manchester Guardian*, 13 October 1936

> How did Harrowgate welcome the Jarrow marchers?

SOURCE 10 – SPEECHES ON THE MARCH

'There were four main speakers. Alderman Thompson (Mayor) spoke about Jarrow's plight in general. "First we lost the Steelworks and 3,000 men lost their jobs. Then we lost our shipyard and another 5,000 were out of work." Councillor David Riley developed the economic theme. Poor towns like Jarrow had to subsidise their own poverty because a higher rate (local tax) had to be levied to cover substantial unemployment benefits that were being paid out. The third speaker, Councillor Paddy Scullion, dealt with the impact of unemployment on the health of the community. Finally, Ellen Wilkinson, the town's Member of Parliament, spoke. She concentrated her attack on the complacency – or cruelty – of the Government and the inertia of its leaders.'

D. Dougan, Jarrow March, 1936

> List the main points made by the speakers.

Wilkinson also replied to the local Bishop of Durham, Dr Henson, who criticised the marchers' 'revolutionary policy' and said they used 'the method of organised mob pressure'. She responded by saying, 'All legal methods in and out of Parliament have been tried... For the Bishop of Durham to stigmatise as "revolutionary" the quiet exercise of our constitutional right to offer a petition to Parliament is dangerous in these days.'

Government View

While the March was in progress, the Government made its views known about the Jarrow March (and others that were in progress at the same time). 'The British Cabinet has chosen the same moment to announce these marches on London are "altogether undesirable"... The country is governed by a parliamentary system which allows every area to put forward its grievances through its elected members, and "processions to London cannot claim to have any constitutional influence on policy".' (*The Irish Times*, 16 October 1936). The men rejected these views and continued their march.

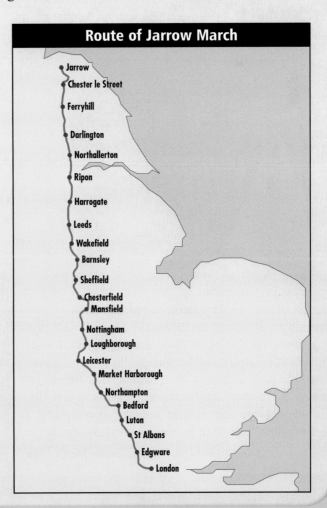

Route of Jarrow March

- Jarrow
- Chester le Street
- Ferryhill
- Darlington
- Northallerton
- Ripon
- Harrogate
- Leeds
- Wakefield
- Barnsley
- Sheffield
- Chesterfield
- Mansfield
- Nottingham
- Loughborough
- Leicester
- Market Harborough
- Northampton
- Bedford
- Luton
- St Albans
- Edgware
- London

London and Home

After twenty-three days marching and two weekend rests, they reached London on Saturday, 31 October. They were led into the city by Ellen Wilkinson, by Jarrow's Mayor, eleven councillors and a Labrador mascot dog.

But their crusade made **little immediate impact** on those in power. The marchers held a demonstration in Hyde Park on 1 November but there were only 3,000 to 5,000 in attendance, compared to 250,000 some days later for a National Hunger March.

Their M.P., Ellen Wilkinson, presented the Jarrow petition to Parliament on 4 November but the Prime Minister, Stanley Baldwin, refused to meet a delegation of marchers. (See Source 13 – Petition to Parliament).

The men were disappointed with the whole process: 'We got turned down. We got a cup of tea, they gave us a cup of tea. When we got turned down in the House of Commons, that was it… You knew you were finished.'

The marchers returned to Jarrow by train. They were welcomed by cheering and shouting crowds; *'Never before in the history of the town has there been such an exhibition of mass enthusiasm,'* reported the *North Mail*.

The next day they got a shock when the Unemployment Assistance Board reduced their unemployment benefit by between four and 11 shillings a week – because they had not been available for work.

SOURCE 11

Jarrow marchers playing the harmonica.

> How did playing the harmonica help the marchers?

SOURCE 12 – OPPOSITION TO THE MARCH

'... the Labour Party Conference in Edinburgh rebuked Ellen Wilkinson for organising the march, on the grounds that hunger marches were associated with Communist organisations, such as the NUWM, and their use might lead to disorder ...'

Stevenson and Cook, *The Slump. Society and Politics during the Depression*

> Why did the Labour Party not help the Jarrow marchers?

SOURCE 13 – PETITION TO PARLIAMENT

'The presentation of petitions was followed by a question from Ellen Wilkinson to the Prime Minister, Mr. Stanley Baldwin, asking how many resolutions he had received since 1 July regarding the position of Jarrow. He replied that he had received 66 resolutions, eight letters, one telegram and five postcards. And that was that… It seemed such a let-down… They [the men] had expected something more dramatic, a debate, a discussion, a statement, but they were left with – nothing.'

D. Dougan, Jarrow March 1936

> Why was the petition to Parliament 'such a let-down'?

? CASE STUDY QUESTIONS

1. How many people took part in the march?
2. What happened each day?
3. What happened at the end of the march each day?
4. What happened when the marchers got to London?

WHAT CAN YOU TELL ABOUT THE SOURCES?

WHAT INFORMATION CA YOU GET FROM THE SOURCE?

| Analysing Documents: Cartoons | What is the purpose of the cartoon? | Who is the intended audience? | Whose viewpoint does it represent? | What stereotypes can you identify in this cartoon? | What techniques or devices does the artist use? Caricature? Symbolism? Ridicule? | Is the cartoon a primary or a secondary source? | Explain your answer in each case. |

- Describe the action that is taking place.
- What does 'EUROPE' represent in the cartoon?
- How are the marchers represented?
- What is its message? Is it effective?
- What groups would agree/disagree with the cartoon's message? Why?
- Explain your answer in each case.

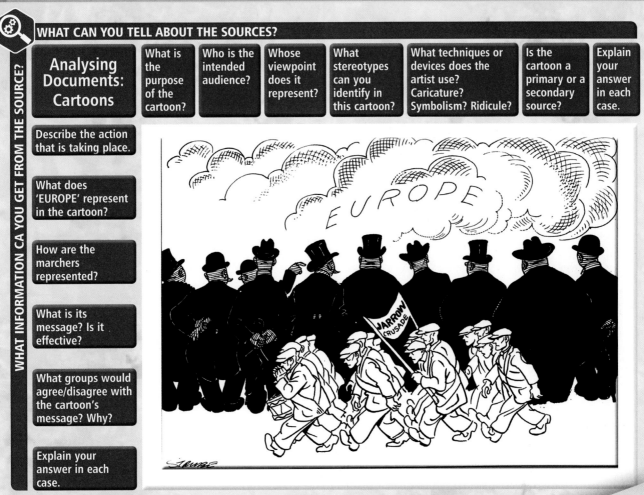

'They marched right back again / They were not asked the reason why / They didn't scream and ...' Artist: Sidney 'George' Strube, Published: *Daily Express*, 04 Nov 1936.

Assessment

The Jarrow March or Crusade achieved its **first aim** of presenting a petition to Parliament. In contrast to other similar marches, it didn't alienate the general public. Instead it achieved a certain fame through its organised and orderly manner. Indeed, in recent decades the symbolism of the Jarrow Crusade has been used for propaganda purposes, often by those who were opposed to it at the time, such as the Labour Party and the TUC.

Jarrow Council proposed a bill which would allow the council to create new industries. Even though the bill eventually became law in 1939, it did little to help the town's unemployment problems.

The March failed in its **main aim** of getting the government to provide jobs for the area. Jarrow's economy improved in the next few years but this had little to do with the crusade. Instead private industry, partly driven by rearmament as the Second World War approached, gradually filled the gap for the unemployed of Jarrow.

In 1938, a ship-breaking yard and engineering works were set up, and a year later a steelworks. There was also a tube factory established in part of the old Palmer's site which produced casings for shells and bullets. The approach of the Second World War also gave a boost to shipbuilding in other areas along the Tyne.

SOURCE 14 – ARRIVAL OF THE JARROW MARCHERS IN LONDON

The Arrival of the Jarrow Marchers in London, Viewed from an Interior, by Thomas Cantrell Dugdale

What is the painting saying about the Jarrow March?

 CASE STUDY QUESTION

Was the march a success?

 EXAM QUESTIONS

1. What were the causes and consequences of the Jarrow March, October 1936?
2. Why did the Jarrow March (October 1936) take place and what did it achieve?
3. How did the Jarrow March reflect the social and economic problems of industrial England in the 1930s?

However, the Jarrow Crusade had an **impact** beyond the confines of the town. Along with the other hunger marches, it sparked the conscience of the middle classes. The march, more than any of the other marches, symbolised the **despair** of unemployed men and depressed areas. As the (London) *Times* said, 'The Jarrow march is, indeed, a symbol of the feeling of neglect and unmerited poverty and dependence which pervades the distressed areas.' (Quoted in *The Irish Times*, 27 October 1936)

The effect of mass unemployment in the 1920s and 1930s contributed to the setting up of the **Welfare State** in Britain after the Second World War. *'The legacy of bitterness and suffering caused by mass unemployment helped spur the creation of the Welfare State.'* (Stevenson and Cook, *The Slump. Society and Politics during the Depression*)

During the Second World War, the British government published the **Beveridge Report**. The report attacked the five 'giant evils' of illness, ignorance, disease, squalor and want. It recommended a minimum standard of living *'below which no one should be allowed to fall'*. The report became the basis of the Welfare State, which introduced reforms in social welfare, health and education to provide for people *'from the cradle to the grave'*.

Differences between Jarrow and the prosperous South-east of England	
Jarrow	**London and the South-east of England**
Older industries	Newer industries
Unemployment in 1934: 67.8%	Unemployment in 1936: 5%
Long-term unemployed: 26%	Long-term unemployed: 6%
Depressed area	(National unemployment 23%)
Falling living standards	Many new houses/Growth of suburbs
Poverty	Leisure time in cinema, dancehalls and sports stadiums
Sickness	
Infant mortality rate: 114 per 1,000	Infant mortality rate: 51 per 1,000

WEB RESOURCES

Jarrow March – http://en.wikipedia.org/wiki/Jarrow_March

Jarrow – http://www.bbc.co.uk/history/british/britain_wwone/jarrow_01.shtml

With the Jarrow marchers – http://century.guardian.co.uk/1930-1939/Story/0,6051,127027,00.html

The Depression of the 1930s – http://www.bbc.co.uk/schools/gcsebitesize/history/mwh/britain/depressionrev1.shtml

Ellen Wilkinson – http://en.wikipedia.org/wiki/Ellen_Wilkinson

Ellen Wilkinson – http://spartacus-educational.com/TUwilkinson.htm

DOCUMENTS-BASED QUESTION

Case study to which the documents relate:

The Jarrow March, October 1936
Study the documents and answer the questions below.

DOCUMENT A

In this edited extract Ellen Wilkinson, M.P. for Jarrow, who took part in the Jarrow March, October 1936, writes of a typical day on the march.

One day's tramp was much like another. The one thing that mattered was the weather. The men were up at 6.30 a.m., the cooks having got up earlier to prepare the breakfast. They had all slept together on the bare boards of a school or drill hall or, if lucky, on straw-filled mattresses. When men sleep in their clothes, it is difficult to keep spruce; but they manage it. Daily shaves were the order. Parade was at 8.45 a.m., with everything packed for the road. I joined them then, having taken whatever hospitality was offered the night before, usually in the home of the secretary of the local Labour party.

Source: Ellen Wilkinson, *The Town That Was Murdered: the Life Story of Jarrow*
(London: Victor Gollancz, 1939)

DOCUMENT B

This edited extract discusses conditions leading to the Jarrow March in October 1936, together with the government response.

Since the mid-nineteenth century shipbuilding in Jarrow had provided work for about 10,000 men. As a result of the Depression, orders for ships came to an end and in 1934 the National Shipbuilding Security Ltd closed down the shipyard. This left 67.8% of the workforce unemployed. In October 1936, the Labour M.P. for Jarrow, Ellen Wilkinson, with some others, organised the Jarrow March. Two hundred of the town's unemployed walked to London, a distance of 291 miles, to present a petition to parliament, hoping that the government would do something to improve the situation in Jarrow. As the marchers neared London, they noticed the prosperity of the area compared with the town of Jarrow. The march was widely reported, particularly in the Daily Herald newspaper, and gained a good deal of public sympathy. However, the marchers drew a very poor response from the government. They were informed that they should return to Jarrow and seek work for themselves.

Source: David Taylor, *Mastering Economic and Social History* (London: Macmillan Press, Ltd., 1988)

1. (i) From Document A, where did the men sleep if they were lucky?
   (ii) According to Document A, what took place at 8.45 a.m.?
   (iii) From Document B, what was the level of unemployment in Jarrow in 1934?
   (iv) From Document B, what did the marchers notice as they came near to London?
   (v) According to Document B, how did the government respond to the Jarrow marchers?

2. (i) Do both documents agree that Ellen Wilkinson took part in the march to London? Refer to both documents in your answer.
   (ii) Which document, A or B, deals with the reasons for the Jarrow March? Explain your answer, referring to both documents.

3. (i) From Document A, did Ellen Wilkinson share the workers' accommodation? Give a reason for your answer.
   (ii) Why is Document B a secondary source?

4. Why were there many social and economic problems in Britain during the 1930s?

Case study to which the documents relate:

The Jarrow March, October 1936

Study the documents and answer the questions below.

DOCUMENT A

J.B. Priestley was an English writer who travelled around England in 1933. The following is an edited extract from his book, *English Journey* (London, 1934).

Jarrow is dead. As a real town, it can never have been alive. Even at its best, when everybody was working, it must obviously have been a mean little conglomeration of narrow monotonous streets of stunted and ugly houses, a barracks cynically put together so that shipbuilding workers could get some food and sleep between shifts. Now Jarrow is a derelict town. There is no escape from its prevailing misery, for it is entirely a working class town.

Why has nothing been done about decaying towns and their workless people? I know that doles have been given out, means tests applied, training places opened, socks and shirts and old books distributed by the Personal Service League and the like; but I am not thinking of feeble gestures of that kind. I mean something constructive and creative.

Why has there been no plan for these areas, these people? The dole is part of no plan. The Labour Exchanges stink of defeated humanity. The whole thing is unworthy of a great country that has given the world some nobly creative ideas. We ought to be ashamed of ourselves.

DOCUMENT B

Ellen Wilkinson, M.P. for Jarrow, helped lead the Jarrow March in 1936. The following is an edited extract from her book, *The Town That Was Murdered* (London, 1939).

The poverty of Jarrow is not an accident, a temporary difficulty, a personal fault. It is the permanent state in which the vast majority of the citizens of any capitalist country have to live. This is the basic fact of the class struggle which not all the well meant efforts of the Personal Service League can gloss over. Class antagonism cuts as deeply to the roots of capitalist society as it ever did.

Men are regarded as mere instruments of production, their labour a commodity to be bought and sold. In capitalist society, vast changes can be made which sweep away the livelihood of a whole town overnight, in the interest of some powerful group, who need take no account of the social consequences of their decisions. Jarrow's plight is not a local problem. It is the symptom of a national evil.

It is time that the workers took control of this country. It is time that they planned it, organised it, and developed it so that all might enjoy the wealth which we can produce. In the interest of this land we love, that is the next job which must be done.

1. (i) What workers are mentioned in document A?
   (ii) How is the misery of life in Jarrow shown in document A?
   (iii) According to document B, what is the permanent state of the majority of citizens in a capitalist country?
   (iv) What is the next job to be done, according to document B?

2. (i) Do both documents mention social and economic problems of the inter war years? Give reasons for your answer, referring to both documents.
   (ii) Do the documents agree that efforts to resolve the problems have been ineffective? Give reasons for your answer, referring to both documents.

3. (i) Does the writer of document A propose a solution to the problems to which he refers? Give reasons for your answer, referring to the document.
   (ii) What are the strengths of document B as a historical source? Support your answer by reference to the document.

4. What were the aims of the Jarrow March and to what extent were they achieved? (2017)

In this section, you should understand:
- The role of radio and cinema in the inter-war years and during the Second World War.
- The role of Bing Crosby.
- The role of Charlie Chaplin.

In the 1920s the American economy boomed. It was a time of mass-production and new advertising. This prosperity formed the basis of the **Roaring Twenties** – a time of fun, music and good times. Very quickly, some of these **American influences** spread to Britain and to continental countries, such as France and Germany.

Popular culture, especially in music, dance and cinema, was heavily influenced by American trends. America dominated the music and cinema industries; it shared a common language with Britain which helped to spread its culture; silent cinema and music were able to cross national boundaries; American soldiers based in Europe during the First World War brought jazz music; and as a wealthier country, America used modern technology to initiate new developments in radio and cinema.

The motor car had a great influence on society in the 1920s and 1930s. Even before Henry Ford introduced mass-production techniques in his factory, the car was popular – it represented freedom and adventure. It influenced people's way of life and the shape of towns.

Popular Culture

Popular culture of the 1920s and 1930s was associated with radio, cinema, jazz and sport. In these decades, the entertainment industry expanded rapidly:
- the working week shortened,
- there were more women working,
- average wages rose so spending power increased,
- holidays with pay became more common by the late 1930s.

Much of the extra time and money was spent on entertainment and leisure. This was helped by the influence of the **motor car** which gave greater mobility. **Mass-production** reduced the cost of consumer goods and loans made them easier to buy. The **Great Depression** only slowed down the spread of these trends but it did not stop them.

The popular culture of the 1920s and 1930s was a **young culture**. It reflected a **difference** in generations between young and old, sons and daughters and their parents. It was also very much a **city culture**, as rural areas in both Britain and the continent remained conservative.

Popular Culture: This term refers to activities, styles and aspects of the way of life which are enjoyed by ordinary people or the majority of people. This can include music, dance, clothes, advertising, sport and entertainment generally.

251

? QUESTIONS

1. What were the Roaring Twenties?
2. What was popular culture?
3. Why did the entertainment industry expand at this time?

Popular culture was spread rapidly in Europe by the two new forms of **mass-entertainment**: radio and cinema. Cinema had begun before the First World War (1914–18) but radio was almost entirely new.

Radio

Radio in Britain

In Britain radio was first broadcast in 1922, and four years later the **British Broadcasting Corporation** (BBC) got a **monopoly** (control) of radio broadcasting. In this way Britain differed from America where competitive commercial radio was more widespread.

As well as being a source of entertainment and news for all the family in the 1920s and 1930s, the radio became part of the furniture.

By the 1930s, the quality of radio reception had improved, the cost of radios had fallen rapidly and the radio unit was often like a piece of furniture in the living room. Radio licences increased from 36,000 in 1922 to 8 million by the late 1930s. By 1939 34 million Britons or 75 per cent of British families were able to receive radio broadcasts. Those who were excluded were largely the poorer people who could not afford the licence fee or the radio.

The BBC wanted to maintain **high standards** and set a good moral tone in its broadcasting. Its programmes were mainly news, information and entertainment. It believed in broadening the interests of the public, and very quickly it developed educational programmes.

It also responded to listener surveys which it carried out in the 1930s. These showed that variety shows, light orchestral music, dance bands and sport were its most popular programmes.

During the 1930s the BBC faced competition from stations such as Radio Luxembourg which broadcast more popular music into the country. When the **Second World War** broke out, Radio Luxembourg was taken over by Nazi Germany in 1940, and the BBC regained its monopoly. It broadcast programmes such as 'Music While You Work', over factory loudspeaker systems aimed at boosting morale and keeping industry going.

? QUESTIONS

1. What were the two new forms of mass entertainment?
2. Who controlled radio in Britain?
3. How popular was radio in Britain?

Radio in Weimar and Nazi Germany

Radio spread rapidly in **Weimar Germany**. The stations were in the hands of private companies but they were controlled by the Post Office and a Broadcasting Commissioner. The number of listeners rose from 10,000 in 1924 to over 4 million by 1932, second only to Britain in Europe.

Programmes were non-political in content, and geared towards entertainment and education. The Weimar government failed to use the radio to support democratic processes and the Weimar Republic. This was in contrast to the later use of radio by Goebbels.

Radio use continued to increase rapidly under **Nazi Germany**. By 1942, 70 per cent of households had a radio, a higher proportion in the cities and towns than in the countryside. This was influenced by the sale of the cheaper **People's Radio**. The Nazis also used street loudspeakers and wireless sets in restaurants to reach a wider audience. Nazi radio wardens 'encouraged' people in their apartment blocks to listen to Party-organised broadcasts. Hitler used the radio frequently to reach a mass audience – in his first year in power, for example, he broadcast fifty times to the German people. (See 'The Totalitarian State – Propaganda and Terror', pp. 208–13)

The Nazis changed the focus of radio content by moving away from serious classical music to light music to attract listeners. Music occupied 70 per cent of broadcasting time by 1937, most of that was light music. This was largely light operas along with folk music and military marches which continued to be the focus during the Second World War. The Nazis' control of radio, their emphasis on light classical music and their limiting of non-Aryan composers meant that foreign jazz and swing was largely excluded from German radio. (See 'All That Jazz', p. 258)

The Influence of Radio

- Radio was a new form of entertainment, cheaper than theatre and cinema. It boosted popular music, and the music industry soon realised that radio helped the sales of records. Jazz, swing and general dance band music were suited to the light entertainment needs of the radio. The radio popularised the names of **American artists** such as **Bing Crosby**, Benny Goodman and Glenn Miller.

- It helped to form a more **unified national culture** in Britain and other countries in Europe, already being fashioned by the national press, the railways and mass education.

- It also kept people **better informed** – and more quickly informed – with its news programmes. In Britain, the death of George V, Edward VIII's abdication message and Chamberlain's news of war with Germany were first carried over the airwaves.

- Governments and politicians realised very quickly the **propaganda value** of radio. The British government gave the BBC a radio monopoly in Britain and tried to discourage people from listening to other radio stations such as Radio Luxembourg which broadcast into Britain.

- Stanley **Baldwin**, Prime Minister of Britain on three occasions between the wars, was the first prime minister to master radio. During the General Strike in 1926, for example, he made personal radio broadcasts to the country in which he appealed to the people to trust him.

  "I am a man of peace. I am longing, and looking and praying for peace. But I will not surrender the safety and the security of the British Constitution… Cannot you trust me to ensure a square deal and to ensure even justice between man and man?"

  These broadcasts contributed to the government's victory over the trade unions. (see 'The General Strike, 1926', pp. 234–35)

- In Weimar Germany, the government refrained from using the radio to support the Republic and its democratic ideals in the 1920s. In contrast, in Nazi Germany, Goebbels realised the **propaganda** value of radio in ensuring Nazi control. Radio broadcasts brought into people's homes the Nazi ideals of national pride, patriotism,

QUESTION

List four major influences of radio and explain them. Provide evidence from both Britain and Germany.

pride in Hitler and in the Aryan race. (See above and 'The Totalitarian State – Propaganda and Terror', pp. 208–13)

- Newspapers were affected by the arrival of this competitor for news. Now the newspapers had to become more sensational and scandalous to compete with radio news.

Cinema

Sound movies arrived in 1927 when Al Jolson starred in The Jazz Singer.

Even though cinema had been popular before the 1920s, it expanded enormously in that decade and in the 1930s. The huge expansion centred on **Hollywood**, a suburb of Los Angeles, with its all-year-round sunshine. Thousands of silent, black and white movies were produced to satisfy the huge demand for them. Technological change brought about the advent of sound films – the 'talkies' – in 1927, when **Al Jolson** featured in *The Jazz Singer* which gave an added boost to cinema. Then Disney produced the first animated film, *Steamboat Willie*, in 1929, introducing **Mickey Mouse**. In the 1930s, colour films also became available. British audiences depended on mostly American films because the First World War led to a fall-off in the production of British films. It was not until the 1930s that British films made an impact again, helped by the **Cinematograph Films Act of 1927** which forced cinemas to show a quota of British-produced films.

The Popularity of Cinema in Europe

Cinema was as popular in Europe as it was in America. In **Britain**, the small cinemas – or **flea-pits**, as they were called – of the pre-First World War era expanded rapidly in the 1920s and 1930s. A huge number of **super-cinemas** which could hold up to 3,000 people were built in the main cities, particularly London. They had plush seats with space for an orchestra, or an organist, up front to accompany the film. But the introduction of sound soon made these redundant.

Going to the **pictures**, or the **flicks** as they were called in Britain, was the most popular form of entertainment in the 1930s. By 1939, 50 per cent of the people went to the cinema once a week, and 25 per cent went twice a week. Not surprisingly, almost one billion cinema admission tickets were bought each year by the end of the 1930s and cinema was by far the **most popular** paid-for leisure activity.

Rudolf Valentino, Italian-born star of American movies, who was idolised by women. He was widely mourned after his early death in 1926.

It was entertainment for **all classes**, even the unemployed. As George Orwell wrote in *The Road to Wigan Pier*: *'Even people on the verge of starvation will readily pay two pence to get out of the ghastly cold of a winter afternoon.'* For others it was a form of escapism – *'a private day-dream of yourself as Clark Gable or Greta Garbo.'*

The most popular **genres** (categories) were adventure, comedy, thrillers and costume dramas, along with films with an imperial theme. British actors such as **George Formby** and **Gracie Fields** were popular with the audiences as well as American actors such as **Clark Gable**, **Fred Astaire** and **Ginger Rodgers**.

Cinema in Germany

In **Weimar Germany**, cinema too became popular in the 1920s. The number of cinemas increased from about 2,300 in 1918 to over 5,000 in 1930, with Germany having the most cinemas of any country in Europe. The film industry produced some famous movies such as *The Cabinet of Dr Caligari* (1920). But American influences became more pronounced during the decade with **Charlie Chaplin's** films such as *The Gold Rush* (1926) becoming very popular. Nevertheless, Germany still produced outstanding films such as its first talking picture, *The Blue Angel*, with Marlene Dietrich who was later to achieve fame in Hollywood.

Cinema in Nazi Germany

Cinema attendance continued to increase during the Nazi years, rising from 250 million in 1933 to one billion by 1942 during the Second World War. But German cinema suffered when some important directors and actors fled the country to Hollywood with the arrival of the Nazis.

CHARLIE CHAPLIN
(CHARLOT)

KEY PERSONALITY: CHARLIE CHAPLIN

Charlie Chaplin was the greatest actor of the silent movies, but his talent went well beyond that.

He was born in **London** of mixed French-Irish parents. He had a difficult early life, experiencing poverty and the workhouse. After playing music halls and theatres in England, he was signed up for a **film career** in America. He began working in films in 1914 and was already a well-established star by the beginning of the 1920s. When he visited Europe at that time, he was hailed as a hero and swamped by huge crowds.

By now he had developed the style which made him famous – **the tramp**. This was the *'little fellow'*, as he said himself, with the tight jacket, the baggy trousers, the over-sized shoes, the bowler hat and the cane. He combined **humour** with **sadness**; he was the underdog who appealed to everybody.

He had great success with *The Kid*, *The Gold Rush* and *The Circus* in the 1920s. He wrote, directed, produced and acted in these films, as he did with later ones. In *The Kid* it was said, *'There are almost as many tears as laughs in this movie.'* *The Circus* resulted in Chaplin being presented with a special award at the first Academy Awards. But *The Gold Rush* is regarded as his greatest film.

When the silent era ended, Chaplin refused to go along with **sound**; instead, he maintained the tramp as his main character in *City Lights* (1931) and *Modern Times* (1936). In *City Lights*, Chaplin portrayed the tramp who was in love with a blind flower girl and wanted to raise money for her eye operation. *Modern Times* – 'a satire on certain phases of our industrial life', he said – was a reflection on the effects of the Great Depression and the effects of capitalism. Both movies showed his sympathy for workers and the poor against the advance of technology. *The Great Dictator* (1940) was his **first talking** film. In it he warned against the rise of Hitler's power in Europe. His political comments here, which seemed to be urging America to join the war, led to criticism.

More serious was his support for **Russian War Relief**. Given the suspicion of Communism in America, it was indeed likely that he would be accused of being a **Communist**. His lifestyle of three marriages and three divorce cases was also criticised. In 1947, he was called before Senator Joe McCarthy's **Senate Committee on Un-American Activities**. He was able to show he wasn't a Communist. But a number of years later, while on a trip to Europe with his family, he was informed that his re-entry permit had been cancelled.

Chaplin spent the remainder of his life in Switzerland. In 1972, he returned to America once more when he was awarded a special honorary Oscar *'for the incalculable effect he has had in making motion pictures* **the art form of this century'**.

Develop notes on the role of Charlie Chaplin in cinema, 1920–45.

The Nazis ensured that the public were given a mixture of love stories, comedies, historical adventures, military and crime thrillers. But they often included a political or social message, since Hitler and Goebbels were fully aware of the propaganda value of film. Some were definitely political such as the anti-British film on the Boer War, *Ohm Kruger*, or the anti-Semitic, *Jud Suss*. Very often the leadership role of Hitler was highlighted indirectly, or directly in **Leni Riefenstahl's** *Triumph of the Will* on the Nuremberg Rally.

During the **Second World War**, the most successful films highlighted background themes on the war such as the suffering of women separated from their husbands during the war, rather than war action. This was left to the newsreels. (See 'The Totalitarian State – Propaganda and Terror', pp. 208–13)

Develop notes on the role of Bing Crosby in radio and cinema, 1920–45.

KEY PERSONALITY: BING CROSBY

Bing Crosby was born in Washington State, America, of Irish descent. He went to university but wanted to be a **singer**, so he headed for California in the mid-1920s. He quickly began a remarkable career, which gave him outstanding success as a singer, a recording artist, a radio and film star; and later, a TV star, to a lesser extent. Bing Crosby began his **recording career** in 1926 and became the most successful recording artist of the twentieth century. His relaxed singing style – his **crooning** – along with his wide range of songs from romantic ballads to Jazz classics appealed to the people. His hits in the 1930s included *Brother Can You Spare a Dime, Red Sails in the Sunset* and *Alexander's Ragtime Band*. But his biggest hit came in 1942 with *White Christmas*, the most successful single of all time.

He first appeared on **radio** in 1928 and very quickly realised how radio could promote his records. From 1931 he had his own show, singing live on CBS and NBC with sponsored radio programmes.

His **film career** was even more successful. For 15 years in the 1930s and 1940s he was a **top, box office attraction**. He usually played light-hearted comedy or musical roles. But he won an **Oscar for Best Actor** in 1944 for his portrayal of Father O'Malley in *Going My Way*. It was during the 1940s that he began the **Road** movies with Bob Hope – the first was *Road to Singapore* – and the movie format lasted into the 1960s.

During the **Second World War** he contributed to the **war effort** by entertaining at military camps and promoting government war bonds. He also took his radio show to Europe and broadcast from England, France and Germany. At the end of the war a magazine poll voted him the individual who had done most for soldiers' morale.

When Bing Crosby died in 1977, President Carter of America paid a **fitting tribute** to him. He described him as '*a gentleman, proof that a great talent can be a good man despite the pressures of show business.'* He was '*successful, yet modest; casual but elegant.'*

The Influence of Cinema

- Cinema was the **most popular** form of entertainment in the 1920s and 1930s. It added a new world of **romance** and **adventure**.
- The **stars** of the new cinema influenced the **lifestyle** of the young in particular. The films influenced fashions, mannerisms, the perfume women wore, the hairstyle of men and, even sometimes, slang. One Welshman complained that the nice local accents were broken by 'such words and phrases as *"Attaboy!"*, *"Oh, Yeah"* and *"Sez you".'*
- In this way, cinema spread **American culture** to Britain and the continent of Europe.
- Cinema used **sex** to sell itself. It contributed to the **gap** between the younger and older generations. In the years before the First World War, sex was not mentioned. But in

But his involvement in the Bayonne Affair – where he floated a loan of 200 million francs based on the false evaluation of the municipal pawnshop in Bayonne – led to his end. After the scheme collapsed in December 1933, he was wanted by the police. He went missing, but in January 1934 he shot himself.

Corruption

It was soon clear that Stavisky had many friends in high places. The right wing went on the attack. They said that Stavisky had been murdered to hide the names of his friends in the police, politics and business. The right-wing groups – particularly those known as the **Leagues** – used the Affair to blame parliamentary democracy. They were supported by the right-wing press who worked to undermine confidence in the Third Republic. During January 1934, there was nightly rioting in Paris against the government, often ringing with the shouts of *'Down with the Robbers'* or *'Hang the Deputies'*.

The Prime Minister, **Chautemps**, attempted a cover-up. He refused to hold an inquiry, but he had to resign when it became known that the public prosecutor was his brother-in-law – the man responsible for the 19 postponements of Stavisky's earlier trial. It now seemed that the governments of the Third Republic were not just incompetent because they could not solve the economic crisis, but they were also corrupt.

Riots

When the new Prime Minister, **Edouard Daladier**, sacked the Prefect of Police, this resulted in a major street demonstration. On that day, 6 February 1934, a huge rally close to the Chamber of Deputies turned into rioting and a battle with the police. The rally and riots were largely organised and led by the Leagues, in particular **Action Française** and **Solidarité Française**. The strongest of the Leagues, **Croix de Feu**, was involved in the protest but did not participate as actively in the rioting. Fourteen rioters were killed and 236 wounded, and one policeman was killed and about 100 injured in six hours of rioting. The rioting led to the immediate **resignation of Daladier**. But it also resulted in a counter-strike a few days later organised by the left wing and trade unions to show that workers were prepared to defend the Republic.

Attempted Coup?

The **riots of 6 February** shocked republican politicians who saw this as an attempt to overthrow the Republic. A later Investigating Committee concluded, *'the Sixth of February was a revolt against Parliament, an attempt against the regime.'* However, the left wing greatly exaggerated the possibility of a Fascist takeover of France, similar to Italy and Germany:

● The groups were **not co-ordinated** and they **lacked a leader** like Hitler or Mussolini.

Stavisky (left) at his trial for corruption (top) and anti-Stavisky demonstrators in riots in Paris (below).

267

? QUESTIONS

1. How was France affected by the Great Depression?
2. How did the French government deal with the Great Depression?
3. What were the Right-wing Leagues and how serious a threat were they?
4. What happened in the Stavisky Affair?

- Many of the groups had **small membership**.
- Unemployment was not as severe in France.
- Parliamentary democracy had a stronger tradition.

But the riots reflected serious dissatisfaction with the Third Republic and its failure to solve the economic, social and political problems.

The Popular Front Government

One effect of the riots of February 1934 and the rise of the Leagues was the coming together of left-wing parties; **the Socialists**, **Communists** and the **Radical Party**, to form the **Popular Front**. The main motivation came from the Communists who were ordered by Moscow to change policy – the rise of Nazism in Germany, and the failure of socialists and Communists to combine to stop Hitler, forced a change in Communist thinking. Now they wanted to **co-operate with other parties** to resist the rise of Fascism.

On Bastille Day, 14 July 1935, almost 400,000 people marched together in Paris and were addressed by the leaders of the three parties. In early 1936 they published a programme for government:

- They wanted **economic and social reform** and the **abolition** of the Leagues.
- In foreign policy they favoured **collective security** and **the League of Nations**.
- Their **slogan** was *'Bread, Peace and Liberty'* and they attacked *'the two hundred families'* who represented organised wealth in France.

The Popular Front won the 1936 general election with a clear majority of seats over the right-wing parties. The Socialists became the largest party and the Socialist leader, **Léon Blum**, became Prime Minister.

Sit-in Strikes and the Matignon Agreement

The victory of the Popular Front raised the hopes of workers who expected the factories would be handed over to them. A spontaneous wave of **sit-in strikes** swept the country. As industry ground to a standstill, the new government was faced with its first serious problem. Blum called a conference of employers' representatives and the CGT (the trade union federation) in the **Hotel Matignon**, the official residence of the Prime Minister. Fear of widespread revolution forced the employers to make significant concessions in the **Matignon Agreement**:

- An **increase in wages** of about 12 per cent.
- The establishment of a **forty-hour working week** and **holidays with pay**.
- The **nationalisation** (government ownership) of the armaments industry and government control of the Bank of France.

For the moment both the workers and employers were pleased: the workers because they had made great gains and the employers because they had avoided a revolutionary situation.

Pause in Reforms

But economic problems continued. The government borrowed to pay for the cost of some of its proposals and the franc lost value in relation to other currencies. This forced the government to **devalue the franc**. Even though this reduced export prices, inflation and unemployment remained high in France and industrial production stayed well below the 1929 level. In March 1937, Blum called a **pause** in the programme of reforms of the Popular Front government.

Collapse of the Popular Front

Blum now proposed to use **decree laws** to bring in economic policies. But his proposals were turned down by the Senate and he resigned in June 1937. *'I have had enough,'* he said. *'Everything I attempted to do has been blocked.'* Further Popular Front governments, including another period with Blum as Prime Minister, failed to resolve France's difficulties. In April 1938, the Popular Front government finally collapsed and a conservative **Government of National Defence** headed by Edouard Daladier of the Radical Party replaced it.

Challenges facing
France, 1920–45 (1)
* Post-war recovery
* Political instability
* Financial crisis
* The Great Depression
* Industrial unrest
* The Right-wing Leagues
* The Stavisky Affair

Government of National Defence

The new government suspended the reforms of the Popular Front and brought in economic policies favoured by the business classes. The government allowed some industries to break the 40-hour week and they cut government spending. This led to conflict with the trade unions. However, the government had a clear victory over the **CGT** who organised a **one-day strike** for November 1938. The government, encouraged by the right-wing press, organised troops and police, and intimidated public sector workers who were forced not to join the strike. After the strike, workers were fired and disciplined and the CGT lost members once again. The left wing was weakened even more.

Problems Continue

By 1939, all the main problems that French society had suffered from in the inter-war years still remained.

Population: The loss of 1.3 million men in the First World War and the falling birth rate meant there was a shortage of labour and, by the end of the 1930s, soldiers. However, the use of migrant labour increased **social and political tensions**.

  Agriculture: Agriculture stayed inefficient. It was protected by a system of tariffs so that farm prices were higher than elsewhere.

  Industry: Industry also suffered from small-scale production. These small producers kept prices up and their large number prevented the implementation of social and economic reforms by the government. They were supported by richer financiers and industrialists.

  Summary: Overall, France was economically backward with a great deal of class conflict. The biggest section of society was comprised of small producers, traders and farmers. The governments of the Third French Republic followed policies which suited

QUESTIONS

1. Why was the Popular Front government formed?
2. What was their policy?
3. What caused sit-ins and strikes and how were they settled?
4. What other problems did France face in the 1930s?

EXAM QUESTION

How and why was France faced with political instability in the 1920s and 1930s?

their interests. They wanted low taxes and little social reform. This caused political instability which led to the many changes of government between 1920 and 1939. It also prevented the many improvements and reforms in French society which would have better prepared the country for the Second World War.

Foreign Policy

French Security and the Peace Treaties

At the Paris Peace Conference (1919) after the First World War, **Clemenceau**, the French Prime Minister, tried to ensure the **security** and **safety** of France by demanding harsh measures on Germany. (See the Treaty of Versailles p. 129) But Clemenceau failed in his demand that Germany should give up all land west of the Rhine River.

Helping with reconstruction in post-war France: subscribe to the National Loan.

Many French people were therefore concerned that the Treaty did not provide enough security for France – after all France had been invaded twice in 50 years by Germany. They had little confidence in the League of Nations. As well as this, American and British guarantees to help France in future wars against German aggression collapsed when the American Senate rejected the Treaty of Versailles. France felt betrayed.

Protecting France

French foreign policy was guided by **French fear** of a revived Germany. The French army was the largest in Europe and there was no threat from the much-reduced German army but this still did not provide security. The government tried to provide greater security by two principal methods: (i) isolating Germany, and (ii) enforcing the terms of the Treaty of Versailles.

Isolating Germany

To provide better security, France made a series of **military treaties** which attempted to encircle Germany. By isolating Germany, France hoped to keep it weak. Treaties with Belgium (1920) and Poland (1921) began the encirclement. These were followed in 1924 with an alliance with Czechoslovakia, which linked France to the **Little Entente** of Czechoslovakia, Yugoslavia and Romania.

French Occupation of the Ruhr

But also the French people wanted to enforce all the terms of the **Treaty of Versailles** on Germany. The question of **reparations** was the one which caused the most trouble during the 1920s.

Poincaré, a hard-line Prime Minister, believed firmly in the rightness of the French case. When Germany failed to pay some of the instalments due under reparations, Poincaré ordered a French army takeover of the **Ruhr**, the industrial heart of Germany (1923). The Ruhr occupation dragged on due to passive German resistance and French relations with Britain and America were embittered. In 1924, the Germans agreed to revised payments under the **Dawes Plan** and the French troops were withdrawn.

For many French people this was **not a satisfactory outcome**. In the first place, the occupation showed that France was not strong enough on its own to enforce the Treaty of Versailles. Secondly, the cost of sending in French troops resulted in increased taxation and the decline in the value of the franc. This contributed to the **defeat of Poincaré** and the **Bloc National** in the general election of 1924.

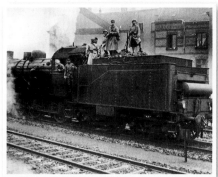

French occupation of the Ruhr in Germany: French gunboats arriving (top) and French troops on German trains (below).

QUESTIONS **?**

1. What was the foreign policy of the French government in the 1920s?
2. Why did France occupy the Ruhr?

Briand and French Foreign Policy

In spite of many changes of government between 1925 and 1932, French foreign policy during this time was largely in the hands of one man, **Aristide Briand**. He realised that it was not possible for France to get support for forcing Germany to adhere to the terms of the Treaty of Versailles. He also realised that he had to come to some agreement with Germany. He believed that by bringing Germany fully into the political and economic life of Europe, Germany would be so dependent on other European countries that she would not go to war with France again.

Briand was fortunate that the German Foreign Minister, **Gustav Stesemann**, also wanted European acceptance of Germany. In the **Locarno Pact** (1925), France and Germany, with British and Italian support, pledged to accept the borders established between them by the Treaty of Versailles. Germany was also invited to join the League of Nations. French people were delighted with the pact and Briand was given a hero's welcome when he returned to Paris.

QUESTIONS **?**

1. What were the aims of French foreign policy under Briand?
2. How successful was Briand in foreign policy?
3. Why did the French build the Maginot Line?

The Locarno Pact was followed by the **Kellogg-Briand Pact** (1928). Briand and Kellogg, the US Secretary of State, agreed, along with 63 other countries, including Germany, to renounce the use of war as an instrument of national policy.

After these successes, Briand continued to work for better relations with Germany. The **Young Plan** (1929) further eased German reparation payments. In 1930, five years ahead of schedule, French troops left the Rhineland.

Rows of posts in front of the Maginot Line, the French defensive line facing Germany.

Maginot Line

However, in spite of these improvements in Franco-German relations, the French still felt insecure. In 1929, they began the building of the **Maginot Line** – a huge line of fortifications along the German border. When it was completed in 1934, it gave the

French a greater sense of security. But by that time also the **Great Depression** was affecting France, German reparations were cancelled in 1932, and Hitler became German Chancellor in January 1933.

Foreign Policy in the 1930s

French foreign policy in the 1930s was still haunted by a feeling of insecurity. Their fear of Germany dictated their agreements and alliances. Initially, however, the arrival of Hitler to power in 1933 did not create any greater insecurity in France. Few French people realised how much Hitler hated France or the nature of Hitler's expansionist policies. Instead they believed his assurances of peace and his support for the Locarno Pact. Indeed, in 1934 France entered a **Four Power Pact** along with Britain, Italy and Germany to guarantee peace.

Soon after the Four Power Pact a new foreign minister, **Louis Barthou**, changed the emphasis of French foreign policy. He maintained a firm line towards Germany and he believed that only an efficient **system of alliances** could protect France. He reinforced French ties with Poland and the Little Entente (Czechoslovakia, Hungary and Romania). He also began talks with Italy and the Soviet Union.

France and Italy

When Barthou was assassinated in 1934, his successor, Pierre Laval was more interested in an agreement with **Mussolini** in Italy. In 1935 he signed the **Rome Agreements** which ended differences between the two countries. Laval next agreed to the **Stresa Front** (1935) which brought Britain, Italy and France together. Their fear of Germany led them to reaffirm the Locarno Pact to contain Germany and guarantee the borders. France had maintained the isolation of Germany – but very soon French foreign policy was in ruins.

Turning Points in French Foreign Policy

The Invasion of Ethiopia: Mussolini's invasion of **Ethiopia** (Abyssinia) in late 1935 had a major impact on French foreign policy. At the League of Nations, Laval had to agree with sanctions on Italy but he opposed British plans to include oil in the sanctions. He then privately persuaded the British Foreign Secretary, **Sir Samuel Hoare**, to agree that Ethiopia should be given to Italy. When news of the **Hoare-Laval Plan** leaked out it led to Hoare's resignation and, soon after, to Laval's also. The Stresa Front collapsed and the League of Nations was defeated. As one historian concluded, *'France was left alone to defend herself as best she could against a restless, aggressive Germany which very soon ... would be stronger on land and in the air than she.'*

Hitler breaks Versailles: Hitler's breaches of the Treaty of Versailles clearly showed the **weakness** of French foreign policy. The French failed to act as Hitler introduced conscription, created the Luftwaffe and expanded the navy in agreement with the British. But the **greatest defeat** for French foreign policy occurred when Hitler took advantage of a rift between France and Britain, and a weak government in France, to **remilitarise the Rhineland** in 1936.

The French refused to act against Hitler on their own, partly because of a **defeatist attitude** in the army and in the right-wing press. The Minister of War expressed this view at a cabinet meeting, *'The Foreign Minister talks of entering the Rhineland... There are risks in this. The present state of the French army does not allow us to run risks.'* Instead they looked to Britain for support. But the British were following a **policy of appeasement** and allowed Hitler break the Treaty of Versailles in order to avoid a major war. France was now dependent on weak Eastern European countries and on ties with Britain.

France and Britain: France had to follow Britain's policy of appeasement even though it allowed Germany to get stronger:

- France needed Britain's resources for rearmament.
- France also needed the British army to fit into their war plan against Germany. The French army with the help of the British intended to block the Germans west of the Maginot Line.

Therefore, for the remainder of the 1930s, the French government made efforts to maintain good relations with Britain.

The Spanish Civil War: French foreign policy was next tested by the **Spanish Civil War** where a Popular Front republican government was attacked by a nationalist army backed by Germany and Italy. Blum, the leader of the French Popular Front government, opted for **non-intervention** in the war because of social and political divisions in France – the Right and Left were bitterly divided – and the need to maintain relations with Britain who also favoured non-intervention. Once again French foreign policy had failed.

More Failures

By now French foreign policy was effectively tied to the British. Neither country made any serious protest when Hitler took over Austria in **Anschluss** (March 1938). But the biggest French sell-out came when Hitler demanded the **Sudetenland** from Czechoslovakia. The French Prime Minister, **Daladier**, attended the **Munich Conference** (September 1938) along with Hitler, Mussolini and Neville Chamberlain, the British Prime Minister. Daladier signed the **Munich Agreement** which forced Czechoslovakia to hand over the Sudetenland to Germany in spite of French agreements with Czechoslovakia. **Daladier** was supported in this policy of appeasement by a majority of French people so as to avoid a European war. The right wing in particular looked on Hitler as less of a danger than Russian Communism.

The Approach of War – Peace at All Costs

During 1939 the French government tried to avoid war at all costs. But France was now tied to Britain and British opinion was changing. After Hitler took over the **rest of Czechoslovakia** (March 1939), Britain gave a formal guarantee of help to Poland. France also agreed to follow Britain. The French and British tried to form a pact with Soviet Russia against Germany. But this was destroyed by the **Nazi-Soviet Pact** (August 1939). Even when Germany invaded Poland on 1 September 1939, the French still tried to break their commitments. However, they had no choice but to go along with Britain and both declared war on Germany on 3 September 1939.

QUESTIONS ?

1. How was each of the following a turning point in French foreign policy in the 1930s: (i) invasion of Ethiopia (ii) Hitler breaks Versailles (iii) the Spanish Civil War?
2. What part did France play in relation to the Munich Conference and Poland?

World War II – The Defeat of the Third French Republic, May–June 1940

Why was France defeated?

Instead of uniting France against the German danger, the beginning of the Second World War divided the country further. Because of the Nazi-Soviet Pact, **French Communists** opposed the French war against Germany. They were directed by Moscow to denounce the war as an imperialist war. They also attempted to undermine French morale. On the other hand, the right wing developed a **peace party**, one of whose members was **Pierre Laval**, who favoured a separate peace with Germany.

German Invasion

It was a divided France which faced the German blitzkrieg of May 1940. The Daladier government fell in March 1940 so a new government led by **Paul Reynaud** faced the German invasion. But the defeat of France was mainly due to **faulty military strategy** which could not cope with the German blitzkrieg tactics of speed and mobility. The French High Command still thought in terms of the First World War. On hearing of the German attack, they sent their best troops, along with the **British Expeditionary Force** (BEF), into

German troops occupying Paris in May 1940 (top) and Hitler posing with the Eiffel Tower in the background.

Belgium. They were easily cut off by the German tanks who raced across from the Ardennes and reached the English Channel in ten days. (See Chapter 25, The Second World War pp. 289–93.)

French Surrender

The government left Paris and eventually went to Bordeaux. **Reynaud** wanted to continue the fight in North Africa but the Army Commander and the cabinet were opposed to this so he was forced to resign. He was replaced by **Marshal Pétain**, hero of the First World War, who sued for peace. On 22 June, France signed an **armistice** with Germany in the same railway carriage in Compiègne in which Germany had surrendered in 1918:

- France was now divided into an **Occupied Zone** (northern and western France) and an **Unoccupied Zone** (southern or Vichy France).

- The French army was reduced to 100,000 men.
- France had to pay the cost of German occupation.

This was a humiliating end for the Third French Republic.

EXAM QUESTION (?)

Why was France defeated in 1940?

Vichy France, 1940–44

The new French government was based in the town of **Vichy**. **Pétain** was head of government but **Laval** played a dominant role in the government. He got the Parliament to agree to abolish itself and the Third Republic. The Vichy government replaced the Third Republic with a **corporate state** similar to Mussolini's where the interests of the employers, workers and the State were represented. Pétain replaced Parliament with a **Veterans' League** of ex-soldiers. He also restored the influence of the Catholic Church to education and he protected the better-off classes. The Vichy government introduced **anti-Semitic laws** and rounded up Jews for deportation to Germany. Over 75,000 of these died in the Holocaust.

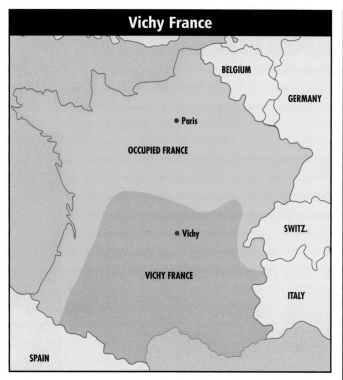

Timeline – French foreign policy, 1920–45

—1919 Treaty of Versailles
—1920 Treaty with Belgium
—1921 Treaty with Poland
—1923 Invasion of Ruhr
—1924 Little Entente
—1925 Locarno Pact
—1928 Kellogg-Briand Pact
—1929 Maginot Line begun
—1934 Four Power Pact
—1935 Stesa Front; Invasion of Ethiopia
—1936 Remilitarisation of Rhineland; Spanish Civil War
—1938 Munich Conference
—1940 Defeat of France; Vichy France

Collaboration

Laval believed that Germany was going to win the war and he wanted France to adjust to the new order in Europe. In October 1940, Pétain and Laval met Hitler. Afterwards, Laval said, *'I enter into the way of collaboration.'* In April 1942, he became Prime Minister. Laval continued to look for a role

French troops released by the Germans praised Pétain and Laval: Vichy France exchanged three French workers for each freed French soldier.

KEY CONCEPT
COLLABORATION is co-operating with the enemy especially when they have taken over your own country.

for France in the new Europe which he believed the Germans were creating. He wanted France to be the **favourite province of Germany**. Both he and Pétain thought that the only alternative to collaboration was direct Nazi rule.

German Policy towards Vichy

But Vichy collaboration did not win greater respect from the Germans. Instead, Hitler looked on Vichy France as a cheap way of policing the area and as a source of raw materials and foodstuffs for the war. The Vichy government paid very large occupation costs. They also agreed to the conscription of French workers for the German war industry in return for the release of some French prisoners of war. Further, they put down the French Resistance which attacked supply routes to Germany.

In November 1942, Vichy France lost most of the little power it had. On 11 November, Hitler ordered his army to take over Vichy France when American and British troops invaded North Africa and took over Vichy-controlled Morocco and Algeria. A Vichy government continued to exist in France until 1944, but only in name.

French Resistance

While those in charge of Vichy collaborated with Germany, a French Resistance movement opposed German occupation in many different ways: collection of military intelligence; helping British airmen to escape; distribution of anti-German leaflets; boycotting Germans in public or in bars; sabotage of railways or guerrilla attacks on German soldiers. German treatment of those who were caught was ruthless; they were arrested, tortured and often executed. Sometimes there were even mass executions as in the town of **Oradour-sur-Glane** where 642 men, women and children were massacred.

The French Resistance planning another ambush.

Resistance Grows

In the early months of the German occupation, Resistance was sporadic, usually carried out by small groups. But gradually groups such as **Combat**, **Franc-Tireur**, **Liberation Nord** and **Front National** developed. The Resistance got a huge boost in June 1941 when Hitler invaded Soviet Russia. Then the **French Communists**, who up to this had been neutral towards Germany, became the most active leaders of the Resistance. A further boost to the Resistance came when French workers were being conscripted to work in German war industries. This enlarged the Resistance as many of the young men took to the hills and forests.

Co-ordination of Resistance

As the war progressed there was greater co-ordination between the Resistance groups. Eventually, the leadership of the French Resistance was taken over by **General Charles de Gaulle**. In 1940, on the fall of France, de Gaulle escaped to London where he set up the **Free French**. He wanted all patriotic Frenchmen to join him. However, he struggled to receive recognition from **Churchill** and the British who found him difficult to deal with. The **Americans** were even more hostile and accepted Vichy France as the legitimate French government.

Instead, de Gaulle was able to create unity among the many resistance groups through his representative, **Jean Moulin**, who was parachuted into France. He first created links between the northern and southern resistance groups. Then he persuaded the Communists to accept de Gaulle as a replacement for Pétain when liberation came.

General de Gaulle, leader of the Free French, led a triumphant march down the Champs Élysées after Paris was recaptured by the Allied forces.

Challenges facing France, 1920–45 (2)
- Foreign policy
- Security
- Reparations and the Ruhr
- Relations with Germany in 1920s
- Turning points in foreign policy in 1930s
- Weakness of foreign policy and the approach of war
- Defeat of France
- Vichy France – collaboration and resistance

De Gaulle Takes Over

The Americans saw little role for the Resistance as they planned the Normandy landings (1944). However, the Resistance increased their attacks but very often at the expense of huge reprisals by the Germans. When Paris was liberated in August 1944, American troops were accompanied by French troops as they took over the city. De Gaulle ensured that he was recognised by all as leader of France when he led a triumphal march from the Arc de Triomphe to Notre Dame.

Revenge on Collaborators

After the Liberation, the Resistance took revenge on the collaborators. About 9,000 were executed without trial and there was a danger these executions would get out of control. But de Gaulle's government began the **systematic punishment** of the collaborators. They arrested and tried 125,000 people over the next two years; about 90,000 were punished, about half of these were imprisoned, and 767 were executed after trial. Some of these included the leaders of Vichy France including **Laval**, but **Pétain's** death sentence was commuted to life imprisonment. By taking control of the punishment of the collaborators, de Gaulle's government contained the violence and established the authority of the State.

Women collaborators' heads were shaved.

Assessment of Resistance

Overall, the numbers involved in the Resistance were relatively small – about 2 per cent of the adult French population. However, the Resistance played a major role in boosting French morale. It helped wipe out the memory of Vichy collaboration. Even though the military impact of Resistance was small, it kept alive the hope that Germany would be defeated. (See also Chapter 26, pp. 312–19, for information about the home front in Germany and Britain during the war.)

QUESTIONS

1. What actions did the French Resistance undertake?
2. Who organised the resistance?
3. Was it successful?
4. What happened to collaborators after the war?

HOMEWORK EXERCISES

ORDINARY LEVEL

1. Study the extracts on French security and answer the following questions.

   What France wanted from Germany, after two damaging invasions in fifty years was above all security. As
   M Clemenceau [the French Prime Minister] told the Paris [Peace] Conference in January 1919: 'If a new war should take place, Germany would not throw her forces upon Cuba or upon Honduras, but upon France; it would always be upon France.'

   J. Terraine, The Mighty Continent: View of Europe in the Twentieth century

   France is, and will remain, the ... enemy of Germany.

   A Hitler, Mein Kampf

   A. (i) How many times did Germany invade France in 50 years?
   (ii) What did France want from Germany?
   (iii) According to M Clemenceau, who would Germany attack in a new war?
   (iv) Does Hitler's attitude support Clemenceau's view?

B. Write a **paragraph** on one of the following:
   (i) The French occupation of the Ruhr
   (ii) French foreign policy in the 1930s
   (iii) The Stavisky Affair
   (iv) The German invasion and the downfall of France's Third Republic, May 1940

C. Write a **long answer** on one of the following:
   (i) French policy towards Germany, 1920–39
   (ii) Pierre Laval and Vichy France
   (iii) Collaboration and resistance in France during the World War II

HIGHER LEVEL

2. How successful were French governments in solving the internal and external problems that the country faced in the 1920s?

3. What caused the downfall of France in 1940 and what were the consequences of that downfall?

4. What problems did the Third Republic of France encounter between 1920 and 1940? (2007)

5. Why was France unstable during the period 1920 to 1940? (2009)

6. What were the main challenges facing France, 1920–45? (2012)

7. What were the fortunes of France during the period 1920–45? (2014)

In this section, you should understand:
• How Hitler's foreign policy caused the Second World War.

Hitler's Aims

In 1939, the Second World War began when Germany invaded Poland. Hitler's aims in foreign policy and the aggressive way in which he carried them out were the main causes of the war.

Hitler had **three main aims** in foreign policy:

1. He wanted to **destroy the Treaty of Versailles** – to rearm the German army, navy and air force; to remilitarise the Rhineland; to form Anschluss (union) with Austria; to change the borders on the east with Poland.
2. He wanted to create a **Greater Germany** (Grossdeutschland) by uniting all German-speaking people.
3. He wanted to create **Lebensraum** – living space in Eastern Europe to make Germany self-sufficient in food and raw materials for his master race. *'The new Reich must ... obtain by the German sword, sod for the German plough and daily bread for the nation.'* (*Mein Kampf*)

> **KEY CONCEPT**
> **LEBENSRAUM** Hitler believed that having additional living space would strengthen Germany by making it self-sufficient in food and raw materials. He wanted the living space in Eastern Europe, particularly Russia. This idea of lebensraum became the basis of German foreign policy during Hitler's Third Reich.

> **QUESTIONS** ?
>
> 1. List the three aims of Hitler's foreign policy.
> 2. What was Greater Germany?
> 3. What was *Lebensraum*?

Hitler's Successes

After coming to power in 1933, Hitler **proceeded cautiously** in foreign policy for the first year. He wanted to be seen as a man of peace while he consolidated his power at home. He withdrew from the **Disarmament Conference** and the **League of Nations** but he was able to blame it on France's refusal to disarm like Germany. He was part of the **Four Power Pact** of Britain, France, Italy and Germany itself to preserve the peace of Europe. He formed a ten-year **Non-Aggression Pact** with Poland. This broke the isolation of Germany which France had achieved. A further success was the **Saar**

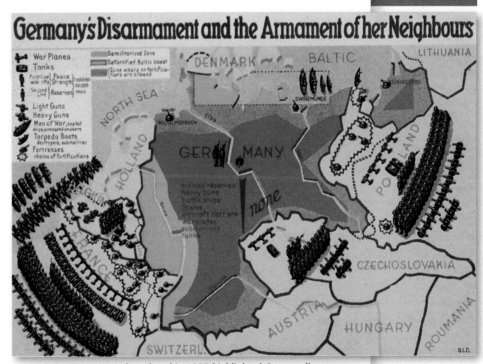

A German postcard produced in 1935 highlighted German disarmament compared to that of her neighbours. The aim of the postcard was to show British people that Germany had been treated unfairly by the Treaty of Versailles. How does it get this message across?

279

Plebiscite (vote of the people). In the Treaty of Versailles (1919), the Saar had been given to France for 15 years to extract coal. Now the people of the Saar voted to become part of Germany.

Setback

But Hitler also suffered a setback. The **union** of Austria with Germany (Anschluss) was one of his main aims. Austrian Nazis were encouraged and helped by Hitler. In 1934, they murdered the Austrian Chancellor, **Dollfuss**, in an attempted Nazi coup (or takeover). Hitler was ready to invade the country, but Italy feared a German takeover. The Italian leader, **Mussolini**, rushed troops to the Austrian border and Hitler backed down.

Destroying Versailles

By 1935, Hitler had consolidated his power at home. He began **a more aggressive foreign policy** by breaking the terms of the Treaty of Versailles. Initially, the terms he broke applied directly to Germany. In early 1935, Hitler began German **rearmament**. He introduced conscription (compulsory military service) and announced the existence of the **Luftwaffe** (air force), which had been set up secretly. Hitler's actions led to the formation of the **Stresa Front** (1935) by **Britain, France and Italy** because of fear of German expansion.

However, within a few months, Britain undermined the Stresa Front and helped Hitler dismantle the Treaty of Versailles further by agreeing to the **Anglo-German Naval Agreement** (1935). This allowed Hitler to increase his navy up to thirty-five per

cent of the British navy, but have the same amount of
submarines (U-boats) as the British. France was very upset by
the agreement because they had not been consulted. But
Hitler was delighted. He felt that Britain was prepared to
allow German breaches of the Treaty of Versailles and this
encouraged him to try again.

Luftwaffe pilots receiving orders: in the background is
a Stuka dive bomber which became an important part of
German military success in the early years of the Second
World War.

Italian Invasion of Abyssinia

In October 1935 Mussolini invaded Abyssinia. Abyssinia
turned to the **League of Nations** for help. The League
imposed economic sanctions on Italy but these sanctions
excluded oil. However, the League failed to take any other effective
action. At the same time, Britain and France secretly agreed the
Hoare-Laval Plan (called after the British and French foreign
ministers) to give most of Abyssinia to Italy. When news of this plan
leaked out, it was dropped and it led to the resignation of both
foreign secretaries. Abyssinia was quickly and easily defeated by the
modern technology of Italy.

The invasion of Abyssinia had a number of important **results**:

- Britain and France fell out over the **Hoare-Laval Plan**.
- British and French support for sanctions upset Mussolini and the
  Stresa Front broke up.
- On the other hand, Hitler supported Mussolini and this brought
  them **closer together**.
- The **weaknesses of the League of Nations** were shown up. They showed that
  collective security – countries working together to protect other countries – did not
  seem to work:
  - **Economic sanctions** did not work because they did not apply to non-members
    such as the US and Germany.

Signing the Pact of
Steel between Italy
and Germany: they
were committed to
help each other in
war.

Timeline: The Build-up to the Second World War					
	Hitler withdrew from the League of Nations and the Disarmament Conference	Hitler remilitarised the Rhineland The Spanish Civil War began			Hitler took over the rest of Czechoslovakia The Nazi-Soviet Pact Hitler invaded Poland
1933	**1934**	**1935**	**1936**	**1938**	**1939**
Hitler came to power in Germany		Hitler began rearmament The Anglo-German Naval Agreement Mussolini invaded Abyssinia		Anschluss with Austria The Munich Conference Hitler took over the Sudetenland	

THE GOOSE-STEP
"GOOSEY GOOSEY GANDER,
WHITHER DOST THOU WANDER?"
"ONLY THROUGH THE RHINELAND—
PRAY EXCUSE MY BLUNDER!"

Hitler had an important success when he remilitarised the Rhineland in 1936. A British cartoon commented on the remilitarisation (left) – what is the message of the cartoon? German troops crossing the Rhine (above).

- The League had **no army** to enforce its decisions.
- The **absence** of the US was a major weakness since it was the most powerful country in the world.

Remilitarisation of the Rhineland, 1936

Hitler took his next gamble. He was encouraged by his early success to remilitarise the Rhineland. The remilitarisation of the Rhineland was banned by the Treaty of Versailles and agreed to by Germany in the **Locarno Pact** (1925).

Hitler **timed** his action well. He took advantage of the crisis in 1936 over Abyssinia between Italy, Britain and France. He also said that Germany was under threat because of a recent agreement between France and Russia. In March 1936 he moved about 10,000 troops, backed up by police, into the Rhineland.

The **League of Nations** condemned his action but did nothing else because of the Abyssinian crisis. France was the country most threatened by the remilitarisation but it failed to act. The Left and Right were bitterly divided; and France did not get British support. Instead, Britain looked on the remilitarisation as the Germans going into their **own back garden**.

Hitler had gambled and won. The remilitarisation of the Rhineland allowed him to build the **Siegfried Line** – a line of fortifications along the Franco-German border – and this prevented France invading Germany. It also protected his back as he turned his attention to Eastern Europe.

The Siegfried Line: the German defensive line which ran along the Franco-German border.

The Influence of the Spanish Civil War

The **Spanish Civil War** (1936–9) broke out between the Republican government and the Nationalist army led by Franco. Hitler and Mussolini gave help to Franco by providing ships, planes, equipment and soldiers. This help ensured victory for Franco.

Mussolini's dispute with Britain and France over Abyssinia and the events of the Spanish Civil War led Hitler and Mussolini to form the **Rome-Berlin Axis** (November 1936). They made an agreement over Austria (Hitler gave up his claim to the German-speaking people of the South Tyrol); in return Mussolini agreed to Hitler's takeover of Austria. One month later, Germany and Italy joined with Japan in the **Anti-Comintern Pact** to stop the spread of Communism.

The Hossbach Memorandum and Plans for War

In November 1937 Hitler met his senior military commanders. The **Hossbach Memorandum**, notes taken at the meeting by Colonel Hossbach, recorded Hitler's plans for the future. That future depended on getting **lebensraum** (living space) for food and raw materials. He believed that his first objective must be to overthrow Austria and Czechoslovakia. He used the same tactics in both cases of **outside pressure** combined with **internal disruption**.

Hitler surveys a German military parade showing the strength of rearmament.

Hitler could feel confident of success because, by this time, Germany was rearming quickly. The army was expanded from 100,000 in 1933 to 750,000 by 1939, with 1 million reserves; large numbers of tanks were produced; the navy was equipped with new battleships and submarines; and the Luftwaffe had about 4,500 aircraft. The other European powers had been overtaken because their rearmament began later. Hitler believed that the latest Germany could go to war was 1943–5 because after that other countries would have caught up with it.

Anschluss with Austria, 1938

Hitler took a special interest in Austria where he was born. He encouraged the Austrian Nazi Party to demand union with Germany (Anschluss). He demanded of the Austrian Chancellor, **Dr Schuschnigg**, that the Nazi Party be legalised and that the Nazi, **Dr Seyss-Inquart**, be appointed Minister of the Interior. Schuschnigg had to agree. However, Schuschnigg decided to hold a **plebiscite** (referendum or vote of the people) on union with Germany, knowing that the Austrian people would reject it. But Hitler

Growth of the German Armed Forces

SOLDIERS

WARSHIPS

AIRCRAFT

? **QUESTIONS**

1. What was the significance of the remilitarisation of the Rhineland?
2. How did the Spanish Civil War influence foreign affairs in the 1930s?
3. What was the Hossbach Memorandum and why is it so important?
4. Explain Anschluss.

acted before the plebiscite. He forced the resignation of Schuschnigg. Seyss-Inquart then invited the German army into Austria to *'help preserve the peace'*. Austria was taken over and Hitler returned triumphantly to Vienna on 15 March 1938. One month later a Nazi-supervised referendum produced a 99.75 per cent vote in favour of Anschluss.

Anschluss consolidated Germany's relations with Italy. Hitler was grateful to Mussolini for allowing the German takeover; *'Tell Mussolini I will never forget him for this,'* he said. The British did not try to stop the union because they felt that the Austrians and Germans had a right to be united.

The Sudetenland, 1938

Across the border from Germany was the **Sudetenland**, a German-speaking part of Czechoslovakia which included 3 million Germans. The Sudeten Germans complained they were discriminated against. Their leader, **Konrad Henlein**, demanded to be united with Germany. He was encouraged and supported by Hitler who sent troops to the border.

But the Czechs had a modern army and strong defences. They also had a military alliance with France, while Britain and Russia promised support. They were prepared to resist the German threats, so Europe seemed on the verge of war during the summer of 1938.

Hitler received a great reception after he entered the Sudetenland, the German-speaking part of Czechoslovakia, which he took over in 1938.

France favoured action but Britain was cautious. **Neville Chamberlain**, the British Prime Minister, expressed his views; *'How horrible, fantastic, incredible it is that we should be digging trenches and trying on gas masks here because of a quarrel in a faraway country between people of whom we know nothing. I am myself a man of peace to the depths of my soul.'*

The Munich Agreement

The **Munich Conference** was organised to prevent war. **Chamberlain, Daladier (France), Mussolini and Hitler** met in Munich (September 1938) to decide the future of the Sudetenland. The Soviet Union was not invited, and neither was Czechoslovakia. The four leaders agreed that the Sudetenland should be given to Germany and Czechoslovakia had to give in. Chamberlain returned home with **peace for our time** and a hero's welcome. In France the view was, *'We can go back to work and sleep soundly again.'*

Once again Hitler had gambled and won. His tactics of taking Europe to the brink of war had succeeded. This crisis encouraged Hitler to believe that neither Britain nor France would back up their words with action. Now Germany was in a much stronger position – in taking over the Sudetenland, Germany had taken most of Czechoslovakia's heavy industries and defences.

Chamberlain, the British Prime Minister, believed that the policy of appeasement was working. What do the photos tell us about the response of the British people?

QUESTIONS

1. Where was the Sudetenland?
2. What did Hitler want to do with the Sudetenland?
3. Why was Europe on the verge of war in the summer of 1938?
4. What was agreed at the Munich Conference and why was that important?

Britain, France and the Policy of Appeasement

Britain's policy towards Hitler was characterised by **appeasement**. Britain believed that if they gave in to Hitler's demands, this would prevent a European war. Instead they believed in the League of Nations and disarmament as the best way of achieving peace. This policy was mainly associated with Neville Chamberlain, but it was supported by all sections of the British people:

- Many British leaders had fought in the First World War and they did not want to see the horrors of war repeated.
- Many British people felt that Germany had been too harshly treated by the Treaty of Versailles; they believed that Hitler's demands were reasonable.
- Hitler and Nazi Germany was seen as a barrier to the spread of Communism from the Soviet Union.
- Britain was not ready for war – the politicians did not want to cut spending on social welfare programmes to pay for rearmament.

EXAM QUESTION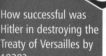

How successful was Hitler in destroying the Treaty of Versailles by 1939?

Winston Churchill was the main opponent of appeasement. By now on the Conservative backbenches, he warned about the threat from Hitler. He opposed the Anglo-German Naval Agreement (1935). Instead, he said Britain should rearm to meet the danger from the Fascist dictator. He also wanted Britain to build up its defences, and he warned about German air superiority.

European leaders – Chamberlain (Britain), Mussolini (Italy), Daladier (France) and Hitler (Germany) – agreed at the Munich Conference to hand over the Sudetenland to Germany.

He campaigned against appeasement in 1938. He looked on the Munich Agreement as 'a total and unmitigated defeat', and a surrender to Hitler. He warned that the rest of Czechoslovakia would soon be 'engulfed in the Nazi regime'. Instead, he wanted collaboration with the Soviet Union. For the moment, however, Churchill was in a minority. (See Key Personality: Winston Churchill, p. 296).

The **French government and people** also longed for peace and supported appeasement for many of the same reasons as Britain. But France was also affected by the **Maginot mind** – the belief that France could defend itself behind the **Maginot Line**, the huge system of fortifications built along the eastern border with Germany. (See Chapter 23, Politics and Administration in France: The Third Republic, 1920–40 and the Vichy State, 1940–44.)

The Destruction of Czechoslovakia, March 1939

In March 1939 Hitler took over the rest of Czechoslovakia. Britain and France only protested. This clearly showed **the weaknesses** of the policy of appeasement. However, this was also the first non-German area taken over by Hitler. British policy began to change. Prior to this, the British believed that Hitler's aims were limited; now they knew he sought European domination. It was clear that Poland would be Hitler's next target.

Poland and the Polish Corridor

The Treaty of Versailles had separated East Prussia from the rest of Germany by the **Polish Corridor** – a narrow strip of land which gave Poland access to the sea through the port of **Danzig**. (See map of Hitler's Foreign Policy and German Expansion, 1933–9, p. 280) In 1939, Hitler demanded the return of Danzig and a road and rail link to East Prussia through the Polish Corridor. Poland rejected Hitler's demands.

In March 1939, Britain and France agreed to support Poland against *'any action which clearly threatened Polish independence'*. But after years of appeasement, Hitler did not believe that Britain and France would act. Hitler also made his own agreement – the **Pact of Steel** with Italy, 1939. This was a military alliance in which each country would help the other in war. Europe was divided into two armed camps and once again it faced the prospect of war.

QUESTIONS

1. What was the policy of appeasement?
2. Why did Chamberlain follow a policy of appeasement?
3. Why did France support appeasement?

The Nazi-Soviet Pact, 1939

However, the key to the safety of Poland was the **Soviet Union**.

Stalin was worried about the safety of Russia since Hitler came to power. He wanted an alliance with Britain and France during the Sudetenland crisis, but now he did not trust them after the Soviet Union was not included in the Munich Conference. Instead,

Ribbentrop, the German Foreign Minister, and **Molotov, the Soviet Foreign Minister**, stunned the world when they agreed a **ten-year non-aggression pact**. The arch-enemies of Fascism and Communism also secretly agreed to divide Poland between themselves.

The **Nazi-Soviet Pact** was very important to Hitler. He feared that if he invaded Poland, he would be involved in a two-front war against Russia in the east and France and Britain in the west. Now the Pact allowed him to attack Poland without Russia intervening. It also gave Stalin time to prepare his army. Later Stalin said, *'We secured peace for our country for eighteen months which allowed us to make military preparations.'*

SOMEONE IS TAKING SOMEONE FOR A WALK

A British cartoon depicting the Nazi-Soviet Non-Aggression pact, 1939. Who are the two people? What is the message of the cartoon?

QUESTIONS ?

1. What were the terms of the Nazi-Soviet Pact?
2. Why was the Nazi-Soviet Pact important for both Hitler and Stalin?
3. Why did Hitler invade Poland?

The War Begins

Hitler believed everything was now in his favour. He had the non-aggression pact with Russia; the Siegfried Line protected him from attack in the west; he believed Britain and France would not fight, and if they did they were too far away to help Poland; and he had Poland surrounded on three sides. He also had the strongest army in Europe.

But Poland still refused to give in to his demands, so on 1 September 1939 Hitler **invaded** the country. To his surprise, Britain and France backed Poland and declared war on Germany on 3 September.

British and French opinion had changed quickly after the Munich Conference. They felt Hitler could not be trusted and they backed rearmament. There was a determination to face war if it was necessary.

In a radio broadcast, Chamberlain expressed his own views and those of many other people.

'[Hitler] gave his word [and] he broke it … Can you wonder his word is, for us, not worth the paper it is written on!'

The Causes of the Second World War

Hitler's Aims and Methods

- Hitler wanted to create a Greater Germany with living space (lebensraum) in the east.
- He broke the terms of the Treaty of Versailles.
- He used outside pressure and internal disruption to take over Austria and Sudetenland.
- When he took over the rest of Czechoslovakia, Britain and France supported his next target, Poland.

Weakness of the League of Nations

The League could not stop Mussolini and Hitler (and Japan in Asia) from taking over other countries:

- Economic sanctions were not effective.
- There had to be unanimous agreement among the members for action.
- The US was not a member and other powers were members for short periods.
- The League did not have an army to enforce decisions.

Isolation of the US

America was the strongest country but it followed a policy of isolation:

- It was only interested in affairs on its own continent.
- It did not want to send troops to fight in faraway wars.
- America rejected the Treaty of Versailles and did not become a member of the League of Nations.
- In the 1930s America passed the Neutrality Acts which stopped aid or trade with warring countries.

Policy of Appeasement

Britain and France followed this policy:

- They believed that if they gave in to Hitler's small demands they would stop a European war.
- The policy was influenced by:
  - Their experiences of the First World War.
  - In Britain they believed that Germany had been harshly treated by the Treaty of Versailles.
  - They wanted a strong Germany to stop the spread of Communism.

HOMEWORK EXERCISES

ORDINARY LEVEL

WONDER HOW LONG THE HONEYMOON WILL LAST?

1. This **London Evening Standard** cartoon (2 September 1939) comments on the non-aggression pact between Nazi Germany and Stalin's Russia which had been signed in Moscow ten days earlier. Study it and answer the questions that follow.

   A. (i) What event is depicted?
   (ii) Where and when did that event take place?
   (iii) Who are the 'bride' and 'groom'?
   (iv) What symbol of Nazi Germany or Stalin's Russia is shown on the wedding cake?
   (v) What action did Hitler take, in June 1941, that ended the relationship depicted in the cartoon?
   (vi) Is this cartoon propaganda? Explain your answer.

   B. Write a **paragraph** on **each** of the following.
   (i) The Policy of Appeasement
   (ii) The Nazi-Soviet Pact and the invasion of Poland

   C. Write a **long answer** of the causes of the Second World War.

HIGHER LEVEL

2. Were the foreign policies pursued by Hitler and Mussolini the main cause of World War II?

3. To what extent did Hitler's foreign policy, 1933–39, contribute to the outbreak of World War II? (2012) (2015)

4. Why did war break out in Europe in 1939?

The Nazi State at War

The Invasion of Poland, 1939

At dawn on 1 September 1939, the German invasion of Poland began. The German army employed the bold new tactics of **Blitzkrieg or lightning war**, based on surprise and speed. The **Luftwaffe**, led by Stuka dive-bombers, attacked the Polish Air Force, knocking most of the planes out of action on the ground. Within two days the air force had ceased to exist and the Luftwaffe had **control of the air**.

At the same time, the **Panzer (tank) units** advanced rapidly into Poland. They bypassed the main Polish army units. They worked with the air force and used a **pincer movement** to cut off the supply and communication lines of the Polish army. Following behind the Panzers, **the infantry units** broke down any remaining resistance.

Within a week, German units were on the outskirts of Warsaw, others then progressed halfway into Poland. As part of the secret clauses of the **Nazi-Soviet Pact**, the Soviet army attacked from the east, almost three weeks into the war. Warsaw held out until 27 September but the Polish government had fled to Romania long ago. Poland had been **humiliated** in a month. (See map p. 290.)

The results of the invasion: Britain, France and even Hitler were surprised by the speed of the victory. A country of 33 million with an army of 1.7 million was crushed before it could fight back.

The cost to Germany was 10,000 killed and 20,000 wounded. In accordance with their pre-war Pact, Poland was divided between Germany and the Soviet Union. Within a few months the victorious countries had executed 18,000 Poles for **offences**, and the Germans began the process of herding Jews into **ghettoes**.

Hitler reviewing troops going into Poland on 1 September 1939.

Victims of German success in Poland: Polish Jews being rounded up for the Warsaw ghetto.

QUESTIONS

1. What was Blitzkrieg?
2. How successful was the German invasion of Poland?

289

German Invasion of Poland, September 1939

German Army
Soviet Army

LATVIA
LITHUANIA
Baltic Sea
EAST PRUSSIA
Danzig
Berlin
River Vistula
GREATER GERMANY
Warsaw
Lodz
River Oder
POLAND
Krakow
SLOVAKIA
HUNGARY
ROMANIA
SOVIET UNION

Soviet Union occupied Eastern Poland, 17 September 1939

German Forces invaded Poland, 1 September 1939

The West

Meanwhile in the West virtually nothing happened. Hitler left just enough forces to defend the **Siegfried Line** knowing that the French and British would be slow to **mobilise** (get their armies ready). Hitler, on the other hand, was triumphant. He had Central and Eastern Europe at his mercy. He offered peace to the British and French, which they rejected.

? **QUESTIONS**

1. How successful was the Soviet Union in the Russo-Finnish War?
2. What was the Phoney War?

The Winter War – The Russo-Finnish War

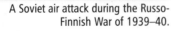

A Soviet air attack during the Russo-Finnish War of 1939–40.

Stalin, the Russian leader, was concerned about the future defences of **Leningrad**. He wanted Finland to hand over some territory to Russia to strengthen Leningrad. When the Finns refused, Russia **invaded** Finland on 30 November 1939. This appeared an unequal contest – a country of 180 million with an army of 1 million and much greater numbers of tanks and planes, against a country of 3 million with just over 30,000 soldiers. However, much to the surprise of the Russians, the Finns held out for over three months, finally surrendering in March 1940. The Russian army could not progress in the snow, while the Finns used ski patrols to ambush and harass them. The Finns had built a strong defence line – the **Mannerheim Line** – and this held up the Russians. But the main reason for the slow progress of the Russians was **Stalin's purges** in the 1930s which weakened the Soviet officer corps.

The Phoney War

While the Russo-Finnish War was in progress, the western front experienced the **phoney war** – a period of seven months after the defeat of Poland when there was no fighting along the western front between France, Britain and Germany.

The French took up a **defensive position** along the **Maginot Line**.

Both the Allies and the Germans waited and built up supplies and armaments for the next round of fighting.

The Invasion of Denmark and Norway, April 1940

The invasion of **Denmark and Norway** brought the phoney war to an end. Hitler needed Norway to protect valuable **Swedish iron ore** supplies which came through the Norwegian port of **Narvik** in winter. The loss of Swedish ore would cripple his war effort. Hitler also saw the value of the long **Norwegian coast** which could be used for sheltering ships and submarines. Britain was also planning to take Norway but when Hitler became aware of these plans he got there before them.

First, however, Hitler captured **Denmark** in less than a day. At the same time his warships transported troops to attack and capture six Norwegian cities, including Trondheim and Bergen. He also used **paratroopers** to take bridges and airfields. But British and French forces also landed, particularly around Narvik. The **Luftwaffe** gave the Germans an advantage and eventually the British and French troops had to be evacuated. Hitler imposed **Vidkun Quisling**, a Norwegian Nazi, in government but a Nazi official soon replaced him due to his incompetence.

Results: Hitler's success in Norway undermined the position of **Neville Chamberlain**, the British Prime Minister. **Winston Churchill** replaced him as Prime Minister the day Hitler began his new campaign, the attack on France. Churchill told the House of Commons, '*I have nothing to offer but blood, toil, tears and sweat.*'

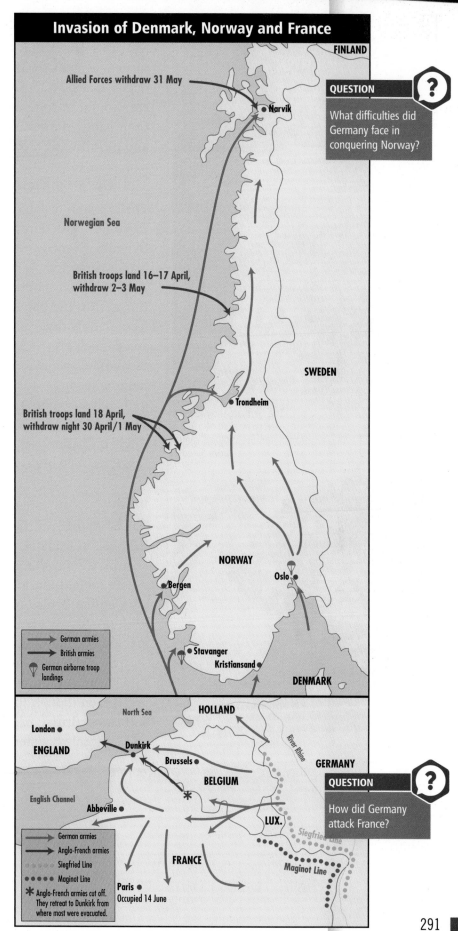

Invasion of Denmark, Norway and France

FINLAND

Allied Forces withdraw 31 May

Narvik

Norwegian Sea

British troops land 16–17 April, withdraw 2–3 May

British troops land 18 April, withdraw night 30 April/1 May

Trondheim

SWEDEN

NORWAY

Oslo

Bergen

Stavanger

Kristiansand

DENMARK

German armies
British armies
German airborne troop landings

North Sea

HOLLAND

London

ENGLAND

Dunkirk

Brussels

BELGIUM

GERMANY

River Rhine

English Channel

Abbeville

LUX.

Siegfried Line

German armies
Anglo-French armies
Siegfried Line
Maginot Line
✳ Anglo-French armies cut off. They retreat to Dunkirk from where most were evacuated.

FRANCE

Maginot Line

Paris
Occupied 14 June

QUESTION ❓

What difficulties did Germany face in conquering Norway?

QUESTION ❓

How did Germany attack France?

The German army invaded Norway in April 1940 to protect iron ore supplies coming from Sweden.

The German army moves into Paris during their invasion of France.

The Invasion of France, May 1940

Now that Hitler had safeguarded his northern side, he again turned to plans for **invading France**. Hitler was presented with a war plan by **General Manstein** which he ordered to be carried out in spite of the objections of the Army High Command. Manstein's plan took full advantage of the **speed** and **mobility of blitzkrieg**.

The Invasion Begins

The invasion began on 10 May 1940. Early that morning 2,500 Luftwaffe aircraft attacked airfields in Holland, Belgium, France and Luxembourg, destroying many enemy planes. The right wing of the German army swung into Belgium, easily capturing the huge Belgian fort at Eben Emael. But the Belgian attack, and the takeover of Holland, were mainly **decoys**. At the first signs of the attack the British and French armies advanced into Belgium. This ideally suited the main German attack which came through the **Ardennes** mountains and forests. Here **General Guderian's** Panzer units advanced rapidly towards **Sedan**, breaking through the French lines. After this they moved westwards towards the English Channel, cutting off the British and French armies in Belgium. (See map p. 291.)

Dunkirk

The British Expeditionary Force (BEF) and the French army fell back to Dunkirk when they realised what was happening. Fortunately for the 300,000 soldiers in Dunkirk, Hitler ordered a halt to the advancing tanks. This breathing space allowed the British to put **Operation Dynamo** into action. With the **Royal Air Force** (RAF) defending the air, 860 boats and ships crossed and recrossed the English Channel over a period of about 10 days to rescue 300,000 soldiers, two-thirds English and one-third French. The British army had been saved even though they lost many tanks, trucks, heavy guns and rifles. British propaganda turned the defeat into victory and a morale booster at home.

THE MAIN ALLIES AND AXIS POWERS	
Allies	**Axis Powers**
Britain	Germany
France	Italy (after June 1940)
Soviet Union (after June 1941)	Japan (after December 1941)
US (after December 1941)	

The Fall of France, June 1940

The remainder of the French army, aided by 100,000 British troops, continued the fight for the next few weeks. But they had no hope against the overwhelming superiority of the Germans. They advanced southwards and took the Maginot Line from the rear.

Eventually the outstanding German successes enticed **Mussolini** into the war. He failed to honour the Pact of Steel when the war broke out in September 1939. Now he wanted to share in Hitler's glory. On 10 June, he invaded southern France. He said, *'I need a thousand dead in order to take my seat at the table with the victors.'*

British and French troops being rescued at Dunkirk in Operation Dynamo.

WHY WAS GERMANY SO SUCCESSFUL IN 1939–41? – SUMMARY

1. The Military Balance
Germany had a **stronger army** than either Poland, Norway, France or Britain:
- In 1939, it had 125 divisions compared to 80 for the French and 4 for the British.
- It had over 4,000 aircraft compared to 1,200 French and 1,700 British. Its planes were faster and better armed than the French.

2. Military Tactics
Germany had better military tactics. Its **use of blitzkrieg** explains why the enemy countries collapsed so quickly. Tanks and aeroplanes worked together for a rapid advance, cutting off the enemy supplies. Paratroopers were also used behind enemy lines. In contrast, the Poles and French used tanks in the same way as in the First World War in support of the infantry, and therefore slowly.

3. Failure to Help Poland
France failed to act when Hitler invaded Poland. At the time France had a far greater army along its border with Germany. But the French military leaders still believed in a defensive stance, as had been used in the First World War.

4. Failure to Act Decisively against Norway
The British and French realised the importance of Norway for German iron ore supplies coming from Sweden. They planned to cut them off, but they delayed their attack and gave Hitler the chance to get there before them.

5. The Weakness of France
France had failed to prepare fully for the war. It was late rearming, it neglected its air force and the new methods of fighting. Its war plan, which involved invading Belgium, was a failure. Its people were divided between Left and Right. (See *Why was France Defeated?* p. 274.)

6. The British Expeditionary Force
The British Expeditionary Force (BEF) of almost 400,000 men was tied to the French war plan. It was attached to the left wing of the French army and followed the French into Belgium. Soon they retreated to Dunkirk when they realised that the German army was about to cut them off in Belgium.

7. The War at Sea
Germany had success in the War at Sea early in the war. (See pp. 295–97.)

8. The War in the Desert
The German army had success in the War in the Desert up to 1941. (See pp. 297–98.)

9. Failure – The Battle of Britain and the Blitz
The German army failed to invade and conquer Britain. (See pp. 294–95.)

Hitler the man-eater, a propaganda cartoon in 1942: what is its message?

? **QUESTION**

1. How successful was the invasion of Denmark and Norway?
2. What were the results of the Fall of France?

? **EXAM QUESTION**

How and why was the German army so successful between 1939 and 1941?

Armistice

The French government survived for another couple of weeks. They moved from Paris to Bordeaux. A new Prime Minister, **Marshal Pétain**, a hero of the First World War, sought an **armistice** with Germany. Hitler ensured that the armistice was signed on 21 June in the same railway carriage, and in the same place in Compiègne, where Germany had signed its surrender in 1918 at the end of the First World War. Now Germany dictated the terms to France:

- The Germans controlled the north and west of France while the rest, **Vichy France**, was under French government control.
- The French army was **disarmed** and **demobilised**.
- France had to **pay** the cost of occupation.

Results: The defeat was a disaster and shame for France. The country and its army had been destroyed in 40 days. The British navy destroyed the French fleet at **Mers-el-Kebir** in Algeria to ensure it did not get into German hands. The future of France rested with either the Vichy government or with **General de Gaulle's Free French** movement which he set up in London. Hitler and his allies now ruled most of Europe from the Atlantic seaboard to the border with the Soviet Union.

The Battle of Britain, August–September 1940

Hitler now planned the invasion of Britain – **Operation Sealion**. He had between 20 and 45 divisions ready to be transported across the English Channel. But he needed **control of the air** to protect the ships and barges. He knew the **Luftwaffe** had to defeat the **RAF**. This was the Battle of Britain.

Winston Churchill urged on the British people,

'We shall defend our island whatever the cost may be... Let us therefore brace ourselves to our duty and so bear ourselves that if the British Commonwealth and Empire last for a thousand years men will still say, "This was their finest hour."'

The Battle

The Battle of Britain was fought in a number of **stages**. First, Hitler began by attacking ships in the English Channel to draw the RAF into battle. Then he followed this with attacks on the **airfields** and **radar stations**. The RAF was stretched as pilots not only from Britain but also from Commonwealth countries (Australia, Canada, New Zealand), as well as Poland and Czechoslovakia, battled against wave after wave of German planes. On **Eagle Day** (13 August) the Luftwaffe sent in five waves of bombers and fighters. This pattern was followed on many other days. However, even though the RAF pilots were exhausted, they were inflicting heavy losses on the Luftwaffe.

The RAF Spitfires matched the speed and manoeuvrability of German fighter planes in the Battle of Britain.

In spite of some success against the RAF, Hitler changed his target to the **bombing of London** in September in response to a British attack on Berlin. He hoped to break the **morale** of the civilian population. London was attacked 24 times that month and people took to living in cellars and in the Underground. From November onwards, the Luftwaffe raided only at night because of the heavy daytime losses. But this was not successful either. London was protected by 1,500 barrage balloons, 2,000 anti-aircraft guns and, most importantly, 750 Spitfire and Hurricane fighter planes. Instead, the bombing of London relieved pressure on the RAF and the airfields. In the middle of September Hitler **postponed** the invasion of Britain and by October he **called it off**. He had lost the Battle of Britain.

The **Battle of Britain** was Hitler's first defeat. Britain now became the centre of resistance to Hitler.

Churchill surveys the rubble in London during the Blitz bombing campaign.

The Blitz

The aerial bombing of British cities, known as the **Blitz**, continued after the Battle of Britain. The Blitz lasted from September 1940 to May 1941. From November onwards, the Luftwaffe raided only at **night** because of the heavy daytime losses. In that period, Luftwaffe bombers not only attacked London, which was bombed many more times, but also industrial cities such as Coventry, Manchester, Birmingham and Liverpool. The Luftwaffe dropped 35,000 tonnes of bombs and lost 650 aircraft. By May 1941, 43,000 people in Britain had been killed and 1.4 million had been made homeless. By that time Hitler needed the Luftwaffe to lead the attack on Russia. (See The Home Front in Britain, pp. 317.)

Why did Britain Win the Battle of Britain?

- The British **Spitfire** and **Hurricane** fighter planes were a match for the German **Messerschmitts** and easily defeated the slow **Stuka**. The Luftwaffe lost nearly twice as many planes as the RAF.
- Hitler made a mistake in changing tactics to bombing London because this relieved pressure on the RAF.
- Churchill rightly praised the **pilots** of the RAF; *'Never in the field of human conflict was so much owed by so many to so few.'*
- **Radar** helped in this battle by giving advance warning of attack. British fighters were able to conserve fuel while German fighters had limited time over Britain.

What was the importance of the War at Sea?

The War at Sea played a vital role in deciding who won the war. Britain was dependent on supplies reaching the country from its empire and above all, from the US. **President Roosevelt** of America responded to urgings from **Churchill** and provided the vital supplies:

- In September 1940, he gave **50 warships** to Britain.
- In January 1941, under the **Lend-Lease Act** Roosevelt could supply military equipment to Britain without payment.

QUESTIONS

1. Why was the Battle of Britain fought?
2. Why did Britain win?
3. What was the significance of the Battle of Britain?
4. What was the Blitz?
5. What did Britain do to cope with the Blitz?

EXAM QUESTION

What part did Churchill play in the Second World War?

Develop notes on Winston Churchill's role in British history, 1920–45.

KEY PERSONALITY: WINSTON CHURCHILL

Winston Churchill had a **long career** in politics behind him when the Second World War broke out in 1939. He was **Chancellor of the Exchequer** from 1924 to 1929 (see pp. 233–35) but he failed to get a cabinet seat in the 1930s, his 'wilderness years'. In the 1930s he warned against the danger of the Nazis and was opposed to the policy of appeasement (see pp. 285–86). In 1939, Neville Chamberlain appointed Churchill to the War Cabinet in charge of the Royal Navy (Lord of the Admiralty). Churchill proposed the mining of Norwegian waters to prevent Germany getting iron ore supplies through Narvik. But disagreement in cabinet delayed the implementation of the plan (Operation Wilfred) and then it was too late to prevent the successful German invasion of Norway.

Churchill succeeded Chamberlain as Prime Minister in May 1940. He took over at a time when Britain needed **strong leadership** during the Battle of Britain and the Blitz. He resisted Foreign Secretary Halifax's proposal that there should be a **negotiated peace** with Hitler after Dunkirk and the Fall of France.

Churchill was the **ideal war leader**. He spoke with enthusiasm, inspiring British people to resist. He also had great energy. In 1943 he travelled 40,000 miles, at the age of 70, to encourage and co-ordinate efforts to defeat Hitler. He **worked well** with the American President, Roosevelt. He was delighted with the **Lend-Lease Act** which gave military goods to England without payment. He strengthened the relationship with the US when he met Roosevelt in Newfoundland in 1941 and they agreed the **Atlantic Charter**. He attended the **Allied Conferences** in Casablanca, Teheran, Yalta and Potsdam and so was involved in the **major decisions** in running the war, and the peace after the war (see Wartime Alliances, p. 302 (and Churchill in the Home Front, p. 319).

After the war, Churchill, as a leader of the Conservative Party, was defeated in the general election in Britain. He continued to advocate the US-British link, now in opposition to Communism and **the Iron Curtain**. He also called for European unity.

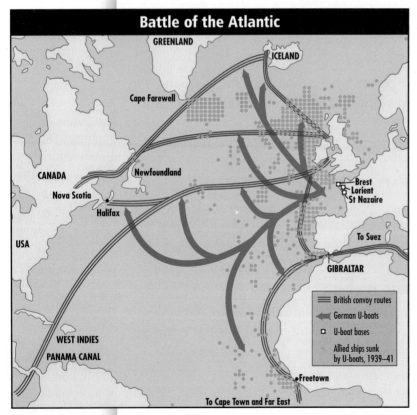

Battle of the Atlantic

GREENLAND
ICELAND
Cape Farewell
CANADA
Newfoundland
Nova Scotia
Halifax
USA
Brest
Lorient
St Nazaire
To Suez
GIBRALTAR
WEST INDIES
PANAMA CANAL
Freetown
To Cape Town and Far East

=== British convoy routes
◄── German U-boats
□ U-boat bases
▨ Allied ships sunk by U-boats, 1939–41

When the war began, Britain faced danger from **commerce-raiders** such as the **Admiral Graf Spee**, and the **Scharnhorst**. These operated in the North and South Atlantic attacking convoys coming from the US or West Africa. The most powerful of these ships was the **Bismarck** but it too was sunk like most of the others. The threat from these had been alarming and spectacular, but not serious.

A much more serious threat came from the **U-boats**. From the middle of 1940, German U-boats were able to use bases in Norway and France to advance into the North Atlantic. **Wolf packs** (groups of U-boats) moved out from strongly protected submarine lairs. They had considerable success in attacking convoys of ships protected by destroyers. In April–June 1941, for example, the U-boats sank 1 million tonnes of Allied shipping.

Allied Counter-measures

Allied losses were at their highest in 1942, but by 1943 counter-measures by the Allies began to work – greater protection for the convoys with more warships, the use of **Ultra** to crack the German navy codes and follow the path of the submarines, the use of long-range aircraft, depth charges, sonar, a huge programme of shipbuilding to replace sunken ships and the entry of the US into the war in December 1941. By 1943 the Allies had won the war at sea, but in the process over 2,700 Allied merchant ships and 100 warships had been sunk by the U-boats.

QUESTIONS **?**

1. What role did the War at Sea play in the Second World War?
2. How did technology influence the War at Sea?

German Involvement in the Mediterranean and the Balkans

The War in the Desert – Italian and German Failure in North Africa

Italy Loses its African Empire

At the start of the war, Italy had an African empire that included Libya, Ethiopia and Somaliland. But defeat at the hands of the British army meant that Italy lost its empire by 1941.

The Battle of El Alamein

British successes forced Hitler to send **Rommel** (the Desert Fox) and the **Afrika Korps** to Libya in April 1941. Rommel recaptured all the territory lost by the Italians along the North African coast into Egypt. Churchill now installed **Montgomery** as commander of the Eighth Army. He prepared for the **Battle of El Alamein** by using information obtained from breaking German codes.

Montgomery defeated Rommel at the Battle of El Alamein in October 1942. Over the next few months, Rommel was forced to retreat to Tunisia. He was in great danger here when a new Allied army – the **Americans** – under **Eisenhower**, landed in Algiers (in **Operation Torch**). Rommel was recalled to Germany, and the Desert War ended in an Allied victory (May 1943).

Rommel, the Desert Fox (left), and his Afrika Korps were sent to North Africa by Hitler to help the Italians.

Results of the Desert War: Victory for the **Axis Powers** (Germany and Italy) would have given them control over Egypt and the Suez Canal and access to oil in Saudi Arabia. Instead, this was the first victorious Allied campaign; it was a **turning point** in the war. The Axis powers lost control of North Africa. In contrast, the Allies maintained their grip on the Mediterranean Sea, and they prepared for the invasion of Italy.

The War in Eastern Europe

Germans and Italians in the Balkans

In October 1940, **Mussolini** attacked Greece from Albania. He wanted to impress Hitler but the attack failed. Germany had to come to Mussolini's rescue. In the process, Bulgaria, Yugoslavia and Greece were occupied by the Germans (1941). The **British** who had helped the Greeks were expelled from the mainland, and their naval base in **Crete** was captured. Germany ensured **control of the Balkans** so that Hitler was protected from attack when he invaded Russia.

The Stalinist State at War

Operation Barbarossa – The German Invasion of Soviet Russia, 1941

Hitler's Reasons

Both Hitler and Stalin knew that the Nazi-Soviet Pact (1939) only postponed the day when they would go to war with each other. Hitler wanted the **open spaces** of Eastern Europe and Russia to provide the oil, grain and the living space (lebensraum) for his master race. In the process he wanted to **destroy Communism** in Russia. *'The fight which is about to begin is a war of extermination,'* he said.

German contacts with the Soviet army in Poland, and the poor performance of the Russians against Finland in the Winter War (1939–40) convinced Hitler that, *'We have only to kick in the door and the whole rotten structure will come crashing down.'* Hitler was sure he *'would not make the same mistake as Napoleon.'*

German tanks and troops advanced rapidly using blitzkrieg tactics in the invasion of the Soviet Union (Operation Barbarossa).

The Invasion Begins

The invasion code-named **Operation Barbarossa** had to be postponed from mid-May to 22 June because Hitler had to help Italy in the Balkans. This delay proved to be crucial to the outcome of the plan.

Three million men, 4,000 aircraft and 3,000 tanks began the invasion in a **three-pronged attack** towards **Leningrad** in the north, **Moscow** in the centre, and **Kiev** in the south.

German Success

The Germans were very successful. The Russian landscape with its rolling countryside was ideal for blitzkrieg (lightning war). In 18 days the Germans advanced 400 miles and the Russians lost 2,000 aircraft, 1,500 tanks and 300,000 prisoners. In the north **Leningrad** was put under siege, in the centre the Germans got to within 15 miles of **Moscow**, and in the south they captured and advanced beyond **Kiev**.

The German advance was so rapid that **Stalin** was surprised by its speed. He did not believe the warnings of invasion he got beforehand. His initial reaction was confusion and fear as he shut himself up in the Kremlin for three days. But once he overcame his depression, he provided the **strong leadership** which Russia needed to overcome the invasion.

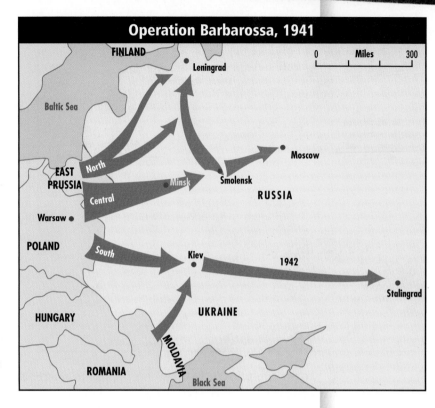

Russian Retreat

The Soviet (Red) army lost heavily in men and machines even though it tried to avoid direct clashes with the Germans. However, the Red army was kept **intact** and retreated in an **orderly fashion**. The Russians also used a **scorched earth policy** – destroying crops, buildings and bridges. They kept pressure on the German army as **Communist guerrilla fighters** harassed the enemy lines.

But the Germans' advance ran into trouble – they had bad maps, the autumn rains brought mud and soon these were changed to snow. Radiators burst, petrol solidified and soldiers froze. Night temperatures fell to minus 40 degrees. The Germans were halted short of **Moscow** by the severe winter and a Russian counter-offensive led by **Marshal Zhukov**.

A victorious German soldier with a burning Russian house in the background.

The Battle of Stalingrad, 1942–43

In 1942, the Germans began the offensive again. This time they concentrated their attack in the south towards **Stalingrad** and **the oilfields of the Caucasus**. The Germans were running short of oil but instead of concentrating solely on the Caucasus,

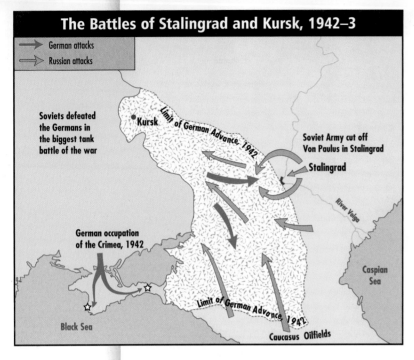

The Battles of Stalingrad and Kursk, 1942–3

→ German attacks
⇒ Russian attacks

Soviets defeated the Germans in the biggest tank battle of the war

• Kursk

Limit of German Advance 1942

Soviet Army cut off Von Paulus in Stalingrad

▪ Stalingrad

River Volga

German occupation of the Crimea, 1942

Caspian Sea

Limit of German Advance 1942

Black Sea

Caucasus Oilfields

Hitler sent part of his army to attack Stalingrad. By dividing his forces, Hitler failed to achieve either target.

The German attack on **Stalingrad** was slowed down by vicious street fighting. The Germans captured most of the city but the Russians held on to a small area of land along the River Volga. Each night more men and supplies were ferried across the river. Then in November 1942, the Russian general, **Marshal Zhukov**, broke through the German lines to the north and south of Stalingrad. His attack trapped the German Sixth Army under **von Paulus** in Stalingrad. Hitler refused permission for von Paulus to attempt a breakout. Instead, efforts to break through to von Paulus failed so the Battle of Stalingrad continued over the winter. But he was forced to surrender, against Hitler's wishes, in February 1943. (See map of The Battles of Stalingrad and Kursk, 1942–43.)

This was a **major turning point** in the war in the east. At the same time the **siege of Leningrad** was lifted after 900 days. From now on the Russians went on the offensive. In July 1943 they won the **Battle of Kursk** where more tanks were involved than in any other battle in history. A year later in the **Battle of Minsk** a much larger Red army again defeated the Germans.

Tough street-by-street fighting in the Battle of Stalingrad (left): the German commander Von Paulus eventually had to surrender (right).

WHY WERE THE GERMANS DEFEATED IN RUSSIA?

1. **The delay in starting the campaign** in 1941 meant that Hitler did not have enough time to capture Moscow before the autumn rains and winter snow slowed progress.

2. **Relocation of factories:** Stalin gave orders between 1939 and 1941 to dismantle many factories and move them over the Ural Mountains out of the range of German planes. Tank, plane and munitions production kept going during the invasion.

3. **German use of terror** – the SS executed thousands of Jews, thousands of Soviet prisoners-of-war were killed or allowed to die, and the civilian population were terrorised behind the German lines – rather than crushing the people, these actions ensured greater resistance from the Russians.

4. **Stalin used the call of nationalism** to motivate the Russian people to resist. In a message to the Russian people, he said, *'The war you are waging is a war of liberation, a just war.'* Stalin set an example in the **Great Patriotic War** by staying in the **Kremlin** in Moscow during the war.

A Soviet war poster encourages the production of armaments.

The War Turns

By 1942, the war had turned against Hitler. From now on the defeat of Germany was only a matter of time:

- In December 1941, Hitler had made the mistake of **declaring war** on the US. After the Japanese attack on Pearl Harbor which brought America into war in the Pacific Ocean and Asia, America and Germany were still at peace. But Hitler **underestimated** the power of the US – he saw it as corrupt because of its mixture of races and the influence of the Jews. By declaring war on the US, Hitler gave Roosevelt the opportunity to make Hitler's defeat in Europe the **main objective** of US policy.

- All of Hitler's plans up to 1942 were based on his belief that he would achieve his goals with **short wars**. But Germany's failure to defeat Britain and Russia meant the country had to mobilise for a **long war** and her resources would not match those of Russia and America.

Hitler looks at himself in the mirror during the Battle of Stalingrad in this Soviet cartoon. What is the message of the cartoon?

QUESTIONS

1. Why did Hitler invade the Soviet Union?
2. How successful was the invasion?
3. How did the Russians cope with the invasion?
4. What happened at the Battle of Stalingrad?
5. Why was Germany defeated and the Soviet Union successful in Operation Barbarossa?

EXAM QUESTION

How was 1942 a turning point in the Second World War?

Wartime Alliances, 1939–45

A Soviet cartoon (1942): The Big Three will tie the enemy in knots. What is the message of the cartoon?

Axis Powers

Germany, Italy and Japan formed the **Axis Powers**. Germany and Italy joined together in the Pact of Steel before the war, but Mussolini did not join the war until Germany had largely defeated France in June 1940. Japan signed the Anti-Comintern Pact (against Communism) with Germany before the war, so in September 1940 the three countries – Germany, Italy and Japan – agreed the **Tripartite Pact** and became known as the **Axis Powers**.

However, Japan did not join the war until it attacked Pearl Harbor in December 1941. Hitler declared war on the US as part of the Tripartite Pact, but this was a disastrous mistake. Now the US could take part in ground, air and naval campaigns against Germany and help Britain and the Soviet Union.

Germany's alliance with Italy contributed to the defeat of Germany in the war. Hitler had to help Mussolini's weak forces several times.

- Rommel was sent to North Africa to help the Italians there and was eventually defeated.
- Hitler delayed the invasion of the Soviet Union (Operation Barbarossa) to help Italy in the Balkans, which contributed to his defeat in the Soviet Union.

Allied Conferences

The leaders of Britain, Russia and America worked together to defeat Hitler. **Churchill**, the British Prime Minister, realised that Britain could not defeat Nazi Germany on its own. He worked tirelessly to maintain good relations with Roosevelt of the US and Stalin of the Soviet Union. He met Roosevelt nine times and Stalin five times during the war. Up to 1941 Britain was largely alone, but when Hitler invaded Russia, Churchill formed the Anglo-Russian Alliance with Stalin. This provided supplies for Russia through Lend-Lease.

Churchill and Roosevelt formed a strong bond, even before America entered the war. Afterwards these leaders, along with Stalin, met at a series of key conferences which decided the shape of the war and made arrangements for the peace settlement after the war.

Lend-Lease

Even before the US entered the war, Britain depended on that country for **Lend-Lease** (March 1941), a programme whereby the US supplied Britain (and later other countries) with war supplies. This enabled Britain to survive until the US was brought into the war after the attack on Pearl Harbor (December 1941).

The Atlantic Charter, 1941

Also before US involvement in the war, Britain's relationship with the US was strengthened by the **Atlantic Charter** (August 1941). Roosevelt and **Churchill** met in Newfoundland and issued the charter, which set out their view of the post-war world. In this, they made *'known certain common principles … on which they base their hopes for a better future for the world'*.

● All people have the right to decide their own form of government.

● All people should live their life in freedom from fear and want.

● There should be improved economic conditions and social welfare.

● All nations should abandon the use of force.

Churchill hoped his meeting with Roosevelt would 'get the Americans into the war'. It did not because the American people were opposed to entering the war until after the Japanese bombing of Pearl Harbor (December 1941). Nevertheless, Churchill was satisfied that the meeting strengthened the relationship between Britain and the USA.

Casablanca Conference, January 1943

Roosevelt and Churchill met again in Casablanca in North Africa. Stalin, who was not present due to the serious war situation in Russia, urged them to open a second front in the west. This would relieve pressure on the Soviet Army.

Roosevelt and **Churchill** agreed on co-ordinating Allied military strategy against the Axis powers for the next year. Instead of opening a second front in France, they agreed on the invasion of Sicily and Italy to knock Italy out of the war. This was in line with **Churchill's** invasion sequence of North Africa (which had already happened), then Italy and finally France.

They also agreed:

● To organise a major anti-submarine campaign

● To organise the bombing of Germany.

They also sought the **unconditional surrender** of Germany.

Teheran Conference, November–December 1943

At the Teheran (Iran) Conference, Roosevelt, **Churchill** and Stalin (the Big Three) met together for the first time. The issue of the **second front** was central to the conference. Stalin was annoyed at what he saw as the long delay in opening the **second front** in the west. **Churchill** favoured an invasion in the Balkans. But Roosevelt and the Americans favoured the invasion of France. Other decisions also favoured Stalin. They decided:

● to plan the **D-Day landings** for May 1944

● to form a **new organisation for peace** after the war to replace the League of Nations

● Russia would get part of Poland after the war as a **buffer zone**

● in compensation, **Poland** would get part of Germany – the decisions concerning Poland were kept secret.

Allied leaders at the Yalta Conference (February 1945): Churchill (Britain), Roosevelt (USA) and Stalin (USSR).

Yalta Conference, February 1945

Roosevelt, **Churchill** and Stalin met at Yalta in the Crimea. This was the most controversial conference. Stalin was in a strong position in the war (he occupied most of Eastern Europe) and Roosevelt was sick. Many of the decisions favoured the Soviet Union. They decided:

- the **Polish-Russian border** would follow the partition line agreed between Stalin and Hitler in 1939
- the **Polish-German border** would follow the line of the Oder-Neisse rivers
- countries liberated by the Allies would have free elections
- the **United Nations** would be formed
- Germany would be divided into **four Occupation Zones** after the war (US, British, French and Russian)
- Germany would pay **reparations**, mainly to the Soviet Union
- the Soviet Union would declare war on Japan three months after defeating Hitler.

Potsdam Conference, July–August 1945

Truman, **Churchill**/Attlee and Stalin met in Potsdam, outside Berlin. The war in Europe was over, but the Japanese were still fighting in Asia. In America, Roosevelt died in April 1945 and he was replaced by President Truman; in Britain **Churchill** lost the general election so during the Conference Clement Attlee replaced him as Prime Minister.

The tension, which eventually developed into the Cold War, was evident. This was not helped by the revelation that America had the atomic bomb. They failed to agree on major issues. They decided:

- Nazi war criminals would be prosecuted,
- Nazis were to be dismissed from government posts. This was part of a process of **denazification** which would be imposed on German society.
- the Council of Foreign Ministers would draw up peace treaties with the Axis Powers,
- German reparations would include machinery and equipment from factories. But Truman wanted to ensure that Germany would not be treated as harshly as it had been by the Treaty of Versailles (1919). So the occupying countries would only be able to take reparations from their own zones.

? QUESTIONS

1. What alliances were formed by the Axis Powers?
2. Who were the participants in each of the following conferences:
   (i) Casablanca
   (ii) Tehran
   (iii) Yalta
   (iv) Potsdam?
3. What were three main agreements in each conference?

The Technology of Warfare

The Air War

In 1941, the Blitz on British cities ended as Hitler concentrated on the invasion of Russia. But it was not until after America joined the war in December 1941 that the Allies began the **systematic bombing** of Germany. Roosevelt and Churchill decided at the Casablanca Conference (1943) that the main aim of the strategic bombing was: *'The progressive destruction and dislocation of the German military, industrial and economic system, and the undermining of the morale of the German people to a point where their capacity for armed resistance is fatally weakened.'*

Lancaster bomber.

THE TECHNOLOGY OF WARFARE

Technology played a vital role in the Second World War. As the war developed into a total war, all aspects of life – political, economic and propaganda as well as technological – were needed to ensure victory. Technological developments were needed to stay **one step ahead of the enemy** or **sometimes to catch up**.

The First World War (1914–18) was dominated by artillery, machine guns and trenches. But two new weapons – **tanks and aeroplanes** – which played a small part in the First World War, dominated the Second World War.

In between the wars, **military thinkers** came up with new strategies to make use of the new technology. German commanders, for example, favoured the use of tanks and planes together for greater speed and mobility. This was their **blitzkrieg** (lightning war) tactics.

There was also the **opposite development** between the wars, when France and Germany used the latest technology to construct huge fortifications, the Maginot Line and the Siegfried Line. But the Second World War showed that the new defensive fortifications were no match for the new faster tanks and planes:

- Tanks and planes **speeded up warfare** and made it **more destructive**.
- Tanks were used together to drive in behind the enemy troops and cut them off (blitzkrieg) (pincer movements). The Germans used these tactics to great effect in the invasions of Poland and France.
- During the war tanks developed quickly. The **German Panzers** were successful at the beginning of the war. But they came up against stronger **Russian tanks** (T-34) so the Germans had to build a tank with stronger armour and more powerful guns (Tiger).
- **Aeroplanes** were used to get **control of the air**. Aeroplanes could be used to bomb enemy troops and ships. They could also be used to bomb cities and industries. Planes were also used to **transport** troops and supplies quickly. But motor transport (trucks) and railways were much more important for transport.
- During the war there were **rapid technological developments** in air warfare:
  - Much **larger bombers** were made which could carry more bombs, and fly faster and further.
  - Long-range **fighter planes** (Mustang) were developed to protect the bombers.
- **Air navigation** was very dependent on technological developments. The Germans used the **Knickbein** system when bombing Britain. On the other hand, the Allies developed the **Oboe** to allow them to bomb through cloud and smoke.

New Weapons: The most significant developments in air warfare came **too late** to affect the outcome of the war. Both sides developed **jet aircraft** which were far faster than existing aircraft. The Germans also developed the **V1 flying bomb** and the **V2 rocket**. The V1 was no faster than an aeroplane so the British were able to defend against it. But the V2 was unstoppable.

Weapons of defence were just as important as weapons of attack. **Radar** (RAdio Direction And Range) was first developed by the British and it played a vital role in the **Battle of Britain**. Just as important, but much more secret, was the use of **Ultra** to crack the secrets of the German **Enigma** coding machine. This influenced land battles as well as the **war at sea**. Here Germany built larger and more powerful **submarines** which could stay at sea longer. These were countered by **Sonar** which tracked the movements of U-boats under the water.

By the end of the war, technology had developed the ultimate weapon which made all others obsolete – the **Atomic bomb**. Developed secretly in the US as the **Manhattan Project**, it was used against Hiroshima and Nagasaki to end the war against Japan.

In answering questions on the technology of warfare, you may use information on various campaigns – e.g. the invasions of Poland, France and Russia; the Battle of Britain and the Blitz; D-Day; war in the air; or the war at sea – to show how the technology was used.

QUESTIONS

1. How were tanks and planes used in Blitzkrieg?
2. What new weapons were developed during the Second World War and what was their impact?
3. What role did technology play in some of the key battles and campaigns of the war?

EXAM QUESTION

What role did technology play in the Second World War?

Day and Night Bombing

The British and the Americans took **two different approaches**. British Bomber Command under Air Marshal Harris used **area bombing** of German cities at **night**. The British used Lancaster and Stirling bombers. On the other hand, the **Americans** used **precision bombing** by **daytime** because they had better bombers, the **Flying Fortresses**. However, they suffered huge losses at the hands of German fighters and anti-aircraft guns. By the **middle of 1944** the Allies had complete control of the air. They were helped by technological developments with better navigational and bomb sighting equipment, and the protection of the long-range fighter, the Mustang.

The German city of Dresden was heavily bombed by the Allies in February 1945.

Most major German cities were attacked, in particular those in the **Ruhr** industrial area: so also was **Hamburg**. Sixty per cent of the homes were damaged or destroyed, 40,000 people were killed and a million people fled the city.

What were the effects of the Air War?

- The Allies disrupted factory production but the Germans quickly started up again.
- The most effective targets were the oil refineries. German oil production declined in 1944 and this hit the tanks and aircraft.
- The Allies lost a great deal of aircraft and men. About 30,000 aircraft were lost and 180,000 British and US airmen were either injured or killed.
- Hundreds of thousands of German civilians were killed and German morale was weakened.

? QUESTIONS

1. What role did the Air War play in the Second World War?
2. How did technology influence the Air War?

The Invasion of Italy, 1943

After defeating the Germans and Italians in North Africa, the Allies turned to Italy. They wanted to knock a weakened Italy out of the war.

In July 1943, in **Operation Husky**, an American army under **Patton** and a British army under **Montgomery** landed and captured Sicily in 39 days. The fall of Sicily led to the dismissal of **Mussolini** as Prime Minister by **King Victor Emmanuel**. The new government, led by **Marshal Badoglio,** imprisoned Mussolini and began secret negotiations with the Allies.

Catching Italian warships: what is the message of this cartoon?

German Defences

However, when the Italian government signed an armistice with the Allies, the Germans took over Rome and continued the fighting. American and British armies then invaded mainland Italy. They advanced northwards until they were held up by the strong German defensive line, the **Gustav Line**, centered on **Monte Cassino**. It took a number of attacks and the heavy bombing of the monastery on Cassino before the Allies broke through. In June 1944, Rome fell.

The Allies then advanced into northern Italy, capturing a second German defence line, the **Gothic Line**. In the meantime, Hitler's commandos rescued Mussolini and he set up the so-called **Salo Republic** in the north. But his capture by Italian resistance fighters led to his execution in April 1945.

The Success of D-Day – The Normandy Landings, June 1944

The Americans and British knew that if they were to defeat Hitler they had to invade France. Stalin, the Russian leader, was pressing them to open a **second front**. The decision to invade was made at the **Teheran conference** between Roosevelt, Churchill and Stalin. Later, **General Eisenhower** was appointed Supreme Commander of the Allied Expeditionary Force to carry out the invasion plan, code-named **Operation Overlord**.

The Allies fooled the Germans into thinking that the invasion would occur around Calais. Instead they chose the beaches of Normandy because they were not as well defended and they gave direct access to Paris.

D-Day Landings

THE BEACHES ON D-DAY

The Invasion

On 6 June 1944, around 5,000 ships landed over 150,000 soldiers, 6,000 tanks and armoured vehicles on five beaches in Normandy. They were protected by Allied control of the air, and they were helped by paratroopers dropped behind the German lines. Over the next few days the Allies extended their control out from the beaches. (See D-Day Landings map.)

Allied reinforcements and supplies were brought in through **mulberry piers** – artificial harbours towed across the English Channel. Oil supplies were brought by

The Allies bring in supplies on Omaha Beach after the success of the D-Day landings in Normandy (June 1944).

PLUTO – an undersea pipeline that crossed from England to France. The surprise landing, control of the air and the huge resources of the Allies ensured victory on D-Day and afterwards.

By August 1944, the Allies broke out of Normandy and headed for Paris. The city was liberated on 24 August. Two days later **General de Gaulle**, leader of the Free French, marched in triumph down the Champs Élysées. He claimed France for the French and for himself.

Advance on Germany

? QUESTIONS

1. How successful was the Allied invasion of Italy?
2. How did the Allies plan and carry out the invasion of France on D-Day?

Britain's part in the Second World War in Europe

- Intro: Appeasement/ Poland/Declaration of war
- Invasion of Norway
- Downfall of Chamberlain/Churchill took over
- Defending France and Dunkirk
- Battle of Britain and the Blitz
- War at Sea/Ultra
- Churchill and Wartime Alliances
- Britain and the War in the Air
- The Home Front
- Invasion of Italy
- Invasion of France/ D-Day
- Overall impact of war on Britain

By 1944, the Allies were advancing on Germany from **three sides**. (See map of Allied Advance on Germany from Three Sides.) The advance progressed as follows:

1. In the **east**, the Russians moved into Poland in March 1944. However, they refused to help the **Warsaw Uprising** organised by Polish resistance fighters. Over 200,000 Poles were killed as the Germans crushed the Uprising. A few months later, in early 1945, the Russians took Warsaw and set up a Communist-controlled government. This was the first of the **Communist satellite states** in Eastern Europe which were to last for 45 years.

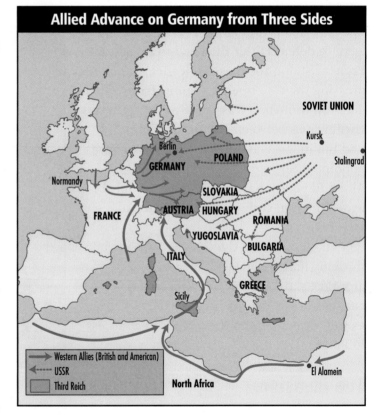

Allied Advance on Germany from Three Sides

SOVIET UNION

Kursk

Berlin

GERMANY · POLAND

Normandy

Stalingrad

FRANCE

SLOVAKIA

AUSTRIA · HUNGARY

ROMANIA

YUGOSLAVIA

BULGARIA

ITALY

GREECE

Sicily

El Alamein

North Africa

→ Western Allies (British and American)
⇢ USSR
▭ Third Reich

2. In the **west**, the British and Canadians pushed into Belgium and captured the sites of the **V1 flying bombs** and the **V2 rockets**. American progress was halted temporarily when the Germans attacked at the **Battle of the Bulge** in December 1944. But the attempt failed, with a huge loss of German lives. A few months later the British and Americans crossed the Rhine.

3. In the **south**, there was slower progress in Italy because of the mountains and the German defence lines. But by April 1945 the Germans there surrendered.

Hitler's Suicide

As the Americans and British advanced across Germany and the Russians attacked Berlin, Hitler committed suicide in his own bunker, along with his former mistress and then wife, **Eva Braun**, and close associate, **Goebbels**. On 7 May 1945, the German government, now led by **Admiral Doenitz**, surrendered unconditionally. The Allies had won **Victory in Europe**.

The Soviet army then joined in the **war against Japan**. But, by then, the Japanese army had been weakened and the first atomic bomb had been dropped on Hiroshima. The Russians overran **Manchuria** and captured 500,000 Japanese troops before Japan surrendered.

A Russian soldier raised the Soviet flag over the Reichstag in Berlin.

EXAM QUESTION ❓

How and why did the Second World War end?

WHY DID GERMANY LOSE THE WAR?

Short war to Total war: Hitler planned for a series of short wars, using Blitzkrieg, to achieve his targets. In between the wars, he would build up his resources. But the war turned into a long war where all the resources of a country were needed (total war), and Germany could not match the resources of the Allied Powers.

Failure to defeat Britain: Hitler's failure to defeat the British at Dunkirk, and in the Battle of Britain, meant that Britain continued to be a centre of resistance in the west when he turned to attack Russia.

Greater resources: Hitler attacked the Soviet Union and declared war on America, two countries with far greater resources than Germany:

- **Population:** The combined population of Britain, Russia and America was 344 million; Germany and her allies 181 million.
- **Army, navy, air force:** the Allies had 27.5 million; Germany and her allies had 17.5 million.
- **Oil production:** the Allies produced 2,200 million barrels a year; Germany and her allies 60 million barrels a year.
- **Military equipment:** Russia alone produced 24,700 tanks, 25,400 aircraft; Germany produced 9,300 tanks and 14,700 aircraft.
- **America** became the **arsenal of democracy** – under **Lend-Lease**, US war supplies were given free to her allies; America gave Britain $31 billion dollars and Russia $10 billion of supplies; America produced 300,000 aircraft and 86,000 tanks.

Italy's role: Because of the weakness of the Italian army, Hitler had to send Rommel and the Afrika Korps to Africa to help the country, and delayed the beginning of Operation Barbarossa to help the Italians in the Balkans. Hitler assumed that he would defeat Russia before winter set in, so he did not make adequate preparations for it.

Hitler's role: Hitler's over-confidence in his ability as a military leader. He supported the use of Blitzkrieg at the beginning of the war and this provided Germany with success. But as the war went on he made a number of mistakes, such as his refusal to allow von Paulus to break out of Stalingrad before he was fully encircled.

Brutal treatment: The Germans treated the people of the occupied countries badly and this increased their opposition to the Nazis.

The war at sea: The Allies won the war at sea and kept the sea route to America open.

Bombing raids: The Allied heavy bombing of Germany disrupted the economy and reduced civilian morale.

The success of D-Day: This opened the second front and the Allies advanced on Germany from east and west.

In answering the question 'Why did Germany lose the war?', you may also use information in relation to the main campaigns of the war, e.g. the Battle of Britain and the Blitz; the invasion of Russia; D-Day; war in the air; or war at sea to explain how Germany lost each battle or campaign.

The Results of the Second World War

1. Death and Destruction

The war resulted in huge loss of life and destruction of cities and countryside. The Soviet Union had about 20 million soldiers and civilians killed, as much as the total loss for all countries in the First World War. In total, between 40 and 50 million soldiers and civilians were killed in the war. Cities, towns and villages were devastated by aerial bombing and by street fighting. Russia and Poland were the worst affected. In Russia alone 1,700 towns, 70,000 villages and 40,000 miles of railway track were either totally or partially destroyed.

2. Refugees

There were about 20 million refugees at the end of the war:

- Most left home because of the dangers of war to seek refuge in a safer place. The largest group of these was about **10 million Germans** who left their homes in Eastern Europe, fleeing from the advancing Soviet army. They moved to the British, French and American Occupation Zones in Germany.
- **Other refugees** included those taken to Germany as **forced labour**. Some were trying to return to their home country.
- **Jewish refugees** left Europe after the war and headed for Palestine. They later founded the state of Israel.

Camps were constructed after the war to house them and they were helped by the United Nations or by Allied troops. Many died from cold, hunger or disease.

3. Political Effects

- **Fascism** and **Nazism**, which had dominated the history of the 1930s, were largely wiped out.
- **Germany** was divided in two, east and west. It remained divided for the next 45 years.

The war is over: German troops captured during the D-Day landings (left), people waiting for bread in Berlin (right).

- **The Growth of Superpowers:** The **Soviet Union** replaced Germany as the strongest European power and it developed as a **superpower**. It spread its influence over satellite states in Eastern Europe, where it established Communist governments. The **US** became the other superpower after the war.
- The **conflicting ideologies** (political ideas and systems) of the two superpowers led to **the Cold War** which dominated post-war foreign policy until the fall of Communism in Russia in 1991.
- The other European powers, particularly Britain and France, lost the power they had before the war. They also lost their colonies in a process of **decolonisation** during the 1950s and 1960s.
- The horror of the war encouraged political leaders to create **organisations** that would prevent another war. The failure of the League of Nations led to the setting up of the **United Nations** to sort out disputes between countries peacefully. In Europe, leaders pushed for **European unity** and this led to the founding of the **European Economic Community** (1958).

4. Scientific and Technological Effects

During the war huge efforts were made by all sides to use new technology to win the war. The new technology was often used for peaceful purposes after the war:

- Improvements in **aircraft** led to a huge expansion in air travel after the war.
- The invention of the V2 rocket, and the engineers who worked on it, became the inspiration for the US and Russian **space programmes**.
- The invention of the atomic bomb led to a **nuclear arms race** and this became a key factor in relations between the superpowers during the **Cold War**.

HOMEWORK EXERCISES

1. Develop notes on Britain's part in the Second World War.

ORDINARY LEVEL

2. Study the cartoon of The Big Three on p. 302 and answer the following questions.

   A. (i) Who are the Big Three countries? (ii) Which country produced the poster? Give a reason for your answer. (iii) What message it is trying to get across? (iv) Give one example of how the countries co-operated in the war against Hitler.

   B. Write a **paragraph** on one of the following. (i) Blitzkrieg tactics in World War II (ii) The Invasion of France, May 1940 (iii) The war at sea

   C. Write a **long answer** on one of the following. (i) German success in World War II, 1939–41 (ii) Operation Barbarossa and Soviet victory (iii) Wartime alliances (iv) How effective a wartime leader was Winston Churchill between 1940 and 1945? (v) The technology of war in World War II (vi) Why did Germany lose World War II?

HIGHER LEVEL

3. How significant was the role played by the Soviet Union in World War II? (2007)

4. What challenges faced the Soviet Union in peace and war, 1924–45? (2014)

5. What part did technology play in World War II? OR What developments took place in the technology of warfare during the period 1920 to 1945? (2006)

6. How effective a wartime leader was Winston Churchill?

7. What did you learn about World War II from your study of one or more of the following: (i) wartime alliances (ii) collaboration/resistance (iii) the technology of warfare? (2009)

8. How well did Britain overcome the challenges it faced in the Second World War?

In this section, you should understand:
- The Home Front in Germany and Britain.
- The role of collaboration and resistance (including Vichy France, Chapter 23, Politics and Administration in France: The Third Republic, 1920–40, and the Vichy State, 1940–44, pp. 274–78).

Hitler's Europe – Nazi-occupied Europe

By the end of 1941, Germany and her allies extended their control over most of the continent of Europe – from the Atlantic seaboard to central Russia. (See map showing Nazi-occupied Europe.) Germany had to organise and mobilise all the resources at her

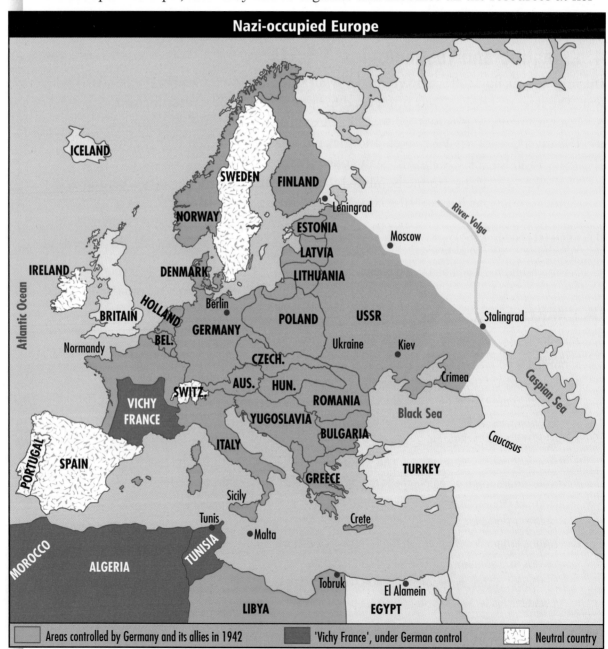

Nazi-occupied Europe

| Areas controlled by Germany and its allies in 1942 | 'Vichy France', under German control | Neutral country |

disposal. This meant that all the conquered lands were forced to support the German war machine. The war had become a **total war**.

The Home Front in Germany

Germany had to gear herself entirely for the war. **Civilians** were as much a part of the war as soldiers. Many had to work in war industries producing weapons and ammunition for the front. As the war went on these included many **women**, even though the Nazis did not approve of women workers. They also included foreign workers who were mostly **forced labour** from the occupied countries. By 1944, these amounted to 7,500,000. Added to these were 2 million **prisoners of war** who were forced to work in factories, mines or farms.

Forced labour in a German concentration camp.

Germany suffered from **food shortages** so food had to be rationed, but some could get supplies on the black market. Civilians experienced the direct effects of war, especially from 1942 onwards. The Allies began to bomb German cities by day and by night. Thousands of civilians were killed as cities and towns were wrecked. These bombings and the food shortages made life in Germany very difficult by the end of the war (see pp. 308–09).

Economic Control

The Germans exploited the lands they took over by a variety of means:

- The cost of supporting the occupying troops was borne by the conquered people e.g. France.
- Almost all exports from the occupied lands were sent to Germany. This included most of the food. In Denmark and Holland, for example, all the dairy and poultry produce went to Germany.
- Consequently, food was **rationed** and this resulted in **inflation** (price rises).
- **Compulsory Labour Service** (forced labour) was used in local projects or sent to Germany – 600,000 were sent from France alone.

Repression

Germany imposed a harsh rule on its own people as well as those of the occupied lands. German rule in the east, in Poland and Russia, was brutal from the start. In the west, in France and Holland, for example, it became as brutal when the war turned against Germany and when the resistance became more active. Most of the repression was carried out by **Himmler's Gestapo** and the **SS**. Hostages were taken, and there were shootings or mass deportations to **concentration camps**. By 1944, there were **20 main camps** and **165 subsidiary camps** holding anybody the Nazis believed was opposed to their regime.

> **KEY CONCEPT**
> **LEBENSRAUM** Hitler believed that having additional living space would strengthen Germany by making it **self-sufficient** in food and raw materials. He wanted the living space in Eastern Europe, particularly Russia.

GERMAN DAILY RATION OF FOOD	
Jam	0.25 oz
Butter, fat	1.25 oz
Sugar	1.25 oz
Meat	2.5 oz (if it could be obtained)
Coffee	0.25 oz

313

Transporting Jews to concentration camps.

KEY CONCEPT
HOLOCAUST This is the word used to describe the Nazi's attempt to exterminate the Jews during the Second World War. It resulted in the death of about 6 million Jews.

KEY CONCEPT
ANTI-SEMITISM is the hatred for, and persecution of, the Jews. This hatred was based on religious and economic factors. Anti-Semitism became an important part of Nazi racial views which saw the Jews as an inferior race. It led to the Nuremberg Laws against the Jews, and later the Holocaust during the Second World War.

KEY CONCEPT
HERRENVOLK This was the Nazi idea of the Germans as a master race, superior to all other races.

Sometimes there were **extreme reprisals**. In Czechoslovakia, the men of the village of **Lidice** were shot and the women sent to concentration camps when Czech guerrilla fighters (partisans) ambushed and killed **Reinhard Heydrich**, the Nazi Protector of Czechoslovakia, in May 1942. Similar action was taken against the village of **Oradour-sur-Glane** in France in 1944, when the SS killed 642 people (see p. 276).

The Jews in the Holocaust

Some groups of people were subjected to even more repression, in particular the Jews. This was driven by **anti-Semitism**. Hitler and the Nazis believed in the superiority of the **Aryan** race, and the need to protect it from **inferior races**, especially the Jews. The Nazis believed this could only be done by **extermination**.

The organisation given the task of eliminating the Jews was the **SS**. Its leader, Himmler, was a firm believer in Nazi **racial ideas**.

As Germany conquered more countries, the Germans took over more Jewish communities. To the 3 million Jews in Poland were added about 4 million more in other parts of Eastern Europe, particularly the Soviet Union. The Nazis first proposed to expel the Jews from Europe after the war to the island of **Madagascar** off the coast of Africa. But planning for this was dropped after a while.

Nazi Concentration Camps

At the same time, the Nazis were herding Jews into **ghettoes**, the most notorious of which was the **Warsaw ghetto**. They were walled into the ghettoes in crowded conditions which got worse as the war progressed. In Russia, **Special Action Units** following the German army carried out **mass executions** of the Jews, such as the 33,000 killed in the Ukraine.

The Final Solution

In early 1942, Hitler and the Nazis decided to exterminate the Jews. The organisation of the **Final Solution** was planned at the **Wannsee Conference**, chaired by **Reinhard Heydrich**. The extermination was conducted in concentration camps in Poland, especially in **Auschwitz-Birkenau**. After various experiments to get the most efficient method of killing, the SS decided on **gas chambers**, camouflaged as shower rooms, using **Zyklon-B**, a poisonous gas.

Victims of the Final Solution.

Jews were rounded up from all over Europe, including France and Holland, and sent to the camps in Poland. Some feared, or even knew, what was going to happen to them, but most went to their deaths still not realising what was happening. Once they got to the camps, the weak were separated from the able-bodied. The latter were worked until they too were weak. The weak were gassed, and their bodies were buried in mass graves or incinerated in ovens. (See also The Nazis and the Jews: Anti-Semitism and the Holocaust, pp. 217–18.)

Resistance

In the first years of the war, resistance was scattered. Very often it was just passive resistance such as deliberately misunderstanding orders. The German army had come so quickly and with such force that it took time for resistance to be organised. After that, resistance grew because of:

- **National pride** – doing something for their country.
- The **brutality of the German invader**, particularly the use of forced labour.
- The involvement of **Communists** after Hitler's invasion of Russia.

Resistance took many forms; publishing an underground press, sheltering and smuggling allied airmen, ambushing, passing on intelligence and in some cases open warfare.

Results: Resistance was more effective in Eastern Europe than in Western Europe. In the west it was no more than a **nuisance value** rather than a barrier to German operations. It was weak when it was not backed by Allied troops (see pp. 276–78).

In the east, however, resistance had a definite impact on German operations. In **Yugoslavia**, for instance, **Tito's** partisans created considerable difficulties for German forces. In **Russia**, it is estimated that 150,000 partisans (or guerrilla fighters) were active behind German lines by 1942, cutting communications and holding down German troops. But even here resistance forces had their greatest effect when they were working with Allied forces, especially when Germany was weakening.

German Resistance

There was also resistance in **Germany**, particularly after 1941. Those such as **student groups** like the **White Rose** in Munich favoured **passive resistance**. But the most dangerous resistance came from within the German army. Here senior officers planned to overthrow Hitler's regime. A number of efforts were made to assassinate Hitler but the most serious was the **July Plot** in 1944. **Count von Stauffenberg** placed a bomb in

QUESTIONS

1. What was total war?
2. How did Germany gear up for total war?
3. How did Germany deal with occupied countries?
4. What plans did the Nazis have for the Jews?
5. What was the Final Solution?

EXAM QUESTION

How did anti-Semitism and the Holocaust affect Europe, 1920–45?

KEY CONCEPT

RESISTANCE This was the act of resisting when enemy troops have taken over the country. The Resistance was usually a secret or underground organisation involved in sabotage against the occupying forces and collaborators.

Villagers bring in fresh food to Russian guerrillas.

? QUESTIONS

1. Why did resistance to Hitler grow?
2. How effective was resistance to Hitler?
3. Who resisted in Germany?

KEY CONCEPT
COLLABORATION
This is co-operating with the enemy especially when they have taken over your own country.

? QUESTIONS

1. Who collaborated with the Nazis?
2. Why did people collaborate with the Nazis?
3. What happened to collaborators after the war?

Hitler's headquarters but Hitler escaped with minor injuries. The leaders of the plot were hanged with piano wire.

Collaboration

Collaboration (or active help) was needed by the Nazis to ensure control of the occupied countries or satellite states. There was active collaboration in many countries under Nazi control, though very little in Poland or Russia.

Sometimes collaborators were members of **minority German communities** in countries such as Slovakia or Romania. In other countries they were members of **pre-war Fascist parties** who now believed that victory would gain them a share of the spoils. In Norway, Quisling held power briefly. In France these groups were active in the German-controlled area as well as in Vichy France. There was also **official collaboration**, as in Vichy France, and in Denmark where local or native governments collaborated with the Germans.

Why Did People Collaborate?

Collaborators had many **reasons** for working with the Nazis. Some admired the German **New Order**; others liked the Nazi control of trade unions and the protection of private property. Some traded with the Germans to make a living. Young women became friendly with German soldiers. These might supply cigarettes or stockings, or the women were attracted to them. Others had more specific reasons. In France, criminal gangs helped the Germans in the hope that their own crimes would be ignored. Still others in France used hatred of the English as an excuse.

Hitler was quite sure that he wanted collaborators and their countries for the benefit of Germany. He used collaborators to do **police work** or to send **recruits** to fight Bolshevik (Communist) Russia. In the latter case a number of countries contributed, including French and Dutch volunteers.

After the war was over, the collaborators were **punished** severely: by death, shaving of the hair in the case of women, or imprisonment. Collaboration became a shame on the country so the punishment of the collaborator was a way of regaining self-respect for the country. (See also Vichy France, p. 275.)

A French collaborator is punished.

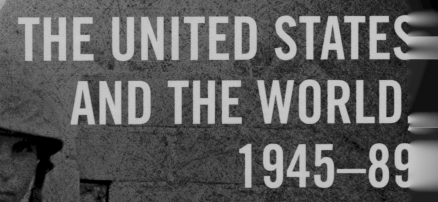

③ THE UNITED STATES AND THE WORLD 1945–89

In this section, you should understand:
- The structure of the US government.
- The roles of the President.
- The domestic policies of the presidents and the growth of the imperial presidency.
- The role of Truman and Johnson.

Structures and Tensions

The United States of America won its independence from Britain in the late eighteenth century. The leaders of the new America drew up a constitution which laid out the basic laws of the country. The new government was:

- A **representative democracy** – the people elected leaders who acted on their behalf.
- A **republic** which had a President, rather than a King, at its head.
- A **federal system** or structure with a central (or national) government in the capital, Washington, sharing power with state governments.

You can refer to this map when states and cities are mentioned in the text.

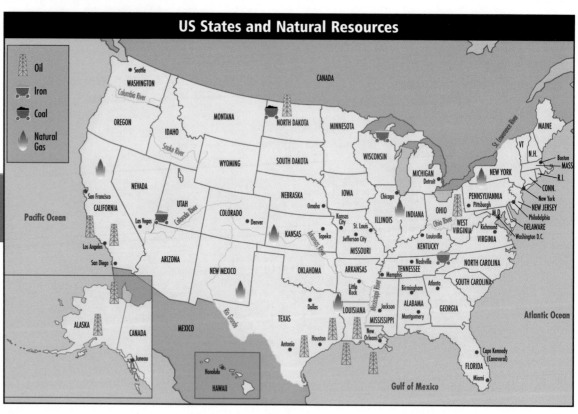

US States and Natural Resources

Federal and State Powers

The Constitution gave some powers to the **federal** (or central) government and some to the **states**. In general, the **federal government** controls war and peace, taxation, interstate and foreign trade and foreign relations. The **states**, on the other hand, provide education, regulate trade within the state, maintain the police and levy local taxes. This **separation of power** between the federal and state governments creates **tension** between the two, but it was one way to avoid an abuse of power. The second way was to separate the powers within the federal government.

Separation of Powers

The eighteenth-century leaders did not want any branch of government to have too much power, so they devised a **separation of powers** between three separate branches – the **legislative** (which passed laws), the **executive** (which carried out the laws) and the **judicial** (which examined the laws). The separation of powers created a system of **checks and balances** which allowed each branch to have some control over the other two branches. This prevented any one branch becoming too powerful.

The Legislative Branch

Congress is the **legislative** or **lawmaking** branch of government. The power of passing laws is shared by the two houses of Congress – the House of Representatives and the Senate – based on Capitol Hill in Washington. The two Houses have a system of checks and balances – each House must co-operate and compromise with the other to get laws passed.

Congress has many important powers – to declare war, raise taxes and pay for the armed forces, and it can **impeach** (bring charges against) any member of the executive branch who may have committed a crime.

The **House of Representatives** has 435 members who serve for two years. They represent the people of a congressional district. The House of Representatives has a special role in taxation – all bills (proposed laws) for raising revenue (money) must begin in the House.

> **KEY CONCEPT**
> **SEPARATION OF POWERS** In the US Constitution, each branch of government has different (separate) powers so that no one branch can have too much power. The power to make laws is divided between the President, Congress and the Supreme Court. Power is also divided between the federal (national) government and the state governments.

POLITICAL PARTIES

There are two main political parties in the US – the **Democratic Party** and the **Republican Party**. They are organised at national and local level, where they are run by county and state committees. Every four years the parties hold national conventions to choose Presidential and Vice-Presidential candidates and to decide a **platform**. This is a statement of the policies of the party which will guide elected representatives.

The Republican Elephant, symbol of the Republican Party.

In general, the **Democrats** favoured federal government intervention in economic and social affairs. On the other hand, the **Republicans** were opposed to government intervention and preferred to give more power to the individual states. Third parties have developed in the US but they have never lasted very long. After the Second World War, the Southern Democrats formed the **States' Rights** or **Dixiecrat Party** to protest at giving **civil rights** to black Americans. At a later stage, in the late 1960s, the American **Independence Party**, led by George Wallace, opposed **racial integration** (the coming together of the races). Very often those parties drew attention to important social and political issues.

The Democratic Donkey, symbol of the Democratic Party.

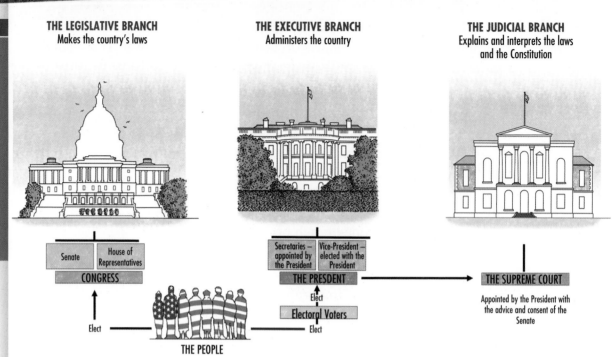

QUESTIONS

1. What type of government structure does the US have?
2. How and why is there a separation of powers?
3. What is the function of each branch of the US government?
4. What two main political parties rule the US?

THE LEGISLATIVE BRANCH
Makes the country's laws

THE EXECUTIVE BRANCH
Administers the country

THE JUDICIAL BRANCH
Explains and interprets the laws and the Constitution

Senate | House of Representatives
CONGRESS

Secretaries – appointed by the President | Vice-President – elected with the President
THE PRESIDENT
Elect
Electoral Voters

THE SUPREME COURT
Appointed by the President with the advice and consent of the Senate

THE PEOPLE
Elect

The branches of the federal government. What is the function of each?

The Houses of Congress on Capitol Hill, Washington showing the US Senate (left) and the House of Representatives (right).

Members of the US Supreme Court.

The **Senate** is much smaller, with 100 members – two from each state, regardless of the population size. Each senator is elected for a six-year term, with elections held for one-third of the senators every two years. The Senate has special responsibility for approving treaties with foreign countries; it is more influential than the House of Representatives in foreign affairs.

The Judicial Branch

The highest court in the US is the **Supreme Court**. Its principal function is to review laws passed by Congress or the state governments. It has the power to declare laws **unconstitutional** (or invalid). Judges are appointed by the President, and Presidents can therefore influence the general direction of the judgments of the Supreme Court.

The Executive Branch

The President of the US is elected every four years on the first Tuesday after the first Monday of November. Presidents can only serve for two terms. The successful candidate takes office after **inauguration** (the ceremony for swearing in the President) on 20 January of the following year. On that day the incoming President takes an oath of office: *'I do* *solemnly swear that I will faithfully execute the office of President of the United States, and will to the best of my ability, preserve, protect, and defend the Constitution of the United States.'*

The White House, home of the US President in Washington, District of Columbia.

Roles of the President

The President has **six main functions** or roles:

- Chief executive
- Commander-in-chief
- Foreign policy director
- Legislative leader
- Party leader
- Head of state

Chief Executive

As chief executive or chief administrator of the country, he or she has to enforce the laws of the country and prepare a national budget. The President is assisted by the **Cabinet**. These are the heads of the government departments who are appointed by the President with the approval of Congress. As the power of the President grew, more departments were formed to run the country. Since 1945, six new departments were added, including Defense, Education and Transportation.

Commander-in-Chief

The President is commander-in-chief of the US army, navy and air force. In this way, he or she is responsible for the **defence of the country**. He or she appoints the top military officers with the approval of Congress. Only the President can decide on the use of nuclear weapons.

Foreign Policy Director

The President can make treaties, appoint ambassadors and meet foreign diplomats. The **Secretary of State** is usually responsible for foreign policy, but some Presidents have been more active than others in this area.

Legislative Leader

The President can propose laws for Congress in his **State of the Union** address, given to the Houses of Congress in January each year. He or she has a large influence on laws passing through Congress. He or she has to work to ensure the support of Congress for his or her proposals. The President can also issue **Executive Orders**, which do not need Congressional approval.

> **KEY CONCEPT**
> **PRESIDENTIAL BUREAUCRACY** As the influence of the President and the federal government grew, so did the bureaucracy (civil service) which had to implement the policies. The President expanded the number of Cabinet posts and departments, also increasing the number of agencies to carry out presidential policy.

> Up to the present time, all US Presidents have been men. Hillary Clinton failed in her attempt to become the first female President in the 2016 election. However, she has opened up opportunities for potential female candidates in future elections.

Party Leader

The President is **leader** of his party. He works to form the party's policies on all major issues. The President is in a strong position if his party is in control (is in the majority) in the House of Representatives and in the Senate.

Head of State

This is mostly a ceremonial role where the President attends functions and meets the representatives of foreign countries.

The Presidency from Roosevelt to Reagan

Presidential Salary	
Date	**Salary ($)**
1789	25,000
1873	50,000
1909	75,000
1949	100,000
1969	200,000
2001	400,000

Introduction

The power of US Presidents has grown from being largely honorary at the end of the eighteenth century to being the most powerful person in the US (and the world) in the second half of the twentieth century:

- The rise of the power of US Presidents has depended very much on **individual** Presidents. Some have been stronger leaders than others.
- It also depended on the circumstances of the time. Very often in times of crisis such as the American Civil War, the First and Second World Wars, the Great Depression and the Cold War, the power of the President has been expanded to lead the country.
- Presidential power has also grown because **American society** has become more complicated, with greater problems. Presidents have been given more powers to solve these problems. Sometimes this has happened because Congress failed to take action itself.
- It also depended on **political beliefs**. Some Presidents believed in active government, while others believed in less active government, often giving power back to the individual states.
- The President is listened to because of his position, so his policies are more likely to be acted upon. As one President called it, this was the *'bully pulpit'*. When a President raises issues, it will be more likely to become part of national debate.
- Some historians have argued that the power of the President is the *'power to persuade'*. In other words, the power of the President rests on **bargaining and persuading Congress** (House of Representatives and the Senate) to carry out presidential policies. Because of the separation of powers, the President has to negotiate and bargain with other groups.
- The President is the only **unifying force** in a political system where power is so scattered. He speaks for the US, more than any of the other branches of government.

Some historians have called this the growth of the **imperial presidency**, whereby more and more power was **centralised** in the hands of the President.

? QUESTIONS

1. What are the six main functions of the US President?
2. What is the imperial presidency?

The Roosevelt Presidency

By the time President Roosevelt (FDR) died in April 1945, he had expanded the power of the presidency considerably. He was the longest-serving President and he was faced with two major crises – the Great Depression and the Second World War.

In trying to solve these problems, he was able to extend presidential power. In Roosevelt's view, *'The presidency is pre-eminently a place of moral leadership.'* This was the rise of the **imperial presidency**, when more power was **centralised** in the hands of the President.

During the Great Depression, as part of Roosevelt's **New Deal** policies, the government took a more active interest in the economy. Roosevelt set up many emergency agencies *'to promote the general welfare'* (US Constitution). This was the beginning of the American **welfare state**. Even though the Supreme Court limited the spread of the New Deal policies by declaring some of them unconstitutional, others expanded the power of the federal government.

In 1939, Roosevelt created the **Executive Office** to control the work of the many agencies that operated directly for the White House.

During the Second World War, Roosevelt extended federal government control over manufacturing. In foreign policy, he took part in the wartime conferences with Churchill (Britain) and Stalin (Soviet Union). He gave general direction to US foreign policy.

Roosevelt provided a direct link with the public (people) by speaking over the radio in his *'fireside chats'*. He was also the first President to speak on television. This increased his **popularity**.

Recent Presidents of the US		
Franklin D Roosevelt	1933–45	Democrat
Harry S Truman	1945–53	Democrat
Dwight Eisenhower	1953–61	Republican
John F Kennedy	1961–63	Democrat
Lyndon Johnson	1963–69	Democrat
Richard Nixon	1969–74	Republican
Gerald Ford	1974–7	Republican
Jimmy Carter	1977–81	Democrat
Ronald Reagan	1981–9	Republican
George Bush Sr	1989–93	Republican
Bill Clinton	1993–2001	Democrat
George Bush Jr	2001–2009	Republican
Barack Obama	2009–2017	Democrat
Donald Trump	2017–	Republican

The construction of the Grand Coulee Dam was part of President Roosevelt's New Deal policy to revive the US economy in the 1930s.

The Truman Presidency

Truman was **Vice-President**, so he became President when Roosevelt died in office (April 1945). Truman was a strong and honourable leader, with sympathy for the less well-off in society. He was a straight-talking person who liked simple food and pleasures. Truman was prepared to take decisive action when it was necessary. *'The buck stops here'* was a sign he displayed on his desk to show how he viewed his responsibility as a President.

Truman's Domestic Policies

- Truman was more successful in his foreign than in his domestic policies. This was partly because he faced opposition to the latter in Congress.
- **Housing:** Truman was faced with a **serious housing shortage** as thousands of demobilised soldiers returned home. Working through the Federal Housing Administration (FHA), Truman made loans from the banks more easily available. The construction industry responded by increasing house construction from 117,000 units in 1944 to 1.7 million units in 1950. In this way, house construction became a key component in boosting the post-war US economy (see p. 379).
- **Inflation and wages:** In spite of demands from industry and business to ease price controls, Truman continued the Office of Price Administration (OPA) which had been set up during World War II to control prices and wages. This **limited inflation** to 7 per cent over the first ten months after the war. In relation to **wages**, Truman had to resolve huge strikes in the electrical, car, and steel industries, and later in the mining

and railway industries. He sought increased legal powers from Congress to control industries vital to the national interest. But Congress resisted and Truman was forced to use mediation to solve the strikes.

- **Congress:** Truman had difficulties with Congress. When he became President, Southern Democrats (Dixiecrats) disagreed with his **21-point programme** for social reform, so he failed to get it passed in Congress. Then the Republicans got control of Congress in the 1946 elections and they were opposed to greater government power.

- **The 1948 presidential election:** The Republican candidate, Thomas Dewey, was the favourite to win this election because the Democrats were divided between Truman, Strom Thurmond, a Dixiecrat candidate, and Huey Wallace, a Progressive candidate. But Truman won because he travelled 22,000 miles on his **'whistle stop'** tour to meet people all over the country. His style pleased ordinary people, who said, *'Give 'em hell, Harry!'* He won with the support of organised labour and working-class Americans, as well as the support of black Americans because of his views on civil rights, housing, health care and education.

- **Fair Deal:** After his re-election, Truman wanted to build on Roosevelt's New Deal. He proposed a **Fair Deal** – to increase the minimum wage, improve health care, set up public works schemes and expand social security. He had some success – there was better social security, more public housing and slum clearance. But other proposals were rejected by Congress. Even though Democrats won a majority in the 1948 elections, Southern Democrats (Dixiecrats) combined with Republicans to reject further government involvement in education and health care.

> Develop notes on Truman's domestic and foreign policies.

KEY PERSONALITY: HARRY S TRUMAN

Harry Truman, a Democrat, was the thirty-third President of the United States of America (1945–53). He was elected a Senator in 1934 and again in 1940. He became Vice-President to President Roosevelt in 1944. When Roosevelt died in April 1945, Truman became President while the Second World War was still in progress. He told reporters he thought that *'the moon, the stars and all the planets had fallen on me.'*

However, he was inspired by the history and biographies which he had read. He believed in the role of **strong and honourable leadership.** On his desk he had a sign, *'The buck stops here',* which reflected his view of his responsibility as President. Truman was also a straightforward person who liked simple food and pleasures.

Truman was faced with two immediate problems when he became President – one was relations with Stalin and the Soviet Union and the second was how to defeat Japan. After Germany was defeated, he met Stalin at **Potsdam** (July 1945) along with the British Prime Ministers, Churchill and Attlee (who replaced Churchill) (See p. 304).

Very soon, relations with the Soviet Union deteriorated. Truman believed in a **policy of containment** – keeping Communism from expanding further. This remained **US foreign policy** for the rest of the Cold War (see p. 339).

In 1948–9, Truman was faced with the **Berlin Crisis** and Airlift (see p. 342).

In domestic policy, Truman wanted to add to the New Deal of Roosevelt, but Congress (House of Representatives and Senate) blocked many of his ideas. However, he was re-elected in 1948 in a very close contest with Thomas Dewey, (see p. 328). During his last few years in office, he also experienced the growth of **McCarthyism** – anti-Communist hysteria – which he disliked (see p. 364).

- **Economy:** The US economy was prosperous after the Second World War, so unemployment did not rise above 4 per cent (see p. 379). Truman set up the **Council of Economic Advisers** and passed the **Employment Act**, which showed that the US accepted more government involvement in the economy. Truman also passed the **GI Bill**, which gave loans for education, housing and business to veterans – 8 million veterans were helped by 1955. There was major economic growth in US by 1950 and this continued after Truman.

Based on early election results in the 1948 Presidential election, the Chicago Daily Tribune ran a headline 'Dewey defeats Truman'. Here Truman laughs at the mistaken headline.

- **Civil rights:** Truman set up the **President's Committee on Civil Rights**. Their report outlined a widespread pattern of segregation and discrimination. In 1948, Truman called on Congress to pass laws on civil rights, including a call to outlaw lynching. Congress failed to act. So later in 1948, Truman issued Executive Orders that ended racial discrimination in federal employment and he desegregated (ended racial segregation) the US armed forces.

- **McCarthyism and the Red Scare:** There was a growth of Communist hysteria in the US after the Second World War due to the Cold War. The House Un-American Committee (HUAC) and the actions of Senator Joe McCarthy (McCarthyism) in looking for Communists in the US heightened tensions. Even though Truman disliked McCarthy, his own actions played on the fear of Communism, e.g. passing the Truman Doctrine and the Marshall Plan. He also set up **Federal Loyalty Boards** to remove people believed to be disloyal to the US government.

The Eisenhower Presidency

Eisenhower became President in 1953. He had been a very successful Supreme Allied Commander in Europe during the Second World War; in particular he was in overall charge of the D-Day landings in 1944. He was now leader of the Republican Party, which favoured cutting back taxes and cutting back **big government**.

Ike, as he was known, had a **limited view** of the presidency. He believed that the functions of the President were very different from those of the legislature and that Roosevelt and Truman had taken over some of the powers of Congress. But he still opposed efforts to pass a constitutional amendment which would reduce the power of the presidency to negotiate agreements and treaties with foreign powers.

Business-dominated Cabinet

In domestic affairs, Ike believed in what he called **dynamic conservatism** – less government intervention in the economy along with continued federal support for individual welfare. He appointed a very business-dominated cabinet – *'eight millionaires and a plumber [a union leader]'*, it was said. He encouraged business by granting tax reductions. He also transferred the control of offshore oil deposits to the states, which opened the way to private development.

QUESTIONS ?

1. What did Truman mean by the phrase *'The buck stops here'*?
2. How successful was Truman in dealing with
   (i) Congress
   (ii) the 1948 presidential election
   (iii) the Fair Deal
   (iv) the economy
   (v) McCarthyism and the Red Scare?

For Truman's foreign policy, see Chapter 20, pp. 339–45. See also McCarthyism, pp. 364–65 and The Red Scare, pp. 410–13.

How successful was Harry Truman as President of the United States?

- Potsdam, Atomic bomb, end of WWII
- Policy of containment
- Truman Doctrine, Marshall Plan
- Berlin Blockade
- 1948 Presidential election
- Korean War
- Domestic policy – 21-point programme, Fair Deal, relations with Congress, economy
- Dealing with the Red Scare and McCarthyism

Dwight Eisenhower acknowledges his nomination as the Republican candidate in the 1952 Presidential election. Eisenhower won the election and served two terms as President until 1961.

For Eisenhower's foreign policy, see Chapter 28, p. 345.

QUESTIONS

1. What were Eisenhower's views on big government and the power of the presidency?
2. What was dynamic conservatism?
3. Why did Eisenhower's prestige decline?

Ike and Congress

However, he did not attempt to repeal the social welfare laws implemented by Roosevelt and Truman; instead, he extended social security and unemployment benefits and raised the minimum wage. Ike worked equally well with **Republicans** and **Democrats** in Congress. He got much of his legislation through Congress. They were largely uncontroversial, so he got 73 out of 83 Bills passed. It was during Eisenhower's presidency that significant **civil rights events** occurred – Brown v. Board of Education, the Montgomery Bus Boycott and Little Rock, Arkansas (see p. 419). These led Eisenhower to pass the **1957 Civil Rights Act** which imposed fines and imprisonment for interfering with a citizen's right to vote. However, trial was by jury and there were all-white juries in the southern states so this limited the effect of the Act.

But Eisenhower's **prestige declined** in his second term from 1956–60 due to a number of factors:

- There was a short economic recession.
- The rise of the civil rights agitation.
- The success of the Sputnik.
- Corruption among some officials.
- The shooting down of the **U-2 spy plane** by the Soviets and the resulting collapse of the Paris Summit.

By 1960, some accused Eisenhower of not making full use of presidential power.

The Kennedy Presidency

John F Kennedy was elected America's youngest President after a hard-fought campaign against Richard Nixon. He appointed **Lyndon Johnson** as his Vice-President. He tried to imitate the New Deal by talking about a **New Frontier** which would *'get America moving again'*. He wanted to take a strong stand against the Soviet Union, and at home tackle poverty, civil rights, health and education.

But Kennedy faced problems with the **conservative coalition** in Congress between Republicans and Southern Democrats. He was able to increase spending on defence and space because of competition with Soviet space successes and another Berlin crisis. By doubling **NASA's** budget, he laid the foundation for the **space project** which eventually fulfilled his promise to have a man on the moon by the end of the 1960s. He had little difficulty getting these passed because much of the spending benefited the southern states. Kennedy's extra spending on largely military purposes gave a boost to the economy which had gone into recession in the last few years of the Eisenhower presidency.

Kennedy and Congress

However, he postponed a cut in taxes which was eventually brought in by his successor, Lyndon Johnson, because he feared failure in Congress. Kennedy did not want to send proposals to Congress which he thought would not pass. This would make him look weak and ineffective and it would damage his chances of re-election. But he was partly to blame himself because he did not work very hard at improving relations with Congress.

Kennedy was able to use the power of the presidency to win a battle against one of America's largest corporations, **US Steel**. He wanted to control inflation (price rises) and he got companies to control wages and price rises. But US Steel raised their prices, which would affect car and defence industries and other areas of the economy. Kennedy threatened an FBI investigation of US Steel and he also threatened to withdraw government contracts. These actions forced US Steel to back down. This victory helped control inflation but it also showed the **power of the presidency** and federal government.

President Kennedy and his wife Jackie pictured in their car on their way to an event in 1962.

Congress Blocked Policies

Poverty was a serious problem in the US by the early 1960s and Kennedy wanted to tackle it. He got agreement with Congress for a school- and job-based training programme, but he failed to get Congress's support for a huge public works programme. He also failed to get a health care programme passed, as well as a proposal to set up a Department of Urban Affairs to tackle the problems of the cities. However, even though the conservative coalition did not like what they saw as federal interference in certain areas, they agreed to $4.88 billion aid for slum clearance and public housing projects.

Kennedy was slow to act on **civil rights**. During his presidency, the Freedom Rides, James Meredith and the University of Mississippi, and King and Birmingham, Alabama highlighted serious civil rights issues (see pp. 420–422). But Kennedy feared that the conservative coalition in Congress would block any proposal. Instead Kennedy was forced to act mainly through his brother Robert, as Attorney-General, to support desegregation. He introduced a **Civil Rights Bill** in 1963 but knew it would be difficult to get it passed. He was assassinated before it came to a vote in Congress. Kennedy's time in government was short and historians still debate what might have happened if he had been re-elected in 1964.

The Johnson Presidency

When President Kennedy was assassinated in November 1963, his Vice-President, Lyndon Johnson, succeeded him. Johnson was able to use the shock of the assassination to continue the work of JFK. He supported the ideas of the **New Frontier** in trying to tackle poverty, health care and civil rights.

FDR was Johnson's hero. Johnson believed that the **power of the federal government** should be used to improve the lives of the people. He wanted to create a **Great Society**. He believed that economic progress gave government the means to improve the lot of its people. He was helped by a huge presidential victory in 1964 and by Democratic control of Congress. The 1964 Congressional elections weakened the conservative coalition which had dominated since the 1930s.

KEY CONCEPT
LIBERALISM was the political belief that was concerned with personal freedom and social progress. Liberals favoured gradual reform of political and economic matters. US liberals favoured government intervention in the economy.

QUESTIONS

1. What was the New Frontier?
2. How did Kennedy deal with Congress?
3. Why was he able to spend money on NASA?
4. How successful was Kennedy in tackling poverty and civil rights?

For Kennedy's foreign policy, see p. 343 and pp. 345–49.

Domestic Policies

Johnson won the 1964 presidential election because:

- He campaigned on peace in Vietnam – Barry Goldwater, the Republican candidate, was a 'hawk', with a more aggressive policy on Vietnam.
- He got the sympathy of the American people after Kennedy's assassination – he wanted to carry on Kennedy's work.
- He outlined his **Great Society programme** – it was a strong social policy, including civil rights for black Americans; Goldwater was seen as right wing and too conservative (Goldwater's slogan – *'In your heart you know he's right'* – was added to by the Democrats – *'In your guts you know he's nuts'*).

What is your view of Johnson's idea of *The Great Society*?

A SPEECH BY PRESIDENT JOHNSON ON *THE GREAT SOCIETY*, MAY 1964

'The Great Society rests on abundance and liberty for all. It demands an end to poverty and racial injustice, to which we are totally committed in our time. But that is just the beginning.

The Great Society is a place where every child can find knowledge to enrich his mind and to enlarge his talents. It is a place where leisure is a welcome chance to build and reflect, not a feared cause of boredom and restlessness. It is a place where the city of man serves not only the needs of the body and the demands of commerce but the desire for beauty and the hunger for community.

It is a place where man can renew contact with nature. It is a place which honours creation for its own sake and for what it adds to the understanding of the race. It is a place where men are more concerned with the quality of their goals than the quantity of their goods.'

Johnson was a dealmaker who could get Congress to play almost any tune he wanted.

Johnson and Congress

Johnson **centralised control** in the White House. He showed his gifts as a negotiator in his dealings with **Congress**. In 1965, Congress felt it was the *'Three B Congress'* – bullied, badgered and brainwashed. He got **60 bills** passed before and after his re-election.

Civil Rights

Johnson ensured the passage of two major laws which ended the legal basis for discrimination and increased the powers of the President and the executive. He felt he had to introduce an even stronger Civil Rights Act than that proposed by President Kennedy. He worked hard to ensure that a combination of liberal Democrats and moderate Republicans supported the Act.

- **Civil Rights Act 1964**, which banned discrimination on grounds of race, religion, sex or national origin. It gave powers to the federal government to investigate cases. It proposed to cut federal funding from programmes that discriminated.
- As a result of the **Selma to Montgomery March** (p. 422), he introduced the **Voting Rights Act 1965** which gave powers to the federal government to supervise state elections, mainly in the southern states because of their history of discriminating against black people.
- He used **affirmative action** to ensure that the companies working on federal contracts reserved a certain quota of jobs for minority groups.

KEY PERSONALITY: LYNDON JOHNSON

Lyndon Johnson (LBJ as he was called) was a Democrat and thirty-sixth President of the US (1963–9). After a brief career as a teacher, he became an assistant to a US Congressman. He was later elected to the House of Representatives in 1937, and to the Senate in 1948. He soon became **Senate majority leader** and showed his ability to get laws passed. He was able to use his powers of persuasion, which were very important later.

He became Vice-President to President Kennedy in 1960 but he was not part of the Kennedy inner circle in the White House. Everything changed suddenly when President Kennedy was assassinated in Dallas in November 1963, and Johnson became President.

Johnson wanted to create a **better and fairer society**. He used the goodwill after the assassination of Kennedy to get a series of laws passed – the **Civil Rights Act 1964** and the **Voting Rights Act 1965**. This outlawed racial discrimination in jobs, voting and education (see p. 424).

He had an overwhelming victory over **Barry Goldwater**, a Republican, in the 1964 presidential election. He also saw more liberal Democrats elected to Congress. Johnson was able to bring in many laws as part of his **Great Society** programme. These included **Medicare** (for older people) and **Medicaid** (for poorer people) (see p. 333).

However, even though he had more interest in domestic affairs, his presidency from 1964 onwards was dominated by the **Vietnam War**. (see Case Study: Lyndon Johnson and Vietnam, 1963–68, pp. 350–62).

Johnson expanded US involvement in Vietnam after the **Tonkin Bay** incident in August 1964.

Most Americans still supported the President in the war. But after the **Tet Offensive** in early 1968, more and more people said America should withdraw. He barely won the New Hampshire Democratic primary election in 1968 against the anti-war Democrat, **Eugene McCarthy**. This prompted Johnson to cut back the bombing of North Vietnam and organise peace talks with the North Vietnamese. He also declared he was not standing for re-election. But he had begun the process which reduced American involvement and eventually led to peace under the next President, Richard Nixon, in 1973.

> Develop notes on Johnson's domestic and foreign policies.

> **Johnson's personality:** *'He'd come on just like a tidal wave sweeping all over the place. He went through walls. He'd come through the door, and he'd take the whole room over. Just like that. Everything.'*

War on Poverty

'(Johnson) was imbued with real concern for the poor and the deprived.' (Woods) He used presidential power to begin **a war on poverty**. He set up the **Office of Equal Opportunity** to coordinate the war on poverty.

- He set up schemes or programmes:
  - To improve employment prospects.
  - To give money to provide cheap housing and rent aid.
  - To provide grants for slum clearance.
  - To educate poor students in public schools.
- **Healthcare** – he set up the first federally funded healthcare system – **Medicare** and **Medicaid** – a proposal which previous Presidents had failed to get passed.

Johnson showed the federal government could tackle poverty. He also involved the **federal government** in creating national parks and many other conservation measures, limiting car pollution and supporting arts and culture.

The economy: Johnson continued Kennedy's boost of the economy. He ensured the passage of a tax bill proposed by Kennedy. The tax cuts, and also increased military spending, both helped the economy to grow – there was a huge increase in GNP (gross national product) in the following year (1964–65) and unemployment was reduced to

List some facts from this extract.

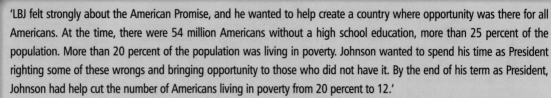

'LBJ felt strongly about the American Promise, and he wanted to help create a country where opportunity was there for all Americans. At the time, there were 54 million Americans without a high school education, more than 25 percent of the population. More than 20 percent of the population was living in poverty. Johnson wanted to spend his time as President righting some of these wrongs and bringing opportunity to those who did not have it. By the end of his term as President, Johnson had help cut the number of Americans living in poverty from 20 percent to 12.'

Source: http://www.lbjlibrary.org/exhibits/social-justice-gallery)

How successful was Lyndon B Johnson as President of the United States?

- Style of presidency; dealings with Congress
- 1964 Presidential election
- Great Society – war on poverty
- Civil rights
- Economy
- Vietnam War
- Space programme
- A Tragic Presidency?

4.5 per cent. But during Johnson's presidency, the cost of the Vietnam War increased rapidly and this damaged the US economy – inflation rose and there was a budget deficit. There was less money available for the war on poverty and the Great Society. As Martin Luther King said, 'The promises of the Great Society have been shot down on the battlefields of Vietnam.'

However, in a period of 18 months, as a *New York Times* columnist wrote, Johnson had passed more reform legislation (laws) than most Presidents had put through in two full terms in office. In doing so, he extended the power of the presidency.

For Johnson's foreign policy, see Case Study: Lyndon Johnson and Vietnam, 1963–8, pp. 350–62. For Johnson's role in the Space Programme, see pp. 466–67.

The Nixon Presidency

Richard Nixon became President in 1969 after he defeated his main opponent, the Democratic candidate Hubert Humphrey (as well as George Wallace of the American Independent Party), in November 1968.

Nixon and Congress

But the **Democrats** still dominated Congress as they did under Johnson, so Nixon's plans to follow a conservative domestic policy were not always successful:

- In spite of Nixon's opposition, in 1970 **Congress** lowered the voting age from 21 to 18.
- Congress also passed many environmental laws to control pollution from industry, power companies and from cars.
- Nixon's plan to end direct payments to the poor was rejected by Congress.
- Congress also increased social security benefits.

QUESTIONS

1. What was Johnson's attitude to the role of government?
2. What was the Great Society?
3. How did Johnson deal with civil rights?
4. How successful was he in relation to poverty?
5. How well did he deal with the economy?

Nixon and the Supreme Court

Nixon also had difficulty with the **Supreme Court**. He wanted to prevent further desegregation in schools in Mississippi. But the Supreme Court demanded more school integration and supported bussing children between black and white areas. However, Nixon was eventually able to appoint **more conservative judges** to the Court. He was also successful with his revenue-sharing plan to hand back power to the states for more control over the finances of social welfare matters.

EXAM QUESTION

How does Johnson's domestic policy compare with Truman's?

But by the early 1970s, Congress was concerned at the growth in the power of the presidency. In spite of his difficulties with Congress and the Supreme Court, Nixon's term in office was the high point of the **imperial presidency** (centralising government powers). More than any other President, Nixon concentrated powers in the presidency:

- He refused to spend money that Congress had allocated for health and the environment.
- He increased US involvement in Cambodia and Laos without approval from Congress.
- Congress began proceedings to impeach Nixon. He refused to co-operate, claiming **executive privilege.**
- He also claimed **executive powers** when he refused to hand over tapes of White House conversations on the **Watergate affair** (a Republican organised break-in at Democratic National Committee headquarters and subsequent cover-up).

President Nixon shaking hands with supporters in Ohio in 1972.

However, the **Supreme Court** ruled against him and he had to hand over the tapes. Nixon then resigned rather than be impeached.

Limiting the Powers of the President

Because of events in the Vietnam War and the Watergate scandal, Congress began to limit the power of the President. Congress passed a series of laws to control presidential powers and to make the federal government more accountable:

- They set limits to political contributions for elections.
- They gave power to individuals to see government files on themselves.
- They passed the **Ethics in Government Act** to require senior government officials to declare their wealth.
- They made the CIA report to Congress.

The **War Powers Act 1973** and the **Budget Reform Act 1974** restored the powers of Congress in declaring war and in budgeting.

The Ford Presidency

Nixon was succeeded by his Vice-President, Gerald Ford. He found himself in conflict with Congress. He wanted to increase military and space spending and reduce spending on social welfare programmes. He vetoed 18 Bills coming from Congress. Congress tried to overrule his veto on nine occasions but only succeeded in having the necessary two-thirds majority on three occasions.

The Carter Presidency

Jimmy Carter defeated Ford in the 1976 presidential election. He was a former governor of Georgia and an outsider to Washington politics. He promised a **new style** of presidency but, as an outsider, he failed to persuade Congress. He came across as being arrogant. However, he did have **some success** – he raised the minimum wage and provided money to clean up toxic waste sites. But he was not a decisive leader and his

QUESTIONS

1. Why did Nixon have trouble passing laws in Congress?
2. What changes did he make to the Supreme Court?
3. How was Nixon's term the high point of the imperial presidency?
4. How did Congress limit the power of the president?

For **Nixon and the economy** see Chapter 32, The Declining Economy – Domestic Recession, p. 389.

foreign policy was a failure. He cancelled the SALT II agreement after the Soviet Union invaded Afghanistan and he failed to rescue American hostages in Iran.

President Reagan and his wife, Nancy, waving and clapping hands in victory at Reagan's first inauguration as President in January 1981.

The Reagan Presidency

Ronald Reagan defeated Carter in the 1980 presidential election. This election also gave control of the Senate to the Republicans. Reagan became a two-term President when he won re-election in 1984.

Reagan's term in office is sometimes called the **Reagan Revolution**. He wanted to restore the **prestige** of the presidency. Reagan was helped by being a good communicator, and was especially good at using **television**.

Reduce Big Government

Reagan wanted to reduce the role of **big government**. He believed that *'Government is not the solution to our problem. Government is the problem.'* He wanted to dismantle the welfare state which had existed since Roosevelt's New Deal in the 1930s.

Reagan increased defence spending and cut taxes for businesses and people on high incomes. He cut federal (government) spending on welfare programmes and aid to big cities, which hit the poor.

His economic policies were called **Reaganomics** – a promise to cut spending, reduce government regulation (control) of industry and lower taxes. In the economy he did this with major tax cuts and by reducing federal spending on 300 programmes. He persuaded the Democrat-controlled House of Representatives to pass these. However, Reagan also began a massive build-up of US armed forces, which only increased government spending.

In **social policy**, Reagan wanted to give the **states** more responsibility for welfare. He also wanted to reduce the federal government by giving money to the states to use as they saw fit. But Congress refused to pass these plans.

Reagan mainly targeted the **health programme** – Medicare and Medicaid – with cutbacks. Reagan also believed that people did not need federal government intervention in their lives and he put this into practice when getting the private sector to do some of the job training. He gave less money to libraries, public radio, museums, national parks and education.

For more on **Reagan and the economy**, see **Reaganomics**, p. 391.

QUESTIONS

1. What was the Reagan Revolution?
2. What was Reagan's attitude to big government?
3. What was Reaganomics?
4. How did Reagan deal with Medicare and Medicaid?

For Reagan's foreign policy, see Chapter 30, pp. 377–78.

THE VOTER

BY EDWARD SOREL

IN '64 I VOTED FOR JOHNSON BECAUSE HE PROMISED PEACE.

BUT HE BETRAYED ME. HE ESCALATED THE WAR!

IN '68 I VOTED FOR NIXON BECAUSE HE PROMISED AN END TO BIG GOVERNMENT.

BUT I WAS FOOLED AGAIN. HE BUGGED PHONES, OPENED MAIL AND DOUBLED THE WHITE HOUSE STAFF.

IN '76 I VOTED FOR CARTER BECAUSE HE PROMISED TO CUT MILITARY EXPENDITURES.

BUT INSTEAD HE KEPT RAISING THE MILITARY BUDGET YEAR AFTER YEAR!

FINALLY I FIGURED IT OUT! I REALIZED THAT POLITICIANS ALWAYS DO THE OPPOSITE OF WHAT THEY PROMISE.

SO I VOTED FOR REAGAN.

BUT HE'S DOING EXACTLY WHAT HE SAID HE'D DO!!

HOMEWORK EXERCISES

ORDINARY LEVEL

1. Study the cartoon, 'The Voter', on p. 337 and answer the following questions.

   A. (i) Why did The Voter vote for Johnson? Was he happy with his vote?

   (ii) Why did The Voter vote for Nixon? Was he happy with his vote?

   (iii) Why did The Voter vote for Carter? Was he happy with his vote?

   (iv) After these votes, what did The Voter conclude?

   (v) Is The Voter happy with his vote for Reagan?

   (vi) What are the strengths and weaknesses of cartoons as sources for historians?

   B. Write a **paragraph** on one of the following.

   (i) The separation of powers in the US Constitution

   (ii) The roles of the US President

   (iii) Harry Truman's domestic policies

   (iv) Johnson's domestic policy

   C. Write a **long answer** on how the power of the presidency increased from Roosevelt to Nixon.

HIGHER LEVEL

2. How did the US Presidency develop from Roosevelt to Reagan? (2011)

3. How well did Harry Truman or President Lyndon Johnson handle the challenges he faced? (2012)

4. What were the successes and failures in the presidency of Lyndon Johnson? (2010)

5. Which president was more successful in his handling of US foreign policy, Harry Truman or Lyndon Johnson? Argue your case, referring to both. (2013)

6. Who was the greater president, Truman or Johnson? Argue your case, referring to both in your answer. (2016) (*Note: include both domestic and foreign policy in your answer.)

7. From Roosevelt to Reagan, would you agree that American presidents always acted for the good of America? Argue your case, referring to more than one president. (2017)

In this section, you should understand:
• US foreign policy in relation to Berlin, Korea, Cuba and Vietnam.
• Truman's role in US foreign policy.
• Case Study: Lyndon Johnson and Vietnam, 1963–8.

US Foreign Policy and the Cold War

Truman Takes Over – Using the Atomic Bomb

When Truman took over as President after the death of Roosevelt in April 1945, the Second World War was still in progress. One month later, war concluded in **Europe** (May 1945) but the war against **Japan** continued until August 1945.

In July 1945, Truman met **Stalin** face to face for the first and only time. This was at **Potsdam** in Germany, where little was agreed (see p. 304). Truman could not afford to be seen to be weak when dealing with Stalin, particularly as some thought too much had been given away by **Roosevelt** at the **Yalta Conference** (February 1945). At Potsdam, Truman issued a warning to Japan to surrender unconditionally or face *'prompt and utter destruction'*.

President Truman stands in the middle and shakes hands with both the Russian leader, Stalin, and British leader, Churchill, at the Potsdam Conference, 1945.

When Japan refused to surrender, Truman decided to bomb **Hiroshima** on 6 August, followed three days later by the bombing of **Nagasaki**. About 130,000 people were killed, mostly civilians, and as many again died over the next five years from the effects of radiation. Japan surrendered on 15 August, six days after the bombing of Nagasaki.

Why did Truman decide to drop the Atomic Bomb?

There were many **reasons** for Truman's decision to drop the atomic bomb. As commander-in-chief of the armed forces, he felt it was his duty to put an **end to the fighting**. He believed that this was the only way to stop the fighting as soon as possible. Otherwise it would involve a **land invasion** of Japan, which would result in the loss of hundreds of thousands or even millions of American and Japanese lives. Truman saw how the Japanese had fiercely defended the Pacific islands; they also used **kamikaze pilots** and some regarded them as *'savages, ruthless, merciless and fanatic'*.

Truman's decision to use the atomic bomb had huge effects on US foreign policy. Now nuclear weapons could wipe out all people, especially after the USSR developed its own bomb in 1949. The US–USSR competition in the Cold War led to an **arms race** with wide political and economic effects. This was supported by a **policy of deterrence** – to maintain a strong nuclear force so that the Soviet Union would be deterred from attacking the US.

QUESTIONS ?

1. Why did Truman decide to drop the atomic bomb on Hiroshima and Nagasaki?
2. What effect did this decision have on US foreign policy?

? QUESTIONS

1. Why did Truman mistrust the Soviet political system?
2. What advice on foreign policy did senior officials give Truman?
3. How did events in Europe and Asia seem to confirm this?
4. What was the message of Kennan's Long Telegram?
5. What did Churchill mean by the 'iron curtain'?

US Foreign Policy and the Soviet Union: Truman Doctrine and Marshall Plan

How did US Foreign Policy develop under Truman?

When Truman took office, he had very little knowledge or experience of foreign affairs. However, he had **definite views** – he disliked dictatorships and countries which behaved aggressively toward other countries. These views led to his mistrust of the Soviet political system.

Because of his inexperience, Truman relied on his **senior officials** for advice:

- By 1946 they believed that the Soviet Union could **not be trusted**.
- Instead of acting defensively, the Soviet Union was acting **aggressively**.
- The Soviet Union should be faced with **firmness** so that war would not break out again.
- The US should **not appease** Russia like Hitler had been appeased before the Second World War. In Truman's view, *'Unless Russia is faced with an iron fist and strong language another war is in the making ... I'm tired of babying the Soviets.'*

Stalin's actions seemed to confirm these conclusions. Stalin imposed a **Soviet-controlled puppet government** in Poland, as well as controlling Bulgaria and Romania. In a major speech **Stalin** said that *'monopoly capitalism caused the Second World War'* and that it should be replaced by Communism to avoid future wars. Soon afterwards, **spies** were arrested in Canada for trying to steal atomic secrets for the Soviet Union. These events confirmed to Washington officials that *'The ultimate aim of the Soviet foreign policy is Russian domination of a Communist world.'*

Kennan's Long Telegram and the Policy of Containment

Crucial to the development of US foreign policy at this time was **George Kennan's Long Telegram** (February 1946). Kennan was based in the US embassy in Moscow and was one of the few well-trained experts in Russian history and language. In Kennan's view, the Russians were using Communism as a cover for military growth, oppression at home and expansion abroad. He concluded that the only way to deal with Soviet Communism was to **contain it** – *'firm, vigilant containment'*.

This secret memo was reinforced a few weeks later by **Winston Churchill's** speech in Missouri (March 1946), where he referred to the **Iron Curtain** descending across the continent of Europe and called for firmness against the Soviet Union. *'From what I have seen of our Russian friends and allies during the war, I am convinced that there is nothing they admire so much as strength, and there is nothing for which they have less respect than weakness, especially military weakness.'*

These ideas shaped the new **policy of containment** developed under Truman – **that the US should contain Communism where it existed and not allow it expand any further**.

Winston Churchill delivers his 'Iron Curtain' speech in Fulton, Missouri.

Truman Doctrine and Marshall Plan

Truman was influenced by these arguments. Over the next year he took a progressively firmer stand against the Soviet Union. In 1947 he passed the **National Security Act** which unified the armed forces under the Secretary of Defence. This Act also set up the **CIA** (Central Intelligence Agency) and the **National Security Council** (NSC) to advise the President on foreign policy.

However, it was Britain's failure to continue helping Greece and Turkey which led to the full development of US foreign policy. America believed that the downfall of **Greece** and **Turkey** would lead to the **spread of Communism** all along the Mediterranean and into Iran, which provided much of Western oil. Truman played up the Communist threat to ensure congressional support for $400 million of military aid to Greece and Turkey. In his speech to Congress, he said, *'I believe that it must be the policy of the Unites States to support free people who are resisting attempted subjugation by armed minorities or by outside pressures.'* This became known as the **Truman Doctrine**.

A ceremony welcoming delivery of new freight wagons for West Germany, bought from Czechoslovakia with European Recovery Program (Marshall Aid) money. The sign reads 'America helps rebuild Europe'.

The Truman Doctrine was complemented by the **Marshall Plan** (European Recovery Program) to give economic aid to Western Europe. Truman said they were *'two halves of the same walnut'*. Marshall, the Secretary of State, said in his speech at Harvard University announcing the Plan, *'Our policy is directed not against any country or doctrine, but against hunger, poverty, desperation, and chaos.'* Truman and Marshall hoped that Marshall Aid would rebuild the European economy and strengthen Western Europe to stand up to Communism. It would also help Europe to import American goods.

Its passage through Congress was eased when Stalin refused to accept any economic aid for Russia and when he forced Eastern European countries to refuse it also. Stalin felt the Plan was part of a US plot to encircle the USSR and undermine Communism.

Effects of Truman Doctrine and Marshall Plan

The effect of the Plan was to speed up the economic recovery of Europe after the war. It showed that the US was not going back to **isolationism**, as it did after the First World War. Instead it was still committed to Europe. **Internationalism** – the belief that America should become involved in treaties and commitments with other countries – was now stronger in the country. The success of the Marshall Plan encouraged the US government to believe that they could undertake further schemes thinking that American strength would carry them through. The **Second World War** had changed American foreign policy for the future. After the war, the US favoured intervention. **As one political leader said, *'Pearl Harbor** drove us to the conclusion that peace was indivisible.'* This is why many people supported **internationalism** after the war. Now people wanted the US to lead the democratic and capitalist world.

> **KEY CONCEPT**
> **INTERNATIONALISM**
> The belief that America should become involved in treaties and commitments with other countries

? QUESTIONS

1. What was the Truman Doctrine?
2. What was the Marshall Plan?
3. What was Stalin's attitude to the Marshall Plan and how did that help Truman?
4. What was the difference between isolationism and internationalism?
5. How did the Second World War affect post-war US foreign policy?

Both the Truman Doctrine and the Marshall Plan highlighted **tension** between the US and the USSR. By 1948, the **Cold War** was fully established. For the next 40 years all US policies revolved around the enmity between the US and the USSR. This influenced the arms race, patrolling by US fleets, round-the-clock flights by Strategic Air Command, the growth of the military in US life and the build-up of the defence industry.

US Foreign Policy and Berlin

Very soon Truman was faced with a new challenge. In June 1948, Stalin began the **blockade** of West Berlin. He responded to American policy in Germany. The wartime allies had agreed to divide Germany into **four zones** and Russia was allowed take **reparations** from the country. But soon the US gave Marshall Aid to rebuild their own zone. The US and its allies, especially Britain, now believed that the economic recovery of Germany was necessary for the economic recovery of Europe. It was also necessary to build up Germany as a barrier to the expansion of Communism. On the other hand, Stalin feared that a prosperous West Germany would undermine Communism in Eastern Germany.

What do you think are the two most important points made by Truman in this extract?

EXTRACTS FROM TRUMAN'S SPEECH TO CONGRESS ANNOUNCING THE TRUMAN DOCTRINE

The foreign policy and the national security of this country are involved. The United States has received from the Greek Government an urgent appeal for financial and economic assistance. The very existence of the Greek state is today threatened by the terrorist activities of several thousand armed men, led by Communists, who defy the government's authority at a number of points…

The United States must supply that assistance.

The peoples of a number of countries of the world have recently had totalitarian regimes forced upon them against their will.

At the present moment in world history nearly every nation must choose between alternative ways of life. The choice too often is not a free one.

One way of life is based upon the will of the majority, and is distinguished by free institutions, representative government, free elections, guarantees of individual liberty, freedom of speech and religion, and freedom from political oppression.

The second way of life is based upon the will of a minority forcibly imposed upon the majority. It relies upon terror and oppression, a controlled press and radio, fixed elections, and the suppression of personal freedoms.

I believe that it must be the policy of the Unites States to support free people who are resisting attempted subjugation by armed minorities or by outside pressures.

End of US nuclear monopoly
The US nuclear monopoly came to an end soon after the Berlin Blockade ended. In 1949, the Soviet Union developed its own atomic bomb. This forced Truman to sanction the development of an even larger nuclear bomb – the Hydrogen bomb. Truman also approved a NSC document (NSC–68) which favoured the massive build up of US conventional and nuclear arms.

'We Are Going to Stay, Period'

Stalin was hoping to force the US out of West Berlin. But Truman did not want to abandon Berlin. It would mean a huge victory for Communism. It would also undermine the **policy of containment**. He was encouraged by his advisers to hold firm. The American commander in Berlin wrote, *'When Berlin falls, Western Germany will be next. If we mean to hold Europe against Communism, we must not budge.'* Truman agreed. He said, *'We are going to stay, period.'*

This resulted in a **huge airlift** by the US and British air forces which kept West Berlin going until Stalin lifted the blockade in May 1949. The Americans had won and containment had worked. The blockade also resulted in the establishment of **NATO** (North Atlantic Treaty Organization) in 1949. The US and Canada joined with 10 Western European countries. The US believed it needed to strengthen Europe militarily against the Soviet Union. This was the **first** time the US formed a **peacetime military alliance**. Under the terms of NATO, an attack on one was an attack on all. It resulted in the deployment of US troops to bases in Western Europe.

Berlin – Centre of Conflict

Berlin continued to be a centre of conflict in the Cold War during the 1950s. At this time, West Berlin and West Germany prospered, and their prosperity attracted a constant stream of immigration from East Berlin into the West, where there was a strong demand for labour. This had a serious effect on the East German economy, since many of these people were skilled workers.

The East German government put pressure on the Soviet Union to act. The leader of the Soviet Union, Khrushchev, believed he could overcome the new young American President, John F Kennedy. They met in Vienna and Khrushchev demanded that the US withdraw from Berlin within six months. Kennedy responded by increasing military spending and calling up reserves. He said, *'We seek peace, but we shall not surrender.'*

The Berlin Wall was built in 1961 to prevent migration of workers from East Berlin to West Germany.

The Berlin Wall

Kennedy was successful, as Khrushchev backed down. Instead, East Germany and the Soviet Union built the Berlin Wall, which divided East and West Berlin. Building the wall eased tensions between both sides by stopping the flow of migrants, but now the US was able to point to East Berlin as a prison for its people.

When President Kennedy visited Berlin in June 1963, he made clear the Western viewpoint:

> *'There are many people in the world who really don't understand, or say they don't, what is the great issue between the Free World and the Communist world. Let them come to Berlin. There are some who say that Communism is the way of the future. Let them come to Berlin. And there are some who say in Europe and elsewhere we can work with the Communists. Let them come to Berlin.'*

US Foreign Policy and Korea

In 1949, China became Communist after a long civil war. This encouraged America to fear the further spread of Communism in Asia. It also led Republicans at home to

QUESTIONS

1. Why did Stalin blockade Berlin?
2. Why did the US and the allies want to stay in Berlin?
3. How was the US successful in the Berlin Blockade?
4. Was this a victory for containment?
5. Why was there tension over Berlin in the 1950s?
6. Why did Khrushchev and Kennedy clash?
7. Why was the Berlin Wall built and what effect did it have on US–USSR relations?

accuse Truman of *'losing China'* by weak policies. American opinion was fully convinced of the danger of Communism, spurred on by **Senator Joe McCarthy** and events in Europe and around the world. Therefore, it was not surprising that the US viewed the invasion by North Korea of South Korea in the same way. This was seen as **another test** of the policy of containment.

US Marines halted on an icy trail in subzero temperatures in North Korea by Red Chinese soldiers after they crossed the Yalu River from China.

There was little or no anti-war movement during the Korean War (unlike the Vietnam War) – it was limited, as one historian said, to pacifists 'talking to themselves' or to 'a few Communists or die-hard isolationists.' Over 80 per cent of Americans supported the war in Korea when it began. After that, public opinion varied from a low of 39 per cent back up to a high of 81 per cent depending on how American forces were doing – low when the Chinese army drove them back, high when the Americans invaded at Inchon (see p. 366).

North Attacked the South

After the Second World War, Korea was divided along the **thirty-eighth parallel** between a Soviet-backed North and a US-supported South. This was meant to be a temporary arrangement until elections were held. The US went ahead with its elections in the South but the Soviet Union did not go ahead with elections in the North. Shortly after (in 1950), North Korea attacked and drove the South Koreans into one corner of the country.

Truman had no choice but to intervene. Firstly, South Korea had suffered an unprovoked attack. Also, he believed that the Soviet Union was behind the attack – if he did not stop them, they would *'swallow up one piece of Asia after another'*. He did not want to repeat the mistake of Munich where European powers gave into Hitler. *'I had to act as commander-in-chief and I did,'* he said. In this way **Truman bypassed Congress.** This was an increase in presidential power which was later used by Kennedy, Johnson and Nixon in Vietnam.

Truman immediately responded to the invasion by committing the US in the name of the **United Nations** (UN) to come to the rescue of South Korea. Truman got UN backing through a UN Security Council vote, when the Soviet Union was temporarily absent due to a dispute over recognition of Communist China.

US Success and Defeat

The US forces, led by **General MacArthur** and aided by troops from 12 other countries, were very successful. MacArthur invaded at **Inchon** behind North Korean lines and the North Korean invasion collapsed. By October, the North Koreans were pushed back behind the thirty-eighth parallel. America had been successful; this was another victory for the policy of containment.

But the US overreacted and invaded the North, easily taking it over in spite of Chinese warnings. This resulted in a Chinese invasion with 250,000 soldiers. They drove the Americans and their allies back and recaptured **Seoul**, the capital of South Korea. But in bitter and slow fighting the US eventually pushed them back to the thirty-eighth parallel again.

MacArthur pressed for an attack on China and even the use of the **atomic bomb**. Truman had to dismiss him, but fighting dragged on for two more years. By 1953, the leadership of the USSR and the US had changed – Stalin died in Russia and Eisenhower was elected President of America. Eventually **peace** was agreed and the border was fixed on the thirty-eighth parallel. America lost over 50,000 soldiers and the war cost $20 billion.

Effects of the Korean War on US Foreign Policy

The war affected US foreign policy. Truman saw the need for strengthening the US military position in South-East Asia. He began by signing treaties with **Japan** and the **Philippines** (1951). He also formed a defence pact with **Australia and New Zealand** (ANZAC Pact). These were extended by Eisenhower, who formed the **South-East Asia Treaty Organization** (SEATO). This meant increased involvement of the US in Asian affairs. It also meant an **expansion of containment**, which led to increased military spending. The war also worsened relations with **China** for two decades. The US was now more closely tied to hateful regimes in Taiwan and South Korea.

The war also affected **US policy in Europe**. The US felt that the defence of Western Europe needed to be strengthened. This led to US demands that West Germany should be allowed to rearm, and that the country should become a member of NATO. This eventually happened when West Germany became a member in 1955.

QUESTIONS ?

1. How was the invasion of South Korea by North Korea a challenge to the policy of containment?
2. How did Truman respond and why?
3. How successful was the US in Korea?
4. What were the effects of the Korean War on US foreign policy?

US Foreign Policy under Eisenhower

Eisenhower maintained the general **policy of containment** laid out by his predecessor, Truman. He believed in the **Domino Theory** – that if any country fell to Communism, other countries nearby would do so also. He relied more on nuclear weapons rather than conventional weapons to back up his case. He thought a **policy of deterrence** would work against the Soviet Union. If he maintained a powerful nuclear arsenal, then this would deter the Russians from attacking. But he also followed a **policy of peaceful co-existence** with the Russians and their new leader, **Khrushchev**. He hoped that both sides could get along peacefully with each other. But his policy here was upset when a U-2 spy plane was shot down over Russia.

Gary Powers on trial in Moscow for spying after his U-2 spy plane was shot down over the USSR.

QUESTIONS ?

Explain these terms in relation to Eisenhower's foreign policy: (i) domino theory (ii) policy of deterrence (iii) policy of peaceful co-existence.

US Foreign Policy and the Cuban Missile Crisis

Background

A number of factors heightened Cold War tension in the early 1960s and contributed to the Cuban Missile Crisis in 1962. First there was talk about a **missile gap** – that the USSR had overtaken the US in missile production. The military-industrial complex, which hoped for greater defence spending, encouraged this. There was also increased anti-Communism caused by **Castro's Communist takeover** of Cuba. Many newspapers and magazines, such as *Time* and *Newsweek*, contributed to this. So did the new President, John F Kennedy.

At his **inauguration speech**, President Kennedy said, 'We shall pay any price, bear any burden, meet any hardship, support any friend, oppose any foe to assure the survival and success of liberty.' He followed this with a number of anti-Communist speeches. 'The enemy is the Communist system itself ... increasing in its drive for world domination.' He too supported the view that there was a missile gap.

Flexible Response

Kennedy took an active interest in foreign policy, even more so than domestic policy. He had his own ideas about that policy. In spite of his view about a missile gap, he thought the US was over-reliant on nuclear weapons. Instead he wanted a policy of **flexible response** in order to be able to respond quickly to regional conflicts. He also supported the development of **counter-insurgency forces** (counter-terrorism) such as the Green Berets. These policies led to increased defence spending.

Kennedy also believed in firm and decisive action; he believed this displayed a certain **toughness**. This contributed to Kennedy's support for an attempt to overthrow Castro through an invasion in the **Bay of Pigs** in April 1960. This was a disastrous failure which was a huge embarrassment for the Kennedy government.

A Russian cargo ship carrying missiles to Cuba during the Cuban Missile Crisis, September 1962.

Soviet Views

Another factor in the development of the Cuban Missile Crisis was the attitude of **Khrushchev**, the Soviet leader. He pledged USSR aid to 'wars of national liberation'. He was aggressive toward Kennedy when they met in **Vienna** in June 1960 and they failed to agree over East Germany. Khrushchev thought he was dealing with a weak and indecisive leader. Thereafter both increased military spending at home. It led to the building of the **Berlin Wall** to stop the flow of refugees from East Berlin to the West. This led to a further heightening of tension between the two sides.

The Soviet Union gave increased support to Cuba, including the building of **missile bases** in the summer of 1962. Their range of over 1,000 miles meant that they could hit the major US cities. **U-2** flights revealed that the missile sites were nearly ready.

American Reaction

Kennedy set up an **Executive Committee** (ExComm) to deal with the missile crisis. Over a period of 13 days the world was on the brink of a third world war. There were various opinions in ExComm on what the US policy should be. Some advised an **invasion** of Cuba, while others advised **air strikes** on the missile bases. The more moderate members said that the US should agree to **demilitarise** Cuba, including withdrawing US forces from their naval bases in **Guantanamo**, and also remove their missiles from Turkey.

Kennedy believed he could not appear to be weak, so he did not agree with the ideas of the moderates. He also rejected air strikes because they would not succeed in knocking out all the sites. Instead he decided on a **blockade** of Cuba to stop any further Soviet equipment reaching the island. He informed Khrushchev and later the public on television. The naval blockade demonstrated US will to resist Soviet pressure, but it also gave Khrushchev a way out.

There was huge **tension** in the US and worldwide. Some Soviet ships turned around, while others without weapons agreed to be searched. Kennedy demanded the dismantling of the missile bases. On the other hand, Khrushchev wanted the US to end the blockade and agree not to invade Cuba. He also wanted the US to dismantle their missile sites in Turkey.

Kennedy publicly agreed to lift the blockade and to call off any invasion. But privately he assured the Soviets of the future dismantling of the Turkish sites. In return Khrushchev agreed to dismantle the Soviet missile bases.

The Cuban Missile Crisis

USA

US naval blockade of Cuba

Approaching Soviet ships

Cuban missile sites

CANADA

Boston

New York

Chicago

Washington

UNITED STATES OF AMERICA

Salt Lake City

Denver

Atlantic Ocean

Range of long – range missiles (3,200 km)

Range of short – range missiles (1,600 km)

New Orleans

Cape Canaveral (space research)

Miami

MEXICO

CUBA

BAHAMAS

Havana Guantanamo

Bay of Pigs

What is the most important point illustrated by this map?

Diplomatic Victory

While some US military leaders were angry that America did not strike, Kennedy's steady handling of the crisis earned him praise. One journalist said it was *'perhaps the greatest personal diplomatic victory of any US President in our history'*. It led to the establishment of a **hotline** between Moscow and Washington to improve future communications between the leaders and to lessen the dangers of nuclear war. It also led to a **Test Ban Treaty**, which banned nuclear testing in the air, in space or underwater.

QUESTIONS (?)

1. What factors heightened Cold War tensions in the early 1960s?
2. What was Kennedy's attitude to these tensions?
3. What were the main causes of the Cuban Missile Crisis?
4. How did Kennedy react to the Cuban Missile Crisis?
5. How successful was he?

US Foreign Policy and the War in Vietnam

How Did the USA Become Involved in Vietnam?

Under Truman

The US became gradually involved in Vietnam. After the Second World War, **Truman** supported the French Empire in Indo-China (Vietnam, Cambodia and Laos) in its battle against **Ho Chi Minh** and the Vietminh. He believed the Vietminh were backed by Stalin and the USSR and he looked on his support for the French in Cold War terms. By backing the French he believed he was containing Communism and following the **Truman Doctrine**. (See How Did US Foreign Policy Develop under Truman?, p. 340)

Under Eisenhower

President **Eisenhower** increased US involvement because he believed in the **Domino Theory** – that if Indo-China fell to Communism, so would all the other countries around it. He sent in the first military advisers. After the French defeat, there was a peace agreement in Geneva which set up four countries – Laos, Cambodia, North Vietnam and South Vietnam. The US, however, refused to hold elections in the South because they feared a victory for the Communists. Instead they backed **Ngo Dinh Diem** in South Vietnam, sent in aid and increased the number of military advisers to 1,500 by 1960.

But Diem was an **unpopular leader**. He was a Catholic leader in a mainly Buddhist country, and he favoured placing Catholics in positions of power. He failed to introduce land reforms demanded by the Buddhist peasants (farmers) so rents remained high. Diem imposed a repressive regime and he was accused of corruption and torture. All these aspects of his rule increased his unpopularity. Instead, popular support went to the South Vietnamese Communists, called the **Vietcong**. These were supported by Ho Chi Minh, who was backed by the Soviet Union and China.

The Americans continued to believe in Vietnam as a **Cold War conflict**. They failed to see it as a **nationalist uprising** seeking independence. Their failure to do this led them to become more and more involved in Vietnam.

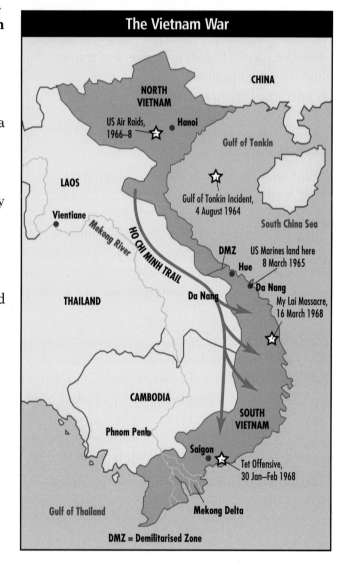

The Vietnam War

US Air Raids, 1966–8

Hanoi

CHINA

NORTH VIETNAM

Gulf of Tonkin

LAOS

Vientiane

Gulf of Tonkin Incident, 4 August 1964

South China Sea

Mekong River

HO CHI MINH TRAIL

DMZ

Hue

US Marines land here 8 March 1965

Da Nang

Da Nang

My Lai Massacre, 16 March 1968

THAILAND

CAMBODIA

Phnom Penh

SOUTH VIETNAM

Saigon

Tet Offensive, 30 Jan–Feb 1968

Gulf of Thailand

Mekong Delta

DMZ = Demilitarised Zone

> **How and why the US became more involved in Vietnam**
> - Cold War
> - Containment/Domino Theory
> - Impact of McCarthyism and the Red Scare
> - What Truman did and why
> - Weakness of French/ Geneva Agreement
> - What Eisenhower did and why
> - Weakness of South Vietnamese government
> - Guerrilla war/Support of Vietcong by North Vietnam
> - What Kennedy did and why
> - What Johnson did and why/full involvement

Kennedy Increases US Involvement

Kennedy believed he had to take a strong stand in South-East Asia since he had already accused the previous Eisenhower government (administration) of being soft. He believed in the **Domino Theory** too and was a strong supporter of the **policy of containment**. His advisers were equally strong in standing up to Communism in South-East Asia. However, Kennedy did not want to get the US militarily involved, so he refused to send troops to Vietnam. But financial aid increased and there was a large increase in US advisers to 16,000 by 1963. It seemed inevitable that they would get involved in the fighting. Indeed, some of the so-called advisers were soon involved.

Kennedy believed in developing a **flexible response** to combat Communist

QUESTIONS ?

How and why did
(i) Truman and
(ii) Eisenhower involve
the US in Vietnam?
How and why did
Kennedy increase US
involvement?

expansion. This involved the US sending in Special Forces to train the South Vietnamese army in **counter-insurgency** (counter-terrorism) methods. But very often their tactics resulted in losing rather than winning the support of the people. Diem's government introduced the **Strategic Hamlet Programme** to herd peasants into armed and protected villages to counter the Vietcong. This only upset the peasants more. Actions by Diem against Buddhist monks in 1963 worsened the situation. Soon after, **Diem was assassinated** in an internal army coup which led to more political uncertainty in Vietnam. Even though the US knew about the plot, they did not attempt to stop it. A few weeks later Kennedy himself was assassinated in Dallas. Kennedy's Vice-President, **Lyndon Johnson**, was sworn in as the new President.

HOMEWORK EXERCISES

ORDINARY LEVEL

1. This is an edited extract from a televised speech by President John F Kennedy on 22 October 1962 during the Cuban Missile Crisis. Read it and answer the questions that follow.

   The government, as promised, has maintained the closest surveillance [watch] of the Soviet military build-up on the island of Cuba. Within the past few weeks, unmistakable evidence has established the fact that a series of offensive missile sites is now in preparation.

   The urgent transformation of Cuba into an important strategic base is an explicit threat to the peace and security of all the Americas. This secret, swift build-up of Communist missiles cannot be accepted by this country.

   A. (i) When, where and by whom was this speech made?
   (ii) What country is responsible for the military build-up?
   (iii) What specific threat to the Americas is identified?
   (iv) According to Kennedy, what attitude does the United States have towards the build-up of Communist missiles?
   (v) Identify a statement which is a *cause*, and a statement which is a *consequence* in the above extract.
   (vi) How did the Cuban Missile Crisis come to an end? (2010)

   B. Write a **paragraph** on one of the following.
   (i) Truman and the development of US foreign policy towards the Soviet Union
   (ii) The role of US foreign policy in (a) the Berlin Crisis, 1948 (b) the Korean War, 1950–53 and (c) the Cuban Missile Crisis, 1962

   C. Write a **long answer** on how the US became so heavily involved in Vietnam in the 1960s.

HIGHER LEVEL

2. How effective was the US policy of containment in relation to at least two major crises of the Cold War?

3. During the period 1945–89, what was the importance for US foreign policy of one or more of the following: Berlin; Korea; Cuba? (2010) (2015)

CASE STUDY Lyndon Johnson and Vietnam, 1963–68

Johnson and Vietnam

Instead of withdrawing from Vietnam, the new President, Lyndon Johnson, increased the number of US advisers by 30 per cent. Not only did Johnson support the **policy of containment** and the **Domino Theory**, he believed that **US credibility** was at stake. He thought that if the US did not stand up for their ally – South Vietnam – nobody would trust them in future. Johnson's advisers, who also advised Kennedy, believed in a **military solution** to the problem. Even when doubts crept in a few years later about US policy, Johnson's **domineering personality** discouraged them from giving an alternative view. Johnson was concerned about how future generations would judge him so he did not want to be 'the first President to lose a war'.
(See Sources 1 to 4)

After Kennedy

Johnson followed Kennedy's policy on Vietnam; *'I swore to myself that I would carry on.'* He approved **NSAM 273**, a National Security Agency memo, which said the US government should 'assist the people and Government of South Vietnam to win their contest against the externally directed and supported Communist conspiracy.' He then approved the transfer of secret operations against North Vietnam from the CIA to the army. Next, in March 1964, he approved **NSAM 288** which said the US should use greater force, including air strikes against North Vietnam. However, Johnson did not want to escalate the war immediately because he was involved in the presidential election campaign.

SOURCE 1 – THE BLIND LEADING THE BLIND

Four Presidents entangled in Vietnam.

Can you identify the four Presidents? What is the message of the cartoon?

SOURCE 2 – JOHNSON'S SPEECH

'Most of the nations of Asia cannot by themselves and alone resist the growing might and grasping ambition of Asian Communism. Our power, therefore, is a vital shield. And an Asia so threatened by Communist domination would imperil the security of the US itself. Moreover, we are in Vietnam to fulfil one of the most solemn pledges of the American nation. Three Presidents over 11 years have promised to help defend this small and valiant nation. We cannot now dishonour our word.'

Speech by President Johnson in 1965

SOURCE 3 – PHONE CALL

'I don't think it's worth fighting for and I don't think we can get out. I don't see that we can ever hope to get out of there once we are committed. It's just the biggest damn mess.'

President Johnson in a private phone conversation in 1964

SOURCE 4 – LESSONS FROM MUNICH

'We learned from Hitler at Munich that success only feeds the appetite of aggression.'

President Johnson

What factors influenced Johnson's policy on Vietnam? Do Sources 1 to 4 explain all the reasons for his policy?

The 1964 Presidential Election

In the 1964 presidential election, Johnson was faced by **Barry Goldwater**, a Republican candidate. Goldwater wanted a 'total victory' in the war against world Communism. In relation to Vietnam, he suggested that atomic weapons should be used to 'defoliate' North Vietnam. Johnson, on the other hand, campaigned as a **candidate of peace**. 'We are not about to send American boys nine or ten thousand miles away from home to do what Asian boys ought to be doing for themselves,' he said. 'We don't want to get … tied down to a land war in Asia.' However, Johnson soon began to realise that:

- Limited American aid was not working.
- The Vietcong were extending their hold on the country.
- The South Vietnamese government was not strong enough to stop them.

Johnson was faced with **two alternatives**: either withdrawing the US from Vietnam or else committing huge numbers of US troops to the country.

CASE STUDY QUESTIONS

1. How did Johnson campaign in the 1964 presidential election campaign?
2. What did he begin to realise about Vietnam?
3. What two alternatives did he face?

SOURCE 5 – JOHNSON'S VERSION OF TONKIN

'The initial attack on the destroyer Maddox, on August 2, was repeated today by a number of hostile vessels attacking two US destroyers with torpedoes. The destroyers and supporting aircraft acted at once on the orders I gave after the initial act of aggression. We believe at least two of the attacking vessels were sunk. There were no US losses.'

President Johnson's television address, 4 August 1964

SOURCE 6 – TONKIN GULF RESOLUTION

'… Whereas naval units of the Communist regime in Vietnam, in violation of the principles of the charter of the United Nations and of international law, have deliberately and repeatedly attacked United States naval vessels lawfully present in international water, and have thereby created a serious threat to international peace…'

Extract from 'The Tonkin Gulf Resolution', 7 August 1964, in the Pentagon Papers

---

The Gulf of Tonkin and Change in US Policy

During the election campaign in 1964, a dramatic change occurred in US policy. In August 1964, North Vietnamese boats fired on the **USS Maddox** while it was patrolling in the **Gulf of Tonkin**, but they were easily driven off. A couple of days later, the **Maddox** and the **Turner Joy** were patrolling in the Gulf when they reported being fired on again. They returned fire but later investigators cast doubts on their account of what happened. Some historians suggest that the US patrols were deliberately set up to provoke a North Vietnamese response. At

SOURCE 7 – *WHY DID JOHNSON ESCALATE THE WAR?*

Johnson's decisions were based on complicated political and military considerations. LBJ steered a middle course: The 'hawks' in Congress and in the military wanted him to engage in massive bombing of enemy cities, threaten to use nuclear weapons, and even threaten to invade North Vietnam. This might have led to Chinese entry into the war, as had happened in the Korean War, or even Soviet engagement. 'Doves' in Congress, the State Department, and even Vice President Hubert Humphrey wanted Johnson to negotiate with Hanoi for a 'neutral' South Vietnam and eventual reunification with the North. The President's 'middle way' involved a commitment of U.S. ground forces, designed to convince the regime in Hanoi that it could not win, and some punishing bombing campaigns, after which serious U.S. negotiations might ensue.

Kent Germany, Associate Professor of History, University of South Carolina, Lyndon B. Johnson: Foreign Affairs

How did the 'hawks' and 'doves' differ? Was Johnson more a 'hawk' or a 'dove'?

any rate, the incident was used by President Johnson to escalate US involvement in the war. (See Sources 5, 6 and 7)

Congress passed the **Tonkin Resolution** after Johnson gave a deliberately misleading account of the incident. This resolution gave Johnson almost unlimited power to wage war. This allowed the President to take 'all necessary measures, including the use of military force' to protect US interests in South-East Asia. It also allowed the US to attack North Vietnam, because Johnson claimed North Vietnam was supplying the Vietcong in South Vietnam.

The Escalation of the War, 1965–68

But Johnson waited until after his re-election before he took action. In response to an enemy raid on an American air base in South Vietnam early in 1965, he gave the go-ahead for **Operation Rolling Thunder**. This operation launched massive air assaults on North Vietnam to stop them helping the Vietcong. He also announced a $1 billion aid programme for the South. (See Sources 8, 9, 10 and 14)

SOURCE 8 – JOHNSON'S VIEW

'We have kept our guns over the mantle and our shells in the cupboard for a long time now. I can't ask our American soldiers out there to continue to fight with one hand tied behind their backs.'

President Johnson at a meeting with his top advisers, February 1965, after the attack on a US air force base in which eight soldiers were killed

Then he began a huge **build-up** of ground forces. In March 1965, the first US Marines landed in **Da Nang**, to protect the US air base there. By the end of the year the US had over 180,000 soldiers in Vietnam. A year later this had increased to over 350,000 and it was a half a million by the end of 1967. By the end of 1968 the war was costing $30 billion a year. (Source 15)

In the meantime, Johnson rejected offers by the North Vietnamese government to negotiate on the basis of their **Four Points**. In turn, the US announced its **Fourteen Points** in January 1966 to form the basis of negotiations, but these were rejected by North Vietnam. (Source 10)

? CASE STUDY QUESTIONS

1. What was Operation Rolling Thunder?
2. How quickly did Johnson escalate the war?

The Fighting

The US army used a variety of tactics to fight against the Vietcong and the North Vietnamese, including:

- In **search-and-destroy missions**, the US army tried to clear areas of suspected Vietcong, and villages suspected of helping the guerrillas were destroyed. In **Operation Cedar Falls** (1967), an area north of Saigon was cleared. But only a

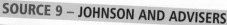

SOURCE 9 – JOHNSON AND ADVISERS

President Johnson meets with advisers in the Cabinet Room of the White House (May 1967).

few Vietcong were found. Instead, 6,000 peasants were evacuated and their villages and land destroyed, thus making enemies of the people the US were supposed to be helping. It was also one of these missions which caused the **My Lai Massacre** in 1968, though news of it did not become public until after Johnson left office.

- Success in search-and-destroy missions was based on **body counts** or **kill ratios**. These were often **inaccurate** because soldiers could not distinguish between villagers and guerrillas. 'If it is dead and Vietnamese, it's VC.'

- The US air force dropped **napalm** (jellied explosives) and **defoliants** (chemicals) on the forests of South Vietnam. The purpose was to clear away the cover of the forest. But instead it made South Vietnamese people angrier at the US conduct of the war.

- The US air force dropped a greater **tonnage of bombs** over North and South Vietnam between July 1965 and December 1968 than the Allies did in Europe in the entire Second World War. However, these failed to undermine the will of the North Vietnamese people and the Vietcong.

- The US relied heavily on **helicopters**. While these provided a quick response and great mobility, the approaching noise meant that the Vietcong could escape from any surprise attacks.

- **Free fire zones** were laid out between the villages in which anybody there was regarded as a target.

- The US attempted to create a better South Vietnamese army, but this failed.

- Most US soldiers were only drafted to serve for a year. This made it difficult to create and maintain 'team spirit'. It also meant that no sooner had they built up the experience to cope with the conditions, than they were flown home.

> **SOURCE 10 – SUMMARY OF NORTH VIETNAMESE FOUR POINTS FOR ENDING THE WAR, 1965**
>
> 1. Withdrawal of the US military from South Vietnam.
> 2. Neutrality of North and South Vietnam pending their reunification.
> 3. The organisation of South Vietnam based on the programme of the Vietcong.
> 4. The peaceful reunification of Vietnam without foreign intervention.

Why, do you think, would Johnson reject these Four Points?

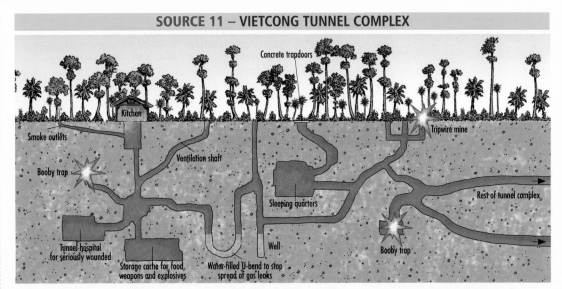

SOURCE 11 – VIETCONG TUNNEL COMPLEX

Concrete trapdoors
Kitchen
Tripwire mine
Smoke outlets
Booby trap
Ventilation shaft
Sleeping quarters
Rest of tunnel complex
Tunnel hospital for seriously wounded
Well
Booby trap
Storage cache for food, weapons and explosives
Water-filled U-bend to stop spread of gas leaks

Underground tunnel complex dug by the Vietcong. The total tunnel network estimated to be 240km long.

What difficulties did these tunnels pose for US soldiers?

Johnson took a close interest in the progress of the war. On Tuesdays, he met with his advisers and they decided the military targets for the bombers. Each morning the first information he looked for was the number of US personnel killed the previous day.

SOURCE 12 – THE EFFECTS OF BOOBY TRAPS

Pulaski tripped on a booby trap, and it blew the hell out of him. Evidently, the enemy stole the explosives or something. The explosion blew one leg off about midway between the knee and the groin, and the other leg was blown off at the calf. The explosion left his body naked.

A US soldier's description of what happened to a fellow soldier

> What effect would booby trap bombs have on US soldier morale?

SOURCE 14 – MEMO FROM SECRETARY OF DEFENSE MCNAMARA

'With the situation continuing to deteriorate (in 1965), McNamara wrote a decisive memo in late July. It laid out three options: "cut our losses and withdraw," "continue at about the same level," or "expand promptly and substantially the U.S. pressure." ... He recommended the third. It would lead to "considerable cost in casualties and material" but would "offer a good chance of producing a favourable settlement in the longer run."'

Quoted in J Patterson, *Grand Expectations: The United States 1945–74*

> What did McNamara favour? Which was McNamara – a 'hawk' or a 'dove', do you think?

SOURCE 13A – A SOLDIER IN VIETNAM

Seven months later, I found myself in Vietnam (1966) (after volunteering). What I found in Vietnam, however, was not at all what I had been taught to expect. The American people had been told that we were defending a free democracy. What I found was a military dictatorship rife with corruption and venality and repression. The premier of South Vietnam openly admired Adolf Hitler. Buddhist priests who petitioned for peace were jailed or shot down in the streets. Officials at every level engaged in blatant black-marketeering at astronomical profit and at the expense of their own people. And the government was clearly devoid of the support of the vast majority of the Vietnamese people.

Source: W. D. Erhart, *In the Shadow of Vietnam, Essays 1977-1991*, McFarland, Jefferson, North Carolina, 2011

SOURCE 13B – AN OFFICER IN VIETNAM

We have seen the creation of a new empire by North Vietnam. We have seen Laos occupied by the North Vietnamese government. We have seen Cambodia robbed and starved by Cambodian Communists and then occupied by the North Vietnamese. We were right to resist terror and war being inflicted on a poor and backward people. The South Vietnamese government had many faults, but Ho Chi Minh and his Communist Party have left a trail of cruelty, famine and tyranny. I maintain in the face of all accusers that we who served in Vietnam did so when our only thought was duty and our only cause was freedom.

Source: David Donovan, *Once a Warrior King; Memories of an Officer in Vietnam*, McGraw-Hill, New York, 1985

> How useful are these sources a evidence soldiers' attitudes the war?

SOURCE 15 – STATISTICS ON THE VIETNAM WAR

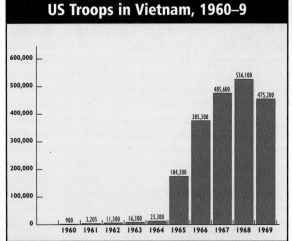

US Troops in Vietnam, 1960–9

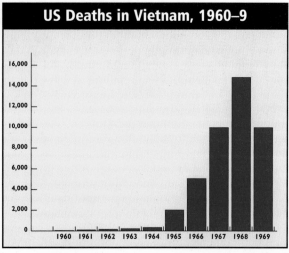

US Deaths in Vietnam, 1960–9

> What is the main conclusion you would draw from this source?

WHAT CAN YOU TELL ABOUT THE SOURCES?

WHAT INFORMATION CA YOU GET FROM THE SOURCE?

Analysing Documents: Photographs	Are photographs **primary** or **secondary** sources?	Are these photographs **objective**?	How would these photos **compare** with eyewitness accounts of the same incidents as historical sources?	What **effects** do you think these photos would have on **US public opinion**?	Are photographs of limited value to historians because they only show a moment in time?

Why were the villagers **rounded up** in 1?

Who was **executed** in 2?

Who set the houses on **fire** in 3?

What was the **name** of the massacre in 4?

What do these photographs show about the **nature of war**?

How **useful** are these photos for understanding the US role in the Vietnam War?

Explain your answer in each case.

Progress of the War

Johnson claimed that the bombing was aimed at military targets, but films showed otherwise. Johnson also claimed that the US was winning the war and that it would be over soon. His commander in Vietnam, **General Westmoreland**, always believed that if only he got more soldiers, he would win the war. But the use of **strategic bombing** failed to cripple a predominantly agricultural country, and the use of **artillery** and search-and-destroy missions failed in a **guerrilla** war.

But Americans still largely supported the **President's handling** of the war. In 1964, 85 per cent of Americans supported the country's policy in Vietnam. But this began to decline as America became more involved in the war, and an **anti-war**

Timeline of Johnson and US involvement in Vietnam War

—1963	(November) President Kennedy assassinated; Johnson became President
—1964	(August) Gulf of Tonkin Incident; Tonkin Resolution Johnson re-elected President
—1965	Operation Rolling Thunder – air bombardment of North Vietnam US Marines land at Da Nang (South Vietnam) – first US combat troops
—1965–67	Growth of US forces to over half a million
—1968	(January) Tet Offensive in South Vietnam (March) My Lai Massacre Johnson ordered partial halt to bombing of North Vietnam; proposed peace talks; announced he would not seek re-election Paris peace talks began
—1969	(January) Nixon became President of US

However, Nixon hoped to improve relations with China, increase US–China trade, put pressure on North Vietnam in the peace negotiations and to play off China and the USSR against each other. It also helped Nixon in the presidential election year of 1972 because television pictures of his visit to the **Great Wall** of China were beamed back to the US. In spite of Nixon's claim that *'This was the week that changed the world'*, his visit was mainly symbolic.

However, Nixon did successfully play off China and the USSR. The Soviets feared that they would be isolated, so two months after his visit, Nixon had a summit meeting in **Moscow** with **Brezhnev**, the Soviet leader. This was the first visit by a serving American President to the Kremlin. The leaders agreed on the **Strategic Arms Limitation Treaty** (SALT I). This treaty put a limit to the number of ICBMs (intercontinental ballistic missiles) and submarine-based missiles for five years. Even though there was still much scope for developing other types of nuclear weapons, **SALT I** showed that both sides realised the dangers of the arms race. The two countries signed a further agreement to work together for **peaceful co-existence**, *'to do their utmost to avoid military confrontation and to prevent the outbreak of nuclear war'*. This was a significant victory for the policy of détente, which was strengthened by **Brezhnev's visit** to the US in 1973.

Arab-Israeli War, 1973 – Its Impact on Détente

However, détente was put to a **severe test** when Egypt and Syria attacked Israel in October 1973 (in the Arab-Israeli – Yom Kippur – War). The USSR had supported Egypt and Syria before the war and the US supported Israel. There was a danger that détente would be destroyed. **Kissinger** was sent to Moscow to work out a truce. The Israelis refused to agree and the Soviets said it should be enforced by the two superpowers. Nixon disagreed and put the US on **nuclear alert**. One year after SALT I, détente seemed to be collapsing, but both sides backed down and a truce was agreed.

Chile and the CIA

In spite of Nixon's visits to China and Russia, it was clear that Cold War tensions were still strong. Some accused Nixon of mainly undertaking his visits for **election purposes** in the election year of 1972. Indeed, Nixon's treatment of **Chile** showed he was still the Cold War warrior. He tried to prevent the election of the socialist **Salvador Allende** as President of Chile. When that failed, he used the CIA to undermine Allende's rule and this led to Allende's overthrow and assassination in 1973. In this way, Nixon was following the traditional **policy of containment**.

QUESTIONS

1. How did Nixon improve relations with (i) China and (ii) the Soviet Union?
2. What effect did the Arab-Israeli War have on the policy of détente?
3. What incidents or events show that Nixon was still a Cold War warrior?

Ford and Détente

President Ford, who succeeded Nixon after he resigned over the Watergate scandal, continued the policy of **détente**. He relied on Henry Kissinger as his Secretary of State and this provided continuity of policy. Ford met **Brezhnev** in Vladivostok in 1974 and agreed on a second round of SALT talks.

Détente took another major step when Ford and Brezhnev, along with 33 other government leaders, signed the **Helsinki Agreement** in 1975. They agreed to:

QUESTIONS

1. How did Ford continue the policy of détente?
2. How did Congress oppose some of Ford's foreign policy?

President Ford (right) and the Soviet leader, Leonid Brezhnev, share a toast at their final dinner in Vladivostok after the Strategic Arms Limitation Treaty (SALT) talks in 1974.

- Respect each others' borders, which applied particularly to Europe.
- Allow freedom of travel, and encourage trade and cultural links.
- Respect human rights.

But Congress was opposed to other aspects of Ford's policies. It refused to send military aid to the collapsing **South Vietnamese government**, which was attacked by North Vietnam in 1975. It also rejected his proposals to send arms and equipment to anti-Communist forces in **Angola**. Congress feared that the US would be dragged into another foreign war.

Carter's Foreign Policy and SALT II

Carter's foreign policy differed from that of Nixon and Ford. He wanted a foreign policy based on **moral principles** – based on honour and right. But Carter was very **inexperienced** in foreign policy. Because he relied for advice on two different points of view – that of his Secretary of State, **Cyrus Vance**, as well as his Secretary of Defense, **Zbigniew Brzezinski** – his policy was often inconsistent.

He wanted to reduce arms but he was also critical of the Soviet Union for its treatment of **dissidents** (political protestors) in Czechoslovakia and the Soviet Union itself. This criticism upset the Russians and this put détente under pressure. Further difficulties were caused between the two superpowers when Carter arranged a peace agreement between **Egypt and Israel** in 1978 without involving the Soviet Union (the Camp David Agreement).

Soviet leader, Brezhnev, holds a signed copy of the SALT II Treaty as he stands beside President Carter of the US in June 1979 in Vienna.

QUESTIONS

1. How did Carter's foreign policy differ from Nixon's and Ford's?
2. What was SALT II?
3. What actions did Carter carry out that undermined détente?

SALT II

The SALT talks continued slowly and once again the US played the **China card** when the Chinese leader, **Deng Xiaoping**, visited the US. The Soviet Union feared isolation again and soon an agreement on arms limitation – **SALT II** – was reached with the US in 1979. This put a limit (on missiles and bombers) of 2,400 per country. But this did not stop the USSR installing SS-20 missiles in Eastern Europe and the US countering with Pershing missiles. SALT II was also criticised in the US, where the liberals said it did not go far enough while the conservative right wing said it went too far.

However, even the limited agreement was halted when the USSR invaded **Afghanistan** in December 1979 and Congress **refused to ratify** the treaty. In his State of the Union speech, Carter said the Soviet invasion was *'the most serious threat to peace since the Second World War'*. He caused relations with the Soviet Union to deteriorate by suspending grain sales to that country and by boycotting the **Olympic Games** in Moscow in 1980. This was the end of détente.

Reagan and Star Wars

By the late 1970s and the early 1980s, Cold War tensions between the US and USSR increased:

- The **Soviet invasion** of Afghanistan confirmed to the US that the Soviet Union had not changed since 1945 – it was still aggressive and expansionist.
- Reagan introduced an **aggressive tone** to his foreign policy – he wanted military superiority over the Soviet Union, which he said was **the evil empire** aiming for world domination.

Reagan began a huge **arms build-up**. Over $550 billion a year was spent on conventional and nuclear weapons. New weapons such as the **stealth bomber** were developed. At the same time, however, Reagan was prepared to discuss **arms reduction**. But because of mistrust between the two sides, the **Strategic Arms Reduction Talks** (START) which began in 1982 failed.

In 1982, Reagan wrote a **private letter** which explained his approach to the Soviet Union.

> *'I don't underestimate the imperialist ambitions of the Soviet Union... I want more than anything to bring them into realistic arms-reduction talks. To do this they must be convinced that the alternative is a build-up militarily by us. They have stretched their economy to the limit to maintain their programme. They know they cannot match us in an arms race if we are determined to catch up. Our true ultimate purpose is arms reduction.'*

To achieve this he was prepared to tolerate huge **budget deficits**.

The following year Reagan announced that the US was developing the **Strategic Defense Initiative** (SDI), popularly called **Star Wars**. This was a plan to develop a **defence shield** in space which would destroy any missiles fired at the US. Some scientists doubted if the US could develop such a shield. Others said they could and that it would make all Soviet missiles obsolete.

Star Wars and Relations with the Soviet Union

SDI was a barrier to US–Soviet agreement when **Reagan and Gorbachev**, the new Soviet leader, met in **Geneva** and **Reykjavik**. Gorbachev objected to extending the arms race into space, while Reagan said the US would share the Star Wars technology. But Gorbachev did not believe him. However, agreement was eventually reached in 1987 when they signed the **Intermediate-range Nuclear Forces Treaty** (INF) in Washington. This led to the dismantling of the Soviet SS-20 missiles and the US Pershing missiles in Europe. But Reagan still refused to abandon the Star Wars project.

Some historians believe that **Reagan's tough policy** and his increase in armaments forced the Soviet Union to see that it could not compete. Others think that the **growing understanding** between Reagan and Gorbachev was more important. At any rate, it was clear that Gorbachev wanted to reform the Soviet Union and reduce arms, and Reagan was prepared to negotiate. A further improvement in relations occurred between the two states when Reagan visited **Moscow** in 1988.

QUESTIONS

1. Why did Cold War tensions increase between the US and the USSR in the late 1970s and early 1980s?
2. Why did Reagan begin a large arms build-up?

US President Ronald Reagan shakes the hand of a baby held by Soviet leader Mikhail Gorbachev during a tour of Moscow's Red Square in 1988. The Kremlin and Lenin's tomb are in the background on the left.

The Policy of Containment – A Successful Policy?

Shortly after, however, **Gorbachev's reform** movement led to a process which caused the collapse of the Soviet empire in Eastern Europe (1989) and finally the **downfall of Communism** in Russia (1991). The US policy of containment **contributed** to this downfall. It forced the Soviet Union to maintain huge spending on armaments which would have been better used in improving the economy and social conditions in the USSR. Ultimately the USSR could not compete with the spending of the stronger US economy. But reforms to reduce military spending in the USSR undermined Communism and led to its collapse and the **end of the Cold War**. The US became the world's most dominant power.

One of the authors of the policy of containment in the 1940s assessed the **cost of the victory** of that policy:

> 'We paid with 40 years of enormous and unnecessary military expenditures [spending]. We paid through the cultivation of nuclear weaponry to the point where the vast and useless nuclear arsenals had become a danger to the very environment of the planet... We paid all this because we were too timid to negotiate.'

But those who supported the policy of containment also argued that it **avoided war** with the Soviet Union and discouraged or **prevented** a Soviet invasion of Western Europe.

? QUESTIONS

1. What was Star Wars?
2. How did Star Wars affect relations between the US and the USSR?
3. When Communism collapsed in the Soviet Union in 1991, did that mean the policy of containment was successful?

HOMEWORK EXERCISES

ORDINARY LEVEL

1. Study the extract from President Reagan's letter on p. 377 and answer the following questions.
   A. (i) What is meant by 'the imperialist ambitions of the Soviet Union'?
      (ii) What does Reagan want the Soviets to do?
      (iii) How does he intend to make them do what he wants?
      (iv) What is the purpose of an arms race as far as he is concerned?
      (v) How successful was his policy?
   B. Write a **paragraph** on the effects of the Vietnam War on the US.
   C. Write a **long answer** on how and why the US withdrew from Vietnam.

2. Study the extract from one of the authors (George Kennan) of the policy of containment on p. 378 and answer the following questions.
   A. (i) What does he say the cost of the Cold War is?
      (ii) What is the result of the 'cultivation of nuclear weaponry'?
      (iii) This was written when the Cold War came to an end. Does the author agree with his views in the 1940s? Explain your answer fully. (See Kennan's Long Telegram, p. 340.)
   B. Write a **paragraph** on SALT.
   C. Write a **long answer** on how US foreign policy under Reagan helped to bring about the end of the Cold War.

HIGHER LEVEL

3. What were the significant developments in US foreign policy, 1973–89? (2007)

4. How successful was the US in trying to contain the spread of Communism, both internally and externally?

5. What part did one or more of the following play in US foreign policy: Korea; Cuba; SALT; Star Wars (2012)

6. What was the significance of the Moon landing (1969) and/or Star Wars?

In this section, you should understand:
- The causes of the boom.
- The role of the multinational corporation.
- The military-industrial complex.
- The impact of demographic growth.

The Boom

During the Second World War the US economy entered a boom period which lasted until the end of the 1960s. After the war was over some Americans feared the return of the Great Depression, but this did not happen.

Instead the US economy **grew rapidly** in the late 1940s and through the 1950s and 1960s. Indeed, the economy more than doubled in size between 1945 and 1960. Throughout this time unemployment remained low, and inflation averaged only 2.5 per cent a year from 1951–70 as the US enjoyed *'the greatest prosperity the world has ever known'*. In the process, the US became the **world's dominant economic power**. The US population in the late 1940s was only 7 per cent of the population of the whole world, yet the country produced half the world's manufacturing output and possessed over 40 per cent of the world's income.

By the end of the 1960s many Americans had become homeowners, high consumers and were well educated. Generally Americans were much better off. By 1960, for example, families could buy about 30 per cent more than they could in 1950.

Huge spaghetti junctions and large highways (motorways), as shown here in California, were symbols of the economic boom in the US in the post-war years.

US Production as % of the World's Production (Late 1940s)	
Steel	57
Electricity	43
Oil	62
Cars	80

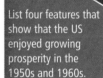

QUESTION

List four features that show that the US enjoyed growing prosperity in the 1950s and 1960s.

What Caused the Boom?

The Influence of the Second World War on the US Economy

The huge expansion in **war industries** eliminated the high unemployment of the Great Depression of the 1930s. It also brought millions of **women** into the workforce. Family earnings increased during the war and so did **savings** because there was nowhere to spend the money. By 1945, there was $140 billion in private savings. These savings were used after the war to boost **consumer spending**.

The war also increased **government revenue** as more people were brought into the tax net. In 1940, the government collected $7 billion in tax. This rose to $51 billion by 1945. This paid for war expenses, along with borrowing. The economy grew enormously because of the extra spending. The US economy almost **doubled** during the war, even allowing for inflation.

KEY CONCEPT
ECHNOLOGICAL
DEVELOPMENT is
the application or use
of scientific discoveries
in industry.

QUESTION

How did each of the
following factors in
the Second World War
help the US economy
to grow: (i) war
industries (ii) mergers
(iii) new technology
(iv) no war damage
(v) exports?

Companies also benefited from the war as their profits increased, especially those on government contracts. Many companies grew much bigger because of **mergers** (joining of companies). By the end of the war, three-quarters of manufacturing industry was controlled by 100 companies (or corporations). These companies had the resources to develop **new technology** which kept American companies ahead of their competitors. (See also The Multinational Corporation, 1945–68, pp. 381–83)

America also benefited from the war in another way. The US mainland was **undamaged** during the war, so the country did not have to spend money on reconstruction like European and Asian countries. The US also benefited by **exports** to these areas. In the case of countries in Western Europe, for instance, Marshall Aid funds were used by those countries to buy in American goods.

Public Investment

US government spending (or public investment) increased dramatically from $10 billion in 1940 to $580 billion in 1980. Much of government spending went on the huge military budget; from 1945–70, 60 per cent of all federal spending went on **defence**. But there was also increased spending on **highways** (roads), **education** and **welfare**. This gave a huge boost to the economy. Its importance can be seen in the mild recessions of 1953–4 and 1957–8, which were mainly due to cutbacks in government spending.

The **defence spending** was due to Cold War rivalries. A conscript army was maintained, some of it abroad in Western Europe and Asia. The US was directly involved in **two major wars** – the Korean War and the Vietnam War, as well as a number of smaller conflicts. There was also huge spending on **weapons research and development** – military aircraft, missiles, ships, submarines and space exploration. The US also benefited from sales of its weapons to other countries. This led to the growth of many **corporations** and involved many thousands of workers. States in the south and south-west, from Florida to California – known as the **Sun Belt** – flourished. The latter benefited most from the new high-tech and defence industries.

A group of people watch as an ICBM (Intercontinental ballistic missile) rises into launch position at a compound in Coney Island, New York.

Government was also involved in other areas of the economy. The **Employment Act** stated that the federal government should try to achieve maximum employment, production and purchasing power. Many government economists followed **Keynesian economic ideas**, which stated that government spending had a large influence on economic growth and employment.

In 1944, the government passed the **GI Bill of Rights**. This gave aid to veterans to buy houses, start businesses and educate themselves. By 1956, about 8 million veterans benefited from further education. This helped the economy grow through the provision of increased **skills** and a boost to the **construction industry** (more schools and colleges).

Government investment in the **Highways Act 1956** had an important influence on economic growth. Over 15 years the government invested $43 billion in major roads crossing the continent. This gave an immediate boost to construction and employment in the various states involved. But it also gave an indirect boost to the car industry and to interstate trade and commerce.

The government spent a great deal on the **social welfare programme** put in place by the New Deal in the 1930s. This was added to during the 1950s and especially during President Johnson's **Great Society** programme in the 1960s. By the end of the 1960s this had the effect of reducing the amount of poverty in the country.

Other Factors

● The American economy also benefited from **cheap energy** (oil) and **technological advances**.

● There were significant advances in research and development – these increased **productivity** (output per worker) and **real per capita income**. Output per worker rose by about 35 per cent in each decade.

The rapid technological expansion occurred in electronic and electrical companies, tobacco, soft drinks, chemicals, plastics and pharmaceutical industries. The number of scientists and engineers involved in industrial research grew six times between 1945 and 1961. Some inventions were more influential than others. In particular, **transistors**, which were invented at the end of the 1940s, were used in machines from computers to hearing aids. In another example, **medicine**, it was estimated that 80 per cent of drugs prescribed in 1956 had been developed in the previous 15 years. (See also Demographic Growth, pp. 385–88 and Affluence and Consumerism, p. 394)

The Development of the US Industrial Structure

The Multinational Corporation, 1945–68

After the Second World War one of the features of the changing American economy was the **concentration of economic power** in business and industry. In 1945, there were over 300 recorded mergers in manufacturing and mining; this had increased to over 2,000 in 1969. These mergers created very large companies or corporations. In 1955, 30 per cent of manufacturing sales was controlled by just 50 of over 300,000 manufacturing companies.

Some of these companies became **multinational corporations** – that is, they built and operated factories or plants outside the US. Some of the largest were Exxon, Standard Oil, Ford and General Motors. They operated on a worldwide scale because they bought raw materials from a variety of countries and sold their products in these and other countries. In the process, the US became the **world's largest overseas investor**. In 1950, foreign investment amounted to $19 billion, but this increased to over $160 billion by 1973. It was estimated that by the end of the 1960s over 1,200 US companies had manufacturing or marketing subsidiaries abroad. They became a form of **economic imperialism**.

However, US **foreign investment declined** in the late 1970s and into the 1980s as the US economy itself was in trouble. Between 1945 and the 1960s, the US accounted

QUESTIONS

1. After the war, where did the government increase spending and investment?
2. How did defence spending boost the economy?
3. How did Keynesian economic ideas help?
4. What was the impact on the economy of (i) the GI Bill of Rights (ii) the Highway Act (iii) the social welfare programme?

Causes of Economic Boom, 1945–69

● Impact of WWII
● Government investments
● Military-industrial complex
● Cheap energy
● New technology
● Population growth/ consumer society
● Multinational corporations
● Globalisation

QUESTION

What other factors boosted the US economy in this period?

KEY CONCEPT
CORPORATE CAPITALISM was part of the economic, political and social system based on private property, business and industry. The large companies or corporations which controlled the system wanted to make increased profits.

? QUESTIONS

1. How was there a concentration of economic power in the US economy after the war?
2. What are multinational corporations and how do they operate?

for most of the world's foreign investment, but by 1980 this had declined to less than half. The type of investment also changed. By the 1980s most US multinationals were investing in service industries – banking, fast food, hotels and financial services – as US home industry changed to more service-orientated industries.

Causes of Multinational Expansion

The expansion of the US multinational corporation was due to a number of factors:

The McDonald's Museum in Des Plaines, Illinois. This is a replica of the first corporate McDonald's opened in 1955. The McDonald's Corporation became a large multinational business with franchised outlets all over the world.

- Many businesses became **successful** in the home market in the US and these businesses tended to invest abroad.
- US multinationals had **advantages** of greater technology, higher productivity and better management skills compared to European or Asian competitors.
- The multinational corporations developed partly in response to the **growth of world markets** – it became easier to control widespread operations by improvements in communications and transportation.
- Another factor in the rise of the American multinational was the **huge investment in research and development**, which paid off with many new products. However, the costs of exporting these were high, so it was easier to build a factory in or near the foreign market to cater for that market.
- Federal **tax laws** encouraged firms to invest abroad. US firms were liable for tax in the host country, but not in the US unless their earnings were brought back to the US. The attraction of host countries was **lower corporation tax** than the US.
- The federal government also helped by **insuring companies** against losses in politically unstable countries, particularly in South America.
- The **US dollar** became the world's main currency.
- The growth of the **European economy** in the 1950s and 1960s, especially the development of the European Economic Community (EEC), provided another prosperous market.

A number of factors influenced the **pattern** of US foreign investment. Most of the foreign investment was in Western Europe and Canada. In Western Europe most of the investment was in **manufacturing**, but in some of the less developed countries there was investment in producing raw materials. This concentration of investment in a couple of areas was caused by a number of factors:

- The spread of Communism in Eastern Europe and Russia excluded these areas.
- The growing **independence movements** (or decolonisation) in Africa and Asia created unstable political conditions which put off investors. This was sometimes followed by the **nationalisation** (government ownership) of industry and raw materials.
- **Japan** deliberately kept out foreign investment.

Concerns about Multinationals

The growth of the multinational corporation caused **concern** over the ability of the US government and foreign governments to control their operations. These corporations were able to take advantage of host country economic policies designed to build up their own economies. Some were involved in **transfer pricing** where they were able to avoid making profits in high-tax countries. The US government, **supported** by Congress, was also concerned about the growth of the huge corporations because they wanted to maintain **competition**. They feared that a smaller number of companies would control the prices of products to increase their profits.

Foreign investment became increasingly important to corporations and this can be seen in the use of **bribes to politicians**. These were illegal payments to political campaign (election) funds, and also to federal government officials. By 1976, 150 corporations admitted to involvement in these activities. Exxon, Lockheed Aircraft and Gulf Oil Corporation were some of the major corporations involved.

The Growth of US Foreign Investment ($ Billions)	
1950	11.8
1960	31.8
1968	64.8
Cars	80

QUESTIONS ?

1. What caused the expansion of multinational corporations?
2. Why was most US financial investment in Western Europe and Canada?
3. Why are some people concerned about the influence of multinational corporations?

Globalisation

The growth of US multinational corporations was one part of the **globalisation** process – the closer **integration** of the world's economies and growing **interdependence** between different places. Through this growing integration, the fortunes of the US economy affected other parts of the world. US multinational corporations were part of the growing **internationalisation** in both trade and politics. They spread new ideas, especially cultural values, to other countries. Indeed, their success depended on a world based on **consumer** goods, particularly American goods, such as **Coca-Cola, IBM** and **Levi's jeans**. They were part of the **Americanisation** of the world, with similar pop music – jazz and rock 'n' roll – and films. Critics accused them of spreading American culture and undermining local cultures. In spite of the increasing popularity and acceptance of American products in Europe, Americanisation also gave rise to **anti-American feelings** in some countries.

The growing popularity of Levi's worldwide was one example of the Americanisation of the world. Levi's and other products were part of the globalisation process.

Global Trade System

The growth of the multinational corporations was eased by the development of a number of international agreements and organisations which created conditions for free trade. Some historians suggest that the US set up a trade system that suited their interests:

- The **International Monetary Fund** was established in 1946 to promote international co-operation in finance and to encourage stability in exchange rates. The US dollar became the cornerstone of the currency market.
- The **World Bank** provided loans for development programmes.

KEY CONCEPT
GLOBALISATION is the spread of institutions, organisations and culture on a worldwide or global scale. It is usually associated with the spread of trade and industry by large companies or corporations to many different countries. Goods, services and culture gradually become the same in all parts of the world.

- At the same time, the **General Agreement on Tariffs and Trade** (GATT) was signed in 1947. This began a process of reducing tariffs on goods which was continued with further agreements, or **rounds**, in later years, such as the Kennedy Round in the 1960s.

This structure made greater trade and globalisation possible.

Supporters and Critics of Globalisation

The intense conflict between those who favoured globalisation and those who opposed it did not come until the 1990s. However, the arguments of the debate were outlined long before in the 1970s and 1980s.

- **Supporters**: Those who favoured globalisation argued that increased world trade reduced worldwide poverty. By boosting economic growth, they said it helped poorer countries catch up with richer countries. They also pointed out that less developed countries increased their share of world trade. Supporters also said that when industry was set up in foreign countries, it improved the skills of the local workforce.

- **Critics**: Critics of globalisation argued against that. They said larger US corporations invested in poorer countries only because they made greater profits from lower wages. They said freer trade only opened markets for the benefit of multinational corporations. They also argued against the spread of American culture.

This globalisation increased the wealth of the better-off states (initially the US and later Western Europe and Japan) at the expense of the less developed world – adding to the growing rift between the **richer** and **poorer** countries. Some regarded globalisation as a form of **imperialism**.

The Military-Industrial Complex

Another aspect of the US industrial structure which developed in the 1950s and 1960s was the **military-industrial complex**. In 1961, in his farewell speech to the American people, President Eisenhower warned about the dangers of the **complex**, whose influence was felt in *'every city, every State house, every office of Federal Government'*. This was the **link** (or connection) between the Department of Defense and the major corporations which provided military equipment. He was concerned that the political leadership might not be able to control this powerful and growing combination.

Eisenhower was concerned that its influence would undermine the values of the **republic** and the **democratic process**. He feared its influence would dominate domestic and foreign policy, heightening tensions with the Soviet Union. He was afraid that it would favour an **aggressive anti-Communist policy** and not favour peaceful co-existence. The Cold War threatened to make the military too powerful in American life, and that was a potential threat to freedom of education and scientific research. He urged Americans to guard against its increased power.

The **corporations** involved in the military-industrial complex included McDonnell Douglas, Lockheed and Boeing. The generals and admirals benefited from increased money for the armed forces. The complex also included the **politicians** whose

QUESTIONS

1. What is globalisation? How did the US set up a trade system to suit its own interests?
2. What did (i) supporters and (ii) opponents of globalisation say about it?

KEY CONCEPT

IMPERIALISM occurs when one country has a great deal of power or influence over others, especially in political and economic affairs. Sometimes the imperial power may actually take over the weaker countries.

McDonnell Douglas war plane

states or cities benefited from armaments contracts and the growth of the armaments industry. This involved the space programme by the end of the 1950s. In the early 1960s, 22 of the 50 states in the US had a great dependency on military spending. However, it was not only selfish gain which motivated politicians and army commanders. They firmly believed in keeping the US strong in its struggle against Communism.

QUESTIONS **?**

1. What is the military-industrial complex?
2. Why was President Eisenhower concerned about it?
3. Who benefitted from the military-industrial complex?
4. What was the missile gap and how did it influence President Kennedy's policies?

The Missile Gap

The relationship between lobbyists (for the arms industry), politicians and arms contractors became known as the **Iron Triangle** and its influence posed problems for political leaders. In the Presidential election of 1960, John F. Kennedy campaigned on the issue of the **missile gap** between the USSR and the US. This suited arms contractors and army leaders, who encouraged talk of a missile gap, even though there was none, in the hope of increased military spending. They used their influence with members of Congress. This was one of the factors – along with heightened Cold War tensions – which encouraged Kennedy to increase defence spending by over 10 per cent for each year from 1961–3 when he became President. (See also p. 330)

Demographic Growth: Population Increase and Movement

One of the most significant aspects of post-war American history was the rapid growth in population and its geographic distribution. The US population increased from 131 million in 1940 to 226 million in 1980 – an increase of 95 million (or almost 75 per cent). Each decade from 1940–80 saw large percentage increases in population – the largest occurring during the 1950s, when the population grew by almost 20 per cent.

	Growth of US Population (Millions)		
	Population (millions)	**% Urban**	**% Rural**
1940	131.7	56.5	43.5
1950	150.7	64.0	36.0
1960	179.3	69.0	31.0
1970	203.2	73.5	26.5
1980	226.5	73.7	26.3
1990	250.0	–	–

Causes

Birth and Death Rates

The most important cause of the rising population was the increased **birth rate**. The birth rate increased after the Second World War with the return of 12 million servicemen and the improving economy. This caused the post-war **baby boom** which lasted into the 1960s. There were 3.5 million births in 1947 and 4.3 million births in 1960.

Along with the increased birth rate, there was a decline in the **death rate** due to **better food** and improvements in **medicine**. New drugs such as **penicillin** controlled sickness and disease. The new polio vaccine eliminated polio, and tuberculosis, which was once a serious killer, was controlled by new medicines and improved living standards. Even when the birth rate declined in the 1970s and 1980s, there was still a further decline in the death rate so that the population continued to rise.

Immigration

Immigration also contributed to population growth, though to a much lesser extent. In all, about 11 million immigrants came to the US between 1940 and 1980. Some were refugees from mainly Eastern and Central Europe after the Second World War. Others came in after the Hungarian Rising in 1956 and after Castro took over Cuba in 1959. In total, refugees amounted to about 20 per cent of all immigration.

Greater numbers of immigrants came from **Canada** and **Mexico**. In the latter case, this was because of a shortage of **farm labour** in the south-west states. Legal Mexican immigrants were far outnumbered by **wetbacks** – those who swam across the Rio Grande to get to the US. By the 1970s, America was experiencing large **Asian immigration**, but this was controlled by new immigration laws (1965) which allowed in people with special skills or qualifications. However, the overall impact of immigration was small between 1945 and 1980 so that the proportion of foreign-born people living in the US declined to 5 per cent in 1970. But the new immigration of the 1970s and 1980s pushed that proportion up again by 1990.

Birth and Death Rates (Per Thousand of Population)		
	Birth Rate	**Death Rate**
1940	19.4	10.8
1950	24.1	9.6
1960	23.7	9.5
1970	18.4	9.5
1980	15.9	8.9
1990	16.7	8.6

Illegal Mexican immigrants are escorted back across the border into Mexico.

Impact of Population Growth on the Economy
- More workers
- Greater demand
- Encouraged investment

Population Structure and Mobility

The increase in the birth rate and the decline in the death rate changed the **age structure** of the population. There were now **more younger people** and **more older people**. The younger people became the **teen market** – the so-called Pepsi Generation – for clothes, music, cars and increased college places. This contributed to the **general consumer boom** of the 1950s and 1960s, which itself was caused by a growing, wealthier population. In the case of the increased numbers of older people, there was greater federal spending on health and welfare to cater for their needs. (See pp. 394–97)

The rapidly growing economy created **greater mobility** in the population. There was movement from cities to the suburbs and from the countryside to the cities, both within states and between states. By 1960 over 60 per cent of the population lived in cities of half a million or more; this increased to over 75 per cent by 1980. The spread of these cities, particularly from Washington through New York to Boston, created the idea of a **conurbation** or **megalopolis** – a vast sprawling built-up area. At the same time the farm population declined rapidly in the US. Increased farm mechanisation and farm size resulted in the farm population dropping from 7 million in 1935 to less than 2 million by 1980.

% of US Population Foreign-born	
1940	8.8
1970	4.8
1990	7.9

? **QUESTIONS**

1. Explain how (i) birth and death rates and (ii) immigration caused rapid population increase in the US after the Second World War.
2. How did the population structure change and what were its effects?

Growth of Suburbs

Within the cities there was huge movement from the inner or central city to the **suburbs,** helped by new roads, the widespread use of cars and cheaper houses. It was here that the vast new housing estates and new towns, such as Levittown in Long Island, were created. Between 1950 and 1970, American cities lost population to their suburbs, ranging from 10 per cent in New York to 35 per cent in Detroit, and the overall population of the suburban areas grew by 35 million.

The growth of the suburbs had a number of **social consequences**:

- The people of the suburbs were **white and middle class**. This left the centre of the city to the poor and the wealthy.

- It also **divided the races**, as blacks migrating from the South largely took over the central city areas. No blacks were allowed to buy houses in Levittown.

- The suburbs were mainly for living in, so that huge **traffic jams** were caused by people commuting to work. It wasn't until the 1970s that significant numbers of people both lived and worked in their communities as schools, churches, shops, businesses and industries developed.

- **Businesses declined** in the city centre – some newspapers, cinemas, hotels and shops closed and buildings decayed. The decay was contributed to by the failure of urban renewal projects and housing projects.

- Some criticised the sameness or **conformity** of the suburbs – Mam, Dad, two kids and the dog. '*Suburbs are small, controlled communities where for the most part everyone has the same living standards, the same weeds, the same number of garbage cans, the same house plans, and the same level in the septic tank.*' They saw it as a **threat to individualism**. Some criticised them as places where everyone '*buys the right car, keeps his lawn like his neighbours, eats crunchy breakfast cereal and votes Republican*'. William Whyte in *The Organization Man* said that white suburbs had some good points, but he also said that they were similar to a large corporation which threatened to squash the individual drive or spirit that made America great.

- Later observers noted that the suburbs **provided houses** when there was a shortage. They also noted that **individualism** did break out, so that with additions and changes no two houses looked the same.

Levittown, New York, which sprang up from potato farmland in Long Island in the late 1940s. The builders, Levitt and Sons, used mass production methods to keep down costs. The suburbs of US cities expanded rapidly in the post-war decades.

Interstate Mobility

There was also mobility from **state to state**. By 1960, one-quarter of Americans were living in a different state to the one they were born in. The greatest beneficiaries of the movement were the states of the **Sun Belt** in the south and south-west, from California on the west coast to Florida on the east coast. The new people were largely following the spread of the new high-tech industries, though the elderly who moved to Florida and Arizona followed the sun. As a result of this movement, California became the most populous state in the US.

There was also the opposite movement from the southern states, with the large migration of **black Americans** to the north and north-west. Between 1940 and 1970, 4.5 million blacks left the South for the North. This migration changed the population structure in the cities. In 1950, there was no city in the US with a majority black population. By 1970 there were four, and a number of others had significant black populations. **Washington, DC**, which was three-quarters white in 1940, became three-quarters black by 1970. This movement of blacks to the cities coincided with the movement of whites to the suburbs. It highlighted the **racial differences** between the central cities and the suburbs.

(?) QUESTIONS

1. Why did the suburbs grow and what were the social effects of this?
2. What was interstate mobility?

Suburban homes in the mid-1950s, the desire of many middle-class Americans.

HOMEWORK EXERCISES

ORDINARY LEVEL

1. Study the graphs below and answer the questions that follow.

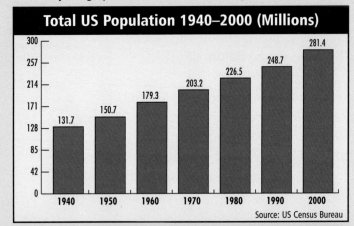

Total US Population 1940–2000 (Millions)

Year	Population
1940	131.7
1950	150.7
1960	179.3
1970	203.2
1980	226.5
1990	248.7
2000	281.4

Source: US Census Bureau

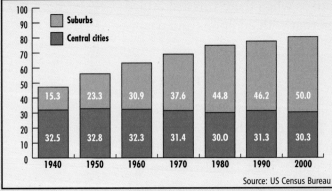

Distribution of Population in Cities Between Central Cities and Suburbs, 1940–2000 (Per Cent)

Suburbs / Central cities

Year	Suburbs	Central cities
1940	15.3	32.5
1950	23.3	32.8
1960	30.9	32.3
1970	37.6	31.4
1980	44.8	30.0
1990	46.2	31.3
2000	50.0	30.3

Source: US Census Bureau

A. (i) By how much did the US population grow between 1940 and 1990?
(ii) Which decade between 1940 and 1990 had the fastest population growth?
(iii) What caused the growth in population?

(iv) How did this growth in population affect the US economy?
(v) How did the distribution of population change in the metropolitan (city) areas between 1940 and 1990?
(vi) What caused the change in population in (iii)?

B. Write a **paragraph** on one of the following.
(i) Government investment in the US economy
(ii) The multinational corporation
(iii) The military-industrial complex

C. Write a **long answer** on the following.
What caused the US economic boom after the Second World War?

HIGHER LEVEL

2. Why did the US experience an economic boom in the 1950s and 1960s?

3. What changes occurred in the US population after 1945 and how did those changes impact on US society and economy?

4. To what extent did the US economy experience both success and decline during the period, 1945–89? (2012) (See also Chapter 32)

5. Why did the United States experience an economic boom, 1945–68, and what was its impact on society? (2010)

6. What were the significant developments in the US economy, 1945–89? (2014) (See also Chapter 32)

7. What were the strengths and weaknesses of the US economy, 1945–89? (2016) (See also Chapter 32)

8. What were the achievements of the US economy, 1945–68, and what factors limited its growth, 1968–89? (2017) (See also Chapter 32)

In this section, you should understand:
- The reasons for the declining economy.
- The role of international competition.

The booming American economy of the 1950s and the 1960s began to show signs of decline by the late 1960s.

During the 20 years prior to 1965, the US experienced economic stability and increasing output and employment. Minor recessions were corrected by government policy. Many came to believe that this would continue.

However, in 1965 these conditions began to change. The cost of the **Vietnam War** led to inflation (price rises). This was worsened by the **Oil Crisis** in 1973, which quadrupled the price of oil. The **Iranian Revolution** of 1979 further increased the cost of oil. Between 1981 and 1983, the US experienced its worst economic recession since the Great Depression of the 1930s.

The Economic Consequences of the Vietnam War

In 1966, President Johnson said to Congress, *'I believe that we can continue the Great Society while we fight in Vietnam.'* Like most Americans at the time, Johnson believed that the American economy was powerful enough to pay for both. In the late 1960s, President Johnson increased spending on the Great Society programme and on the Vietnam War.

Budget Deficit

Balancing the federal budget was the normal target of US governments in the 1950s. Deficit budgeting began under President Kennedy – but it was on a small scale.

Part of the prosperity of the 1960s was due to increased government spending. But this increased spending was not matched by increased taxes. Indeed, in 1964 the Johnson government brought in tax cuts, so government revenue (taxes) did not equal spending. This caused a **budget deficit**.

There was a federal deficit in previous years. But throughout the 1960s, under the influence of Keynesian economics, the budget was in deficit every year from 1961–8. However, these deficits were small compared to the 1970s and 1980s. The average deficit in the 1960s (1 per cent of GDP) doubled in the 1970s and doubled again in the 1980s. Since the government did not increase taxes to pay for the deficit, it **borrowed**. This put more money into the economy, which caused **inflation** (price rises).

QUESTIONS (?)

1. Why was there a budget deficit?
2. How did the government cover the deficit? What caused inflation?

389

In spite of US prosperity, there were also scenes of squalor like this one, typical of Washington slums.

QUESTION

How were each of the following affected in the recession: (i) prices (ii) labour costs (iii) unemployment (iv) balance of payments?

Domestic Recession

From 1965, **prices rose**. They had risen only 2 per cent in each of the years 1963–65. But they increased to 3 per cent in 1966 and reached over 6 per cent by the early 1970s. Inflation increased dramatically after the **Yom Kippur War** in 1973, rising to 12 per cent in 1974. The US backed Israel in the war and as a result Arab countries responded by imposing oil sanctions on the US, and increasing the price of oil. The **Iranian Revolution** of 1979 worsened the situation further (see graph).

Labour costs also rose. This was partly due to wage rises, but it was also due to the fall in productivity (output per worker).

The US also faced increased **unemployment** which began about 1969. In 1971, there were 7 million unemployed and the average duration of joblessness rose from nine weeks to 12 weeks. The winding down of the war contributed to unemployment as demobilised soldiers ('veterans') sought jobs at a time when defence industries were cutting back. As a result unemployment doubled between 1968 (3 per cent) and 1974 (6 per cent).

By 1975–76, after the impact of the Oil Crisis of 1973, unemployment rose to 8.5 per cent. Unemployment hit teenagers, women, blacks and other minority groups hardest. During the 1970s the US was hit by both unemployment and inflation troubles. Unemployment averaged over 6 per cent compared to 4 per cent during the 1960s. Inflation went from over 2 per cent to 13 per cent. The combination of unemployment and inflation became known as **stagflation**.

The US **balance of payments** (the balance of imports and exports) also worsened. At the end of the 1940s, the US held large gold reserves. But during the 1950s and early 1960s the US gave over $140 billion in economic and military aid abroad. This was mostly balanced by US exports, but gradually the US gold reserves fell to one-third of what they had been. By the end of the 1960s, US imports were greater than exports so the US had a huge deficit (shortage).

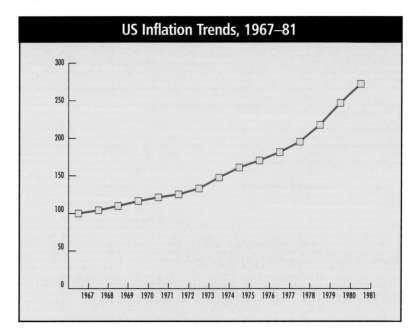

Government Reaction

Nixon took measures to improve the economy in the early 1970s, as he was faced with **stagflation**. Nixon's immediate solution – **rising interest rates** – drove the US economy into recession. In 1971, he put a **freeze** on wages and prices for three months, later making them voluntary. He also abandoned the **fixed exchange rate system** set up after the Second World War. The US dollar was the backbone of the system. The US dollar was **devalued**, which made exports cheaper and imports dearer. Nixon also placed a **tariff** (taxes) on imported Japanese cars. But these actions only led to temporary improvements so that inflation and unemployment continued to be high during the 1970s.

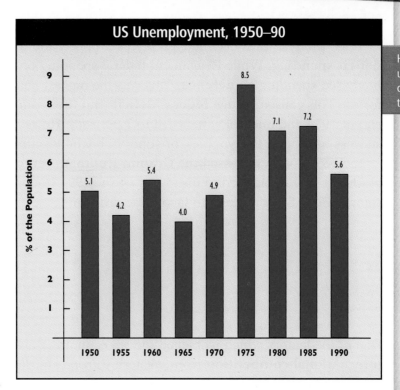

How did trends in unemployment compare in each of the decades?

The economic policies followed by **Ford** and **Carter** did not help the economy either. Ford cut government spending, while Carter tried the opposite. When Carter increased government spending, this only added to inflation, as well as increasing imports, including foreign cars.

By 1980, inflation had reached 13 per cent and interest rates were 20 per cent. The Iranian Revolution led to a doubling of the price of oil and Carter was given powers to ration petrol. At the same time, the states reacted against **big-spending governments**. This began in California, where a state referendum passed Proposition 13, which cut state taxes.

Japanese imported cars.

Reaganomics

When Ronald Reagan became President in 1980, he rejected Carter's economic policies. In his **Program for Economic Recovery**, he wanted to create employment and growth through improvements in productivity and output. He intended to do this with major **tax cuts** of 25 per cent to encourage people to work and to reduce government spending. Reagan believed in what was called **supply-side economics**. He said cutting personal and business taxes would boost the economy and create jobs. Business and industry would put money they would have paid in taxes into the economy. This would create jobs and increase the overall tax take.

The economy grew under Reagan but not because of what he did with cutting taxes and spending programmes. Instead the Federal Reserve Board kept **control of the**

QUESTIONS

1. What was Reagan's economic policy?
2. What were the effects of his policy?

money supply and this brought down inflation from 14 per cent in 1980 to 3.5 per cent in 1984. Interest rates declined, oil prices dropped and the economy expanded due to **deficit spending**. While Reagan cut federal spending on 300 domestic programmes, he increased spending on **defence**. This was the biggest peacetime build-up of US armed forces. This caused a huge **federal deficit**. But the economy grew by 10 per cent by the end of 1984 and unemployment fell to 7 per cent. However, much of the economic success benefitted the 'yuppies' or super rich who became richer.

In 1985, Congress passed the **Gramm-Rudman Act** to reduce the federal deficit gradually. It was planned to disappear by the 1991 Budget. But the next President, George Bush Sr, continued to face these problems when he took office in 1989.

International Competition – Impact on U.S. Economy

One of the factors which worsened the US economy in the 1970s and the 1980s was **international competition** from Western Europe and Japan. While the US remained the largest economy, other economies were catching up. Between 1966 and 1987, other economies grew faster than the US (3.3 per cent), e.g. the Japanese (6.5 per cent) and the West Germans (13 per cent). These countries also invested more of their income in business.

The increased international competition led to more imports coming into the US, the decline of some manufacturing industry, rising unemployment and a worsening balance of payments.

Growth of Japan and West Germany

One of the competing economies was the **Japanese**, which grew faster than the US economy in the 1970s. Japanese productivity also grew faster than the US. In manufacturing, the average output per worker grew at three times the US average between 1960 and 1973. Some believed that Japanese success was due to their management style.

Another country was **West Germany**, which led the Western European challenge to the US. West Germany recovered rapidly in the 1950s, aided by the Marshall Plan and its own economic policies of free trade, government support for industries, large firms and cartels, the banking sector and skilled workers. Between 1965 and 1979, German productivity grew faster than the US. The West German economy depended more on exports (30 per cent of manufacturing output) compared to the US (7 per cent) and Japanese (11 per cent). West Germany was the world's leading exporting country because it spent less on consumer goods and paid its employees less than the US.

Even though the US economy was still much larger than the Japanese or the West German's, these countries had improved their position. In particular, they closed the gap in chemicals, machinery, communications equipment, cars and trucks. They competed against the US in a global market and in the US domestic market.

The US share of **world trade** also declined from 25 per cent in 1948 to 15 per cent in 1964 and 10 per cent by 1970. The US was no longer the largest trading bloc – the EEC was. The US was no longer the fastest-growing economy – Japan was. US imports amounted to 6 per cent in the early 1960s; by 1970 this had risen to 16 per cent.

Some claimed that the US was going through a process of **deindustrialisation** – as shown by the decline of such basic industries such as steel and the shift out of manufacturing to the service industry, the transfer of manufacturing facilities abroad, the loss of some foreign markets and the increased share of the domestic market taken by foreign goods.

However, the decline was only relative; the US economy continued to be far larger than the others.

CAUSES OF ECONOMIC DECLINE, 1969–89 – SUMMARY

- Johnson paid for **Vietnam War & Great Society** without rising taxes – greater deficit – borrowing – greater money supply – inflation
- **Stiff competition** from cheaper, high-quality goods especially from Japan & Germany – US slow to change policies – Japanese government subsidised certain industries – percentage of foreign cars rose from 4 per cent to 17 per cent during 1960s, 33 per cent by 1980 – greater US trade deficit
- **Oil** – after Yom Kippur War 1973 – OPEC sanctions on US – Oil price increase – inflation 5 per cent 1972 – 10 per cent at end 1973
- **Structural unemployment** – slow increase in US productivity – industrial workers' jobs filled by robots or computers or lost altogether due to foreign competition
- **Failure of government/presidential policies to solve economic problems** (Nixon, Ford, Carter, Reagan)

HOMEWORK EXERCISES

1. Study the cartoon below (which dates from 1989) and answer the following questions.

A.
- (i) What is the newspaper headline on the left referring to?
- (ii) What is the newspaper headline on the right referring to?
- (iii) What is the message of the cartoonist?
- (iv) How effective is the cartoonist at getting his message across?
- (v) Is this propaganda? Explain your answer.

B. Write a **paragraph** on the economic consequences of the Vietnam War.

C. Write a **long answer** on one of the following:
- (i) How and why the US economy declined in the 1970s and 1980s?
- (ii) How the US governments coped with the decline in the economy in the 1970s and 1980s?

HIGHER LEVEL

2. Why did the US economy decline from the mid-1960s and how successful were government policies in trying to solve the economic problems?

3. What was the impact on the US economy of one or more of the following: the multinational corporation; the military-industrial complex; international competition from Japan and Europe? (2013)

4. What were the significant developments in the US economy, 1945–89? (2014) (See also Chapter 31)

5. What were the strengths and weaknesses of the US economy, 1945–89? (2016) (See also Chapter 31)

In this section, you should understand:
• Affluence and the consumer society.
• The role of leisure.
• The role of work.
• The changing role of women and the family.
• The role of Muhammad Ali, *The Organization Man* and Betty Friedan.

Affluence and Consumerism

KEY CONCEPT
CONSUMERISM is the stage in industrial society when a great deal of goods are bought and sold. It is also called the consumer society.

Post-war US culture was characterised by a desire (demand) for **consumer goods**. This was based on the **affluence** (wealth) and **productivity** of the country. In the 1950s, US gross national product (GNP) grew from $318 billion in 1950 to $488 billion in 1966. Average household incomes were twice that of the 1920s, and a whole new middle class was created, amounting to 60 per cent of American families. In the 1940s and 1950s the average working week was reduced by 10 per cent while real wages rose. This increased wealth led to the growth of a **mass consumer culture**. But there were other factors involved as well.

The growth of **consumerism** was partly fuelled by the rapidly **rising population**. Between 1950 and 1960 the population grew by 29 million, boosted by the post-war **baby boom** which lasted into the 1960s. This increased demand for houses, schools, household appliances, cars and so on.

The increased spending was financed by **wartime savings**. But consumers were also encouraged to spend with **low-interest loans** or **instalment payments**; *'Buy Now, Pay Later'* was the slogan. **Credit cards**, first introduced in 1950, also made money more easily available. Not surprisingly, private debt more than doubled in the 1950s.

Advertising persuaded people that they needed all these products for the **Good Life**. People were presented with a whole range of new goods – electric clothes dryers, Polaroid cameras, vacuum cleaners and refrigerators.

A sign of affluence: the growth of consumerism – a middle-class American family with food for a year.

Cars on sale at a dealership in the 1960s.

Cars, Fast Food and Houses

There was a huge expansion in **car sales** because a car represented status and freedom, as well as being necessary for work and shopping. There were 2.1 million new car sales in 1946 but this increased to 8 million by 1956. By 1960, there were over 70 million cars registered in the US. By 1974, this increased to over 130 million. Only a small proportion were imported cars. The growth of the car industry led to the expansion of gas (petrol) stations, roadside motels and restaurants. It also contributed to expanding the suburbs and suburban shopping centres. The latter increased from eight in 1946 to over 4,000 by the end of the 1950s.

The growth of **fast-food outlets** also reflected the new consumer society. **McDonald's** created a food production line to increase efficiency and reduce costs. Their successful operation, begun in San Bernardino, California in 1955, was later franchised throughout the US. They were generally based in the new suburbs and along the new highways. They influenced the change in eating habits of Americans who, before this, rarely ate out because of the expense.

Cars and Household Appliances (% Ownership in Population)					
	Cars	Radios	Televisions	Fridges	Washing Machines
1940	58	81	–	71	–
1946	–	88	0.002	–	–
1950	–	95	9	91	73
1960	75	95	87	90	70
1970	79	99	98	100	73
1980	86	99	98	100	75
1990	84	99	98	100	75

There was a also a huge expansion in **house construction**, partly to compensate for the lack of it during the war. The **GI Bill of Rights** guaranteed mortgages for veterans, and the **Housing Act 1949** committed the federal government to building subsidised housing for poorer families. Fifteen million houses were built in the US between 1945 and 1955 and many of these were in suburbs. By 1960, 60 per cent of Americans owned their own homes. They were aided by mass production techniques in housing, which created vast new towns but also reduced the cost of housing. The new houses had to be fitted out with **household goods**, increasing the demand for washing machines, dishwashers and furnishings as people's lives became more comfortable.

Television

Television was part of the consumer demand, but it also caused it. By 1948, few Americans had seen television, as only 172,000 families had a set. But then a huge boom in television sales began. By 1952, there were over 15 million television sets and by 1960 over 90 per cent of houses owned at least one set. This expansion continued as colour replaced black and white, so that by 1970 almost 40 per cent of houses had colour sets.

Television dominated **home life**. Household activities stopped as families tuned into their favourite programmes. Forty-four million people saw an episode of *I Love Lucy*, a weekly comedy show in 1953. By 1960, 50 per cent of Americans listed television as their favourite leisure

Increased sales of televisions were part of the growing consumer demand, but it also caused it by advertising other products of the consumer society.

This big General Electric Spacemaker gives you almost twice as much room inside...

GENERAL ⊛ ELECTRIC

The new kitchen with the large fridge and freezer well stocked with food.

? QUESTION

What role did television play in economic and social life?

activity. It also contributed to the spread of the **consumer culture** or **consumerism** by advertising and standardising tastes. It helped create the **mass market** and thus reinforced the rising consumerism of the 1950s and 1960s. **Advertisers** saw the potential of television. They geared their ads in the 1950s to young, middle-class families. *'We are after a specific audience, the young housewife ... with two to four kids who has to buy clothing, the food, the soaps and the home remedies.'*

There was also a new **teenage market** for records, record players, jukeboxes and clothes. Teenagers earned money working part time in shops or fast-food outlets or got increased allowances from their more prosperous parents. Sales of records of the new rock 'n' roll jumped three times in six years between 1954 and 1960. But teenagers also wanted **cars**. By 1958, 6 million teenagers had licences to drive, and about 1.5 million of them owned cars.

Critics of the Consumer Society

Critics of the new mass consumer culture said it was **tacky** and **showy**. They disliked the ugly roadside hoardings, criticised the mass entertainment of the movies and Disneyland and laughed at the huge **gas-guzzling** cars with their flashy designs – *'like jukeboxes on wheels'*, they said. In his book *The Affluent Society*, J. K. Galbraith said Americans were too concerned with materialism. He said more money should be spent on improving the quality of life.

A more effective critic of **consumerism** and the **corporate capitalism** which gained from it was **Ralph Nader**. He was a graduate of Harvard Law School who began a one-man campaign against the giants of American business and industry. His book, *Unsafe at Any Speed*, highlighted defects in a General Motors car and led to improvements in

The consumer advocate, Ralph Nader, with a young girl demonstrating the automobile airbag in 1977. Nader's Raiders led many campaigns to improve laws to protect the consumer.

? QUESTION

What did critics of the consumer society say about it?

motor safety. But this one-man operator was soon joined by his **Nader's Raiders** – young lawyers and researchers – as they investigated the food industry, federal commissions, pollution and much more. Their campaigns led to many laws to protect the consumer.

Equally strong criticism came from Michael Harrington's book *Other America*, where he highlighted the **poverty** in the midst of affluence. Whatever the spending of the middle classes, he pointed out that more than 20 per cent of the US population lived below the **poverty line** (the amount of money needed to maintain a family at a minimum standard of living).

The consumer culture was rejected by the **Beat generation** of the 1950s and the **counter-culture** of the 1960s. The **Beats** (or Beatniks) rejected middle-class consumerism and followed a **bohemian** way of life. They were generally in their thirties and forties but their numbers were small – no more than a thousand or so – and their movement didn't last long. But their message was spread wider through witty poems, books and songs. In the 1960s, the **hippies** rejected consumer culture by wearing army surplus gear and second-hand clothing.

Yuppies of the 1980s

The consumer culture took a downturn as the American economy worsened in the late 1960s and 1970s. However, consumerism and the consumer culture were by then established trademarks of the American economy and an integral part of economic progress. Consumer spending revived again in the **1980s** when new wealth was created out of stock market speculation. More than 100,000 millionaires were created each year and this fuelled a new surge in consumer spending. The **yuppies** (young upwardly mobile professionals) of the 1980s spent their money on luxury goods such as imported quality cars, designer clothes, expensive hi-fi equipment or they fitted out a home gym. Their attitude was expressed in 1987 by Gordon Gekko in the film *Wall Street* when he said, '*greed is good*'.

In spite of its critics, the consumer culture provided people with a more comfortable life, especially better food and housing than had existed before. It also increased employment to provide those products. All this encouraged even greater expectations that other aspects of the American way of life could be improved.

Leisure

In the 1950s, *Business Week* magazine said, '*Never have so many people had so much time on their hands – with pay.*' This was the key to the huge expansion of the leisure industry, which had begun in the early twentieth century but expanded enormously after the Second World War.

Sport

Sport benefited enormously from the greater demand for leisure time activities. Increased wealth, the greater amount of leisure time, the use of the car and the television increased the popularity of sport. It was estimated that 35 million attended football matches, including college football, in 1953; this was followed by 15 million at major league baseball matches and over 2 million at professional basketball matches. But television also popularised sport, just as radio had done in the 1920s and 1930s. Fifty million watched the football playoff in 1958 and the success of this, and later playoffs, gave rise to the launch of the **Super Bowl** in 1966 as a marketing device to heighten interest in football. By now, of course, many sportsmen were professionals, making a good living from their chosen sport.

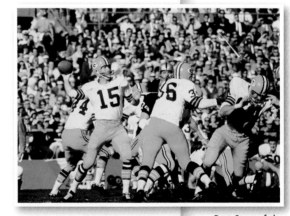

Bart Starr of the Green Bay Packers passing the ball in the 1968 Superbowl against Oakland Raiders. The Super Bowl is watched by millions of Americans.

The changing pattern of **golf** playing illustrated how sport responded to the greater demand. Before the Second World War, golf was played by the **privileged few** in private clubs. But in the 1950s, spurred on by television and the example of President Eisenhower, who loved to play golf, the sport was taken over by the **middle classes**. From the late 1950s to the 1970s there was a huge **construction boom** in golf courses. Six thousand golf courses were built in those years to cater for the new participants. In the process, too, golf had to gradually open its doors to **black people**. However, the building of new golf courses slowed down due to increased construction and land costs. But in 1988 – the centenary year of golf in America – 20 million people played over 400 million rounds of golf on over 12,000 courses.

Weekly Hours of Recreation and Work, 1975		
	Men	Women
Working on the job	33.1	16.9
Working in the house and shopping	13.5	30.1
Total recreation	33.3	31.9
Television	14.8	14.0
Sports, entertainment, travel, hobbies	14.0	13.9
Meals out, gardening, movies, bars	4.5	4.0

Changing work practices influenced the forms of leisure people enjoyed. Before the Second World War, workers experienced hard labour with longer working hours. Leisure time was relaxing, watching a game or listening to radio. After the war, **mechanisation** made tasks easier and more routine, which did not offer enough stimulation for workers; *'I felt so stifled, my brain wasn't needed anymore,'* said one. This

KEY PERSONALITY: MUHAMMAD ALI

Muhammad Ali was born **Cassius Clay** in Louisville, Kentucky in 1942. He took up **boxing** at 12, and over the next six years fought 108 fights as an amateur. In 1960, at the age of 18, he won an **Olympic gold medal** in Rome. He returned to a victory parade in Louisville.

However, Louisville was then part of the **segregated south** and so even though he was an Olympic champion, Clay was refused service at a local restaurant. Clay was openly critical of the treatment of his fellow blacks or African-Americans – some time later he threw his Olympic medal in the river as a protest.

Soon after his Olympic victory, Clay became a **professional heavyweight boxer**. His success depended on dedicated training, his **dancing** style of boxing and his constant talk. He used his speed and mobility to dance his way to victory – it was said that *'he floated like a butterfly and stung like a bee'*. He invented what was later called the **Ali Shuffle**, a rapid foot movement which confused his opponents. His constant talking both inside and outside the ring was also part of his style – he even predicted the rounds in which he would defeat opponents: *'To prove I'm great he will fall in eight.'* He became known as the **Louisville Lip** which got him great publicity, but it also turned some people against him.

In 1964, Clay defeated **Sonny Liston** to become Heavyweight Champion of the World for the first time. Also, at this time he came under the influence of **Malcolm X**, the black Muslim leader. After the Liston fight, Clay announced he was converting to the Muslim religion and becoming a member of the **Nation of Islam**. He changed his name to Cassius X, to signify the former slave status of blacks, and later to **Muhammad Ali**. When Malcolm X left the Nation of Islam, or Black Muslims as they were also called, Ali did not follow him.

Ali continued his successful career as heavyweight champion by defending his title against all-comers. In 1967, however, his career changed dramatically when he was called up for the **draft** (military service) in **Vietnam**. He refused to go on religious grounds, as a practising Muslim minister. *'I ain't got no quarrel with the Vietcong,'* he said. Ali's refusal to join the army caused huge controversy. His boxing licenses were revoked, he was stripped of his title and his passport was taken away. He was jailed, but let out on bail while he appealed against his conviction through to the Supreme Court.

Public opinion began changing against the war, and Ali made his comeback after two and a half years. In 1970, he defeated Jerry **Quarry**, the Great White Hope. However, he lost to the champion, Joe **Frazier**, as a result of his long layoff. But, soon after, the **Supreme Court** reversed his conviction and upheld his position as a conscientious objector.

Ali continued to fight. His most famous victories were the **Rumble in the Jungle** against George **Foreman**, who had beaten Frazier; this was followed by his great fight – the **Thrilla in Manila** – against Frazier. Ali then lost his title to Leon **Spinks** before winning it back a third time. He retired at 38 in 1979, probably the greatest heavyweight boxer of all time.

Ali was also involved in **politics** – he supported Jimmy Carter's presidential campaign in 1980 and worked for the release of four US hostages captured in Lebanon. Ali was diagnosed with **Parkinson's disease** in 1982.

1. How successful was Muhammad Ali as an amateur boxer?
2. How and why did he protest against segregation?
3. How successful was he as a professional boxer?
4. How did the Nation of Islam influence him?
5. Why did he protest against the Vietnam War?

? EXAM QUESTION

What did Muhammad Ali contribute to American culture?
(2011)

led to greater participation in sports. In addition to just watching the popular sports, there was also increased **participation** in more extreme sports such as skiing, skydiving, mountain biking, surfing as well as mountain and rock climbing. The new work practices also led to the growth of fitness clubs and the sale of sports equipment.

Television as Leisure

But in spite of the growth of sports and other leisure activities, **television was the main source of leisure** – *'the piece of furniture that stares back at you,'* said comedian Bob Hope. Record audiences watched *I Love Lucy* and 65 million people watched *Peter Pan* in 1955. Successful radio programmes moved over to television, such as the *$64,000 Question* (a quiz show) and *Gunsmoke* (a Western series). The first **soap operas** appeared in 1956 and they were targeted at women. Many shows portrayed middle-class families in suburban homes. To ease the burden on the working mother, inside or outside the home, companies produced **TV dinners** and 25 million were sold in 1955.

But not everybody was happy with these developments. Critics said television was *'chewing gum for the mind'*. Some blamed increased violence and changing behaviour patterns on television.

Movies, Books and Musicals

Movies went into decline in the 1950s and 1960s. The weekly audience was down to 36 million from a high of 86 million in 1946. The rise of television – entertainment at home – and the movement of people from the city centres where the cinemas were located contributed to the decline. Movies fought back with new **technological advances** – widescreen format, improved colour, the drive-in cinema and **epics** such as *Ben Hur* and *The Ten Commandments*. But they failed to stop the decline. Movies had to wait until the 1970s before they experienced rising numbers again as teenagers and those in their twenties increased its popularity.

Drive-in movies became popular in the 1950s. There were over 3,000 in the US in 1951. This one in Utah covered 22 acres.

Book publishing boomed, helped by the **paperback revolution**. Americans bought 50 per cent more books in the 1950s compared to the previous decade. Publishers put their success down to television. They said Americans stayed at home to watch their favourite programmes and when the show was over, it was *'too late to go out and too early to go to bed'*. So they read books ranging from *Peyton Place* (a mixture of adultery, drunkenness, greed and murder) to self-help guides such as *The Power of Positive Thinking*.

Musicals were also popular in the 1950s. They packed theatres to see *Guys 'n' Dolls*, *The King and I*, *West Side Story* and the most successful of all, *My Fair Lady*. All these became successful films in later decades. But the costs of production, the movement of the middle classes from the city centres and the attraction of other forms of entertainment contributed to the **decline of theatre and musicals** in the 1960s and 1970s.

The leisure industry also catered for **younger people**. The television stations had children's shows in the mornings. The Disney company used television to promote its

QUESTIONS

1. Why did the leisure industry grow in the 1950s and 1960s?
2. How did changing work practices influence leisure?
3. How important was television as a source of leisure?

first **Disneyland**, built in California in 1955. It created Fantasyland, Frontierland and Main Street USA, as well as attracting 4 million visitors in its first seven weeks. Later, **Walt Disney World** was built in Florida on the same successful pattern. There were also new fads or gimmicks aimed at the youth market and some of these, such as Frisbees and hula-hoops, were very successful. By the late 1970s and the 1980s **computer games** became a huge attraction which fuelled a new industry.

The Role of Work

Work was highly valued in American society in the 1950s and 1960s. Some said America's success was based on the **work ethic** – a code of behaviour which valued thrift, discipline, hard work and individualism. Work was important for a good life. *'Work made men useful.'*

The work ethic was part of the **American Dream** – work provided the means of improving a person's life. Americans believed that individuals were rewarded for their work according to their merits and not according to their birth, family ties or length of service.

Unemployment

For 20 years up to the end of the 1960s there was plenty of work for everybody. Unemployment remained low, and there was much part-time work available for students. It was not until the **1970s** that unemployment became a serious issue in America. As the economy declined due to the impact of the Vietnam War and the two oil crises of the 1970s, US unemployment grew to 10 per cent.

Unemployment in the US was higher among women than men, higher among blacks than whites, higher among young than adults and higher among less educated and skilled compared to more educated and higher skilled.

Decline of Manufacturing Work

But the **nature of the work** also changed. In the 1950s, manufacturing industry (blue-collar work) was an important part of US employment – in steel mills, factories and engineering works. But this began to change as the service industry (white-collar work) became more important. By the 1960s and 1970s, the service industry occupied three-quarters of the labour force. This change in the type of work opened up opportunities for women in the workforce – their numbers increased.

The **structure** of the workforce also changed:

- By 1947, 28 per cent of the US labour force was **female**. This expanded in the 1950s and 1960s until it reached over 40 per cent by 1977. They were mainly older women returning to the workforce after their children reached school age.
- Workers became **younger** with a growing population. The under-35 age group grew from 37 per cent of the workforce in 1960 to 50 per cent by 1977.
- The workforce was also better **educated**. Between 1958 and 1977 the percentage of college graduates in the workforce more than doubled. But black male participation in the workforce fell – from 85 per cent in 1954 to 71 per cent in 1977.

The Assembly Line

Work in the American manufacturing industry followed the **assembly line system** devised in the early twentieth century by Henry Ford to produce his Model T cars. This involved the production of many identical parts and their assembly into finished products. His system cut the time involved in manufacturing goods and their cost. This increased worker **productivity** (output per worker).

New York commuters pack this station in the city as they head out to the suburbs after work. Many of them were employed in the growing service industries.

It also meant the replacement of skilled workers by cheaper unskilled labour. The production was dictated by the speed of the assembly line, which caused conflict between workers and management. It also created dull, repetitive work on the assembly line, and this bored the workers. Managers reported **absenteeism** and **poor workmanship** on the assembly line.

By the 1950s the manufacturing industry was divided into unskilled workers, a large body of supervisors and production managers and an office management staff of accountants, engineers and chemists, as well as distribution and sales staff.

The Organisation of Work

A **scientific approach** to the organisation of this work developed. It was based on the ideas of Frederick **Taylor**, an American mechanical engineer. He emphasised the job of **management**.

His view was that the job of management was to decide the best way for the worker to do the job and to provide incentives for good work. Out of his ideas, **time and motion studies** developed.

These ideas led to the development of **industrial psychology**. This said that the attitudes of workers to their jobs and toward the company was just as important as the assembly line. The managers should try to improve motivation by rotating jobs and making them more challenging. This led to the new study of industrial relations to ensure that management and workers sorted out their problems.

Automation

Throughout the post-war period there was increased **mechanisation** and **automation**. Some argued that the introduction of automatic machinery would cause mass unemployment. But the alarm and panic caused by these predictions was eased as time went by and other industries grew to provide employment for displaced workers.

Automation increased efficiency and quality control. It also provided the basis for higher wages and more leisure time. The increased production changed worker–employer pay negotiations as productivity was now included to the advantage of the worker.

Example of automation.

KEY CONCEPT
TECHNOLOGICAL DEVELOPMENT is the application or use of scientific discoveries in industry.

QUESTIONS

1. How was the work ethic part of the American Dream?
2. How and why did the nature of work change?
3. What role did the assembly line play?
4. How did the role of each of the following change: (i) manager (ii) blue-collar workers (iii) migrant workers?

EXAM QUESTION

What were US attitudes to work and changes in the role of work in the post-war decades?

The role of the **manager** also changed. Originally managers were often recruited from the factory floor or supervisory staff, but now more and more managers were recruited from university graduates. This frequently involved further on-the-job training. Management promotion often meant moving to another city in the US.

Blue-collar workers often changed jobs. On average over a 25-year period of working, they changed to very different jobs five times. The most skilled and the least skilled workers were the most mobile – the skilled because they could avail of higher pay elsewhere, the least skilled because they did not have any particular attachment to their work.

Migrant work also played its part, though at a declining rate. About 600,000 were involved annually in the 1950s; this declined to about 400,000 in the 1960s. This was largely because of improvements in the economy and the demand for permanent labour. Migrant workers were mainly young, male and often from the southern states of the US. They were usually employed in agricultural work and followed the ripening of the crops from citrus fruits in Florida to vegetables further north. Their work was casual, hard and badly paid.

Criticisms of Work

In the 1950s, there were criticisms of the changing nature of work. In *The Organization Man*, William Whyte said that corporations were forcing **middle managers** to conform to the values of the company. He said that this was getting rid of individuality and experimentation. Instead, loyalty and obedience to the corporation had become more important. (See Key Personality: *The Organization Man*, p. 403)

Trade Unions

Union members grew in the US during the Second World War. The workers were organised by the **American Federation of Labor** (AFL) and by the **Congress of Industrial Organizations** (CIO), which merged in 1955. But unions faced difficulties after the war. The **Taft-Hartley Act 1947** gave greater government control of unions:

- Closed shop agreements in which employers only hired union labour were outlawed.
- Workers' right not to join a union was protected.

While the numbers joining unions increased up to the early 1960s, the percentage of workers who belonged to unions declined throughout the post-war years. Thirty-five per cent of workers were unionised in 1954, but this started to decline, reaching 27 per cent by 1970. There was a more rapid decline in the 1980s during the economic recession. By the early 1990s only 15 per cent of workers were in unions.

The overall decline in union membership was due to:

- A shift from blue-collar to white-collar work.
- Anti-union laws in the states.
- Union corruption in the late 1950s.
- Regulations on picketing tightened.
- Inter-union squabbles.
- Growth in part-time work.

QUESTIONS

1. What did the Taft-Hartley Act do?
2. What proportion of workers were trade union members by the 1990s?
3. Why did trade union membership decline?

KEY PERSONALITY: *THE ORGANIZATION MAN*

In 1956, **William H. Whyte** wrote *The Organization Man*. Whyte was a journalist with *Fortune* magazine and he was critical of many developments in US society.

Whyte was an admirer of the spirit and freedom of the **individual**. The (Protestant) work ethic valued hard work, thrift and a competitive struggle. He was concerned that it was being crushed by organisations.

Whyte was concerned about the impact of the organisation on the individual. His views highlighted the role of **corporate culture** (the values, ideas and ways of doing things) in the operation of companies and other organisations. The corporate culture brought pressures on the managers to conform for the good of the company.

Whyte's typical organisation men were **middle managers** in large organisations (especially companies). The **organisation man** did not only **work** for the organisation, he also **belonged** to it. The organisation man conformed to the **culture** of the company, mainly to get **promoted** in his career.

The organisation man believed that his own well-being was linked to the well-being of the company. Many assumed that they would work for the company all their lives. **Loyalty, reliability and obedience** were important characteristics of the organisation man. These guaranteed job security and long-term careers.

Top managers worked very long hours – 50 to 60 hours a week – and more in work-related entertaining and reading. They looked on this as part of the job and promoted those who thought like themselves.

'*We have, in sum, a man who is so completely involved in his work that he cannot distinguish between work and the rest of his life – and is happy that he cannot.*'

The organisation had layers of **bureaucracy**. Each layer had certain power and the organisation man knew his place in this set-up. He knew he had to **conform**. He could not show creativity, experimentation, enterprise or independence.

In the world of organisation man, he was the breadwinner and his wife kept house. He lived in the suburbs and took the train to work each day. '*This is the new suburbia, the packaged villages that have become the dormitory of the new generation of organisation men.*' He wore a suit to work – he was also *The Man in the Gray Flannel Suit*. His wife availed of new **household appliances** which speeded up housework. This gave time for coffee mornings with friends – the so-called *Kaffeeklatsch*.

1. Who wrote *The Organization Man*?
2. What were the main ideas of *The Organization Man*?
3. What was corporate culture?
4. What was the role of *Organization Man's* wife?

The Changing Role of Women and the Family

The Role of Women

In the 1940s and 1950s the **traditional role** of women was still popular. This was the role of woman as wife and mother. This view was reinforced by television programmes and films. However, at the same time **economic and social influences** were at work which eventually changed the traditional role.

Women at Work

In 1940, only 25 per cent of women over 14 were at work – this was the same as in 1910. They were mostly young, unmarried and poor. Many were blacks or foreign-born whites. The Second World War and the post-war era changed all that. By 1970, there were over 31 million women at work, 43 per cent of the workforce. Married women now outnumbered single women, and a large proportion were over 35. The greatest growth

More women went out to work. Many worked in the new service industries but some worked in factories such as the women seen here supervising the spinning machines at this nylon factory in South Carolina.

was among well-educated, middle-class wives. These changes were partly **caused** by the growth of the tertiary (or service) industry, labour-saving devices in the home and cultural change (**the feminist movement**).

But women were still a **depressed class** as they continued to experience **prejudice**. There was still the view that *'For the sake of every member of the family, the family needs a head. This means Father, not Mother.'* The *Atlantic Monthly* expressed the view that *'What modern woman has to recapture is the wisdom that being just a woman is her central task and greatest honor.'* They were still discriminated against in employment and wages. Relatively few were in skilled crafts or the professions. In 1973, 34 per cent had clerical jobs and 22 per cent were in service occupations. These were generally low-paid and low-prestige jobs. They were also paid much less than men doing the same job.

Weekly Hours of Housework		
	Meals and Washing-up	Laundry	Cleaning
1925–7	24	6	9
1965	15	n/a	n/a
1975	10	1	7

The Women's Movement

The civil rights movement provided the spur to the **women's movement**. In 1963, **Betty Friedan** published *The Feminine Mystique*. This attacked the idea that women could only get satisfaction and fulfilment when rearing children and minding the house. Her views sparked off a national debate. (See Key Personality, Betty Friedan, p. 405)

Friedan took a further step when she founded the **National Organization for Women (NOW)** in 1966 *'to take action to bring American women into full participation in American society'*. Its main aim was to end sexual discrimination in employment. It later developed other issues such as child care centres, legal abortion and paid maternity leave. It sponsored the **Equal Rights Amendment (ERA)**, which guaranteed sexual equality. NOW depended on legislation and the law to improve the position of women. It publicised its message with demonstrations and protests. In 1977, thousands of women took part in a 2,610-mile marathon walk from New York to Houston, Texas to publicise the first National Women's Conference.

Radical feminists were more aggressive than Friedan. They wanted to overthrow society, which they saw as male dominated. They burned bras, attacked advertising that *'demeaned women'* and insisted that men help with housework. They invaded men's bars and restaurants or picketed the Miss America Pageant. They developed feminist publishing houses, health organisations and child care centres. These were women-run organisations. Some disliked all men. They expressed this in bumper stickers – *'Don't Cook Dinner Tonight, Starve a Rat Today'.* They were a small number but they got a great deal of publicity.

> **KEY CONCEPT**
> FEMINISM is the belief that women should be treated as equal to men with the same rights and opportunities.

Success

The women's movement had considerable **success**. **The Civil Rights Act 1964** outlawed discrimination on the basis of sex. The federal and state governments passed equal opportunities laws, and presidential Executive Orders did away with the legal basis for discrimination. President Johnson signed an Executive Order requiring employers on federal contracts to take **affirmative action** to ensure more women and underprivileged minorities were hired. Skilled trades, such as carpenters and electricians, as well as professions were opened up to women; the numbers of women accountants grew more rapidly than men.

KEY PERSONALITY: BETTY FRIEDAN

Betty Friedan was born in 1921 and graduated from Smith College, Massachusetts in 1942 with a degree in **psychology**. It was at Smith that she developed a questioning of authority and a belief in social change. In 1949, she married Carl Friedan – becoming a housewife, mother of three children and an occasional freelance writer.

In 1963, Friedan published *The Feminine Mystique*, which sold 3 million copies in a year. She based her ideas on a questionnaire which she issued in 1957 to fellow graduates of Smith College at a 15-year reunion. She discovered that they were as unhappy with their lives as she was with her own. This led her to a series of studies resulting in *The Feminine Mystique*. This book inspired the women's movement.

The 1950s was the period of growing **suburbanisation** and the **baby boom**. *The Feminine Mystique* concentrated on the white **middle-class wife** who lived in the suburbs. The main idea of the book was that women were victims of a set of values and culture (the feminine mystique) which said they would find their fulfilment through their husbands and children. Friedan said women were in a trap and to escape they must finally exercise *'their human freedom and recapture their sense of self'*.

Friedan said women were not being given a chance to develop their talents. Women were expected to stay in the kitchen and nursery, get involved in voluntary community work, look pretty and get frustrated. She called it **The Problem That Has No Name** *'which is simply the fact that American women are kept from growing to their full human capacities'*. Friedan said that the media (press, TV, radio and cinema) manipulated women in order to keep them at home to sell them their vacuum cleaners and dishwashers.

'The feminine mystique has succeeded in burying millions of American women alive.' She felt women were not complete in themselves. *'The problem lay buried, unspoken, for many years in the minds of American women... Each suburban wife struggled with it alone. As she made her beds, shopped for groceries, matched slipcover material, ate peanut butter sandwiches with her children, chauffeured Cub Scouts and Brownies, lay beside her husband at night – she was afraid to ask even of herself the silent – "Is this all?"'*

She claimed that suburban women were **frustrated and unhappy**, comparing them to the prisoners of a Nazi concentration camp – they had become *'Dependent, passive and childlike'*. She criticised the second-class status of women. She emphasised that women could find happiness in careers outside the family.

More recent **critics** have questioned her account of her own life in *The Feminine Mystique*, claiming it is unreliable and misleading. Some claimed she was bad-tempered, selfish and arrogant. Her 21-year marriage was troublesome; *'Although her marriage was violent, ... she and Carl were a match; she egged him on, and she gave as good as she got...'* Their marriage ended in divorce in 1969.

Some have also raised doubts about her **sources** and the questionable research methods of the sources she used. They said the experts she quoted were unreliable. However, Friedan and her book helped to change not only the thinking but also the lives of many American women. Her book coincided with other developments which were making women reconsider their role in society.

In 1966, Friedan co-founded the **National Organization of Women** (NOW), which campaigned to achieve equality of opportunity for women. She was also a founding member of the **National Women's Political Caucus** in 1971, which fought to ratify the **Equal Rights Amendment**, but lost. Ten years later, she wrote *The Second Stage*, which assessed the current state of the women's movement. She said that feminists must reclaim the family and deal with child care, maternity leave and flexible work arrangements. She disagreed with the extreme feminists – *'the disrupters of the women's movement'*, she called them – who were advocating *'lesbianism and the hatred of men'*.

1. How did university influence Betty Friedan?
2. What were the main ideas of her book, The Feminine Mystique?
3. What was 'The Problem That Has No Name'?
4. What role did Friedan play in the women's movement?

EXAM QUESTION (?)

What criticisms did Betty Friedan make of US society?

Femisist protest.

Greater participation in education was the key to success. **Yale and Princeton**, two of America's most prestigious universities, opened their doors to women. In 1950, from 5 per cent to 8 per cent of students in medical, law and business schools were women – by the mid-1980s this had grown to 40 per cent.

Legalised **abortion** was a very controversial issue. Seventeen states made abortion easier. As a result, in 1970 there were 200,000 legal abortions, which was 10 times greater than in 1968. In 1973, the Supreme Court, in the *Roe v. Wade* decision, upheld a woman's right to abortion in the early stages of pregnancy.

Women also became more successful in **politics**. There were women mayors elected in Chicago, San Francisco and San Jose (California). The first woman governor was elected in Connecticut.

The Limits of Success

But women still held few of the **top jobs**. In 1970, only 5 per cent of the country's 3 million managers and executives were women. The **ERA** passed Congress but there was stiff opposition in the states and it failed to get ratified before its deadline.

Poorer Women

The benefits of the women's movement were confined mainly to middle- and upper-class women. Hardly any of the benefits trickled down to poorer women. **Race**, **class** and **gender** operated against them. Poor, black or Hispanic women still suffered. A third of black families were headed by women who apart from being single were also jobless. Women without skills or training were usually stuck in dead-end, low-paying jobs; but so were men in a similar situation. Between 1955 and 1981, women's earnings fell from 64 per cent to 59 per cent of men's, and even by the late 1980s only climbed back to 62 per cent. 80 per cent of all women workers were employed in the lowest-paying jobs and women comprised 70 per cent of the adult poor.

Traditionalists

Some women were still **traditionalists**. They believed that women's place was in the home as wife and mother. They attacked the women's liberation movement. They were part of the rising new political force in the 1970s and 1980s – the conservative New Right which developed in response to the social problems of the time. **Phyllis Schlafly** headed this movement, whose main aim was to *'Stop the ERA'* – and they did.

The Family

Marriage rates grew and remained high after the war. Many married young in the 1950s – the average age for men was 22 and 20 for women. Public opinion polls showed that young people expected to marry and raise children. Divorce rates dropped sharply after

? QUESTIONS

1. What was the traditional role of women?
2. How did the proportion of women in the workforce change?
3. What was the women's movement?
4. What were the limits to their success?
5. How were poorer women affected? Who were the traditionalists?

? EXAM QUESTION

What were the successes and failures of the women's movement in the US between the 1950s and the 1980s?

1947. Despite more liberal divorce laws in the 1950s, the divorce rates remained lower in the 1950s and early 1960s than since 1942. Illegitimacy rates also remained stable.

The **change in family life** came in the 1960s. Family life changed as the role of mother and father changed. With more women at work outside the home, fathers had to take a greater share of family and housekeeping duties. Increased social pressures led to the break-up of families. Families also became more isolated due to **mobility** – from city centre to suburbs, or from state to state. Connections to the extended family of grandparents and uncles and aunts were weakened or broken.

Divorce and Illegitimacy

In these circumstances, **divorce** and **illegitimacy rates** rose sharply. The divorce rate rose from 9.2 per 1,000 married couples in 1960 to 11.2 per 1,000 married couples in 1968. This was partly caused by more women at work who now had the resources to break away from unhappy marriages. The instability of marriage and the sexual revolution contributed to the rise of **trial** marriages or partnerships.

Illegitimacy rates also rose quickly after 1963. In 1963, 23 per cent of births among blacks were illegitimate and 2 per cent among whites. This rose to 30 per cent among blacks and 3 per cent among whites by 1970. By 1990, almost 30 per cent of all births were illegitimate. The sexual liberation of the 1960s and the increased use of drugs and alcohol were blamed for the change.

By the 1970s and 1980s there were concerns that the break-up of family life would cause **further social problems** in the years ahead. In 1965, the **Moynihan Report** argued that the biggest single cause of poverty in the US was the instability of black marriages, as black husbands abandoned their families. He argued that government policy should help to establish a *'stable family structure'*.

QUESTION

How did the nature of the family change in the 1960s?

Rise of Illegitimate Births		
	Totals	% of All Births
1940	89,500	3.5
1950	141,600	3.9
1960	224,300	5.3
1970	398,700	10.7
1980	665,800	18.4
1990	1,165,400	28.0

HOMEWORK EXERCISES

ORDINARY LEVEL

1. Study this edited extract from *The 1960s: A Decade of Change for Women* and answer the questions that follow.

   In the 1960s, deep cultural changes were altering the role of women in American society. More females than ever were entering the paid workforce, and this increased the dissatisfaction among women regarding huge gender disparities in pay and advancement and sexual harassment at the workplace. One of the most profound changes was happening in the bedroom. By the end of the Sixties, more than 80 percent of wives of childbearing age were using contraception after the federal government in 1960 approved a birth control pill. This freed many women from unwanted pregnancy and gave them many more choices, and freedom, in their personal lives.

   Gradually, Americans came to accept some of the basic goals of the Sixties feminists: equal pay for equal work, an end to domestic violence, curtailment of severe limits on women in managerial jobs, an end to sexual harassment, and sharing of responsibility for housework and child rearing.

   One in 5 women with children under 6 and nearly one fourth of women whose children were over 16 held paid jobs in the Sixties. Their pay, however, was 60 percent of the male rate. Though equal pay legislation passed in 1963, that did not solve the problem of low pay in jobs that were classed as female.

   Over time, the feminist trends of the Sixties took hold and over the subsequent decades changed relationships between the genders. 'Most young women, at least in the middle class, expected to have access to the same careers and to receive the same compensation as men,' wrote historians Maurice Isserman and Michael Kazin in *America Divided: The Civil War of the 1960s*. 'It was no longer surprising to see women leaders in formerly 'men's' fields like television production (Oprah Winfrey), diplomacy (Secretary of State Madeleine Albright), or the Supreme Court (Justices Sandra Day O'Connor and Ruth Bader

   Ginsburg). Even conservative Republicans recruited female candidates and urged them to be as aggressive on the stump as men.'

   Source: US News, https://www.usnews.com/news/articles/2010/03/12/the-1960s-a-decade-of-change-for-women

   A. (i) Give an example of the 'deep cultural changes' that altered the role of women in society.
      (ii) What were the basic goals of 'the Sixties feminists'?
      (iii) How did the female pay rate compare with the male pay rate?
      (iv) How were relationships changed between the genders?
      (v) In what other ways was America divided in the 1960s?

   B. Write a **paragraph** on one of the following.
      (i) The consumer society in the US
      (ii) The role of television in leisure
      (iii) The *Organization Man*

   C. Write a **long answer** on one of the following.
      (i) How and why was there a huge expansion of leisure in the US after the Second World War?
      (ii) How did the role of women in the US change between the 1950s and the 1980s?

HIGHER LEVEL

2. How and why was there a huge expansion of leisure in the US after the Second World War?

3. To what extent were Betty Friedan and Marilyn Monroe typical of women in the US between 1945 and the 1980s? (See p. 415 for Marilyn Monroe)

4. What was the American Dream and to what extent was it reflected in life in the US, 1945–89? (See also p. 413; also Chapter 35)

5. In what ways did the life and work of Betty Friedan reflect the changing role of women and family in modern America? (2013)

6. What criticisms did Betty Friedan or Norman Mailer make about life in the US? (2015)

In this section, you should understand:
- Why these years were regarded as the age of consensus.
- The Red Scare.
- The role of Hollywood and the American Dream.
- The role of Marilyn Monroe.

The Age of Consensus

The period from the early 1950s to the mid-1960s is often regarded as an **age of consensus** in American history. The majority of Americans seemed to agree on many of the same things.

The affluence of the 1950s created a growing **optimism** in America about the ending of class, religion and racial divisions. Some talked about a **post-industrial society** which provided a consensus about American society and how it would develop:

- There was a feeling that ethnic divisions were declining – the **melting pot** was working and people were becoming part of the American way of life.
- There was a rise of **patriotism** in the prevailing Cold War conditions.
- Organised **religion** grew stronger.
- There was agreement to **oppose Communism**.
- Many believed there were opportunities to be had for everybody. This was the **American Dream** that hard work was the key to success; that people could improve in society and their children would do better than themselves. America was the land of opportunity. It rested on the idea that Americans could move up in society.

Overall, Americans were **confident** of their place in the world. This confidence was based on American prosperity – the affluent society. The people generally had very little fear of or concern for the future – only their health and the danger of war and the Soviet threat. Americans were **optimistic** – their athletes expected victory; their economists expected economic growth; doctors expected to cure diseases and social problems too could be solved. They expected to be the best in the world.

Economic System

The new economic prosperity was supported by the **New Economics**. *'American capitalism works, and in the years since the Second World War, quite brilliantly,'* said the respected economist John Kenneth Galbraith. Based on the ideas of the English economist, **J M Keynes**, it was felt that **US governments** could manage the economy and end economic depressions. They would keep down unemployment and inflation and create economic growth and prosperity.

The American **free enterprise** (capitalist) system created **abundance**, which would lessen social injustice. They believed the economy would continue to grow and this would satisfy people's needs. They believed it was creating greater equality in society; indeed, everybody was becoming better off. The prosperity of the 1950s was so widespread that some claimed that everybody was now middle class.

No Left Wing

There was **no left wing** (socialism) in politics. No party wanted great social and economic change and supported the interests of the disadvantaged (the poor) against the rich or more powerful groups in society.

There was also consensus in **foreign policy**. Americans believed that foreign affairs were more important than domestic matters. They also believed that the **policy of containment** should be followed everywhere – not only in Europe, but also in South-East Asia. This meant America should intervene wherever necessary to defend the **Free World** against the spread of Communism. Americans now supported **internationalism** over isolationism.

Looking Back

Looking back from the 1960s, people remembered the calmness of the 1950s. In fact, it took the 1960s to show that much of the calmness of class, race and religion of America in the 1950s was **superficial**. The cracks began to appear openly in the troubled 1960s. Apart from that, not everybody in the 1950s shared the view of harmony and consensus. They pointed to problems with suburban growth and the consumer society. They also pointed to the unspoken poverty, but for most people all this was covered over.

? QUESTIONS

1. Why were the years from the early 1950s to the mid-1960s known as the age of consensus (agreement)?
2. Why were people happy with the New Economics?
3. Why did some people say everybody was now middle class?
4. What was the consensus in foreign policy?

The Red Scare

There was a steady build-up of **anti-Communism** in the US after the Second World War. It traced its origins to the **Communist Revolution** in Russia in 1917. The victory of the Communists there created fear in the West and in the US that Communists would take over property and establish a **totalitarian system** of government. Some called it the **Red Menace**.

Even though the US and the Soviet Union worked together during the Second World War, the alliances created to fight Hitler and Japan quickly broke down as the Cold War spread. A series of incidents and events in the late 1940s and early 1950s increased anti-Communist feeling in the US. These gave rise to the belief that the US was **infiltrated** by Communist sympathisers and spies:

A member of the House Un-American Activities Committee (HUAC) reading a newspaper in 1953 which claimed that the actress Lucille Ball was registered as a Communist in the 1930s.

- Six hundred **US government documents** were found in a raid on the office of a Communist magazine in America.
- Canada announced it had caught a **network of spies** working for the Soviet Union.
- Truman played up the **fear of Communism** to get congressional support for the Truman Doctrine, the Marshall Plan and to set up the National Security Council to advise on security matters. By exaggerating the Communist threat abroad, Truman heightened fears about Communists in America.
- Truman also passed **Executive Order (EO) 9853** to get federal Loyalty Boards to remove employees if *'reasonable grounds existed for the belief that the person involved is disloyal to the government of the US'*. States passed their own anti-Communist laws and employees had to take loyalty oaths or lose their jobs.

- The development of the **first Soviet atomic bomb** in 1949, the takeover of **China** by Communists and the beginning of the **Korean War** in 1950 all heightened tension in relation to Communism.
- The main **newspapers** – the *New York Times* and the *Washington Post* – and **magazines** – *Time* and *Newsweek* – were strongly anti-Communist. Their message was that America was losing the Cold War.
- The **Catholic Church** in America was strongly anti-Communist. So also were the **Protestant Evangelical preachers** such as **Billy Graham**. He preached that, *'The world is divided into two camps! On the one side we see Communism has declared war against God, against Christ, against the Bible, and against all religion...'*
- The **Internal Security (McCarron) Act 1950** was passed – all Communist organisations had to register and no Communist could be employed in defence projects.

KEY CONCEPT
PUBLIC OPINION
The views and attitudes of the people. This is measured in elections or in between elections in opinion polls. In a democracy, political parties have to get elected so they have to pay attention to public opinion.

QUESTIONS ?

1. What was (i) the Red Menace and (ii) the Red Scare?
2. List some events that gave Americans the idea that their country was infiltrated by Communists. Who encouraged the spread of anti-Communism?

HUAC (House Un-American Activities Committee)

As part of the growing fear of Communism, the HUAC began hearings in 1947 to investigate subversive activities in the US. Witnesses were asked, *'Are you now or have you ever been a member of the Communist Party?'* Witnesses were also expected to *'name names'*, that is, give names of other alleged Communists. Witnesses could not plead the **Fifth Amendment**, which says nobody has to implicate (connect) himself or herself to a crime. The Committee took the view that this was an admission of guilt. Gradually the constitutional rights of Americans were being whittled away.

The House Un-American Activities Committee in action in Washington investigating Communist activities in the film (movie) industry.

HUAC and Hollywood

In 1947, and again from 1951–54, HUAC concentrated on **Hollywood**. HUAC claimed Hollywood was infiltrated by Communists. They disliked the influence movies had over **public opinion**. Actors and actresses who failed to co-operate were blacklisted and some were jailed.

In 1947, the **Hollywood Ten** refused to discuss their political views with HUAC. They were jailed for terms of four to 10 months for contempt of Congress. They were supported by prominent Hollywood actors and actresses who formed the **Committee for the First Amendment** (which guaranteed free speech in the US Constitution). But very soon a public backlash saw support for the Ten disappearing. Some towns boycotted films in which supporters of the Ten appeared. On one occasion, stones were thrown at the screen when Katherine Hepburn, one

Prominent film stars Lauren Bacall and Humphrey Bogart head for the Capitol Building in Washington to protest at the hearings by HUAC into the film industry.

of the Committee for the First Amendment, appeared. Under this pressure, Hollywood producers and directors withdrew support from the Ten, who were often blacklisted during the 1950s.

Between 1951 and 1954, 90 actors, actresses, producers and directors were questioned by HUAC. The Committee cited over 300 people in Hollywood as Communists, and these were blacklisted by the studios. They looked with suspicion on anybody with **liberal views**.

Even the actors' union, the **Screen Actors' Guild**, headed by **Ronald Reagan**, later US President, co-operated in *'naming names'* and blacklisting alleged Communists.

? **QUESTIONS**

1. What was HUAC?
2. Why did HUAC question actors and actresses?

Alger Hiss, accused of Communist spying, takes an oath during hearings of the House Un-American Activities Committee (HUAC) in Washington in 1948.

The Rosenbergs, Ethel and Julius, separated by a wire screen as they are transported to prison after their conviction for spying in 1953. They were later executed.

The Hiss Case

One of the HUAC members was **Richard Nixon**, later President of the US. Nixon rose to fame over the **Alger Hiss** case. Hiss was a graduate of two of America's most famous universities and he served in the State Department, where he had been one of President Roosevelt's closest advisers. He was brought before the HUAC in 1948, where he denied he had been a Communist. But constant cross-questioning by Nixon, who was supplied with information by the FBI, broke Hiss down. Hiss was later charged with perjury and found guilty, and Nixon became a national hero.

The Hiss case encouraged people to believe that Communists could be found in high places. This was reinforced when **Julius and Ethel Rosenberg** were arrested for spying. They were part of a spy ring which passed **atomic secrets** to the Soviet Union. The Rosenbergs were tried, found guilty and executed by electric chair in 1953.

Effects of the Red Scare

Education too was affected by the Red Scare. Some feared that schools and universities would be used for Communist propaganda. They warned about the *'little Red schoolhouse'* and wrote articles saying that *'your child is their target'*. In high schools, **600 teachers** lost their jobs because they were accused of being Communists; blacklists ensured they did not get jobs elsewhere. HUAC demanded reading lists from universities and colleges, and some university lecturers who were alleged to be Communists were fired.

The Red Scare affected **other aspects** of American life in the 1950s and 1960s. **Movies** and **books** reflected the main thinking. Some wartime films had praised Soviet resistance to the German invaders. Now in the Cold War, Hollywood wanted to confirm its loyalty. Communists were portrayed in 50 films and many documentaries as traitors and spies. *The Iron Curtain, I Was a Communist for the FBI* and *My Son John* were examples of films where the Communists or **Reds** were uncovered and defeated. Books reinforced this thinking.

KEY CONCEPT
LIBERALISM was the political belief that was concerned with personal freedom and social progress. Liberals favoured gradual reform of political and economic matters. US liberals favoured government intervention in the economy.

Civil liberties suffered, particularly **free speech**. Federal workers faced severe loyalty tests. They could be brought before Boards to answer for their views, and dismissed if *'reasonable doubt'* existed about their suitability. The **FBI**, headed by **J. Edgar Hoover**, was virulently anti-Communist. The organisation kept records on suspected Communists, used surveillance and tapped phones. They leaked information about the activities of *'subversives'* to the press, which heightened tensions.

All these actions generated an **atmosphere of fear**. Librarians took books off their shelves in case they would come under suspicion themselves. People were afraid that innocent comments would be reported to the FBI. **McCarthyism** was the high point of the Red Scare. The overall feeling of fear helped McCarthy to maintain his position for so long and, in the end, he was largely responsible for his own downfall. (See '1. McCarthyism (and the Red Scare)' in Chapter 29, pp. 363–65.)

These demonstrators made clear their views during the trial of the Rosenbergs.

Hollywood – The American Dream

The American film industry was dominated by Hollywood. The studio system which grew up in the 1920s and 1930s controlled both the production (making) and the distribution (showing) of films. Movies enjoyed huge audiences up to and including the Second World War.

However, after the war, the studios declined. But Hollywood still held its attractions. For many there was still the desire to go to Hollywood to become a **star**. For most people it was an illusion because very few reached stardom. However, Hollywood continued to have great appeal, and stories of actors and actresses, such as **Marilyn Monroe**, who made it to the top inspired others.

The **success story** was also the theme of many Hollywood films, which needed a **good ending** to satisfy popular taste. Hollywood made everybody's dream come true – some called it the Dream Factory.

Decline and Change

But Hollywood went through huge changes in the 1950s and 1960s. This was brought on by:

- Declining ticket sales due to television.
- Government anti-trust laws.
- Suburban living and new forms of leisure.

Declining sales led to a cutback in production: box office receipts declined from over $1.6 billion in 1946 to $1.3 billion in 1956 – a drop of nearly 20 per cent. The revenue (income) of the 10 leading companies fell by a quarter, while profits fell by three-quarters.

The number of people employed in Hollywood – the majority were craftsmen – fell from over 22,000 in 1946 to 13,000 in 1956. Actors, writers, directors and producers were taken off long-term contracts.

Hollywood was also affected by the **anti-trust lawsuit** against the studios by the US government. In 1948, the **Supreme Court** ruled that the studios could not control both

QUESTIONS

1. What was the Hiss case?
1. How were (i) education (ii) movies and books (iii) civil rights affected by the Red Scare?

production and distribution. This forced the studios to sell off their cinemas and to stop the practice of block booking and price fixing. This created a boom in **independent productions**. The major studios provided the money and studio space for independent directors and handled their films afterwards.

Attack on Hollywood

The **HUAC** (House Un-American Activities Committee) hearings also affected Hollywood. The hearings, which were hunting for Communists in Hollywood, led to the blacklisting of actors, actresses and others. The HUAC hearings, along with McCarthyism and the general Red Scare, eliminated **liberalism** in Hollywood. They also affected the **content** of movies. Prior to this, some films showed an interest in social problems, and some of them were box-office successes. But after the hearings, film producers were rarely involved in social comment. Instead, Hollywood emphasised **pure entertainment**. They also produced some anti-Communist films – about 50 were made in the late 1940s and early 1950s – but they were not successful. (See Chapter 37, 'The Mass Media in Modern American Culture', pp. 453–56.)

The Star System and New Technology

Publicity poster for *On The Waterfront*, a film starring 1950s star Marlon Brando.

While there were **fewer movies** in the 1950s, the quality was still maintained. *From Here to Eternity, On the Waterfront, Bridge over the River Kwai* and *A Streetcar Named Desire* all became classics. There were also some outstanding Westerns, such as *High Noon, The Searchers* and *Shane*.

Hollywood developed the **star system** in the 1920s and 1930s to sell their movies. The lives and actions of movie stars were given great publicity. In the 1950s, male stars such as Cary Grant, Robert Mitchum, James Stewart, Gary Cooper and Marlon Brando were matched by the female stars such as Marilyn Monroe, Grace Kelly, Debbie Reynolds, Lana Turner and Doris Day. (See Key Personality: Marilyn Monroe, p. 415)

Hollywood also tried to innovate. They tried to give the audiences *'something television can't'*. The first of these was improved **colour** (colour was already used in the 1930s) – next came **Cinerama** and **3-D**. But these had short-term success, and could not compare with the success of **CinemaScope**. The huge costs of production and the new technology which could not be afforded by smaller companies ensured that Hollywood was still dominated by **about 10 major companies**.

Foreign Markets

But Hollywood also looked for other markets. It increased its sales **abroad**, particularly as most of the European film industry had collapsed during the Second World War. Hollywood was encouraged by the US government, which saw American films as important **propaganda** weapons during the Cold War – *'ambassadors of goodwill'*, in Truman's words.

Very soon the major companies began to **invest abroad** in genuine locations and to take advantage of lower labour costs and tax benefits. In 1949, Hollywood made 19 films abroad; in 1969 it made 183. Not surprisingly, Hollywood films dominated much of the Western European market. By the 1960s, half of Hollywood's revenue came from abroad. This compensated for declining revenues at home.

KEY PERSONALITY: MARILYN MONROE

Marilyn Monroe, Hollywood sex symbol of the 1950s, was born **Norma Jean Mortenson** in 1926 to a single mother. Her mother's single status and mental illness meant that Marilyn spent many of her early years in **orphanages and foster homes**. *'The whole world around me at the time was kind of grim. I had to learn to pretend in order to ... block the grimness,'* she said. One of her foster parents encouraged her, *'Don't worry Norma Jean. You're going to be a beautiful girl when you grow big ... an important woman, a movie star.'* Monroe herself said Jean Harlow, star of the 1920s, was her idol.

Monroe experienced a **failed teenage marriage**. But she was spotted by a photographer while working in a factory during the Second World War. He advised her to join a **modelling** agency. By 1947, she had appeared on the cover of 33 national magazines. She was spotted by 20th century Fox, one of the big studios, and **changed her name** to Marilyn Monroe. However, for the next few years she only got **small parts** in movies. It was at this time that she also posed nude for a calendar.

Gradually, however, her career took off in the early 1950s. She starred in a series of hits such as *Niagara*, *The Seven Year Itch*, *Gentlemen Prefer Blondes*, *Bus Stop* and *Some Like It Hot*. *The Seven Year Itch* had the famous skirt-blowing scene. She was partly helped by the controversy surrounding her earlier nude appearance in a calendar. Hollywood exploited this to achieve **sex-symbol** status for her.

Monroe, however, had an **unhappy life**. Her second marriage to **Joe DiMaggio**, a former baseball star, was a failure which only lasted a year. *'I didn't want to give up my career, and that's what Joe wanted me to do most of all.'* A third marriage to playwright **Arthur Miller** was also a failure and ended in divorce. She also had affairs with other movie stars, such as **Robert Mitchum** and **Frank Sinatra**. There were also reports of affairs with **President John F Kennedy** and his brother, **Robert**.

Marilyn Monroe suffered two miscarriages while married to Miller. She was also taking **tranquilisers**. She was sometimes difficult to work with and had a record of being late for work.

On 4 August 1962, she died from an **overdose** of sleeping pills. Controversy still surrounds her death. Even without any evidence, many believe that the US government was involved to cover up affairs with Robert and JFK. Her fame continued long after her death. Indeed, her death contributed to that fame. In 1999, she was named the Number One Sex Star of the Twentieth century. Elton John composed *'Candle in the Wind'* as a tribute to her.

She once said, *'I knew I belonged to the public and to the world, not because I was talented or even beautiful, but because I had never belonged to anything or anyone else.'*

1. What kind of an upbringing did Marilyn Monroe have?
2. How successful was she as an actress?
3. What made her life unhappy?

Some Benefits from Television

Even though Hollywood suffered from declining audiences due to television, television provided **benefits** in other ways. Small independent production companies made low-budget programmes for television, usually half an hour in length. The series *I Love Lucy* was the most successful example of this.

Hollywood soon realised it had to **co-operate** with the new medium, television. The major companies began to show regular filmed programmes. By the end of the 1950s most of the prime-time shows came from Hollywood. This replaced live broadcasting on TV.

415

Hollywood also supplied old **feature films** and **shorts** for television. Older films became features of **movie nights** on the main television channels. Very soon networks competed with each other for film rights. In 1966, ABC paid $2 million for *Bridge on the River Kwai*. When it was shown on ABC in September 1966, it created history by having an audience of 60 million.

By the 1960s, television had become an important **market** for movies. Indeed, film projects were now assessed partly on their potential for television. Television distribution usually took place about 18 months after films were shown in the cinemas.

There was also the **made-for-television movie**, which relied on low-budget production costs. In this way advertising covered the costs of production. By the late 1960s, there was a glut of films being shown on television so that film companies and television networks suffered losses. This resulted in companies cutting back operations. Ten years later, Hollywood was making half the number of films it made in the 1960s.

By the 1970s and 1980s, huge prices were being paid by the networks for the television rights to show films such as *Alien* ($15 million). By the end of the 1970s, pay TV, cable, satellite and video provided outlets for Hollywood productions. As well as this, new **marketing techniques** tried to exploit other areas of leisure. Books and soundtracks as well as the merchandising of toys, games and clothing all created new income for Hollywood.

? QUESTIONS

1. What changes did Hollywood introduce?
2. How did television provide benefits to Hollywood and the film industry?

HOMEWORK EXERCISES

ORDINARY LEVEL

1. Study this cover from a *Captain America* comic book (1954) and answer the questions that follow.

A. (i) Who is Captain America going to 'defy'?
   (ii) How are the Communists portrayed on the cover?
   (iii) Is the cover propaganda? Explain your answer.

B. Write a **paragraph** on one of the following.
   (i) The age of consensus
   (ii) The origins and effects of the Red Scare

C. Write a **long answer** on Marilyn Monroe and the Hollywood film industry.

HIGHER LEVEL

2. How and why did the Red Scare develop in the US in the late 1940s and the 1950s?

3. To what extent was the period from the early 1950s to the mid-1960s an age of consensus in American history?

4. How successful was the Hollywood film industry in adapting to changing circumstances from the 1940s to the 1980s?

5. What did one or more of the following contribute to American culture: Marilyn Monroe; Muhammad Ali; Billy Graham? (2011)

In this section, you should understand:
• How and why desegregation occurred.
• The role of Martin Luther King.
• Case Study: The Montgomery Bus Boycott, 1955–56.
• The causes and effects of urban poverty (the war on poverty).
• The spread of drugs and crime.

Racial Conflict

Background

The **American Constitution** (1791) said that *'all Men were created equal, that they are endowed by their Creator with inalienable rights'*. But the Constitution allowed **slavery**, which was not abolished until the American Civil War in the 1860s. Even after the abolition of slavery, black America did not have civil, political and social equality. An important episode in American history is the struggle of black Americans to achieve these rights.

Jim Crow Laws

Once the Civil War was over, whites in the **southern states** used their power to make the blacks second-class citizens. They did this by passing **Jim Crow** laws, which introduced the **segregation** of blacks and whites. The laws stated that blacks and whites had to use **separate** public facilities such as toilets, benches and schools. They were supported by a Supreme Court ruling in the 1890s that upheld separate but equal treatment.

Blacks were also banned from voting. In addition, they suffered from violence and intimidation, particularly by the **Ku Klux Klan**, a **white supremacist** group, and some were even **lynched**.

The Second World War was a **major turning point** for blacks. Thousands of blacks served in the armed forces and worked in the war industries in defence of democracy and freedom. But after the war they were still second-class citizens in their own country. However, **conditions had now changed**, and over the next 40 years black Americans (and other ethnic minorities) gradually, and often painfully, won civil and political equality.

The Conditions of Change

● By 1945, many black Americans had **migrated** from the South (where they worked on subsistence farming) to northern cities. This continued into the 1950s and

A segregated drinking fountain in use in the American South.

KEY CONCEPT
DISCRIMINATION means treating a group of people differently because of their colour, religion, sex, age etc.

White tenants trying to prevent black Americans from moving into a government housing project in Detroit.

417

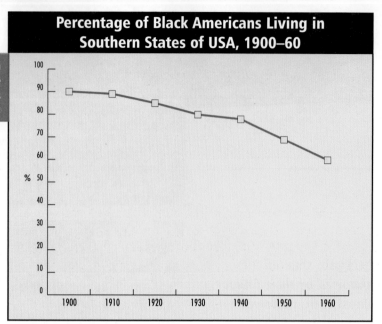

Percentage of Black Americans Living in Southern States of USA, 1900–60

What are the main conclusions to be drawn from this graph?

1960s, so many benefited from the greater prosperity (affluence) of the times. Others migrated to southern cities. Because blacks were **concentrated in cities**, they were easier to organise.

- Black **education** had expanded in the North and South with more schools, colleges and universities. This progress continued over the next 40 years. A new, **educated black leadership** emerged.

- Blacks also depended a great deal on their **Christian churches** and on **Christian leadership**. Some of their most important leaders were clergymen and these gave them unity and a belief to carry on.

- When black Americans returned from the **Second World War**, they had **higher expectations** for greater civil and political rights and they were not prepared to accept less.

- There was a decline in colour prejudice as **whites** believed less and less that blacks should be denied equal opportunity simply because they were black. This was part of **liberalism** or liberal ideas. This was helped by leaders such as President Roosevelt and his wife, Eleanor, during the war.

- The development of the **Cold War** from the late 1940s onwards had a significant influence on the progress of black rights. The US portrayed itself as the leader of the **Free World** against evil Communism. This position was difficult to maintain when the **Old South** continued segregation and legal discrimination against blacks. If the US wanted to maintain respect in Europe and the new countries of Africa and Asia, it would have to reform itself.

- The influence of the **mass media**, especially television, which became widespread in the 1950s, was very important. All Americans became aware of the issues affecting black Americans. Very often television highlighted the brutal and oppressive treatment of blacks in various incidents in the South.

- Blacks themselves were **better organised**. The **NAACP** (National Association for the Advancement of Colored People), founded in 1909, fought a series of successful Supreme Court challenges to laws in the South. The NAACP was later joined by other organisations such as **CORE** (Congress of Racial Equality) who worked in different ways for racial desegregation.

? QUESTIONS

1. What were (i) the Jim Crow laws (ii) segregation (iii) the Ku Klux Klan?
2. What were the conditions of change in post-war USA which helped black Americans win civil and political equality?

Conditions of Change		
Migration to the cities	World War II expectations	Better educated black leadership/ Christian churches
Influence of mass media	Better organisation – NAACP, CORE	White liberalism

The Process of Desegregation

The army

One of the first areas to be desegregated was the **armed forces** – army, navy and air force. President Truman issued an **Executive Order** in 1948 ending segregation in the armed forces. This process was speeded up by the **Korean War** when it was easier to organise mixed units of blacks and whites. By 1954, the armed forces were desegregated, though the officer class was largely white.

Education

A much more difficult and controversial area was education. The battle here was carried on by the NAACP, who took test cases all the way to the **Supreme Court.** In 1953 a new Chief Justice, **Earl Warren**, was appointed by President Eisenhower. Over the next 16 years his Court provided a succession of judgments which opened up not only education, but many other areas of life.

One of the most important decisions was ***Brown v. The Board of Education, Topeka, Kansas*** in 1954. Here the Court said, *'We conclude that in the field of public education the doctrine of separate but equal has no place. Separate education facilities are inherently unequal.'* It declared state laws which required public school segregation **unconstitutional**. In a follow-up judgment, it said that public schools should be integrated *'with all deliberate speed'*.

In spite of the Supreme Court ruling, there was huge **resistance** to **integration** (mixing people of different colours) in the South, where **17 states** had segregated education. White **Citizens Councils** and **governors** all over the South resisted and they were sometimes backed up by a revived **Ku Klux Klan**. This resistance led to conflict, as in **Little Rock, Arkansas** in 1957, where angry whites tried to prevent desegregation.

Central High, Little Rock: In Arkansas the state's Board of Education planned a process of desegregation for September 1957. But when **nine black students** attempted to enter the **Central High School** in Little Rock, National Guardsmen stopped them. But the governor was forced to withdraw the National Guards and the students entered the school under police protection. Very soon an angry mob attacked the school. Newspaper coverage highlighted the incidents and forced **President Eisenhower** to send 1,000 federal troops. These had to stay on guard for a few months until tempers cooled.

Ku Klux Klan.

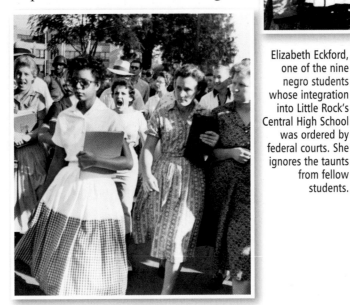

Elizabeth Eckford, one of the nine negro students whose integration into Little Rock's Central High School was ordered by federal courts. She ignores the taunts from fellow students.

? QUESTIONS

1. What is desegregation?
2. How did each of the following help in the process of desegregation (i) the army (ii) Earl Warren (iii) Brown v. Board of Education, Topeka (iv) Little Rock (v) James Meredith

THE MURDER OF EMMETT TILL

Emmett Till, a 14 year old boy from Chicago, was brutally murdered in Money, Mississippi in August, 1955, because he said, 'Bye baby' to a white shop assistant. His battered body was visible in an open coffin and photographs were later published in newspapers and magazines. 'These photographs quickly became a symbol of the violence that simmered just under the surface of segregated communities in the South.' (*Eyes on the Prize*) Later, Bob Dylan wrote a song, 'The Death Of Emmett Till', about the murder and the trial, in which two white men were acquitted. The murder and trial highlighted the issue of civil rights and the treatment of black Americans, especially for whites living in the Northern cities of the US.

Bussing: Although legal segregation in the South was ended by the *Brown* case, **segregated housing** in other parts of America resulted in separate black and white schools. Supreme Court decisions supported the bussing of black and white students across cities to achieve a **racial balance** in public schools. In the North, this resulted in widespread resistance – even rioting in Boston and Detroit – because black students were moved from inner-city ghettoes to suburban schools and vice versa. Eventually the Supreme Court softened compulsory bussing.

However, while these and other legal battles were won, by 1964 only 2 per cent of blacks attended multiracial schools in 11 southern states. Even in the North, by the late 1980s two-thirds of black children attended public schools where they formed over 50 per cent of the students. This indicated that in spite of Supreme Court judgments there were other social and political conditions which hindered desegregation. In part this was caused by **white middle-class families** sending their children to private schools and leaving the public schools to black students.

University of Mississippi: In 1962, **James Meredith**, a 29-year-old air force veteran, attempted to attend the all-white University of Mississippi. He was opposed by the governor, who believed in state power over federal power: *'We must either submit to the awful dictate of the federal government or stand up like men and tell them.'* Meredith was only admitted when President Kennedy sent federal marshals to protect him. However, a few days later, a white mob attacked the university and two onlookers were killed. Regular army troops had to be sent in to control the situation.

Transport: Transport was also segregated in some parts of the South. Blacks had to sit at the back of buses and whites at the front. The battle to desegregate transportation was highlighted by the **Montgomery Bus Boycott**, 1955–56. (See Case Study: The Montgomery Bus Boycott, 1955–56; pp. 432–40.)

The Civil Rights Protest Continued

Lunch counter protests: Non-violent protest became an important part of the methods used to change segregation. It was used in 1960 in the lunch counter protests. A group of black students sat at a **whites only** lunch counter. The first protest took place in an all-white Woolworth's cafeteria in **Greensboro, North Carolina**, led by four black students. **Martin Luther King** visited the students to encourage them. Their action set off a widespread lunch counter protest in 54 cities in the Old South, involving up to 70,000 students in these sit-ins. These protests were highlighted in the press and on television. Their success in **desegregating lunch counters** led to greater student involvement, largely led by the SNCC (Student Nonviolent Coordinating Committee).

The Freedom Riders: In 1961, black and white college students took **interstate buses** to test that the law against segregating interstate buses was being applied. One bus was firebombed and other Freedom Riders were attacked by crowds. Once again, the **media** highlighted the issues and forced the federal government to enforce desegregation on interstate buses.

Albany, Georgia: The **SNCC**, who wanted full desegregation, first targeted this city. Older black leaders in the city invited **King**, who led a march and got agreement from the city authorities. However, as soon as King left the agreement was reneged on – the city refused to desegregate the schools and closed the public parks. King had failed to gain national publicity over the situation in Albany because the police deliberately did not attack the protestors. King looked on the Albany Movement as a failure.

Birmingham, Alabama: In the case of the lunch counter protests and the Freedom Riders, the protestors encouraged a **white backlash** against their actions to get national and world media coverage. This was also the case in Birmingham, Alabama in 1963 when **Martin Luther King** used school children as demonstrators. The overreaction of

KEY PERSONALITY: MARTIN LUTHER KING

Martin Luther King was born in Atlanta, Georgia, the son of a **Baptist** minister. He was encouraged by his father to enter the Baptist ministry instead of law or medicine, which was his preference. He studied for the ministry and completed his education at Boston University, where he was a awarded a PhD in 1955.

At the same time, he was appointed pastor of a Baptist church in **Montgomery**, Alabama. It was here that he came to national prominence as leader of the **Montgomery Bus Boycott**, 1955–56 (see Case Study: Montgomery Bus Boycott, pp. 432–40)

Soon after, King founded the **Southern Christian Leadership Conference**. He made good use of his gifts as a powerful and moving speaker to publicise the problems of blacks. In the early 1960s, he was involved in many **non-violent demonstrations** against segregation and he was arrested several times. He was involved in leading demonstrations in **Birmingham**, Alabama, over segregated hotels and restaurants. Late in 1963, he led 200,000 people in a civil rights march in Washington. It was here he made his 'I Have a Dream' speech (see p. 422).

In 1964, he was awarded the **Nobel Peace Prize** and he also saw the passing of the **Civil Rights Act 1964**. He was also involved in the **Selma to Montgomery** march to highlight voting discrimination against blacks (see p. 422). This led to the passage of the **Voting Rights Act 1965**, which gave power to the federal government over voter registration (see p. 424).

However, by now King's leadership was being challenged by younger, **more radical** (extreme) black leaders, such as **Malcolm X**. King himself became more critical of other **social and economic problems** faced by blacks. He was also investigated by the **FBI**, who were trying to uncover any **dirt** to undermine his campaign. He became very critical of the **Vietnam War**, which he believed was taking money away from the reform programmes to help the poor. He was planning a **Poor People's March** on Washington when he was assassinated in Memphis, Tennessee in 1968 on the balcony of a motel by a hired assassin, **James Earl Ray**. His death gave rise to widespread riots in the black areas of many American cities.

Develop notes on the role of Martin Luther King in US history, 1945–68.

the police chief, **Eugene 'Bull' Connor**, and his men when they used **dogs and water cannon** was featured on television.

Washington: Soon after, in August 1963, a huge peaceful rally of 250,000 civil rights protestors marched in Washington to advance their cause. It was here that **Martin Luther King** made his famous **'I Have a Dream'** speech.

Mississippi Freedom Summer: Only 5 per cent of blacks were registered to vote in Mississippi compared to 30 per cent over the South generally. As well as this, 70 per cent of blacks in the state were illiterate. The Student Nonviolent Coordinating Committee (SNCC) organised Freedom Summer in 1964 to promote black voter registration. Many white activists from the North came south to help. There was resistance from the Ku Klux Klan and the police. White segregationists murdered three student activists (two of them white). Mississippi Freedom Summer attracted widespread publicity.

Selma to Montgomery March: In 1965, half of the population of Selma County, Alabama were black, but only 1 per cent of blacks were registered to vote. Efforts by black leaders to register black voters were stopped by police and state troopers in **Selma**. When they attempted to march from Selma to Montgomery, the state capital, to protest, they were attacked by state troopers. But this shocking violence was covered by national **television**. President Johnson sent National Guardsmen to Selma to protect the marchers, who were now joined by **Martin Luther King** and other black leaders. Three thousand began the march in Selma and this had increased to 25,000 by the time the march reached Montgomery. This march won support for the **Voting Rights Act**, which became law in August 1965 (see p. 424).

Martin Luther King acknowledges the crowds at the Lincoln Memorial during the March in Washington in August 1963 when he made his 'I Have a Dream' speech.

EXTRACTS FROM MARTIN LUTHER KING'S SPEECH IN WASHINGTON, AUGUST 1963

'…I say to you today, my friends, that in spite of the difficulties and frustrations of the moment, I still have a dream. It is a dream deeply rooted in the American dream.

I have a dream that one day this nation will rise up and live out the true meaning of its creed: "We hold these truths to be self-evident: that all men are created equal." I have a dream that one day on the red hills of Georgia the sons of former slaves and the sons of former slave owners will be able to sit down together at a table of brotherhood. I have a dream that one day even the state of Mississippi, a desert state, sweltering with the heat of injustice and oppression, will be transformed into an oasis of freedom and justice. I have a dream that my four children will one day live in a nation where they will not be judged by the colour of their skin but by the content of their character. I have a dream today….

With this faith we will be able to transform the jangling discords of our nation into a beautiful symphony of brotherhood. With this faith we will be able to work together, to pray together, to struggle together, to go to jail together, to stand up for freedom together, knowing that we will be free one day.'

King goes North

Martin Luther King next turned his attention to the Northern ghettoes. Here the problem for blacks was social and economic inequality (see 'Urban Poverty', pp. 426–28). King and the Southern Christian Leadership Conference (SCLC) decided that they would concentrate first on Chicago in 1966 to highlight the problems of bad housing, poor facilities and discriminatory house-selling practices. But the SCLC campaign led to conflict with the police and with white neighbourhoods. King's own family suffered from the poor conditions, living in a small apartment. Overall, King's Chicago campaign was a failure and it showed him the difficulties of trying to overcome social and economic inequality.

The Poor People's Campaign, 1968

King now took a more radical approach to tackling the social and economic problems of blacks. He planned a **Poor People's Campaign** which would include a national civil disobedience campaign, occupying government buildings and boycotting businesses. He demanded that the government spend $30 billion a year to combat poverty.

But by now the civil rights movement was dividing. Martin Luther King's influence began to decline. In March 1968, he was shot by a **white assassin in Memphis**. His assassination sparked off huge **rioting** and **looting** in 130 cities across the US. Sixty-five thousand troops were called out to quell the riots, in which 35 people were killed.

Black Power and Black Panthers: Blacks were also demanding more than civil rights. *'What use is a mouthful of civil rights and a empty stomach?'* said an unemployed black youth. Large proportions of the unemployed were black. They were **frustrated** by the slow progress of racial integration, the poverty of the **black ghettoes** and by white violence against civil rights marchers.

Out of this grew a more **radical** (extreme) black voice. Led by **Malcolm X**, the radical black movement advocated violence and supported **black nationalism**. They advocated **Black Power**, which expressed a growing pride in being **African-American**. They sought the development of a separate black identity. The Black Power slogan was adopted by many different groups. The most extreme of these were the **Black Panthers**, who wanted to gain Black Power *'through the barrel of a gun'*.

They differed from **Martin Luther King** who sought white and black integration and who wished to respect the democratic tradition of the US. In contrast, **Malcolm X** sought separation of blacks and whites – he wanted black self-determination, where blacks would rule themselves.

Bad social and economic conditions in inner-city ghettoes, combined with a growing violence, led to **race riots** in a number of cities, ranging from **Harlem** in New York to **Watts** in Los Angeles to Chicago between 1965 and 1968. (See 'Urban Poverty', pp. 426–28.)

QUESTIONS

1. What part did each of the following play in the process of desegregation: (i) lunch counter protests (ii) the SNCC (iii) Freedom Rides (iv) Albany, Georgia (v) Birmingham, Alabama (vi) 'I Have a Dream' speech (vii) Mississippi Freedom Summer (viii) Selma to Montgomery?
2. What divisions occurred in the civil rights movement in the late 1960s?
3. What was black nationalism?

The Government and Civil Rights

The federal government was concerned about racial conflict and about the image which US racial segregation gave to the world. In opposition to southern state governments, the federal government played a vital role in getting civil rights for blacks and other minority groups:

- Both Truman and Eisenhower ended segregation in the armed forces.
- In the **Civil Rights Act 1957**, Eisenhower set up a Civil Rights Commission to investigate places where blacks were denied the vote.

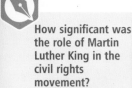

How significant was the role of Martin Luther King in the civil rights movement?

- Montgomery Bus Boycott – role in
- His style and his message – non-violent direct action
- Organisation – role of SCLC
- Exploiting white hatred
- Others using non-violent strategy – CORE/SNCC
- Influence on Civil Rights Act 1964
- Voter registration campaign – Selma march, Voting Rights Act 1965
- Impact on northern ghettoes/challenge from Malcolm X
- Other factors to balance King's role – NAACP; SNCC; limited role in education

President Johnson signing Civil Rights Act or Voting Rights Act.

- Kennedy brought in the **Civil Rights Bill** but it was not until Johnson became President that it was passed. The **Civil Rights Act 1964** outlawed discrimination in public places, including restaurants, theatres, sport stadiums and cinemas. It also set up the **Employment Opportunities Commission** to outlaw job discrimination.
- The **Voting Rights Act 1965** organised **voters' registration** and banned literacy tests for voter registration.
- In 1968, another Civil Rights Act – popularly known as the **Fair Housing Act** – was passed. This prohibited discrimination concerning the sale, rental and financing of housing based on race, religion, national origin and sex.
- The government extended **affirmative action** by ensuring that companies on federal contracts had to provide jobs for minorities.

Reagan, however, tried to withdraw federal support for the civil rights programme. He appointed more **conservative judges** to the Supreme Court. He also dismantled some of the welfare programmes set up under the **New Deal** and the **Great Society**, which had mostly benefited blacks.

Black Success

Many African-Americans benefited from the civil rights struggle as a new economic and social black leadership was created – in sports, films, politics and music. In the 1960s, Diahann Carroll and Sidney Poitier in television and movies, **Muhammad Ali** in boxing, Bill Russell and Wilt Chamberlain in basketball and the Motown stars in popular music became national and international figures. More blacks were registered to vote and more were elected to state and federal Houses of Congress. The first black mayor was elected in Springfield, Ohio in 1966. The next year saw the first black senator elected to the US Senate for almost 100 years. This was accompanied by a much greater white acceptance of blacks. Opinion polls showed clear majorities of whites in support of desegregation.

However, this still left a large number of blacks in **poverty**. Black society itself became divided. Around 40 per cent of black society achieved a **middle-class lifestyle** during the 1970s, but about 30 per cent were still below the poverty line. The condition of these blacks was a class issue as much as it was a race issue.

Chicanos and Native Americans

Chicanos (Mexican-Americans) and Native Americans (American Indians) were encouraged by the civil rights movement to fight for their rights. Chicanos were used

QUESTIONS

1. What steps were taken by each of the Presidents from Truman to Johnson in granting civil rights?
2. What did Reagan do to slow down civil rights and conditions for black Americans?

legally and illegally as farm labourers in the US. They suffered general white hostility, particularly in California and Florida. In the early 1960s, **Cesar Chavez** used non-violent methods of **boycotting** to gain improved working and living conditions for agricultural labourers.

Native Americans were even worse off. They suffered from over 100 years of discrimination and repression. By the end of the 1960s, their 1 million members suffered the worst education and housing and the highest disease and death rates among any ethnic group in the US. Some founded the **American Indian Movement** (AIM) and took over Alcatraz Island and government buildings to highlight their conditions. This worked. The **Indian Self-Determination Act 1975** was passed, which gave Indians control of their reservations. Other laws gave Indians **religious freedom** and **educational support**. Tribes also won legal battles to get the return of lands taken from them in the past by the federal government.

QUESTIONS

1. How did black Americans make progress in society?
3. How did conditions improve for (i) Chicanos (ii) Native Americans?

The Achievements of the Civil Rights Movement		
	Key Events	**Positive Outcomes**
Education	Brown v Board of Education, Topeka – segregated education not equal education	Slow integration of schools esp. in the South; in 1968, 58 per cent of black students still in segregated schools
	Johnson's Higher Education Act 1965	By early 1970s, four times more black students in colleges and universities
Transport	Montgomery Bus Boycott	Desegregation of buses in Montgomery; slow progress in other cities of South
	Freedom Rides	Desegregation of interstate buses
Desegregation of Public Places	Lunch counter protests/sit-ins	By 1963, 200 cities had desegregated restaurants.
	Civil Rights Act 1964	Federal government forced cities – 214 Southern cities by 1965 – to desegregate public places, e.g. restaurants, parks, toilets
Voting Rights	Voting Rights Act 1965	230,000 more black people registered to vote in South – slow
		Very effective in North – increase from 4 million in 1960 to 6 million in 1965 First elected black mayor in 1966 By 1980 proportion of elected black officials similar to black population
Jobs and Income	Fair Employment Practice laws	Applied to government jobs and companies working for the government – overall slow progress – by early 1960s, black unemployment twice the national average Income of black workers half national average income Black unemployment reduced by late 1960s
Housing	Fair Housing Act 1968 prohibited discrimination in the housing market	Ineffective because poor enforcement/white resistance
General support for civil rights	Increased public support among whites for black civil rights; but still white resistance to fair housing	

Urban Poverty

Background

In the 1950s and early 1960s, most Americans were happy with their way of life. The affluence (wealth) of the country led people to believe that if poverty existed, it was only in **small pockets**. Then in 1962, Michael Harrington wrote *The Other America*, which revealed the poverty behind the affluence – 40 million Americans were living in poverty. This was about 25 per cent of the population.

Traditionally, poverty in America was associated with rural poor blacks in the South. But since the Second World War a number of changes had occurred that created the problem of **urban poverty**.

A street scene in East Harlem, New York.

Causes – Black Ghettoes

During the 1940s and 1950s, there was **huge movement of black Americans** from the South to the northern cities. They fled poverty, racial discrimination, white violence and lynching to find a better life in the urban North. They sought jobs in the booming manufacturing industries. They concentrated in the inner areas or the centre of cities.

At the same time, there was **movement of whites** from the cities to the suburbs. This was often accompanied by a movement of industry to the suburbs. This left many decayed and abandoned buildings and factories in the centre. This was also a time of change in industry. As **manufacturing declined** in the 1950s and 1960s, so did the need for unskilled – mostly black – labour.

Instead of the better life for many migrant black families, the inner cities became places with high concentrations of unemployment, poverty, low educational levels and poor housing. They became **black ghettoes**.

Taxes and Housing

The movement of the whites to the suburbs had another result: it deprived cities of **tax revenue** which could be used to maintain streets, schools and public areas. In spite of federal funding, many cities were in **financial trouble**. In 1975, New York City was almost bankrupt and was only saved by huge federal funding.

The cities were made worse by government **housing policies**. The cities built over 2 million new houses by the early 1970s but this was not enough to house people. These public housing projects were often a cause of further problems because the high rise apartments only included the **very poorest people** and those with **serious social problems**. The government also provided billions of dollars from the 1940s for slum clearance, or **urban renewal**, as it was called. This often meant replacing the old tenements with office blocks and luxury apartments, which increased the number of homeless.

QUESTION

What was Michael Harrington's estimate of the amount of poverty in the US in 1962?

War on Poverty

In the 1940s and 1950s, Presidents Truman and Eisenhower had increased **social security payments** and established a **minimum wage**. President Kennedy continued on the same path, but he also provided federal money for **school and job-based training**.

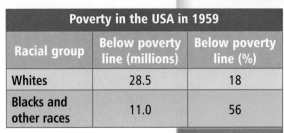

Poverty in the USA in 1959		
Racial group	**Below poverty line (millions)**	**Below poverty line (%)**
Whites	28.5	18
Blacks and other races	11.0	56

The federal government established a **poverty line** in 1964 – this was an income level below which people were regarded as poor. This included more than half the black population, almost half of female-headed families and a third of elderly people.

President Johnson wanted to use government resources to improve the condition of poor people as part of his **Great Society** programme. He believed that a **war on poverty** would give people a chance to help themselves. He set up the **Office of Economic Opportunity**. This organised:

- **Head Start** – where children went to preschool classes.
- **Job Corps** – to provide skills for inner-city youth.
- **Community Action Programs** which set up clinics and law centres.

He also provided $1 billion to help poor students in **public schools**, but this was often spent by school boards on middle-class children instead. He also gave $3 billion to fund low- and middle-income **housing** as well as rent aid. He set up **Medicare** for the elderly and **Medicaid** for the poorer welfare recipients.

Johnson's war on poverty had some success. The number of people below the poverty line dropped from 40 million in 1959 to 28 million in 1968 and 25 million in 1970. This was also helped by the growth in the economy in the 1960s. When the economy took a downturn in the 1970s and 1980s, government spending was cut back and this, along with rising unemployment, made urban poverty worse.

1. What conclusions can you draw from these figures?
2. What actions did the government take to combat poverty?
3. How successful were the actions?

Urban Riots

However, before Johnson's policy could have any effect, riots broke out in 1965 in **Watts**, **Los Angeles**. These were sparked off by an incident between a young black driver who was drunk and a white policeman. The rioters looted and burned shops and businesses and threw bottles and stones at police. Thirty-four people were killed, almost all black, and over 900 were injured and 4,000 arrested.

Watts was the beginning of a series of urban riots that lasted from 1965–8 and affected many US cities – Chicago, Cleveland, San Francisco, Newark (New Jersey) and Detroit. There were 38 riots in 1966, in which seven people were killed, 400 injured and 3,000 arrested. In 1967, the worst year, there were 164 riots. The two most serious riots – in Newark (New Jersey) and Detroit – resulted in 23 and 34 dead respectively and thousands of buildings looted and burned.

National Guardsmen with fixed bayonets moving against rioters in Detroit in 1967, in one of the most serious riots of those years.

427

Causes

Many **causes** were given to explain these riots:

- There was a **concentration of poverty and unemployment** in these areas, and most of the rioters were poor or working class. They were class riots every bit as much as they were racial riots.

- But for others there were **rising expectations** – much of the legal discrimination against blacks had been overcome and the civil rights movement had given hope of a better life to blacks. But now there were other social and economic **barriers to improvement**. Indeed, blacks were better off on average than the 1950s, when there was no violence. The black ghettoes in Detroit and Watts were better off than those in other cities.

> 'You go into a local store in Watts. Besides the rats and the roaches, the food was rotten. There would be some Jewish guy or white guy standing there saying, "The Hell with you, you're going to have to buy this anyway." Those were the first places people went, to burn down the store. What we didn't have in Watts wasn't civil rights. It was jobs, housing and education. It was a positive image of ourselves. We didn't know what they were complaining about in the South.'

> (A Watts rioter)

- There was also a concentration of **young people**, especially young men – the group most likely to be involved in violence.

- **Malcolm X** – Martin Luther King was not the hero of the young rioters. Instead of the message of non-violence, they preferred the message of Malcolm X. He wanted blacks to be black, he preached black nationalism and spoke about inequality. *'I'm not going to sit at your table and watch you eat,'* he said, *'with nothing on my plate and call myself a diner.'* Some preached a message of black power with violence.

- There was growing tension between the **police and black youths**. Most of the riots were sparked off by incidents between white police and black residents.

- The influence of **television**, which made people aware of what was happening elsewhere and spread a general discontent.

- There were also growing levels of **violence in society** generally and guns were easy to get.

Malcolm X, speaking at a Black Muslim rally in 1961, preached a message of black nationalism.

QUESTIONS

1. Where did urban riots first break out?
2. Where did they spread to?
3. What caused the riots?

Drugs and Crime

Poverty, unemployment and slum conditions were major causes of crime in the US. But they were not the only causes. There was also:

- The widespread availability of guns – almost one gun per person in a population of 250 million.
- Drug addiction and the cost of drugs.
- Inadequate number of police.

Crime levels began to rise after the Second World War. However, they jumped rapidly from the early 1960s onwards. Violent crime, for example, trebled between 1960 and 1977. The problem was more serious in the US than elsewhere. Compared with other industrialised countries, the US had the highest rate of reported murders, rapes and robberies.

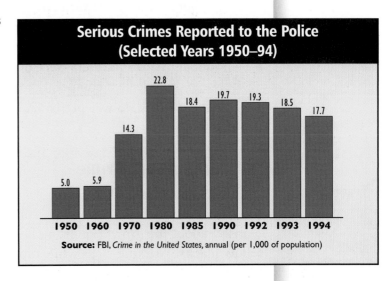

Serious Crimes Reported to the Police (Selected Years 1950–94)

1950	1960	1970	1980	1985	1990	1992	1993	1994
5.0	5.9	14.3	22.8	18.4	19.7	19.3	18.5	17.7

Source: FBI, *Crime in the United States*, annual (per 1,000 of population)

Rising crime was largely an **urban** phenomenon. In the 1970s, 30 per cent of all reported crimes in America took place in the **six largest cities**. But these cities only contained 12 per cent of the country's population. New York, a city with a population roughly equal to Sweden's, had 20 times more murders.

Criminals tended to be **young, male, poor and black**. In 1975, three-quarters of all people arrested for violent crime were males under 25. But the average age of criminals dropped in the 1980s. Crime was largely confined to a small proportion of society. US criminologists estimated that two-thirds of all violent crimes were committed by 7 per cent of the people. These people were habitual offenders with a number of arrests. Crime also paid, particularly in relation to burglaries, where arrest and conviction rates were very low.

Drugs

By the 1970s, much crime was **drug related**, as the US became the largest **consumer** of illegal drugs. This pattern began in the late 1950s and grew more rapidly in the 1960s, partly encouraged by being fashionable among pop and film stars. By 1990, 6 per cent of all Americans were drug addicts, but many more had experienced drugs. Surveys showed that 44 per cent of high school students had taken drugs at least once, and about 12 per cent were frequent users.

By the 1980s, drug trafficking had become a huge **multinational business** operated by **organised crime**. There were Columbian cartels linked with the Mafia and Jamaican, Puerto Rican, black or Mexican gangs in various cities across the US. Most of the drugs originated in poorer countries such as Columbia, Peru, Turkey and Afghanistan. Poorer peasants were dependant on the cash they got for their crops. In

A warning sign to drug dealers, users and gang members, posted in a New York street around 1970.

some places, guerrilla groups depended on the money from drug sales to fund their war against a local government.

Drugs were linked to **other crimes** and **problems**:

- Many drug addicts began to steal to feed their habit until they were stealing up to 90 per cent of what they spent on drugs.
- About half the US murders were drug related. These were often caused by gang wars between drug dealers competing for territory.
- The spread of AIDS was partly caused by dirty needles being shared among drug addicts.

Concerns about Crime

? **QUESTIONS**

1. What caused crime in the USA? Explain each of the following in relation to urban crime: (i) crime levels (ii) young, male, poor, black.
2. How widespread was drug abuse?
3. How did drug trafficking become a multinational business?
4. In what ways were drugs related to other crimes and problems?

In the US, many **feared** the spread of crime. By the late 1960s, **crime in the streets** was the country's main problem according to opinion polls. Blacks as well as whites worried about the growth of crime because blacks were often the targets of crime from fellow blacks. Working-class whites were angry about crime – it led to increased racial tension. A white resident of Brooklyn, New York said, *'You can't walk anywhere. It's because these people don't know how to live. They steal. They got no values. They say it's history. It's not history, it's the way they live. They live like animals.'*

The **US government** reacted to the people's concerns. Crime became an issue in presidential and congressional elections. Government policies tried to tackle the causes of crime by investing in job-training schemes and improving education and housing. They also tried to **crack down** on crime by increasing penalties, building more prisons and putting more police on the street.

Similar approaches were tried in the case of **drug trafficking**. In 1986, President Reagan increased funding for police and increased penalties for drug traffickers. He also proposed **economic sanctions** against drug-producing countries to force them to deal with the problem there.

HOMEWORK EXERCISES

1. Study this edited extract from 'Letter from Birmingham Jail', April 1963, and answer the questions that follow.

> **While in Birmingham jail, Alabama, for participating in demonstrations against segregation, Martin Luther King, Jr, wrote a letter in response to a statement issued by eight white Southern religious leaders.**
>
> *WHILE confined here in the Birmingham city jail, I came across your recent statement calling our present activities 'unwise and untimely.' ... I think I should give the reason for my being in Birmingham, since you have been influenced by the argument of 'outsiders coming in.' I have the honour of serving as President of the Southern Christian Leadership Conference, an organisation operating in every Southern state, with headquarters in Atlanta, Georgia. .... Several months ago our local affiliate here in Birmingham invited us to be on call to engage in a nonviolent direct-action programme if such were deemed necessary. We readily consented, and when the hour came we lived up to our promises. ... Beyond this, I am in Birmingham because injustice is here. ... just as the Apostle Paul ... carried the gospel of Jesus Christ to practically every hamlet and city of the Greco-Roman world, I too am compelled to carry the gospel of freedom beyond my particular hometown. ... Moreover, I am cognizant [aware] of the interrelatedness of all communities and states. ... Injustice anywhere is a threat to justice everywhere. ... Never again can we afford to live with the narrow, provincial 'outside agitator' idea. Anyone who lives inside the United States can never be considered an outsider. You deplore the demonstrations that are presently taking place in Birmingham. But I am sorry that your statement did not express a similar concern for the conditions that brought the demonstrations into being. I am sure that each of you would want to go beyond the superficial social analyst who looks merely at effects and does not grapple with underlying causes. I would not hesitate to say that it is unfortunate that so-called demonstrations are taking place in Birmingham at this time, but I would say in more emphatic terms that it is even more unfortunate that the white power structure of this city left the Negro community with no other alternative.*
>
> Source: The Atlantic Monthly, https://www. theatlantic.com

   A. (i) Why did Martin Luther King write this letter?

   (ii) What organisation was he President of?

   (iii) In what way was he acting like the Apostle Paul?

   (iv) Why were the demonstrations taking place in Birmingham at this time?

   (v) Is the letter propaganda? Explain your answer.

   B. Write a **paragraph** on desegregation in education in the US.

   C. Write a **long answer** on the causes of urban poverty in the US and how the government tried to combat poverty.

HIGHER LEVEL

2. How successful were black Americans in their attempts to achieve civil and political rights from 1945 to the 1980s?

3. What caused urban poverty in the US and what were its effects?

4. During the period 1945–89, what was the impact of one or more of the following on American society: (i) racial conflict (ii) urban poverty (iii) organised crime? (2006)

5. What were the main developments in race relations in the US, 1945–68? (2013)

CASE STUDY: The Montgomery Bus Boycott, 1955–56

Introduction

Montgomery was the capital of the state of Alabama in the Deep South. It was a city of 70,000 whites and 50,000 blacks. It enforced **Jim Crow** by having segregated schools and other public facilities. Most blacks were employed in **low-paid, unskilled jobs**; 60 per cent of black women worked as domestics and 50 per cent of black men worked as domestics or labourers. The **average income** of blacks was half that of whites. (Source 1)

The **bus company** followed the pattern of the rest of the city. It employed no blacks as drivers. It also segregated buses, with blacks sitting at the back and whites at the front. Black passengers often complained about verbal abuse from the white bus drivers. (Source 2)

SOURCE 1 – NEGROES' MOST URGENT NEEDS

FOLLOWING ARE A FEW OF THE MOST URGENT NEEDS OF OUR PEOPLE. IMMEDIATE ATTENTION SHOULD BE GIVEN EACH OF THESE. WHAT IS YOUR STAND TOWARD THEM?

1. The present bus situation. Negroes have to stand over empty seats of city buses, because the first ten seats are reserved for whites who sometime never ride. We wish to fill the bus from the back toward the front until all the seats are taken. This is done in Atlanta, Mobile, Alabama and in most of our larger southern cities.

2. Our parks are in a deplorable state.

3. Sub-division for housing [of Negroes stopped]

4. [Civil service] Jobs for qualified Negroes [not open to them]

5. Negro representation on all boards affecting Negroes

6. Congested areas, with inadequate or no fireplugs

7. Lack of sewage disposals make it necessary to resort to outdoor privies [toilets] which is a health hazard

Gentlemen, what is your stand on these issues? What will you do to improve these undemocratic practices?

Very truly yours,

Montgomery Negroes

Inez Jessie Baskin Papers, in the Alabama Department of Archives and History, Montgomery

> Apart from segregated bus seating, what other problems had black people in Montgomery?

SOURCE 2 – CODE OF THE CITY OF MONTGOMERY

Section 10. Separation of races – Required.

Every person operating a bus line in the city shall provide equal but separate accommodation for white people and negroes on his buses, by requiring the employees in charge thereof to assign passengers seats on the vehicles under their charge in such manner as to separate the white people from the negroes, where there are both white and negroes in the same car ...

Section 11. Some powers of persons in charge of vehicle; passengers to obey directions.

Any employee in charge of a bus operated in the city shall have the powers of a police officer while in actual control of any bus, for the purpose of carrying out the provisions of the preceding section, and it shall be unlawful for any passenger to refuse or fail to take a seat among those assigned to the race in which he belongs, at the request of any such employee in charge, if there is such a seat vacant.

Alabama Department of Archives and History, Montgomery

> In your own words, what do Sections 10 and 11 mean?

Rosa Parks

One of those who used the buses regularly was **Rosa Parks**, a 42-year-old black woman. She worked as a **seamstress** in a downtown department store. She was also a member of the local **NAACP** (National Association for the Advancement of Colored People). She had been put off a bus in the mid-1940s for refusing to do as she was told. She had recently completed a workshop on race relations.

On 1 December 1955, she boarded a bus after a day's work and some shopping. She took a seat in the black section at the rear. When all the seats filled up, she was told by the driver to get up and give her seat to a white man – but she refused. The driver called the police and Rosa Parks was arrested for breaking city laws. She had to appear in court four days later. (Sources 3, 4 and 5)

SOURCE 3

Rosa Parks being fingerprinted in Montgomery after being charged with violating segregation laws.

SOURCE 4 – WHY MRS PARKS WAS CHOSEN

'Mrs Parks was a married woman. She was morally clean, and she had a fairly good academic training ... If there was ever a person we would've been able to [use to] break the situation that existed in the Montgomery city line, Rosa L. Parks was the woman to use ... I probably would've examined a dozen before I got there if Rosa Parks hadn't come along before I found the right one.'

E. D. Nixon, quoted by Gary Younge in *The Guardian*, 16 December 2000

Why was Rosa Parks an ideal person to challenge the laws?

 CASE STUDY QUESTIONS

1. How were blacks discriminated against in Montgomery?
2. What discrimination took place in buses?
3. How did Rosa Parks break segregation laws?
4. Why was Rosa Parks chosen by the NAACP to fight her case?

SOURCE 5 – NOT YIELD ONE INCH

'The City Commission, and we know our people are with us in this determination, will not yield one inch but will do all in its power to oppose the integration of the Negro race with the white race in Montgomery, and will forever stand like a rock against social equality, intermarriage and mixing of the races under God's creation and plan.'

Statement from the Montgomery City Commission at the start of the boycott, quoted in M. Walker, *Makers of the American century*

What is Montgomery City Commission opposed to?

SOURCE 6 – THE WEAPON OF PROTEST

'Since it had to happen, I'm happy it happened to a person like Mrs Parks, for ... nobody can doubt the height of her character. Nobody can doubt the depth of her Christian commitment... And you know my friends, there comes a time when people get tired of being trampled on by the iron feet of oppression. The only weapon that we have in our hands this evening is the weapon of protest. If we were incarcerated behind the iron curtains of a Communistic nation, we couldn't do this... But the great glory of American democracy is the right to protest for right ... We are not wrong in what we are doing. If we are wrong, the Supreme Court of this nation is wrong. If we are wrong, God almighty is wrong.'

Martin Luther King, speaking at a public meeting at the beginning of the boycott

Summarise Martin Luther King's views in Sources 6 and 7.

Organising the Boycott

Local black leaders decided to take action. **E. D. Nixon** was leader of the Montgomery NAACP and **Jo Ann Robinson** was leader of the Women's Political Council of Montgomery.

Nixon asked Parks if the NAACP could use her case to fight for desegregation, even though it might put her life in danger. She discussed it with her husband and mother and decided to let the NAACP go ahead with a lawsuit to contest the constitutionality of the segregation law.

Robinson, along with the Women's Political Council, decided to ask blacks to **boycott** the buses on the following Monday, the day of Parks's trial. They issued 35,000 leaflets to spread the word. The boycott decision was supported by **black ministers** in their church sermons on Sunday.

The organisers looked around for a **leader**. They found one in **Martin Luther King**, a 26-year-old clergymen who had come to Montgomery just a year before. King was an inspirational leader and an outstanding speaker. As one historian wrote, 'As King spoke in a singsong cadence [tone, lilt], his followers would cry and clap and sway, carried away by the magic of his oratory.' He became President of the **Montgomery Improvement Association** (MIA), which was set up to lead the boycott. (Sources 6, 7, 8 and 9)

King was inspired by the teachings of the leader of Indian independence, **Mahatma Ghandi**, and **Reinhold Niebuhr**, a theologian. From these people he adopted the method of **non-violent protest**. This belief spread to others and it gave his followers a strong feeling of unity and determination.

In court on Monday, 5 December, Parks was convicted and was fined $10. Her lawyer appealed against the conviction. But the bus boycott that day was successful. Most blacks supported it in spite of great inconvenience.

SOURCE 7 – THIS IS NOT A WAR

'There are those who would try to make this a hate campaign. This is not a war between the white and the Negro but a conflict between justice and injustice ... We must use the weapon of love.'

Speech by Martin Luther King

SOURCE 8 – MARTIN LUTHER KING SPEAKING

'Martin Luther King spoke in a very soft, rich voice, and as he was going along, you'd get the feeling ... that here was a person who really cared... He was able to make all of us – the washerwoman, the domestic, the teenager – feel like he was talking directly to each of us.'

Inez Jessie Baskin, quoted in P. Jennings and T. Brewster, *The century*

> What were Martin Luther King's strengths as a speaker?

SOURCE 9 – COMMUNIST VIEW

'No day passed but the Italian Communists pointed to events in our South to prove that American democracy was a "capitalist myth" ... No man has ever waged the battle for equality under our law in a more lawful and Christian way than you have.'

Clare Booth Luce, American ambassador to Italy, wife of the founder of Time magazine, January 1957 in a private letter to Martin Luther King, quoted in M. Walker, *Makers of the American century*

> Why did the writer praise Martin Luther King?

 CASE STUDY QUESTIONS

1. What was the boycott and who organised it?
2. What was Martin Luther King's role?
3. What was King's philosophy (set of beliefs)?

Continued Boycotting

After the success of the **Monday boycott**, the Montgomery Improvement Association decided to continue with the boycott until the bus company gave in to its demands:

- That black drivers be employed on the buses.
- That drivers should be courteous to passengers.
- That seats should be filled on a first come, first served basis.

The policy of boycotting was **risky** because it needed widespread support. Blacks would have to walk to work or co-operate with sharing cars. But boycotting also had **advantages**:

- It allowed people to take action without violence.
- It could create a sense of solidarity.
- It would hit the bus company because it would lose money.
  (Sources 10 and 11)

SOURCE 10

Blacks walking to work during the Montgomery Bus Boycott.

During the boycott, the **MIA** held weekly mass meetings with sermons and music to **mobilise** the black community. The Association's leaders, including King, negotiated with the Montgomery City leaders. They also co-ordinated legal challenges to the city's bus segregation laws. The MIA also supported the boycott financially by passing the plate at meetings to collect money and getting further support from other northern and southern civil rights organisations.

SOURCE 11 – ORGANISING THE TRANSPORT

'One of the first practical problems that the ex-bus riders [had experienced] is that in finding some way to get around the city. The first thing that we decided to do was to use a taxi, and they had agreed to transport the people for just ten cents, the same as the buses. Then the police commission stopped this by warning the taxis that they must charge a minimum of forty-five cents a person. Then we immediately got on the job and organised a volunteer car pool. And almost overnight over three hundred cars were out on the streets of Montgomery. [applause] They were out on the streets of Montgomery carrying the people to and from work from the various pickup and dispatch stations. It worked amazingly well. Even Commissioner Sellers had to admit in a White Citizens Council meeting that the system worked with 'military precision.' [applause] It has continued to grow and it is still growing.

Since that time we have added more than twenty station wagons to the car pool and they're working every day, all day, transporting the people. It has been an expensive project. Started out about two thousand dollars or more a week, but now it runs more than five thousand dollars a week. We have been able to carry on because of the contributions coming from the local community and nationally, from the great contributions that have come from friends of good will all over the nation and all over the world. [Applause]'.

Martin Luther King speaking in San Francisco in June 1956, to gather support for the Boycott.

> How does this source show that the boycott was well organised?

In organising the boycott, black leaders collected money to buy station wagons for a private **taxi service**. Some of the money came from local black workers (who donated 20 per cent of their wages), the NAACP, the United Auto Workers' Union, sympathetic whites and the Montgomery Jewish community. The leaders set up a **Transportation Committee** to form **car pools**, while some black workers took bicycles or walked to work. When local insurance agents tried to cancel **insurance** for the car pool, the boycotters insured with Lloyds of London. (Sources 14 and 15)

The **black churches** played a vital role in organising the boycott. The churches raised $30,000 for the car pool, and the churches became the despatch centres where people gathered to wait for rides. During the year, 24 ministers were arrested for helping the boycott.

SOURCE 12 – A PROTEST OF THE PEOPLE

'The amazing thing about our movement is that it is a protest of the people. It is not a one-man show. It is not the preachers' show. The masses of this town, who are tired of being trampled on, are responsible.'

Jo Ann Robinson, 1955

Why was the protest 'not a one-man show'?

 CASE STUDY QUESTIONS

1. What were the demands of the Montgomery Improvement Association?
2. What advantages did boycotting have as a method of protest?
3. How did blacks get to work?
4. What role did black churches play in the Montgomery Bus Boycott?

 WHAT CAN YOU TELL ABOUT THE SOURCES?

WHAT INFORMATION CA YOU GET FROM THE SOURCE?

| Analysing Documents: Cartoons | What does the information about the sources tell you? | How does the circled information on the second cartoon help you? | Are there aspects of the first cartoon that you think should be circled? | Are cartoons primary or secondary sources? | Are cartoons objective? | Are there symbols used in these cartoons? | Do the artists use any of the following to persuade you: exaggeration; caricature; positioning? |

What is each of the cartoons about?

What is passive resistance?

Who is the 'somebody from outside'?

What is segregation?

What is the message of the cartoons?

Why does the cartoonist want to convey this message?

What do the cartoons tell you about the Montgomery Bus Boycott?

Do you agree with the views of these cartoonists on the Montgomery Bus Boycott?

'Somebody From Outside Must Have Influenced Them'

A cartoon by Herb Block (Herblock) which appeared in the *Washington Post*, the most widely circulated daily newspaper in Washington, in 1956. Herblock supported civil rights for black Americans.

A cartoon by Laura Gray which first appeared in *The Militant*, a socialist newspaper published in the US, 13 February 1956.

White Opposition

City authorities tried to undermine the protest. When black-owned taxis (cabs) took customers for 10 cents a trip – the same as a bus fare – the city authorities threatened to shut them down. At the same time, the **Ku Klux Klan** became active. They marched in the streets and poured acid on cars involved in the car pooling. The homes of King and other leaders were bombed. (Sources 13 and 14)

The **police** also interfered. Those involved in car pools were stopped regularly by police trying to find any excuse to disrupt the boycott. **King** was arrested for doing 30 miles an hour in a 25-mile-an-hour zone. In February 1956, 89 blacks, including King, were arrested under an old law banning boycotting. Black **churches** were bombed.

But the boycott held out during 1956 in spite of great pressure. This was partly helped by the increasing outside interest, both in America and abroad. Television and newspapers publicised the boycott and the local white reaction to it.

One local white supporter wrote; *'All the big newspapers have people here and the Radio and TV and* Figaro *and the* Manchester Guardian *and that of course is a big factor in giving the Negroes the feeling that they have support all over the world and certainly the papers in the rest of the country have done a good job of coverage.'* (Virginia Durr)

> ### SOURCE 13 – LISTEN, NIGGER
> 'Listen, nigger. We've taken all we want from you. Before next week, you'll be sorry you ever came to Montgomery.'
>
> Late-night phone caller speaking to Martin Luther King, quoted in P. Jennings and T. Brewster, The century

> ### SOURCE 14 – WE WANT TO LOVE OUR ENEMIES
> 'We believe in law and order. Don't get panicky. Don't do anything at all. Don't get your weapons. He who lives by the sword will perish by the sword. Remember, that is what God said. We are not advocating violence. We want to love our enemies. We must love our white brothers no matter what they do to us.'
>
> Martin Luther King, after his house was bombed

Compare the views expressed in Source 13 with those in Source 14.

Supreme Court Judgment

At the same time, the lawsuit by the NAACP was proceeding through the law courts. The Montgomery NAACP leaders decided that Rosa Parks's case might get bogged down in the state courts. Instead they filed a federal case, *Browder v. Gayle*. Browder was another Montgomery woman, also a NAACP activist, who had been arrested like Rosa Parks eight months earlier, while Gayle was the Mayor of Montgomery. The case eventually reached the **Supreme Court** in Washington. The Court ruled on 13 November 1956 that the city laws relating to buses violated (broke) the Constitution. It said that the seating arrangements must stop on 20 December.

When the city officials gave in, King and his Montgomery Improvement Association called off the boycott. On 21 December 1956, 381 days after it began, King and other civil rights leaders took seats at the front of the bus. But this led to a new round of violence when snipers shot at buses, and churches and houses were bombed. However, this **white backlash** soon quietened down.

After it was over, King appeared on the front cover of *Time* magazine, which regarded him as the **American Ghandi**. He was also invited to the independence ceremony for the African country of Ghana.

? CASE STUDY QUESTION

What did the supreme court decide?

Conclusion

The **significance** of the Montgomery Bus Boycott:

- The success of a **well-organised and peaceful resistance** set an example for further action against segregation. Many historians regard it as the beginning of the modern civil rights movement.

- This was a **new method** of non-violent protest that blacks could use to promote civil rights, and not just the NAACP (National Association for the Advancement of Colored People) way of testing the laws.

- **Non-violent protest** was also used by James Meredith in the University of Mississippi, and in the Lunch Counter Protests and the Freedom Rides. It was also used in the Selma to Montgomery March.

- The boycott involved **local black leaders** and **followers** who had to face violence and pressure. The organisation and commitment involved was a source of great pride to black people all over America.

- It saw the rise to prominence of **Martin Luther King**. Following on from this, he founded the **Southern Christian Leadership Conference** in 1957, which became prominent in fighting for civil rights for blacks. Luther King became the accepted leader of black America. He used his influence to ensure that the Civil Rights Act 1964 and the Voting Rights Act 1964 were passed into law.

- The boycott got support from the **press and television**, especially outside the South, and highlighted the issues for northern whites. This method was also used by Martin Luther King in Birmingham, Alabama.

- It highlighted the role of the **black churches and religious leaders** in the fight for civil rights.

- The boycott was eventually ended by a **Supreme Court decision**; on its own it might have failed to force the Montgomery city officials to change.

- It also **failed to end Jim Crow** in other areas of Montgomery life; schools, hotels and theatres were still segregated and bus drivers were still white.

- **Rosa Parks** lost her job and had her life threatened several times. She and her husband left Montgomery in 1957 and settled in Detroit,

---

SOURCE 15 – THERE LIVED A GREAT PEOPLE

'If you will protest courageously and yet with dignity and Christian love, when the history books are written in future generations the historians will pause and say, "There lived a great people – a black people – who injected new meaning and dignity into the veins of civilisation."'

Martin Luther King, 1956, quoted in P. Jennings and T. Brewster, *The century*

Why was the Montgomery Bus Boycott successful?
- Parks – ideal 'victim'
- Strong leadership – King, MIA, NAACP, WPC, role of churches
- Alternative means of transport
- Unity among blacks, mass support
- Financial support
- National media interest
- Use of federal courts/Supreme Court decision

What did the Montgomery Bus Boycott (1955–56) contribute to the civil rights movement? (2010)
- Rise of Martin Luther King (and later SCLC)
- Non-violent methods/direct action (and later examples)
- Black organisation and tactics/ Christian churches
- NAACP and legal route
- Role of media
- Successful outcome/city transport
- Limitations of MBB success

CASE STUDY QUESTION

What were the main conclusions of the Montgomery Bus Boycott and what was their significance?

EXAM QUESTION

In what ways did the Montgomery Bus Boycott, 1955–56, advance the cause of the civil rights movement? (2007)

where she worked as an administrative assistant in a politician's office. In 1994, she was **attacked** and beaten by a young black man who wanted money. Two years later she was awarded the **Presidential Medal of Freedom**.

WEB RESOURCES

The Montgomery Bus Boycott, http://www.montgomeryboycott.com/

Using Primary Sources in the Classroom, Civil Rights Movement Unit

Lesson 1: Riding the Bus - Taking a Stand

http://www.archives.state.al.us/teacher/rights/rights1.html

Martin Luther King, An Extraordinary Life, http://projects.seattletimes.com/mlk/?utm_source=redirect&utm_medium=vanityURL&utm_campaign=redirect

Eyes on the Prize, http://www.pbs.org/wgbh//amex/eyesontheprize/

Teaching the Montgomery Bus Boycott, http://civilrightsteaching.org/resource/teaching-the-montgomery-bus-boycott/

Civil Rights, http://www.lbjlibrary.org/exhibits/civil-rights/

DOCUMENTS-BASED QUESTIONS

1. Study the documents below and answer the questions that follow (2009).

DOCUMENT A

Martin Luther King recalling the first morning of the Montgomery bus boycott.

Fortunately, a bus stop was just five feet from the house. We could observe the opening stages [of the boycott] from our front window. And so we waited.

I was in the kitchen, drinking my coffee, when I heard [my wife] Coretta say, 'Martin, Martin, come quickly!'

I put down my cup and ran toward the living room. As I approached the front window, Coretta pointed joyfully to a slowly moving bus: 'Darling, it's empty!'

I could hardly believe what I saw. I knew that the South Jackson line, which runs past our house, carried more Negro passengers than any other line in Montgomery, and that the first bus was usually filled with domestic workers going to their jobs. Would all the other buses follow the pattern that had been set by the first? Eagerly we waited for the next bus. In fifteen minutes it rolled down the street, and like the first it was empty. A third bus appeared, and it too was empty of all but two white passengers.

I jumped in my car and, for almost an hour, I cruised down every major street and examined every passing bus. At the peak of the morning traffic, I saw no more than eight Negro passengers.

Instead of the 60 per cent co-operation we had hoped for, it was becoming apparent that we had reached almost 100 per cent. A miracle had taken place.

C. Carson (ed.), The Autobiography of Martin Luther King Jr.

DOCUMENT B

Joe Azbell, of the *Montgomery Advertiser*, reporting from Holt Street, Montgomery, later the same day.

As I drove along Cleveland Avenue, en route to the Holt Street Baptist Church, Monday night, I could see Negroes by the dozens forming a file, almost soldierly, on the sidewalk. They were going to the protest meeting at the church. They were silent people, bundled in overcoats, performing what appeared to be a ritual. I parked my automobile a block from the church and noted the time was six forty-five. Already cars were strung out for six or seven blocks in each direction. In fact, the area around the church looked like Cramton Bowl at the Alabama state football game. Except for one thing: these people were stony silent.

The passion that fired the meeting was seen as the thousands of voices joined in singing. Then there followed a prayer by a minister. It was interrupted a hundred times by 'yeas' and 'uhhuhs' and 'that's right'. At several points there was an emotionalism that the ministers on the platform recognized could get out of control. The meeting was much like an old-fashioned revival [religious meeting]. It proved beyond a doubt that there was a discipline among Negroes that many whites had doubted. It was almost a military discipline combined with emotion.

S. Burns (ed.), Daybreak of Freedom: The Montgomery Bus Boycott

Black Communities

Religion played an important part in the lives of black communities. **Baptism** and **Methodism** were especially influential in the rural South. Religious leaders and church buildings were important in the **social life** of the community. The civil rights movement was spearheaded by religious leaders such as **Martin Luther King** and **Ralph Abernathy**. When many blacks **migrated** to northern and southern cities, so did their churches. In the huge change in social life from rural to urban, from agriculture to industry, religion provided a constant source of **stability**, in church buildings which were often small and intimate.

The **Islamic tradition** also developed among the black community in northern cities. The **Black Muslims** (Nation of Islam) grew from about 1,000 members in 1946 to about 100,000 members in 1960. They rejected the term **Negro** (they said it was a slave term) for black. They enforced strict rules of behaviour and called for separate black development. Their most outstanding spokesman in the 1960s was **Malcolm X**. But they attracted high-profile members such as **Muhammed Ali**, the world heavyweight boxing champion, and their message spread well beyond their own members. When Malcolm X split with the leadership of the Black Muslims in 1965, he was assassinated. In spite of this crisis, Black Muslims still appealed to sizeable numbers of blacks.

Elijah Muhammad, leader of the Black Muslims, addressing their National Meeting in 1966 with Muhammed Ali beside him.

QUESTIONS

1. What role did religion play among black Americans?
2. How did Islam spread among black Americans?

The Mass Media in Modern American Culture

The spread of many aspects of modern American culture was dependent on the mass media which itself was an integral part of that culture. **Newspapers** and **movies** continued as important elements of the mass media, but the new medium, **television**, became the dominant aspect of the mass media.

KEY CONCEPT
MASS MEDIA is a medium of communication (newspapers, magazines, radio and television) which reaches a large audience or the mass of the people.

Newspapers

Newspaper circulation expanded rapidly in the decades before the Second World War. But in the second half of the twentieth century the coming of television influenced both their **content** and **circulation**. Americans turned more to television for their daily news, so newspapers had to change. There was a greater concentration of ownership as some newspapers were bought out. The number of US cities with more than one daily newspaper dropped. By 1960, over 80 per cent of cities had only one daily newspaper. As a result, the number of newspapers in the country also dropped to about 1,500. While the daily circulation of newspapers remained steady, the population rose by 90 per cent, so that a smaller proportion of people bought newspapers.

Newspaper Circulation (Millions)	
1949	53
1965	59
1995	57

Newspaper Influence

Nevertheless, the influence of newspapers remained strong. Newspaper **investigations** played an important role in monitoring government policy. The *New York Times* broke the story of the Pentagon Papers, which revealed the deceit of American foreign policy in relation to Vietnam. Some years later, Woodward and Bernstein, two journalists working for the *Washington Post*, revealed the corruption at the centre of the Nixon Administration and the conspiracy over the Watergate Affair. The impact of these revelations was to roll back the powers that **presidents** (the imperial presidency) had accumulated over the previous 40 years.

There was no **national daily newspaper** in the US until the 1980s due to the vast size of the country and the different time zones. But early in the decade, *USA Today*, the first daily national newspaper, was published. Its style of short articles and colour made it a success. It was soon followed by the *Wall Street Journal* and the *New York Times* with national editions of their own newspapers using satellite transmission and regional printing.

QUESTIONS

1. How did the popularity of television change the content and circulation of newspapers?
2. What influence did newspapers still have?

Movies

Movies too declined in post-war America. This was partly caused by the **movement of population** from the city centres (where cinemas were located) to the suburbs. But it was also caused by the rise of **television**. (See also Hollywood – The American Dream pp. 413–16)

The film industry, largely based in Hollywood (Los Angeles), responded by building drive-ins, using wide screens, 3-D and stereo sound. The film industry also responded to changes in popular culture. As a commercial operation, it needed to satisfy the mass market. Therefore, new productions were aimed at the popular taste.

Westerns were popular, as were **Cold War** stories. So too were spectacular shows such as *The Ten Commandments* and *Ben Hur*. These reinforced popular images of brave men, gentle women and the evils of Communism. However, some films broke with general consensus, such as the anti-war movie *Paths of Glory*, or *Rebel without a Cause*, which highlighted rebellious youth.

But these failed to reverse the decline. However, these figures underestimate the influence and role of movies in modern American culture. From the 1950s, many movies (films) were rerun on television and some were made for television only. By the 1970s and 1980s, videos and pay TV channels such as **Home Box Office** (HBO) widened the audience and the influence of films.

During this time, Hollywood maintained a **code of conduct** in relation to portraying sex or violence on screens. This was not relaxed or eased until 1966, after which films became more obscene, violent and sexual to reflect the more turbulent 60s. *Bonnie and Clyde*, which featured a couple of young robbers on the run from the law, and *The Wild Bunch* were early examples which reflected the changes.

The 1970s saw the appearance of many young directors, such as **Francis Ford Coppola**, whose *Godfather* series told the story of a Mafia family. These directors followed the pattern of **realistic portrayals** of life. But there were also **action movies**, such as *Star Wars* and *Raiders of the Lost Ark*, which harked back to the earlier decades of the cinema. Very often some of the best movies were directed by **independent directors** outside the Hollywood studio system which controlled the film industry. This, along with new suburban cineplexes (multiple-cinema complexes), helped to attract a growing younger audience back to the cinema.

Television

Television grew **rapidly**. In 1948, fewer than 200,000 families had televisions. But this boomed in the next few years to 15 million by 1952 and 35 million in 75 per cent of homes by 1955. By 1960, 90 per cent of homes had televisions. Colour took over in the 1960s. It was not until the late 1970s that **cable** began to spread – only 12 per cent of homes had cable in 1974, but by 1990 about 70 per cent had cable television.

The use of **satellite transmissions**, beginning with Telstar and Early Bird in the 1960s, made national live broadcasts possible. Their link-up with cable TV gave rise to new channels geared to specific **mass audiences**, such as **MTV** (Music Television) and **CNN** (Cable News Network), which both began in 1981. But some feared that the effect of the wider range of channels specialising in religion, sport and business might lead to a **splintering of society** and reduce the overall national feeling of identity. However, as others pointed out, there was also the likelihood of **oversaturation**. As pop star Bruce Springsteen sang:

> *'I can see by your eyes friend you're just about gone*
> *Fifty-seven channels and nothin' on...'*

Star Wars, one of the most successful action and science fiction movies of the 1970s.

QUESTIONS

1. How did movies react to the rise of television?
2. What themes were common in movies?
3. How did the Hollywood code of conduct change?
4. What different types of movies or genres became popular in the 1970s?

Television and Family Life

Television became the centre of the **family life**, influencing the time of meals, sometimes even what was eaten in the form of TV dinners. Television provided many hours of **leisure** – some said too much because it produced a **lazy lifestyle**. To cater for **mass audiences**, television went for general interest programmes, variety entertainment, quiz shows, sitcoms and talk shows. Some criticised the **mindlessness** of these programmes. Even before television became very popular, the President of Boston University said in 1950, *'If the television rage continues ... we are destined to have a nation of morons.'*

Television affected other aspects of **American life**. Along with movies it reinforced the **image** of the white, suburban, middle-class family. In this way it also reflected the woman's role as a housewife. *'A career is just fine,'* said Debbie Reynolds in *The Tender Trap*, *'but it is no substitute for marriage.'* Television also increased the value and attractiveness of **advertising** and in this way contributed to the growing consumer society. The advertisers *'had a more potent force available for selling purposes. Radio was abandoned like the bones at a barbecue.'*

Since television depended largely on **sponsorship**, the advertisers had a huge influence on what was shown on television. One of the most influential and provocative

Choosing a TV dinner from the freezer: the popularity of television influenced the time of meals.

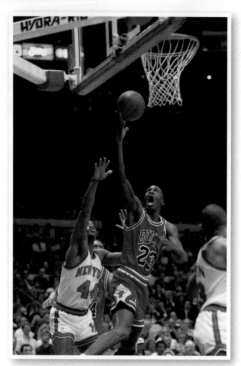

Television raised the profile of sports stars, including Michael Jordan, one of the all-time great basketball players.

current affairs programmes of the early 1950s was changed to an occasional documentary before it was dropped when the sponsoring company withdrew its support.

Televised **sport** was ideal for the mass audiences. Television money paid for more **professionalism** in sport, especially by the 1970s and 1980s, when multi-million-dollar contracts became normal. But it also dictated breaks in sport to cater for advertising. It also raised the profile of black and Hispanic sports stars, such as **Michael Jordan** in basketball and **Muhammed Ali** in boxing. In its entertainment programmes, it had to change gradually to reflect **the racial mix of society** by moving from blacks as servants and slaves to portraying them with a fuller role in society.

Television and Politics

Television also influenced **politics** by shaping **public opinion**. It contributed to the downfall of **Senator Joe McCarthy** when his bullying style was shown up badly by live television broadcasts at the Army-McCarthy hearings in 1954. Television also influenced the outcome of **presidential elections**, particularly the very close 1960 race between John F. Kennedy and Richard Nixon. Kennedy's performance on the first live television presidential debates and his youthful image helped to give him a narrow victory.

It influenced politics in another way. By increasing the **costs of campaigning**, it opened politicians to charges of influence when they got money from businesses to cover their costs. Television could not deal with more complicated problems, so it tended to **simplify issues**. In this way advertisers and political consultants emphasised the importance of **sound bites** – short, snappy comments which caught attention – rather than serious discussion.

Television had a large influence on the progress of the **civil rights movement**. It exposed to national and international audiences police efforts to prevent school desegregation in Little Rock, Arkansas in 1957, **Bull Connor** and his police force's brutal treatment of black protestors in Birmingham, Alabama and the police violence against the Selma-Montgomery marchers. It brought **Martin Luther King** to national prominence as a black spokesman. In this way television encouraged northern liberal white support for civil rights and it provoked government action.

In the 1960s and 1970s, Americans watched the first **living room war** as they saw action from Vietnam. But producers at NBC, ABC and CBS cut out **bloody incidents** from evening news broadcasts. This helped shield the public from the horrors of war. For the most part television gave the **government's version** of the war – that America was winning – until the Tet Offensive in early 1968. After this, television played an important role in the growth of anti-war opinion. Just like the newspapers, television felt betrayed by government misinformation.

KEY CONCEPT
PUBLIC OPINION
The views and attitudes of the people. This is measured in elections or in between elections in opinion polls. In a democracy, political parties have to get elected so they have to pay attention to public opinion.

? QUESTIONS

1. How rapidly did television grow?
2. What changes occurred to television broadcasting in the 1960s and 1970s?
3. What influence did TV have on family life?
4. How did TV influence other aspects of American life?
5. What role did sport play in television?
6. How did TV Influence (i) politics (ii) civil rights campaign (iii) the Vietnam war?

Mass Higher Education

Expansion of Higher Education

There was a **huge interest** in education in post-war America. Dozens of books on education and educational articles were published. This reflected parents' higher aspirations for their children. A more complex and technical world also demanded higher levels of education. The booming economy of the 1950s created a strong demand for college-educated students by corporations providing large salaries.

Aerial view of Harvard University.

Colleges and universities faced problems of coping with the increased demand for places. Enrolment grew because of veterans attending under the **GI Bill of Rights**. It fell off slightly during the Korean War, but grew rapidly again afterwards when the post-war **baby boomers** reached college age. By the time the GI Bill was wound up in 1956, 8 million had benefited. University enrolment also grew because of the **greater prosperity** – college fees grew slower than family incomes. As well as this, full employment made part-time jobs more easily available for students who needed to fund some of their education.

Enrolment went from 1.5 million (16 per cent of the 18–21 age group) in 1945 to 7.9 million (over 40 per cent) in 1970. Of those in college in 1970, 60 per cent of whites and 75 per cent of blacks came from families with no previous experience of higher-level education. In 1970, 26 per cent of workers were college educated; this increased to 46 per cent by 1989. To cope with this increase, the **number** of colleges and universities grew – from 1,500 in 1940 to over 2,000 in 1960, and over 3,000 in 1975.

College and University Numbers (Millions)	
1945	1.5
1950	2.3
1960	3.6
1970	7.9
1975	9.7

Problems

Because of the rapid increase, the **quality** of the universities and colleges varied from the high-flying ones such as **Yale** and **Harvard** to colleges which offered courses in anything. Some even accused these colleges of **dumbing down** education.

Universities also grew in **size** – 39 had over 20,000 students each in 1969. This made them more **bureaucratic** and **impersonal**. This led to conflict between the strict campus regulations about lifestyle and behaviour inherited from olden days and the youth of the 1960s, some influenced by a culture of long hair, untidy clothes, rock music, drugs and the sexual revolution.

This contributed to **mass campus uprisings** in the mid-1960s, partly spurred on by opposition to the Vietnam War and to the **draft**. The first protest – the **Free Speech Movement** at the University of California at Berkley in 1964 – was due to college attempts to restrict political activity on campus. In 1965, 25,000 students marched through Washington to protest against the Vietnam War. The **campus riots** spread over the next few years, with over 200 major university demonstrations in 1968. The climax of the demonstrations was a pitched battle between students and the Chicago police and National Guards outside the Democratic Convention being held in Chicago in late 1968.

There was also more widespread **criticism of American society**, in particular the economic system and the role of the universities as part of it. The **New Left**, in particular **Students for a Democratic Society** (SDS), argued that acceptance of large **research grants** from government and corporate industry posed a threat to independent scholarship. The **Massachusetts Institute of Technology** (MIT), for example, was part of the military-industrial complex. Even *Time* magazine worried about the development. *'Is the military about to take over US science lock, stock and barrel?'*

The universities responded to these criticisms by relaxing entry requirements and changing courses to reflect changes in society, such as introducing black studies and women's studies, as well as abolishing officer training courses.

(See also Chapter 29, 'The Anti-war Movement', p. 366.)

James Meredith tying to gain admission to University of Mississippi

Racial Conflict

Universities also became the scene of **racial conflict**. In southern universities, blacks, like James Meredith at the University of Mississippi, had to battle to gain entry to all-white universities. In other places, some colleges and universities had **special admission policies** for blacks and other minority groups in the 1960s. This was part of the government's **affirmative action** programme which increased black enrolment. However, it also caused a white complaint of **reverse discrimination** that they were failing to gain admission to university because of special schemes for blacks, and not on the basis of merit or ability. In 1978, a white Californian student challenged his failure to get into medical school because of the admissions policy. The Supreme Court ruled in his favour, and declared that **other factors** along with ethnic and racial background had to be considered in admissions policies.

There was a **decline** in student political activity after 1973. This was due to the ending of the Vietnam War and the draft and also to worsening economic conditions, which concentrated minds on jobs. The reduction in federal support, higher costs of courses and the fact that a degree did not guarantee a good job reduced enrolments. As a result of cutbacks in colleges, some even closed.

? QUESTIONS

1. Why did higher education expand in the 1950s and 1960s?
2. What problems did universities experience as they expanded?
3. What did critics say about the role of universities?
4. How did universities become centres of racial conflict?

HOMEWORK EXERCISES

ORDINARY LEVEL

1. Read this extract on Billy Graham and answer the following questions.

   *Graham gained further exposure and stature through nationally publicised crusades in Los Angeles, Boston, Washington, and other major cities from 1949 to 1952, and through his **Hour of Decision** radio programme, begun in 1950. Stunningly successful months-long revivals in London (1954) and New York (1957), triumphant tours of the Continent and the Far East, the founding of **Christianity Today** magazine (1956), the launching of nationwide television broadcasts on ABC (1957), and a public friendship with President Dwight Eisenhower and Vice-President Richard Nixon firmly established him as the acknowledged standard-bearer for evangelical Christianity. As Graham's prestige and influence grew, particularly among 'mainline' (non-evangelical) Christians, he drew criticism from fundamentalists who felt his cooperation with churches affiliated with the National and World Council of Churches signalled a compromise with the corrupting forces of modernism.*

   Source: Billy Graham, 1918– , http://www.christianitytoday.com/history/people/evangelistsandapologists/billy-graham.html

A. (i) In what cities did Graham hold crusades?
   (ii) How did his radio programme, *Hour of Decision*, help him?
   (iii) How was he established as 'the acknowledged standard-bearer of evangelical Christianity'?
   (iv) Why did fundamentalists disagree with Billy Graham?
   (v) Explain 'evangelicals' and 'fundamentalists'.

B. Write a **paragraph** on one of the following.
   (i) Religion in modern American culture.
   (ii) The role of newspapers, movies and television in the US mass media during the post-war decades.

C. Write a **long answer** on Billy Graham and the religious revival in the US.

HIGHER LEVEL

2. What was the impact of the post-war religious revival on modern American society?

3. What was the impact of the mass media on modern American society?

4. What was the impact of the expansion of higher education on modern American society?

5. What was the contribution of religion and/or the mass media to modern American culture? (2013)

In this section, you should understand:
• The advances in military technology.
• The advances in space technology.
• The advances in information technology.
• How advances in military and information technology helped space technology.
• Case Study: The First Moon Landing, 1969.

Advances in Military Technology

In the second half of the twentieth century, America led most advances in military technology. Its involvement in a series of wars – hot and cold – its powerful economy, advanced research and technology, its superpower status and public opinion have all contributed to continuous advances in military technology:

- The **wars** provided the reason for developing weapons and the final testing of them.
- The **economy** provided the resources to fund the development of military technology.
- **Research and development** came up with new ideas and built them.
- **Superpower status** needed to be maintained.
- American **public opinion** supported the strengthening of the military.

> **KEY CONCEPT**
> **TECHNOLOGICAL DEVELOPMENT** is the application or use of scientific discoveries in industry.

Nuclear Weapons

The most spectacular and dangerous advances in military technology occurred in **nuclear weaponry**. Already during the Second World War, the US had developed the atomic bomb in the **Manhattan Project**. When they dropped the bombs on Hiroshima and Nagasaki in August 1945, the atomic age truly began.

These bombs were delivered on board **B-29 bombers**. In the post-war era, the US began to develop more powerful planes, particularly after the USSR exploded its own atomic bomb in 1949. Now the US needed a plane that could attack the USSR directly. This became the **B-52 Stratofortress**, which entered service in 1955. The B-52 was the backbone of Strategic Air Command for the next 35 years, with 650 in operation at its peak in 1963. It had a dual role both in delivering atomic bombs and in conventional bombing, as in Vietnam.

At the same time, President Truman gave the go-ahead for a crash programme to develop the **hydrogen bomb** (H-bomb), largely in response to the USSR's A-bomb and to counteract the possibility that the USSR would develop a hydrogen bomb itself. **Computer technology** played a key role in the development of nuclear bombs. The US tested its first H-bomb in the Pacific Ocean in 1952. The explosion sent a radioactive cloud 25 miles into the sky and developed a crater one mile wide.

Rockets

The development of **rockets** gave much greater precision to nuclear warfare. They were also much more difficult for the enemy forces to shoot down. US rocket development was boosted enormously when the best German staff working on rockets of the Second World War, and headed by **Werner von Braun**, surrendered to US troops. The US also captured some of the rockets (the V2s), which they tested in America between 1945 and 1951.

The US used their experience of these rockets to develop short- and medium-range missiles such as the **Snark** and **Corporal**. These were developed to supplement the long-range bomber, not replace it. By the 1960s, the US had replaced earlier rockets with the **Pershing**, which had a range of 400 miles (640 kilometres) and was based in Europe. They could all carry either nuclear or conventional warheads.

ICBM

The development of **intercontinental ballistic missiles** (ICBMs) began in the mid-1950s. President Eisenhower speeded up the arms race with his preference for nuclear missiles over conventional ones. He said nuclear weapons gave *'more bang for the buck'*. The development of the H-bomb, the improved rocket guidance systems and new rocket fuels made building the ICBMs possible. The launching of the **Russian** *Sputnik* into space made it necessary. Now Americans feared the Russians would attack from space.

The first ICBM rocket was the **Atlas**, launched in 1958, followed by **Titan** and later by the **Minuteman**, which could be fired from an **underground silo**. Further development of the Minuteman gave it a longer range (7,000 miles) and **multiple warheads** (MIRV).

At the same time, the navy developed the **Polaris missile**, which could be fired from nuclear-powered submarines. By the 1970s, these were being replaced by the **Poseidon**, with a longer range and carrying MIRV warheads.

A Polaris missile being tested off the coast of Florida in 1963.

Warning Systems

The similar development of Soviet planes and missiles made it necessary for the US to develop an **early warning system** to detect an attack and to initiate counter-attacks. The US worked with Canada to develop the **DEW** (Distant Early Warning) system – a series of radar stations stretched across northern Canada and Alaska. The US also developed **airborne search radars** such as AWACS (Airborne Warning and Control System), which are constantly in the air. In 1960, they launched the first **reconnaissance satellite**, SAMOS, which provided early warning.

In the 1980s, President Reagan announced his **Strategic Defence Initiative** (SDI) – popularly known as **Star Wars** – which would be able to defend US territory against Soviet attack by launching intercepting missiles from space. However, the huge costs involved in developing such a missile defence system ($1,000 billion) and the end of the Cold War meant that this was not developed by the end of the 1980s.

Conventional Technology

In spite of President Eisenhower's wish in the 1950s to cut back on spending on conventional weapons, these were not neglected either. In fact, the awesome power of nuclear bombs made their use unlikely and the US was involved in a number of conventional wars – the Korean War, 1950–3 and the Vietnam War in the 1960s, for example.

QUESTIONS

1. What factors influenced advances in US military technology?
2. How were atomic bombs delivered?
3. How important was the B-52?
4. What was the significance of the H-bomb?
4. Why were rockets developed?
5. What were ICBMs? How and why were ICBMs developed?
6. What warning systems were developed?

See pp. 340–47 for US relations with the Soviet Union

To cope with this kind of fighting, the US continued with the development of planes, a variety of missiles such as air-to-air or surface-to-air, tanks, reconnaissance aircraft, chemical and biological warfare, aircraft carriers and submarines. In spite of the huge advances in military technology, **tactics and strategy** remained much as they were, and these weapons were used in the same way as in the Second World War. As well as this, the **Vietnam War** showed that superior technology did not guarantee victory in fighting unconventional **guerrilla warfare**.

Air War

The development of the **jet engine** at the end of the Second World War increased the speed and range of aircraft. Fighter aircraft were equipped with missiles to attack enemy aircraft, but also other missiles to attack tanks, troops, fuel depots and airfields. These aircraft included the McDonnell F-4 (1958) and the Northrop F-5 (1959). By the late 1950s, supersonic air-to-air missiles such as the **Sidewinder**, **Phoenix** and **Falcon** were developed to cope with faster aircraft.

Bomber aircraft were also developed with greater range and accuracy, including the **B-29 Superfortress** (1943) and the **B-52 Stratofortress** (1955). They were used in the **Korean War** and in **Vietnam**, where they **carpet-bombed** areas of the Vietnamese jungle. But they had to wait for the development of computer-controlled, radar-guided bombs in the 1990s to increase their accuracy and effectiveness.

Reconnaissance aircraft were also developed, especially the supersonic **U-2**, which was involved in spying over the USSR and also over Cuba before and during the Cuban Missile Crisis (see pp. 345–47). In more recent decades, **drones** or **pilotless aircraft** were developed for spying.

Helicopters

The **helicopter** was one of the most significant developments in military technology. After their use in the Second World War, helicopters came into their own in the **Korean War**. They were used for scouting and troop-carrying, as well as search and rescue. Their ability to evacuate casualties from particularly difficult countryside was given as a reason for the reduced death rate. In the Vietnam War, **helicopter gunships** became symbolic of the action there. They were fast, heavily armed and used in support of ground troops. However, they were also **noisy** and the Vietcong could hear them coming some distance away.

To combat the power and speed of enemy aircraft, **surface-to-air missiles** were developed to replace conventional artillery. The US army and navy developed separate types – the army developed the **Hercules**, which had a range up to 85 miles, while the navy developed the **Terrier** and the **Sea Sparrow**. But as well as these, the **Redeye**, a shoulder-mounted missile, was developed for ground troops. All these used various methods such as radar and heat seeking to guide their missile on to the target.

Aircraft Carriers

The growing significance of air war increased the importance of **aircraft carriers**. These gave mobility and rapid response to cater for small and larger-scale wars. The advent of jet aeroplanes after the Second World War meant that aircraft carriers had to be larger and stronger. It also led to the development of the **catapult** (a British device) to cater for larger and faster planes.

Carriers, such as the Valley Forge, played crucial roles in the **Korean War**. Fighter planes took off from carriers based in the Sea of Japan to bomb North Korean forces. Other carriers were used on blockade duty off the west coast of North Korea. Carriers also were vital in the **Vietnam War**. They were deployed in the South China Sea and supported combat operations over South Vietnam and bombing operations over North Vietnam. The fighter aircraft from aircraft carriers *Saratoga* or

Aircraft carriers gave increased mobility to the US armed forces, who could respond rapidly to small or large conflicts.

Independence, for example, supported troops on the ground, attacked enemy troops or bombed military targets near Hanoi.

The *Enterprise* (1961), a nuclear-powered aircraft carrier, was the most powerful of the new carriers, with great speed, manouverability and endurance. It was equipped with a wide range of military technology to meet the needs of modern warfare – radar, missile guidance, guided missiles and sophisticated communications equipment. She also saw action during the **Vietnam War**.

Land War

Tank development proceeded similarly to the Second World War. The essential design of the tank remained the same, but there were significant improvements in engines, suspension and firepower. By the 1960s and 1970s the **M60** and **MBT-70** tanks had gun launchers to fire missiles as well as conventional shells.

To cope with the vast range and power of the new weaponry developed against them, the **soldiers** also had improved military technology. Apart from the Redeye missile, they were equipped with heavy machine guns, anti-tank grenade launchers, recoilless rifles with armour-piercing bullets and night-viewing glasses. Soldiers also had to be equipped to meet new threats from **chemical** and **biological** warfare.

Permanent War Economy

The huge advances in US military technology from 1945 onwards cost a great deal of money. Indeed, so much money was spent on weapons and the military that some claimed America was a **permanent war economy**. On average, 10 per cent of national income was spent each year on such technology.

Most of the money was spent on a small number of companies – General Dynamics, Lockheed, IBM, Boeing and a few others. Their manufacturing plants were located largely in the states of the **Sun Belt** in the south and south-West of the US, from California to Florida.

This led to the development of what **President Eisenhower** called the **military-industrial complex** – the link between the Defense Department, industries, certain states and their political representatives. He warned about the danger of the military-industrial complex and its influence on government policy, in particular its interest in pushing for an aggressive foreign policy. (See Chapter 31, p. 384.)

QUESTIONS

1. What was conventional military technology?
2. Why did the US need to develop such technology?
3. Was it always successful?
4. What developments took place in air warfare?
5. What role did aircraft carriers play?
6. How did tanks change? How did soldiers cope with tanks?

KEY CONCEPT
MILITARY-INDUSTRIAL COMPLEX was the combination of the armed forces, the politicians who supported them and the industries who supplied them. They had a strong influence on government decisions.

QUESTION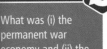

What was (i) the permanent war economy and (ii) the military-industrial complex?

Advances in Space Technology

Rockets and Soviet Competition

A Russian postcard celebrates Yuri Gagarin's successful voyage as the first man in space.

During the 1950s there were considerable developments in **rockets**. But these were mainly to power nuclear missiles. Then, in 1957, the Russians sent a modified rocket into space called *Sputnik*. In contrast, the Americans' first attempt to send a rocket into space – the *Vanguard* – was destroyed by an explosion on its launch pad a few months after the *Sputnik's* success. According to the press, it was a case of '*Flopnik*' and '*Kaputnik*'.

This – and later Russian **firsts**, such as Yuri Gagarin becoming the first man in space – shocked the Americans. They had believed that American technology was superior to the Russians' and the Russian successes were a severe blow to American **morale**. They also saw the Russian successes as a danger to national security, a very important consideration in the middle of the **Cold War**.

NASA (National Aeronautics and Space Administration) was set up in 1958 to catch up to, and beat, the Russian space technology. The Americans launched their first satellite, *Explorer I*, also in the same year. In 1961, President Kennedy, inspired by Cold War competition and Yuri Gagarin's success, promised that the Americans would have a man on the moon '*before the decade is out*'. During the 1960s the Americans spent $25 billion to achieve that aim.

Mercury and Gemini Projects

This was done in stages. First the **Mercury Project** sent Americans into space. The first was **Alan Shepard** in 1961, a month after Gagarin. This flight lasted 15 minutes. Five more flights followed, including *Freedom 7* in February 1962, in which **John Glenn** orbited Earth three times.

In the **Gemini Project**, two-man flights were organised to test **rendezvous** and **docking** techniques – this included space walks. The US also used the **Surveyor** space flights to test soft landings on the moon, as well as photographing and testing the surface. Then a series of **Lunar Orbiter** craft photographed possible landing sites for manned flights to the moon. By now American technology had overtaken the Russians'.

Rockets and Space Technology

The developments in rocket technology helped space technology. Rockets developed as missiles were adapted to send satellites into space. **Atlas rockets** powered the Mercury Project to put Americans into space. **Titan rockets** powered the Gemini Project of two-man flights. **Saturn rockets** were specially designed for the Apollo Missions to land on the moon, orbit and return. (See also p. 474)

Man on the Moon

The next stage was the development of a **three-man spacecraft**. This was the **Apollo Mission**. In 1968, *Apollo 8* made a successful manned orbit of the moon, sending back

---

(?) QUESTIONS

1. How did rocket technology help the space programme?
2. How and why did the US and USSR compete in the space race?
3. What role did NASA play in the US space programme?

Computers and the Moon Landing
The *Apollo 11 mission* to the moon in 1969 had two onboard computers, one in the command module, the other in the lunar module. They were the first computers to use integrated chips. They were used for navigation and controlling the engines. The control centre in Houston used mainframe computers.

television pictures for millions of viewers at Christmas. Later missions tested the operation of the lunar module. In July 1969, *Apollo 11*, with **Neil Armstrong, 'Buzz' Aldrin** and **Michael Collins** on board, lifted off from Cape Kennedy, Florida for the moon. On 20 July 1969, Neil Armstrong stepped out of the lunar module, *Eagle*, to become the first man to set foot on the moon. (See Case Study: The First Moon Landing, 1969 pp. 473–83)

Later Apollo missions continued with further **landings** – in some of which the astronauts used a moon buggy to get around – and scientific investigations of the moon until 1972.

- *Apollo 12*, later in 1969, collected soil samples from the moon, took photographs and set up scientific experiments.

- *Apollo 13* took off in 1970 but ran into difficulties when an oxygen tank burst. The astronauts had to cancel their planned landing on the moon. Instead they had to use the power of the lunar module to bring them back to Earth.

- *Apollo 14* (1971) carried out the mission intended for Apollo 13. They landed in a rugged part of the moon and set up scientific experiments and collected rock samples.

- **The crew of *Apollo 15*** (1971) spent almost three days on the moon. They used a **moon buggy** to travel away from their spacecraft. They collected some of the oldest samples of moon rock and set up further experiments. They also launched a **lunar mini-satellite** to send back data about the moon's environment. This was the first crew which did not have to be quarantined.

- *Apollo 16* (1972) and *Apollo 17* (also 1972) followed the same pattern as previous moon visits.

- *Apollo 17* was the last of the missions to the moon.

Space advances during the Johnson Presidency

- First American space walk
- First use of fuel cells for electrical power
- First space rendezvous between two spacecraft
- First space docking
- Unmanned surveyor rockets to the moon to test landing
- Testing Saturn rocket and re-entry shield
- First manned flight around the moon

Timeline on Advances in Space Technology	
—1948	US launched captured V2 rocket
—1957	USSR launched the first ICBM
—	USSR launched *Sputnik 1*; Space Race began
—	USSR launched *Sputnik 2* with a dog, Laika, on board
—	Failure of US *Vanguard* rocket launch
—1958	US launched *Explorer 1*
—	NASA established to organise US space programme
—	First US ICBM launched, *Atlas*
—1960	Launch of first US weather satellite
—1961	USSR sent first man into space, Yuri Gagarin, in Vostok 1 and orbited Earth
—	US sent first American, Alan Shepherd, into space in Freedom 7 in a sub-orbital flight
—	President Kennedy's speech on sending an American to the moon and back 'before the decade is out'
—1962	John Glenn orbited Earth three times
	Telstar, US communications satellite, beams first live transatlantic telecast
—1962–63	Further Mercury missions
—1963	First woman in space, Valentina Tereshkova of the USSR
—1966–68	Star Trek series on television
—1966	First soft landing on the moon by USSR
—1967	The Outer Space Treaty
—1969	Apollo 11 mission on the first Moon landing
—1969–72	Further Apollo missions (12-17) to the moon; successful except for *Apollo 13*
—1971–86	USSR first space station programme
—1973	Skylab, first US space station
—1975	*Viking* missions to Mars
—1977	*Voyager* missions to other planets
—1981	First successful flight by space shuttle, *Columbia*
—1986	Explosion of space shuttle, *Challenger*, stopped use of space shuttles for 3 years

THE SPACE RACE AND THE COLD WAR

Cold War rivalry and suspicion, competition between Democrats and Republicans, public opinion and the strength of the US economy were **important factors** in influencing the Space Race.

In the mid-1950s, President **Eisenhower** had little interest in having a space race but he was forced to set up NASA due to Cold War rivalry and the work of Lyndon Johnson.

After the success of Sputnik 1 in October 1957, **Lyndon Johnson**, then Democratic Senate Majority Leader, set up hearings of the Senate Armed Services Committee on US unpreparedness for space. Johnson and his Democratic senators laid the blame for US failure on the Republican Eisenhower. Johnson argued that the country 'that would conquer outer space would dominate the world of the future'. The 'Free World Must Control Space, Johnson tells Senate Group', announced *The Washington Post*. Johnson said the control of space was the first aim of the Soviet Union's national policy. Johnson's campaign led to the founding of **NASA** (the National Aeronautics and Space Administration) in 1958 and to a huge increase in spending on the space programme.

The **Presidential election campaign in 1960** heightened Cold War tensions. **Johnson** warned that the Russians 'will be dropping bombs on us from space like kids dropping rocks onto cars from freeway overpasses'. **John F. Kennedy** added to the fear by stating that the country that controlled space would control Earth, like in the past control of the seas gave control of the continents.

This was reinforced by the statements of **Khrushchev**, the Soviet leader, who said that 'Russian space successes and American space failures proved the superiority of Communism over capitalism, as well as the inevitability of Communism's world triumph through the process of peaceful economic and technological competition.' (quoted in the *New York Times*, July 1969)

However, when **Kennedy** became President, he had little interest in the space programme. He put **Johnson**, now the Vice President, in charge of it, and Johnson continued to work on developing the space programme. He used his influence, along with others, to ensure that the **Manned Spacecraft Centre** was based in **Houston**, Texas, his home state.

Soviet success in sending **Yuri Gagarin** into space in April 1961 (and the Bay of Pigs disaster soon after) forced Kennedy to change his mind on space quickly, with Johnson's support. He announced a huge increase in spending on the space budget and made his promise, 'before the decade is out, of landing a man on the moon and safely returning him to earth' (May 1961). US public opinion also supported this plan.

When Johnson became President, he continued his support for the space programme. During his Presidency the US made huge strides in preparing for landing men on the moon and returning them safely to earth (see box). He renamed Cape Canaveral Space Centre the **Kennedy Space Centre**.

However, Johnson's **Great Society** and the **Vietnam War** forced him to reduce space rivalry, and cut spending.

By now also, public opinion saw 'reaching the moon before Russia does' as much less important than earlier in the decade. With each successful step in the Mercury, Gemini and Apollo programmes, the US caught up to and passed out the Soviet technological lead, so the people were **less afraid** of the Soviet threat from space.

Johnson got agreement with the Soviet Union on the **Outer Space Treaty** in 1967. This said that there would be no nuclear weapons in space, and neither country would claim ownership of the Moon, regardless of which country got there first. Johnson provided enough resources for NASA to continue its moon planning but after that spending on space development decreased.

Some historians claim that 'a single man, Lyndon Baines Johnson, 'LBJ', is primarily responsible for both starting and ending 'The Space Race'.' (Wasser)

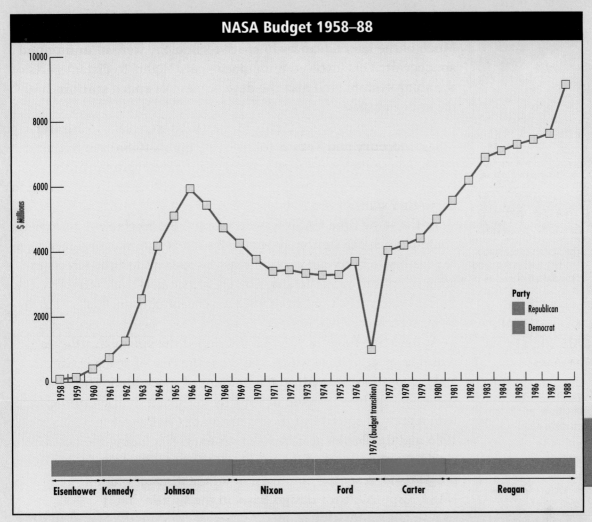

NASA Budget 1958–88

Party
Republican
Democrat

Eisenhower | Kennedy | Johnson | Nixon | Ford | Carter | Reagan

1976 (budget transition)

What conclusions can you draw from the graph on NASA's budget?

'LET'S SEE, WE'VE GOT TO GET SOME OF YOU SLIMMED DOWN'

ENGELHARDT

ARMS
SUBSIDIES
SPACE
WELFARE
BUDGET REDUCTIONS

Source: The Philadelphia Inquirer, 9 June 1968

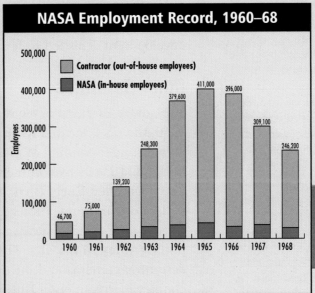

NASA Employment Record, 1960–68

Contractor (out-of-house employees)
NASA (in-house employees)

Year	Contractor
1960	46,700
1961	75,000
1962	139,200
1963	248,300
1964	379,600
1965	411,000
1966	396,000
1967	309,100
1968	246,200

Compare this graph with the graph on NASA's budget. What conclusions can you draw?

Source: NASA Historical Data Book

The Skylab space station orbits the Earth during the Skylab 4 mission in 1973–74.

IMPACT OF ADVANCES IN SPACE TECHNOLOGY ON US SOCIETY

- Developed **new technologies** which benefitted society
- Boost to **US economy**, jobs, sun belt, military-industrial complex
- Increased US **national debt** and **budget deficit**
- Resources taken from **other government programmes**
- **The Moon Landing – Victory** in the Space Race
- **Satellites** for weather forecasting, communications, spying, GPS for navigation; conduct of war; study Earth/ozone layer/rainforests
- Public debate on **arguments for and against** space exploration
  - **For:** victory for capitalism over Communism; undermined Soviet Communism; boosted economy through increased government spending; more than 400,000 employed; boost for scientists; technological spin-offs bettered society
  - **Against:** Too expensive, took resources from other government programmes which could improve society – health care, education, housing; done to boost politicians; space debris from older satellites

Space Stations and Space Shuttles

Much of the later advances in space technology were in **unmanned spacecraft**. This involved unmanned space flights to distant parts of the **solar system**, and also the development of **space stations** and the **space shuttle**.

A succession of space flights in the 1970s were sent to **Jupiter**, **Mars**, **Mercury** and **Venus**, followed by flights to **Saturn** in the 1980s. These flights were mostly scientific investigations of the surface and atmosphere of these planets, with the main aim being to try to find signs of life.

At the same time NASA was developing the **Skylab** programme to maintain a space station above the Earth. Skylab was designed as a laboratory to carry out experiments in space, to test the effects of long periods of weightlessness on crew members and to observe the sun. Skylab was launched in 1973 and eventually crashed to Earth in western Australia in 1979.

At the same time the US also developed the **space shuttle** – a reusable space vehicle which could cut the cost of space research and exploration and reduce the amount of space litter. The first successful flight was made in 1981 by the space shuttle *Columbia* with a crew of seven. But the explosion of *Challenger* in January 1986 and the deaths of its seven astronauts (including the first US civilian in space) raised doubts about the organisation of the space programme. A special commission on the disaster did not hold NASA responsible for design flaws in the shuttle, but it recommended that the agency be reorganised. By the end of the 1980s there was declining public interest and declining support from Congress for space flights. **Budget cutbacks** limited research and development. This led to fewer manned space flights.

Other Satellites

The advances in space technology led to other developments. In 1960, the US launched its first **weather satellite**, which gave much greater understanding of global weather patterns. This was followed in the mid-1960s by commercial **communications satellites**; the first was called **Early Bird**. These provided a faster, worldwide system of communications by television, radio and phone.

In military and security, the US competed with the Russians by putting **spies in the sky**. These were satellites which used high-definition cameras and infrared technology to survey each other's country in great detail. But President Reagan's plan for the **Strategic Defense Initiative** (SDI), or Star Wars as it was called, was too ambitious for its time. This would have developed a space technology to intercept incoming Soviet missiles by exploding them before they reached America.

Advances in Information Technology

Information technology (IT) is the equipment and methods used to handle information. The information is collected, processed and stored. As the twentieth century progressed, more and more information needed to be handled to organise a more complex society. The development of the computer was central to the new information age and the development of modern information technology.

The needs of the **American government** and **military** in the middle of the century were crucial to the development of the computer. Their need to handle vast amounts of data concerning atomic weapons gave a spurt to the development of the early computers. They linked with **business** (mostly IBM) and **universities** to design and build the first US computers.

This was the ENIAC, the first general purpose computer, which was based at the US Proving Ground in Maryland. It weighed 30 tonnes and it was 8 feet high, 3 feet deep and 100 feet long.

First Computers

Computers developed rapidly during and after the Second World War. **Mark 1** was developed in 1943 through co-operation between Harvard University and IBM (International Business Machines). But this used **mechanical switches** to do its calculations. Much faster was **ENIAC**, which was the first **all-electronic computer**. It was developed for the army for calculations of thermonuclear fusion. Both machines were huge – ENIAC weighed 30 tonnes – and were very expensive. They needed a team of operators to work them.

One of those who contributed to the development of computers was **John von Neumann**, a Hungarian-born mathematician working in the US. He devised the logic which became the basis for the **mainframe computers**, particularly those built by IBM. His work led to the development of **EDVAC**, which influenced the building of IBM mainframe computers. They next developed **UNIVAC 1**, which became the first commercially available computer. It was used to count the US Census in 1951 and the presidential election results in 1952.

Invention of the Transistor

However, computers were still very large. This began to change after the invention of the **transistor** in 1947 by **William Shockley** at Bell Telephone Research Laboratories. It was mostly made of silicon and it replaced the electronic valves, produced no heat, eliminated miles of wiring, was very small and cheap to produce. In 1958, Seymour Cray designed the **first fully transistorised** computer. IBM produced its own version a year later.

The spread of this new form of information technology was gradual. Twenty computers were sold in 1954, but this rose to 1,000 in 1957 and 2,000 in 1960.

Further advances in integrated circuits in the early 1960s led to the development of the **microchip**. Now the entire workings of the computer could be put on a few

QUESTIONS (?)

1. What is information technology?
2. What led to the development of computers?
3. What were the main steps in the development of computers?
4. What was the importance of the invention of (i) the transistor and (ii) the microchip?

microchips. Smaller, personal computers became possible with the development of **Intel's microprocessor** in 1971. (See also The Role of Computers in the Moon Landing p. 477)

Personal Computers

The first **personal computer** (PC) was produced in 1975, but its use was mainly confined to electronic engineers. Two years later, however, **Steve Jobs** and **Steve Wozniak** introduced the **Apple II**, which brought personal computers within the range of small business, families and schools. Shortly afterwards, **IBM** entered the personal computer market and the market expanded dramatically in the 1980s. The development of new operating systems, begun by Apple and later spreading to others, in particular **Bill Gates** of **Microsoft**, made computers much more user friendly. The number of computers rose quickly from less than 2 million to over 65 million in 1991.

Computer Industry

By 1958, the US produced about $1 billion worth of computer equipment. Ten years later, this had grown to almost $5 billion, and to $17 billion by 1978. This was all part of the move away from heavy manufacturing to the **high-technology industries**, which also included genetic engineering, lasers and fibre optics. In 1952, 50 per cent of workers were employed in manufacturing industry; by 1992 this had fallen to 20 per cent.

By 1990, the US had the **largest computer industry** in the world, employing 1 million people with a revenue of $100 billion. Companies such as Dell, Compaq, Apple and Microsoft dominated hardware and software production. It also had the greatest number of computers – 50 million – half of the world's computers, compared to Japan with 11 per cent and Europe with about 25 per cent.

However, the industry split between the high-cost **research and development** side and the **production** side. Research and development was largely confined to **core areas** in the US – Silicon Valley in California, the Route 128 corridor around Boston and the Research Triangle in North Carolina. On the other hand, much of the routine production and assembly functions were transferred to **peripheral locations**, particularly in Asia. This is how **multinationals** in information technology have developed. In this way, they have increased the gap between the **haves** and the **have-nots** on a worldwide scale.

The Internet

In 1969, fear of a Cold War nuclear attack resulted in the beginning of the **internet**. This was the Defense Department's Advanced Research Project Agency (**ARPANET**) to allow military scientists to communicate over computers in the event of a nuclear explosion. It was expanded in 1986 to the National Science Foundation to include researchers at American universities. By the late 1980s, the **internet**, as it had become known, was widely used by businesses and individuals. But the huge expansion of the internet, or the World Wide Web as part of it, did not come until the early 1990s.

Impact of Information Technology

- By the late 1980s, computers had made a huge impact on **all aspects of American life**, from home to shopping and from work to entertainment.

- They played an important role in the **Moon Landing** (p. 477).

- They caused a rapid **rise in productivity**. Indeed, they caused a debate about the danger of **technological unemployment**.

- Some point to the fact that the Fortune 500 companies in the US shed over **4 million jobs** in the 1980s. These used information technology to replace workers with machines. At the same time, these companies' sales and assets grew, and their **chief executives** increased their own income by six times. This increased the gap between the rich (haves) and poor (have-nots) within America during the 1980s.

- Others argue that the fears that computer technology would replace people are exaggerated. They say that while some industries have declined, others have replaced them.

- An **example** of how the computer and information technology industries have made many people extremely **wealthy** is Bill Gates of Microsoft. Gates dropped out of college, founded Microsoft and produced the **MS-DOS** and Windows operating systems for IBM computers. By the age of 32 in 1987, he was worth $1 billion.

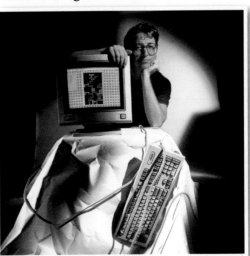

Bill Gates, founder of Microsoft, which invented the operating system running most personal computers.

- Information technology had a major influence in the **globalisation** of industry, finance and culture. Computers speeded up communications and the transfer of money and made it easier to transmit television channels worldwide.

- There was a **greater concentration of industry** because of the expense of the new technology, which only the largest corporations could afford.

- Computer technology gave rise to a debate about the **invasion of privacy** and **dangers to democracy** of storing information on people. The US government passed a law to protect the privacy of individuals.

KEY CONCEPT

GLOBALISATION is the spread of institutions, organisations and culture on a worldwide or global scale. It is usually associated with the spread of trade and industry by large companies or corporations to many different countries. Goods, services and culture gradually become the same in all parts of the world.

QUESTIONS

1. How was the personal computer developed? How did the computer industry grow?
2. How did the computer industry divide? How and why was the internet developed?
3. How did developments in information technology influence American life?

HOMEWORK EXERCISES

ORDINARY LEVEL

1. In this edited extract from his memoir, *A Reporter's Life* (1997), the veteran American reporter, Walter Cronkite, recalls the early days of the US space project. Read it and answer the questions which follow. (2016)

> The American test site was set up on a remote snake-infested swamp called Cape Canaveral on the Florida coast. As the test site grew, so did the nearby villages until they resembled every boomtown ever – cheap hotels, bars, girlie joints, their wares proclaimed in gaudy neon.
>
> A spirit of high adventure permeated the place. While the rest of the population dealt with a succession of problems – civil rights, assassination, Vietnam – everyone at the Cape was looking up, up into the skies.
>
> Source: Walter Cronkite, *A Reporter's Life* (New York: Ballantine Books, 1997).

A. (i) Where was the test site set up?
   (ii) What problems occupied the rest of the American population?
   (iii) Mention one way in which the villages resembled boomtowns.
   (iv) How is it suggested that there was an air of optimism at Cape Canaveral?
   (v) Why was the 1969 Moon landing an important event?
   (vi) How useful and reliable are memoirs as sources for historians?

B. Write a **paragraph** on one of the following.
   (i) Advances in military technology
   (ii) Advances in information technology

C. Write a **long answer** on the following.
   (i) How technology influenced the development of space exploration in the US from the 1940s to the 1980s.
   (ii) How did the United States achieve a Moon landing in 1969 and what was its importance?

HIGHER LEVEL

2. How and why was there a huge expansion in military technology in the US from 1945 to the 1980s?

3. What was the impact of advances in rockets in the US on the post-war decades?

4. What was the importance of one or more of the following: **(i)** McCarthyism **(ii)** the Moon landing, 1969 **(iii)** developments in information technology? (2006)

5. During the period 1945–89, what advances were made by the Americans in military, space and information technology? (2015)

Introduction

The Russian space successes in the late 1950s and early 1960s surprised and shocked the US. The country was going through its greatest economic boom and its technology appeared to be well in advance of all other countries. Then the Russians proved otherwise.

To counter the Soviet success, the US set up **NASA** (National Aeronautics and Space Administration) in 1958 to take charge of US space exploration. Now the space race became fully part of Cold War rivalry. It forced **President Kennedy** to commit the US to landing a man on the Moon before the end of the 1960s. (See The Space Race and the Cold War, p. 466) (Source 1)

SOURCE 1 – MAN ON THE MOON

'...if we are to win the battle that is now going on around the world between freedom and tyranny, the dramatic achievements in space which occurred in recent weeks should have made clear to us all, as did the Sputnik in 1957, the impact of this adventure on the minds of men everywhere, who are attempting to make a determination of which road they should take ... I believe this nation should commit itself to achieving the goal, before this decade is out, of landing a man on the Moon and returning him safely to earth.'

President Kennedy's Special Message to Congress, 25 May 1961

What does President Kennedy mean by the phrase 'the minds of men everywhere, who are attempting to make a determination of which road they should take'?

? CASE STUDY QUESTIONS

1. How did the USSR space success influence the US?
2. What did Kennedy say about landing a man on the Moon?

The Apollo Programme

The Apollo Program was developed to land the first man on the Moon. The first six Apollo missions were unmanned. They were used to test the giant **Saturn** rocket. But soon after, it hit disaster. In 1967, three astronauts in *Apollo 7* died when a fire broke out in the spacecraft on the launch pad. The next three missions successfully tested various aspects of the Moon journey:

- *Apollo 8* undertook an important mission in December 1968 by orbiting around the Moon and returning.
- *Apollo 9* practised docking the command ship and the lunar module in Earth's orbit.
- *Apollo 10* went to the Moon to test the lunar module further by flying to within 15 kilometres of the Moon's surface before rejoining the command module.

US military, space and information technology

Cold War rivalry/ political decisions/ public opinion influencing the Moon landing Project

Factors Influencing the Moon Landing Project

US economy

Leadership and organisation/ experience

NASA AND THE MILITARY-INDUSTRIAL COMPLEX
THE TOP 5 INDIVIDUAL CONTRACTS AWARDED BY 1968

1. To develop, and test the Apollo command and service modules (North American Rockwell Corp.)
2. To develop the Apollo lunar module (Grumman Aircraft Engineering Corp.)
3. To design, develop and fabricate one stage of the Saturn V vehicle and provide launch support services (Boeing Co. Aerospace Division)
4. To design, develop and fabricate a second stage of the Saturn V vehicle and provide launch support services (North American Rockwell Corp.)
5. To design, develop and fabricate another stage of the Saturn V vehicles and provide launch support services (McDonnell Douglas Corp.)

The Role of Technology in the Apollo Programme

In the Apollo programme, NASA had to overcome many technological problems to get men on the Moon and back. NASA worked with many different **private companies** to develop these technologies.

The **Saturn V rocket** was developed in the US mostly by German engineers led by **Werner Von Braun**. It needed enormous power to lift-off, and it had three stages to carry its payload into orbit.

But there were **many other technologies** needed to solve other problems.

- They developed **special photography** to select a suitable landing site, similar to CAT and MRI scanning used in hospitals today.
- They developed **freeze-dried food** to feed astronauts on an extended voyage to the Moon.
- **Cool suits** were used to keep astronauts at a comfortable temperature while they were on the Moon.
- They also developed **boots** for better shock absorption and stability on the Moon's surface.
- **Cordless power tools** were developed to help gather Moon rock.
- They also developed a **heart conditioner** to maintain the heart on long space voyages, **insulation barriers** of aluminium foil to protect instruments and astronauts from radiation and **water purification technology** to maintain a fresh water supply.

Without these advances in technology, the US would not have been able to put men on the Moon and return them safely. (See The Role of Computers, p. 477)

'*Apollo really did drive our industry. We were asking people to do things that were probably 10 or 20 years faster than they otherwise would have done. And they knew it. They stepped up to it and succeeded. Today's cell phones, wireless equipment, iPads and so on are a result of the fact that the country did this hi-tech thing and created this large portfolio of available technologies.*'

(*The Guardian*, 16 December 2012)

Apollo 11

Apollo 11 was destined to make the first Moon landing. It was powered by the most powerful Saturn rocket yet, 111 metres tall. It had three **modules** (parts) to it:

- The **command module** (called Columbia) to carry the astronauts to the Moon and back.
- The **service module** which held the rockets and fuel needed for the Moon journey.
- The **lunar module** (Eagle) to land on the Moon. It had four landing legs, each with a large footpad to prevent it from sinking into the lunar soil.

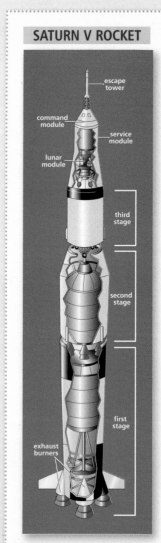

SATURN V ROCKET

escape tower
command module
service module
lunar module
third stage
second stage
first stage
exhaust burners

What role did each of the modules play?

At the top was the **launch escape tower** to allow the astronauts to escape from the command module if there were problems on the launch pad.

The Astronauts

The three astronauts were selected some years before:

- **Neil Armstrong**, the commander, was a pilot in the Korean War and later a test pilot. He flew in Gemini 8 in 1966.
- **Edwin 'Buzz' Aldrin** was also a pilot in Korea. He flew in Gemini 12 when he also walked in space. He was pilot of the lunar module.
- **Michael Collins**, also a pilot, flew in Gemini 10. He was the pilot of the command module.

The astronauts went through intensive training. They practised in **simulators**, similar to the Apollo spacecraft. They also experienced **weightlessness** in underwater tanks and in special aeroplane flights. Armstrong practised flying the **Lunar Module**, on one occasion narrowly escaping death when he ejected out of the module as it burst into flames.

THE ASTRONAUTS

'**Neil Armstrong:** Devoted to duty, he has little time for anything but his job and sets himself apart from people except for his family and close friends. He has been described as a modern day soldier of fortune because he likes to be where the excitement is, whether as a test pilot of the X-15 rocket plane or flying 78 combat missions during the Korean War.

Edwin 'Buzz' Aldrin: The young man seemed to know everything in his chosen profession. West Point honours graduate, Distinguished Flying Cross with Oak Leaf cluster, 56 combat missions in Korea with two MiGs shot down and one damaged, but, at the age of 33, his blond hair already thinning, he was back in school ...

The crew of *Apollo 11* ready to go to the moon; Neil Armstrong, Michael Collins and Edwin 'Buzz' Aldrin.

Writing the dissertation [study, thesis] that won him a Doctor of Science degree in Astronautics, he dedicated it to "the men in the astronaut programme".

Michael Collins: How will he feel about acclaim after the flight? "I've really enjoyed the programme immensely. This job is the most fascinating in the world. On the other hand, I say in all candour [truth] that I appreciate remaining anonymous, and I'll do the best I can to keep that going. I like to live a normal private life."'

The Irish Times, 16 July 1969

The Launch

On 16 July 1969, the three astronauts ate a large breakfast of steak, eggs, toast and orange juice in the Kennedy Space Center in Florida. They then dressed in bulky **spacesuits** and went aboard the command module, **Columbia**, two hours before take-

SOURCE 2 – LARGEST TURNOUT IN HISTORY

'An estimated 750,000 to one million persons witnessed the launching [at Cape Kennedy] ... The turnout was the largest in history to witness a space launch ... Traffic was tied up even further with about 160 members of the Poor People's Campaign, with four mules, who marched about one mile along the highway to emphasise the plight of the nation's hungry.'

New York Times News Service, *The Irish Times*, 17 July 1969

Why did the Poor People's Campaign attend the launch?

off. Aldrin sat in the centre, with Armstrong on his left and Collins on his right. Thousands of spectators watched the launch some distance from Apollo, while millions more watched on television.

The Journey

At 9.32 a.m. Apollo was cleared for take-off. Saturn 5 had **three rocket stages** – each one was jettisoned (dropped off) when its fuel was used up (see Source 8 and The Launch). It was loaded with 2,000 tonnes of fuel which it burned at a rate of 15 tonnes a second:

- At 3 minutes, the **launch escape tower** was jettisoned; now the astronauts could see out from the command module.
- At 9 minutes the second-stage rocket was jettisoned.
- At 11 minutes Apollo and its three astronauts reached Earth's orbit. It was ready for its journey to the moon.

THE LAUNCH – 1

The Apollo rocket breaks free from its moorings at launch time.

Can you identify the escape tower and the command module?

THE LAUNCH

escape tower is jettisoned

second stage separates

first stage separates

The launch – escape tower is jettisoned and rocket takes off

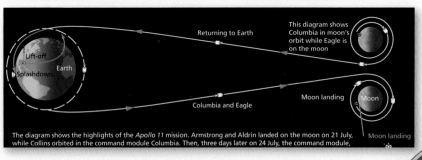

THE JOURNEY TO THE MOON AND BACK

Returning to Earth

This diagram shows Columbia in moon's orbit while Eagle is on the moon

Lift-off

Earth

Splashdown

Columbia and Eagle

Moon landing

Moon

Moon landing

The diagram shows the highlights of the *Apollo 11* mission. Armstrong and Aldrin landed on the moon on 21 July, while Collins orbited in the command module Columbia. Then, three days later on 24 July, the command module,

Briefly explain the diagram in your own words.

Apollo 11 badge

CASE STUDY QUESTIONS

1. What was the purpose of the Apollo programme?
2. What was tested by (i) *Apollo 8* (ii) *Apollo 9* (iii) *Apollo 10*?
3. What were the three modules of *Apollo 11* and what were their roles?
4. Who were the astronauts of *Apollo 11* and how experienced were they?

At this point, **Collins** separated the command module from the third-stage rocket, then reconnected with the lunar module before heading for the moon. On the **journey**, the astronauts checked the lunar module, participated in live television broadcasts and rested in sleeping bags. They did not have to wear their spacesuits except at certain stages of the voyage, such as the launch and re-entry. Their food included bacon strips, peaches, chicken, salmon and beef stew and they had drinks of coffee and orange juice. The food was **freeze-dried** and sealed in small plastic bags and sometimes had to have water added. On 19 July, they reached the Moon.

THE ROLE OF COMPUTERS IN THE MOON LANDING

The **Saturn** rocket had its own computer to guide it into Earth orbit; NASA's computers on the ground helped with navigation corrections. The **command module** (CM) and the **lunar module** (LM) each had their own computer; the CM computer navigated between the Earth and the moon, while the LM controlled the landing, ascent and rendezvous again with the command module. Other **ground computers**, which cost $3.5 million each and were as large as cars, monitored the astronauts' health and maintained communication between Earth and the lunar module.

WHAT INFORMATION CA YOU GET FROM THE SOURCE?

WHAT CAN YOU TELL ABOUT THE SOURCE?

Analysing Documents

- Is this a **primary** or a **secondary** source?
- How **useful** and **reliable** are public speeches as sources for historians of the Moon landing?
- What evidence is there in the document that President Kennedy is trying to convince his audience that space exploration is worthwhile? Is that propaganda?
- How **persuasive** is the document in putting the case for space exploration?
- Do you think this speech was given before or after he spoke about committing the US to putting men on the Moon and bringing them back to Earth?
- Explain your answer in each case.

- What **reasons** does President Kennedy give for choosing the Moon as a goal?
- How many **satellites** in the previous 19 months were American?
- How did American satellites **compare** to those of the Soviet Union?
- What were the **functions** of some of these satellites?
- What was the **direct benefit** of the 'space effort' itself'?

President Kennedy's Address at Rice University, Houston, Texas on the Nation's Space Effort, 12 September, 1962

There is no strife, no prejudice, no national conflict in outer space as yet. Its hazards are hostile to us all. Its conquest deserves the best of all mankind, and its opportunity for peaceful cooperation may never come again. But why, some say, the Moon? Why choose this as our goal? And they may well ask why climb the highest mountain? Why, 35 years ago, fly the Atlantic? … We choose to go to the moon in this decade and do the other things, not because they are easy, but because they are hard, because that goal will serve to organise and measure the best of our energies and skills, because that challenge is one that we are willing to accept, one we are unwilling to postpone, and one which we intend to win, and the others, too … Within these last 19 months at least 45 satellites have circled the Earth. Some 40 of them were 'made in the United States of America' and they were far more sophisticated and supplied far more knowledge to the people of the world than those of the Soviet Union … Transit satellites are helping our ships at sea to steer a safer course. Tiros satellites have given us unprecedented warnings of hurricanes and storms, and will do the same for forest fires and icebergs … And finally, the space effort itself, while still in its infancy, has already created a great number of new companies, and tens of thousands of new jobs.

Address at Rice University on the Nation's Space Effort, 12 September 1961, John F. Kennedy Presidential Library and Museum, Historical Sources, www.jfklibrary.org

Moon Landing

The next day, 20 July, Armstrong and Aldrin went into the lunar module, *Eagle*. They separated from Collins in the command module and landed in the **Sea of Tranquility**. On the final descent, Armstrong noted that the automatic landing system was taking *Eagle* towards a crater with large boulders. He coolly took over manual control and continued over the crater, landing in a flat plain beyond. *Eagle* had only about 30 seconds' worth of fuel left at touchdown. Then he reported back to Earth, 'Contact light on. Engine off. The *Eagle* has landed.' When Armstrong came out of the module and stepped on the Moon, he said, 'That's one small step for man, one giant leap for

SOURCE 3 – ONE SMALL STEP FOR (A) MAN

QUESTION: 'Mr. Armstrong, many would agree that you gave the most eloquent and enduring speech when you stepped onto the Moon, and I think if you could share with us how and when did you compose the "one small step"? And could you settle it for once and for all, was there an "a" before the word "man"?'

ARMSTRONG: 'I didn't think about that until after landing, but after landing I … actually having been somewhat surprised at the fact that we were able to make a successful touchdown, I realised I actually was going to have to say something. But it … there wasn't anything very complicated: when you just think about stepping off, why, it seemed to follow.'

'The "a" was intended. I thought I said it. I can't hear it when I listen on the radio reception here on Earth, so I'll be happy if you just put it in parenthesis [word in brackets].'

Apollo 11 thirtieth anniversary press conference in Cape Kennedy Space Center, 1999

Apollo 11 Moon Landing Timeline

— 16 July *Apollo 11* launched from Kennedy Space Centre, Florida

— 19 July *Apollo 11* entered lunar orbit

— 20 July Lunar module, *Eagle*, landed on the Moon
Armstrong and Aldrin walked on the Moon
Command module, *Columbia*, piloted by Michael Collins, orbited the Moon

— 21 July Lunar module lifted off from the Moon
Lunar module and command module docked
Lunar Module jettisoned
Command module began return to Earth

— 24 July *Apollo 11* splashed down in the Pacific

SOURCE 4 – ROCK SAMPLES AND SCIENTIFIC EXPERIMENTS

'The temporary inhabitants of Tranquility Base collected enough pieces of the Moon early yesterday to keep scientists happy for months. They also established a remote geophysical observation station that should benefit science … The two scientific instruments left on the Moon were a laser mirror and a seismometer. The laser reflector will help scientists to reduce the error in Earth-Moon distances to about six inches. The seismometer is designed to see if the Moon has tremors … [and to measure] meteor impacts.'

The Irish Times, 22 July 1969

What was the scientific benefit of the experiments on the Moon?

Do you agree with President Nixon's statement that 'this is the greatest week in the history of the world since creation'?

SOURCE 5

'It has only been eight days – just a long week – and this is the greatest week in the history of the world since creation. Because as a result of what happened in this week the world is bigger infinitely.'

President Nixon speaking to the astronauts in their mobile quarantine laboratory on board *USS Hornet*, *The Irish Times*, 25 July 1969

mankind.' Aldrin followed later and they planted an **American flag**, stiffened with wire. (See Source 3)

The **spacesuit** for walking on the Moon was similar to the suit for the launch, except that it had an extra layer for added protection. They also had special underwear cooled by plastic tubing filled with water. Their backpack, or **Portable Life Support System** (PLSS), supplied cooling water for the underwear and oxygen to breathe. Their helmets had a plastic shell, and two visors for added protection.

They spent 21.5 hours on the surface conducting **scientific experiments** and **collecting rock samples**. They were able to walk quite easily on the moon without having to take the kangaroo-like steps they thought they would have to. They also placed a **metal plaque** on the moon, commemorating the landing: 'Here men from the planet Earth first set foot upon the Moon, July 1969 AD. We came in peace for all mankind.' (Source 4)

SPACESUIT TECHNOLOGY

Portable life support system – backpack with 4-hour supply of oxygen

Bubble helmet with sun visors

Controls for oxygen and radio

Gloves with layers of material to prevent cutting; also flexible to pick up objects

A water-cooled undergarment

Lunar overshoes to resist extreme heat and cold

The Return

When Eagle took off from the Moon, the descent stage of the module was left behind. The lunar module then docked with Columbia. After Armstrong and Aldrin returned to the command module, Eagle was detached and left to float in the Moon's orbit.

The command module returned to Earth, protected by its **heat shield** as it came through the Earth's atmosphere. Parachutes then slowed down the entry speed. The command module splashed down in the **Pacific Ocean**, one thousand miles south-west of Hawaii, on 24 July, one mile from the target area. The capsule landed upside down in the sea, but it was soon righted. The astronauts were taken on board the **USS *Hornet*** and placed into quarantine for 21 days in case they brought back any dangerous germs. Their mission had lasted eight days. The quarantine chamber was taken to Houston Space Center, Texas. (Source 5)

SOURCE 6 – COMING HOME

'What they have done is to push outward not only into space, but into untapped reserves of hope. A generation or so from now their contribution will move into a more settled perspective. By then, there may be interplanetary space stations and hotels on Mars. But the men on the Moon began it all.'

Editorial, *The Irish Times*, 22 July 1969

What is your view of the *Irish Times* editorial?

Russia

2017 What was the impact of war and revolution on Russia, 1900–20?

2016 ---

2015 How did economic crises and wars affect Tsarist Russia?

2014 ---

2013 During the period 1871–1920, what were the main developments in one or more of the following: church/state tensions in Italy; anti-Semitism in France; economic crises in Tsarist Russia?

2012 During the period 1900–1920, how was Russia affected by war and revolution?

2011 ---

2010 What were the main challenges facing Russia during the period 1871–1920?

2009 ---

2008 ---

2007 Why was there an economic and political crisis in Tsarist Russia in the years after 1900?

2006 To what extent did one or more of the following contribute towards crises in Russia: anti-Semitism; industrialisation; the impact of war?

World War I

(Case Study: Women in the workforce during World War I)

2017 What did you learn about World War I and the post war Peace Settlement from your study of one or more of the following: Douglas Haig; women in the workforce; Woodrow Wilson?

2016 What did you learn about World War I from your study of the conduct of war and/ or the literature of war?

2015 During the period 1871–1914, how did one or more of the following contribute to international tensions: colonial rivalry; the naval policy of Wilhelm II; Serbia and its neighbours?

2014 What did you learn about World War I and the post-war Peace Settlement from your study of one or more of the following: the conduct of the war; women in the workforce; Woodrow Wilson?

2013 To what extent did colonial rivalries contribute to international tensions, 1871–1914?

2012 What did your learn about World War I from your study of the conduct of war and/ or women in the workforce during World War I?

2011 What were the main international tensions in Europe, 1871–1914?

How did the literature of World War I reflect both the conduct of war and changing attitudes towards it?

2010 What was the impact of World War I on economy and society in Europe?

2009 What did you learn about World War I from your study of one or more of the following: Douglas Haig; Wilfred Owen; women in the workforce?

2008 What were the causes of World War I?

2007 What role did President Woodrow Wilson play in the affairs of Europe in the years up to 1920?

Why was Wilfred Owen honoured, both as a soldier and as a poet, following his role in World War I?

2006 How did the literature of World War I reflect changing attitudes towards the war?

Church-State Relations/Anti-Semitism

2017 ---

2016 ---

2015 How did European states manage relations with the churches and/or religious minorities such as the Jews during the period 1871–1914?

2014 What was the impact of anti-Semitism in France and Russia, 1871–1920?

2013 During the period 1871–1920, what were the main developments in one or more of the following: church/state tensions in Italy; anti-Semitism in France; economic crisis in Tsarist Russia?

2012 ---

2011 What problems were posed by church-state relations in Germany and/or anti-Semitism in France?

2010 ---

2009 What was the impact of anti-Semitism in France and/or in Russia, 1871–1914?

2008 How did European states manage relations with the churches and/or religious minorities (e.g. the Jews) in the period 1870–1914?

2007 ---

2006 To what extent did one or more of the following contribute towards crisis in Russia: anti-Semitism; industrialisation; the impact of war?

Other

(Case Study: The invention and early history of the motor car)

2017 ---

2016 What was the contribution to European affairs of one or more of the following: Pope Leo XIII; Marie Curie; Rosa Luxemburg?

2015 During the period 1871–1920, what developments took place in one or more of the following: the motor car; science and technology; medicine?

2013 During the period 1871–1920, what were the main developments in one or more of the following: church/state tensions in Italy; anti-Semitism in France; economic crisis in Tsarist Russia?

How did the invention and early history of the motor car affect Europe?

2012 What was the contribution to European affairs of one or more of the following: Pope Leo XIII; Rosa Luxemburg; Woodrow Wilson?

2011 What did you learn about science/technology/medicine from your study of one or more of the following: the Krupp family; the invention and early history of the motor car; Marie Curie?

2010 How was national identity expressed through literature and the arts during the period 1871–1920?

2008 During the period 1871–1920, what were the key developments in one or more of the following: science; technology; medicine?

SOME COMMENTS FROM THE CHIEF EXAMINER'S REPORTS 2006 AND 2011 ON ANSWERING THE HIGHER LEVEL EXAMINATION PAPER:

- Too many candidates showed over-reliance on their knowledge of the Case Studies in answering questions which were partly related to a Case Study, e.g. 'What were the strengths and weaknesses of Éamon de Valera as a political leader?' (2011); 'To what extent did Lenin and/or Stalin bring about social and economic change?'(2011)
- Some candidates ignored the date parameters of the question or of the Topic.
- Some candidates offered historical content which was irrelevant to the set question, e.g. 'What were the main characteristics of the Nazi state in Germany, 1933–1939?' (2011), where many wrote about Hitler's foreign policy rather than on the main characteristics of the Nazi state.
- Questions which examined the perspective, Culture, Religion and Science proved to be the least popular and earned a low average mark.
- Students should adopt time-management strategies to ensure full, but not excessive, coverage of the Documents-based question in the examination.
- Students should be prepared to engage in historical argument as part of their engagement with examination questions.

ORDINARY LEVEL

Sample Case Study and Key Personality Questions

Case Studies

What was the naval policy of Kaiser Wilhelm II, and how did it affect relations with Britain?

What part did women play in World War I?

How did women contribute to the workforce during World War I, 1914–18?

What were the main developments in the invention and early history of the motor car?

Key Personalities

How successful was Otto von Bismarck as Chancellor of Germany?

What steps did Otto von Bismarck take in foreign policy of church-state relations in Germany?

Why is Marie Curie important in the development of science and medicine?

What was the importance of Karl Benz and/or the Krupp family for the industrial development of Germany?

What part did Douglas Haig play in World War I?

Why was the career of Pope Leo XIII important in the history of the Catholic Church?

How did Pope Leo XIII try to ease social tensions in industrial Europe?

How did the activities of Rosa Luxemburg influence events in Germany in the years before 1920?

What did you learn about World War I from your study of Wilfred Owen?

Other Topics

Church/State tensions in Germany

Colonial rivalries

The Paris Peace Conference

Industrialisation in Germany

Anti-Semitism in France and/or Russia

The Second International

Serbia as a fulcrum of Great Power rivalry

Past Exam Questions by Topic on Dictatorship and Democracy in Europe, 1920–1945

Compulsory Documents-study Question

2017 (Case Study: The Jarrow March, October 1936)Contextualisation: What were the aims of the Jarrow March and to what extent were they achieved?

2016 (Case Study: The Nuremberg Rallies) Contextualisation: What did the Nuremberg Rallies and/or Joseph Goebbels contribute to Nazi propaganda?

Communism in Russia

(Case Study: Stalin's Show Trials, 1936–38)

2017 ---

2016 ---

2015 How did Mussolini and/or Stalin use propaganda and terror to remain in power?

2014 What challenges faced the Soviet Union in peace and war, 1924–45?

2013 How did Stalin transform the Soviet economy and/or use show trials to consolidate his power?

2012 What were the main characteristics of Stalin's rule in Russia?

2011 To what extent did Lenin and/or Stalin bring about social and economic change?

2010 How effective were the internal and external policies of Josef Stalin?

2009 How did dictators use propaganda and/or terror to maintain their power?

2008 What did Lenin and Stalin contribute to communism in Russia?

2007 How significant was the role played by the Soviet Union in World War II?

2006 To what extent did Stalin transform the society and economy of the Soviet Union?

Fascist Italy/Nazi Germany

(Case Study: The Nurenberg Rallies)

2017 ---

2016 (Case Study: The Nuremberg Rallies)

2015 What were the social and economic problems facing Germany, 1920–39, and how were they dealt with? How did Mussolini and/or Stalin use propaganda and terror to remain in power? To what extent did Hitler's foreign policy, 1933–39, contribute to the outbreak of World War II?

2014 How did Church-State relations develop under Mussolini and Hitler?

2013 What were the characteristics of fascist regimes in Europe in the inter-war period?

2012 To what extent was Hitler's foreign policy, 1933–1939, responsible for the outbreak of World War II?How did anti-Semitism and the Holocaust affect Europe, 1920–1945?

2011 How effective were the internal and external policies of Benito Mussolini?What were the main characteristics of the Nazi state in Germany, 1933–1939?

2010 What were the main developments in church-state relations under Hitler and Mussolini?

2009 How did dictators use propaganda and/or terror to maintain their power?

2008 What contribution did Joseph Goebbels and/or Leni Riefenstahl make to Nazi propaganda?

2007 What were the main characteristics of the Nazi state in Germany between 1933 and 1939?

2006 During the inter-war period, what conditions in Europe contributed to the growth of fascist regimes?

Economic and Social Problems in the Inter-war Years
(Case Study: The Jarrow March, 1936)

2017 (Case Study: The Jarrow March, October 1936)

2016 ---

2015 What were the social and economic problems facing Germany, 1920–39, and how were they dealt with? What were the economic and social problems of Britain during the inter-war years and/or what was the impact of World War II on its civilian population?

2014 How did the Jarrow March (1936) illustrate the social and economic problems facing Britain during the inter-war period?

2013 What were the challenges facing Britain in peace and war, 1920–1945?

2012 ---

2011 What did one or more of the following achieve in Britain during the period 1920–1945: J. M. Keynes; those who took part in the Jarrow March, October 1936; Winston Churchill?

2010 How successfully did German governments deal with the social and economic problems of the period 1920–1939?

2009 What were the main social and economic challenges facing Britain, 1920–1945?

2008 Which had greater social and economic problems during the inter-war years, Britain or Germany? Argue your case, referring to both countries.

2007 What were the causes and consequences of the Jarrow March, October 1936?

2006 How successfully did Britain deal with the social and economic problems of the inter-war period?

Anglo-American Popular Culture

2017 ---

2016 ---

2015 ---

2014 ---

2013 What did you learn about radio and cinema, 1920–1945, from your study of one or more of the following: Charlie Chaplin; Leni Riefenstahl; Bing Crosby?

2012 ---

2011 ---

2010 What was the impact of Anglo-American popular culture on Europe, 1920–1945?

2009 ---

2008 ---

2007 ---

2006 ---

Third Republic and Vichy France

2017 ---

2016 ---

2015 ---

2014 What were the fortunes of France during the period 1920–45?

2013 ---

2012 What were the main challenges facing France, 1920–1945?

2011 ---

2010 ---

2009 How was France unstable during the period, 1920–1940?

2008 What was the impact of World War II on the civilian population of Britain and/or France?

2007 What problems did the Third Republic of France encounter between 1920 and 1940?

2006 ---

World War II

Society During World War II

SOME COMMENTS FROM THE CHIEF EXAMINER'S REPORTS 2006 AND 2011 ON ANSWERING THE HIGHER LEVEL EXAMINATION PAPER:

- Too many candidates showed over-reliance on their knowledge of the Case Studies in answering questions which were partly related to a Case Study, e.g. 'What were the strengths and weaknesses of Éamon de Valera as a political leader?' (2011); 'To what extent did Lenin and/or Stalin bring about social and economic change?'(2011)
- Some candidates ignored the date parameters of the question or of the Topic.
- Some candidates offered historical content which was irrelevant to the set question, e.g. 'What were the main characteristics of the Nazi state in Germany, 1933–1939?' (2011), where many wrote about Hitler's foreign policy rather than on the main characteristics of the Nazi state.
- Questions which examined the perspective, Culture, Religion and Science proved to be the least popular and earned a low average mark.
- Students should adopt time-management strategies to ensure full, but not excessive, coverage of the Documents-based question in the examination.
- Students should be prepared to engage in historical argument as part of their engagement with examination questions.

ORDINARY LEVEL

Sample Case Study and Key Personality Questions

Case Studies

How did the Nuremberg Rallies and/or Leni Riefenstahl contribute to the Nazi regime?

Why did Stalin set up show trials and did they achieve his desired result?

What were the economic and social conditions in Britain that led to the Jarrow March in October 1936?

Why did the Jarrow march take place, October 1936, and what did it achieve?

Key Personalities

Would you agree that the leadership of Mussolini was a disaster for Italy?

What developments took place in church-state relations in Italy under Mussolini?

What did Charlie Chaplin and/or Bing Crosby contribute to entertainment?

Winston Churchill – How successful was Winston Churchill as a wartime leader between 1940 and 1945?

Lenin

How did Joseph Goebbels and/or Leni Riefenstahl use the German mass media to promote the Nazi movement?

What social and economic changes did Lenin and/or Stalin bring about in Russia?

Other Topics

Anti-Semitism and the Holocaust

Vichy France/France during World War II

Church-state relations in Fascist Italy and/or Nazi Germany

Technology of warfare, 1920–45

Collaboration and Resistance during World War II

The growth in radio and cinema, 1920–1945

The Battle of Stalingrad

Past Exam Questions by Topic: The United States and the world, 1945–1989

HIGHER LEVEL

Compulsory Documents-study Question

2009 (Case Studies – The Montgomery Bus Boycott, 1955–56) Contextualisation: How important was the Montgomery bus boycott to the American civil rights movement?

2008 (Case Studies – Johnson and Vietnam, 1963–68) Contextualisation: Why was President Johnson unable to win the war in Vietnam?

US Politics

2017 From Roosevelt to Reagan, would you agree that American presidents always acted for the good of America? Argue your case, referring to more than one president.

2016 Who was the greater president, Truman or Johnson? Argue your case, referring to both in your answer.

2015 ---

2014 What were the strengths and weaknesses of Lyndon Johnson as a political leader?

2013 ---

2012 How well did President Harry Truman or President Lyndon Johnson handle the challenges he faced?

2011 How did the US Presidency develop from Roosevelt to Reagan?

2010 What were the successes and failures of the presidency of Lyndon Johnson?

2009 ---

2008 ---

2007 ---

2006 ---

US Foreign Policy

(Case Study: Lyndon Johnson and Vietnam, 1963–68)

2017 ---

2016 ---

2015 During the period 1945–89, what was the importance for US foreign policy of one or more of the following: Berlin; Korea; Cuba?

2014 ---

2013 Which president was more successful in his handling of US foreign policy, Harry Truman or Lyndon Johnson? Argue your case, referring to both.

2012 What part did one or more of the following play in US foreign policy: Korea; Cuba; SALT and Star Wars?

2011 Why did the US lose the Vietnam War and/ or what was the significance of the Moon landing?

2010 What was the importance for US foreign policy of one or more of the following: Berlin; Korea, Cuba?

What were the successes and failures of the presidency of Lyndon Johnson?

2009 ---

2008 (Case Studies – Johnson and Vietnam, 1963–68)

2007 What were the significant developments in US foreign policy, 1973–1989?

2006 Which had the greater impact on the United States: involvement in Korea or involvement in Vietnam? Argue your case referring to both.

Domestic Factors in US Foreign Policy

2017 ---

2016 During the period 1945–89, what was the impact on US society of McCarthyism and/or the anti-war movement?

2015 ---

2014 ---

2013 ---

2012 ---

2011 ---

2010 ---

2009 ---

2008 ---

2007 How did McCarthyism and/or the anti-war movement affect US foreign policy, 1945–1972?

2006 What was the importance of one or more of the following: McCarthyism; the Moon landing, 1969; developments in information technology?

US Economy

2017 What were the achievements of the US economy, 1945–68, and what factors limited its growth, 1968–89?

2016 What were the strengths and weaknesses of the US economy, 1945–89?

2015 ---

2014 What were significant developments in the US economy, 1945–89?

2013 What was the impact on the US economy of one or more of the following: the multinational corporation; the military-industrial complex; international competition from Japan and Europe?

2012 To what extent did the US economy experience both success and decline during the period 1945–1989?

2011 ---

2010 Why did the United States experience an economic boom, 1945–1968, and what was its impact on society?

2009 ---

2008 ---

2007 ---

2006 ---

Troubled Affluence
(Case Study: The Montgomery Bus Boycott, 1955–56)

2017 What was the contribution of Martin Luther King to the events of the Montgomery Bus Boycott and to other aspects of US life?

2016 ---

2015 Why did the Montgomery Bus Boycott (1956) take place, how was it carried out, and to what extent was it successful?

2014 Why did race relations remain a major issue in the US, 1945–89?

2013 What were the main developments in race relations in the US, 1945–1968?

2012 What was the significance of one or more of the following in US history: Hollywood, 1945–1968; the Montgomery Bus Boycott; religion in modern American culture?

2011 What was the contribution of Martin Luther King to US affairs?

2010 ---

2009 (Case Studies – The Montgomery Bus Boycott, 1955–56)

2008 ---

2007 In what ways did the Montgomery Bus Boycott, 1955–56, advance the cause of the civil rights movement?

2006 During the period, 1945–1989, what was the impact of one or more of the following on American society: racial conflict; urban poverty; organised crime?

Advances in Technology
(Case Study: The Moon Landing, 1969)

2017 ---

2016 What was the significance of the Moon landing (1969) and/or Star Wars?

2015 During the period 1945–89, what advances were made by the Americans in military, space and information technology?

2014 How did the Americans achieve a successful Moon landing in 1969 and what was its importance for the US?

2013 ---

2012 ---

2011 Why did the US lose the Vietnam War and/or what was the significance of the Moon landing?

2010 What was the impact of the Moon landing on US domestic and foreign affairs?

2009 ---

2008 ---

2007 ---

2006 What was the importance of one or more of the following: McCarthyism; the Moon landing, 1969; developments in information technology?

Other

2017 How did one or more of the following challenge widely-held views in the US: Norman Mailer; Betty Friedan; Muhammad Ali?

2016 ---

2015 What was the American Dream and to what extent was it reflected in life in the US, 1945–89?

2014 ---

2013 What was the contribution of religion and/or the mass media to modern American culture?

2012 What was the significance of one or more of the following in US history: Hollywood, 1945–1968; the Montgomery Bus Boycott; religion in modern American culture?

2011 What did one or more of the following contribute to American culture: Marilyn Monroe; Muhammad Ali; Billy Graham?

ORDINARY LEVEL

Sample Case Study and Key Personality Questions

Case Studies

What problems did President Johnson encounter in dealing with Vietnam?

How was it possible for the United States to achieve a Moon landing in 1969 and what was its importance?

Why was the Montgomery Bus Boycott (1956) so important to the story of the civil rights movement?

Key Personalities

How successful was Lyndon Johnson as a political leader at home and abroad?

What part did President Truman play in the history of the United States?

How did Senator Joe McCarthy influence the direction of foreign policy in the United States?

What did Norman Mailer and/or Marilyn Monroe contribute to American culture?

Betty Friedan and the changing role of women

How and why did Billy Graham become such a popular religious leader in the United States?

Other Topics

Urban poverty, drugs and crime

The United States and Cuba

Youth culture in modern America

The 'red scare' in post-war United States

Muhammad Ali

INDEX OF KEY PERSONALITIES

2. (a) In humans there are two types of cell division: mitosis and meiosis. The table gives several statements about cell division. Tick one box in each row if the statement is true for mitosis only, for meiosis only or for both mitosis and meiosis. The first row has been completed for you.

2 identical daughters → → 4 non aden daughters.

(4 marks)

Statement	Mitosis only	Meiosis only	Both mitosis and meiosis
Used for growth and replacement of cells	✔		
Used for production of gametes		✓	
Before the parent cell divides each chromosome is copied			✓
Produces genetically identical cells	✓		
Halves the chromosome number		✓	

(b) Cystic fibrosis is an inherited disease caused by a mutated allele for the CFTR protein found in lungs and other tissues. A couple, neither of whom had cystic fibrosis, came from families that both had a history of the disease. The couple were concerned that they might have children who were affected. They underwent genetic testing and were found to be heterozygous for the cystic fibrosis gene.

(i) Using F for the normal allele and f for the mutated allele, state the genotype of both parents.

(1 mark)

...........Ff...

Watch out!

You need to use capital and lower case letters clearly. Watch out for this when the letters S and s are used to represent the alleles.

You must use the Punnett square in your answer to show how genetic information is inherited, as it tells you to in the question.

Make sure that you fully answer the question – do not forget to give the percentage probability of the couple's children having cystic fibrosis.

Maths skills This question asks you to give the percentage probability of a couple's children having cystic fibrosis. The probability is 1:4. You need to do ¼ ×100 to get a percentage probability.

(ii) Predict the percentage probability of the couple's children having cystic fibrosis. Use the Punnett square.

(2 marks)

....

....

(c) Two proteins, DAZL and PRDM14, are involved in the development of sperm cells. Mutations in these genes are associated with an increased risk of developing testicular cancer. Almost 100% of all testicular cancers can be completely cured if diagnosed early.

Explain how the Human Genome Project has made it possible to improve early diagnosis of diseases, such as testicular cancer in men with a family history of testicular cancer.

(3 marks)

....

....

....

....

....

....

(Total for Question 2 = 10 marks)

Hint

In this question, **explain** means that you need to give reasons why the Human Genome Project has made it possible to improve early diagnosis of disease. Use your own knowledge **and** information from the question.

Hint

The question states 'such as testicular cancer, in men with a family of testicular cancer'. You need to relate your answer to this.

LEARN IT!

The base sequence of an individual is the order of bases in their DNA. DNA is a large, double-stranded molecule made of nucleotides. Each nucleotide has one DNA base.

Explore

The Human Genome Project involved lots of scientists working together in order to work out the order of the bases on all of the chromosomes. The results are being used to treat diseases and make new medicines. What are the advantages and disadvantages of this project?

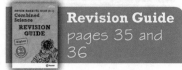

Revision Guide
pages 35 and 36

3. A man has an infection of disease-causing bacteria. He has not been immunised against these bacteria. Figure 1 shows how the number of these bacteria changes after a doctor gives the man a 7-day course of antibiotics.

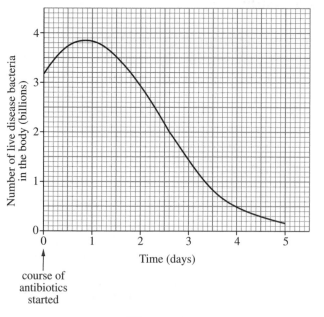

Figure 1

(a) Which of these is a typical feature of non-communicable diseases?

(1 mark)

☐ **A** a pathogen is involved

☐ **B** cases are often localised

☐ **C** cases may be widely distributed

☐ **D** number of cases varies rapidly

(b) Use the graph to determine:

(i) the time taken for the number of live bacteria to begin to fall after starting the course of antibiotics

(1 mark)

....

(ii) the maximum number of live disease bacteria in the man's body.

(1 mark)

....

(c) State whether the man has a communicable or a non-communicable disease. Give a reason for you answer.

(2 marks)

....

....

....

....

(d) The doctor suspected that the illness was caused by a bacterium rather than by a virus. Give **two** reasons that explain why the doctor was correct.

(2 marks)

....

....

....

....

(e) The man was told to take the antibiotics for the full seven days, even if he began to feel better.

   (i)   Explain why antibiotics can be used to treat bacterial infections.

(2 marks)

....

....

....

....

   (ii) Give **two** reasons why it was important that the man did not stop taking the antibiotics early.

(2 marks)

....

....

....

....

LEARN IT!

Pathogens cause infectious diseases. Different pathogens cause different diseases.

Hint

You should be able to name the different types of pathogens – viruses, bacteria, fungi and protists. Make sure you can give examples of the symptoms that different pathogens cause.

Hint

You need to use your knowledge about antibiotics to explain why they can be used to treat bacterial infections in animals.

Explore

Antibiotics kill only bacteria – they do not kill viruses. There are different types of antibiotics. Why must the correct type of antibiotic be used?

Revision Guide
page 45

Hint

Use the axes titles to help you to state the relationship between alcohol consumption and relative risk.
When you explain the relationship you should use numbers from the graph **and** use your knowledge.

This graph shows a **positive correlation** between alcohol consumption and relative risk. This means that as alcohol consumption increases, the relative risk increases.

(f) Figure 2 shows the results of two studies into the effect of alcohol consumption on the risk of developing liver disease. One group (solid line) consisted only of males and the other group (dotted line) consisted only of females.

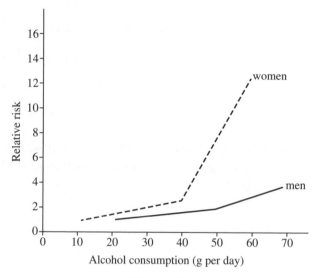

Figure 2

State and explain the relationship between alcohol consumption and relative risk of liver disease for men.

(3 marks)

....

....

....

....

....

....

(Total for Question 3 = 14 marks)

4. Figure 3 shows a bacterial cell and a plant cell.

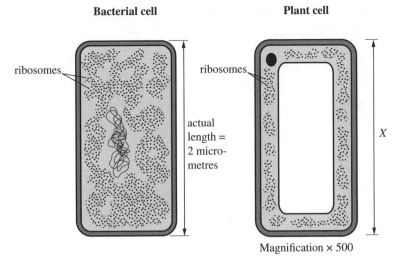

Figure 3

(a) (i) Both types of cell contain ribosomes. State the function of a ribosome.

(1 mark)

....

(ii) The plant cell contains mitochondria but the bacterial cell does not. State **two** other ways in which the plant cell is different to the bacterial cell.

(2 marks)

....
....
....
....

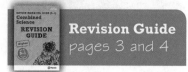

Revision Guide
pages 3 and 4

Maths skills To calculate the actual length of the cell you need to rearrange the formula:

magnification =

$$\frac{\text{image size}}{\text{real size}}$$

Maths skills There are 1000 mm in a metre and 1000 micrometres in a millimetre.

To divide by 1000 move the decimal point three places to the left; to multiply by 1000 move the decimal point three places to the right.

Maths skills Remember to show all of your working out – even if you don't get the answer correct, you may still get some marks for your working out.

(b) Although the cells are drawn the same size, the magnifications are different. The actual length of the bacterial cell is two micrometres.

Calculate the actual length, X, of the plant cell. Give your answer in micrometres, to one decimal place. Show your working.

(3 marks)

(Total for Question 4 = 6 marks)

Revision Guide
pages 14 and 15

5. Figure 4 shows a percentile chart developed by the US Government to monitor the growth of males between the ages of 2 and 20 years. It can be used to monitor both weight and height.

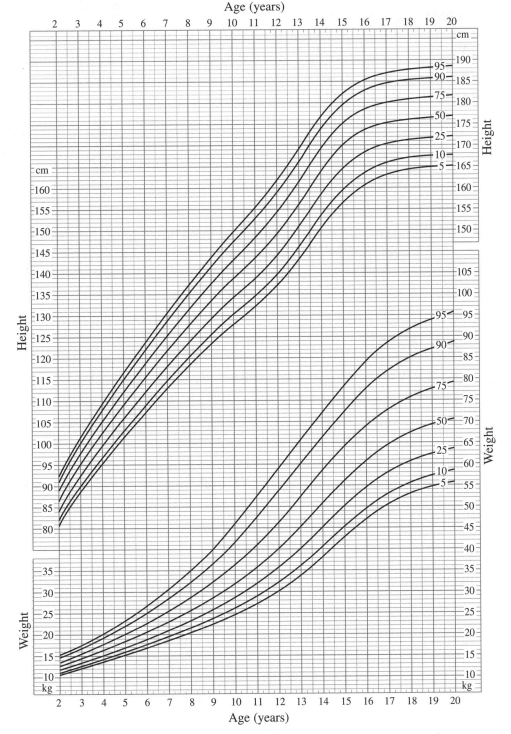

Figure 4

Hint

Growth is a measure of a permanent increase in size – this can be an increase in mass or an increase in length. Growth charts can be used to monitor increases in weight and height of children.

Hint

You need to say what is being measured by the doctor or nurse **and** say when the measurements should be made. You should then say how the doctor or nurse should use the measurements with the chart.

Hint

You should read the sentence at the top of the chart carefully. You will need the information to answer the question fully.

(a) Describe how a doctor or nurse could use this chart to monitor the growth of a boy from the age of 2 to 16 years.

(3 marks)

....

....

Hint

The question has told you to use different symbols for boy A and boy B. Make sure that you use the correct symbols. You should not make the symbols too big on the chart.

Hint

You are told only to plot the height and weight of both boys on the chart. You are not told to join the points. Just do as the question tells you to. There is 1 mark per set of points correctly plotted.

Hint

You need to look at the plotted points for each of the boys. For each boy you need to say what the positions of the points tell you about their development.

Explore

Percentile charts are used to monitor the growth rate of children. Children who are growing too quickly or too slowly can be identified using them. What determines a child's growth rate?

(b) The table shows the weight and height records of two boys, A and B, from the ages of 4 to 16.

Age (years)	Height (cm)		Weight (kg)	
	Boy A	Boy B	Boy A	Boy B
4	102	105	18	17
8	127	132	32	27
12	148	155	56	42
16	170	179	83	60

(i) Plot the height and weight of both boys on the chart in Figure 4. Use '+' for Boy A and 'o' for Boy B.

(4 marks)

(ii) Explain what your plotted points show about the development of the two boys.

(4 marks)

....

....

....

....

....

....

(Total for Question 5 = 11 marks)

6. Figure 5 shows the neurones and other parts of the body involved in the response to touching a sharp object.

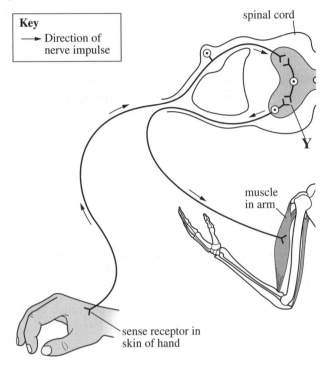

Figure 5

Revision Guide
pages 17 and 18

LEARN IT!

Reflex reactions are rapid, involuntary reactions that protect us from harm or damage.

Hint

You need to remember the order of the neurones in a reflex arc. Remember that the reflex arc starts with a receptor and finishes with an effector. Receptor cells sense stimuli. An effector can be a muscle or a gland.

(a) Identify which of the following describes the correct sequence of events following touching a sharp object.

(1 mark)

Hint

Electrical impulses pass along sensory neurones first.

☐ **A** sensory receptor → sensory neurone → motor neurone → relay neurone

☐ **B** sensory receptor → muscle → motor neurone → relay neurone

☐ **C** sensory receptor → relay neurone → sensory neurone → motor neurone

☐ **D** sensory receptor → sensory neurone → relay neurone → motor neurone

Hint

You only need to
give the name for
this question, you do
not need to give any
further information.

Hint

There are gaps
between each type of
neurone – these are
called synapses. The
electrical impulses
cannot pass across
the synapses, so
chemicals called
neurotransmitters
diffuse across the
synapse, carrying the
information from one
neurone to the next.

Explore

You need to be
able to explain the
structure and function
of the axon, dendron
and myelin sheath
and the role of
neurotransmitters. Try
drawing and labelling a
diagram, writing on the
role of each of these.

(b) (i) State the name of the structure labelled Y on the diagram.

(1 mark)

....

(ii) Describe the events that occur at point Y that allow the
impulse to be passed on from one neurone to the next.

(3 marks)

....
....
....
....
....
....

*(c) Stem cell therapy has been suggested as a possible treatment for patients with spinal cord injuries. Explain how stem cell therapy could be used in the future to treat spinal cord injury. In your answer you should discuss the sources of stem cells as well as the ethical implications.

(6 marks)

Revision Guide
page 16

Hint

Explain means that you have to give reasons for something happening. The word 'because' is useful in explain questions.

Discuss means you should consider all aspects of the sources of stem cells as well as the ethical implications of the different sources.

....
....
....
....
....
....
....
....
....
....
....
....
....
....
....
....
....
....
....
....
....

Explore

There are different types of stem cells. Try to name three different types. Where is each type found, and what are their uses?

(Total for Question 6 = 11 marks)

TOTAL FOR PAPER = 60 MARKS

Combined Science
Paper 2: Biology

Time allowed: 1 hour 10 minutes

Answer ALL questions. Write your answers in the spaces provided.

1. (a) A student carried out an investigation into osmosis in potato pieces. The student cut five pieces of potato, weighed them and then placed them into different concentrations of salt solution. After one hour the student removed the potato pieces from the salt solution and weighed them again. The student's results are shown in the table.

Concentration of salt solution (mol dm⁻³)	Initial mass of potato (g)	Final mass of potato (g)	Percentage change in mass (%)
0.0	5.2	5.4	
0.25	5.6	5.6	
0.5	5.6	5.4	−3.6
1.0	5.0	4.6	−8.0
1.5	5.2	4.2	

(i) Complete the table by calculating the percentage change in mass of the potato pieces. Give your answers to 1 decimal place.

(3 marks)

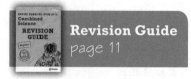

Revision Guide
page 11

(ii) Describe **one** way in which the student could improve the experiment.

(1 mark)

....

(iii) Use your results from part (i) to estimate the solute concentration of the potato cells.

(1 mark)

....

(b) Figure 1 shows the part of the lung where gas exchange takes place.

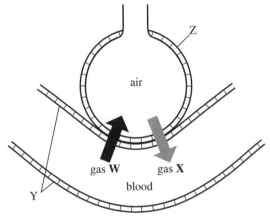

Figure 1

(i) State the name of the structures labelled 'Y' and 'Z' in the diagram.

(2 marks)

Structure Y is the ....

Structure Z is the ....

Biology Paper 2

🧪 **Practical skills** Improving the experiment should make it more accurate and repeatable. Accurate results are close to the true value. The experiment is repeatable if you do the same method again, using the same equipment, and get the same results.

Hint

You need to give a number for the solute concentration of the potato cells and give the correct units.

 Revision Guide pages 10 and 63

LEARN IT!

You should be able to explain how the alveoli of the lungs are adapted for the diffusion of oxygen into the blood and carbon dioxide out of the blood. Diffusion is the movement of particles from where they are at a higher concentration to where they are at a lower concentration.

Hint

State means that you should just give the name. You do not need to describe or explain.

(ii) Which one of the following methods describes how gases W and X move in the directions shown?

(1 mark)

☐ **A** diffusion

☐ **B** osmosis

☐ **C** breathing

☐ **D** respiration

(iii) State the name of gas W.

(1 mark)

....

(c) A scientist recently estimated that the average human lung has 480 million alveoli and that 1 million alveoli have a surface area of 0.15 m^2.

Calculate the total surface area of one human lung.

(2 marks)

(Total for Question 1 = 11 marks)

Watch out!

This question is asking you to calculate the total surface area of a human lung – that is **one** human lung.

Maths skills Remember to show all of your working out – if you get the answer wrong you could still get some marks.

Explore

Multi-cellular organisms are large and require special organs to exchange substances with their environment. Think about how exchange surfaces in these organs are adapted for their roles.

Revision Guide
page 70

2. Figure 2 shows the heart rate of an adult male over a 24-hour period.

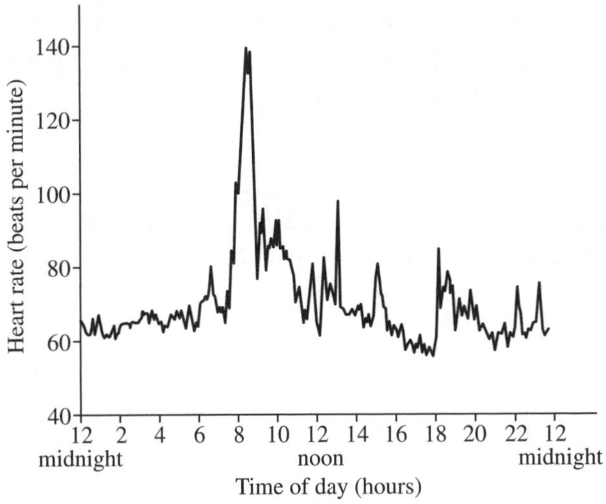

140 ⎤
120 ⎤
100 ⎤
80 ⎤
60 ⎤
40 ⎤

Heart rate (beats per minute)

12   2   4   6   8   10   12   14   16   18   20   22   12
midnight   noon   midnight

Time of day (hours)

Figure 2

(a) (i) Use the graph to estimate this person's resting heart rate.

(1 mark)

Hint

You need to give an approximate value for this person's resting heart rate. You should identify when the man is resting and read off the heart rate.

....

(ii) The man attended a one-hour spinning (indoor cycling) class during the day. Use the graph to estimate the start time of the class.

(1 mark)

Hint

When the man is exercising, the heart rate will increase. You need to find the time when the man started to exercise.

....

(iii) About an hour before the class started the man walked uphill to the gym where the class was held. He then rested until the class started.

Give **one** piece of evidence from the trace that supports this.

(1 mark)

Hint

You need to give numbers from the graph as evidence.

....

....

(iv) The man noticed that his heart rate remained higher than normal for some time after the end of the class.

Explain why his heart rate remained high.

(2 marks)

Hint

Explain means that you have to give reasons for something happening. The word 'because' is useful in explain questions.

....

....

....

Watch out!

You have been given units for stroke volume and heart rate – use these to give the unit for cardiac output.

Maths skills Remember to show all of your working out – if you do not get the answer correct you could still get some marks.

Maths skills You need to use the equation cardiac output = stroke volume × heart rate.

Hint

Suggest means that you need to apply your knowledge to a new situation.

Hint

Your cells are respiring all of the time. When you exercise, **more** respiration occurs, so cells need **more** oxygen and glucose and produce **more** carbon dioxide, water and energy.

Explore

What are the effects of exercise on the body? You need to be able to use terms such as cardiac output, heart rate and stroke volume to describe these effects.

(b) (i) The table shows the stroke volume and heart rate for two people measured while they were at rest. Complete the table by calculating the cardiac output for each person. Include the units for cardiac output.

(3 marks)

	Stroke volume (cm^3)	**Heart rate (beats/min)**	**Cardiac output**	**Units**
Person A	95	52		
Person B	58	72		

(ii) One of these was a trained athlete, the other was untrained. Suggest and explain which is the trained athlete.

(2 marks)

....

....

(Total for Question 2 = 10 marks)

Revision Guide
pages 57 and 58

3. (a) The table lists several hormones, their site of production and target organ(s).

Choose from the following list of words to complete the table.

adrenalin	glucagon	kidney	muscle
oestrogen	ovaries	pancreas	pituitary
progesterone	testes	thyroid

Hormone	Produced in	Target organ
ADH		
	adrenal gland	various organs, e.g. heart, liver, skin
glucagon		
	ovaries	pituitary gland

(4 marks)

(b) (i) Describe what happens in the uterus if an egg is not fertilised.

(2 marks)

....

....

(ii) Explain how a hormone contraceptive pill prevents pregnancy.

(2 marks)

....

....

(iii) Give **one** advantage of barrier methods of contraception compared to hormonal contraception.

(1 mark)

....

LEARN IT!

Hormones are chemical messengers that travel in the bloodstream.

LEARN IT!

You need to be able to explain how chemical contraceptives affect the menstrual cycle and the release of an egg cell (ovulation).

Hint

Don't just give an advantage of barrier methods, make sure that it is an advantage compared to hormonal contraception.

Hint

Before reading the choices in a multiple-choice question, try to answer the question. Then choose the choice closest to your answer.

Always answer multiple-choice questions even if you are not sure of the answer.

(c) Which one of the following statements describes a way in which specialised cells are adapted for their function in reproduction?

(1 mark)

☐ **A** Sperm cells have cilia allowing the sperm cell to swim towards the egg cell.

☐ **B** Sperm cells have an acrosome allowing the sperm cell to swim towards the egg cell.

☐ **C** Ciliated epithelial cells transport sperm cells towards the uterus.

☐ **D** Ciliated epithelial cells transport egg cells towards the uterus.

(Total for Question 3 = 10 marks)

4. The survival of some organisms is dependent on other species. For example, the flea is an animal that feeds on the blood of other animals, including humans.

(a) Which term correctly describes a flea?

(1 mark)

☐ **A** mutualist

☐ **B** parasite

☐ **C** producer

☐ **D** primary consumer

Hint

A parasite feeds on another organism (the host).

(b) An epiphyte is a type of plant that grows harmlessly on another species of plant. The epiphyte obtains its water and nutrients from air, rain and debris that accumulate around it.

The mistletoe is a parasitic plant. Describe how a parasite differs from an epiphyte.

(2 marks)

Watch out!

In parasitic relationships only one of the organisms benefits; the other is harmed. In mutualistic relationships, both organisms benefit. Think about how the bacteria and the plants benefit from the relationship.

....

....

....

....

(c) Nitrogen-fixing bacteria grow in nodules attached to the roots of some plants. The bacteria make nitrogen compounds that can be absorbed by the plant.

(i) Suggest **one** way in which the relationship benefits the bacteria.

(1 mark)

....

Hint

(ii) Explain why the relationship between the bacteria and plants is described as mutalism.

(2 marks)

You need to say what mutualism is, using the information about the bacteria and the plants.

....

....

....

....

Revision Guide
pages 10 and 11

Hint

Focus on how plants obtain each substance.

Explore

You need to be able to describe how some species depend on other species for their survival. Can you give some examples of parasitic and mutualistic relationships?

(d) Plants obtain the substances they need by different processes.

(i) Draw one straight line from each substance to the corresponding process.

(2 marks)

Substance

Mistletoe obtains mineral ions

Epiphyte obtains water

Process

down a concentration gradient

by osmosis

by active transport

by diffusion

(ii) Which of the following correctly describes the function of an enzyme in plants?

(1 mark)

☐ **A** Starch synthase produces starch from glucose.

☐ **B** Starch synthase produces glucose from starch.

☐ **C** Amylase produces starch from glucose.

☐ **D** Amylase produces starch from maltose.

(Total for Question 4 = 9 marks)

5. A group of students were undertaking a survey of an area of land alongside a path that crossed a field and entered a piece of woodland.

Revision Guide
pages 72 and 73

(a) (i) State **two** abiotic factors that might influence the distribution of plant species in the woodland.

(2 marks)

Watch out!

Abiotic factors are 'non-living' factors.
Biotic factors are 'living' factors.

....

....

(ii) State **two** biotic factors that might influence the distribution of plant species next to the path in the field.

(2 marks)

....

....

*(b) Describe how the students should survey the abundance of different plant species growing alongside the path from the field and into the wood.

(6 marks)

....
....
....
....
....
....
....
....
....
....
....
....
....
....

(Total for Question 5 = 10 marks)

6. (a) Figure 3 shows a specialised type of plant cell.

 Revision Guide
pages 1, 2 and
52

```
                    ┌──── F
      companion ──  ●    E
      cell
                          └──── cytoplasm
```

Figure 3

(i) Which specialised plant tissue is shown in Figure 3?

(1 mark)

☐ **A** xylem

☐ **B** phloem

☐ **C** mesophyll

☐ **D** root hair

(ii) Identify the parts labelled E and F.

(2 marks)

E ....

F ....

(b) The companion cells contain large numbers of mitochondria.

(i) What is the function of a mitochondrion?

(1 mark)

☐ **A** to carry out photosynthesis

☐ **B** to carry out respiration

☐ **C** to control the entry of substances to the cell

☐ **D** to control the activities of the cell

(ii) Suggest an explanation for why the companion cell contains large numbers of mitochondria.

(2 marks)

....

....

....

....

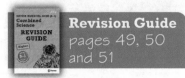

Revision Guide
pages 49, 50 and 51

Watch out!

There are a number of different answers here; you just need to give one factor. BUT you cannot give temperature – they have already given this factor in the question.

Hint

Explain means that you have to give reasons why the rate of photosynthesis changes as temperature is increased. You need to explain what happens as the rate of photosynthesis increases, then decreases, as the temperature increases.

Explore

Photosynthesis is an enzyme-controlled reaction. Use your knowledge of how enzymes work to explain how the rate of photosynthesis changes with a change in temperature.

(c) (i) Temperature can be a limiting factor in photosynthesis. State one other factor that can limit the rate of photosynthesis.

(1 mark)

....

(ii) Figure 4 shows how the rate of photosynthesis changes as temperature is increased.

Figure 4

Explain how the rate of photosynthesis changes as the temperature is increased.

(3 marks)

....
....
....
....
....
....

(Total for Question 6 = 10 marks)

TOTAL FOR PAPER = 60 MARKS

Combined Science
Paper 3: Chemistry 1

Time allowed: 1 hour 10 minutes

Answer ALL questions. Write your answers in the spaces provided.

1. (a) Complete the table below to show the properties of protons, neutrons and electrons.

(4 marks)

Subatomic particle	Relative mass	Relative charge
proton	1	
neutron		
electron		−1

(b) Neon has the atomic number 10. Neon exists as neon-20 and neon-22 atoms.

Explain, in terms of protons and neutrons, why these atoms are isotopes of neon.

(2 marks)

....

....

....

....

(Total for Question 1 = 6 marks)

2. This question is about elements and the periodic table.

(a) Which of these describes the arrangement of elements in the modern periodic table?

(1 mark)

☐ **A** in order of increasing relative atomic mass

☐ **B** in order of increasing relative formula mass

☐ **C** in order of increasing mass number

☐ **D** in order of increasing atomic number

(b) Dmitri Mendeleev (1834–1907) was a Russian chemist who developed a periodic table.

Give **one** similarity and **one** difference between Mendeleev's table and the modern periodic table.

(2 marks)

....

....

....

....

(c) Phosphorus, P, has the atomic number 15. Complete Figure 1 to show the electronic configuration of phosphorus, P.

(1 mark)

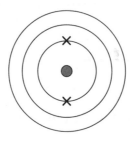

Figure 1

(d) The table below gives the numbers of electrons in atoms of lithium, sodium and magnesium.

Element	Number of electrons in atom
lithium	3
sodium	11
magnesium	12

Explain, in terms of their electronic configurations, why:

(i)   lithium and sodium are placed in group 1

(1 mark)

....

....

(ii)   sodium and magnesium are placed in period 3.

(1 mark)

....

....

(Total for Question 2 = 6 marks)

Hint

What do the electronic configurations of lithium and sodium have in common, and how is this linked to the group number?

Hint

How are the electronic configuration of sodium and magnesium similar and how is this linked to the period number?

Explore

The electronic configuration of an element is related to its position in the modern periodic table. Why didn't Mendeleev organise his table using electronic configurations and atomic numbers?

Revision Guide
pages 91–93

LEARN IT!

The numbers of each ion in the formula for an ionic compound must give equal numbers of positive and negative charges. So there is no overall charge.

Maths skills The numbers of protons, neutrons and electrons in atoms and ions are always integers (whole numbers).

Hint

Remember to take into account the number of electrons lost to form an Al^{3+} ion.

3. The table below gives the formulae of two ions.

Name of ion	Formula of ion
aluminium	Al^{3+}
sulfate	SO_4^{2-}

(a) Which of these is the correct formula for aluminium sulfate?

(1 mark)

☐ **A** Al_3SO_4

☐ **B** $Al_3(SO_4)_2$

☐ **C** $Al_2(SO_4)_3$

☐ **D** Al_2SO_4

(b) The atomic number of aluminium is 13 and its mass number is 27.

Calculate the numbers of protons, neutrons and electrons in an aluminium **ion**.

(3 marks)

protons...

neutrons...

electrons ....

(c) The melting point of aluminium sulfate is 770 °C.

Explain why the melting point of aluminium sulfate is high.

(3 marks)

Hint

Aluminium sulfate is an ionic compound.

....

....

....

....

....

Revision Guide page 103

(d) Aluminium sulfate is soluble in water. It is used in the treatment of water for drinking.

A solution of aluminium sulfate is formed by dissolving 35 g of aluminium sulfate in 250 cm^3 of water. Calculate the concentration, in g dm^{-3}, of this solution.

(2 marks)

Maths skills The volume is given in cm^3 but the concentration is in g dm^{-3}. Remember to convert from cm^3 to dm^3 in your calculation.

(Total for Question 3 = 9 marks)

Revision Guide
pages 94–96

Hint

Covalent bonding does not involve the formation of ions.

Hint

Draw a circle for each atom, overlapping them where you want to show the bonding electrons. For a compound show a solid dot for each electron from one element, and a cross for each electron from the other element.

Watch out!

Make sure you also include dots or crosses for any pairs of electrons not involved in bonding.

Explore

Ionic compounds, giant covalent substances and metals have high melting points and boiling points. Which different strong bonds are broken in these substances during melting and boiling?

4. Air is a mixture of gases, including nitrogen, oxygen and carbon dioxide.

(a) Why does nitrogen have a low boiling point?

(1 mark)

☐ **A** There are weak forces of attraction between nitrogen molecules.

☐ **B** There are weak covalent bonds between nitrogen molecules.

☐ **C** There are weak forces of attraction between nitrogen atoms.

☐ **D** There are weak covalent bonds between nitrogen atoms.

(b) The structure of a water molecule can be shown as:

$$H–O–H$$

The symbol – is used to show a covalent bond.

The electronic configuration of hydrogen is 1 and the electronic configuration of oxygen is 2.6.

Draw a dot-and-cross diagram to show a molecule of water, H_2O.

Show the outer electrons only.

(2 marks)

(c) Figure 2 shows the structures of diamond and graphite.

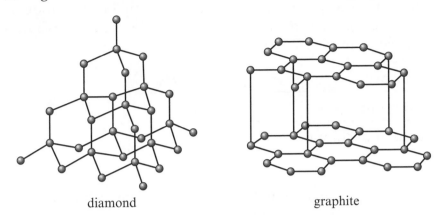

diamond   graphite

Figure 2

Explain, in terms of structure and bonding, why:

(i)   diamond has a very high melting point

(2 marks)

....

....

....

....

(ii) graphite is used as a lubricant.

(3 marks)

....

....

....

....

(Total for Question 4 = 8 marks)

Revision Guide
page 101

5. A student adds magnesium to an excess of dilute hydrochloric acid in an evaporating basin. Magnesium chloride solution and hydrogen gas form. When the reaction is complete, the student carefully evaporates the magnesium chloride solution to dryness. The table below shows her results.

Substance	Mass (g)
magnesium used	2.40
magnesium chloride formed	9.50

Hint

Magnesium and chlorine are the only elements present in magnesium chloride.

(a) Use the information in the table to calculate the mass of chlorine present in the magnesium chloride.

(1 mark)

LEARN IT!

An empirical formula is the simplest whole number ratio of atoms of each element in a substance.

(b) Use the mass of magnesium used (shown in the table) and your answer to part (a) to calculate the empirical formula of magnesium chloride.

(A_r of Mg = 24 and A_r of Cl = 35.5)

(3 marks)

Watch out!

Remember to write down the empirical formula after doing the calculations.

empirical formula ....

(Total for Question 5 = 4 marks)

6. This question is about clean tap water.

(a) Which of these describes clean tap water?

(1 mark)

☐ **A** a pure substance

☐ **B** a simple molecular compound

☐ **C** a mixture of substances

☐ **D** not potable

Revision Guide
pages 105 and 111

 **Explore**

Separation methods include simple distillation, fractional distillation, filtration, crystallisation and paper chromatography. How do each of these work?

(b) Drinking water can be made by the simple distillation of seawater.

(i) State, in terms of the relative energy of water particles, what happens when water is heated.

(1 mark)

....

....

LEARN IT!

There are changes in the arrangement, movement and relative energy of particles during state changes.

(ii) Suggest a reason that explains why producing large volumes of drinking water by simple distillation is expensive.

(1 mark)

....

....

(iii) Tap water contains dissolved salts that may interfere with chemical tests.

Describe why distilled water is suitable for use in such tests.

(1 mark)

Hint

What does tap water contain that distilled water does not?

....

....

Explore

Separation methods
include simple
distillation, fractional
distillation, filtration,
crystallisation and
paper chromatography.
What types of mixtures
can be separated by
each method?

Hint

Include the name of
the substance used in
chlorination.

(b) Fresh water can be made safe for drinking at a water treatment plant. Sedimentation is needed to allow insoluble particles to settle out. Filtration and chlorination are also needed.

(i) Describe why filtration is needed.

(1 mark)

....

....

(ii) Explain why chlorination is needed.

(2 marks)

....

....

....

....

(Total for Question 6 = 7 marks)

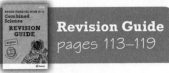

Revision Guide
pages 113–119

7. This question is about acids, alkalis and salts.

(a) Which row in the table correctly identifies a soluble substance and an insoluble substance?

(1 mark)

	Soluble in water	Insoluble in water
☐ A	silver chloride	lead chloride
☐ B	sodium carbonate	calcium sulfate
☐ C	sodium chloride	calcium chloride
☐ D	barium sulfate	barium nitrate

LEARN IT!

All nitrates are soluble, and so are common sodium, potassium and ammonium salts.

(b) Predict whether a precipitate will form when sodium hydroxide solution and iron(III) chloride solution are mixed together. Name the precipitate, if any forms.

(1 mark)

Hint

A precipitate is an insoluble substance formed in a reaction.

....

(c) Copper oxide and potassium hydroxide are examples of bases.

(i) Give a reason why both substances are bases.

(1 mark)

Explore

If you want to make a precipitate **XY**, you can usually use solutions of **X** nitrate and sodium **Y**. How could you make a precipitate of silver chloride?

....

....

(ii) Give a reason why potassium hydroxide is also described as an alkali.

(1 mark)

....

(d) Aqueous solutions can be acidic, neutral or alkaline. Give the pH of a neutral solution.

(1 mark)

....

 **Practical skills** One of the Core Practicals is the preparation of pure, dry hydrated copper sulfate crystals, starting from copper oxide. This is a similar practical. Make sure you include the main steps in your answer.

Hint

Many metal oxides and metal carbonates are insoluble in water.

Explore

What other methods are used to prepare soluble salts?

*(e) Plan an experiment to prepare pure, dry crystals of copper chloride, $CuCl_2$, from an insoluble copper compound and a suitable dilute acid. In your answer, include the names of suitable reagents and describe any essential stages. You may wish to write an equation to help with your plan.

(6 marks)

....
....
....
....
....
....
....
....
....
....
....

(Total for Question 7 = 11 marks)

8. This question is about electrolysis and extracting aluminium.

(a) Which of the following correctly describes the movement of ions during electrolysis?

(1 mark)

- ☐ **A** Negatively charged cations migrate to the positively charged cathode.

- ☐ **B** Positively charged cations migrate to the negatively charged cathode.

- ☐ **C** Positively charged anions migrate to the negatively charged anode.

- ☐ **D** Positively charged anions migrate to the positively charged anode.

(b) Two products form during the electrolysis of a concentrated sodium sulfate solution.

Which row in the table correctly shows what product forms at each electrode?

(1 mark)

	Cathode	Anode
☐ **A**	sodium	oxygen
☐ **B**	sodium	hydrogen
☐ **C**	hydrogen	oxygen
☐ **D**	hydrogen	sodium

Revision Guide
pages 120–123,
128

LEARN IT!

Electrolysis is a process in which electrical energy, from a direct current supply, decomposes electrolytes.

Hint

It may help to work out first if sodium or hydrogen forms at the cathode. Think about the reactivity of sodium and hydrogen.

(c) Predict the product formed at each electrode during the electrolysis of molten zinc chloride.

(2 marks)

cathode ....

anode ....

(d) Aluminium is extracted by the electrolysis of aluminium oxide, dissolved in molten cryolite.

State why aluminium cannot be extracted from aluminium oxide by heating with carbon.

(1 mark)

....

....

(Total for Question 8 = 5 marks)

 Explore

Most metals are extracted from compounds found in ores. How does the method used depend on the metal's position in the reactivity series, and the cost of the process itself?

9. Ammonia is manufactured from nitrogen and hydrogen by the Haber process:

$$N_2(g) + 3H_2(g) \rightleftharpoons 2NH_3(g)$$

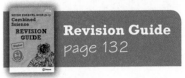

Revision Guide
page 132

(a) Give the meaning of the symbol $\rightleftharpoons$ in chemical equations.

(1 mark)

....

Explore

The nitrogen is extracted from the air and the hydrogen is obtained from natural gas. The reaction between them can reach a dynamic equilibrium. What is a dynamic equilibrium?

(b) State the conditions used in the Haber process:

(i) temperature

(1 mark)

....

(ii) pressure

(1 mark)

....

(iii) catalyst

(1 mark)

....

(Total for Question 9 = 4 marks)

TOTAL FOR PAPER = 60 MARKS

Combined Science
Paper 4: Chemistry 2

Time: 1 hour 10 minutes

Answer ALL questions. Write your answers in the spaces provided.

Revision Guide
page 133

Hint

It may help to work out first if the alkali metals are soft or hard metals.

Watch out!

Make sure you answer multiple choice questions, even if you are not certain that you are correct.

Hint

You need to add whole numbers to the spaces to the left of the formulae. Remember to write the state symbols for all the substances involved to the right of each formula.

Watch out!

Make sure you write about what you would **see** during the reaction, not why the substances react together or the names of any products formed.

1. This question is about the alkali metals, the elements in group 1 of the periodic table.

   (a) Which of these shows the typical physical properties of the alkali metals?

   (1 mark)

   ☐ **A** soft with relatively low melting points

   ☐ **B** soft with relatively high melting points

   ☐ **C** hard with relatively low melting points

   ☐ **D** hard with relatively high melting points

   (b) Sodium reacts with water to produce sodium hydroxide solution, NaOH, and hydrogen gas, H_2.

   (i) Balance the equation for the reaction between sodium and water. Include state symbols.

   (2 marks)

   ..... Na ..... + ... H_2O ..... → ..... NaOH .... + H_2 .....

   (ii) Describe **two** observations seen when a piece of sodium is added to a trough of water.

   (2 marks)

   ....

   ....

   ....

   (Total for Question 1 = 5 marks)

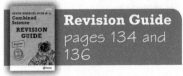
2. This question is about the halogens, the elements in group 7 of the periodic table.

(a) Which row in the table correctly shows the colours and physical states of the halogens at room temperature and pressure?

(1 mark)

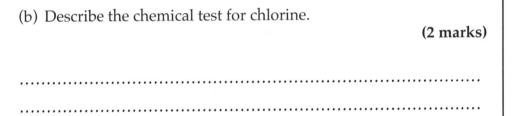

	Chlorine	Bromine	Iodine
A	pale yellow liquid	red–brown liquid	red–brown solid
B	yellow–green gas	purple liquid	purple-black solid
C	yellow–green gas	red–brown liquid	purple-black solid
D	yellow–green gas	purple liquid	red–brown liquid

(b) Describe the chemical test for chlorine.

(2 marks)

....

....

Revision Guide pages 134 and 136

LEARN IT!

The melting points and boiling points of the halogens increase going down group 7.

Practical skills Write down what you would do, including the names of necessary substances, and what you expect to observe.

Hint

A more reactive halogen can displace a less reactive halogen.

Explore

Chemists use displacement reactions, like this one, to determine a reactivity series for the halogens. How can they use displacement reactions to determine a reactivity series for metals?

*(c) A student investigates the reactivity of the halogens. She adds a few drops of a dilute aqueous solution of bromine to potassium iodide solution, and then to potassium chloride solution. Her results are shown in the table.

Mixture	Observation
bromine + potassium iodide	colour change seen
bromine + potassium chloride	no visible change

Explain how the student's observations provide evidence for the order of reactivity of bromine, iodine and chlorine. You should include an equation in your answer.

(6 marks)

....

....

....

....

....

....

....

....

....

....

....

....

....

(Total for Question 2 = 9 marks)

3. A student investigates the rate of reaction between calcium carbonate (marble chips) and excess dilute hydrochloric acid:

$$CaCO_3(s) + 2HCl(aq) \rightarrow CaCl_2(aq) + H_2O(l) + CO_2(g)$$

(a) Which of these would increase the rate of reaction?

(1 mark)

☐ **A** adding water to the acid

☐ **B** increasing the volume of acid

☐ **C** increasing the size of the marble chips

☐ **D** using calcium carbonate powder instead of marble chips

(b) Describe the chemical test for carbon dioxide.

(2 marks)

....

....

....

....

(c) The temperature of the reaction mixture increases during the reaction. Explain what this tells you about the reaction between calcium carbonate and dilute hydrochloric acid.

(2 marks)

....

....

....

....

Revision Guide
pages 139 and 140

Practical skills Remember that you should also be able to suggest practical methods to determine the rate of a given reaction.

Practical skills Write down what you would do, including the names of any necessary substances you might need, and what you expect to observe.

(d) The student measured the volume of carbon dioxide produced until all the calcium carbonate had reacted. Figure 1 shows the results that he obtained at 20 °C.

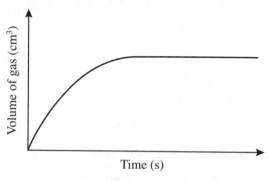

Figure 1

(i) The student repeats the experiment at a higher concentration of hydrochloric acid at 20 °C. Sketch the results he would expect on Figure 1.

(2 marks)

(ii) Explain why increasing the concentration has the effect you showed in part (i) on the rate of reaction. Your answer should be in terms of particles.

(2 marks)

....

....

....

....

(iii) State the effect on the reaction time of increasing the temperature of the reaction mixture.

(1 mark)

....

(Total for Question 3 = 10 marks)

4. Reactions involve energy transfers to and from the surroundings.

(a) Which row in the table correctly shows the overall energy change involved in breaking chemical bonds and forming chemical bonds?

(1 mark)

Revision Guide pages 142 and 143

	Breaking bonds	Forming bonds
☐ A	exothermic	endothermic
☐ B	exothermic	exothermic
☐ C	endothermic	endothermic
☐ D	endothermic	exothermic

Hint

Energy is transferred as heat **to** the surroundings in an exothermic change, and transferred as heat **from** the surroundings in an endothermic change.

(b) Explain what is meant by the term 'activation energy'.

(2 marks)

....

....

Hint

The amount of energy involved differs from reaction to reaction. You need to give a general definition in your answer.

(c) Hydrogen peroxide decomposes to form water and oxygen:

$$2H_2O_2(aq) \rightarrow 2H_2O(l) + O_2(g)$$

The reaction is exothermic.

Complete Figure 2 to show a reaction profile diagram for this reaction. Draw and label the activation energy.

(3 marks)

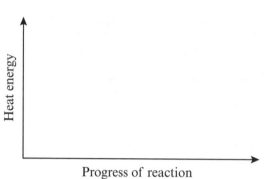

Figure 2

(d) (i) On Figure 2, draw the reaction profile for the same reaction in the presence of a catalyst. Label this line with an **X**.

(1 mark)

(ii) The products formed in a reaction are the same whether or not a catalyst is used. State **two** other features of a catalyst.

(2 marks)

....

....

....

....

(e) Describe the role of enzymes in the production of alcoholic drinks.

(1 mark)

....

....

(Total for Question 4 = 10 marks)

5. This question is about crude oil.

(a) Which of these statements about crude oil is correct?

(1 mark)

☐ **A** It is a renewable resource.

☐ **B** It contains molecules with carbon atoms in rings and chains.

☐ **C** It is a complex mixture of carbohydrates.

☐ **D** At room temperature, it contains only liquids.

(b) Crude oil is separated in fractions using fractional distillation. Figure 3 shows an oil fractionating column and the main fractions obtained from it.

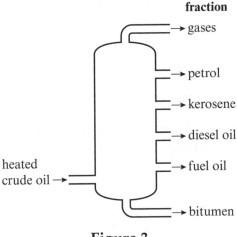

fraction

gases

petrol

kerosene

diesel oil

heated crude oil →

fuel oil

bitumen

Figure 3

(i) Identify the fraction that has the highest boiling point.

(1 mark)

....

(ii) Identify the fraction that is used as a fuel for large ships and some power stations.

(1 mark)

....

(iii) Give a commercial use for the kerosene fraction.

(1 mark)

....

Revision Guide
pages 144 and 145

Hint

A non-renewable resource is being used up faster than it can be replaced.

Watch out!

Make sure you can recall the names and uses of the fractions shown in the diagram.

Explore

How are oil refineries able to separate crude oil into useful fractions by fractional distillation? How does this process work?

Watch out!

'Identify' means you must give an answer using the information given. In these questions, these are the names of crude oil fractions and where they leave the fractionating column.

Hint

This is not the same as a non-renewable resource, although these resources are usually also finite.

Watch out!

'Describe' means you need to give an account of something without giving reasons.

Hint

These include differences in other physical properties of the fractions, and differences between the molecules themselves.

(c) Give **one** industrial use of crude oil, other than as a source of fuels.

(1 mark)

....

(d) State why crude oil may be described as a finite resource.

(1 mark)

....

(e) The substances in crude oil fractions are mostly members of the alkane homologous series.

(i) Describe why alkanes are **hydrocarbons**.

(2 marks)

....

....

(ii) The hydrocarbons in different fractions have different boiling points. State **two** other ways in which they differ.

(2 marks)

....

....

....

....

(Total for Question 5 = 10 marks)

Revision Guide pages 152 and 153

6. This question is about the Earth's atmosphere.

(a) Where do scientists think the gases in the Earth's earliest atmosphere came from?

(1 mark)

☐ **A** the oceans

☐ **B** primitive plants

☐ **C** carbonate rocks

☐ **D** volcanoes

(b) Which gas was the most abundant in the Earth's earliest atmosphere?

(1 mark)

☐ **A** nitrogen

☐ **B** oxygen

☐ **C** argon

☐ **D** carbon dioxide

Watch out!

Read questions carefully. This one is not about today's atmosphere.

(c) Oxygen is found in the atmosphere.

(i) Describe the chemical test for oxygen.

(2 marks)

....

....

Practical skills Write down what you would do, including the names of any necessary substances you might need, and what you expect to observe.

(ii) Explain why the amount of oxygen in the atmosphere increased over millions of years.

(2 marks)

....

....

....

....

Hint

Living organisms released oxygen into the atmosphere. What type of organism were they, and what process was involved?

Hint

Carbon dioxide is a very soluble gas.

Hint

Although humans produce carbon dioxide because of respiration, just like other living organisms, you need to think about other things we do that release this gas.

Explore

There is evidence that human activities are leading to increased levels of carbon dioxide and methane, and that this is a cause of climate change. What evidence is there for this? What are the potential effects of climate change, and how could they be reduced or overcome?

(d) Carbon dioxide is described as a greenhouse gas.

(i) Explain how the formation of oceans affected the amount of carbon dioxide in the atmosphere.

(2 marks)

....

....

....

....

(ii) Human activities increase the amount of some greenhouse gases. Complete the table below.

(2 marks)

Name of greenhouse gas	Main human activity that produces the gas
carbon dioxide	
	livestock farming

(iii) Increasing amounts of greenhouse gases in the atmosphere cause global warming.

Other than an increase in temperature, describe **one** potential effect of global warming on the environment.

(1 mark)

....

....

(Total for Question 6 = 11 marks)

7. This question is about the combustion of hydrocarbon fuels.

   (a) Which row in the table correctly shows the possible products of complete combustion and incomplete combustion of hydrocarbon fuels?

   (1 mark)

Revision Guide
pages 146–148

Hint

Complete combustion happens in a plentiful supply of air or oxygen, but incomplete combustion happens when the supply of air or oxygen is limited.

	Complete combustion	Incomplete combustion
A	carbon dioxide, water	carbon monoxide only
B	carbon dioxide, carbon monoxide, water	carbon monoxide, water
C	carbon dioxide, water	carbon monoxide, carbon, water
D	carbon monoxide, water	carbon dioxide, carbon, water

   (b) Sulfur dioxide is produced when some hydrocarbon fuels burn.

   (i) Name the element that reacts with oxygen to produce sulfur dioxide.

   (1 mark)

   ....

   (ii) Acid rain forms when sulfur dioxide dissolves in water in the atmosphere.

   Describe **one** environmental problem caused by acid rain.

   (1 mark)

Hint

Your answer could be to do with the built environment (such as buildings), or to do with the living environment (such as plants and animals).

   ....

   ....

   (c) Carbon monoxide may be produced during the combustion of hydrocarbon fuels.

   Explain how it acts as a toxic gas.

   (2 marks)

Hint

Carbon monoxide passes into the bloodstream when we breathe it in. What does carbon monoxide do when it gets there?

   ....

   ....

   ....

   ....

   (Total for Question 7 = 5 marks)

   TOTAL FOR PAPER = 60 MARKS

Combined Science
Practice Paper 5: Physics 1

Time allowed: 1 hour 10 minutes

Answer ALL questions. Write your answers in the spaces provided.

1. Robert and Nolly plan to set up an experiment to measure speed. They have a trolley, an inclined ramp, a ruler and a stopwatch.

   (a) Describe a method that the students could use to measure the speed of the trolley using the apparatus above.

   (3 marks)

   ....
   ....
   ....
   ....
   ....
   ....

   (b) Suggest other apparatus that the students could use to improve the precision of the data collected.

   (2 marks)

   ....
   ....

Revision Guide
page 157

Hint

Read the list of apparatus carefully. Use all the apparatus, and nothing else.

Practical skills You could sketch and label a diagram and then say how the apparatus will be used.

Hint

Don't ramble! Give clear, concise points. Use bullet points if you find paragraphs hard.

Hint

There are two marks here; you need two pieces of apparatus.

Practical skills Think about the biggest cause of uncertainty in the experiment then suggest what could be used to get round that problem.

(c) Robert and Nolly then extend their experiment to investigate the influence of another independent variable. The table below shows data collected by the students.

(cm)	Distance (m)	Time (s)	Speed (m/s)
5	1.80	3.2	0.56
10	1.80	2.4	
15	1.80	1.8	1.0
20	1.80	1.4	1.29
25	1.80	1.0	
30	1.80	0.4	4.5
35	1.80	0.2	9.0

(i) Deduce what the new independent variable might be.

(1 mark)

....

(ii) Add the **two** missing entries for the fourth column.

(1 mark)

Hint

The independent variable is the one the person doing the experiment chooses the values of. Look for one which goes up in regular steps.

Hint

Look back at the aim of the experiment at the start of the question to work out what you might need to help with the analysis.

Maths skills You will have to calculate the correct entries. Choose the appropriate formula, write in the values, and then work out the answer.

Hint

Here you get one mark for the units; remind yourself about what these are by looking at the table.

LEARN IT!

$$speed = \frac{distance}{time}$$

Hint

Think about the formula for acceleration. Which variable isn't given in this part of the question?

Explore

There were several energy transfers as the trolley rolled down the ramp and came to a stop. At the top of the ramp it had a store of gravitational potential energy. When it was released, this was transferred to kinetic energy of the trolley. In terms of energy transfers, why does it come to a stop?

(d) Robert and Nolly then release the trolley from a height of 0.02 m and record a time of 4.5 s over a distance of 1.8 m.

(i) Calculate the speed of the trolley. Give the unit.

(3 marks)

(ii) Suggest the additional data that the students would need to collect to be able to calculate the acceleration of the trolley.

(2 marks)

....

....

....

....

(Total for question 1 = 12 marks)

2. (a) A crash test car of mass 1000 kg is driven at the design testing centre to examine impact forces. The car starts from rest and accelerates to its final speed.

Revision Guide
page 164

   (i) Write the equation to calculate the acceleration of the car towards the crash barrier in a time t.

(1 mark)

Hint

You need to know the relationship between acceleration, change in velocity, and time taken.

....

   (ii) The car is accelerated uniformly from 0 m/s to 10 m/s over a time of 20 s.

      Calculate how far the car will travel.

(3 marks)

LEARN IT!

'Uniformly' means at a constant rate.

Maths skills Check that the answer seems reasonable. A car travelling for 20s is unlikely to cover more than 500m, or less than 20m.

Revision Guide
page 159

Hint

Break the question up. It is actually asking for how four things change over the course of the ride.

*(b) The graph in Figure 1 reflects a test ride by a cyclist on a new bicycle. Discuss the test ride and refer to acceleration, constant speed, deceleration and distance covered in your answer.

(6 marks)

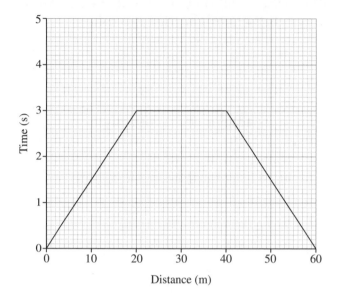

Figure 1

....

....

....

....

....

....

....

....

....

....

....

(Total for Question 2 = 10 marks)

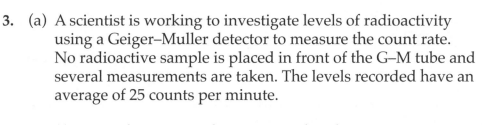

3. (a) A scientist is working to investigate levels of radioactivity using a Geiger–Muller detector to measure the count rate. No radioactive sample is placed in front of the G–M tube and several measurements are taken. The levels recorded have an average of 25 counts per minute.

(i) Give the name of the radiation that the scientist is measuring.

(1 mark)

....

Hint

What kind of radiation is always present, everywhere, every day?

(ii) State **two** sources of this radiation.

(2 marks)

....

....

Hint

Some sources of radioactivity are natural, some are man-made. Think about things that are around us all the time.

(b) The scientist now places a radioactive sample in front of the Geiger–Muller detector and takes some more measurements. The levels recorded now have an average of 200 corrected counts per minute.

(i) Describe what the scientist does to determine the corrected count rate.

(1 mark)

....

....

Practical skills Doing this is like zeroing a top-pan balance before use. There were extra counts that were not from what was being studied, so the scientist got rid of them.

(ii) Explain why the scientist wears a photographic film badge while she carries out her research.

(2 marks)

....

....

Practical skills Whenever you do an experiment, you need to think about safety. How could a film badge help make her safer?

Hint

Mass affects the ionising properties of radiation. Think about how mass varies with different types of radiation.

 Explore

The ionising properties are related to the penetrating powers of the different types of radiation. Can you think how?

Hint

Think of something that will mean the scientist gets a smaller dose of radiation.

(c) Describe the nature of alpha, beta and gamma radiation in terms of ionising properties.

(3 marks)

....

....

....

....

....

....

....

....

(d) Suggest **one** safety precaution the scientist should take when carrying out this experiment.

(1 mark)

....

....

(Total for Question 3 = 10 marks)

4. Figure 2 shows the graph of a radio wave.

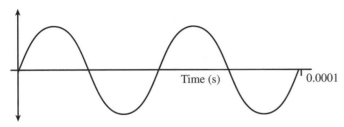

Time (s)   0.0001

Figure 2

Revision Guide
pages 175–176

(a) On the graph:

   (i)   Identify the amplitude of the wave by adding 'A' next to an arrow or marker.

   (1 mark)

   (ii) Identify the time period of the wave by adding 'T' with arrows or markers.

   (1 mark)

   (iii) Determine the time period of the wave.

   (1 mark)

Hint

Amplitude is how tall the wave is.

Hint

How many time periods are shown on the diagram?

Explore

Radio waves travel through a vacuum at the speed of light. How might you be able to set up an experiment to directly measure the speed of a radio wave?

(b) Determine the frequency of the wave shown in the diagram.

(2 marks)

(c) Write the equation linking wave speed, wavelength and time period.

(1 mark)

....

(Total for Question 4 = 6 marks)

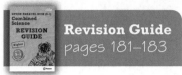

5. Figure 3 shows part of the electromagnetic spectrum.

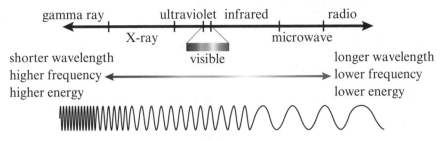

Figure 3

(a) State **one** use for each of the following waves:

    (i) microwaves

                                                     (1 mark)

....

    (ii) ultraviolet

                                                     (1 mark)

....

    (iii) gamma rays.

                                                     (1 mark)

....

(b) Explain which of the waves in (a) is the most damaging to body cells.

                                                     (2 marks)

....

....

....

....

Hint

Electromagnetic waves can travel through a vacuum because they don't require any particles to vibrate.

Maths skills 3×10^8 means 300 000 000. You can think of the 8 as meaning 'move the decimal point 8 places to the right'.

LEARN IT!

speed (v) = frequency (f) × wavelength (λ)

Hint

'Visible light from the Sun travels at' is another way of saying 'The speed of light from the Sun is'.

Maths skills Remember when dividing indices, you subtract them.

Explore

The wavelengths of visible light are usually expressed in nanometres (nm) (1 nm = 1×10^{-9} m). How would you work out the wavelengths of red and violet light in nanometres?

(c) Which one of the following terms best describes the nature of electromagnetic waves?

(1 mark)

- ☐ A longitudinal
- ☐ B mechanical
- ☐ C seismic
- ☐ D transverse

(d) Visible light from the Sun travels at 3×10^8 m/s through space, with approximate frequencies ranging from 4.3×10^{14} Hz (red light) to 7.7×10^{14} Hz (violet light).

(i) Calculate the approximate wavelength of red light.

(2 marks)

wavelength = ... m

(ii) Calculate the approximate wavelength of violet light.

(2 marks)

wavelength = ... m

(e) Suggest three types of EM waves commonly found in communications systems, giving examples of how they are used.

(3 marks)

....

....

....

(Total for Question 5 = 13 marks)

Explore

Radio signals are divided into ground waves, sky waves and space waves as the wavelength shortens. Find out why these different types of wave got their names.

Revision Guide
pages 169, 170
and 173

Maths skills Write down the formula. Put in the values from the question. Calculate the answer. Not all the values given will be needed in this part of the question.

Hint

Any mechanical system, like a lift, has moving parts that rub together. What happens to them?

Maths skills In the formula, only the speed is squared.

---

6. A lift travels between floors in a building. The lift moves from the ground floor to the fourth floor through a height of 15 m in 20 s. The mass of the lift is 750 kg.

(a) Calculate how much energy, in J, the lift gains in moving from the ground floor to the fourth floor. Take g to be 10 N/kg.

(2 marks)

energy gained = ...…........…..... J

(b) As the lift moves upwards, not all of the energy supplied is usefully transferred.

Suggest **one** way in which energy is not usefully transferred.

(1 mark)

....

....

(c) Calculate the kinetic energy, in J, of the lift when it is moving from the ground floor to the fourth floor.

(4 marks)

kinetic energy = ….............. J

(d) Explain why this mechanical process could be described as wasteful. Give an example of wasted energy in this process.

(2 marks)

....

....

....

....

(Total for Question 6 = 9 marks)

TOTAL FOR PAPER = 60 MARKS

Combined Science
Paper 6: Physics 2

Time allowed: 1 hour 10 minutes

Answer ALL questions. Write your answers in the spaces provided.

Revision Guide
page 205

Hint

Remember that W is the same as J/s.

1. (a) A kettle is rated at 2000 W and is designed to operate on a 230 V mains supply. Calculate the charge moved in the kettle in one second. Give correct unit.

   (3 marks)

Hint

Think about how the energy in the heater, the water, and the air around the kettle changes.

charge = ...

   (b) Explain what happens to the energy of the system when the kettle is switched on.

   (3 marks)

   ....
   ....
   ....
   ....
   ....
   ....

(c) Draw an energy transfer diagram to illustrate the energy transferred inside the kettle after it is switched on.

(3 marks)

Hint

Be careful with the widths of the arrows. The larger the energy store, the wider its arrow.

(d) Describe how energy is not transferred usefully while boiling water in the kettle.

(2 marks)

Explore

How does the electric current cause the heater to get hot?

....

....

....

....

(Total for question 1 = 11 marks)

Revision Guide
page 217

Hint

Use the right-hand corkscrew rule: make a thumbs-up sign with your right hand, point your thumb in the direction of the current flow, and your fingers will curve in the direction of the field.

Watch out!

This is similar to a bar magnet, but the field lines are inside the coil as well.

Hint

Remember that the current can be turned off or reversed.

Explore

How does the density of flux lines affect the strength of the magnet?

---

2. (a) Figure 1 shows a current-carrying wire passing through a card.

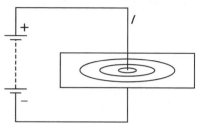

Figure 1

A compass is positioned at various places on the card to determine the direction of the magnetic field round the wire. Explain whether the magnetic field is clockwise or anticlockwise.

(2 marks)

....

....

(b) (i) The wire is now turned into a solenoid. Draw the new magnetic field that this produces.

(4 marks)

(ii) Suggest a use for this device.

(1 mark)

....

(Total for question 2 = 7 marks)

3. An electrical heater supplies electrical energy to a copper block of mass 2000 g at 12 V with a current of 12 A for 2 minutes.

    (a) Calculate the energy supplied to the heater. State the unit.

    (3 marks)

                    energy supplied = ……………… unit ……….

    (b) Calculate the temperature rise for the block of copper when supplied with the energy from (a) (your answer). The specific heat capacity of copper is 385 J/kg K. State the unit.

    (3 marks)

                    temperature rise = …………… unit ……………………

    (c) Suggest why the actual temperature rise may be lower than the predicted value.

    (1 mark)

    ....

    ....

Hint

What do you do when you go outside in the cold and want to reduce your heat loss?

Explore

Consider how you would design an experiment to test which material was best. What equipment would you use? What would you change and what would you keep the same?

(d) (i) Give **one** way to reduce unwanted energy transfer in the heating of a metal block.

(1 mark)

....

(ii) Give an example of a suitable material that could be used.

(1 mark)

....

(Total for question 3 = 9 marks)

4. Deimos, one of the moons of Mars, orbits at a distance of almost 24 000 km from the planet. It is thought that Deimos was once an asteroid from further away and later 'captured' by Mars.

 Revision Guide
page 201

(a) Describe what would have caused Deimos to be 'captured' and become a moon of Mars.

(3 marks)

Hint

What force would be 'capturing' it?

....

....

....

....

....

(b) (i) Name **two** other non-contact forces that act over a distance.

(2 marks)

Hint

Think about what can cause something to be attracted or repelled.

....

....

(ii) Explain what decides the magnitude of the two non-contact forces you have described in (i).

(1 mark)

....

(c) (i) Describe the pair of vertical forces acting when a cyclist sits on a stationary bicycle at traffic lights.

(2 marks)

Hint

Give the type of force and its direction.

....

....

(ii) Describe the horizontal contact forces acting as the cyclist moves off when the traffic light turns green.

(2 marks)

Explore

How does the size of the unbalanced force affect the acceleration?

....

....

....

(Total for question 4 = 10 marks)

Revision Guide
pages 206,
207 and 220

Hint

There are 1.5V between
the right and left side
of the circuit. Consider
how that divides up
between the lamps.

LEARN IT!

Potential difference
is the difference in
potential between two
points.

Hint

As a thermistor gains
heat energy, more
electrons are able to
flow in it. Think how
that will affect the
current, and thus what
must have happened to
the resistance.

Hint

Think of something
where temperature
controls what happens.

5. Figure 2 is a circuit diagram that shows three identical lamps and
one cell.

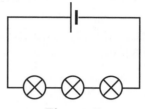

Figure 2

(a) The cell provides 1.5 V. State the potential difference across each
lamp.

(1 mark)

....

(b) Figure 3 shows a circuit to test a thermistor.

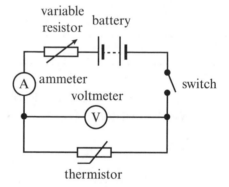

Figure 3

(i) Describe how a thermistor changes the current flowing in
the circuit.

(3 marks)

....

....

(ii) Give a use for a thermistor in a domestic circuit.

(1 mark)

....

(c) Calculate the electrical power of the following domestic appliances that use temperature controls, commonly used in a household circuit:

(i)   a toaster drawing a current of 4 A connected to a 230 V domestic electricity supply

(2 marks)

power = ...W

(ii)   a hairdryer drawing a current of 2 A with a resistance of 300 Ω.

(2 marks)

Explore

Why might a hairdryer need an automatic temperature control?

power = ...W

(Total for question 5 = 9 marks)

Revision Guide
pages 228–230

Practical skills Think about what other equipment you could use, and what other measurements you could take.

6. Two students carry out an experiment to investigate the linear elastic distortion of a thin spring. They add weights to a spring but can only find five weights: one of 0.1 N, one of 0.5 N and three of 1 N. They then measure the final extension. When the spring is unloaded the students find the spring has stretched.

(a) (i) Suggest **two** ways of improving the experiment.

(2 marks)

....

....

....

....

(ii) Suggest a safety precaution that should be used in carrying out this experiment.

(1 mark)

....

(b) The table below shows results from a different experiment for the loading of a 32 mm spring.

(2 marks)

Weight (N)	Length of spring (mm)
0	32
0.1	
	40
0.3	
0.4	48
	52
0.6	56

Hint

Spot the pattern in each column. Then work out the missing numbers.

(i) Complete the missing values in the table.

(ii) Calculate the spring constant for the weight of 2 N resulting in extension 0.026 m.

(2 marks)

force = spring constant × extension

k = ... N/m

(iii) Caitlin and Dinah try to calculate the spring constant from their results but, instead, find a range of values from 7.69–6.78 N/m. Suggest a possible source of error in their data collection that may have resulted in this range of values.

(1 mark)

Practical skills Think about what is difficult to measure accurately in this experiment.

....

Hint

In this graph, the dependent variable is plotted on the x-axis, rather than the y-axis as is usual. This is because it makes the gradient equal to the spring constant, so it is easier than having to find the reciprocal (1/gradient) to calculate the spring constant.

Explore

How could you use the spring and this graph to find out the weight of an object that is less than 0.6 N?

*(c) The students used their results from (b) to produce Figure 4.

Explain how the graph illustrates linear elastic distortion and how the graph could be improved.

Explain how you could extend the experiment to find out the force, which makes the spring change shape permanently. You should refer to the graph in your answer.

(6 marks)

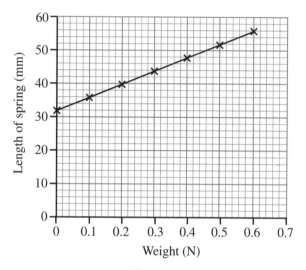

Figure 4

....

....

....

....

....

....

....

....

....

....

....

....

....

....

*..

....

....

....

....

....

(Total for question 6 = 14 marks)

TOTAL FOR PAPER = 60 MARKS

Combined Science
Paper 1: Biology 1

Time allowed: 1 hour 10 minutes

Answer ALL questions. Write your answers in the spaces provided.

1. Catalase is an enzyme found in many different tissues in plants and animals. It speeds up the breakdown of hydrogen peroxide:

hydrogen peroxide → water + oxygen

A group of students carried out an experiment to determine the amount of catalase in different plant and animal tissues. Their method is shown below.

Method

1. Add hydrogen peroxide solution to a test tube.

2. Add a few drops of washing up liquid and shake gently to mix.

3. Add a piece of plant or animal tissue.

4. Measure the height of the foam produced by the oxygen after 30 seconds.

(a) Suggest a reason that explains why the students added a few drops of washing up liquid.

(1 mark)

To produce a foam (with the oxygen). ✓

(b) The students decided to use a water bath to control the temperature. Which temperature would be most suitable to use in their experiment?

(1 mark)

☒ **A** 0 °C ✓

☐ **B** 20 °C

☐ **C** 60 °C

☐ **D** 100 °C

(c) State **two** variables, other than time or temperature, that the students should control in their investigation.

(2 marks)

Alternative answer:
You could also write:
• mass of tissue
• pH of mixture.

volume of hydrogen peroxide ✓

concentration of hydrogen peroxide ✓

(d) The students discovered that raw liver caused foaming in their experiment, but cooked liver did not. Suggest an explanation for these observations.

(2 marks)

Alternative answer:
Denatured is the scientific term but you would still get a mark for saying destroyed or damaged.

Liver contains catalase, ✓ which is denatured by heating. ✓

(e) Explain why catalase will break down hydrogen peroxide, but it will not break down starch.

(2 marks)

The enzyme's active site ✓ fits hydrogen peroxide but not starch. ✓

(Total for Question 1 = 8 marks)

2. (a) In humans there are two types of cell division: mitosis and meiosis. The table gives several statements about cell division. Tick one box in each row if the statement is true for mitosis only, for meiosis only or for both mitosis and meiosis. The first row has been completed for you.

(4 marks)

Statement	Mitosis only	Meiosis only	Both mitosis and meiosis
Used for growth and replacement of cells	✓		
Used for production of gametes		✓	✓
Before the parent cell divides each chromosome is copied			✓ ✓
Produces genetically identical cells	✓		✓
Halves the chromosome number		✓	✓

(b) Cystic fibrosis is an inherited disease caused by a mutated allele for the CFTR protein found in lungs and other tissues. A couple, neither of whom had cystic fibrosis, came from families that both had a history of the disease. The couple were concerned that they might have children who were affected. They underwent genetic testing and were found to be heterozygous for the cystic fibrosis gene.

(i) Using F for the normal allele and f for the mutated allele, state the genotype of both parents.

(1 mark)

Ff (and Ff) ✓

(ii) Predict the percentage probability of the couple's children having cystic fibrosis. Use the Punnett square.

(2 marks)

		Mother's gametes	
		F	f
Father's gametes	F	FF	Ff
	f	Ff	ff

✓

Percentage probability of having a child with cystic fibrosis = 25%. ✓

(c) Two proteins, DAZL and PRDM14, are involved in the development of sperm cells. Mutations in these genes are associated with an increased risk of developing testicular cancer. Almost 100% of all testicular cancers can be completely cured if diagnosed early.

Explain how the Human Genome Project has made it possible to improve early diagnosis of diseases, such as testicular cancer in men with a family history of testicular cancer.

(3 marks)

Being able to determine the base sequence of an individual ✓
means that doctors know if that individual has an increased risk
of testicular cancer, ✓ so he can be monitored more closely
and diagnosed earlier. ✓

(Total for Question 2 = 10 marks)

---

3. A man has an infection of disease-causing bacteria. He has not been immunised against these bacteria. Figure 1 shows how the number of these bacteria changes after a doctor gives the man a 7-day course of antibiotics.

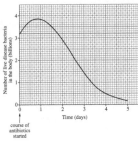

Figure 1

(a) Which of these is a typical feature of non-communicable diseases?

(1 mark)

- ☐ **A** a pathogen is involved
- ☐ **B** cases are often localised
- ☒ **C** cases may be widely distributed ✓
- ☐ **D** number of cases varies rapidly

(b) Use the graph to determine:

(i) the time taken for the number of live bacteria to begin to fall after starting the course of antibiotics

(1 mark)

0.9 days ✓

(ii) the maximum number of live disease bacteria in the man's body.

(1 mark)

3.85 billion ✓

(c) State whether the man has a communicable or a non-communicable disease. Give a reason for you answer.

(2 marks)

The man has a communicable disease ✓ because it is caused
by a bacterium or a pathogen. ✓

(d) The doctor suspected that the illness was caused by a bacterium rather than by a virus. Give **two** reasons that explain why the doctor was correct.

(2 marks)

The number of bacteria decreased and the man felt better
because the antibiotics killed the bacteria. ✓ antibiotics do
not affect viruses. ✓

(e) The man was told to take the antibiotics for the full seven days, even if he began to feel better.

(i) Explain why antibiotics can be used to treat bacterial infections.

(2 marks)

Antibiotics inhibit cell processes in bacteria ✓ but not in the
host organism. ✓

(ii) Give **two** reasons why it was important that the man did not stop taking the antibiotics early.

(2 marks)

Some disease bacteria remain ✓ and these bacteria could
reproduce. ✓

Alternative answer:
You could also say:

The remaining bacteria are more likely to be resistant to the antibiotic and there is a risk of increasing the number of antibiotic-resistant bacteria.

(f) Figure 2 shows the results of two studies into the effect of alcohol consumption on the risk of developing liver disease. One group (solid line) consisted only of males and the other group (dotted line) consisted only of females.

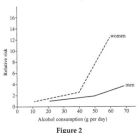

Figure 2

State and explain the relationship between alcohol consumption and relative risk of liver disease for men.

(3 marks)

As alcohol consumption increases risk of liver disease also
increases. ✓ The risk increases much more with alcohol
consumption greater than 50 g per day ✓ because ethanol is
poisonous, particularly to liver cells. ✓

(Total for Question 3 = 14 marks)

4. Figure 3 shows a bacterial cell and a plant cell.

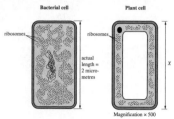

Figure 3

(a) (i) Both types of cell contain ribosomes. State the function of a ribosome.

(1 mark)

Ribosomes make or synthesise proteins. ✓

(ii) The plant cell contains mitochondria but the bacterial cell does not. State **two** other ways in which the plant cell is different to the bacterial cell.

(2 marks)

Plant cells have vacuoles ✓ and chloroplasts ✓ bacterial cells do not.

Alternative answers:
You could also say:

Plant cells:

• have a nucleus

• are much larger.

(b) Although the cells are drawn the same size, the magnifications are different. The actual length of the bacterial cell is two micrometres.

Calculate the actual length, X, of the plant cell. Give your answer in micrometres, to one decimal place. Show your working.

(3 marks)

$$\text{real size} = \frac{\text{image size}}{\text{magnification}}$$

$$= \frac{53}{500} \checkmark$$

$$= 0.106 \text{ mm} \checkmark$$

$$= 106.0 \text{ micrometres} \checkmark$$

(Total for Question 4 = 6 marks)

5. Figure 4 shows a percentile chart developed by the US Government to monitor the growth of males between the ages of 2 and 20 years. It can be used to monitor both weight and height.

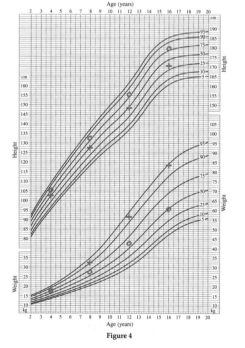

Figure 4

(a) Describe how a doctor or nurse could use this chart to monitor the growth of a boy from the age of 2 to 16 years.

(3 marks)

Measure weight and height ✓ every year or at regular intervals ✓ and plot the results on the chart. ✓

(b) The table shows the weight and height records of two boys, A and B, from the ages of 4 to 16.

Age (years)	Height (cm)		Weight (kg)	
	Boy A	Boy B	Boy A	Boy B
4	102	105	18	17
8	127	132	32	27
12	148	155	56	42
16	170	179	83	60

There is 1 mark per set of points correctly plotted, as shown in Figure 4.

(i) Plot the height and weight of both boys on the chart in Figure 4. Use '+' for Boy A and 'o' for Boy B.

(4 marks)

(ii) Explain what your plotted points show about the development of the two boys.

(4 marks)

Boy A is average or below average height ✓ but in the upper range for weight and is overweight. ✓

Boy B is above average height ✓ and average weight or possibly underweight for his height. ✓

(Total for Question 5 = 11 marks)

6. Figure 5 shows the neurones and other parts of the body involved in the response to touching a sharp object.

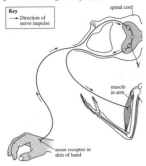

Figure 5

(a) Identify which of the following describes the correct sequence of events following touching a sharp object.

(1 mark)

☐ A sensory receptor → sensory neurone → motor neurone → relay neurone

☐ B sensory receptor → muscle → motor neurone → relay neurone

☐ C sensory receptor → relay neurone → sensory neurone → motor neurone

☒ D sensory receptor → sensory neurone → relay neurone → motor neurone ✓

(b) (i) State the name of the structure labelled Y on the diagram.

(1 mark)

synapse ✓

(ii) Describe the events that occur at point Y that allow the impulse to be passed on from one neurone to the next.

(3 marks)

Nerve impulse reaches the axon terminal. ✓ Neurotransmitter substance is released into the gap. ✓ This is detected by the next neurone, which generates a new impulse. ✓

*(c) Stem cell therapy has been suggested as a possible treatment for patients with spinal cord injuries. Explain how stem cell therapy could be used in the future to treat spinal cord injury. In your answer you should discuss the sources of stem cells as well as the ethical implications.

(6 marks)

Stem cells are unspecialised cells, which can divide and produce differentiated cells. Stem cells can be obtained from embryos or from the patient, when they are called adult stem cells.

Embryonic stem cells are taken from embryos at a very early stage of division; they can be used to repair damaged nervous tissue in the spinal cord. They are easy to extract from embryos and can produce any type of cell, which the patient receives as a transplant. However, embryos are destroyed in this process and some people think embryos have a right to life. There is also a danger of rejection because the transplanted tissue is seen as foreign and could be attacked by the patient's immune system.

If adult stem cells are used, they do not require destruction of embryos and will not be rejected (if taken from the person to be treated). However the types of cells that adult stem cells will differentiate into are limited so they may not be suitable for treating damaged nerve tissue. Stem cell therapy may also increase the risk of cancer.

(Total for Question 6 = 11 marks)

TOTAL FOR PAPER = 60 MARKS

13   14   15

Combined Science
Paper 2: Biology

Time allowed: 1 hour 10 minutes

Answer ALL questions. Write your answers in the spaces provided.

1. (a) A student carried out an investigation into osmosis in potato pieces. The student cut five pieces of potato, weighed them and then placed them into different concentrations of salt solution. After one hour the student removed the potato pieces from the salt solution and weighed them again. The student's results are shown in the table.

Concentration of salt solution (mol dm⁻³)	Initial mass of potato (g)	Final mass of potato (g)	Percentage change in mass (%)
0.0	5.2	5.4	$\frac{5.4 - 5.2}{5.2} \times 100 = +3.8$ ✓
0.25	5.6	5.6	$\frac{5.6 - 5.6}{5.6} \times 100 = 0.0$ ✓
0.5	5.6	5.4	−3.6
1.0	5.0	4.6	−8.0
1.5	5.2	4.2	$\frac{4.2 - 5.2}{5.2} \times 100 = -19.2$ ✓

(i) Complete the table by calculating the percentage change in mass of the potato pieces. Give your answers to 1 decimal place.

(3 marks)

(ii) Describe **one** way in which the student could improve the experiment.

(1 mark)

Use the same shape of potato piece. ✓

(iii) Use your results from part (i) to estimate the solute concentration of the potato cells.

(1 mark)

0.25 mol dm⁻³ ✓

Alternative answers:
You could also:
- use the same surface area of potato pieces
- blot the pieces dry before measuring mass
- keep all the tubes at same temperature
- cover the tubes to prevent solution evaporating.

(b) Figure 1 shows the part of the lung where gas exchange takes place.

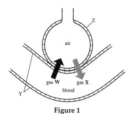

Figure 1

(i) State the name of the structures labelled 'Y' and 'Z' in the diagram.

(2 marks)

Structure Y is the .....capillary wall.✓..........

Structure Z is the .....wall of the alveolus.✓........

(ii) Which one of the following methods describes how gases W and X move in the directions shown?

(1 mark)

☒ **A** diffusion ✓

☐ **B** osmosis

☐ **C** breathing

☐ **D** respiration

(iii) State the name of gas W.

(1 mark)

carbon dioxide ✓

(c) A scientist recently estimated that the average human lung has 480 million alveoli and that 1 million alveoli have a surface area of 0.15 m².

Calculate the total surface area of one human lung.

(2 marks)

480 × 0.15 = 72 m² ✓ ✓

(Total for Question 1 = 11 marks)

2. Figure 2 shows the heart rate of an adult male over a 24-hour period.

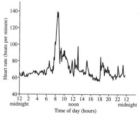

Figure 2

(a) (i) Use the graph to estimate this person's resting heart rate.

(1 mark)

60–65 beats per minute ✓

(ii) The man attended a one-hour spinning (indoor cycling) class during the day. Use the graph to estimate the start time of the class.

(1 mark)

7.30–8.00 am ✓

(iii) About an hour before the class started the man walked uphill to the gym where the class was held. He then rested until the class started.

Give **one** piece of evidence from the trace that supports this.

(1 mark)

Heart rate increases to a peak of about 80 and then falls again shortly before the main peak. ✓

(iv) The man noticed that his heart rate remained higher than normal for some time after the end of the class.

Explain why his heart rate remained high.

(2 marks)

The man's heart rate remained high because extra oxygen is needed to replace oxygen used in the exercise ✓ and to oxidise lactic acid produced. ✓

(b) (i) The table shows the stroke volume and heart rate for two people measured while they were at rest. Complete the table by calculating the cardiac output for each person. Include the units for cardiac output.

(3 marks)

	Stroke volume (cm³)	Heart rate (beats/min)	Cardiac output	Units
Person A	95	52	4940 ✓	cm³/min ✓
Person B	58	72	4176 ✓	cm³/min

person A = 95 × 52 = 4940

person B = 58 × 72 = 4176

units for cardiac output = cm³/min

(ii) One of these was a trained athlete, the other was untrained. Suggest and explain which is the trained athlete.

(2 marks)

Person A is the trained athlete ✓ because he or she had the higher cardiac output. ✓

Alternative answers:
You could also give the reason:
• higher stroke volume
• lower heart rate.

(Total for Question 2 = 10 marks)

---

3. (a) The table lists several hormones, their site of production and target organ(s).

Choose from the following list of words to complete the table.

adrenalin	glucagon	kidney	muscle
oestrogen	ovaries	pancreas	pituitary
	progesterone	testes	thyroid

Hormone	Produced in	Target organ	
ADH	pituitary	kidney	✓
adrenalin	adrenal gland	various organs, e.g. heart, liver, skin	✓
glucagon	pancreas	muscle	✓
oestrogen	ovaries	pituitary gland	✓

(4 marks)

1 mark for each correct row

(b) (i) Describe what happens in the uterus if an egg is not fertilised.

(2 marks)

The uterus lining breaks down ✓ and the lining and unfertilised egg are lost in a menstrual period. ✓

(ii) Explain how a hormone contraceptive pill prevents pregnancy.

(2 marks)

The contraceptive pill releases hormones ✓ that prevent ovulation. ✓

Alternative answer:
You could also write that the hormones thicken mucus at the cervix to prevent sperm passing through.

(iii) Give **one** advantage of barrier methods of contraception compared to hormonal contraception.

(1 mark)

protection against sexually transmitted infections (STIs) ✓

(c) Which one of the following statements describes a way in which specialised cells are adapted for their function in reproduction?

(1 mark)

- ☒ **A** Sperm cells have cilia allowing the sperm cell to swim towards the egg cell. ✓
- ☐ **B** Sperm cells have an acrosome allowing the sperm cell to swim towards the egg cell.
- ☐ **C** Ciliated epithelial cells transport sperm cells towards the uterus.
- ☐ **D** Ciliated epithelial cells transport egg cells towards the uterus.

(Total for Question 3 = 10 marks)

---

4. The survival of some organisms is dependent on other species. For example, the flea is an animal that feeds on the blood of other animals, including humans.

(a) Which term correctly describes a flea?

(1 mark)

- ☐ **A** mutualist
- ☒ **B** parasite ✓
- ☐ **C** producer
- ☐ **D** primary consumer

(b) An epiphyte is a type of plant that grows harmlessly on another species of plant. The epiphyte obtains its water and nutrients from air, rain and debris that accumulate around it.

The mistletoe is a parasitic plant. Describe how a parasite differs from an epiphyte.

(2 marks)

A parasite harms the host ✓ but an epiphyte does not. ✓

(c) Nitrogen-fixing bacteria grow in nodules attached to the roots of some plants. The bacteria make nitrogen compounds that can be absorbed by the plant.

(i) Suggest **one** way in which the relationship benefits the bacteria.

(1 mark)

Bacteria are protected by the plant. ✓

Alternative answer:
You could also write that bacteria get food from the plant.

(ii) Explain why the relationship between the bacteria and plants is described as mutalism.

(2 marks)

The bacteria and plants live together ✓ in a way that benefits them both. ✓

(d) Plants obtain the substances they need by different processes.

(i) Draw one straight line from each substance to the corresponding process.

(2 marks)

Substance	Process
	down a concentration gradient
Mistletoe obtains mineral ions	by osmosis ✓
Epiphyte obtains water	by active transport ✓
	by diffusion

(ii) Which of the following correctly describes the function of an enzyme in plants?

(1 mark)

☒ A Starch synthase produces starch from glucose. ✓

☐ B Starch synthase produces glucose from starch.

☐ C Amylase produces starch from glucose.

☐ D Amylase produces starch from maltose.

(Total for Question 4 = 9 marks)

---

5. A group of students were undertaking a survey of an area of land alongside a path that crossed a field and entered a piece of woodland.

(a) (i) State **two** abiotic factors that might influence the distribution of plant species in the woodland.

(2 marks)

light intensity, ✓ water availability ✓

(ii) State **two** biotic factors that might influence the distribution of plant species next to the path in the field.

(2 marks)

predation or grazing by animals, ✓ competition for light and space ✓

Alternative answers to 5(a)(i): You could also state:

- availability of mineral ions in the soil
- temperature.

Alternative answers to 5(a)(ii): You could also state:

- competition for water
- competition for mineral irons.

---

*(b) Describe how the students should survey the abundance of different plant species growing alongside the path from the field and into the wood.

(6 marks)

To survey the abundance of different plant species growing alongside the path from the field and into the wood the students should use a belt transect. They should use a tape measure to place quadrats at regular intervals alongside the path.

In each quadrat they should count the number of each different plant species or calculate the percentage cover of each different plant species.

At each quadrat position they should record abiotic factors (temperature, light intensity, etc.) and record biotic factors e.g. shade from tree, animals.

They could present the results as a table or a graph.

(Total for Question 5 = 10 marks)

---

6. (a) Figure 3 shows a specialised type of plant cell.

Figure 3

(i) Which specialised plant tissue is shown in Figure 3?

(1 mark)

☐ A xylem

☒ B phloem ✓

☐ C mesophyll

☐ D root hair

(ii) Identify the parts labelled E and F.

(2 marks)

E sieve tube ✓

F sieve plate ✓

(b) The companion cells contain large numbers of mitochondria.

(i) What is the function of a mitochondrion?

(1 mark)

☐ A to carry out photosynthesis

☒ B to carry out respiration ✓

☐ C to control the entry of substances to the cell

☐ D to control the activities of the cell

(ii) Suggest an explanation for why the companion cell contains large numbers of mitochondria.

(2 marks)

Respiration occurs in mitochondria so they supply energy ✓
Energy is used for the active transport of sucrose in translocation. ✓

Alternative answers:
You could also state:
- carbon dioxide concentration
- amount of chlorophyll.

(c) (i) Temperature can be a limiting factor in photosynthesis. State one other factor that can limit the rate of photosynthesis.

(1 mark)

light intensity ✓

(ii) Figure 4 shows how the rate of photosynthesis changes as temperature is increased.

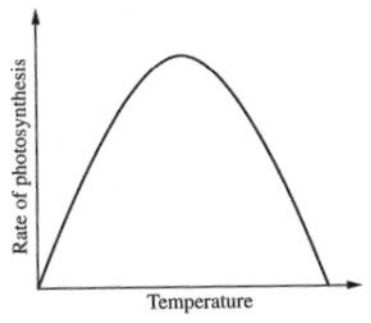

Figure 4

Explain how the rate of photosynthesis changes as the temperature is increased.

(3 marks)

The rate of photosynthesis increases and then decreases ✓ because increasing temperature increases rate of enzyme reactions ✓ but high temperatures denature enzymes so at higher temperatures the rate slows down. ✓

(Total for Question 6 = 10 marks)

TOTAL FOR PAPER = 60 MARKS

28

Combined Science
Paper 3: Chemistry 1

Time allowed: 1 hour 10 minutes

Answer ALL questions. Write your answers in the spaces provided.

1. (a) Complete the table below to show the properties of protons, neutrons and electrons.

(4 marks)

Subatomic particle	Relative mass	Relative charge
proton	1	+1 ✓
neutron	1 ✓	0 ✓
electron	$\frac{1}{1837}$ ✓	−1

Alternative answers to 1(a): You could also give the relative mass of the electron as:
- negligible
- very small
- almost zero, or
- a number less than 1/1500 or 0.00067.

(b) Neon has the atomic number 10. Neon exists as neon-20 and neon-22 atoms.

Explain, in terms of protons and neutrons, why these atoms are isotopes of neon.

(2 marks)

The atoms of each isotope contain 10 protons. ✓ However, neon-20 atoms contain 10 neutrons but neon-22 atoms contain 12 neutrons. ✓

Alternative answer to 1(b): You could also explain that the atoms of each isotope contain the same number of protons but different numbers of neutrons.

(Total for Question 1 = 6 marks)

29

---

2. This question is about elements and the periodic table.

(a) Which of these describes the arrangement of elements in the modern periodic table?

(1 mark)

☐ **A** in order of increasing relative atomic mass

☐ **B** in order of increasing relative formula mass

☐ **C** in order of increasing mass number

☒ **D** in order of increasing atomic number ✓

(b) Dmitri Mendeleev (1834–1907) was a Russian chemist who developed a periodic table.

Give **one** similarity and **one** difference between Mendeleev's table and the modern periodic table.

(2 marks)

Elements with similar properties are arranged in groups in both tables. ✓ However, Mendeleev's table contained fewer elements than the modern periodic table. ✓

Alternative answers: Another similarity is that elements are arranged in periods in both tables.

Other differences include:
- Elements in Mendeleev's table are arranged in order of relative atomic mass, but elements in the modern table are arranged in order of atomic number.
- Mendeleev's table had gaps for undiscovered elements, but the modern periodic table does not.
- The modern periodic table contains group 0 elements, but Mendeleev's table did not.

(c) Phosphorus, P, has the atomic number 15. Complete Figure 1 to show the electronic configuration of phosphorus, P.

(1 mark)

  ✓

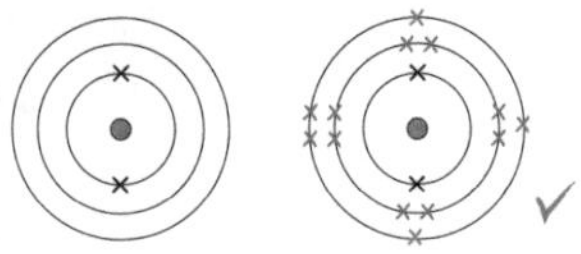

Figure 1

30

(d) The table below gives the numbers of electrons in atoms of lithium, sodium and magnesium.

Element	Number of electrons in atom
lithium	3
sodium	11
magnesium	12

Explain, in terms of their electronic configurations, why:

(i) lithium and sodium are placed in group 1

(1 mark)

Atoms of both elements have one electron in their outer shell. ✓

(ii) sodium and magnesium are placed in period 3.

(1 mark)

Atoms of both elements have three occupied shells. ✓

(Total for Question 2 = 6 marks)

Alternative answer to 2(d)(i): You could also give the electronic configurations of the atoms:
- Lithium is 2.1 and sodium is 2.8.1, **and** the group number is linked to the number of outer electrons.

Alternative answer to 2(d)(ii): You could also give the electronic configurations of the atoms:
- Sodium is 2.8.1 and magnesium is 2.8.2, **and** the period number is the same as the number of occupied shells.

31

---

3. The table below gives the formulae of two ions.

Name of ion	Formula of ion
aluminium	Al^{3+}
sulfate	SO_4^{2-}

(a) Which of these is the correct formula for aluminium sulfate?

(1 mark)

☐ **A** Al_3SO_4

☐ **B** $Al_3(SO_4)_2$

☒ **C** $Al_2(SO_4)_3$ ✓

☐ **D** Al_2SO_4

(b) The atomic number of aluminium is 13 and its mass number is 27.

Calculate the numbers of protons, neutrons and electrons in an aluminium **ion**.

(3 marks)

protons ....13 ✓....

neutrons ....27 − 13 = 14 ✓....

electrons ....13 − 3 = 10 ✓....

32

(c) The melting point of aluminium sulfate is 770 °C.

Explain why the melting point of aluminium sulfate is high.

(3 marks)

Aluminium sulfate contains strong electrostatic forces of
attraction ✔ between oppositely charged ions. ✔ These need
a lot of heat energy to overcome, ✔ so aluminium sulfate has a
high melting point.

....

Alternative answer to 3(c): You could also write that aluminium sulfate contains strong ionic bonds between oppositely charged ions, which need a lot of heat energy to break.

(d) Aluminium sulfate is soluble in water. It is used in the treatment of water for drinking.

A solution of aluminium sulfate is formed by dissolving 35 g of aluminium sulfate in 250 cm³ of water. Calculate the concentration, in g dm⁻³, of this solution.

(2 marks)

volume of water = $\frac{250}{1000}$ = 0.25 dm³

concentration = $\frac{35}{0.25}$ ✔

= 140 g dm⁻³ ✔

Alternative answer to 3(d): You could also show your working out like this:

- concentration = $\frac{35}{250}$ × 1000 ✔ = 140 ✔ g dm⁻³

(Total for Question 3 = 9 marks)

---

4. Air is a mixture of gases, including nitrogen, oxygen and carbon dioxide.

(a) Why does nitrogen have a low boiling point?

(1 mark)

☒ **A** There are weak forces of attraction between nitrogen molecules. ✔

☐ **B** There are weak covalent bonds between nitrogen molecules.

☐ **C** There are weak forces of attraction between nitrogen atoms.

☐ **D** There are weak covalent bonds between nitrogen atoms.

(b) The structure of a water molecule can be shown as:

H–O–H

The symbol – is used to show a covalent bond.

The electronic configuration of hydrogen is 1 and the electronic configuration of oxygen is 2.6.

Draw a dot-and-cross diagram to show a molecule of water, H_2O.

Show the outer electrons only.

(2 marks)

The two marks are for:
- one bonding pair of electrons between each H and O
- two non-bonding pairs of electrons on the O atom.

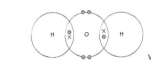

✔✔

(c) Figure 2 shows the structures of diamond and graphite.

diamond   graphite

Figure 2

Explain, in terms of structure and bonding, why:

(i) diamond has a very high melting point

(2 marks)

Diamond has a giant covalent structure. ✔ This contains many
strong covalent bonds, which need a lot of energy to break. ✔

....

(ii) graphite is used as a lubricant.

(3 marks)

The carbon atoms in graphite are arranged in layers. ✔ There
are only weak forces between these layers, ✔ so the layers
easily slide over each other. ✔

....

(Total for Question 4 = 8 marks)

---

5. A student adds magnesium to an excess of dilute hydrochloric acid in an evaporating basin. Magnesium chloride solution and hydrogen gas form. When the reaction is complete, the student carefully evaporates the magnesium chloride solution to dryness. The table below shows her results.

Substance	Mass (g)
magnesium used	2.40
magnesium chloride formed	9.50

(a) Use the information in the table to calculate the mass of chlorine present in the magnesium chloride.

(1 mark)

mass of chlorine

= mass of magnesium chloride − mass of magnesium

= 9.50 − 2.40

= 7.10 g ✔

(b) Use the mass of magnesium used (shown in the table) and your answer to part (a) to calculate the empirical formula of magnesium chloride.

(A_r of Mg = 24 and A_r of Cl = 35.5)

(3 marks)

	Mg	Cl	
mass	2.40	7.10	
A_r	24	35.5	
$\frac{mass}{A_r}$	$\frac{2.40}{24}$ = 0.10	$\frac{7.10}{35.5}$ = 0.20	✔
simplest ratio	$\frac{0.10}{0.10}$ = 1	$\frac{0.20}{0.10}$ = 2	✔

empirical formula ......$MgCl_2$...... ✔

(Total for Question 5 = 4 marks)

6. This question is about clean tap water.

(a) Which of these describes clean tap water?

(1 mark)

☐ **A** a pure substance
☐ **B** a simple molecular compound
☒ **C** a mixture of substances ✓
☐ **D** not potable

(b) Drinking water can be made by the simple distillation of seawater.

(i) State, in terms of the relative energy of water particles, what happens when water is heated.

(1 mark)

When the water is heated, the water particles gain energy and move faster. ✓

(ii) Suggest a reason that explains why producing large volumes of drinking water by simple distillation is expensive.

(1 mark)

A lot of energy is needed to heat the seawater so it boils. ✓

> **Alternative answer:**
> You could also write that a lot of fuel is needed to heat the seawater so it boils.

(iii) Tap water contains dissolved salts that may interfere with chemical tests.

Describe why distilled water is suitable for use in such tests.

(1 mark)

Distilled water does not contain any dissolved salts, so it does not interfere with the chemical analysis. ✓

(b) Fresh water can be made safe for drinking at a water treatment plant. Sedimentation is needed to allow insoluble particles to settle out. Filtration and chlorination are also needed.

(i) Describe why filtration is needed.

(1 mark)

Filtration removes solid particles of insoluble substances in the water that were not removed by sedimentation. ✓

(ii) Explain why chlorination is needed.

(2 marks)

Chlorination involves adding chlorine to the water. ✓ This kills harmful bacteria that might cause disease. ✓

(Total for Question 6 = 7 marks)

7. This question is about acids, alkalis and salts.

(a) Which row in the table correctly identifies a soluble substance and an insoluble substance?

(1 mark)

		Soluble in water	Insoluble in water
☐	**A**	silver chloride	lead chloride
☒	**B**	sodium carbonate	calcium sulfate	✓
☐	**C**	sodium chloride	calcium chloride
☐	**D**	barium sulfate	barium nitrate

(b) Predict whether a precipitate will form when sodium hydroxide solution and iron(III) chloride solution are mixed together. Name the precipitate, if any forms.

(1 mark)

A precipitate of iron(III) hydroxide forms. ✓

(c) Copper oxide and potassium hydroxide are examples of bases.

(i) Give a reason why both substances are bases.

(1 mark)

They both react with acids, forming a salt and water in the reaction. ✓

(ii) Give a reason why potassium hydroxide is also described as an alkali.

(1 mark)

It is a base that dissolves in water. ✓

> **Alternative answer to:** You could also write that potassium hydroxide is a soluble base.

(d) Aqueous solutions can be acidic, neutral or alkaline. Give the pH of a neutral solution.

(1 mark)

pH 7 ✓

*(e) Plan an experiment to prepare pure, dry crystals of copper chloride, $CuCl_2$, from an insoluble copper compound and a suitable dilute acid. In your answer, include the names of suitable reagents and describe any essential stages. You may wish to write an equation to help with your plan.

(6 marks)

> **Alternative answers:**
> You could use copper carbonate instead of copper oxide:
> - $CuCO_3 + 2HCl \rightarrow CuCl_2 + H_2O + CO_2$
> - The evaporating basin could be left aside in a warm place for a few days, instead of heating to evaporate some of the water.

Add about 25 cm³ of dilute hydrochloric acid to a beaker. Warm the acid using a water bath and gauze mat. Add a spatula of copper oxide powder and stir. This is the equation for the reaction that happens:

$CuO + 2HCl \rightarrow CuCl_2 + H_2O$

Carry on adding copper oxide powder until some of it is left still unreacted in the beaker. Filter the mixture to remove the excess copper oxide powder. Pour the filtrate into an evaporating basin. Heat it gently to evaporate some of the water to form crystals. Stop heating and let it cool down. Pour away the excess liquid and dry the crystals with filter paper, or in a warm oven.

(Total for Question 7 = 11 marks)

37

38

39

40

8. This question is about electrolysis and extracting aluminium.

(a) Which of the following correctly describes the movement of ions during electrolysis?

(1 mark)

☐ A Negatively charged cations migrate to the positively charged cathode.

☒ B Positively charged cations migrate to the negatively charged cathode. ✓

☐ C Positively charged anions migrate to the negatively charged anode.

☐ D Positively charged anions migrate to the positively charged anode.

(b) Two products form during the electrolysis of a concentrated sodium sulfate solution.

Which row in the table correctly shows what product forms at each electrode?

(1 mark)

	Cathode	Anode	
☐ A	sodium	oxygen	
☐ B	sodium	hydrogen	
☒ C	hydrogen	oxygen	✓
☐ D	hydrogen	sodium	

(c) Predict the product formed at each electrode during the electrolysis of molten zinc chloride.

(2 marks)

cathode .... zinc ✓ ....

anode .... chlorine ✓ ....

(d) Aluminium is extracted by the electrolysis of aluminium oxide, dissolved in molten cryolite.

State why aluminium cannot be extracted from aluminium oxide by heating with carbon.

(1 mark)

Aluminium is more reactive than carbon ✓ (so carbon cannot reduce aluminium oxide to aluminium).

(Total for Question 8 = 5 marks)

Alternative answer:
You could give the reverse argument instead:

• Carbon is less reactive than aluminium (so it cannot reduce aluminium oxide to aluminium).

9. Ammonia is manufactured from nitrogen and hydrogen by the Haber process:

$$N_2(g) + 3H_2(g) \rightleftharpoons 2NH_3(g)$$

(a) Give the meaning of the symbol $\rightleftharpoons$ in chemical equations.

(1 mark)

The reaction is reversible. ✓

(b) State the conditions used in the Haber process:

(i) temperature

(1 mark)

450 °C ✓

(ii) pressure

(1 mark)

200 atmospheres ✓

Alternative answer:
You could also give the pressure as 20 MPa.

(iii) catalyst

(1 mark)

iron ✓

(Total for Question 9 = 4 marks)
TOTAL FOR PAPER = 60 MARKS

Combined Science

Paper 4: Chemistry 2

Time: 1 hour 10 minutes

Answer ALL questions. Write your answers in the spaces provided.

1. This question is about the alkali metals, the elements in group 1 of the periodic table.

   (a) Which of these shows the typical physical properties of the alkali metals?

   (1 mark)

   ☒ A soft with relatively low melting points ✓

   ☐ B soft with relatively high melting points

   ☐ C hard with relatively low melting points

   ☐ D hard with relatively high melting points

   (b) Sodium reacts with water to produce sodium hydroxide solution, NaOH, and hydrogen gas, H_2.

   (i) Balance the equation for the reaction between sodium and water. Include state symbols.

   (2 marks)

   $\underline{2}$ Na (s) + $\underline{2}$ H_2O (l) → $\underline{2}$ NaOH (aq) + H_2 (g)

   balanced ✓ state symbols ✓

   (ii) Describe **two** observations seen when a piece of sodium is added to a trough of water.

   (2 marks)

   There is rapid fizzing ✓ and the metal may ignite with a yellow flame. ✓

Alternative answers:
You could also write:
- The metal floats.
- The metal moves around.
- The metal melts to form a silvery ball.
- The metal disappears.

(Total for Question 1 = 5 marks)

2. This question is about the halogens, the elements in group 7 of the periodic table.

   (a) Which row in the table correctly shows the colours and physical states of the halogens at room temperature and pressure?

   (1 mark)

	Chlorine	Bromine	Iodine
☐ A	pale yellow liquid	red–brown liquid	red–brown solid
☐ B	yellow–green gas	purple liquid	purple-black solid
☒ C	yellow–green gas	red–brown liquid	purple-black solid ✓
☐ D	yellow–green gas	purple liquid	red–brown liquid

   (b) Describe the chemical test for chlorine.

   (2 marks)

   Damp blue litmus paper ✓ turns red, then bleaches white. ✓

Alternative answer:
You could also write:

Damp starch-iodide paper turns blue-black.

*(c) A student investigates the reactivity of the halogens. She adds a few drops of a dilute aqueous solution of bromine to potassium iodide solution, and then to potassium chloride solution. Her results are shown in the table.

Mixture	Observation
bromine + potassium iodide	colour change seen
bromine + potassium chloride	no visible change

Explain how the student's observations provide evidence for the order of reactivity of bromine, iodine and chlorine. You should include an equation in your answer.

(6 marks)

To obtain the maximum of 6 marks, you must write a clear explanation that links all the ideas together to provide an order of reactivity.

Bromine reacts with potassium iodide solution. A colour change to brown shows that a reaction happens. This is because bromine is more reactive than iodine, so bromine can displace iodide ions:

bromine + potassium iodide → potassium bromide + iodine

Br_2 + 2KI → 2KBr + I_2

Bromine does not react with potassium chloride solution. There is no visible change, showing that a reaction does not happen. This is because bromine is less reactive than chlorine, so bromine cannot displace chloride ions.

Putting it all together, the order of reactivity (from most reactive to least reactive halogen) is chlorine, bromine, iodine.

(Total for Question 2 = 9 marks)

3. A student investigates the rate of reaction between calcium carbonate (marble chips) and excess dilute hydrochloric acid:

   $CaCO_3(s) + 2HCl(aq) \rightarrow CaCl_2(aq) + H_2O(l) + CO_2(g)$

   (a) Which of these would increase the rate of reaction?

   (1 mark)

   ☐ A adding water to the acid

   ☐ B increasing the volume of acid

   ☐ C increasing the size of the marble chips

   ☒ D using calcium carbonate powder instead of marble chips ✓

   (b) Describe the chemical test for carbon dioxide.

   (2 marks)

   Limewater ✓ turns milky ✓ when carbon dioxide is bubbled through it.

Alternative answer:
You could also write that the limewater turns cloudy white.

   (c) The temperature of the reaction mixture increases during the reaction. Explain what this tells you about the reaction between calcium carbonate and dilute hydrochloric acid.

   (2 marks)

   The reaction is exothermic ✓ because heat energy is given out. ✓

(d) The student measured the volume of carbon dioxide produced until all the calcium carbonate had reacted. Figure 1 shows the results that he obtained at 20 °C.

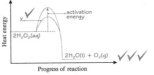

Figure 1

The two marks are for drawing a line which:
- is drawn to the left of the original, starting at origin and with a similar shape but is steeper
- becomes horizontal at the same volume as the original.

(i) The student repeats the experiment at a higher concentration of hydrochloric acid at 20 °C. Sketch the results he would expect on Figure 1.

(2 marks)

(ii) Explain why increasing the concentration has the effect you showed in part (i) on the rate of reaction. Your answer should be in terms of particles.

(2 marks)

Alternative answers: You could also write that the acid particles in the same volume are more crowded so there are more collisions per unit time.

At a higher concentration, there are more acid particles in the same volume ✓ so they collide more frequently with calcium carbonate particles. ✓

(iii) State the effect on the reaction time of increasing the temperature of the reaction mixture.

(1 mark)

The reaction time decreases. ✓

(Total for Question 3 = 10 marks)

48

4. Reactions involve energy transfers to and from the surroundings.

(a) Which row in the table correctly shows the overall energy change involved in breaking chemical bonds and forming chemical bonds?

(1 mark)

	Breaking bonds	Forming bonds
☐ A	exothermic	endothermic
☐ B	exothermic	exothermic
☐ C	endothermic	endothermic
☒ D	endothermic	exothermic	✓

(b) Explain what is meant by the term 'activation energy'.

(2 marks)

Activation energy is the minimum energy ✓ needed for a collision between reactant particles to be successful. ✓

Alternative answer: You could also write that it is the minimum energy needed for a reaction to start.

49

The three marks for part (c) are for drawing:
- a labelled product line below and to the right of the labelled reactant line
- a curve from the reactant line to the product line
- an upwards arrow from reactant line to the top of the curve, labelled **activation energy.**

(c) Hydrogen peroxide decomposes to form water and oxygen:

$$2H_2O_2(aq) \rightarrow 2H_2O(l) + O_2(g)$$

The reaction is exothermic.

Complete Figure 2 to show a reaction profile diagram for this reaction. Draw and label the activation energy.

(3 marks)

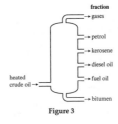

Figure 2

The mark for part (d) (i) is for drawing a curve below the first curve, labelled X.

(d) (i) On Figure 2, draw the reaction profile for the same reaction in the presence of a catalyst. Label this line with an **X.**

(1 mark)

(ii) The products formed in a reaction are the same whether or not a catalyst is used. State **two** other features of a catalyst.

(2 marks)

Alternative answer for part (d)(ii): You could also write that a catalyst is not changed chemically by the end of the reaction.

A catalyst speeds up a reaction. ✓
The mass of the catalyst is unchanged at the end of the reaction. ✓

(e) Describe the role of enzymes in the production of alcoholic drinks.

(1 mark)

Enzymes catalyse the production of alcohol by fermentation. ✓

(Total for Question 4 = 10 marks)

50

5. This question is about crude oil.

(a) Which of these statements about crude oil is correct?

(1 mark)

☐ A It is a renewable resource.

☒ B It contains molecules with carbon atoms in rings and chains. ✓

☐ C It is a complex mixture of carbohydrates.

☐ D At room temperature, it contains only liquids.

(b) Crude oil is separated in fractions using fractional distillation. Figure 3 shows an oil fractionating column and the main fractions obtained from it.

fraction
→ gases
→ petrol
→ kerosene
→ diesel oil
→ fuel oil
heated crude oil →
→ bitumen

Figure 3

(i) Identify the fraction that has the highest boiling point.

(1 mark)

bitumen ✓

(ii) Identify the fraction that is used as a fuel for large ships and some power stations.

(1 mark)

fuel oil ✓

(iii) Give a commercial use for the kerosene fraction.

(1 mark)

It is a fuel for aircraft. ✓

51

Alternative answer to 5(c): You could also write that crude oil is the raw material for making polymers and other substances.

Alternative answers to 5(d): You could also write that:
- Crude oil takes millions of years to form.
- Crude oil is not being made any more.

Alternative answers to 5(e)(ii): You could also write that:
- Their molecules have different sizes OR have different relative formula masses.
- The fractions differ in how easily they are ignited.

(c) Give **one** industrial use of crude oil, other than as a source of fuels.
(1 mark)

Crude oil is a feedstock for the chemical industry. ✓

(d) State why crude oil may be described as a finite resource.
(1 mark)

Crude oil is made extremely slowly. ✓

(e) The substances in crude oil fractions are mostly members of the alkane homologous series.

   (i) Describe why alkanes are **hydrocarbons**.
   (2 marks)

Hydrocarbons are compounds of hydrogen and carbon ✓ only. ✓

   (ii) The hydrocarbons in different fractions have different boiling points. State **two** other ways in which they differ.
   (2 marks)

Their molecules have different numbers of carbon atoms and hydrogen atoms. ✓

The different fractions have different viscosities. ✓

(Total for Question 5 = 10 marks)

---

6. This question is about the Earth's atmosphere.

   (a) Where do scientists think the gases in the Earth's earliest atmosphere came from?
   (1 mark)
   - ☐ **A** the oceans
   - ☐ **B** primitive plants
   - ☐ **C** carbonate rocks
   - ☒ **D** volcanoes ✓

   (b) Which gas was the most abundant in the Earth's earliest atmosphere?
   (1 mark)
   - ☐ **A** nitrogen
   - ☐ **B** oxygen
   - ☐ **C** argon
   - ☒ **D** carbon dioxide ✓

   (c) Oxygen is found in the atmosphere.

      (i) Describe the chemical test for oxygen.
      (2 marks)

Light a splint then gently blow it out. The glowing splint ✓ should relight when placed in oxygen. ✓

      (ii) Explain why the amount of oxygen in the atmosphere increased over millions of years.
      (2 marks)

Primitive plants evolved and grew. ✓ They released oxygen because they carried out photosynthesis. ✓

(d) Carbon dioxide is described as a greenhouse gas.

   (i) Explain how the formation of oceans affected the amount of carbon dioxide in the atmosphere.
   (2 marks)

Carbon dioxide dissolved in the oceans. ✓ This reduced the amount of carbon dioxide in the atmosphere. ✓

   (ii) Human activities increase the amount of some greenhouse gases. Complete the table below.
   (2 marks)

Name of greenhouse gas	Main human activity that produces the gas
carbon dioxide	burning fossil fuels ✓
methane ✓	livestock farming

   (iii) Increasing amounts of greenhouse gases in the atmosphere cause global warming.

   Other than an increase in temperature, describe **one** potential effect of global warming on the environment.
   (1 mark)

Global warming could cause rising sea levels. ✓

(Total for Question 6 = 11 marks)

Alternative answers: You could also write that it could cause:
- climate change
- melting ice caps
- changes in the distribution of plants and animals.

---

7. This question is about the combustion of hydrocarbon fuels.

   (a) Which row in the table correctly shows the possible products of complete combustion and incomplete combustion of hydrocarbon fuels?
   (1 mark)

	Complete combustion	Incomplete combustion	
☐A	carbon dioxide, water	carbon monoxide only	
☐B	carbon dioxide, carbon monoxide, water	carbon monoxide, water	
☒C	carbon dioxide, water	carbon monoxide, carbon, water	✓
☐D	carbon monoxide, water	carbon dioxide, carbon, water	

   (b) Sulfur dioxide is produced when some hydrocarbon fuels burn.

      (i) Name the element that reacts with oxygen to produce sulfur dioxide.
      (1 mark)

sulfur ✓

      (ii) Acid rain forms when sulfur dioxide dissolves in water in the atmosphere.

      Describe **one** environmental problem caused by acid rain.
      (1 mark)

Acid rain can damage stonework such as limestone buildings or statues. ✓

   (c) Carbon monoxide may be produced during the combustion of hydrocarbon fuels.

   Explain how it acts as a toxic gas.
   (2 marks)

Carbon monoxide combines with the haemoglobin in red blood cells. ✓ This reduces the amount of oxygen that can be carried by the blood. ✓

Alternative answers: You could also write that acid rain can:
- damage metalwork such as iron or steel
- harm or kill trees and other plants
- harm or kill aquatic organisms such as fish.

(Total for Question 7 = 5 marks)
TOTAL FOR PAPER = 60 MARKS

Combined Science
Practice Paper 5: Physics 1

Time allowed: 1 hour 10 minutes

Answer ALL questions. Write your answers in the spaces provided.

1. Robert and Nolly plan to set up an experiment to measure speed. They have a trolley, an inclined ramp, a ruler and a stopwatch.

   (a) Describe a method that the students could use to measure the speed of the trolley using the apparatus above.

   (3 marks)

   Choose a distance to be travelled by the trolley, write it down and mark this on the ramp. ✓ Place the trolley at the top of the ramp and let it go. Time how long it takes to cover the marked distance. ✓ Repeat the experiment to reduce the effect of random errors. ✓

   Both distance and timing should be mentioned for the second mark in 1(a).

   (b) Suggest other apparatus that the students could use to improve the precision of the data collected.

   (2 marks)

   light gates ✓ and data logger ✓

   Alternative answer for 1(b): You could also suggest:
   • computer.

(c) Robert and Nolly then extend their experiment to investigate the influence of another independent variable. The table below shows data collected by the students.

Height (cm)	Distance (m)	Time (s)	Speed (m/s)
5	1.80	3.2	0.56
10	1.80	2.4	0.75
15	1.80	1.8	1.0
20	1.80	1.4	1.29
25	1.80	1.0	1.8
30	1.80	0.4	4.5
35	1.80	0.2	9.0

✓

   (i) Deduce what the new independent variable might be.

   (1 mark)

   height ✓

   (ii) Add the **two** missing entries for the fourth column.

   (1 mark)

   $$speed = \frac{distance}{time}$$

   $$\frac{1.8 \text{ m}}{2.4 \text{ s}} = 0.75 \text{ m/s}$$

   $$\frac{1.8 \text{ m}}{1.0 \text{ s}} = 1.8 \text{ m/s}$$

   Both needed for mark.

(d) Robert and Nolly then release the trolley from a height of 0.02 m and record a time of 4.5 s over a distance of 1.8 m.

   (i) Calculate the speed of the trolley. Give the unit.

   (3 marks)

   $s = d \div t$

   $= 1.8 \div 4.5$ ✓

   $= 0.4$ ✓ m/s ✓

   (ii) Suggest the additional data that the students would need to collect to be able to calculate the acceleration of the trolley.

   (2 marks)

   To calculate acceleration of the trolley the students need to calculate the change in acceleration. ✓ The students would need to collect two velocity readings. ✓

   (Total for question 1 = 12 marks)

2. (a) A crash test car of mass 1000 kg is driven at the design testing centre to examine impact forces. The car starts from rest and accelerates to its final speed.

   (i) Write the equation to calculate the acceleration of the car towards the crash barrier in a time t.

   (1 mark)

   $$acceleration = \frac{change \ in \ velocity}{time \ taken}$$ ✓

   (ii) The car is accelerated uniformly from 0 m/s to 10 m/s over a time of 20 s.

   Calculate how far the car will travel.

   (3 marks)

   $$average \ speed = \frac{10-0}{2} = 5 \text{ m/s}$$ ✓

   $distance \ travelled = average \ speed \times time \ taken$

   $= 5 \text{ m/s} \times 20 \text{ s}$ ✓

   $= 100$ ✓ m

*(b) The graph in Figure 1 reflects a test ride by a cyclist on a new bicycle. Discuss the test ride and refer to acceleration, constant speed, deceleration and distance covered in your answer.

(6 marks)

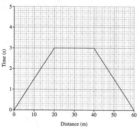

Figure 1

The cyclist accelerates uniformly during the first 20 seconds from 0 m/s to 3 m/s.

Between 20 and 40 seconds of the total ride time the cyclist maintains a constant velocity.

Between 40 and 60 seconds of the total ride time the cyclist decelerates uniformly from 3 m/s to 0 m/s.

The total distance covered is found by calculating the area under the graph.

This is $2 \times (20 \text{ s} \times 3 \text{ m/s})/2 + (20 \text{ s} \times 3 \text{ m/s}) = 60 \text{ m} + 60 \text{ m}$.

The total distance covered is 120 m.

(Total for Question 2 = 10 marks)

---

3. (a) A scientist is working to investigate levels of radioactivity using a Geiger–Muller detector to measure the count rate. No radioactive sample is placed in front of the G–M and several measurements are taken. The levels recorded have an average of 25 counts per minute.

   (i) Give the name of the radiation that the scientist is measuring.

(1 mark)

background radiation ✓

   (ii) State **two** sources of this radiation.

(2 marks)

radon gas ✓ , rocks ✓

(b) The scientist now places a radioactive sample in front of the Geiger–Muller detector and takes some more measurements. The levels recorded now have an average of 200 corrected counts per minute.

   (i) Describe what the scientist does to determine the corrected count rate.

(1 mark)

She subtracts the mean background count rate from the measured count rate. ✓

   (ii) Explain why the scientist wears a photographic film badge while she carries out her research.

(2 marks)

In order to check how much radiation she has been exposed to ✓ to make sure she is safe. ✓

(c) Describe the nature of alpha, beta and gamma radiation in terms of ionising properties.

(3 marks)

Alpha radiation is highly ionising because it is the most massive particle so can easily ionise atoms by knocking off their electrons. ✓

Beta radiation is moderately ionising because although the particles are highly energised they are very small so have less chance of knocking electrons off other atoms. ✓

Gamma radiation is the least ionising because it has no mass. ✓

(d) Suggest **one** safety precaution the scientist should take when carrying out this experiment.

(1 mark)

Store radioactive samples in lead-lined box in safe radioactive store. ✓

(Total for Question 3 = 10 marks)

---

4. Figure 2 shows the graph of a radio wave.

Figure 2

(a) On the graph:

   (i) Identify the amplitude of the wave by adding 'A' next to an arrow or marker.

(1 mark)

   (ii) Identify the time period of the wave by adding 'T' with arrows or markers.

(1 mark)

   (iii) Determine the time period of the wave.

(1 mark)

$T = \dfrac{0.0001}{2}$

$T = 0.00005 \text{ s}$ ✓

(b) Determine the frequency of the wave shown in the diagram.
(2 marks)

$$\text{period} = 0.000\,05 \text{ s}$$

$$\text{frequency} = \frac{1}{\text{period}}$$

$$= \frac{1}{0.000\,05} \text{ s} \checkmark$$

$$= 20\,000 \text{ Hz} \checkmark$$

(c) Write the equation linking wave speed, wavelength and time period.
(1 mark)

$$\text{wave speed} = \frac{\text{wavelength}}{\text{time period}} \checkmark$$

(Total for Question 4 = 6 marks)

5. Figure 3 shows part of the electromagnetic spectrum.

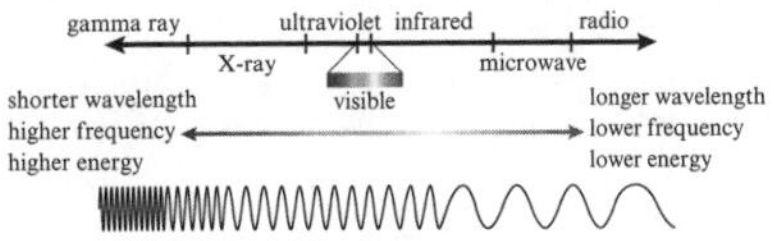

Figure 3

(a) State **one** use for each of the following waves:

   (i) microwaves
(1 mark)

cooking ✓

   (ii) ultraviolet
(1 mark)

security marking ✓

   (iii) gamma rays.
(1 mark)

treating cancer ✓

(b) Explain which of the waves in (a) is the most damaging to body cells.
(2 marks)

Gamma rays are the most damaging ✓ because they carry the most energy and are highly ionising. ✓

> **Alternative answer to 5(a)(i):** You could also state:
> • communications
> • mobile phones.

> **Alternative answer to 5(a)(ii):** You could also state:
> • tanning
> • disinfecting water
> • fluorescent lights.

> **Alternative answer to 5(a)(iii):** You could also state:
> • detecting cancer
> • sterilising food or water.

(c) Which one of the following terms best describes the nature of electromagnetic waves?
(1 mark)

☐ A longitudinal
☐ B mechanical
☐ C seismic
☒ D transverse ✓

(d) Visible light from the Sun travels at 3×10^8 m/s through space, with approximate frequencies ranging from 4.3×10^{14} Hz (red light) to 7.7×10^{14} Hz (violet light).

   (i) Calculate the approximate wavelength of red light.
(2 marks)

$$\lambda = \frac{v}{f}$$

$$\lambda = \frac{3 \times 10^8 \text{ m/s}}{4.3 \times 10^{14} \text{ Hz}} \checkmark$$

wavelength = 6.97×10^{-7} m ✓

   (ii) Calculate the approximate wavelength of violet light.
(2 marks)

$$\lambda = \frac{v}{f}$$

$$\lambda = \frac{3 \times 10^8 \text{ m/s}}{7.7 \times 10^{14} \text{ Hz}} \checkmark$$

wavelength = 3.89×10^{-7} m ✓

> **Alternative answer to 5(d)(i):**
> 7×10^{-7} m

> **Alternative answer to 5(d)(ii):**
> 4×10^{-7} m

(e) Suggest three types of EM waves commonly found in communications systems, giving examples of how they are used.
(3 marks)

Radio waves are used in radio or television. ✓
Microwaves are used in communications, such as mobile phones. ✓
Infrared waves are used for short-range communications. ✓

> **Alternative answer:** You could also suggest satellite transmissions.

(Total for Question 5 = 13 marks)

6. A lift travels between floors in a building. The lift moves from the ground floor to the fourth floor through a height of 15 m in 20 s. The mass of the lift is 750 kg.

   (a) Calculate how much energy, in J, the lift gains in moving from the ground floor to the fourth floor. Take g to be 10 N/kg.

   (2 marks)

   ΔGPE = mass $\times$ g $\times$ change in height

   ΔGPE = 750 kg $\times$ 10 N/kg $\times$ 15 m ✓

   energy gained = ...112 500... ✓ J

   (b) As the lift moves upwards, not all of the energy supplied is usefully transferred.

   Suggest **one** way in which energy is not usefully transferred.

   (1 mark)

   It is transferred to the thermal energy store of the motor. ✓

   (c) Calculate the kinetic energy, in J, of the lift when it is moving from the ground floor to the fourth floor.

   (4 marks)

   $$speed = \frac{distance\ travelled}{time\ taken}$$

   $$= \frac{15\ m}{20\ s} ✓$$

   $$= 0.75\ m/s ✓$$

   KE = ½ $\times$ mass $\times$ speed^2 = ½ $\times$ 750 kg $\times$ (0.75 m/s)^2 ✓

   kinetic energy = ...210.9... ✓ J

   (d) Explain why this mechanical process could be described as wasteful. Give an example of wasted energy in this process.

   (2 marks)

   This process could be described as wasteful because it causes a rise in temperature in parts of the system, and so transfers energy by heating the surroundings which is not useful. ✓

   An example is the rise in temperature of the lift motor. ✓

   (Total for Question 6 = 9 marks)

   TOTAL FOR PAPER = 60 MARKS

Combined Science
Paper 6: Physics 2

Time allowed: 1 hour 10 minutes

Answer ALL questions. Write your answers in the spaces provided.

1. (a) A kettle is rated at 2000 W and is designed to operate on a 230 V mains supply. Calculate the charge moved in the kettle in one second. Give correct unit.

   (3 marks)

   power = 2000 W = 2000 J/s, so energy in 1 second = 2000 J ✓

   $E = Q \times V$

   $Q = \dfrac{E}{V}$

   $Q = \dfrac{2000}{230}$

   charge = ...8.7...... ✓ C / coulombs ✓

   (b) Explain what happens to the energy of the system when the kettle is switched on.

   (3 marks)

   Electrical energy is transferred to the thermal energy store of the heater of the kettle. ✓ The heater of the kettle then transfers energy to the thermal energy store of the water and the kettle jug. ✓ The water and the kettle transfer energy to the thermal energy store of the environment. ✓

   (c) Draw an energy transfer diagram to illustrate the energy transferred inside the kettle after it is switched on.

   (3 marks)

   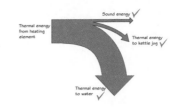

   (d) Describe how energy is not transferred usefully while boiling water in the kettle.

   (2 marks)

   Energy is transferred as sound energy ✓ and in heating the material of the kettle ✓ which is not useful.

   > **Alternative answer:** You could also state that energy is transferred to the environment.

   (Total for question 1 = 11 marks)

2. (a) Figure 1 shows a current-carrying wire passing through a card.

   Figure 1

   A compass is positioned at various places on the card to determine the direction of the magnetic field round the wire. Explain whether the magnetic field is clockwise or anticlockwise.

   (2 marks)

   The direction of the magnetic field will be clockwise ✓ as the current flows from positive to negative. ✓

   (b) (i) The wire is now turned into a solenoid. Draw the new magnetic field that this produces.

   (4 marks)

   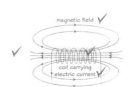

   > Your diagram should be the correct shape; lines of flux very close inside; lines of flux further apart outside; pattern indicated on both sides of the electromagnet.

   (ii) Suggest a use for this device.

   (1 mark)

   speaker ✓

   > **Alternative answers:** You could also suggest:
   > • doorbell
   > • electromagnet.

   (Total for question 2 = 7 marks)

3. An electrical heater supplies electrical energy to a copper block of mass 2000 g at 12 V with a current of 12 A for 2 minutes.

   (a) Calculate the energy supplied to the heater. State the unit.

   (3 marks)

   energy supplied = current × potential difference × time

   = 12 A × 12 V × 120 s ✓

   energy supplied = ...17 280...... ✓ unit ......J...... ✓

   (b) Calculate the temperature rise for the block of copper when supplied with the energy from (a) (your answer). The specific heat capacity of copper is 385 J/kg K. State the unit.

   (3 marks)

   change in temperature = $\dfrac{\text{change in heat energy}}{\text{mass} \times \text{specific heat capacity}}$

   $= \dfrac{17\,280 \text{ J}}{2 \text{ kg} \times 385 \text{ J/kg K}}$ ✓

   temperature rise = ...22.4...... ✓ unit ......K or °C...... ✓

   (c) Suggest why the actual temperature rise may be lower than the predicted value.

   (1 mark)

   Some of the thermal energy is dissipated to the thermal store of the environment. ✓

(d) (i) Give **one** way to reduce unwanted energy transfer in the heating of a metal block.

(1 mark)

You could thermally insulate the block. ✓

(ii) Give an example of a suitable material that could be used.

(1 mark)

cotton wool ✓

(Total for question 3 = 9 marks)

4. Deimos, one of the moons of Mars, orbits at a distance of almost 24 000 km from the planet. It is thought that Deimos was once an asteroid from further away and later 'captured' by Mars.

(a) Describe what would have caused Deimos to be 'captured' and become a moon of Mars.

(3 marks)

The gravitational field of Mars ✓ acts over a large distance. ✓ Whilst travelling at a certain speed, Deimos would come within the gravitational field of Mars and would become attracted by its mass ✓ ; therefore Deimos would settle into an orbit around Mars.

(b) (i) Name **two** other non-contact forces that act over a distance.

(2 marks)

electrostatic ✓ , magnetic ✓

(ii) Explain what decides the magnitude of the two non-contact forces you have described in (i).

(1 mark)

the strength of the field ✓

(c) (i) Describe the pair of vertical forces acting when a cyclist sits on a stationary bicycle at traffic lights.

(2 marks)

the weight of the cyclist and bicycle acting downwards ✓ and the normal reaction force of the road ✓

(ii) Describe the horizontal contact forces acting as the cyclist moves off when the traffic light turns green.

(2 marks)

the forward thrust of the bicycle and the cyclist acting on the bicycle ✓ and the opposing force of friction between the tyres and the road ✓

(Total for question 4 = 10 marks)

5. Figure 2 is a circuit diagram that shows three identical lamps and one cell.

Figure 2

(a) The cell provides 1.5 V. State the potential difference across each lamp.

(1 mark)

Each lamp would have a potential difference of 0.5 V across it. ✓

(b) Figure 3 shows a circuit to test a thermistor.

Figure 3

(i) Describe how a thermistor changes the current flowing in the circuit.

(3 marks)

When the temperature rises ✓ the resistance falls, ✓ allowing more current to flow. ✓

(ii) Give a use for a thermistor in a domestic circuit.

(1 mark)

the thermostat in a central heating system ✓

(c) Calculate the electrical power of the following domestic appliances that use temperature controls, commonly used in a household circuit:

(i) a toaster drawing a current of 4 A connected to a 230 V domestic electricity supply

(2 marks)

$P = I \times V$ so $P = 12\ A \times 230\ V$ ✓

power = 2760 ✓ W

(ii) a hairdryer drawing a current of 2 A with a resistance of 300 Ω.

(2 marks)

$P = I^2 \times R$ so $P = (2 \times 2) \times 300$ ✓

power = 1200 ✓ W

(Total for question 5 = 9 marks)

6. Two students carry out an experiment to investigate the linear elastic distortion of a thin spring. They add weights to a spring but can only find five weights: one of 0.1 N, one of 0.5 N and three of 1 N. They then measure the final extension. When the spring is unloaded the students find the spring has stretched.

(a) (i) Suggest **two** ways of improving the experiment.

(2 marks)

The students could add smaller weights each time ✓ to increase the resolution. They should unload the spring after measuring each extension to check that the spring returns to its original length, which shows distortion is still elastic. ✓

(ii) Suggest a safety precaution that should be used in carrying out this experiment.

(1 mark)

Safety glasses/goggles should be worn. ✓

(b) The table below shows results from a different experiment for the loading of a 32 mm spring.

(2 marks)

Weight (N)	Length of spring (mm)
0	32
0.1	36
0.2	40
0.3	44
0.4	48
0.5	52
0.6	56

✓ ✓

(i) Complete the missing values in the table.

(ii) Calculate the spring constant for the weight of 2 N resulting in extension 0.026 m.

(2 marks)

$F = k \times x$

so $k = \dfrac{F}{x}$

so $k = \dfrac{2}{0.026}$ ✓

$k = $ 76.923 ✓ N/m

(iii) Caitlin and Dinah try to calculate the spring constant from their results but, instead, find a range of values from 7.69–6.78 N/m. Suggest a possible source of error in their data collection that may have resulted in this range of values.

(1 mark)

Parallax error in reading extension. ✓

*(c) The students used their results from (b) to produce Figure 4.

Explain how the graph illustrates linear elastic distortion and how the graph could be improved.

Explain how you could extend the experiment to find out the force, which makes the spring change shape permanently. You should refer to the graph in your answer.

(6 marks)

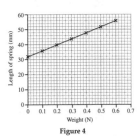

Figure 4

The graph shows that the length of the spring is proportional to the weight added (force) because it is a straight line. For every 0.1 N added the spring extends by 4 mm.

If the students had calculated the extension by subtracting the original length of the spring (32 mm) from the length of the spring after the weights had been added, that would have given the extension. The line would then have gone through the origin (0,0) and shown the relationship between force and extension to be directly proportional.

If the students added progressively more weight the material might permanently change shape. The force would continue to increase but the extension would not increase as much as before. This would mean that the extended or extrapolated line on the graph would start to level off or curve towards the horizontal. The straight line should be labelled 'elastic region'

and the curved line should be labelled 'inelastic region'. The point at which the straight line stopped should be labelled 'elastic limit'.

(Total for question 6 = 14 marks)

TOTAL FOR PAPER = 60 MARKS

78   79   80   81

103

The Periodic Table of the Elements

Key

relative atomic mass
atomic symbol
name
atomic (proton) number

Example:

1
H
hydrogen
1

Group 1	Group 2												Group 3	Group 4	Group 5	Group 6	Group 7	Group 0
																		4 **He** helium 2
7 **Li** lithium 3	9 **Be** beryllium 4												11 **B** boron 5	12 **C** carbon 6	14 **N** nitrogen 7	16 **O** oxygen 8	19 **F** fluorine 9	20 **Ne** neon 10
23 **Na** sodium 11	24 **Mg** magnesium 12												27 **Al** aluminium 13	28 **Si** silicon 14	31 **P** phosphorus 15	32 **S** sulfur 16	35.5 **Cl** chlorine 17	40 **Ar** argon 18
39 **K** potassium 19	40 **Ca** calcium 20	45 **Sc** scandium 21	48 **Ti** titanium 22	51 **V** vanadium 23	52 **Cr** chromium 24	55 **Mn** manganese 25	56 **Fe** iron 26	59 **Co** cobalt 27	59 **Ni** nickel 28	63.5 **Cu** copper 29	65 **Zn** zinc 30		70 **Ga** gallium 31	73 **Ge** germanium 32	75 **As** arsenic 33	79 **Se** selenium 34	80 **Br** bromine 35	84 **Kr** krypton 36
85 **Rb** rubidium 37	88 **Sr** strontium 38	89 **Y** yttrium 39	91 **Zr** zirconium 40	93 **Nb** niobium 41	96 **Mo** molybdenum 42	[98] **Tc** technetium 43	101 **Ru** ruthenium 44	103 **Rh** rhodium 45	106 **Pd** palladium 46	108 **Ag** silver 47	112 **Cd** cadmium 48		115 **In** indium 49	119 **Sn** tin 50	122 **Sb** antimony 51	128 **Te** tellurium 52	127 **I** iodine 53	131 **Xe** xenon 54
133 **Cs** caesium 55	137 **Ba** barium 56	139 **La*** lanthanum 57	178 **Hf** hafnium 72	181 **Ta** tantalum 73	184 **W** tungsten 74	186 **Re** rhenium 75	190 **Os** osmium 76	192 **Ir** iridium 77	195 **Pt** platinum 78	197 **Au** gold 79	201 **Hg** mercury 80		204 **Tl** thallium 81	207 **Pb** lead 82	209 **Bi** bismuth 83	[209] **Po** polonium 84	[210] **At** astatine 85	[222] **Rn** radon 86
[223] **Fr** francium 87	[226] **Ra** radium 88	[227] **Ac*** actinium 89	[261] **Rf** rutherfordium 104	[262] **Db** dubnium 105	[266] **Sg** seaborgium 106	[264] **Bh** bohrium 107	[277] **Hs** hassium 108	[268] **Mt** meitnerium 109	[271] **Ds** darmstadtium 110	[272] **Rg** roentgenium 111								

Elements with atomic numbers 112–116 have been reported but not fully authenticated

*The lanthanoids (atomic numbers 58–71) and the actinoids (atomic numbers 90–103) have been omitted.

Physics Equations List

(final velocity)^2 – (initial velocity)^2 = 2 × acceleration × distance $v^2 - u^2 = 2 \times a \times x$
energy transferred = current × potential difference × time $E = I \times V \times t$
potential difference across primary coil × current in primary coil = potential difference across secondary coil × current in secondary coil $V_p \times I_p = V_s \times I_s$
change in thermal energy = mass × specific heat capacity × change in temperature $\Delta Q = m \times c \times \Delta\theta$
thermal energy for a change of state = mass × specific latent heat $Q = m \times L$
energy transferred in stretching = 0.5 × spring constant × (extension)^2 $E = \frac{1}{2} \times k \times x^2$

Your own notes

Your own notes

Your own notes